Recent titles in the
Wiley Series on Personality Processes
Irving B. Weiner, *Editor*
University of South Florida

The Rorschach: A Comprehensive System. Volume 3: Assessment of Children and Adolescents (Second
Edition) *by John E. Exner, Jr., and Irving B. Weiner*
Understanding and Managing Classroom Behavior *by Sam Goldstein*
Intelligent Testing with the WISC-III *by Alan S. Kaufman*
Handbook of Child Behavior Therapy in the Psychiatric Setting *edited by Robert T. Ammerman and
Michel Hersen*
Handbook of Play Therapy. Volume II: Advances and Innovations *edited by Kevin J. O'Connor and
Charles E. Schaefer*
Handbook of Group Psychotherapy: An Empirical and Clinical Synthesis *edited by Addie Fuhriman and
Gary M. Burlingame*
Psychology and the Streets: Mental Health Practice with Homeless Persons *by Thomas L. Kuhlman*
The Working Alliance: Theory, Research, and Practice *edited by Adam Horvath and Leslie S. Greenberg*
Handbook of Developmental Family Psychology and Psychopathology *by Luciano L'Abate*
A Theory of Personality Development *by Luciano L'Abate*
Anxiety and Related Disorders: A Handbook *by Benjamin B. Wolman, Editor, George Stricker, Co-Editor*
Social Origins of Mental Ability *by Gary Collier*
Symptoms of Schizophrenia *edited by Charles G. Costello*
The Rorschach: A Comprehensive System. Volume I: Basic Foundations (Third Edition) *by
John E. Exner, Jr.*
Symptoms of Depression *edited by Charles G. Costello*
Handbook of Clinical Research and Practice with Adolescents *edited by Patrick H. Tolan and
Bertram J. Cohler*
Internalizing Disorders in Children and Adolescents *edited by William M. Reynolds*
Assessment of Family Violence: A Clinical and Legal Sourcebook *edited by Robert T. Ammerman and
Michel Hersen*
Handbook of Clinical Child Psychology (Second Edition) *edited by C. Eugene Walker and
Michael C. Roberts*
Handbook of Clinical Behavior Therapy (Second Edition) *edited by Samuel M. Turner, Karen S. Calhoun, and
Henry E. Adams*
Psychological Disturbance in Adolescence (Second Edition) *by Irving B. Weiner*
Prevention of Child Maltreatment: Development and Ecological Perspectives *edited by Diane J. Willis,
E. Wayne Holden, and Mindy Rosenberg*
Interventions for Children of Divorce: Custody, Access, and Psychotherapy *by William F. Hodges*
The Play Therapy Primer: An Integration of Theories and Techniques *by Kevin John O'Connor*
Adult Psychopathology and Diagnosis (Second Edition) *edited by Michel Hersen and Samuel L. Turner*
The Rorschach: A Comprehensive System. Volume II: Interpretation (Second Edition) *by John E. Exner, Jr.*
Play Diagnosis and Assessment *edited by Charles E. Schaefer, Karen Gitlin, and Alice Sandgrund*
Acquaintance Rape: The Hidden Crime *edited by Andrea Parrot and Laurie Bechhofer*
The Psychological Examination of the Child *by Theodore H. Blau*
Depressive Disorders: Facts, Theories, and Treatment Methods *by Benjamin B. Wolman, Editor, and
George Stricker, Co-Editor*
Social Support: An Interactional View *edited by Barbara R. Sarason, Irwin G. Sarason, and
Gregory R. Pierce*
Toward a New Personology: An Evolutionary Model *by Theodore Millon*
Treatment of Family Violence: A Sourcebook *edited by Robert T. Ammerman and Michel Hersen*
Handbook of Comparative Treatments for Adult Disorders *edited by Alan S. Bellack and Michel Hersen*
Managing Attention Disorders in Children: A Guide for Practitioners *by Sam Goldstein and Michael
Goldstein*
Understanding and Treating Depressed Adolescents and Their Families *by Gerald D. Oster and
Janice E. Caro*
The Psychosocial Worlds of the Adolescent: Public and Private *by Vivian Center Seltzer*
Handbook of Parent Training: Parents as Co-Therapists for Children's Behavior Problems *edited by
Charles E. Schaefer and James M. Briesmeister*
From Ritual to Repertoire: A Cognitive-Developmental Approach with Behavior-Disordered Children *by
Arnold Miller and Eileen Eller-Miller*

THE RORSCHACH
A COMPREHENSIVE SYSTEM

VOLUME 3: ASSESSMENT OF CHILDREN AND ADOLESCENTS

SECOND EDITION

JOHN E. EXNER, JR.
IRVING B. WEINER

A Wiley-Interscience Publication
JOHN WILEY & SONS, INC.
New York • Chichester • Brisbane • Toronto • Singapore

Library of Congress Cataloging-in-Publication Data:

ISBN: 0-471-55927-X

Printed in the United States of America

10 9 8 7 6 5 4 3 2 1

To Kristan, John, Garrett, Alissa, Chelsie,
Madison, Alexandra, and ??

Series Preface

This series of books is addressed to behavioral scientists interested in the nature of human personality. Its scope should prove pertinent to personality theorists and researchers as well as to clinicians concerned with applying an understanding of personality processes to the amelioration of emotional difficulties in living. To this end, the series provides a scholarly integration of theoretical formulations, empirical data, and practical recommendations.

Six major aspects of studying and learning about human personality can be designated: personality theory, personality structure and dynamics, personality development, personality assessment, personality change, and personality adjustment. In exploring these aspects of personality, the books in the series discuss a number of distinct but related subject areas: the nature and implications of various theories of personality; personality characteristics that account for consistencies and variations in human behavior; the emergence of personality processes in children and adolescents; the use of interviewing and testing procedures to evaluate individual differences in personality; efforts to modify personality styles through psychotherapy, counseling, behavior therapy, and other methods of influence; and patterns of abnormal personality functioning that impair individual competence.

IRVING B. WEINER

University of South Florida
Tampa, Florida

Preface

Personality assessment of youngsters is, at best, a difficult task. Many tests are available for use in collecting data about the psychological functioning of younger people, but the findings always have to be translated at least twice. First, they are interpreted in the context of basic rules that have been developed for dealing with the test data. Then, the resulting interpretations must be re-examined in a developmental framework. The second step is very challenging because of the rapid changes that occur as young people grow and because of the broad range of individual differences that exist at almost every year in the developmental cycle prior to adulthood. This challenge becomes more difficult as the test data become more complex, and probably no test yields more complex findings than the Rorschach.

When the nuclear elements of the *Comprehensive System* evolved during the period from 1968 to 1974, essentially all the research focused on the applications of the test with adults. Gradually, everyone associated with the project became acutely aware that data concerning children were sorely lacking. Several important works concerning the Rorschach and children had been published, including the major contributions of Louise Bates Ames, Mary Ford, and Marguerite Hertz, but none could be applied directly to the new system because of variations in the tactics of administration or the criteria for scoring responses. Thus, it became obvious that the project should be expanded to include the collection of a reasonably large standardization sample of children. That data set could then serve as a reference bank against which findings from other projects could be compared.

Probably no one working on the project fully recognized the massive effort that would be required, or the many-headed monster into which the project would develop. The host of demographic issues concerning the sample seemed easily resolved on paper, but in reality they often posed nearly insurmountable problems, and at several times during the next five years the project seemed doomed.

Most of the early solutions to those problems were due to the perseverance of the first series of regional project directors. Their effort was coordinated from 1974 to 1978 by Antonnia Victoria Leura, and among them they found numerous ways to entice parents to volunteer their children to become involved with the "blotto game." During that first phase of the project, we all learned a great deal about how to convince and reassure school officials, hospital administrators, department heads, and colleagues; and perhaps most of all we learned about parents, who should probably be the exclusive subject of a separate volume. Collectively, this group was able to obtain protocols from more than 1,200 patient and 1,100 nonpatient youngsters by 1978, but the project was far from being complete. Several issues concerning the stratification of the samples remained only partially resolved, and the number of subjects for each age group was considerably less than the targeted goal.

During the period from 1979 to 1983, Eugene A. Thomas coordinated the efforts of the regional project directors, focusing mainly on the refinement of the standardization sample for nonpatient children and the completion of a much needed series of retest studies, most of which have been designed to address the issue of the temporal consistency of the test with younger clients. The people working in this second phase of the project, like their predecessors, put forth a monumental effort, and they were able to add nearly 2,000 new records to the protocol pool and refine the nonpatient sample considerably so that some seemingly respectable normative findings could be published by 1982. Unfortunately, in 1987 we discovered that more than 1,100 of the protocols collected from younger subjects, including nearly 500 from the nonpatient group, were probably invalid because they contained fewer responses than seems to be required to insure temporal stability. Thus, came the task of re-analyzing data from more than 100 studies and restructuring the normative data.

The end product is less than optimal but the composite of findings, from both patient and nonpatient subjects, has yielded considerable information that seems to make the Rorschach somewhat more useful and understandable when working with younger clients. Certainly, we have learned much about the test and about some of the problems involved in researching it, especially with young people. We have learned a great deal about children: that they are delicate and yet sturdy and resilient; that they are very concrete and yet also very creative; that they can avoid a task by some of the most unusual tactics and yet perform well when pressed to the issue. Most of all we've learned to respect them and even envy some of the playful ways that they use to approach life.

Our newfound awareness about youngsters would not have developed without the dedicated efforts of our regional project directors and senior examiners. They include Doris Alinsky, Michael Allen, Jeffrey Berman, Edward Caraway, Eileen Carter, Terry Cross, Roy Fishman, Dorothy Frankman, Christy George, Doris Havermann, Sarah Hillman, Richard Hunt, Geraldine Ingalls, Marianne Johnston, Lester Jones, Mary Lou King, Nancy Latimore, Denise McDonnahue, Andrew Miller, Doris Price, Carmen Penzulotta, George Pickering, Carrie Rustenmeyer, Virginia Reynolds, Louise Stanton, Vicki Thompson, Edward Walker, Robert Wilke, Helen Yaul, and Mark Zimmerman.

Many of the teaching and research assistants at Rorschach Workshops also served in several of the projects, either as examiners or as boilerroom slaves in the data analysis segments. They include Gerald Albrecht, Carol Bluth, Richard Bruckman, Joel Cohen, Michael Colemen, Susan Colligan, Gail Famino, Barbara Ferraro-Mason, Katherine Gibbons, Lisa Hillman, Susan James, Carol (TC) Levantrosser, Beatrice Mittman, Naomi Sadowsky, Sherill Sigalow, Sara Sternklar, and Donald Viglione.

It would be erroneous to consider that this project has reached closure, or that the broader project to develop the *System,* begun in 1968, has been completed. Some good beginnings have been achieved and considerable knowledge about the test and its use with various groups, including children, has unfolded. Hopefully, the younger generation of researchers will strive to expand this knowledge. Some will develop sophisticated and intricate designs that will yield findings to enhance our understanding of the test and how it can be used best to serve those who are its subjects. Others may take on the more difficult task of increasing our knowledge about how young nonpatients respond to the test, and how the variations in performance that exist within each age group can be framed in ways that amplify interpretive accuracy.

JOHN E. EXNER, JR.

Asheville, North Carolina
September 1994

Contents

Tables

PART I

Interpretation and the Younger Client

CHAPTER 1

The Nature and Interpretation
of the Rorschach

The Rorschach assessment of children and adolescents should be guided by three general considerations. First, Rorschach data comprise both objective and subjective features, and best results are achieved when these features are distinguished from each other but also used together in a complementary fashion. Second, Rorschach interpretations can be formulated from either an empirical or a conceptual perspective, but only an adequate integration of these two perspectives fully taps the test's potential to measure personality functioning. Third, accurate evaluation of Rorschach records obtained from young people does not involve any age-specific principles of interpretation, but it does require familiarity with age-level normative data. This first chapter presents these three considerations in further detail.

OBJECTIVE AND SUBJECTIVE FEATURES
OF RORSCHACH DATA

Rorschach tradition is grounded for the most part in an objective approach to the test data. Hermann Rorschach regarded the inkblot test as an experimental procedure for differentiating perceptual differences among pathological groups that might be useful in determining the diagnostic implications of perceptual processes. Ultimately, he also noted that his experimental procedure could help differentiate personality styles. His *Psychodiagnostics* was subtitled *A Diagnostic Test Based on Perception,* and he wrote, "The test cannot be used to probe into the content of the subconscious" (Rorschach, 1921/1942, p. 123).

In this vein, the traditional structural analysis of Rorschach responses, as pioneered in the United States by Beck (1944), proceeds in an objective manner from the coding of perceptual processes to conclusions concerning the implications of particular perceptual styles. For example, whether or not subjects are using the whole blot (*W*) in formulating a response is an objective fact, and the corollaries of *W* emphasis in a record can be examined as objectively as the corollaries of variables drawn from any test that is generally regarded as an objective measure.

When examiners attend to objective features of Rorschach test data, Rorschach responses are taken as representative samples of behavior, and the manner in which subjects deal with the test situation is considered to reflect directly how they deal with other life situations. Thus subjects who respond primarily to peripheral details of the blots and rarely to the whole stimulus are inferred to be individuals who become preoccupied with the details of their experience and fail to grasp the broad significance of situations they encounter. Those whose responses often involve distorted form perception are inferred to misperceive what they observe in other situations as well and consequently to demonstrate poor reality testing. Those who give an unusual frequency of *Anatomy* and *X-ray* responses are inferred to be inordinately concerned with their body and its functions, and so on.

As a departure from examining only objective features of the test data, other Rorschach pioneers came to believe that Hermann Rorschach's focus on observable perceptual phenomena did not fully mine the richness of the inkblot test for illuminating personality processes. Klopfer and Schafer in particular were influential in using psychoanalytic perspectives to elaborate how thematic content in the Rorschach can provide clues to underlying feelings and concerns (Klopfer, Ainsworth, Klopfer, & Holt, 1954; Schafer, 1954). Although some clinicians and researchers continued to concentrate on identifying correlates of formally scored perceptual style in the tradition of Hermann Rorschach, others established a new and less objective tradition that viewed the inkblots not as a perceptual task but as a stimulus to fantasy (see Blatt, 1990; Goldfried, Stricker, & Weiner, 1971, Chap. 13). In this subjective tradition, the most important data in a Rorschach protocol are the subject's fantasy productions, and elaborations of content provide the major basis for drawing inferences about personality functioning.

When examiners attend to subjective features of Rorschach data, responses are taken as symbolic rather than as representative of behavior. Consider, for example, a boy who sees the center detail (*D4*) of Card I as "A lady, sort of old and mean-looking, and she's waving her arms and looking the other way." Objectively, the important elements of this response are the location and developmental quality (*Do*), the determinant and form quality (*Mao*), and the content (*H*), each of which contributes to key aspects of the Structural Summary. Subjectively, however, the significance of this response lies in whatever meaning can be attached to the theme of a woman who is "old," "mean-looking," "waving her arms," and "looking the other way."

The distinction between objective and subjective features of Rorschach data bears a close relationship to the role of *projection* in the formulation of responses. In perceptual terms, projection occurs when people attribute characteristics to a stimulus field on the basis of their internal thoughts, feelings, or need states. The concept of projection entered the Rorschach literature in 1939, when Lawrence Frank suggested that projection may account for idiographic features of perception in general and of Rorschach percepts in particular. Frank's suggestion led to the customary but misleading classification of the Rorschach as a projective test, which it is not, and the common but erroneous belief that all Rorschach responses involve projection, which they do not.

The Rorschach is basically a problem-solving task, not a projective test. The task is to say what the blots might be, other than what they really are, which is 10 inkblots. Subjects can comply fully with the instructions of the test ("What might this be?" "Where do you see it?" "What makes it look like that?") and produce a valid, interpretable protocol without using projection in formulating their responses. At the same time, subjects may choose to embellish some of their answers with products of their fantasy lives, in which case their responses may well be determined in part by projection. In actual practice, Rorschach protocols are likely to vary considerably in how much projection they contain, from records in which only a few responses appear slightly influenced by projection to records in which almost every response seems largely determined by projected fantasy.

The notion that projection plays a variable and often secondary role in the Rorschach has sometimes been regarded as antithetical to psychoanalytic or psychodynamic formulations of test-taking behavior. Such an impression is unfounded, however. Schachtel

(1966), speaking to the nature of Rorschach test data from a distinctly psychoanalytic frame of reference, observed many years ago, "Only a small fraction of the many processes underlying Rorschach responses are of a projective nature" (p. 10). Whatever their theoretical orientation, examiners need to recognize that some or all of the responses in a valid record may involve little or no projection. On the other hand, the responses in a record will typically vary widely in how much projection they involve, and these variations have important implications for the interpretive process.

At this point, an example may clarify the difference between responses in which projection has exerted a negligible or prominent influence. A response to Card I of "The whole thing has the shape of a bat and it's black like a bat" does not attribute characteristics to the stimulus that are not already there. Card I does in fact have the shape of a bat, and it is grey-black in color. As a commonly seen percept using the entire blot and articulating achromatic color, this response may contribute to inferences about personality style, especially if the total number of *W, P,* or *C'* in the record is elevated. However, these inferences will derive from objective features of how the subject has dealt with the Rorschach task, such as using the whole blot, not from any manifestations of projection.

By contrast, consider Card I seen as "A spider reaching out to grab its prey." This response involves an uncommon and inaccurate percept ("spider"), the attribution of movement to a static inkblot ("reaching out"), and the fantasy of imminent victimization ("to grab its prey"). Responses that are inaccurately perceived or embellished in these ways usually involve projection, because they report characteristics that are not present in the stimulus and must therefore have originated in attitudes and concerns internal to the subject. Accordingly, responses in which projection appears to have occurred can extend the interpretive process beyond the boundaries envisioned by Hermann Rorschach and provide clues to underlying personality dynamics.

The broad issue of projection in the Rorschach is elaborated elsewhere within the context of the Comprehensive System (Exner, 1989; 1991, pp. 107–116) and will not be pursued further here. However, further note should be taken of some differences between representative and symbolic interpretations in their implications for the communication of Rorschach findings.

When Rorschach responses are taken as representative of behavior and interpretations are based on objective features of the data, conclusions can be drawn with considerable certainty. Only a modest inferential leap is required to conclude, for example, that people who strive to simplify the Rorschach task and deal with it in an economical fashion (high *Lambda*) are likely to seek simplicity and economy in their dealings with other life situations. Because objectively based interpretations hew closely to observed behavior, examiners can and should express them in definite terms, as in, "This person would rather reflect on his experience than express how he feels about it" (*Introversiveness*), or "This person is seriously impaired in her ability to think logically and coherently" (elevated *Critical Special Scores*).

On the other hand, when Rorschach responses are taken as symbolic of behavior and interpretations are based on subjective features of the data, conclusions are speculative and should be phrased as hypotheses or conjectures rather than as certainties. Whereas people who give numerous *minus* responses *do* perceive their world inaccurately, a boy who sees a mean-looking old lady waving her arms and looking away *could be* revealing several possible underlying concerns. The "old lady" *could be* his mother, his teacher, or perhaps some other important female figure in his life. "Waving her arms" *could be* a greeting or a prelude to some physical violence, and "looking the other way" *could be* an indication of fears of being ignored or of wishes to escape notice. Accordingly, because of the several alternative possibilities usually inherent in symbolic representations, interpretations based on subjective features of the Rorschach are more or less speculative.

To serve well both their clients and the persons to whom they consult, psychodiagnosticians must avoid either understating or overstating their case (see Weiner, 1989). When objective data identify representative features of personality style or status, the interpreter must be prepared to enunciate clearly and without equivocation that this is, indeed, the way the person is: an overincorporator, an ideationally oriented person, a self-centered person, someone who avoids closeness with others, a person prone to circumstantial reasoning, or whatever. On the other hand, when subjective features of the data symbolically suggest aspects of underlying personality dynamics, the interpreter needs to specify that these are alternative possibilities that *may* play a role in the subject's current situation and therefore merit further consideration and exploration.

While recognizing and respecting these differences between representative interpretations based on objective features of Rorschach data and symbolic interpretations of subjective elements of a protocol, examiners need also to include both kinds of interpretation in drawing conclusions. The human condition is complex, and what people are like comprises their dispositions to think, feel, and act in certain ways; their current emotional and attitudinal states; their underlying concerns, self-perceptions, and impressions of the people in their lives; and the cumulative influences, sometimes developmentally constructive and sometimes developmentally arresting, that have made them what they are and what they are likely to become. To paint this broad portrait, Rorschach examiners need to draw on all available sources of data, objective and subjective, and blend them in judicious fashion. Insufficient attention either to structural or thematic characteristics of Rorschach responses wastes valuable information and precludes the fullest possible description of a subject's personality.

EMPIRICAL AND CONCEPTUAL APPROACHES TO RORSCHACH INTERPRETATION

In whatever form they communicate their results, Rorschach interpreters must be prepared to justify their conclusions and hypotheses. To say, "This boy is preoccupied with the details of his experience" or "This girl appears to feel rejected by her mother" is only a first step in conveying what the data mean. The next step consists of explaining how and why Rorschach responses lead to such inferences. When the persons who request these reports ask, "How can you tell from your tests that this adolescent is schizophrenic?" or "What about the Rorschach indicates that this child will respond well to psychotherapy?" they are entitled to clear and denotative answers. Failure to provide good explanations of why test findings mean what they mean is an abdication of professional responsibility, and inability to provide adequate explanations is a demonstration of professional incompetence.

At various times and in various circumstances, psychologists have employed four approaches to explaining their Rorschach interpretations. Two of these, the *Ouija-board approach* and the *authoritative approach,* although sometimes flashy, rarely reflect clinical wisdom or scientific sophistication. The other two approaches consist of *empirical* and *conceptual* perspectives on the interpretive process that, when integrated in informed fashion, serve effectively to indicate how and why Rorschach responses warrant the inferences being drawn from them. Examiners can benefit from recognizing when they may be employing each of these approaches in their practice; they should strive to integrate the empirical and conceptual approaches to the best of their ability.

The Ouija-Board Approach   In the Ouija-board approach, interpreters justify their conclusions by deferring to their intuition, as in such statements as, "It's something I sense about this person" or "I have a feeling about him but I can't say exactly where it comes from." An unusually intuitive, extraordinarily empathic interpreter may work the Ouija-board approach to the Rorschach well and generate accurate and clinically useful hypotheses about a subject's personality functioning. On balance, however, this approach suffers from being insufficiently generalizable, inadequately focused, and professionally embarrassing.

With respect to generalizability, the insights of intuitive clinicians reside in unique personal capacities that allow them to understand their clients' nature. However, unless these clinicians can point to generally observable data that help them arrive at their conclusions, they are incapable of sharing their talents or teaching them to others. Only the individual clients they evaluate benefit from their skills, and these skills make no general contribution to the field. The Ouija-board method thus has little to offer, except when it suggests a starting point for developing hypotheses about the meaning of specific bits of Rorschach data—at which point it becomes a data-based rather than an intuitive approach.

With respect to focus, intuitions tend to come and go, as the inspiration strikes, and rarely yield a comprehensive Rorschach picture of personality. The Ouija-board interpreter may come up with notions about the client's sex role identity when the central referral issue is possible schizophrenia. When asked, "Is this boy schizophrenic?" this clinician may have to say, "I don't have any feelings about that." Or the Ouija-board approach may generate hypotheses primarily about objective facts that could easily be gathered without Rorschach testing, such as, "I think this girl is the middle of three children" or "I have the feeling that this boy has gone through a period of separation from his parents."

As for embarrassment, Rorschach clinicians who aspire to public respect and professional status have everything to lose by resting their case on intuition. The general public is too sophisticated, the professionals with whom psychologists work are too informed, and the field of clinical psychology is too committed to a scientist-practitioner blend for Rorschachers to prosper by cloaking themselves in mysticism. Implications that only experienced Rorschach interpreters can understand the test, that only a self-anointed inner circle can appreciate its message, and that the meanings of the inkblots stand somehow immune to scientific study serve only to isolate Rorschachers from their professional colleagues and group them in the public eye with palm readers and crystal-ball gazers.

The Authoritative Approach   In the authoritative approach, examiners justify their Rorschach interpretations by noting, "So-and-so says so." When authorities who are invoked in this way have presented clear, consistent, and clinically meaningful formulations that have stood the tests of time and validation, interpreters who rely on them will be on solid ground. Indeed, an informed appeal to authority has much to recommend it. Interpreters who keep current with the literature and are broadly familiar with areas of agreement among leading scholars are likely to serve their clients well.

Nevertheless, Rorschachers who rely excessively on appeals to authority risk compromising their own critical judgment and their independent capacity to account for their impressions. Interpreters who are prepared only to cite authority are not prepared to indicate in their own words why an authority is dependable. It may be correct to say that a Rorschach with poor form quality is consistent with schizophrenia, but to say this is so because Weiner (1966) says it is so is inadequate. Such a justification does not indicate Weiner's reasons for saying so, nor does it address other diagnostic possibilities that should be considered when form quality is poor.

Interpreters who depend on authority may fare reasonably well in clinical practice, especially if they choose their authorities carefully and are not required to give direct feedback to clients, referral sources, or adversaries in the courtroom. In giving feedback, however, they will command greater respect and avoid grief under questioning if they can explain, in either empirical or conceptual terms, why certain Rorschach structural and thematic characteristics suggest certain personality patterns.

The Empirical Approach In the empirical approach to Rorschach assessment, interpretations are justified on the basis of research findings. Rorschach practitioners have customarily turned to research findings for guidance in their clinical assessments. To what extent, they ask, do a subject's responses resemble responses typically given by persons with such known characteristics as being schizophrenic, depressed, or conduct disordered? The more similarities that emerge between a subject's responses and research evidence concerning how people with a certain characteristic or condition can be expected to respond, the more reasonable it becomes to conclude that the subject has this characteristic or condition. To continue with the example of schizophrenia, poor form quality suggests the presence of this disorder because of the well-documented fact that schizophrenic patients generally show much poorer form quality than nonschizophrenic individuals.

Unlike the Ouija-board approach and appeals to authority, the empirical approach constitutes a scientifically sound and professionally respectable way of justifying Rorschach interpretations. Moreover, there is good reason to regard adequate empirical foundations as necessary for effective utilization of the Rorschach in personality assessment. Without sufficient quantitative data concerning the normative distribution and other psychometric properties of Rorschach patterns that reflect dimensions of personality along which psychologically normal and abnormal individuals are likely to differ, clinicians are ill-prepared to draw distinctions from the Rorschach concerning what is psychopathological and what is not, what is common and what is not, and what calls for professional intervention and what does not.

For example, suppose that poor form quality is being used in part as a basis for inferring that someone has a schizophrenic disorder. How poor is this person's perceptual functioning? How frequently are people with similarly poor form quality eventually confirmed by all available data to be schizophrenic, and what percentage are found to have some other disturbance? Is this person's level of poor form quality associated with schizophrenia that usually requires treatment in a hospital setting or with schizophrenia that is usually treatable on an outpatient basis? Unless examiners can answer such questions intelligently, their diagnostic inferences and treatment recommendations may not wear well in the face of informed inquiry. Only by supporting their inferences with empirical data can Rorschachers command respect as scientists and as professionals. For clinicians to translate their conclusions into effective and convincing applications of the Rorschach, they need to adduce hard facts that document the reliability, validity, and degrees of certainty of the inferences they draw.

Nevertheless, as necessary as it may be, a strictly empirical approach to Rorschach interpretation is not good enough. Empiricism falls short of providing answers to the question "Why?" Why does a particular subject perceive the inkblots in certain ways, and why do certain ways of perceiving the inkblots help to identify a broad range of normal and pathological conditions? Empirical statements ("The data say so") are sounder and more convincing than appeals to intuition or authority, but they say nothing about the personality processes that link certain kinds of test responses with certain types of diagnostic or descriptive inferences. Whenever such links remain unforged and unspecified, a criterion-valid measuring instrument will stand isolated from general knowledge of normal and abnormal personality functioning. The instrument will work, but no one will know why it works, and there will be no guidelines for relating it to other bodies of theory and research.

The Conceptual Approach   The conceptual approach to Rorschach assessment identifies aspects of personality functioning that link test data with the conclusions drawn from them. In this approach, poor form quality helps to identify schizophrenia because (a) poor form quality, especially with a predominance of *minus* over *unusual* responses, indicates inaccurate perception, (b) inaccurate perception identifies poor reality testing, and (c) poor reality testing is a defining characteristic of schizophrenic disorder (see Chapter 5 of this book). The key to justifying the Rorschach interpretation becomes a personality construct (impaired perceptual accuracy, in this example) that accounts for both the Rorschach finding (poor form quality) and the diagnostic inference drawn (schizophrenic disorder). As elaborated by Weiner (1986), this conceptualization of Rorschach interpretations can guide both research and clinical work in beneficial ways.

Research Benefits   The conceptual approach to Rorschach interpretation opens up intriguing research possibilities that go beyond the empirical investigation of how, for example, schizophrenic and comparison groups differ in their Rorschach form quality. Whether form quality is a good index of perceptual accuracy can be investigated independently of schizophrenia, and whether perceptual inaccuracy is a good index of schizophrenia can be investigated independently of the Rorschach. Positive findings from both kinds of investigation provide a broader basis for the validity of Rorschach perceptual indices of schizophrenia than data derived solely from comparing the Rorschachs of schizophrenic and nonschizophrenic subjects.

In addition, Rorschach findings that rest on a conceptual framework can be related meaningfully to other lines of research on personality processes (e.g., perceptual functioning) and on dimensions of psychopathology (e.g., characteristics of schizophrenia). Such relationships build bridges between study of the Rorschach and mainstream theory and research in behavioral science, and they allow Rorschachers to draw on a vast array of data sources to help them shape their understanding and use of the test. In turn, clinicians and researchers with little direct familiarity with the Rorschach can draw on Rorschach research to enhance their understanding of personality processes and psychopathology.

In this latter regard, Rorschach clinicians who can formulate their interpretations in conceptual terms are well prepared to communicate their impressions to a wide audience. The interpreter who can only say, "I think this boy is schizophrenic because his form level is poor" will have difficulty gaining the ear of anyone outside the Rorschach community. The Rorschach clinician who instead can say, "I think this boy is schizophrenic because he tends to misperceive the meaning of events in his life" will be able to make sense to most reasonably sophisticated people, even if they are unacquainted with the Rorschach or with the nature of psychological disorder.

Clinical Benefits   The conceptual approach can aid clinicians not only in talking about the Rorschach, but also in deciding when and how to use the Rorschach in responding to requests for consultation. From a conceptual point of view, test batteries are selected on the basis of the particular psychological functions that must be assessed to answer the referral question. Accordingly, an examiner's first step after receiving a request for consultation is to think through what features of the client's psychological functioning will provide answers to the questions that have been asked. If one of the questions is whether a young person has a schizophrenic disorder, knowledgeable examiners will recognize that some assessment of reality testing should be included in their evaluation. Working from their clinical knowledge, diagnostic consultants should prepare as full a list as they can of the client characteristics they need to evaluate in order to respond helpfully to the referral question.

If such a list is readily available, Rorschachers can then determine the assessment procedures they should use. If reality testing is on the list, the Rorschach is a likely candidate, not because it measures schizophrenia directly, but because it offers a reliable index of perceptual distortion that helps to identify schizophrenia. If the list includes visual-motor coordination, as it should in cases of possible brain dysfunction or attention deficit hyperactivity disorder, such tests as the Wechsler Intelligence Scale for Children (WISC-R) or various portions of a Reitan or Luria-Nebraska battery would be chosen. The Rorschach might be included to help identify how children with attention deficit hyperactivity disorder are coping with their disability, but its role in answering the diagnostic question would be minimal. If the diagnostic questions concerns retardation, the choice may well be not to use the Rorschach at all. Although the Rorschach reflects numerous features of intellectual style and level, it cannot replace standardized IQ tests as a measure of intellectual ability.

In addition to helping clinicians decide which tests to use, conceptualizing a referral question in terms of psychological functions can indicate when it would be best not to test at all. Suppose the referral question concerns whether young men will perform well in a training program for aviation cadets, as was the case in a once often-cited study by Holtzman and Sells (1954). What personality characteristics have been identified as predicting success in learning to fly? Few if any, except perhaps for a reasonable degree of intelligence and emotional stability. Hence, there is no conceptual basis for attempting to answer this question from the Rorschach, which is a measure of personality functioning. The test should not be used for this purpose, and its failure to answer this question should not be considered relevant its clinical utility.

To set this example in its broader context, Rorschachers need to be wary of referral questions that involve considerable nonpersonality variance. Behavior is, after all, a function of the personality and the environment. The Rorschach measures only the way in which the personality is organized and provides some information about the psychological functioning of the subject. To the extent that environmental circumstances determine outcome, examiners must be very conservative in trying to predict behavior from their test data. Whether a disturbed adolescent is ready to leave the hospital depends in part on how well his or her personality functions are currently integrated, but it also depends on the climate in the young person's home and the availability of adequate outpatient aftercare.

In these and similar cases in which both personality and nonpersonality factors are important to answering a referral question, interpreters drawing on Rorschach findings should keep in mind that the Rorschach by itself can rarely predict behavior. "Will he continue to be disruptive in the classroom?" "Is she likely to make another suicide attempt?" "Would foster home placement be advisable?" These are complex matters concerning which personality functioning, as addressed by Rorschach data, can provide some guidance. With few exceptions, however, Rorschachers responding to such questions will be well advised to draw on numerous other sources of information, to offer statements of probability rather than certainty and, as sometimes is necessary, to explain why no prediction at all can be offered about the client's future behavior. Interpreters may, on occasion, feel strongly that the answer to a referral question rests almost entirely on nonpersonality variance. Then the appropriate decision would be not to test at all.

When the time comes to prepare a report, the conceptual approach provides a useful basis for determining how best to organize and present whatever inferences have been drawn from Rorschach and other test data. Psychodiagnosticians proceeding in terms of concepts can avoid feeling overwhelmed by having obtained more data than they can easily organize. Having formulated the referral question in terms of key personality issues, they can then proceed in systematic fashion to translate relevant personality dimensions into test data that are likely to measure them. The resulting report will then evolve as a series of paragraphs that give substance to this process. Asked about possible schizophrenia, for example, a major section of the report may begin with, "This boy's poor reality testing, as reflected in frequently inaccurate perceptions of the Rorschach stimuli, is consistent with the presence of a schizophrenic disorder," following which the details of the observed perceptual distortion and their implications for schizophrenia can be evaluated.

EVALUATING THE RORSCHACHS OF YOUNGER CLIENTS

Rorschachers who have learned to use the test primarily with adults often hesitate to work with the records of children and adolescents. Any such reluctance is unwarranted, however. Although there is something special about young people, there is nothing special about the Rorschach records they give. Any clinician who understands the Rorschach is well prepared to interpret the protocols of clients of any age. Principles of Rorschach interpretation cut across age groups for the simple reason that Rorschach behavior means what it means regardless of the age of the subject.

To illustrate the universality of Rorschach interpretive principles, consider the relationship between *FC* and *CF* responses. *FC* answers are indicative of well modulated, fairly stable, and rather reserved ways of experiencing and expressing affect, whereas *CF* answers reflect more spontaneous, intense, and labile emotionality. People with a predominance of *FC* over *CF* responses in their records can be expected to restrain their feelings for the most part, to express relatively mild degrees of affect, and to maintain a rather even emotional keel. People with a predominance of *CF* responses, by contrast, typically prefer letting their emotions flow rather than holding them in check.

They tend to be relatively quick to express strong feelings and relatively prone to show rapid fluctuations in their emotional tone from one moment to the next.

These implications of color use apply equally to children, adolescents, and adults, and the same can be said for all interpretable features of Rorschach behavior. The age of the subject becomes important only after the interpreter has arrived at his or her interpretations and is considering the significance or meaning of these inferences in the context of a particular client or referral question. Suppose, for example, that a protocol showing a predominance of *FC* over *CF* responses has been given by a 7-year-old, thereby indicating that the subject is restrained in his or her emotional displays and not much given to spontaneous affective expression. Seven-year-olds normally do not deal with their emotions in such a reserved fashion, and Rorschach evidence of well-modulated affectivity, which might signify adaptive maturity for an adult, probably identifies maladaptive emotional inhibition in a 7-year-old. Conversely, a protocol showing a predominance of *CF* and thereby indicating unreserved and intense emotionality, would be consistent with expectations for a 7-year-old but suggestive of emotional immaturity in an adult.

As this example should clarify, the key to working effectively with the Rorschachs of young people is not learning a special set of interpretive hypotheses, but rather being conversant with the normative data. Nonpatient 7-year-olds give substantially more *CF* answers than *FC* answers (see Table 9), whereas just the opposite is true for adults. For interpretable features of the Rorschach, then, protocols must be evaluated carefully in light of normative data. The wise use of norms allows Rorschach examiners familiar with basic principles of interpretation to evaluate the records of subjects of all ages in a sophisticated and useful manner.

In clinical practice, however, two additional requirements are necessary to ensure accurate evaluation of young people. First the data must be collected properly. This calls not only for an understanding of standard test procedures, but also for familiarity with how best to apply these procedures in particular contexts and with particular subject groups. Chapter 2 discusses special considerations in collecting Rorschach data from younger clients.

Second, assessors working with young people need to be conversant with current knowledge of personality development and developmental psychopathology. To move adequately from descriptions of personality functioning to informed opinions about whether a child is schizophrenic, depressed, conduct disordered, or likely to respond favorably to a particular form of treatment, diagnostic consultants require thorough familiarity with the personality characteristics that identify normality, define various clinical syndromes, or relate to prognosis for alternative kinds of therapy. Accordingly, each of the chapters in Parts II through IV of this book precede discussion of Rorschach data with an overview of information concerning the condition or question that is being addressed.

REFERENCES

Beck, S. J. (1944). *Rorschach's test.* I. *Basic processes.* New York: Grune & Stratton.

Blatt, S. J. (1990). The Rorschach: A test of perception or an evaluation of representation. *Journal of Personality Assessment, 55,* 394–416.

Exner, J. E., Jr. (1989). Searching for projection in the Rorschach. *Journal of Personality Assessment, 53,* 520–536.

Exner, J. E., Jr. (1991). *The Rorschach: A comprehensive system.* Vol. 2: *Interpretation* (2nd ed.). New York: Wiley.

Frank, L. K. (1939). Projective methods for the study of personality. *Journal of Psychology, 8,* 389–413.

Goldfried, M. R., Stricker, G., & Weiner, I. B. (1971). *Rorschach handbook of clinical and research applications.* Englewood Cliffs, NJ: Prentice-Hall.

Holtzman, W. H., & Sells, S. B. (1954). Predictions of flying success by clinical analysis of test protocols. *Journal of Abnormal and Social Psychology, 49,* 485–498.

Klopfer, B., Ainsworth, M. D., Klopfer, W. G., & Holt, R. R. (1954). *Developments in the Rorschach technique.* I: *Theory and development.* Yonkers-on-Hudson, NY: World Book.

Rorschach, H. (1942). *Psychodiagnostics.* Bern: Hans Huber. (Original work published 1921)

Schachtel, E. G. (1966). *Experiential foundations of Rorschach's test.* New York: Basic Books.

Schafer, R. (1954). *Psychoanalytic interpretation in Rorschach Testing.* New York: Grune & Stratton.

Weiner, I. B. (1966). *Psychodiagnosis in schizophrenia.* New York: Wiley.

Weiner, I. B. (1986). Conceptual and empirical perspectives on the Rorschach assessment of psychopathology. *Journal of Personality Assessment, 50,* 472–479.

Weiner, I. B. (1989). On competence and ethicality in psychodiagnostic assessment. *Journal of Personality Assessment, 53,* 827–831.

CHAPTER 2

Rorschach and the Younger Client

Very few children delight in being tested, and for a youngster the Rorschach can be a particularly difficult ordeal. If the adult has a hard time understanding the necessity of puzzling through inkblots, it is even worse for the younger person, who is far less inclined to try to present the "correct" appearance, and far more inclined to defend himself or herself against the intrusions of a stranger; particularly a stranger whose very position evokes ominous assumptions.

Most children and adolescents who are "called" to assessment are very aware of the purpose. Unfortunately, much of their awareness includes negative assumptions. Some of these may be correct, for quite often the input of the psychologist becomes paramount in deciding the future of the subject. Frequently, faulty assumptions are spawned in the home by negative or indifferent parents, but most misconceptions probably are inspired by the many rumors that circulate in even the most sophisticated of educational environments about assessment and those who do it. It would likely be difficult to locate the school or clinic psychologist who has not encountered the very resistant child, frightened by the prospect of being examined by "the person who gets into your head," or "the one who studies the retards."

The typical negative set of younger clients approaching assessment poses difficult but by no means insurmountable problems for the examiner administering the Rorschach. Obviously, it is very important for the examiner to devote sufficient time to easing the mistrust and anxiety of the subject in the testing situation. It is very important to take enough time to explain the purpose of the examination and create a suitable, though not transferential, relationship with the subject. This routine should be marked by honesty. Both the child and the parents have a right to understand the purpose of the assessment and to be informed of the findings. If the examiner has taken appropriate care in introducing the overall assessment process, when it comes time for the Rorschach to be administered, the subject is likely to offer at least a minimal sampling of behaviors or responses. The resulting Rorschach data can be expected to offer a reasonably high yield in terms of understanding the subject, even if the child remains somewhat resistant. The approach of the examiner can be enhanced if he or she understands the task that is put to the subject. This is probably true for any test, but it is of paramount importance in using the Rorschach. The critical aspect of the Rorschach to be understood is the nature of the response and its delivery.

ATTRIBUTES OF THE RESPONSE PROCESS

For decades, most Rorschachers have assumed that what is seen is delivered in the form of responses. The findings of several research projects suggest that is only partially true. The findings of Exner, Armbruster, and Mittman (1978) seem to establish beyond question that subjects, including children, do see many more things than they are willing to report. In this Exner et al. study, subjects were told that the way to take the test was to find as many things as possible during a 60-second exposure for each card. The study included five groups, one of which consisted of nonpatient children between the ages of 11 and 13. All five groups gave significantly greater average numbers of responses than are ordinarily given, and, somewhat surprisingly, the children averaged nearly the greatest number of answers, 94.1.

It had been anticipated in this study that, if more than the usual number of answers were delivered, the bulk of the responses would appear during the second 30 seconds of blot exposure. The rationale for this assumption was that the longer a subject viewed a blot, the greater would be the tendency to find things. The reverse proved to be true. In all groups, including the children, more than two thirds of the total number of answers were given during the first 30-second period. In fact, when the first 30-second period of exposure was subdivided into the first 15 seconds versus the second 15 seconds, the data revealed that slightly more answers were delivered in the first 15 seconds. It had also been postulated that, as the number of responses increased, the form quality of the responses would decrease, yielding a significantly lower $X + \%$ with each subsequent 15-second interval as contrasted with the first 15 seconds. This too proved not to be the case except with adult inpatient depressives and schizophrenics, where some decline did occur in form quality as the minute elapsed. But for children, the form quality actually improved, although not to a statistically significant level.

Possibly the most important feature of the Exner et al. results, for purposes here, is that children drawn from a typically "reluctant" population gave an average of 3.5 answers to each blot during an exposure time of 15 seconds per blot. Obviously this is a far greater number than children usually deliver in a standard administration, and even significantly more than delivered by most adults. A reevaluation of the tape recordings for the children reveals that almost all (18 of 20) subjects gave at least 2 answers during the first 10 seconds of exposure to the blots, and that 12 of the 20 gave an average of 2 answers per blot within a 7-second exposure. These findings are difficult to compare with the response times for children when the test is administered using a standardization format; however, some comparison is possible.

Collectively, in a standard administration, the average number of responses per record for nonpatient children, ages 11 to 13, is 21.03. The average time for the first response per card is 6.8 seconds, and the average total time per card is 21.1 seconds. Although the average total time per card is often inflated because of the examiner's prompting on the first card when only one answer is given, it would appear that, under the experimental instructions of Exner et al., nonpatient children of the same ages as the standardization group gave about one more response in a period of at least one-third less time than is common under standard instructions.

In other words, extrapolating from the number of answers delivered in a 15-second response interval in the experimental condition, the 11-year-old group would have averaged 37 responses per record, whereas under standard conditions, and with an exposure time of at least 8 seconds more, a record of 21 to 23 responses is evoked. Therefore it seems reasonable to assume that children, as do most subjects, both young and old, see considerably more than they articulate. More data concerning the fact that most people probably see many more things in the blots than they articulate are presented in substantially greater detail elsewhere (Exner, 1978, 1991); however, the bottom line appears to be that subjects, including children, will deliver those answers that they think are acceptable, or that, for some psychological reasons, they need to articulate. Stated differently, the response process consists of a complex set of psychological operations that can be conceptualized as involving at least three interrelated phases.

PHASE 1 OF THE RESPONSE PROCESS: INITIAL INPUT

Phase 1 involves the input and initial classification of the stimulus field. The scanning of the field occurs very quickly. The initial scan of most blots occurs in 1 second or less, although the more broken blots, such as Cards III and X, may require as many as 2 seconds (Colligan, 1990; Colligan & Exner, 1985; Exner, 1986). As the scanning of the stimulus field occurs, the perceptual input causes the visual image to be stored in the short-term memory of the subject. This requires little effort, as the field remains in the visual field of the subject. Once the encoding occurs and the image or engram is formed, a translation of the stimulus, or parts of it, begins, prompted by the directions from the examiner (What might this be?). During this first phase of the response process, the classification of the field, or its parts, occurs very rapidly, and several potential answers are created. Some are crude (Stein, 1949), but many are commonplace (Colligan, 1990).

PHASE 2 OF THE RESPONSE PROCESS: SETS OF THE SUBJECT

During the second phase of the response process, the scanning activity continues. This permits a reevaluation of the earlier classifications that have occurred, but more importantly, it is a time during which the sets of the subject toward the test and the testing situation stimulate an evaluation by the subject of the several potential responses that have been created. In part, this evaluation includes judgments about the accuracy of the potential answers. Sometimes, rescanning causes an answer to be refined, and in many instances a potential response is discarded because the stored image is judged to be more like one answer than another. This process of discarding potential answers is influenced considerably by another element. It involves the issue of most appropriate or "correct" answers. These judgments are influenced enormously by the set of the subject regarding the test and the test situation.

As noted earlier, children, like most subjects, are not very enthusiastic about being tested. Except in those instances in which a subject is very strongly influenced by needs and/or an obsessional style to deliver as much as possible, most subjects restrict the number of answers that they give to the Rorschach. For instance, most 13-year-olds give between 17 and 25 answers, whether they are drawn from a patient or nonpatient population, whether they are from urban, suburban, or rural environments, and generally, regardless of the socioeconomic level of their family. This average range of responses is only slightly lower than occurs for adults, and only slightly higher than for significantly younger children. In their 1978 study, Exner et al. demonstrated that adult patients, tested by their own therapists, gave an average of 10 more responses than patients tested by a stranger.

To determine if this same influence appears in younger clients, Leura and Exner (1978) trained 10 volunteer junior high school teachers for four days (two consecutive weekends) in the basics of Rorschach administration (procedures of administration and scoring). Each was then asked to recruit two volunteer students from his or her class, with the criterion for selection being that the students were progressing very well (doing well-above-average work). No effort was made to judge the relationship of the teacher with the student. However, it was assumed that, because the student was doing very well in class, the relationship between the student and teacher was positive. The 20 volunteer students were all 13-year-olds, in seventh-grade classes. They were randomized into two groups, so that each teacher tested one student from his or her own class and one student with whom the teacher had no association. All testing was audiotape-recorded to ensure that no unusual dialogue occurred during the test administration. The protocols were then scored by one of four technicians, none of whom was aware of the purpose of the study. Data were analyzed using a series of F tests for frequencies or *chi*-square analyses when proportions were involved. Table 1 summarizes some of the findings.

These findings are strikingly similar to those reported by Exner et al. in which therapists tested their own patients; that is, significantly more responses are given to the

Table 1.   A Comparison of 28 Variables for Two Groups of 13-Year-Olds—One Group Tested by Their Own Teacher

Variable	Tested by Own Teacher $N = 10$		Tested by Unknown Teacher $N = 10$	
	M	SD	M	SD
R	38.2*	7.1	22.6	5.4
Popular	9.1	2.8	7.7	2.3
Zf	15.7*	4.1	11.2	3.7
Lambda	.49	.37	.74*	.29
M	6.9*	3.1	3.7	2.9
FM	5.8*	2.9	3.9	2.7
m	2.1	0.8	0.9	1.1
Active	9.7*	2.8	5.3	2.1
Passive	5.1	2.7	3.2	1.2
FC	4.1	1.9	2.4	1.7
CF+C	4.3	1.6	2.9	0.8
Sum C	6.7*	2.8	4.2	2.3
Afr	.72	.19	.66	.23
Sum T	1.9	0.9	1.1	0.4
Sum V	0.4	0.6	0.2	0.4
Sum C'	1.5	1.1	1.4	0.7
Sum Y	0.8	0.9	0.7	0.9
Sum Shad	4.5	2.1	3.4	1.6
X+%	.73	.13	.77	.15
3r+(2)/R	.44	.14	.46	.13
Sum 5 Sp Sc	4.2	1.9	3.7	1.6
EA	13.6*	4.7	7.9	2.8
es	12.4*	3.5	8.2	2.3
W	13.9*	3.8	8.2	2.7
Dd	5.9*	2.4	2.1	1.3
Blends	6.2*	2.3	4.1	2.1
Human Content	6.1	2.2	4.9	2.0
Animal Content	17.8*	4.7	8.1	2.6

* = significantly larger mean or proportion, $p < .05$.

examiner who is familiar with the subject, with the major elevations in the structural data occurring in *M,* color responses, and blends, and significant increases in the use of *W* and *Dd* as location areas. Interestingly, with the exception of the location features, the proportion of determinants does not change substantially for the "own-teacher" group compared with controls. In other words, even though they gave significantly more Human Movement and color answers, the proportions of each in relation to *R* are similar for both groups. The largest differences between the groups involve the values for Lambda, *EA,* and *es.* The own-teacher group have substantially lower Lambda values and significantly higher values for *EA* and *es.* Although the *EA* and *es* values are much higher for the own-teacher group, this fact does not change the resulting D Scores. Conversely, those high scores give a false impression concerning accessible resources and ongoing stimulus demands.

Although the relationship between the subject and examiner can form an important set, another element probably forms a more important set for most subjects. It concerns correct or acceptable answers. Every experienced Rorschacher has encountered the subject who seems to need some reinforcement or validation concerning his or her responses. These pleas usually occur in the form of direct questions put to an examiner during the Response Phase of the test, such as "Is that right?" "Do you see it, too?" "What do most people see?" "Am I doing it right?" or "Is that what you want?" These gestures occur much more commonly among children than they do among adults, possibly because children are more influenced by their daily experiences in which "passing" and "failing" are emphasized, or possibly because children reveal their own needs more readily.

Whatever the cause, most subjects are influenced in responding to the Rorschach by some need to "pass the test," or at least to avoid saying anything that might be interpreted to their detriment. Social influence appears to play an important role in this process. For example, when Exner et al. subdivided their adult nonpatient population on the basis of scores on the Minnesota Multiphasic Personality Inventory (MMPI) *K* Scale, which is at least partially a measure of social desirability, they found that those in the high *K* group gave significantly fewer responses than those in the low *K* group. This suggests that, as the need to make socially desirable responses increases, performance on the Rorschach will be marked by more caution and some constriction.

In a related study (Exner & Leura, 1976), it was demonstrated that adult nonpatients were quite willing to endorse responses of a sexual or aggressive content as "easy to see" when they thought those answers were given frequently by successful businessmen, whereas a control group judged the same responses as "difficult to see" when under the impression that they were commonly given by seriously disturbed schizophrenics.

The influence on the response process by elements such as set and the orientation toward making socially desirable responses is probably evoked by the nature of the test itself. It is likely that many or even most examiners have, at one time or another, tried to ease the apparent anxiety or concern of a subject by indicating that the Rorschach is a test in which there are no "right" or "wrong" answers. In reality, that is not true. There is one truly correct answer to each card: *It is an inkblot* (Exner, 1980), and to be sure, it is only an inkblot. Nonetheless, if the subject appeals, "But it's only an inkblot," the examiner will usually reply with something such as, "Yes, it's the inkblot test, but what does it look like—what might it be?"

In this context, the test becomes one involving problem solving. The problem facing the subject requires some violation of reality; that is, defining an inkblot as being something other than an inkblot. Even worse for the subject, there are no guidelines or prior experiences that are directly applicable to this somewhat unusual task; no information about how many things are to be identified, how creative or imaginative one should try to be, or about how others have approached the task; and no warning that later, the subject will be asked to justify his or her responses. The examiner remains ambiguous and noncommittal with phrases such as, "People see all kinds of things."

Thus, the nature of the Rorschach task and the lack of models and/or precise rules leave the subject in a somewhat isolated position. When the subject becomes overly cautious and delivers only one answer to the first card, a prompting occurs: "I think if you'll take your time you'll probably find something else, too." The prompt only serves to make the task more complex and aggravates any sense of caution that may already exist. Thus, the nature of the test tends to arouse sets that may be present within the subject but also stimulates the core psychological makeup of the subject, that is, his or her basic habits or styles. In many instances, those core features override or at least "seep through" some of the guardedness provoked by the sets.

PHASE 3 OF THE RESPONSE PROCESS: FINAL SELECTION OF ANSWERS

Phase 3 of the response process may be the most complex, because it involves the final selection of answers to be delivered and also involves their articulation. It is during this phase that the core psychology of the subject seems to have its greatest impact. In spite of the rescanning and reevaluation of potential answers that has occurred in Phase 2, several seemingly acceptable responses remain, and the subject is still faced with choices. Although the core psychological features have been influential earlier, by orienting scanning procedures or playing a role when potential answers are compared or judged in the context of social acceptability, their role in Phase 3 takes on a new dimension when closure is required and final decisions must be made public.

It is the decision-making requirement that affords sturdiness to the test. It calls into action the variety of psychological response styles that have developed through time and experience in other coping situations. Most people, even children, tend to approach problem solving in ways that are relatively consistent. As the child grows, he or she develops psychological habits that have increasing probabilities of recurring as they prove effective in reducing stress or enabling the person to cope effectively with everyday life situations. Thus, when the subject approaches the problem-solving (what is it), decision-making (what shall I say) task posed in the Rorschach, the operations involved in selecting some responses from a much broader array of possible answers are markedly influenced by these repetitious psychological features.

These styles or traits are manifest regularly in most overt behaviors, and typically they form the basis from which descriptive judgments about a person are made by others. For instance, it is not uncommon to hear a child being identified as "very thoughtful," or "very emotional," or "too impulsive," or "very meticulous," or "hyperactive," and so on. Some judgments such as these may be erroneous because they are formed too hastily, but others, especially those formed over time and based on many observations, can be reasonably accurate. But, however accurate, most such descriptions do not encompass the full breadth of the person. Much richer and more precise information is available if the *covert* perceptual-cognitive-affective operations of the person can be studied.

The Rorschach provides an indirect view of some of the covert operations of the person, mainly because it includes a method of coding or scoring the products of these operations. A large data pool has evolved from which psychological-behavioral correlates have been established for the scoring categories and various clusters or configurations of scores (Exner, 1974, 1978, 1986, 1991, 1993). These findings provide much of the validation data for the Rorschach, and as the research yield has increased, a greater understanding has unfolded about which features of the person are relatively static (traits or styles) and which are more subject to variation under different situations (states).

For example, when viewing Card I, one person may articulate a bat (F), whereas another person, responding to the same stimulus field, may articulate a black bat (FC'), and still another may report a bat in flight (FM^a). Similarly, for Card III, one person may report two people lifting something (M^a), whereas another may describe the same stimulus field as two people looking at each other (M^p); to Card VI, one person may attribute an animal skin that has jagged edges (F), whereas a second person, using the same blot area, may report an animal skin that has a furry appearance because of the different colors (FT). These differences reflect something about the differences that exist among people and in some ways, illustrate different stylistic features. Most single Rorschach codes or scores, however, cannot be interpreted in an isolated manner as defining the presence of a style or feature. It is the accumulation, or redundancy, of codes or scores that begins to suggest the presence of certain psychological features.

For example, some people obviously strive to subdivide the blot and reorganize it meaningfully ($DQ+$), whereas others seem oriented to giving answers that involve only the use of common detail areas of the blots in a simple fashion (DQo). The former may be intellectually bright, or somewhat obsessive, or achievement oriented, whereas the latter may be very conservative, or highly defensive, or even intellectually dull. No final judgment concerning these or other possible hypotheses can be generated from the respective scores for the two variables. Nevertheless, the consistency by which they occur does provide a clue about their respective cognitive approaches to decision making, or at least about the processing of information that will ultimately contribute to decisions.

Typically, it is the unusual frequencies of some kinds of codes or scores, or of interrelated scores, that will signal the presence of marked personality styles. For instance, some people give large numbers of human movement answers and very few chromatic color responses. They are manifesting an introversive style, indirectly reflecting that they prefer to think things through before taking overt action. For others, the reverse may be true. They deliver many chromatic color answers, but very few human movement responses. They are extratensive people who tend to indulge their feelings and prefer a trial-and-error approach in most problem-solving situations.

The repetition of specific kinds of answers does not always reflect a persistent psychological trait or style. Some sorts of answers may represent transient characteristics. For instance, the inanimate movement response (m) has been shown to be highly unstable over time and is apparently a corollary of some kind of psychological experience associated with situational stress. An m response is not expected to appear more than once in most protocols, and when it does, there is a significant probability that the person is experiencing some form of situationally related stress. The same is found for the Y determinant.

Other frequencies for determinants may also be more transient than permanent. For example, it is quite unusual for the subject who gives the Popular "bat" response to Card I to articulate the grey-black features of the blot as relevant to the response. This occurs an average of 1.6 times in each 100 "bat" responses given to Cards I or V by nonpatient adults and even less frequently among children under the age of 14. However, when either of these two Popular "bat" responses is given by 100 inpatient depressives, the frequency with which the grey-black features are articulated soars to 22.3. When these same depressive patients are retested, after their depression has abated, they tend to repeat the Popular "bat" answers to either Card I or Card V with about the same frequency but mention the grey-black features in only 3.8 per 100 bat responses.

Although some psychological characteristics are transient, such as those apparently represented in the *m* and *Y* answers in the Rorschach, many other features become much more consistent as the person grows older and the consistency of his or her response styles, or psychological habits, increases. This accounts for much of the regularity or predictability that characterizes most adults. Children are much less consistent over time than adults; however, some response features do tend to solidify rather early in the developmental process. Thus, when using the Rorschach with the younger client, it becomes vitally important to understand which variables of the test may represent stable characteristics in light of the age of the subject, and which are likely to change over time. Some information concerning this issue may be obtained by studying the reliability or temporal consistency of the numerous test variables with various groups and for some younger subjects retested several times during an 8-year period.

TEMPORAL CONSISTENCY OF RORSCHACH VARIABLES

Numerous temporal consistency studies concerning the Rorschach have been completed with adults, and these studies illustrate that the majority of the variables included in the Comprehensive System are very sturdy over time. Possibly the most extensive of these studies involved the retesting of 100 nonpatients after a 3-year interval. Retest correlations ranged from 0.90 for the Affective Ratio to 0.66 for the Sum of all Grey-Black and Shading responses, with most of the correlations falling between 0.75 and 0.87 (Exner, Armbruster, & Viglione, 1978). In a second long-term study, involving 50 nonpatient adults retested after 1 year, the results were quite similar, with most retest correlations being somewhat higher than those from the 3-year retest (Exner, 1986).

This kind of temporal stability is not expected in the protocols of children, especially over lengthy time intervals. The voluminous literature in developmental psychology illustrates extensive changes that occur in the younger person during relatively brief intervals. This is particularly true for the very young child. The differences between the perceptual-cognitive-affective operations of 5-year-olds and those of 7-year-olds are, ordinarily, many times greater than the differences between the operations of 13- and 15-year-old children.

The lack of consistency in many psychological operations of the child, when viewed over lengthy periods, is illustrated by a temporal consistency study involving retesting of two groups of children after long periods (Exner, 1980). The first consisted of 30 nonpatient children who were administered Rorschachs for the first time shortly after entering the first grade. They included 17 females and 13 males, and all were between the ages of 6 years, 2 months, and 6 years, 5 months. Ten examiners were used in the first testing, with no examiner collecting more than four records. These subjects were retested approximately 24 months later, 6 weeks after entering the third grade, by 10 different examiners with none collecting more than three records. The second group consisted of 25 nonpatient 9-year-olds, 14 females and 11 males, first tested while in the fourth grade and retested approximately 30 months later. Eight examiners were used for both testings, with no examiner taking more than four records or testing the same child twice. The resulting retest correlations for these two groups, plus those for 100 adults retested after 3 years, are shown in Table 2.

The criterion for adequate temporal consistency has been variously defined. Usually, a minimum retest correlation of .75 (accounting for 50% of the variance) is satisfactory if the retest interval is considerable, although requiring a higher minimum correlation (.80 or .85) if the retest occurs after only a brief period. The data in Table 2 reveal that the liberal minimum of .75 occurs in the adult sample for 16 of the 23 variables, but for only 4 of the 23 variables in the retest findings for 6-year-olds retested at 8 years (Popular, Active movement, $X + \%$, and Egocentricity Index), and 4 of the variables in the retests of 9-year-olds retested at age 11 (Active Movement, Afr, Sum T, and $X + \%$). Only 2 variables are consistently high for both groups ($X + \%$ and Active movement). All other variables show considerable diversity in the retest correlations for both groups of children. In other words, the retest data for both groups suggest that the distribution of scores for most variables is very different from that in the first test.

Extrapolation from these findings affirms that long-term predictions based on Rorschach data concerning the psychological organization or activity of children generally are unwarranted. That conclusion is supported by the results of a more elaborate longitudinal study of nonpatient children (Exner, Thomas, & Mason, 1985). This study began

Table 2.   Retest Correlations for 23 Variables for Two Groups of Children and 100 Adults

Variable	Group 1; $N = 30$ 1st Test Age 6 2nd Test Age 8	Group 2; $N = 25$ 1st Test Age 9 2nd Test Age 11	Adults; $N = 100$ 2nd Test after 3 Years
R	.67	.61	.79
Popular	.77	.74	.73
Zf	.55	.68	.83
Lambda	.18	.39	.82
M	.48	.62	.87
FM	.49	.60	.72
m	.13	.09	.31
Active	.86	.81	.86
Passive	.42	.29	.75
FC	.38	.34	.86
CF+C	.27	.35	.79
Sum C	.41	.58	.86
Afr	.51	.79	.90
Sum T	.68	.84	.87
Sum V	—	.91	.81
Sum C'	.68	.51	.67
Sum Y	.09	.17	.23
Sum Shad	.08	.29	.66
X+%	.84	.86	.80
3r+(2)/R	.78	.74	.87
Sum 5 Sp Sc	.60	.56	.88
EA	.19	.45	.85
es	.20	.57	.72

with the testing of 80 eight-year-old subjects, 40 males and 40 females, all between the ages of 8 years, 2 months, and 8 years, 5 months. By agreement with the parents, the child was to be available for retesting at each 2-year interval until the age of 16, in return for which a deposit of $25 would be made on behalf of the child in a savings plan after each test was completed, the funds from which would be available to the child after the 4th retest. Unfortunately, 23 subjects dropped out the study at various intervals, so that only 57 subjects actually were tested five times. Nonetheless, the retest correlations at each interval for the 57 subjects completing the study are impressive when reviewed in light of the issue of long-term predictions. Table 3 shows the retest correlations from one test to the next for 23 Rorschach variables.

The retest correlations for only three variables (Popular, Active movement, $X + \%$) appear to remain stable during the entire 8-year cycle, and even during the 2-year interval between ages of 12 and 14 only seven variables have retest correlations of .75 or greater, representing considerable temporal stability of operations related to them. The number of temporally consistent variables increases to 11 when data for the interval between ages 14 and 16 are reviewed. The results should not be surprising in view of information that has accumulated about the substantial changes that occur during the developmental years. The low retest correlations do not reflect on the validity of the test with children, but they do indicate that Rorschach data collected at

Table 3. Retest Correlations for 23 Variables for Each Two-Year Interval for 57 Subjects Tested Five Times with the First Test Administered at Age 8

Variable	Ages 8 to 10 Test 1 vs. 2	Ages 10 to 12 Test 2 vs. 3	Ages 12 to 14 Test 3 vs 4	Ages 14 to 16 Test 4 vs. 5
R	.61	.57	.76	.80
Popular	.75	.81	.82	.82
Zf	.52	.40	.42	.70
Lambda	.32	.28	.68	.78
M	.53	.47	.69	.77
FM	.64	.60	.51	.81
m	.32	.11	.29	.06
Active	.77	.86	.79	.83
Passive	.62	.75	.71	.78
FC	.63	.39	.76	.73
CF+C	.70	.47	.26	.72
Sum C	.76	.63	.38	.69
Afr	.69	.52	.33	.76
Sum T	.73	.82	.89	.91
Sum V	—	.92	.84	.92
Sum C'	.58	.54	.54	.69
Sum Y	.44	.07	.23	.13
Sum Shad	.64	.51	.63	.71
X+%	.82	.84	.80	.85
3r+(2)/R	.61	.43	.54	.73
Sum 5 Sp Sc	.70	.56	.47	.68
EA	.62	.51	.63	.71
es	.42	.62	.68	.73

one time during the active developmental cycle may not predict very accurately what the Rorschach data for that same subject will be at a much later time.

To what extent then, can Rorschach findings be considered to represent a consistent picture in the psychological makeup and operations of the child? During shorter periods, greater consistency for other variables can be expected. This is illustrated in the retest results for three small samples (Exner, 1986, 1993). The first involved the retest of 35 nonpatient adults after 3 weeks. Six examiners were used for each test with no examiner testing the same subject twice. The second group consisted of 25 8-year-old, third-grade students retested after 7 days (Exner, 1980). Six examiners were involved, with none testing the same subject twice. The third group included 35 nine-year-old, fourth-grade subjects, retested after 3 weeks. They were tested by nine examiners, none of whom tested the same subject twice. The retest correlations for each of the groups are shown in Table 4.

The data for these three groups are remarkably similar and consist mainly of very high retest correlations. This indicates that, for each group, the configuration of the second record was highly similar to that of the first. Among the 8-year-olds retested after 1 week, 20 of the 23 variables have retest correlations of .75 or higher and most exceed .80. Among the 9-year-olds retested after 3 weeks, 18 of the 23 variables have retest correlations of .75 or greater, the same number that are greater than .75 for the adult sample. Thus, although the data presented in Tables 2 and 3 indicate that most Rorschach vari-

Table 4.   Retest Correlations for 23 Variables for Two Groups of Children and 35 Adults

Variable	8-Year-Olds Retested after 7 Days; $N = 25$	9-Year-Olds Retested after 3 Weeks; $N = 35$	Adults Retested after 3 Weeks; $N = 35$
R	.88	.87	.84
Popular	.86	.89	.81
Zf	.91	.92	.89
Lambda	.86	.84	.76
M	.90	.87	.83
FM	.75	.78	.72
m	.49	.20	.34
Active	.91	.91	.87
Passive	.86	.88	.85
FC	.90	.84	.92
CF+C	.89	.92	.83
Sum C	.88	.87	.83
Afr	.91	.91	.85
Sum T	.86	.92	.96
Sum V	.96	.93	.89
Sum C'	.77	.74	.77
Sum Y	.42	.17	.41
Sum Shad	.76	.68	.71
X+%	.95	.92	.87
3r+(2)/R	.94	.86	.90
Sum 5 Sp Sc	.91	.93	.94
EA	.85	.87	.84
es	.74	.70	.59

ables will not be very stable for children over long periods, the data in Table 4 indicate considerable stability for almost all Rorschach variables during relatively brief intervals.

The remaining question is how reliable the Rorschach may be during intervals of less than 2 years, but more than 3 weeks, for different age groups. Thousands of tests would be necessary to answer that question in detail; however, some useful information may be gleaned from retest data collected for two groups of youngsters differing considerably in age at the first testing (Exner, 1980). These groups involved 20 subjects each, with the retest administered between 260 and 290 days (approximately 9 months) after the first test. Ten of the 20 subjects in each group were black or Hispanic, drawn from an inner city population; the remaining 10 subjects in each group were drawn from suburban areas. The main proviso for selection, in addition to parental consent, was that the child was making passing grades in school. The 20 subjects in the first group were between the ages of 7 years, 2 months, and 7 years, 7 months, at the time of the first test. At that time all were in the second grade, and all were in the third grade at the time of the retest. The 20 subjects in the second group ranged in age from 15 years, 3 months, to 15 years, 8 months, at the time of the first test and all were in tenth-grade classes. All were beginning the eleventh grade at the time of the retest.

Twenty-one examiners were used to collect the 80 records in this study, with no examiner collecting more than four protocols and none retesting the same subject. All records were scored by the examiner administering the test, and then 20 of the 40 records from each group were also scored by one of five skilled technicians who had no awareness of the purpose of the study, or that a retest had been involved. Percentage of agreement between scorers for both groups of records range from 83% concerning special scores to 99% regarding issues of location and/or developmental quality. The results for these two 9-month retest groups are shown in Table 5.

The retest data for the 7-year-olds are not remarkably different from those found for the groups of 8- and 9-year-olds retested after 2 years. Only 5 of the 23 variables have retest correlations of .75 or greater. Thus, it must be concluded that considerable change occurs in the psychological organization and activity of the very young child, even during an interval as brief as 9 months. Again, this is not very surprising in light of findings from developmental psychology that indicate very rapid changes usually occur at this age. It is a critical period, when the complexity of the cortex is developing and some of the higher levels of abstraction begin to occur. There is much greater consistency during the 9-month interval for the 15-year-old group than for the 7-year-old group. A .75 or greater retest correlation occurs for 13 of the 23 variables, and in fact, most are .80 or higher. Many of the retest correlations are quite similar to those obtained from adults retested over even longer periods. This suggests that many of the personality features represented by Rorschach variables are stabilizing or have stabilized by the mid-adolescent period.

The composite of these temporal consistency studies provides considerable information that is important when interpreting the Rorschach. First, and most obvious, the data emphasize that children do indeed change over time, and the younger the child, the more change may be expected during relatively brief periods. Therefore, it would be erroneous to assume that test findings developed from a record taken at age 5, 7, 8, or even 10 will yield many indications of things to come. These results also suggest that as subjects age, especially into middle or late adolescence, the likelihood that the results will reflect a more stabilized psychological profile increases, particularly for some variables. The features represented by the $X + \%$ (mediational conventionality) appear to become stable quite early, possibly in the preschool years. On the other hand, the

Table 5.   **Retest Correlations for 23 Variables for Two Groups of 20 Children Each Retested after Approximately Nine Months**

Variable	7-Year-Olds $N = 20$	15-Year-Olds $N = 20$
R	.71	.80
Popular	.88	.83
Zf	.62	.79
Lambda	.24	.76
M	.46	.82
FM	.53	.70
m	.06	.17
Active	.77	.85
Passive	.39	.64
FC	.28	.81
CF+C	.41	.71
Sum C	.37	.70
Afr	.61	.89
Sum T	.75	.87
Sum V	—	.92
Sum C'	.49	.73
Sum Y	.21	.16
Sum Shad	.11	.48
X+%	.86	.83
3r+(2)/R	.70	.86
Sum 5 Sp Sc	.79	.88
EA	.23	.73
es	.18	.64

tendency to solve problems using deliberate ideation, as illustrated by a preponderance of *M* answers (introversive style), may not occur until the mid-adolescent years.

One of the sturdiest features found among the Rorschachs of adults is the *Erlebnistypus,* calculated as the Sum of *M* in relation to the Weighted Sum of Color responses. As noted earlier, Rorschach postulated that subjects giving significantly more *M* responses than the Weighted Sum *C* are introversive people who prefer to delay and think things through before manifesting behaviors. On the opposite side of the coin are persons giving significantly more Weighted Sum of Color responses than *M*. They are extratensive people who tend to involve their emotions in decision making and take a more trial-and-error approach to problem solving. Rorschach's postulates concerning these two basic response styles have been validated by the results of many investigations (Exner, 1978, 1991). These two styles of coping are quite different, although neither appears to be preferable with respect to incidence of psychopathology, effectiveness of coping or problem solving, or a variety of measures of adjustment.

An issue yet to be fully resolved concerns when these styles, which might best be described as *internalization* and *externalization,* actually fall into place in the development of the psychology of the young person. The findings from the 8-year longitudinal study may shed some light on this issue. Only 9 of the 57 subjects completing that study showed an introversive style at age 8, and 6 of the 9 persisted in that style at age 10. Fourteen subjects manifested the introversive style at age 10, as did 15 subjects tested at age 12. Twelve of those 15 subjects had manifest the introversive style at age 10. At age 14, there were 16 introversive subjects in the group, including 14 of the 15 subjects who were introversive at age 12. At age 16, there were 21 introversive subjects, including 15 of the 16 subjects who were introversive at age 14. Conversely, 25 of the 57 subjects gave records indicating extratensiveness at age 8. When the group was retested at age 10, there were 21 extratensives, but they included only 12 of the 25 subjects who were extratensive in the first test. However, at age 12, 21 of the 57 subjects showed an extratensive style, of whom 17 had been extratensive in the age 10 retest; at age 14, 23 subjects were extratensive including 21 who had been extratensive at age 12; and at age 16, 26 of the 57 subjects manifest an extratensive style including 22 who had shown this style at age 14.

These findings suggest that the presence or absence of either style is not very important for the person early in life. In fact, most children probably do not manifest any marked style through most of the developmental years. The data do, however, indicate that, if an introversive style develops early in the developmental span, it is likely to persist, whether or not it is advantageous in coping and problem solving. There are obvious hazards to the premature development of an introversive style. Usually, children younger than ages 11 or 12 do not have enough cortical development to conceptualize issues very thoroughly, especially when more abstract concepts are involved. Thus, if an introversive style develops prematurely, a risk exists for many ideational tactics to become stylized that are overly concrete.

The data from the longitudinal study suggest that most children tend to fluctuate between an extratensive style and the lack of a persistent style (ambient) during most of their developmental years. For instance, 25 of the 57 subjects showed an extratensive style at age 8, but only 12 of the 25 continued to be extratensive at age 10. Similarly, 21 subjects were extratensive at age 12, but they included only 17 who had been extratensive at age 10. At age 14, the sample included 23 extratensives, 21 of whom had been extratensive at age 12, and at age 16, the sample consisted of 26 extratensives, 22 of whom had been extratensive at age 14. Stated differentially, the extratensive style seems to stabilize among nonpatient children at about the age of 12 or 13. These findings seem confirmed by the standardization data for nonpatient children and adolescents. Few of the children in the younger age groups show the characteristics of a prominent coping style, either extratensive or introversive. But, at some time during the teen years, usually between the ages of 13 and 16, the more permanent style does takes form, and, with few exceptions, it does not change over time.

THE ISSUE OF PROJECTION IN THE RORSCHACH

Responses are often articulated in a very idiographic manner. Obviously, what is *articulated* in the response is a critical part of the test process, and this often includes the actual content of the response or the way in which the content is elaborated. Responses often include projected material that develops in Phases 1 or 2 of the process or is incorporated into the answer as it is delivered in Phase 3. Most projected material provides information about self-perceptions, attitudes, or conceptions of the environment and those in it. The interpretation of projected material often contributes much information regarding the idiography of the subject, but it is important to caution against the faulty assumption that every Rorschach answer will have projected features.

The Rorschach situation does not discourage projection. However, unlike tests that are designed to force projection, such as the *Thematic Apperception Test,* in which the subject is asked to create a story that goes well beyond the stimulus field (What is happening? What are the characters feeling or thinking? What led up to the event? What will be the outcome?), the subject taking the Rorschach is simply asked, "What might this be?" This instruction creates somewhat narrow parameters for the subject that are made even more so by the fact that the blots are not completely ambiguous as has often been purported by some in the projective psychology movement. The limited ambiguity of the stimulus fields of the blots plus the nature of the task do not encourage projection. At the same time, they do not prohibit or discourage unique translations or embellishments that almost certainly have some projected properties. As a result, projected features seem to occur in some answers, but not necessarily all answers and, in fact, it is possible for a subject to give a reliable, valid protocol without including any projected material in the responses, although this does not happen often, even in the records of younger clients.

The Rorschach has been erroneously mislabeled as a "projective test" for far too long, and that label has created many faulty inferences about the test process and tactics of interpreting the test data. Projection is only a possibility in the Rorschach. Because the inkblots are far less ambiguous than has been assumed, some answers simply result from classifying the blot or blot area in ways that are compatible with the stimulus field. They are not projections. But, projections can and do occur in spite of the limited ambiguity of the stimuli. There are probably two types of projected responses: One is formed during the Phase 1 operations and the second is formed during the Phase 2 or Phase 3 operations.

Projection and Phase 1   Although the potent stimulus elements within each blot tend to facilitate the formation of certain responses or classes of response, the demands or restrictions created by their characteristics also tend to reduce the likelihood that projection will be involved in most Phase 1 operations. Nonetheless, classifications of blots or blot areas in ways that violate or ignore these prevalent features do occur. Technically, they are minus answers, and if they are not the product of some neurophysiologically related dysfunction in perceptual operations, it seems logical to postulate that they are the result of a mediational activity in which internal psychological sets or operations have superseded a reality-oriented translation of the field. In other words, some form of projection may be involved (Exner, 1989).

Projection and Phases 2 and 3   Although it is likely that projection sometimes plays a role during the Phase 1 classifications of the blot, it seems much more probable that the impact of the process, if it occurs, will be greater during the Phase 2 and 3 operations. During these operations, a process such as described by Symonds (1946) as interpretive projection and by White (1944) and Murray (1951) as imaginative projection becomes involved when the subject overelaborates or departs from the stimulus field. As each potential answer is reviewed, judged, and refined, the circumstance exists during which a subject may embellish the answer.

For example, most children who are shown a toy airplane and asked what it is will answer that it is an airplane. But even within the parameters of that narrow stimulus field, a child might expand the answer by saying, "It's a plane but nobody knows how to fly it." Likewise, most children who are asked, "How much is three times two?" will answer "six," but again, the answer could be embellished in a projected manner with,

"If you bet a lot of sixes in the lotto, you'll have good luck." Such an elaboration reflects something about the person who gives it, because there is nothing in the stimulus field or in the question posed that provokes it.

In each of these examples, the nature of the tasks, that is, identifying an object or multiplying numbers, reduces the probability that projection will occur. It can occur, but usually it will not because the parameters of the task and the field are so narrow. But in the Rorschach, the parameters of both the task and the field are broader. Although the limited ambiguity of the stimulus field and the nature of the task do not encourage projection, they do not prohibit or discourage unique translations or embellishments that almost certainly have some projected properties. As a result, projected characteristics occur in the judgments made concerning some answers in Phase 2, and they continue to be weighed positively during the Phase 3 operations, ultimately appearing in the protocol.

As suggested by Piotrowski (1957, 1969), the majority of answers that include this kind of projection do not require much interpretive translation because of their obvious departure from or overelaboration of the stimulus field such as occurs in many movement responses, or answers in which an object is described with considerable embellishment. In some instances, a single answer that includes projected material can provide a wealth of interpretive information concerning the subject, but that sort of answer is quite rare. In most protocols, it is the redundancy of themes or classes of projected material that generates the greatest interpretive yield. Some responses that appear to have projected features may be nothing more than straightforward translations of the blot stimuli.

For instance, most children give at least one passive movement answer, which has little interpretive significance. However, research concerning high frequencies of passive movement answers has contributed much to the understanding of both passive-dependent and passive-aggressive coping styles, and when passive features are predominant among human movement answers, they signal an abusive use of fantasy as a defensive tactic (Exner, 1978, 1991, 1993). Similarly, most children deliver at least one embellished response containing morbid content (MOR), which alone means little, but data reveal that subjects who give high frequencies of these answers feel more damaged, unwanted, or unqualified and harbor much more pessimism about themselves and their world than do those who do not give many of these kinds of responses (Exner, 1986; Exner & Weiner, 1982). Data concerning aggressive movement answers (AG) indicate that children who give higher-than-average frequencies of such answers manifest significantly more aggressive verbal and nonverbal behaviors, mainly because they have come to regard aggressiveness as a natural element in interpersonal relationships (Exner, 1991, 1993).

When themes or classes of projected material occur with a substantial frequency, it is probably erroneous to think of them as *indirect* representations of the psychological features of people. Instead, as Piotrowski argued, they are probably direct reflections of the feelings and/or behaviors of people.

SUMMARY OF THE RESPONSE PROCESS

The response process involves a complicated set of operations occurring in a relatively brief time span. Each answer that is articulated reflects something about the subject. Some are rather straightforward manifestations of processing and mediational activity that occur directly in accordance with the instructions of the examiner. Others are the products of much more complex activity in which traits, styles, sets, and preoccupations contribute significantly to the selection and articulation of the answer. If additional data were available about the nature of the blot stimuli, it would be easier to glean more precise information concerning which characteristics have contributed to the formulation and selection of specific answers. But even the current state of knowledge regarding blot characteristics often provides sufficient data to address clusters of information logically and translate them in a manner that enhances understanding of the subject's psychological organization and functioning.

COLLECTING THE PROTOCOL

Much of the preceding material emphasizes the importance of the structural data derived from the scoring of the responses. Those responses should be collected in a standardized manner. The appropriate procedures for Rorschach administration have been elaborated elsewhere (Exner, 1990, 1993), but those procedures are so critical to the effective use of the test, especially with younger clients, that some aspects of them warrant emphasis here.

Every examiner should take care to avoid providing any sets about the test, and certainly should avoid reinforcing any particular kinds of responses. Seating should be side by side, except in those rare instances when the examiner feels it important to alter that routine. Such alterations are most likely to occur with the very young child, such as the 5- or 6-year-old who may feel ill at ease sitting in a large chair or working at a table or desk designed for an adult. In such situations, the examiner might decide to test sitting on the floor, standing or, in very unusual circumstances, outdoors. All have been explored, and there is no reason to believe that these somewhat peculiar alterations provoke unusual Rorschachs; that is probably because the examiners using these altered routines have been faithful to the standardized procedures.

It also is always wise to preface any testing, and particularly the Rorschach, with some brief but honest statement about the process so that the subject is aware of the purpose of the examination. Prior to the administration of specific tests, some time should also be devoted to making the client feel at ease with the situation. Ordinarily, this should not take very much time, but quite often children are disturbed by being "looked at," and extra time may be required to stimulate a minimally cooperative attitude. Experience suggests that the more a client understands the assessment procedure, including what will happen after the testing, the more willing the client will be to participate. Thus, the task of the examiner, prior to any testing, is to take some of the mystery out of the process.

The Rorschach consists of 10 inkblots, and there is no reason to avoid calling them inkblots. Most people, even children, have heard of the inkblot test, and children have very often made their own inkblots in the classroom. The nature of the task is also described in a straightforward manner: "What might this be—what does it look like?" Children tend to ask many more questions about the test than do adults and, within reason, the examiner should answer these questions. "Did you make these?" ("No they are printed.") "What do other people see?" ("People see lots of different things.") "What do you see?" ("Let's see what you see, first, and I'll tell you later if you want me to.") "Is that right?" ("If it looks like that to you.") "How many of these are there?" ("Ten.") "Why are you writing everything down?" ("So I can remember what you saw.") There are very few questions asked that cannot be answered directly and honestly. If a question requires a lengthy and involved answer, it is probably best to defer the answer until the test is complete, but in a tactful way. ("Let's finish the test first, and then I'll tell you. In fact, let me write that down so I don't forget.")

Similar caution about avoiding sets must be exercised during the Inquiry. The Inquiry should always be prefaced with an explanation about the process again in a simple, honest, and straightforward manner: "We are going to go back through these now, and I'm going to read to you what you said. And I want you to show me where it is that you see that, and tell me why it looks like that, what is there that makes it look like that to you, so that I can see it just the way you did." It is crucial in the preface to the Inquiry to enlist the cooperation of the subject in identifying whatever he or she saw. The examiner does really want to see it just as the subject did, for when that is the case, the response is scored easily. The importance of introducing the Inquiry adequately cannot be overemphasized. It is a very delicate phase of the test, and if it is approached too casually by the examiner or is misunderstood by the subject, the result can become a nightmare, both in scoring and interpreting the record.

Questioning during the Inquiry should be done as necessary. Under optimal circumstances, the clarity of the preface to the Inquiry and the cooperation of the subject will eliminate the need for any questions, but this is not always the way it goes with children. Sometimes, a simple reminder to the child about the purpose will suffice. ("Wait, now. Remember, I want to see it just the way you did, so show it to me and tell me what there is to make it look like that.") In other instances, a somewhat more forceful prompt is required, ("I don't think I see it yet, help me.") Naturally, any key words offered in the Response or given spontaneously early in the Inquiry should be pursued. ("Wait a minute, you said it looks pretty?" or "I'm not sure why it looks terrible," or "Why does it look as if he's been hurt?" or "What do you mean, bumpy?") The objective in the Inquiry is to clarify what was seen during the response, and care should be taken to avoid prompting a "new look" at the percept. It is frustrating when an examiner has a hunch that a determinant exists but, in spite of nondirective questioning, that hunch does not prove valid. It is tempting to become directive, but to do so can alter the data significantly and evoke a picture of the perceptual-cognitive operations of the subject during the problem-solving task that is quite misleading.

Difficult Clients   When working with a youngster who seems especially resistive or uncooperative, the examiner should first decide whether to proceed with the testing. If the data seem essential to the purpose of the assessment, the examiner must next make a decision about altering the routine, but this decision should not be made hastily. Often the problem is not so much resistance to the test as it is anxiety or hyperactivity that makes it hard to keep the child in one place long enough to administer the test.

When these situations occur, the examiner may decide that the standard procedure might yield an incomplete record; that is, the examiner might not be able to coax the child through the entire test. Ames, Metraux, Rodell, and Walker (1974) have suggested that more useful records may be obtained if the Inquiry is accomplished after each card. The examiners used in developing the standardization data for the Comprehensive System have generally not found this to be the case, and fewer than 5% of the more than 3,000 records collected from children have actually involved this altered procedure.

To study this matter, 40 cooperative children, ages 5 to 7, were randomized into two groups, with one tested in the standardized manner and the second using an Inquiry after each card. The latter group did give significantly more responses (20.4 vs. 16.2 $p < .05$), but the only statistically significant differences that occurred in the structural data were increases in D and F answers (Leura & Exner, 1977). It would seem that the technique of challenging the subject after each card causes the child to oversimplify the stimulus or resist processing and/or articulation of the more complex blot features. Interestingly, most of the elevations in D and F answers occurred in Cards VI through X.

This is not to suggest that the technique of Inquiry after each blot should be abandoned completely, for there are clear instances in which the pretest behavior of the child warns of difficulty and the potential for rejection of the standard Inquiry procedure. The final judgment rests with the examiner, but when there is to be some variation from the standard procedure, he or she must be cautious and introduce the test in a way that makes the requirement of an Inquiry after each card very clear. Again, this will be the exception rather than the rule—even with the young child of 5 or 6—but if such an exception is necessary, the following instructions should be employed at the onset of the test:

> I want you to look at this and tell me what it might be, and I want you to show it to me so that I can see it, too. Show me where it is, and what makes it look like that, because I want to see what you see, just the way you see it.

When this modified procedure is used, questions are sharply limited and usually will be restricted to a reminder about the task such as, "Wait now, I can't see it yet. Help me so I can see what you see," or questions generated from key words spontaneously offered such as, "I'm not sure why they look as if they are in a circus," or "What makes it look pretty to you?" In both instances, the key words "circus" and "pretty" are spontaneously given by the subject. The examiner must be very cautious about pursuing key words offered as a result of some prompting question, for altogether too often, the suggestibility of the child makes him or her vulnerable to any kind of reinforcement, especially in the stress situation posed by the test. Thus, a new question, developed from a seemingly important word delivered in answer to a question, may provoke a new key word, and so on.

This modified technique of conducting the Inquiry during and after the administration of each card is not really satisfactory and should only be used as a last resort, and primarily in those cases where the Rorschach data are deemed essential to the assessment objectives. Nearly 2,100 protocols of nonpatient children were collected for the standardization samples for the Comprehensive System. These records were collected by 147 examiners, of both sexes, and ranging in age from 19 years to 68 years. There was no instance in which the examiner decided to alter the procedure of administration, even though the option existed and he or she had been trained to use the alternative method; and from a variety of anecdotal reports, it is clear that many of the subjects were not very cooperative.

Similarly, more than 1,000 protocols have been collected from patient children by more than 200 examiners. An alteration of standard procedure was employed in only 74 cases at the discretion of the examiners. Sixty-six of those cases involved children under the age of 8 years, 39 of whom displayed marked behavior problems, and the remaining 27 were schizophrenic children drawn from residential treatment centers. As these records were studied separately, it was decided that 24 of the 39 collected from the behavior problem children were probably not very useful as almost all consisted of simplistic Pure F responses. Twelve of the 27 protocols obtained from the schizophrenic children using the modified procedure of administration were also discarded for the same reason.

The Problem of Brief Records   Brief records have been a matter of concern in the Rorschach community for many years, especially to those who test children. The concern focuses on the reliability and validity of the test data. Younger children, both patients and nonpatients, tend toward brief records. For example, nonpatient children ages 5 through 8 average about 18 answers, as contrasted with an average of about 22 responses given by most patient and nonpatient adults. Children who are patients, especially those who are 11 years old or younger, also tend to give fewer answers, and not infrequently, a resistive subject may give fewer than 14 responses.

Exner (1988) has studied the reliability (temporal consistency) of brief protocols for both adults and children, using retest data from 10 studies, 4 of which involved children. The results make it clear that protocols of less than 14 answers are not temporally consistent, even over relatively brief intervals of 3 weeks or less. In other words, the findings show that the overwhelming majority of brief records will not have the level of reliability prerequisite to the assumption of interpretive validity. Records of less than 14 answers are often given by highly resistive subjects who are simply attempting to avoid the many demands of the test situation. In effect, these performances depict subtle refusals to take the test, and there is no easy way to distinguish between the low R record that is valid from one that is not.

Thus, as a rule, protocols in which the number of responses is less than 14 should probably be discarded on the premise that they are unreliable and as such are not interpretively valid. There will be some exceptions. The most common of these exceptions will be the protocols of severely disturbed patients in which the $X + \%$ is extremely low, the $X - \%$ is quite high, and two or three bizarre responses occur, *and for which other data exist confirming the magnitude of the disability*. The second exception involves those brief records in which extremely deviant response patterns, when compared with more modal response patterns, seem likely to persist even if a longer record is taken.

Most brief records are guarded, and tend to include some of the well-known characteristics of guardedness. These include a high Lambda, a profusion of Popular answers, an acceptable $X + \%$, many D locations, a narrow range of blend contents, and a minimum of verbiage in the response and Inquiry. An elaborated brief record that runs in opposite directions from these features of guardedness not only reveals some specific personality characteristics of the subject but often does so more clearly and dramatically than a longer record with similar features. Thus, the young person who gives only 12 answers of which half are minus and do not involve the use of S is likely to have impaired reality testing. Likewise, the brief record that includes six MOR responses conveys a significant indication of pessimistic thinking and negative body imagery. The presence of several *Sex* responses in a brief, presumably guarded record is quite likely to indicate a sexual preoccupation, and so on. Thus, any unusual or dramatic signs of personality disorder that break through the typical guardedness of a brief and otherwise generally invalid record are probably stable, and as such, provide significant information about some of the personality characteristics of the subject.

Unfortunately, brief records occur much more often than might be expected, particularly among the broad spectrum of younger clients. Some brief records from children reflect a form of subtle resistance to the test, but in many other instances, they simply result from following instructions very concretely and failing to generalize from encouragement given during Card I. Some subjects, especially younger children, want to go through the test as quickly as possible, and their haste produces a short record. In many instances, this is because the subject has not been prepared properly for the test or assessment situation. Whatever the cause, a record of less than 14 answers should not be accepted unless it is quite bizarre and/or dramatic in some ways that seem consistent with other information. Ordinarily, the brief record should not even be inquired.

Usually, when a brief record is taken the examiner should consider either of two options. The first is simply to discard the test and rely on other assessment data that are available to evaluate the subject. On the other hand, a second option exists if Rorschach data seem to be of importance to the assessment issue(s) that have been posed. It involves an immediate retest following the response phase of the test. To do so, the examiner should interrupt the standard procedure, which ordinarily means proceeding to describe the purpose of the Inquiry, and explain to the subject:

> Now you know how it's done. But there's a problem. You didn't give enough answers for us to get anything out of the test. So we will go through them again and this time I want you to make sure to give me more answers. You can include the same ones you've already given if you like but make sure to give me more answers this time.

Some subjects seek direction under this new circumstance and ask, "How many should I really give?" The response should depend mainly on whether the examiner feels that the subject has tried to be cooperative. For example, if the subject seems cooperative, it is appropriate to say, "Well, it's really up to you, but you only gave _____ answers and I really need more than that to get anything out of the test." If a subject obviously has been more resistive or guarded, the examiner should be more directive if a question is asked about how many answers are required, such as, "Well, it's up to you but I really need several more answers than you gave."

RETESTING AFTER A BRIEF PERIOD

Most Rorschachers have been reluctant to retest after a brief interval, assuming that the recent exposure to the stimulus figures would generate a very similar verbal record, or that previous exposure to the blots and the test routine would afford the subject opportunities to alter his or her responses in a manner that would change the interpretive outcome. Three studies suggest that this is not the case.

The first of these studies was designed to assess the stability of the major structural variables under a retest condition in which severely disturbed children were encouraged to improve their test performance (Hulsart, 1979). This study used 55 children who were between the ages of 11 and 15, drawn randomly from inpatient and day-care populations of a children's psychiatric unit. All were screened to ensure that none were intellectually deficient or exhibited significant evidence of neurological involvement. The 55 subjects were then randomized into two groups of 27 and 28 subjects and administered the Rorschach by one of eight examiners, none of whom had any awareness of the purpose of the study, using a standard procedure except that each subject was instructed to give two responses per card.

The retest was administered two days later, with each subject tested by a different examiner. The retest was introduced to one group by the project coordinator, who told each subject that the results of the first test had been reviewed by the staff, including the professional regarded as the most significant to the child, and the conclusion reached was, "We felt you did a good job, but we all felt you could do better. We'd like to give you a second chance at this test so we can see the very best you can do." The subjects in the second group were simply informed that at this facility the test is always administered twice.

All protocols were scored by a skilled clinician who had no awareness of which group or which test the protocol might be drawn from, and a randomly selected group of 20 records were also scored independently by a second skilled scorer. The two scorers agreed on 92% of all scores in the 20 selected records. The data were analyzed using a multivariate analysis, Hotelling's $T2$ technique, performed on the vector of mean differences between the groups, plus a series of analyses of variance for specific variables. The results indicated no significant differences for any of the major structural features for either test between or within the groups, even though many of the responses given by the subjects in the experimental group during the second test were quite different from those delivered in the first test.

The findings of the Hulsart study, though intriguing, raise several issues. The subjects were seriously disturbed children, and possibly the instructions to the experimental group were ambiguous, threatening, or both. They were told that they were being given a second chance ". . . so we can see the very best you can do." The key word "best" could have been interpreted in a variety of ways, some of which might not have stimulated the kind of positive motivation on which the hypotheses of the study were predicated. A second issue is that even if the subjects were motivated to improve their performance, their pathology could have been an overriding variable that inhibited any significant alterations in performance. Obviously, if the Hulsart design could be improved, and the findings replicated, it would have a direct bearing on the issue of reliability. This provoked a new design that involved nonpatients as the target population (Exner, 1980).

Sixty nonpatient 8-year-olds, 30 males and 30 females, were recruited for this second study from four third-grade classes in the same school district. They were randomized into two groups, each containing 15 males and 15 females. Each subject was tested twice, with each test being administered on a school day during regular class hours, and no child being tested during play periods. Ten examiners were randomized across the 60 subjects so that no examiner tested any subject twice or more than four subjects from the same class. Each examiner collected a total of 12 records. The examiners were not aware of the true nature of the study. Instead, all functioned under the impression that their respective subjects were part of a larger pool being evaluated in a routine reliability investigation.

The retest for each subject was completed on the third or fourth day after the first testing. All subjects had been recruited, through their parents and school officials, for participation in an examiner training program, and were led to believe that the records would be taken as a matter of practice for the examiners. Thus, each subject anticipated being tested at least twice. No specific additional information was provided to the 30 control subjects prior to the second testing, except to note that a different examiner would be used. The 30 subjects in the experimental group were specifically instructed to give different answers in the second test from those they had given in the first test. They were told that examiners tend to hear the same answers over and over and that their training would be improved by hearing different kinds of responses. All examiners used the standard procedure for administration, except if they had to encourage a subject who gave only one answer to Card I. The standard prompt ("I think if you take your time, you'll find something else, too") was lengthened to include, ". . . and I hope that you'll find at least two things in each one." The retest correlations for the two groups are shown in Table 6.

The retest correlations for the experimental group are remarkably similar to those of the control group for 18 of the 23 individual variables. The main differences between the retest correlations occur in the frequency of Pure *F* answers, with the experimental group giving significantly more Pure *F* in the second record. This produced significantly more disparate Lambda values and inanimate movement responses. The experimental group are significantly more *m* in the second test, and more Grey-Black and Shading responses, thereby producing a substantial difference in the array of values for *es*.

The retest correlations for the control group are very similar to those reported in Table 4 for 25 eight-year-olds retested after 7 days. In fact, none of the retest correlations from these separate studies differs more than .04, even though the children of the two studies were drawn from very different population centers.

Another important set of data in this study concerns shifts in the directionality of five ratios that often are important foundations of interpretation (*EB, eb, EA:es, a:p, FC:CF + C*). Data presented by Exner, Armbruster, and Viglione (1978) reveal that nonpatient adults do not generally shift the directionality for four of these five ratios, except

Table 6.   Retest Correlations for 23 Variables for Two Groups of 30
Children Retested after Three or Four Days, with Experimental
Subjects Instructed to Give Different Answers in the Second Test

Variable	Experimental Group $N = 30$	Control Group $N = 30$
R	.81	.89
Popular	.76	.84
Zf	.89	.87
Lambda	.67	.82
M	.91	.89
FM	.78	.75
m	.27	.48
Active	.94	.90
Passive	.82	.87
FC	.91	.89
CF+C	.83	.87
Sum C	.88	.85
Afr	.92	.91
Sum T	.88	.90
Sum V	—	—
Sum C'	.67	.81
Sum Y	.08	.16
Sum Shad	.44	.71
X+%	.84	.94
3r+(2)/R	.90	.93
Sum 5 Sp Sc	.84	.85
EA	.84	.88
es	.38	.70

for the *eb,* after a 3-year period. However, that kind of sturdiness might not hold for younger children, and especially for those taking the test for a second time under directions to give different answers. Surprisingly, the data on ratio directionality from this instructional set study are very similar to those found for adults for each of the five ratios. Each group tends to remain very stable for directionality for four of the five ratios. In the first test, 15 experimental subjects and 14 control subjects manifest an extratensive *EB* style. In addition, 2 experimental subjects and 1 control subject manifest an introversive style. The remaining 32 subjects from both groups showed an ambient status, which is not unusual for children of this age. In the retest, all 15 experimental subjects and 13 of the 14 control subjects who were extratensive in the first test remained so. One control subject who had been extratensive in the first test was an ambient in the second test. The 3 subjects who had been introversive in the first test remained introversive in the second test. Also in the retest, 7 subjects who had been ambient in the first test became extratensive.

In the first test, 48 subjects from both groups showed a higher *EA* than *es*. In the retest, 47 of the 48 continued to do so. In the first test, 45 subjects gave more active than passive movement. In the retest, 43 of the 45 continued to do so. In the first test, 47 of the 60 subjects gave more *CF + C* answers than *FC* answers. In the retest, all 47 continued to do so, but 7 experimental subjects who had given more *FC* in the first test now gave more *CF + C,* as did two control subjects. Forty-five subjects gave more active than passive movement in the first test. That number increased to 57 in the second test, and included all 45 from the first test plus 12 who had given more passive movement in the first test. The data for the *eb* change most from the first to second tests. In the first test, 48 subjects were higher for the left-side value of the *eb* (*FM + m*) and 12 subjects were higher for the right-side value (*T + C' + V + Y*). In the second test, 21 subjects showed a directionality different from that of the first, with 15 of the changes occurring among experimental subjects.

A critical question is whether the experimental subjects did, in fact, follow directions and give different answers in the second test. For purposes of this study, a same answer was defined as any with identical content to that given in Test 1, using the same or nearly the same location area (identical content meaning same specific content rather than same scoring content category). In other words, a response of two men fighting in Test 1, using the Popular area of Card III, would be considered the same answer as two men working at night, using the same area in Test 2, even though the second response includes a *C'* or *Y* determinant. Conversely, if the answer in Test 2, using the same area, was two women dancing, the responses would be considered to be different. Similarly, a bat, given to the whole of Card I, would be considered the same answer as a bat at night given to the same area in Test 2, whereas a butterfly using the *W* area would be judged a different answer in Test 2 than in Test 1. Data concerning the replication of identical or nearly identical responses in the Test 2 protocols are shown in Table 7.

The data in Table 7 reveal that the two groups gave approximately the same number of answers in both tests, and that the experimental group did generally follow instructions, with more than 85% of their answers in Test 2 being different from the answers they gave in Test 1. Conversely, as is so often the case where a retest occurs after only a very brief interval, the control subjects repeated more than 85% of their answers.

These findings are similar to those reported in the third study by Haller and Exner (1985), in which essentially the same design was used with two groups, each consisting

Table 7.   Total Number of Responses by Card Given by Two Groups of 8-Year-Olds Plus Frequencies and Percentages of Answers Repeated in the Second Testing

Card	Experimental Group N = 30				Control Group N = 30			
	Test 1	Test 2	Repeated	%	Test 1	Test 2	Repeated	%
I	63	66	4	.06	60	62	51	.85
II	61	63	7	.11	64	61	56	.87
III	58	62	6	.10	61	57	49	.80
IV	51	57	9	.17	49	54	42	.85
V	39	34	7	.17	44	47	38	.86
VI	47	44	8	.17	51	48	46	.90
VII	52	50	10	.19	55	51	49	.89
VIII	63	65	9	.14	59	60	53	.89
IX	41	39	11	.14	46	44	43	.93
X	73	71	11	.15	69	65	51	.73
Totals	548	551	77		558	549	478	
Means	18.26	18.36	2.56	.14	18.60	18.20	16.30	.86

of 25 first-admission depressed adults. The retest correlations for the two group are comparable, even though the control subjects repeated about two thirds of their first test answers in the second test, whereas the experimental subjects repeated only about 34% of their first test answers.

SOME CONCLUSIONS

The composite of findings concerning response frequencies, sets, temporal consistency, and experimental manipulation involving instructions provides considerable information about the Rorschach process. It seems clear that most subjects, both adults and children, translate the blot stimuli into many more responses than they will ordinarily deliver when the test is administered under standard conditions. The set of the subject about the test and the examiner also influence how many responses are delivered and which responses that have been formulated will not be delivered.

The composite of temporal consistency studies illustrates that the psychological habits or response styles underlying responses tend to be quite consistent in adults over long periods, but this tendency is equally true for children for briefer periods. Some of these features, such as mediational conventionality, appear to become quite stable or consistent early in the developmental years. Others appear to remain unstable until mid-adolescence or adulthood, and some, mainly related to situational stress, remain unstable indefinitely. In other words, those features that ultimately identify the person as a unique personality become stabilized at different intervals during the developmental period. Undoubtedly, much more change occurs in the psychology of the young child than in the teenager, but considerable change continues for many features, at least into mid-adolescence.

In light of these findings, the Rorschach interpreter must exercise great caution in any attempts to predict from the test data what the child will be like in the distant future. At the same time, even very young children tend to remain consistent in the manifestations of their psychological operations over relatively brief intervals. Thus, the test data provide a picture of the psychological organization and functioning of the subject as he or she is at the moment, mainly in the context of perceptual, cognitive, and decision-making features. At times, however, because of personal verbal elaborations that are projected into responses, the picture includes a glimpse of some of the more private features that distinguish one human being from another.

Used wisely and cautiously, the Rorschach offers the potential for yielding much important information about younger subjects as they are and, for some characteristics, as they will be. The Rorschach highlights both assets and liabilities, and in instances where diagnosis and treatment planning are required, the test data provide an excellent starting point. But, as implied throughout Chapter 1, the data will be as useful as the knowledge and skill of the interpreter. His or her knowledge must include an acute awareness about the test as well as considerable information about personality, development, and psychopathology. An awareness of normative data and the intelligent applications of those data also becomes critical, particularly when working with children. This latter point is crucial. When normative data are used wisely, they contribute much to the portrait of the subject that is developed in the interpretive routine. But normative data can also be easily abused or misapplied, and when that happens, the interpretation can become misleading and erroneous.

REFERENCES

Ames, L. B., Metraux, R. W., Rodell, J. L., & Walker, R. N. (1974). *Child Rorschach responses* (rev. ed.) New York: Brunner/Mazel.

Colligan, S. C. (1990). *Responses of nonpatients to a tachistoscopic presentation of the Rorschach.* XIII International Rorschach Congress, Paris.

Colligan, S. C., & Exner, J. E. (1985). Responses of schizophrenics and nonpatients to a tachistoscopic presentation of the Rorschach. *Journal of Personality Assessment, 49,* 129–136.

Exner, J. E. (1974). *The Rorschach: A Comprehensive System: Vol. 1.* New York: Wiley.

Exner, J. E. (1978). *The Rorschach: A Comprehensive System: Vol. 2. Current research and advanced interpretation.* New York: Wiley.

Exner, J. E. (1980). But it's only an inkblot. *Journal of Personality Assessment, 44,* 562–577.

Exner, J. E. (1986). *The Rorschach: A Comprehensive System: Vol. 1. Basic foundations* (2nd ed.). New York: Wiley.

Exner, J. E. (1988). Problems with brief Rorschach protocols. *Journal of Personality Assessment, 52,* 640–647.

Exner, J. E. (1989). Searching for projection in the Rorschach. *Journal of Personality Assessment, 53,* 520–536.

Exner, J. E. (1990). *A Rorschach workbook for the Comprehensive System,* (3rd ed.). Asheville, NC: Rorschach Workshops.

Exner, J. E. (1991). *The Rorschach: A Comprehensive System: Vol. 2. Interpretation* (2nd ed.). New York: Wiley.

Exner, J. E. (1993). *The Rorschach: A Comprehensive System: Vol. 1. Basic foundations* (3rd ed.). New York: Wiley.

Exner, J. E., Armbruster, G. L., & Mittman, B. L. (1978). The Rorschach response process. *Journal of Personality Assessment, 42,* 27–38.

Exner, J. E., Armbruster, G. L., & Viglione, D. (1978). The temporal stability of some Rorschach features. *Journal of Personality Assessment, 42,* 474–482.

Exner, J. E., & Leura, A. V. (1976). Variations in the ranking of Rorschach responses as a function of situational set [Workshops Study No. 221 (unpublished)]. Rorschach Workshops.

Exner, J. E., Thomas, E. A., & Mason, B. (1985). Children's Rorschachs: Description and Prediction. *Journal of Personality Assessment, 49,* 13–20.

Exner, J. E., & Weiner, I. B. (1982). *The Rorschach: A Comprehensive System: Vol. 3. Assessment of children and adolescents.* New York: Wiley.

Haller, N., & Exner, J. E. (1985). The reliability of Rorschach variables for inpatients presenting symptoms of depression and/or helplessness. *Journal of Personality Assessment, 49,* 516–521.

Hulsart, B. (1979). The effects of a second chance instructional set on the Rorschachs of emotionally disturbed and culturally deprived children. Unpublished doctoral dissertation, Long Island University.

Leura, A. V., & Exner, J. E. (1977). The effects of inquiry after each card on the distribution of scores in the records of young children [Workshops Study No. 247 (unpublished)]. Rorschach Workshops.

Leura, A. V., & Exner, J. E. (1978). Structural differences in the records of adolescents as a function of being tested by one's own teacher [Workshops Study No. 265 (unpublished)]. Rorschach Workshops.

Murray, H. A. (1951). Forward. In H. H. Anderson & G. L. Anderson (Eds.), *An introduction to projective techniques* (pp. xi–xiv). Englewood Cliffs, NJ: Prentice-Hall.

Piotrowski, Z. A. (1957). *Perceptanalysis.* New York: Macmillan.

Piotrowski, Z. A. (1969). A Piotrowski interpretation. In J. E. Exner, *The Rorschach systems* (pp. 297–314). New York: Grune & Stratton.

Stein, M. I. (1949). Personality factors involved in the temporal development of Rorschach responses. *Rorschach Research Exchange, 13,* 355–414.

Symonds, P. M. (1946). *The dynamics of human adjustment.* New York: Appleton-Century-Crofts.

White, R. W. (1944). Interpretation of imaginative productions. In J. McV. Hunt (Ed.), *Personality and the behavior disorders* (pp. 214–251). New York: Ronald Press.

CHAPTER 3

Normative Data and the
Interpretive Process

Any psychological test that is purported to be useful must be supported by data concerning three essential features: (a) reliability, (b) validity, and (c) normative samples. The normative samples are quite important because they provide some reference information against which test results can be studied. In some tests, comparison of results with the normative samples can lead to conclusions quickly and easily. For instance, if all unimpaired 8-year-olds composing a normative sample are able to discriminate the colors blue and yellow, and an 8-year-old who is subjected to that task is unable to do so, the logical deduction is that the child is impaired. This finding does not include information about the specific features of the impairment or the cause, but the conclusion itself is logically inferred by comparing the subject's performance with the normative data. Unfortunately, most normative data cannot be used in such easy applications, particularly when the issues of personality and psychological functioning are involved, for each encompasses some broad parameters. The issue of functioning may be the more difficult of the two. Personality assessment involves a description of the psychological organization of the subject. On the other hand, an assessment of functioning requires a description of the activity of that organization in a broad range of situations. In other words, a subject may function quite effectively in some situations but very ineffectively in others.

Although many characteristics of psychological functioning are easily identified because they are routine, some aspects of functioning are altered by various circumstances. For instance, a person who usually is calm and controlled may become hysterical under unexpected stress, whereas a second person who usually seems poorly controlled in most situations might become very controlled when encountering unexpected stress. Thus, a description of functioning or potential functioning often requires many more logical inferences or predictions than are involved in a basic description of personality organization. Normative data can assist in either task if used wisely, but unfortunately, they are often misused extensively.

The concept *normative* is derived from measurement theory, and, contrary to popular belief, has little to do with the issues of normality and abnormality. Yet, in personality assessment or psychodiagnostic work, the notion of "norms" and the concept of "normal" often become intertwined. This is not necessarily illogical or impractical, provided the interpreter understands that the two are not synonymous and works at keeping the concepts separate. Normative data offer reference points from which to interpret. The concept of normality implies a much different and sometimes nebulous reference point but, nonetheless, is quite important in personality and diagnostic assessment.

SOME ASPECTS OF NORMALITY

How does the normal child appear, physically, behaviorally, and psychologically? For decades, researchers from many disciplines have sought to answer this question, and although much useful information has evolved, the question has not been answered satisfactorily from any perspective. As the data have accumulated, it has become obvious that any attempt to define the normal child must include some rather broad parameters whether the focus is on physical development, behavioral growth, or psychological features. People are diverse and unique. The uniqueness is not difficult to understand: Each person is a product of a union of two people drawn from billions of possible unions, and from these two, one of millions of sperm and one of thousands of eggs unite to form the zygote, which has well over a million genes, the combinations of which create the foundations of the psychological structure that will ultimately reflect the person. And this unique offspring is reared in an environment that is constant only to itself, shaped by billions of stimuli that are perceived and interpreted in an idiosyncratic way.

As children grow older, some of the differences that exist among them tend to lessen, but they never disappear completely. One of the outstanding features of the human being is his or her uniqueness, a special kind of separateness from everyone else. The younger the child, the greater the likelihood of differences, on a broad range, from his or her peers. In any age group, a great range of individual differences will be observed but, generally, the younger the age group to be studied, the more marked the differences. For example, a much larger number of 12-year-olds are neurologically prepared to read than is the case for 6-year-olds. Unfortunately, many 6-year-olds are identified as disabled or even brain damaged because they do not respond to the task of learning to read easily. But many of these children, in fact, possibly most, are neither disabled nor brain damaged. They simply have not developed neurologically at the expected or average rate. With the passage of time, their neurological development becomes sufficient for them to approach tasks that previously were impossible or at least quite difficult. A similar pattern is noted in physical appearance. A large percentage of 16-year-olds appear to be midadolescents, whereas a much smaller majority of 6-year-olds appear to be 6. Some are mistaken for 8-year-olds, and many others are mistaken for 4's. The differences are considerable.

This same kind of broad diversity exists in the psychology of the child. Some are more mature than others for their age. Others are less so. This is true for cognitive, emotional, and social development. There is likely to be much more homogeneity among 16-year-olds for social behaviors than among 7-year-olds, who show great diversity in language development, attitudes, allegiances, and certainly their less-well-developed cognitive operations. Some 7-year-olds can conceptualize time. Others cannot. Some of these children can conceptualize distance. Others cannot, and so on.

The considerable differences that exist among people, and especially among children, have played havoc with attempts to identify the psychologically normal child. The concept has remained elusive, and the word normality has often been tossed about like a ball. Quite often, the psychologist working in the clinical setting has lost sight of the concept altogether and instead reviews all cases in terms of the negatives discovered. No assessment tool, including Rorschach, should be used this way. The interpreter of data, regardless of the data source, should have some baseline or guideline to help him or her judge normal from abnormal features and put these features in the proper perspective with regard to the client. But this requirement also highlights a problem that exists in attempting to define the normal.

Behaviors tend to be regarded quite differently in terms of social acceptability. What may be pathological in one environment can be the norm in another. Consider the streetwise 9-year-old. He is very independent and even malicious at times; he has learned to take advantage of the opportunities presented in the inner city environment. He would probably be considered unusual, at best, in the rural atmosphere in which cooperation and traditional values of peaceful cooperation are the typical framework. But his actions may be normal for his own environment. The reverse may be true also. The youngster reared in the rural environment might be described as inadequate and even pathologically inept if thrust into the harsh, competitive world of the inner city.

The problem with the preceding example is that normality is defined in terms of adaptability to the person's own world. Numerous authors have suggested this, and to some extent it may be appropriate, but this approach raises the issue of conformity. In other words, whoever conforms to the behavioral norms is normal, and whoever does not is abnormal. That kind of conception is, at best, naive, and more likely ridiculous. Carried to the extreme, it suggests that someone living in a pathological environment must also become behaviorally (and possibly psychologically) pathological to be considered normal.

Certainly, any definition or description of the normal person that is based exclusively on external adaptation ignores much hard-won knowledge about human functioning and neglects most of the rich literature that exists about psychopathology. This does not mean that the issue of adaptation should be cast aside in any quest for a criterion of normality. It would be difficult, if not impossible, to define any person as normal who is unable to make effective adaptations to his or her world, especially if that world makes no demands that are alien to the psychological and behavioral features of the individual. Thus, the issue of adaptation, gauged in some relative parameters, can be useful to any understanding of what is normal. But it is quite important to distinguish adaptation from conformity.

Adaptation, used in the broader sense, implies an ability to adjust and coexist with an environment. Conformity implies much more of a commitment to a set of standards or rules that will define limits for behavior. The former implies some flexibility and a greater range of psychological and behavioral boundaries, whereas the latter permits less flexibility and more narrow parameters within which psychological and behavioral functioning can occur. Whereas conformity tends to offer a greater assurance of behavioral adaptation, the psychological strain of this can create an internal chaos that can ultimately be destructive to the individual.

If the problem of defining normality is approached from a more internal perspective, for instance, using a psychobiological framework, the main emphasis is on efficient, survival-oriented, behaviors. In this context, functions are described as normal that serve to promote need reduction and stress avoidance. The focus here is quite individualistic and easily encompasses the full range of differences among people. If the functioning is profitable to the individual with respect to survival or need reduction, it is normal. But just as the adaptation concept of normality overemphasizes external interaction, the psychobiological concept overemphasizes internal interaction. Although some species can function in an isolated existence, where survival can become the main variable in promoting behavior, this is not true for the human. For better or worse, people operate in a social world where rules and pecking orders are not always well defined, and where change is more often the case than regularity.

In fact, most societies tend to be very critical, and even punitive toward those who function mainly in their own self-interest. Many societies have their roots in the philosophical argument that the human, as a special being, has special sensitivities and is naturally oriented toward the total human enterprise. Nonetheless, emphasis on efficient internal interaction cannot be dismissed as irrelevant to the question of normality any more than can the emphasis on adaptation.

It would seem that any set of criteria applied to definitions of normality would include, at the very least, some demand for evidence of both internal and external effectiveness or adaptability. No one assessment procedure, including the Rorschach, will provide all the data necessary for judging whether a person falls into that broad category of normality. Some assessment tactics, such as observation, behavioral assessment, interviewing, and thorough history data, are probably much more viable as indices of external adaptation than any of the standard test techniques. But those tactics offer far less information about the internal workings of the individual than do many of the testing approaches. Negative findings from either source signal some kind of abnormality. In other words, the broad and poorly defined notion of normality provides a vague but important framework for detecting the unusual or the abnormal. It is a general benchmark against which judgments are made. And provided that it does not become too specific, normality as a construct is quite useful. Thus, although we may not be able to define it as specifically as we might wish, the general construct does offer guidelines against which various characteristics, both psychological and behavioral, can be evaluated.

THE NORMATIVE DATA

One form of evaluation that can be used to view the psychological characteristics of the individual is comparison with peers. This kind of evaluation occurs frequently in everyday life. People are judged winners or losers, things are judged best or worst, biggest or smallest, desirable or undesirable, and so on. Most of these judgments imply some sort of continuum with intervals from one end to the other. The reference point, from which judgments of more than and less than, better and worse, can be made is in many cases the center, or the average. In effect, these determinations tend to have more meaning and become more useful when they can be referenced in the context of a series of judgments or evaluations that constitute a set of normative data. Such data can be helpful in understanding the psychological features of a person or they can be very misleading. Numerous problems can occur in creating norms, and even more in their use.

Selecting the Samples Whereas any population can be used to establish a set of norms, those norms are useful only when applied to subjects from the population for which they were established. Because norms are designed to be representative of the features of a group, it would be ideal to include all members of the group in the data pool. But this is usually impractical for any measures that are to be applied to large and diverse populations. Thus, representative samples must suffice, and where universal applicability is involved, sample selection poses many problems. Typically, large numbers are required, but a large sample is not necessarily representative. Test data collected from a randomly selected group of 200 13-year-olds in a single school district might be representative of all 13's in that district, but might not be representative of 13's in other school districts.

Obviously, to generalize from a normative sample of 13-year-olds, the sample should be collected in several school districts that, as a group, appear to include the distribution of those characteristics that exist within the entire population of children that age.

But, as noted earlier, the range of features characterizing people is so broad that to attempt to account for all possibilities in establishing norms is, at best, an enormous problem.

Three general criteria were applied in selecting the samples to be included in the normative data regarding children for the Comprehensive System: (a) that sample sizes would be large enough to ensure that the data would be psychometrically meaningful; (b) that samples would include relatively equal numbers of males and females; and (c) that the samples would be stratified on the basis of geographic distribution and socioeconomic status (SES) to the extent possible for each age.

At the onset, it appeared as though the first two criteria posed no major problems, but the issue of stratification made the task somewhat more difficult. The project was designed to accumulate a minimum of 150 nonpatient protocols at each age, from 5 through 16. Figures from the 1970 Census were used as a reference for the stratification. Thus, optimally, the project would yield at least 75 males and 75 females for each age, of whom 65% would be drawn from urban and suburban areas and 35% from semirural and rural areas. A modified 9-point version of the Hollingshead and Redlich scale was used to estimate SES, wherein each group would consist of 16% SES groups 2 and 3 (middle-upper and lower-upper classes), 18% each from SES groups 4, 5, and 6 (upper-middle, middle-middle, and lower-middle classes), and 10% each from SES groups 7, 8, and 9 (upper-lower, middle-lower, and lowest-lower classes.* Three age groups, 7, 11, and 15, were also targeted to include between 15% and 20% from black and Hispanic populations.

The nonpatient children were recruited through schools and social organizations such as Cub Scouts, Boy Scouts, Girl Scouts, Little Leagues, 4H Clubs, and such. A tangible donation, usually worth less than $300, was provided to the school or organization for their assistance in recruiting subjects. Usually this involved the purchase of library, audiovisual, playground, or athletic equipment. More than 3,100 children indicated a willingness to participate in the project, but parental consent forms were returned for only 2,213 of the volunteers. All subjects with parental permission were tested, with about 75% of the testing done in schools during school hours. Under optimal circumstances, a larger number of records would have been collected from a much larger pool of available subjects, but this was not possible. Almost 30% of volunteer children did not or could not obtain parental permission, which reduced the total pool considerably; and in many instances, the number of volunteer subjects represented a very small proportion of all potentially available subjects, which contributed to the relatively modest sample sizes for each year.

As with the best laid plans, the final standardization sample did not always meet the objectives for the project even though more than 2,200 protocols were collected. When the criteria for male-female distribution and stratification for geographic and SES criteria were applied to the total sample, the result yielded 1,580 seemingly valid protocols across ages 5 through 16 with the number for each year ranging between 105 (age 6) to 150 (ages 9, 11, and 16).

---

* The decision to exclude subjects from the SES 1 group was made after findings, based on an N of 12 children from ages 8, 9, and 10, revealed that all 12 gave significantly longer records, ranging in length from 29 to 52 answers with a mean of 37 responses. The number of words in the basic response was about twice that of other children. Since this SES group (upper-upper) constitutes only a fraction of 1% of the population, the omission is not considered significant; however, if the record of an SES 1 subject is to be interpreted, any application of normative data is, at best, tenuous.

A significant problem concerning brief protocols was discovered about 6 years after the original nonpatient samples had been published (Exner, 1988). Protocols containing less than 14 responses did not show temporal consistency (reliability) and, as such, could not be regarded as valid except in cases involving severe pathology. As a result of this finding, protocols with less than 14 answers were discarded from both the adult and younger client normative samples. Eliminating records of less than 14 responses changed the samples for younger subjects much more than the adult sample. A total of 239 of the 1,580 protocols (15%) were discarded from the 1982 samples because of a low R.

Nearly half of the discarded records were from ages 5 through 8. Thus, the data for those ages changed most, but every age group was affected. Some records of nonpatient children that had not been selected for use in the 1982 tables have been added to replace about 20% of those that had been discarded, but samples for all years remain smaller than the originals, and the discarding and replacement procedure has altered the stratification pattern, based on geographic distribution and socioeconomic level that was applied in the original sample. The revised sample consists of 1,390 protocols.

The 1,390 records were collected by 87 examiners, for an average of 16 protocols each. Actually, 12 examiners collected between 21 and 26 protocols, but no examiner collected fewer than 7 records. The sample represents 84 school districts, from 33 states and the District of Columbia. There are no more than 36 subjects from any single school district, and none contributed more than 10 records for any age group. Most minority subjects were recruited from the northeastern, southwestern, and western United States.

Table 8 provides some demographic data concerning sex, race, socioeconomic level, and geographic distribution by age group.

Table 8.   Distribution of Demographic Variables, by Age, for 1,390 Nonpatient Children and Adolescents

	Age Groups											
	5	6	7	8	9	10	11	12	13	14	15	16
TOTAL	90	80	120	120	140	120	135	120	110	105	110	140
Male	50	46	68	54	72	64	70	63	45	43	53	68
Female	40	34	52	66	68	56	65	57	65	62	57	72
RACE												
White	71	60	106	88	106	97	110	87	80	76	81	107
Black	11	15	9	16	14	11	13	19	20	18	16	21
Hispanic	8	5	5	14	13	12	9	10	8	9	8	11
Asian	0	0	0	2	7	0	3	4	2	3	5	1
SES & GEOGRAPHIC												
Upper	22	17	21	15	21	25	27	19	14	15	20	17
Middle	47	38	63	64	80	63	77	67	68	61	57	84
Lower	21	25	36	41	39	32	31	34	28	29	33	39
Urban	31	21	34	34	45	27	41	34	37	24	43	46
Suburban	26	27	39	42	51	41	51	43	39	44	35	49
Rural	33	32	46	44	44	52	43	43	34	37	32	44

The data pose two challenging issues in providing a useful baseline or normative data against which other records can be compared. First, the size of the samples at each age are modest. Only three age groups (9, 11, 16) include more than 130 subjects and two age groups (5, 6) include less than 100 subjects. Some might suggest that the data for adjacent ages could be combined to create a larger sample that might be more representative, but such a suggestion is not well grounded in the realities of development. Psychological changes occur very rapidly in children, and for most it is unrealistic to assume that representative data for one year will be equally representative for the next year. The literature from developmental psychology emphasizes this point, and, if Rorschach data are considered, the longitudinal study of Exner, Thomas, and Mason (1985) indicates that the test is quite unreliable over 2-year intervals for younger clients, at least to the age of 14. Thus, the age samples must remain separate, but regrettably, the numbers for each age are not terribly impressive when considered in the context of *normative*. Adding to this issue is the fact that the stratification process has, potentially, created a great deal of heterogeneity in the data for each age group.

A second issue regarding these data may be even more important. It has been noted earlier that all subjects were volunteers, with parental agreement, and it has also been noted that in many instances the actual number of volunteers with parental agreement was considerably less than the actual number of potential subjects available in a school or group. This proved to be a particular problem in recruiting children from urban communities. Often, fewer than 20% of children in a class volunteered to participate, and often that percentage was reduced considerably by the failure to obtain parental consent. This raises a question about volunteers versus nonvolunteers. It seems highly likely that those who volunteered probably felt aligned with the school or organization sponsoring the project and were comfortable in it. In addition, the matter of parental consent becomes an issue. Actually, more than 900 subjects who had volunteered for the project did not submit the required parental consent forms. Whether this indicates some concerns by the parents or simply reflects a failure to respond is not known. Hypothetically, the more than 900 subjects in the nonconsent group may be different from the consent group, and of course, there is the issue of the much larger group of nonvolunteer subjects. Are they, indeed, different from the volunteer subjects? The questions concerning volunteering and consent raise the specter that each age sample may represent only the best, or at least the most effectively functioning, of the group recruited. We hope this is not true, but it would be misleading to suggest that the data, by age, represent the typical youngster for a given age. Instead, the data should be regarded as representing children who, for one reason or another, were interested in taking the test and whose interests were supported by their parents. In other words, the data may reflect that group of younger people who tend to adjust well to the demands of their environments and with whom their parents seem reasonably satisfied. This could constitute a large percentage of nonpatient youngsters, but the samples might be skewed in some ways.

Intragroup Differences   Whatever the samples may represent, intragroup differences may make the data even more heterogeneous and less useful. This is a risk that is created whenever a stratification criterion is applied. In other words, adding subclasses together may conceal features that differentiate one subclass from another. In that context, it seemed important to complete a variety of analyses that compared each subgroup by sex, geography, and SES with the other subgroups of the same age, or at times by combining adjacent age groups.

In general, most of the results are inconsequential. Males and females do not differ for any location or determinant scoring, except that females in the age groups 5, 6, and 7 gave a significantly higher *WSumC* than males for the same age groups. Females in the age groups 12, 13, and 14 gave significantly more *Y* responses than males for the same ages. Females in those same age groups also have significantly higher Egocentricity Indices than the males.

The differences are somewhat more marked when SES is reviewed. For ages 5 through 11, the combined group of SES 8 and 9 (middle-lower, lowest lower) gave significantly fewer *M* responses than children of other SES groups regardless of race, sex, or geography. This combined group also has significantly higher mean value for Lambda, although the group does not have a significantly greater proportion of records in which the value for Lambda is 1.0 or greater. For ages 5 through 9, males from the combined SES groups 8 and 9 have significantly lower Egocentricity Indices than children in other SES groups. For ages 13 through 15, children in SES 8 and 9 gave fewer *W* responses than children in the other SES groups.

There are some interesting but unexplainable differences by geographic distribution. For instance, children, ages 10 through 14 from the southwestern and western groups gave more color answers and a significantly higher *WSumC* than children of the same ages from other geographic regions. Children ages 8 through 10 from the northeastern and midwestern regions gave significantly more *C'* answers than children from other regions. Children from the Northeast and Far West ages 5 through 9 gave significantly more *M* answers than children from other regions. In spite of the *M* and WSumC differences that occur by SES and by region for some age groups, the distributions of extratensive, introversive, and ambient subjects by age, SES, and region are not significantly different.

Differences in Verbiage   Although the various subgroups in the total sample may be considered relatively homogeneous with regard to the structural features of the test, this does not necessarily mean that the records for any one age group will read or "sound" the same. In fact, that is not the case. Ten psychology graduate students were asked to sort, independently of each other, the 135 protocols from the 11-year-old sample into the five categories represented in the geographic distribution of the sample (Northeast, Southeast, Midwest, Southwest, and West) by simply reading the records. No scores were available to the sorters. A total of 812 of the 1,350 decisions were correct (60%), suggesting that there is much greater homogeneity in verbiage, by region, than is reflected in the distribution of the structural data.

In a similar procedure, six elementary school teachers were asked to sort 90 protocols that had been selected from the 14-, 15-, and 16-year-old samples into three groupings, guessing in the sort whether the subject was drawn from a rural, urban, or suburban environment. The 90 records included 30 from each of those demographic areas. A total of 369 of the 540 sorts were correct (68%), again suggesting that there is greater homogeneity in verbiage and/or content in each of these three subgroups than is reflected in the structural data. Apparently, these differences occur in verbiage that is not related directly to the score for location or determinants or to the frequencies that occur for the major content categories (*H* and *A*), as there are no significant differences for these categories for any of the groups.

These findings suggest that the test process, while being quite consistent for the perceptual-cognitive operations represented in the structural data, is also markedly influenced by cultural and subcultural factors on a different level; and that these factors may be very important to any investigations aimed at detecting common interpretive meaning and/or principles to be applied to response content.

The findings also highlight the importance of using good judgment when interpreting some of the special scores, especially words and phrases that involve the special scores *DV* and *DR*. This *does not mean* that the scoring should be altered. A *DV* remains a *DV*, as does a *DR*, but in some instances a peculiar misuse of a word or a strange phrase can be common to a subculture. Thus, a substantial number of *DV* and *DR* special scores from one subject may signify notable cognitive slippage, whereas the data for another subject giving the same number of *DV* and *DR* responses might simply reflect some unusual verbiage common to the subculture.

Cross-Cultural Utility of the Norms   The fact cannot be avoided that the normative data are based on an American sample. The extent to which this sample also represents children from a much broader geographic distribution cannot be determined without collecting large samples from a variety of countries; however, some encouragement for the postulate that the data may be cross-culturally consistent is derived from two sources.

The first (Ruiz, Panelos, Thomas, & Exner, 1980) compared 30 protocols drawn randomly from the 10-year-old sample with the records of 30 10-year-olds collected in three Spanish-speaking countries, 9 from Spain, 13 from Mexico, and 8 from Panama. All subjects were in school grades appropriate for their age, and none had any psychiatric history. Only three statistically significant differences were found, two of which are not explained easily. The Spanish-speaking group gave significantly more *W* and *DQv* scores than the American controls. There does not seem to be any logic that accounts for these differences, and they appear to be chance findings. The third difference involves the reporting of *T*. Children in the American sample gave *T* answers more frequently than children in the three Spanish speaking countries. A careful review of the data reveals that most of the *T*-less records in the Spanish-speaking sample were collected in Spain, and traditional Castilian Spanish has no specific word for fur. The word for skin is used interchangeably for skin or fur. Thus, it is likely that this difference is a function of language. A similar lower frequency of *T* responses has been noted in the protocols of nonpatient adults collected in Spain.

The second important source from which to argue that the American sample does have broad applicability is derived from a variety of cross-cultural studies involving nonpatient adults. During the period from 1976 to 1990 more than 900 records have become available from various countries throughout the world including, Argentina, France, China, India, Italy, Japan, Malaysia, Micronesia, Norway, Philippines, and Spain. Although none of these samples is large enough to test against the American nonpatient normative data, the composite of all the non-American samples does permit such an analysis. In general, the distributions of scores for each of the structural variables are similar to those for the American sample. It is obvious that the frequencies for some responses differ in some countries when compared with the American sample. For instance, although the records from 208 nonpatient adults from Spain (Sendin, 1981) show no significant differences for location and determinant distribution, except for a lower frequency of *T* responses, the subjects in the Spanish sample did not give the frequency (one in three) of the *D3* Card IX Popular (human or humanlike figure) necessary to define the answer as Popular as is found in the American sample.

More importantly, when the data for each country are studied separately, most have mean *X + %*'s that are 4% to 10% lower, and *Xu%*'s that are 5% to 9% higher, than the

American sample. This is probably because there are some more commonly given responses in the various countries that replace more frequently given answers by the American group.

These findings might lead some to argue that normative data for the test should be established by country, or language, or even by culture. Such a suggestion is probably not very realistic unless very large samples are available. Instead, it seems more reasonable to suggest that the items in the Form Quality Table be reviewed for frequency. In other words, if a response currently not found in the Table occurs frequently in a given country or culture, the form quality scoring for that answer should be adjusted accordingly. Likewise, if a response that is currently listed in the Form Quality Table as unusual occurs with a high frequency in the nonpatient records for a country or culture, it should be scored as ordinary. This is a very different procedure from that involved in attempting to establish separate normative data.

THE NORMATIVE SAMPLES

Tables 9 and 10 provide the descriptive statistics for the nonpatient samples that have been collected in the standardization project. If studied carefully, they provide interesting food for thought about the developmental process and how it is reflected in the Rorschach. If used cautiously, they will afford some assistance to the interpretive process and to those involved in researching the test with youngsters. However, some important cautions must be exercised.

First, as has been stressed earlier, *it is erroneous to assume that norms define normality.* A deviation from the norm for any score, ratio, or percentage may reflect some kind of *uncommonness,* but that may not be abnormal when viewed in the context of internal and/or external adaptation. Uncommon or unique features are expected in every person, and in many instances, those features contribute substantially to the adaptation of an individual. Protocols in which all critical scores fall within an average range are rare, and when interpreted, many yield findings that suggest the subject may be impoverished or handicapped in some area of internal or external adaptation. On the other hand, many records in which most or even all the critical scores fall outside of the average range yield the interpretive conclusion that the subject seems quite well adjusted.

Second, it is important to recognize the potential limitations of the data, as has been stressed earlier. Although the entire sample totals nearly 1,400 subjects, each age group is modest in size, falling far short of the much larger number that would be optimal for a normative sample. Another issue of concern is the extensive growth changes that can occur within a single chronological year. Many findings from developmental psychology suggest that it is unreasonable to judge all children within a single year by one standard. This appears to be especially true for youngsters of 7 years and under. Subdividing the 5-, 6-, and 7-year-old samples by 6-month intervals might prove very important, but the sample sizes for each year are too small to produce useful subdivisions of the data.

Finally, normative data should never be applied concretely. Exner (1991, 1993) has stressed the importance of making sense out of the available data, that is, using all the findings. For some variables, the means, standard deviations, and range provide meaningful points for comparison. Generally, these three statistics are most useful when the data for a variable are on a normal or parametric distribution; in some instances, however, a variable may be normally distributed and the means and standard deviations can still be misleading.

The most obvious illustration of how these data can be misleading concerns *M* and *WSumC,* both of which are extremely important to the interpretation of any record. If the normative data for both variables are addressed concretely, the conclusion for almost any age group will be that the average or expected values for each are about the same. Review, for instance, the data in Table 8 for 11-year-olds. The means for these variables are nearly the same (*M* = 4.12, *SD* = 1.67, Range = 2 to 7; *WSumC* = 4.02, *SD* = 1.15, Range = 2.5 to 8). If the data are reviewed simplistically, they can be interpreted to mean that most 11-year-olds will have about as much *M* in their record as the Weighted Sum of Color responses. But that is not true. The sample of 11-year-olds consists of 135 subjects, 41 of whom are introversive. They average 5.76 *M* answers (Range = 5 to 8) and a *WSumC* of 4.15 (Range 3.5 to 6). The sample also contains 60 extratensive subjects who average only 2.88 *M* answers (Range = 1 to 4) and a mean *WSumC* of 7.45 (Range = 6 to 8).

Thus, for this age group, the distributions for *M* and *WSumC* are really bimodal, in accord with a particular response style manifested by the youngster at the time the test was administered. Several response styles tend to confound data for some parametric variables in the Rorschach. Not only are *M* and WSumC affected by these styles but variables such as the Affective Ratio and the frequencies for blends and human contents can also be affected. The adult normative data have been studied extensively with regard to the impact of these styles, and separate norms have been published concerning those findings (Exner, 1991, 1993). Although this approach is impractical for children because of the small samples for each age group, those using the normative tables should be acutely aware of the parametric variables that might be misleading because of a possible bimodal distribution.

Another form of misuse of normative data, especially data for younger clients, concerns the variables that are not parametric or normally distributed. Many Rorschach variables are in this category. Typically, they include those for which the range of scores includes less than 5 points, such as 0 to 4, 2 to 6, and so on. These are the nonparametric variables of the test, and often the distribution of scores will fall on a *J-Curve,* that is, one in which most of the scores will fall on one or two points of the distribution. Data concerning the means and standard deviations for these variable are, essentially, useless. Any intelligent use of normative findings for variables such as these will focus on the range and the median and modal values and include special attention to the values for skewness and kurtosis. The grey-black variable, the shading variables, the *FD* determinant, most of the content variables, some of the *DQ* scores, and most of the special scores fall into this category.

The normative tables have been organized so that brackets enclose the standard deviations for most of these variables. In fact, consideration has been given to the notion of deleting the data for the mean and standard deviation for these variables for the nonpatient tables, but this idea was discarded to avoid penalizing those interested in the data for research purposes. Nonetheless, even though means and standard deviations are shown for the nonparametric variables of the test, they will be disregarded by the conscientious interpreter. In many instances, the frequency data shown in Table 10 will provide a more valuable basis from which to interpret than will the table of descriptive statistics.

Table 9. Descriptive Statistics for 1,390 Nonpatient Children and Adolescents by Age

Variable	Mean	SD	Min	Max	Freq	Median	Mode	SK	KU
				5-Year-Olds ($N = 90$)					
R	17.64	1.44	14.00	20.00	90	18.00	18.00	−0.83	−0.25
W	9.97	1.65	7.00	12.00	90	9.00	11.00	0.24	−1.35
D	7.10	2.61	3.00	12.00	90	8.00	6.00	−0.83	−0.24
Dd	0.58	[0.65]	0.00	2.00	44	0.00	0.00	0.70	−0.53
S	1.40	[1.14]	0.00	3.00	64	1.00	0.00	0.14	−1.39
DQ+	5.47	1.43	2.00	8.00	90	5.50	4.00	0.35	−1.29
DQo	10.72	2.07	7.00	13.00	90	12.00	13.00	−1.25	0.05
DQv	1.37	[0.62]	0.00	4.00	83	1.00	1.00	0.36	−0.63
DQv/+	0.09	[0.29]	0.00	1.00	8	0.00	0.00	2.94	6.78
FQX+	0.00	0.00	0.00	0.00	0	0.00	0.00	—	—
FQXo	11.54	2.50	6.00	15.00	90	13.00	13.00	−0.70	−0.52
FQXu	3.59	1.96	1.00	7.00	90	4.00	1.00	0.13	−1.19
FQX−	1.46	0.64	0.00	3.00	86	1.00	1.00	0.04	−0.19
FQXNone	0.87	[0.62]	0.00	2.00	63	1.00	1.00	0.36	−0.63
MQ+	0.00	0.00	0.00	0.00	0	0.00	0.00	—	—
MQo	1.13	0.34	1.00	2.00	90	1.00	1.00	2.19	2.88
MQu	0.38	0.66	0.00	2.00	25	0.00	0.00	1.53	1.00
MQ−	0.19	[0.39]	0.00	1.00	17	0.00	0.00	1.62	0.63
MQNone	0.00	[0.00]	0.00	0.00	0	0.00	0.00	—	—
S−	0.91	[0.69]	0.00	3.00	62	1.00	1.00	0.45	−0.83
M	1.70	1.00	1.00	4.00	90	1.00	1.00	1.26	0.36
FM	5.00	0.95	4.00	7.00	90	5.00	4.00	0.32	−1.20
m	0.78	0.80	0.00	3.00	49	1.00	0.00	0.43	−1.32
FM + m	5.78	1.19	4.00	9.00	90	6.00	5.00	0.65	0.50
FC	0.71	0.46	0.00	1.00	64	1.00	1.00	−0.95	−1.13
CF	3.02	1.41	1.00	6.00	90	3.00	3.00	0.53	−0.20
C	0.67	[0.62]	0.00	2.00	63	1.00	1.00	0.36	−0.63
Cn	0.00	[0.00]	0.00	0.00	0	0.00	0.00	—	—
FC + CF + C + Cn	4.40	1.10	2.00	6.00	90	4.00	4.00	−0.39	−0.11
WGSum C	4.38	1.09	2.50	6.50	90	4.00	4.00	0.27	−0.73
Sum C'	0.63	[0.48]	0.00	1.00	57	1.00	1.00	−0.56	−1.72
Sum T	0.83	[0.48]	0.00	2.00	57	1.00	1.00	0.42	2.42
Sum V	0.00	[0.00]	0.00	0.00	0	0.00	0.00	—	—
Sum Y	0.36	[0.33]	0.00	2.00	20	0.00	0.00	−0.65	2.71
SumShd	1.77	0.97	0.00	2.00	57	2.00	2.00	−0.56	−1.72
Fr + rF	0.38	[0.45]	0.00	2.00	29	0.00	0.00	1.01	−1.00
FD	0.28	[0.63]	0.00	1.00	16	0.00	0.00	1.77	0.58
F	6.98	1.26	4.00	9.00	90	6.00	6.00	0.19	−0.35
PAIR	9.08	1.96	5.00	11.00	90	9.00	11.00	−0.91	−0.29
3r(2)/R	0.69	0.14	0.33	1.00	90	0.60	0.64	0.28	0.57
LAMBDA	0.86	0.15	0.36	1.25	90	0.75	0.60	0.76	−0.52
EA	5.08	1.34	2.50	8.50	90	5.50	5.00	−0.24	−0.75
es	7.04	1.14	5.00	9.00	90	7.00	7.00	0.10	−0.60
D	−0.24	0.43	−1.00	0.00	90	0.00	0.00	−1.21	−0.55
AdjD	−0.20	0.40	−1.00	0.00	90	0.00	0.00	−1.53	0.33
a (active)	6.28	0.95	5.00	8.00	90	6.00	6.00	0.38	−0.70
p (passive)	1.20	1.37	0.00	4.00	49	1.00	0.00	0.82	−0.60
Ma	1.42	0.67	1.00	3.00	90	1.00	1.00	1.32	0.47
Mp	0.28	0.45	0.00	1.00	25	0.00	0.00	1.01	−1.00
Intellect	0.17	0.38	0.00	1.00	90	0.00	0.00	1.82	1.34
Zf	10.08	2.18	8.00	14.00	90	10.00	14.00	0.15	−1.52
Zd	−1.13	2.60	−5.00	4.50	90	−1.75	−2.50	0.70	0.09
Blends	2.86	1.92	0.00	5.00	77	3.00	5.00	−0.21	−1.56
Col Shd Bl	0.18	[0.56]	0.00	1.00	5	0.00	0.00	1.81	−2.37

Note: Standard Deviations shown in brackets indicate that the value is probably unreliable and/or misleading and should not be used to estimate expected ranges. Ordinarily, these variables should not be included in most parametric analyses.

Table 9. (Continued)

Variable	Mean	SD	Min	Max	Freq	Median	Mode	SK	KU
				5-Year-Olds ($N = 90$)					
Afr	0.88	0.13	0.50	1.00	90	0.90	0.80	−0.65	−0.08
Popular	4.66	1.69	3.00	10.00	90	4.00	4.00	0.55	−0.94
X + %	0.67	0.10	0.47	0.83	90	0.68	0.72	−0.27	−0.68
F + %	0.84	0.13	0.50	1.00	90	0.83	0.83	−0.62	0.28
X − %	0.09	0.04	0.00	0.21	86	0.07	0.11	−0.03	−0.18
Xu%	0.23	0.10	0.06	0.40	90	0.22	0.06	0.08	−1.42
S − %	0.49	[0.46]	0.00	1.00	52	0.50	0.00	0.02	−1.83
Isolate	0.17	0.06	0.11	0.27	90	0.17	0.11	0.58	−0.88
H	2.19	0.50	1.00	3.00	90	2.00	2.00	0.38	0.34
(H)	1.46	0.50	1.00	2.00	90	1.00	1.00	0.18	−2.01
Hd	0.36	0.48	0.00	1.00	32	0.00	0.00	0.61	−1.66
(Hd)	0.46	0.57	0.00	2.00	13	0.00	0.00	1.42	1.54
Hx	0.00	[0.00]	0.00	0.00	0	0.00	0.00	—	—
All H Cont	4.00	1.15	2.00	6.00	90	4.00	3.00	0.41	−0.90
A	10.69	2.32	6.00	14.00	90	11.00	12.00	−0.88	−0.28
(A)	0.37	[0.48]	0.00	1.00	33	0.00	0.00	0.56	−1.72
Ad	0.71	[0.60]	0.00	2.00	57	1.00	1.00	0.23	−0.57
(Ad)	0.00	[0.00]	0.00	0.00	0	0.00	0.00	—	—
An	0.37	[0.49]	0.00	3.00	18	0.00	0.00	0.46	2.01
Art	0.17	0.38	0.00	1.00	15	0.00	0.00	1.82	1.34
Ay	0.00	[0.00]	0.00	0.00	0	0.00	0.00	—	—
Bl	1.13	[0.46]	0.00	2.00	86	1.00	1.00	0.54	1.30
Bt	0.28	0.45	0.00	1.00	25	0.00	0.00	1.01	−1.00
Cg	3.73	1.35	2.00	6.00	90	3.00	3.00	0.62	−0.92
Cl	0.58	[0.74]	0.00	2.00	42	0.00	0.00	1.21	0.83
Ex	0.22	[0.51]	0.00	2.00	16	0.00	0.00	2.31	4.54
Fi	0.22	[0.51]	0.00	2.00	16	0.00	0.00	2.31	4.54
Fd	0.41	[0.53]	0.00	2.00	21	0.00	0.00	2.16	2.38
Ge	0.00	[0.00]	0.00	0.00	0	0.00	0.00	—	—
Hh	0.71	0.65	0.00	3.00	61	1.00	1.00	−0.48	1.96
Ls	2.68	0.63	2.00	4.00	90	3.00	3.00	0.38	−0.65
Na	0.36	[0.51]	0.00	2.00	19	0.00	0.00	1.42	−0.39
Sc	0.52	[0.43]	0.00	2.00	37	0.00	0.00	1.35	3.58
Sx	0.00	[0.00]	0.00	0.00	0	0.00	0.00	—	—
Xy	0.00	[0.00]	0.00	0.00	0	0.00	0.00	—	—
Idio	0.14	0.35	0.00	1.00	13	0.00	0.00	2.06	2.28
DV	1.16	[1.05]	0.00	4.00	83	1.00	1.00	1.00	0.57
INCOM	1.96	[0.70]	0.00	4.00	76	1.00	1.00	0.06	−0.93
DR	0.11	[0.21]	0.00	1.00	9	0.00	0.00	4.50	18.63
FABCOM	0.89	[0.57]	0.00	3.00	72	1.00	1.00	−0.02	0.06
DV2	0.00	[0.00]	0.00	0.00	0	0.00	0.00	—	—
INC2	0.09	[0.29]	0.00	1.00	8	0.00	0.00	2.94	6.78
DR2	0.09	[0.29]	0.00	1.00	8	0.00	0.00	2.94	6.78
FAB2	0.22	[0.42]	0.00	1.00	20	0.00	0.00	1.36	−0.16
ALOG	0.61	[0.50]	0.00	1.00	57	0.00	0.00	0.37	−1.91
CONTAM	0.00	0.00	0.00	0.00	0	0.00	0.00	—	—
Sum6 Sp Sc	6.88	2.01	3.00	9.00	90	6.00	5.00	0.45	−0.65
Sum6 Sp Sc2	0.40	[0.58]	0.00	2.00	32	0.00	0.00	1.12	0.30
WSum6	14.88	4.68	4.00	22.00	90	14.00	7.00	−0.10	−1.05
AB	0.00	[0.00]	0.00	0.00	0	0.00	0.00	—	—
AG	1.23	0.67	0.00	3.00	82	1.00	1.00	0.60	0.74
CFB	0.00	0.00	0.00	0.00	0	0.00	0.00	—	—
COP	1.08	0.52	0.00	3.00	81	1.00	1.00	0.10	0.67
CP	0.23	[0.81]	0.00	1.00	2	0.00	0.00	3.38	11.55
MOR	0.78	[0.75]	0.00	2.00	53	1.00	0.00	0.39	−1.10
PER	0.18	0.41	0.00	2.00	21	0.00	0.00	0.69	4.73
PSV	0.63	[0.48]	0.00	1.00	57	1.00	1.00	−0.56	−1.72

Table 9. (Continued)

Variable	6-Year-Olds (N = 80)								
	Mean	SD	Min	Max	Freq	Median	Mode	SK	KU
R	18.91	0.98	14.00	20.00	80	19.00	20.00	−0.23	−1.25
W	10.79	1.17	7.00	10.00	80	11.00	9.00	−0.56	−1.16
D	7.94	1.01	7.00	11.00	80	7.00	8.00	−1.38	2.27
Dd	0.30	[0.46]	0.00	1.00	24	0.00	0.00	0.89	−1.24
S	0.79	[0.76]	0.00	3.00	51	1.00	1.00	1.09	1.67
DQ+	4.42	0.59	3.00	5.00	80	4.00	4.00	−0.46	−0.66
DQo	11.31	1.35	9.00	13.00	80	11.00	13.00	0.11	−1.45
DQv	2.54	[1.19]	1.00	5.00	80	3.00	3.00	0.14	−0.89
DQv/+	0.45	[0.64]	0.00	1.00	38	1.00	1.00	−1.18	−0.63
FQX+	0.00	0.00	0.00	0.00	0	0.00	0.00	—	—
FQXo	13.39	1.22	12.00	16.00	80	14.00	14.00	0.25	−0.92
FQXu	4.01	1.29	3.00	7.00	80	4.00	4.00	0.75	−0.32
FQX−	0.94	0.50	0.00	6.00	66	0.00	0.00	0.21	−2.01
FQXNone	0.74	[0.48]	0.00	2.00	68	1.00	1.00	−0.58	−1.70
MQ+	0.00	0.00	0.00	0.00	0	0.00	0.00	—	—
MQo	1.96	0.75	1.00	3.00	80	2.00	2.00	0.06	−1.22
MQu	0.00	0.00	0.00	0.00	0	0.00	0.00	—	—
MQ−	0.23	[0.67]	0.00	1.00	6	0.00	0.00	1.24	4.12
MQNone	0.00	[0.00]	0.00	0.00	0	0.00	0.00	—	—
S−	0.42	[0.78]	0.00	0.50	11	0.00	0.00	0.98	3.15
M	1.96	0.75	1.00	3.00	80	2.00	2.00	0.06	−1.22
FM	4.52	0.81	4.00	8.00	80	5.00	4.00	−1.25	2.76
m	1.40	1.48	0.00	4.00	51	1.00	0.00	0.81	−0.72
FM + m	5.92	0.99	7.00	10.00	80	8.00	8.00	1.11	0.35
FC	1.11	1.09	0.00	3.00	42	2.00	0.00	0.07	−1.72
CF	3.51	0.94	1.00	5.00	80	3.00	3.00	−0.36	0.83
C	0.94	[0.48]	0.00	2.00	68	1.00	1.00	−0.58	−1.70
Cn	0.06	[0.09]	0.00	1.00	1	0.00	0.00	4.15	35.81
FC + CF + C + Cn	5.56	1.63	1.00	7.00	80	6.00	6.00	−0.94	0.29
WGSum C	5.02	1.42	1.00	6.50	80	5.50	5.50	−1.23	1.26
Sum C'	0.58	[0.50]	0.00	1.00	46	1.00	1.00	−0.31	−1.95
Sum T	0.83	[0.22]	0.00	1.00	69	1.00	1.00	−1.21	6.12
Sum V	0.00	[0.00]	0.00	0.00	0	0.00	0.00	—	—
Sum Y	0.54	[0.48]	0.00	1.00	37	0.00	0.00	0.70	−1.55
SumShd	1.95	0.88	0.00	3.00	76	2.00	2.00	−0.18	−0.89
Fr + rF	0.28	[0.40]	0.00	2.00	17	0.00	0.00	1.83	0.35
FD	0.48	[0.68]	0.00	1.00	29	0.00	0.00	1.49	2.34
F	5.77	1.47	3.00	10.00	80	4.00	4.00	3.10	10.34
PAIR	9.61	1.79	5.00	12.00	80	10.00	11.00	−0.88	0.30
3r(2)/R	0.67	0.15	0.25	0.90	80	0.66	0.60	0.38	0.61
LAMBDA	0.79	0.17	0.18	1.50	80	0.78	0.65	−1.56	0.64
EA	6.98	1.42	2.00	8.50	80	6.00	5.00	0.85	1.77
es	7.87	1.00	8.00	11.00	80	7.00	6.00	0.13	−1.52
D	−0.41	0.59	−2.00	0.00	80	0.00	0.00	−1.11	0.28
AdjD	−0.21	0.41	−2.00	0.00	80	0.00	0.00	−1.43	0.05
a (active)	6.03	1.27	5.00	9.00	80	6.00	5.00	0.43	−1.17
p (passive)	1.85	1.90	1.00	6.00	80	2.00	1.00	0.51	−1.49
Ma	0.98	0.84	0.00	2.00	51	1.00	0.00	0.05	−1.59
Mp	0.99	1.35	0.00	3.00	29	0.00	0.00	0.70	−1.44
Intellect	0.96	0.51	0.00	2.00	80	1.00	1.00	−0.06	0.93
Zf	10.15	1.44	6.00	12.00	80	11.00	9.00	−0.45	−1.21
Zd	−1.38	2.20	−5.00	1.00	80	0.00	0.00	−0.91	−0.93
Blends	2.16	0.49	1.00	3.00	80	2.00	2.00	0.38	0.64
Col Shd Bl	0.44	[0.64]	0.00	1.00	18	0.00	0.00	2.13	4.67

Note: Standard Deviations shown in brackets indicate that the value is probably unreliable and/or misleading and should not be used to estimate expected ranges. Ordinarily, these variables should not be included in most parametric analyses.

Table 9. (Continued)

	6-Year-Olds ($N = 80$)								
Variable	Mean	SD	Min	Max	Freq	Median	Mode	SK	KU
Afr	0.87	0.26	0.25	1.11	80	0.82	0.78	−0.76	−0.36
Popular	5.02	1.43	4.00	9.00	80	5.00	5.00	0.14	−0.70
X + %	0.71	0.07	0.45	0.84	80	0.70	0.60	−0.30	−0.89
F + %	0.74	0.25	0.50	1.00	80	0.75	0.75	0.63	1.02
X − %	0.11	0.07	0.00	0.25	80	0.06	0.08	0.21	−1.78
Xu%	0.18	0.09	0.16	0.35	80	0.18	0.15	0.49	−0.48
S − %	0.25	[0.67]	0.00	0.00	28	0.33	0.20	0.88	2.13
Isolate	0.24	0.08	0.12	0.39	80	0.22	0.15	0.31	−1.21
H	2.63	1.14	1.00	4.00	80	3.00	3.00	−0.47	−1.24
(H)	0.78	0.50	0.00	1.00	66	1.00	1.00	−0.31	−1.95
Hd	0.64	0.62	0.00	2.00	45	1.00	1.00	0.43	−0.63
(Hd)	0.23	0.63	0.00	1.00	16	0.00	0.00	1.28	3.16
Hx	0.00	[0.00]	0.00	0.00	0	0.00	0.00	—	—
All H Cont	4.28	0.68	2.00	6.00	80	4.00	4.00	0.22	−0.83
A	8.24	0.96	6.00	10.00	80	8.00	8.00	−0.06	0.32
(A)	0.30	[0.46]	0.00	1.00	24	0.00	0.00	0.89	−1.24
Ad	0.95	[0.22]	0.00	1.00	76	1.00	1.00	−4.21	16.12
(Ad)	0.00	[0.00]	0.00	0.00	0	0.00	0.00	—	—
An	0.33	[0.50]	0.00	1.00	11	0.00	0.00	0.99	2.02
Art	0.96	0.51	0.00	2.00	68	1.00	1.00	−0.06	0.93
Ay	0.00	[0.00]	0.00	0.00	0	0.00	0.00	—	—
Bl	0.25	[0.44]	0.00	1.00	20	0.00	0.00	1.18	−0.63
Bt	1.52	0.60	0.00	2.00	76	2.00	2.00	−0.84	−0.25
Cg	1.02	0.70	0.00	3.00	49	1.00	1.00	0.47	−0.68
Cl	0.11	[0.32]	0.00	1.00	9	0.00	0.00	2.50	4.36
Ex	0.20	[0.40]	0.00	1.00	16	0.00	0.00	1.53	0.35
Fi	0.64	[0.48]	0.00	1.00	51	1.00	1.00	−0.58	−1.70
Fd	0.58	[0.50]	0.00	1.00	46	1.00	1.00	−0.31	−1.95
Ge	0.05	[0.22]	0.00	1.00	4	0.00	0.00	4.21	16.12
Hh	1.26	0.55	1.00	3.00	80	1.00	1.00	2.01	3.16
Ls	1.27	0.78	0.00	3.00	80	1.00	1.00	2.21	3.84
Na	0.81	[0.75]	0.00	2.00	49	1.00	1.00	0.32	−1.14
Sc	0.69	[0.57]	0.00	2.00	51	1.00	1.00	0.08	−0.59
Sx	0.00	[0.00]	0.00	0.00	0	0.00	0.00	—	—
Xy	0.00	[0.00]	0.00	0.00	0	0.00	0.00	—	—
Idio	0.15	0.36	0.00	1.00	12	0.00	0.00	2.00	2.04
DV	0.26	[0.24]	0.00	2.00	35	0.00	0.00	0.68	1.87
INCOM	2.35	[0.48]	2.00	3.00	80	2.00	2.00	0.64	−1.63
DR	0.78	[0.56]	0.00	2.00	36	0.00	0.00	0.57	2.76
FABCOM	0.58	[0.50]	0.00	1.00	46	1.00	1.00	−0.31	−1.95
DV2	0.00	[0.00]	0.00	0.00	0	0.00	0.00	—	—
INC2	0.15	[0.36]	0.00	2.00	13	0.00	0.00	1.94	2.56
DR2	0.00	[0.00]	0.00	0.00	0	0.00	0.00	—	—
FAB2	0.20	[0.45]	0.00	1.00	10	0.00	0.00	1.74	0.96
ALOG	0.64	[0.48]	0.00	1.00	51	1.00	1.00	−0.58	−1.70
CONTAM	0.00	0.00	0.00	0.00	0	0.00	0.00	—	—
Sum6 Sp Sc	6.63	1.38	2.00	8.00	80	6.00	5.00	−0.03	−1.54
Sum6 Sp Sc2	0.72	[0.98]	0.00	2.00	20	0.00	0.00	1.94	2.05
WSum6	13.30	5.03	4.00	20.00	80	13.00	10.00	−0.33	−1.71
AB	0.00	[0.00]	0.00	0.00	0	0.00	0.00	—	—
AG	0.30	0.56	0.00	3.00	20	0.00	0.00	1.74	2.11
CFB	0.00	0.00	0.00	0.00	0	0.00	0.00	—	—
COP	2.40	0.54	0.00	3.00	76	2.00	2.00	−4.21	16.12
CP	0.18	[0.30]	0.00	1.00	2	0.00	0.00	2.73	11.95
MOR	0.60	[0.57]	0.00	3.00	37	0.00	0.00	0.55	2.15
PER	0.23	1.06	0.00	3.00	14	0.00	0.00	0.78	3.24
PSV	0.64	[0.77]	0.00	2.00	28	0.00	0.00	1.21	3.85

Table 9. (Continued)

| | 7-Year-Olds ($N = 120$) | | | | | | | | |
Variable	Mean	SD	Min	Max	Freq	Median	Mode	SK	KU
R	19.93	1.25	14.00	24.00	120	19.00	19.00	−0.10	−0.50
W	10.33	2.01	5.00	12.00	120	9.00	9.00	0.02	−1.34
D	9.09	2.86	7.00	15.00	120	9.00	7.00	0.07	−1.77
Dd	0.82	[0.32]	0.00	3.00	74	0.00	0.00	0.42	2.91
S	1.44	[1.06]	0.00	4.00	102	2.00	2.00	−0.49	−0.38
DQ+	6.48	0.80	6.00	9.00	120	6.00	6.00	0.11	−0.41
DQo	11.15	0.98	10.00	13.00	120	11.00	11.00	0.36	−0.92
DQv	1.63	[0.58]	0.00	3.00	89	2.00	1.00	0.28	−0.71
DQv/+	0.28	[0.45]	0.00	1.00	33	0.00	0.00	1.02	−0.98
FQX+	0.00	0.00	0.00	0.00	0	0.00	0.00	—	—
FQXo	14.37	1.46	12.00	18.00	120	15.00	14.00	0.24	−1.28
FQXu	2.08	0.69	1.00	3.00	120	2.00	2.00	−0.10	−0.86
FQX−	1.99	1.27	0.00	4.00	117	2.00	1.00	0.36	−1.18
FQXNone	1.10	[0.30]	0.00	3.00	72	1.00	1.00	2.70	5.38
MQ+	0.00	0.00	0.00	0.00	0	0.00	0.00	—	—
MQo	2.51	1.16	2.00	6.00	120	3.00	2.00	1.25	0.67
MQu	0.56	0.34	0.00	1.00	13	0.00	0.00	2.20	4.96
MQ−	0.45	[0.22]	0.00	2.00	28	0.00	0.00	2.18	11.75
MQNone	0.00	[0.00]	0.00	0.00	0	0.00	0.00	—	—
S−	0.12	[0.32]	0.00	1.00	14	0.00	0.00	2.42	3.91
M	3.02	1.22	2.00	6.00	120	3.00	2.00	1.15	0.12
FM	5.92	1.20	3.00	7.00	120	6.00	6.00	−1.11	0.14
m	1.06	0.40	0.00	2.00	114	1.00	1.00	0.52	3.35
FM + m	6.08	1.14	5.00	8.00	120	7.00	8.00	−0.80	−0.79
FC	2.17	0.93	1.00	4.00	120	2.00	2.00	0.27	−1.82
CF	3.19	0.98	1.00	6.00	120	3.00	3.00	−0.71	0.47
C	0.99	[0.30]	0.00	3.00	72	0.00	0.00	2.70	5.38
Cn	0.00	[0.00]	0.00	0.00	0	0.00	0.00	—	—
FC + CF + C + Cn	6.15	1.39	4.00	10.00	120	5.00	5.00	0.70	−1.11
WGSum C	4.97	1.14	3.00	7.00	120	4.00	4.00	0.16	−1.17
Sum C'	1.25	[0.86]	0.00	2.00	87	2.00	2.00	−0.51	−1.47
Sum T	0.93	[0.78]	0.00	2.00	110	1.00	1.00	0.42	4.14
Sum V	0.00	[0.00]	0.00	0.00	0	0.00	0.00	—	—
Sum Y	0.23	[0.42]	0.00	1.00	37	0.00	0.00	1.33	−0.23
SumShd	2.48	1.12	1.00	4.00	120	3.00	3.00	−0.05	−1.37
Fr + rF	0.30	[0.39]	0.00	2.00	22	0.00	0.00	2.70	5.38
FD	0.13	[0.70]	0.00	1.00	14	0.00	0.00	1.31	−2.94
F	7.62	1.60	3.00	10.00	120	7.00	8.00	−0.68	−0.31
PAIR	9.73	1.94	7.00	12.00	120	9.00	8.00	0.03	−1.75
3r(2)/R	0.65	0.12	0.33	0.90	120	0.62	0.60	0.14	0.28
LAMBDA	0.79	0.16	0.20	1.25	120	0.70	0.62	−0.17	−0.32
EA	7.48	1.04	4.00	9.00	120	8.00	7.00	−0.41	−1.07
es	8.56	1.67	4.00	12.00	120	8.00	7.00	0.01	−0.98
D	−0.53	0.67	−2.00	0.00	120	0.00	0.00	−0.92	−0.32
AdjD	−0.47	0.58	−2.00	0.00	120	0.00	0.00	−0.79	−0.35
a (active)	6.97	1.24	4.00	8.00	120	7.00	8.00	−1.00	−0.19
p (passive)	3.03	1.28	2.00	6.00	120	2.00	2.00	0.91	−0.50
Ma	2.82	0.87	2.00	5.00	120	3.00	2.00	0.84	−0.07
Mp	0.20	0.40	0.00	1.00	24	0.00	0.00	1.52	0.31
Intellect	0.27	0.44	0.00	1.00	120	0.00	0.00	1.07	−0.87
Zf	11.51	1.46	10.00	15.00	120	11.00	14.00	−0.08	−1.14
Zd	−1.04	2.41	−3.50	3.00	120	−1.00	−3.50	0.39	−1.46
Blends	5.11	0.65	3.00	7.00	120	4.00	5.00	−0.72	0.74
Col Shd Bl	0.36	[0.64]	0.00	1.00	20	0.00	0.00	2.12	8.35

Note: Standard Deviations shown in brackets indicate that the value is probably unreliable and/or misleading and should not be used to estimate expected ranges. Ordinarily, these variables should not be included in most parametric analyses.

Table 9. (Continued)

					7-Year-Olds ($N = 120$)				
Variable	Mean	SD	Min	Max	Freq	Median	Mode	SK	KU
Afr	0.79	0.09	0.45	0.83	120	0.67	0.75	0.02	−1.21
Popular	4.75	0.79	2.00	8.00	120	6.00	4.00	−0.35	−0.16
X + %	0.74	0.09	0.45	0.89	120	0.71	0.72	−0.62	−0.39
F + %	0.66	0.17	0.33	0.88	120	0.63	0.88	−0.08	−0.98
X − %	0.12	0.07	0.05	0.30	107	0.09	0.12	0.33	−1.09
Xu%	0.14	0.08	0.05	0.28	120	0.11	0.11	−0.68	−0.56
S − %	0.15	[0.14]	0.00	0.50	24	0.00	0.00	2.60	5.18
Isolate	0.25	0.05	0.17	0.35	120	0.25	0.25	0.41	−1.08
H	1.87	0.79	1.00	3.00	120	1.00	1.00	0.65	−1.10
(H)	1.64	0.88	0.00	3.00	93	2.00	2.00	−0.29	−1.00
Hd	0.38	0.49	0.00	1.00	45	0.00	0.00	0.52	−1.76
(Hd)	0.74	0.87	0.00	3.00	63	1.00	0.00	1.15	0.71
Hx	0.00	[0.00]	0.00	0.00	0	0.00	0.00	—	—
All H Cont	4.63	0.89	2.00	7.00	120	5.00	4.00	0.17	−0.94
A	9.26	0.77	8.00	10.00	120	9.00	10.00	−0.48	−1.16
(A)	1.18	[0.81]	0.00	2.00	90	1.00	2.00	−0.35	−1.39
Ad	0.68	[0.79]	0.00	2.00	57	0.00	0.00	0.65	−1.10
(Ad)	0.05	[0.22]	0.00	1.00	6	0.00	0.00	4.18	15.75
An	0.37	[0.48]	0.00	1.00	44	0.00	0.00	0.56	−1.72
Art	0.10	0.30	0.00	1.00	12	0.00	0.00	2.70	5.38
Ay	0.17	[0.37]	0.00	1.00	20	0.00	0.00	1.81	1.30
Bl	0.48	[0.45]	0.00	2.00	43	0.00	0.00	1.02	−0.98
Bt	2.11	0.56	1.00	3.00	120	2.00	2.00	0.03	0.12
Cg	1.15	0.36	1.00	2.00	120	1.00	1.00	1.98	1.97
Cl	0.38	[0.57]	0.00	1.00	21	0.00	0.00	2.78	6.10
Ex	0.41	[0.64]	0.00	2.00	19	0.00	0.00	2.46	4.84
Fi	0.48	[0.50]	0.00	1.00	57	0.00	0.00	0.10	−2.02
Fd	0.20	[0.40]	0.00	1.00	24	0.00	0.00	1.52	0.31
Ge	0.00	[0.00]	0.00	0.00	0	0.00	0.00	—	—
Hh	1.45	0.88	0.00	3.00	58	1.00	1.00	0.73	1.40
Ls	1.21	0.93	0.00	3.00	92	1.00	1.00	0.93	1.59
Na	0.96	[0.77]	0.00	2.00	82	1.00	1.00	0.07	−1.31
Sc	1.54	[1.14]	0.00	4.00	96	1.00	1.00	0.39	−0.62
Sx	0.00	[0.00]	0.00	0.00	0	0.00	0.00	—	—
Xy	0.00	[0.00]	0.00	0.00	0	0.00	0.00	—	—
Idio	0.53	0.59	0.00	2.00	57	0.00	0.00	0.64	−0.53
DV	1.39	[0.49]	1.00	2.00	120	1.00	1.00	0.45	−1.83
INCOM	1.39	[0.58]	0.00	2.00	114	1.00	1.00	−0.34	−0.71
DR	0.46	[0.63]	0.00	2.00	56	0.00	0.00	1.06	0.06
FABCOM	0.49	[0.46]	0.00	3.00	55	0.00	0.00	0.93	−1.16
DV2	0.00	[0.00]	0.00	0.00	0	0.00	0.00	—	—
INC2	0.29	[0.57]	0.00	1.00	13	0.00	0.00	2.58	5.05
DR2	0.10	[0.34]	0.00	1.00	7	0.00	0.00	2.98	7.45
FAB2	0.08	[0.26]	0.00	1.00	9	0.00	0.00	3.27	8.83
ALOG	0.48	[0.49]	0.00	2.00	55	0.00	0.00	0.52	−1.76
CONTAM	0.01	0.09	0.00	1.00	1	0.00	0.00	10.95	120.00
Sum6 Sp Sc	5.92	1.25	1.00	7.00	120	5.00	5.00	−0.31	−0.12
Sum6 Sp Sc2	0.18	[0.26]	0.00	1.00	19	0.00	0.00	3.27	8.83
WSum6	12.18	4.66	1.00	29.00	120	10.00	4.00	0.86	0.69
AB	0.00	[0.00]	0.00	0.00	0	0.00	0.00	—	—
AG	1.20	0.40	1.00	2.00	120	1.00	1.00	1.52	0.31
CFB	0.00	0.00	0.00	0.00	0	0.00	0.00	—	—
COP	1.57	0.59	0.00	4.00	108	2.00	2.00	−0.06	−0.28
CP	0.00	[0.00]	0.00	0.00	0	0.00	0.00	—	—
MOR	1.64	[0.58]	1.00	3.00	120	2.00	2.00	0.23	−0.70
PER	2.22	0.57	1.00	4.00	120	1.00	2.00	2.51	4.94
PSV	0.54	[0.50]	0.00	1.00	65	1.00	1.00	−0.17	−2.01

Table 9. (Continued)

				8-Year-Olds (*N* = 120)					
Variable	Mean	SD	Min	Max	Freq	Median	Mode	SK	KU
R	18.73	2.46	14.00	23.00	120	18.00	16.00	0.21	−1.57
W	10.03	1.01	6.00	11.00	120	11.00	8.00	0.55	−1.05
D	7.00	1.28	7.00	11.00	120	7.00	7.00	0.41	−1.12
Dd	1.70	[0.84]	0.00	3.00	104	1.00	0.00	0.40	−1.47
S	1.73	[0.58]	1.00	3.00	119	2.00	2.00	0.08	−0.43
DQ+	6.80	1.74	4.00	10.00	120	6.00	6.00	0.64	−0.57
DQo	11.27	1.40	9.00	14.00	120	12.00	12.00	−0.04	−0.68
DQv	0.90	[0.62]	0.00	3.00	99	1.00	1.00	0.50	−0.59
DQv/+	0.17	[0.25]	0.00	1.00	19	0.00	0.00	3.56	11.07
FQX+	0.00	0.00	0.00	0.00	0	0.00	0.00	—	—
FQXo	13.22	1.83	10.00	17.00	120	13.00	12.00	0.44	−0.37
FQXu	3.47	1.37	2.00	6.00	120	4.00	2.00	0.24	−1.34
FQX−	1.72	0.76	1.00	4.00	120	2.00	1.00	0.53	−1.07
FQXNone	0.43	[0.48]	0.00	1.00	43	0.00	0.00	0.73	−1.53
MQ+	0.00	0.00	0.00	0.00	0	0.00	0.00	—	—
MQo	3.12	1.62	1.00	6.00	120	2.00	2.00	0.68	−0.97
MQu	0.20	0.40	0.00	1.00	24	0.00	0.00	1.54	0.38
MQ−	0.07	[0.25]	0.00	1.00	10	0.00	0.00	3.56	11.07
MQNone	0.00	[0.00]	0.00	0.00	0	0.00	0.00	—	—
S−	0.13	[0.34]	0.00	1.00	29	0.00	0.00	2.21	3.00
M	3.38	1.85	1.00	7.00	120	3.00	2.00	0.79	−0.49
FM	4.72	1.37	3.00	8.00	120	4.00	4.00	0.71	−0.30
m	0.57	0.50	0.00	3.00	57	0.00	0.00	0.14	−2.05
FM + m	5.28	1.56	3.00	8.00	120	5.00	4.00	0.20	−1.29
FC	1.80	0.84	1.00	3.00	120	2.00	1.00	0.40	−1.47
CF	2.73	0.78	1.00	4.00	120	3.00	3.00	−0.38	−0.01
C	0.43	[0.48]	0.00	1.00	43	0.00	0.00	0.73	−1.53
Cn	0.00	[0.00]	0.00	0.00	0	0.00	0.00	—	—
FC + CF + C + Cn	4.87	0.72	3.00	6.00	120	5.00	5.00	−0.90	1.37
WGSum C	4.13	0.77	3.00	6.00	120	4.00	3.50	0.80	0.22
Sum C'	1.30	[0.89]	0.00	3.00	102	1.00	1.00	0.92	−0.26
Sum T	1.08	[0.60]	0.00	2.00	107	1.00	1.00	0.76	2.58
Sum V	0.00	[0.00]	0.00	0.00	0	0.00	0.00	—	—
Sum Y	0.92	[0.85]	0.00	2.00	68	1.00	0.00	0.37	−1.54
SumShd	2.90	1.47	1.00	5.00	120	2.00	2.00	0.18	−1.46
Fr + rF	0.33	[0.48]	0.00	1.00	33	0.00	0.00	0.73	−1.53
FD	0.53	[0.34]	0.00	2.00	39	0.00	0.00	2.21	3.00
F	6.98	1.64	5.00	10.00	120	7.00	7.00	0.67	−0.58
PAIR	7.97	1.19	6.00	10.00	120	8.00	8.00	0.07	−0.60
3r(2)/R	0.62	0.12	0.30	0.90	120	0.67	0.60	0.28	0.39
LAMBDA	0.77	0.27	0.29	1.35	120	0.65	0.70	0.91	−0.21
EA	7.51	1.45	4.00	11.50	120	7.00	6.50	0.48	−0.31
es	8.18	2.51	4.00	12.00	120	7.00	6.00	0.07	−1.31
D	−0.22	0.64	−2.00	1.00	120	0.00	0.00	−1.38	2.44
AdjD	−0.15	0.61	−2.00	1.00	120	0.00	0.00	−1.82	4.40
a (active)	6.73	1.63	4.00	10.00	120	6.00	6.00	0.15	−0.34
p (passive)	1.93	1.30	0.00	5.00	112	2.00	1.00	0.89	0.20
Ma	3.12	1.66	1.00	6.00	120	3.00	2.00	0.52	−1.01
Mp	0.37	0.45	0.00	2.00	46	0.00	0.00	1.08	−0.86
Intellect	0.46	0.98	0.00	1.50	120	0.00	0.00	2.46	3.15
Zf	11.27	1.49	10.00	15.00	120	12.00	11.00	0.28	−1.27
Zd	−0.70	1.93	−4.50	5.00	120	−1.00	0.00	1.23	3.73
Blends	4.88	1.03	3.00	6.00	120	5.00	5.00	−0.54	−0.82
Col Shd Bl	0.30	[0.40]	0.00	1.00	34	0.00	0.00	1.54	0.38

Note: Standard Deviations shown in brackets indicate that the value is probably unreliable and/or misleading and should not be used to estimate expected ranges. Ordinarily, these variables should not be included in most parametric analyses.

Table 9. (Continued)

Variable	Mean	SD	Min	Max	Freq	Median	Mode	SK	KU
				8-Year-Olds (N = 120)					
Afr	0.69	0.09	0.36	0.90	120	0.68	0.63	0.64	0.00
Popular	5.68	0.80	3.00	7.00	120	6.00	6.00	−0.57	−1.22
X + %	0.69	0.07	0.45	0.82	120	0.67	0.63	0.44	−0.76
F + %	0.59	0.07	0.43	0.71	120	0.60	0.60	−0.47	0.10
X − %	0.10	0.04	0.05	0.25	120	0.09	0.06	0.82	−0.25
Xu%	0.20	0.06	0.13	0.32	120	0.18	0.13	0.86	−0.07
S − %	0.06	[0.15]	0.00	0.50	24	0.00	0.00	2.38	4.02
Isolate	0.23	0.04	0.14	0.27	120	0.24	0.19	−0.66	−0.44
H	1.87	1.03	1.00	4.00	120	1.00	1.00	0.66	−1.06
(H)	1.47	0.62	1.00	3.00	120	1.00	1.00	1.00	0.00
Hd	0.27	0.45	0.00	1.00	32	0.00	0.00	1.08	−0.86
(Hd)	1.20	0.55	1.00	3.00	120	1.00	1.00	2.69	6.06
Hx	0.00	[0.00]	0.00	0.00	0	0.00	0.00	—	—
All H Cont	4.80	1.92	3.00	9.00	120	4.00	3.00	0.89	−0.41
A	9.27	1.45	7.00	12.00	120	9.00	8.00	0.35	−1.06
(A)	1.73	[0.58]	1.00	3.00	120	2.00	2.00	0.08	−0.43
Ad	0.33	[0.48]	0.00	1.00	40	0.00	0.00	0.73	−1.53
(Ad)	0.13	[0.34]	0.00	1.00	16	0.00	0.00	2.21	3.00
An	0.20	[0.40]	0.00	1.00	24	0.00	0.00	1.54	0.38
Art	0.59	0.64	0.00	1.00	13	0.00	0.00	2.41	4.58
Ay	0.10	[0.35]	0.00	1.00	4	0.00	0.00	4.87	11.65
Bl	0.33	[0.48]	0.00	1.00	40	0.00	0.00	0.73	−1.53
Bt	1.45	0.65	0.00	3.00	118	1.00	1.00	0.77	0.10
Cg	1.80	1.18	1.00	4.00	120	1.00	1.00	0.92	−0.92
Cl	0.13	[0.34]	0.00	1.00	16	0.00	0.00	2.21	3.00
Ex	0.43	[0.34]	0.00	2.00	35	0.00	0.00	2.20	3.13
Fi	0.33	[0.48]	0.00	1.00	40	0.00	0.00	0.73	−1.53
Fd	0.20	[0.40]	0.00	1.00	41	0.00	0.00	1.54	0.38
Ge	0.00	[0.00]	0.00	0.00	0	0.00	0.00	—	—
Hh	0.45	0.36	0.00	3.00	48	0.00	0.00	1.01	2.11
Ls	0.93	0.25	0.00	1.00	112	1.00	1.00	−3.56	11.07
Na	0.80	[0.40]	0.00	1.00	96	1.00	1.00	−1.54	0.38
Sc	2.45	[0.62]	1.00	3.00	120	3.00	3.00	−0.68	−0.46
Sx	0.00	[0.00]	0.00	0.00	0	0.00	0.00	—	—
Xy	0.00	[0.00]	0.00	0.00	0	0.00	0.00	—	—
Idio	0.53	0.62	0.00	2.00	56	0.00	0.00	0.74	−0.40
DV	1.33	[0.71]	0.00	2.00	104	1.00	2.00	−0.58	−0.80
INCOM	2.07	[0.45]	1.00	3.00	120	2.00	2.00	0.32	2.18
DR	0.47	[0.62]	0.00	2.00	48	0.00	0.00	1.00	0.00
FABCOM	0.55	[0.89]	0.00	3.00	84	1.00	1.00	1.63	1.78
DV2	0.07	[0.25]	0.00	1.00	7	0.00	0.00	3.56	11.07
INC2	0.13	[0.34]	0.00	1.00	15	0.00	0.00	2.21	3.00
DR2	0.00	[0.00]	0.00	0.00	0	0.00	0.00	—	—
FAB2	0.13	[0.34]	0.00	1.00	16	0.00	0.00	2.21	3.00
ALOG	0.73	[0.45]	0.00	1.00	88	1.00	1.00	−1.08	−0.86
CONTAM	0.00	0.00	0.00	0.00	0	0.00	0.00	—	—
Sum6 Sp Sc	6.15	1.96	2.00	10.00	120	6.00	5.00	0.74	0.52
Sum6 Sp Sc2	0.33	[0.48]	0.00	1.00	27	0.00	0.00	0.73	−1.53
WSum6	14.33	5.12	5.00	28.00	120	14.00	13.00	0.72	1.86
AB	0.00	[0.00]	0.00	0.00	0	0.00	0.00	—	—
AG	0.93	0.58	0.00	4.00	96	1.00	1.00	−0.00	0.11
CFB	0.00	0.00	0.00	0.00	0	0.00	0.00	—	—
COP	1.93	1.01	1.00	4.00	120	2.00	1.00	0.55	−1.05
CP	0.08	[0.40]	0.00	1.00	2	0.00	0.00	3.17	16.45
MOR	1.13	[0.34]	1.00	3.00	120	1.00	1.00	2.21	3.00
PER	0.33	0.48	0.00	2.00	40	0.00	0.00	0.73	−1.53
PSV	0.46	[0.78]	0.00	2.00	18	0.00	0.00	2.74	9.86

Table 9. (Continued)

Variable	Mean	SD	Min	Max	Freq	Median	Mode	SK	KU
				9-Year-Olds ($N = 140$)					
R	20.53	2.46	14.00	26.00	140	21.00	19.00	0.41	0.57
W	10.33	1.57	6.00	12.00	140	11.00	9.00	0.55	0.05
D	9.00	1.28	7.00	13.00	140	9.00	8.00	0.41	0.84
Dd	1.20	[0.84]	0.00	4.00	102	1.00	0.00	0.40	3.47
S	1.73	[0.58]	0.00	4.00	108	2.00	1.00	1.78	3.43
DQ+	6.40	1.94	3.00	12.00	138	7.00	6.00	0.64	2.57
DQo	11.67	1.80	7.00	14.00	140	11.00	10.00	−0.04	−0.68
DQv	1.61	[0.65]	0.00	4.00	72	1.00	0.00	0.50	−0.59
DQv/+	0.45	[0.65]	0.00	1.00	23	0.00	0.00	3.56	11.07
FQX+	0.26	0.31	0.00	1.00	5	0.00	0.00	4.18	13.67
FQXo	14.22	1.83	10.00	18.00	140	14.00	12.00	0.44	−0.37
FQXu	3.49	1.37	2.00	6.00	140	4.00	2.00	0.24	−1.34
FQX−	2.04	0.76	1.00	3.00	140	2.00	1.00	0.53	−1.07
FQXNone	0.38	[0.48]	0.00	2.00	31	0.00	0.00	0.73	−1.53
MQ+	0.00	0.00	0.00	0.00	0	0.00	0.00	—	—
MQo	3.12	1.62	1.00	6.00	140	2.00	2.00	0.68	−0.97
MQu	0.20	0.40	0.00	1.00	22	0.00	0.00	1.54	0.38
MQ−	0.37	[0.25]	0.00	2.00	7	0.00	0.00	3.27	10.61
MQNone	0.00	[0.00]	0.00	0.00	0	0.00	0.00	—	—
S−	0.13	[0.34]	0.00	1.00	29	0.00	0.00	2.21	3.00
M	3.12	1.85	1.00	7.00	140	3.00	2.00	0.79	−0.49
FM	4.22	1.47	3.00	9.00	140	4.00	4.00	0.71	0.64
m	0.67	0.58	0.00	3.00	66	0.00	0.00	0.14	3.65
FM + m	5.64	1.86	2.00	9.00	140	6.00	4.00	0.20	0.59
FC	1.89	0.86	0.00	3.00	131	2.00	1.00	0.40	2.47
CF	2.79	0.78	1.00	4.00	140	3.00	2.00	−0.38	2.01
C	0.43	[0.48]	0.00	2.00	22	0.00	0.00	0.73	2.53
Cn	0.00	[0.00]	0.00	0.00	0	0.00	0.00	—	—
FC + CF + C + Cn	4.15	0.72	3.00	9.00	140	6.00	5.00	−0.90	1.37
WGSum C	5.13	1.07	2.50	7.50	140	4.00	3.50	0.80	0.22
Sum C'	1.16	[0.79]	0.00	4.00	104	1.00	1.00	0.92	1.66
Sum T	0.97	[0.63]	0.00	2.00	123	1.00	1.00	0.24	3.58
Sum V	0.00	[0.00]	0.00	0.00	0	0.00	0.00	—	—
Sum Y	0.83	[0.85]	0.00	3.00	102	1.00	1.00	0.37	−1.76
SumShd	2.96	1.27	1.00	6.00	140	2.00	2.00	0.18	−1.46
Fr + rF	0.42	[0.43]	0.00	1.00	26	0.00	0.00	0.73	2.53
FD	0.63	[0.34]	0.00	1.00	64	0.00	0.00	2.45	3.13
F	9.14	1.84	5.00	11.00	140	8.00	8.00	0.67	−0.58
PAIR	8.97	1.69	5.00	12.00	140	9.00	8.00	0.07	−0.60
3r(2)/R	0.57	0.12	0.30	0.88	140	0.60	0.55	0.18	0.54
LAMBDA	0.81	0.37	0.29	1.45	140	0.85	0.70	0.91	0.21
EA	8.25	1.95	4.00	11.50	140	8.00	6.50	0.38	0.56
es	8.60	2.59	4.00	13.00	140	7.00	6.00	0.07	1.31
D	−0.18	0.54	−3.00	1.00	140	0.00	0.00	1.18	1.44
AdjD	−0.10	0.41	−2.00	1.00	140	0.00	0.00	−1.32	3.44
a (active)	6.26	1.23	3.00	11.00	140	7.00	6.00	0.12	0.30
p (passive)	2.51	1.40	0.00	5.00	76	2.00	1.00	0.89	0.70
Ma	2.72	1.36	1.00	6.00	134	3.00	2.00	0.52	−1.01
Mp	0.27	0.45	0.00	1.00	61	0.00	0.00	1.28	1.86
Intellect	1.03	0.98	0.00	1.00	140	0.00	0.00	2.68	10.89
Zf	11.16	1.54	7.00	15.00	140	11.00	11.00	0.28	0.47
Zd	0.40	2.03	−4.50	6.00	140	0.00	0.00	0.23	0.73
Blends	4.38	1.23	2.00	7.00	140	5.00	5.00	−0.44	−0.92
Col Shd Bl	0.90	[0.56]	0.00	3.00	59	0.00	0.00	1.04	0.34

Note: Standard Deviations shown in brackets indicate that the value is probably unreliable and/or misleading and should not be used to estimate expected ranges. Ordinarily, these variables should not be included in most parametric analyses.

Table 9. (Continued)

Variable	Mean	SD	Min	Max	Freq	Median	Mode	SK	KU
				9-Year-Olds ($N = 140$)					
Afr	0.79	0.13	0.38	1.05	140	0.76	0.68	−0.44	0.03
Popular	5.78	0.63	4.00	7.00	140	6.00	5.00	−0.52	−1.02
X + %	0.74	0.09	0.53	0.90	140	0.76	0.71	−0.02	0.64
F + %	0.70	0.08	0.43	1.00	140	0.75	0.67	−0.37	0.15
X − %	0.09	0.06	0.05	0.25	140	0.07	0.09	−0.32	0.25
Xu%	0.17	0.07	0.10	0.33	140	0.18	0.15	0.81	−0.15
S − %	0.06	[0.15]	0.00	1.00	29	0.00	0.00	1.34	4.22
Isolate	0.16	0.05	0.06	0.32	140	0.14	0.17	−0.67	−0.34
H	2.87	1.03	0.00	6.00	138	2.00	2.00	0.66	−1.06
(H)	1.32	0.61	1.00	3.00	140	1.00	1.00	0.84	1.25
Hd	0.57	0.40	0.00	2.00	46	0.00	0.00	1.58	0.36
(Hd)	0.74	0.58	0.00	2.00	62	0.00	0.00	1.60	4.06
Hx	0.00	[0.00]	0.00	0.00	0	0.00	0.00	—	—
All H Cont	5.50	1.62	2.00	8.00	140	5.00	4.00	0.59	−0.41
A	8.28	1.59	5.00	13.00	140	9.00	8.00	0.35	0.06
(A)	0.73	[0.68]	0.00	3.00	101	1.00	1.00	0.28	1.63
Ad	0.53	[0.98]	0.00	2.00	80	1.00	1.00	−0.63	2.73
(Ad)	0.23	[0.39]	0.00	1.00	13	0.00	0.00	3.27	4.00
An	0.36	[0.60]	0.00	3.00	34	0.00	0.00	2.54	2.38
Art	0.32	0.71	0.00	2.00	31	0.00	0.00	1.38	3.09
Ay	0.13	[0.28]	0.00	1.00	11	0.00	0.00	3.94	8.28
Bl	0.33	[0.48]	0.00	1.00	28	0.00	0.00	1.03	1.33
Bt	1.45	0.65	0.00	3.00	129	1.00	1.00	0.97	1.10
Cg	1.84	1.08	1.00	4.00	133	1.00	1.00	0.92	1.92
Cl	0.16	[0.39]	0.00	1.00	40	0.00	0.00	2.01	3.34
Ex	0.26	[0.54]	0.00	1.00	21	0.00	0.00	1.93	4.06
Fi	0.69	[0.68]	0.00	1.00	68	0.00	0.00	0.33	2.73
Fd	0.18	[0.46]	0.00	1.00	15	0.00	0.00	2.54	4.38
Ge	0.00	[0.00]	0.00	0.00	0	0.00	0.00	—	—
Hh	0.59	0.36	0.00	1.00	49	0.00	0.00	2.11	2.07
Ls	0.93	0.59	0.00	3.00	107	1.00	1.00	−0.28	0.83
Na	0.70	[0.48]	0.00	2.00	96	1.00	1.00	−0.54	1.38
Sc	1.55	[0.72]	0.00	3.00	102	2.00	1.00	0.68	2.46
Sx	0.00	[0.00]	0.00	0.00	0	0.00	0.00	—	—
Xy	0.00	[0.00]	0.00	0.00	0	0.00	0.00	—	—
Idio	0.63	0.42	0.00	1.00	48	0.00	0.00	0.84	1.40
DV	1.01	[0.61]	0.00	2.00	97	1.00	1.00	−0.08	2.80
INCOM	1.37	[0.75]	0.00	3.00	81	1.00	1.00	0.32	2.18
DR	0.67	[0.72]	0.00	2.00	91	1.00	1.00	−0.73	2.00
FABCOM	1.05	[0.89]	0.00	3.00	102	1.00	1.00	0.63	1.68
DV2	0.07	[0.21]	0.00	1.00	6	0.00	0.00	1.56	12.07
INC2	0.11	[0.59]	0.00	1.00	7	0.00	0.00	1.27	11.40
DR2	0.00	[0.00]	0.00	0.00	0	0.00	0.00	—	—
FAB2	0.05	[0.39]	0.00	1.00	3	0.00	0.00	0.68	13.00
ALOG	0.61	[0.49]	0.00	1.00	56	0.00	0.00	1.08	3.86
CONTAM	0.00	0.00	0.00	0.00	0	0.00	0.00	—	—
Sum6 Sp Sc	5.95	2.16	1.00	9.00	140	6.00	6.00	0.74	0.52
Sum6 Sp Sc2	0.27	[0.51]	0.00	2.00	14	0.00	0.00	0.63	6.53
WSum6	13.06	4.72	3.00	26.00	140	12.00	11.00	0.92	0.86
AB	0.00	[0.00]	0.00	0.00	0	0.00	0.00	—	—
AG	1.37	0.78	0.00	4.00	128	2.00	1.00	0.67	1.11
CFB	0.00	0.00	0.00	0.00	0	0.00	0.00	—	—
COP	2.03	1.14	0.00	5.00	136	2.00	2.00	0.18	1.05
CP	0.00	[0.00]	0.00	0.00	0	0.00	0.00	—	—
MOR	0.87	[0.64]	0.00	4.00	116	1.00	1.00	−0.41	1.87
PER	1.16	0.78	0.00	6.00	99	1.00	1.00	0.73	−1.53
PSV	0.26	[0.61]	0.00	2.00	29	0.00	0.00	1.04	4.14

Table 9. (Continued)

Variable	Mean	SD	Min	Max	Freq	Median	Mode	SK	KU
				10-Year-Olds ($N = 120$)					
R	20.97	1.92	18.00	25.00	120	19.00	19.00	0.85	−0.39
W	9.52	0.87	9.00	12.00	120	9.00	9.00	1.59	1.46
D	10.10	1.48	8.00	13.00	120	10.00	9.00	0.31	−1.32
Dd	1.35	[0.44]	0.00	3.00	119	0.00	0.00	1.17	−0.64
S	1.48	[0.70]	1.00	3.00	107	1.00	1.00	1.12	−0.08
DQ+	7.68	0.96	3.00	9.00	120	8.00	7.00	−0.48	−0.18
DQo	12.07	1.78	9.00	17.00	120	12.00	11.00	0.08	0.01
DQv	0.53	[0.50]	0.00	2.00	64	1.00	1.00	−0.14	−2.02
DQv/+	0.38	[0.28]	0.00	1.00	36	0.00	0.00	3.05	7.45
FQX+	0.30	0.50	0.00	1.00	11	0.00	0.00	4.04	9.15
FQXo	15.80	1.98	13.00	21.00	120	15.00	15.00	0.81	0.33
FQXu	2.95	0.79	1.00	4.00	120	3.00	3.00	−0.54	0.12
FQX−	1.58	1.03	0.00	6.00	104	2.00	2.00	1.74	6.56
FQXNone	0.13	[0.34]	0.00	1.00	29	0.00	0.00	2.19	2.82
MQ+	0.08	0.21	0.00	1.00	2	0.00	0.00	4.80	13.25
MQo	3.23	1.48	1.00	6.00	120	3.00	3.00	0.22	−0.78
MQu	0.25	0.44	0.00	1.00	30	0.00	0.00	1.17	−0.64
MQ−	0.17	[0.37]	0.00	2.00	21	0.00	0.00	1.81	1.30
MQNone	0.00	[0.00]	0.00	0.00	0	0.00	0.00	—	—
S−	0.12	[0.32]	0.00	1.00	14	0.00	0.00	2.42	3.91
M	3.65	1.63	1.00	7.00	120	4.00	3.00	−0.04	−0.69
FM	5.53	1.46	3.00	7.00	120	6.00	7.00	−0.43	−1.38
m	1.08	0.28	1.00	2.00	120	1.00	1.00	3.05	7.45
FM + m	6.62	1.40	4.00	8.00	120	7.00	8.00	−0.56	−1.06
FC	2.55	0.96	1.00	4.00	120	2.00	2.00	0.44	−1.03
CF	3.68	1.29	2.00	6.00	120	3.50	5.00	0.14	−1.27
C	0.13	[0.34]	0.00	2.00	29	0.00	0.00	2.19	2.82
Cn	0.00	[0.00]	0.00	0.00	0	0.00	0.00	—	—
FC + CF + C + Cn	6.37	1.50	4.00	8.00	120	7.00	8.00	−0.41	−1.30
WGSum C	5.16	1.25	3.00	7.00	120	5.00	4.00	−0.23	−1.26
Sum C'	0.79	[0.85]	0.00	4.00	73	1.00	1.00	0.41	0.44
Sum T	0.98	[0.39]	0.00	2.00	106	1.00	1.00	−0.16	3.86
Sum V	0.02	[0.13]	0.00	1.00	2	0.00	0.00	7.65	57.43
Sum Y	0.43	[0.65]	0.00	2.00	34	0.00	0.00	0.82	−0.37
SumShd	1.83	1.32	1.00	6.00	120	3.00	4.00	0.06	−1.16
Fr + rF	0.35	[0.36]	0.00	1.00	36	0.00	0.00	1.98	1.97
FD	0.67	[0.58]	0.00	2.00	78	1.00	1.00	1.33	0.81
F	6.38	2.04	3.00	12.00	120	5.50	5.00	0.57	−0.73
PAIR	9.62	1.36	6.00	12.00	120	9.00	9.00	−0.29	0.09
3r(2)/R	0.54	0.07	0.29	0.68	120	0.52	0.47	−0.71	6.30
LAMBDA	0.49	0.23	0.19	1.11	120	0.36	0.36	0.90	−0.23
EA	8.81	1.36	4.00	11.00	120	9.00	7.00	−0.37	1.09
es	8.45	1.90	5.00	12.00	120	8.00	7.00	−0.33	−0.89
D	−0.15	0.44	−2.00	1.00	120	0.00	0.00	−1.89	5.07
AdjD	−0.12	0.49	−2.00	1.00	120	0.00	0.00	−1.17	3.81
a (active)	7.15	1.37	6.00	11.00	120	8.00	7.00	0.32	−0.74
p (passive)	3.27	0.66	1.00	4.00	120	2.00	2.00	1.46	1.91
Ma	2.82	1.09	1.00	5.00	120	3.00	3.00	−0.10	−0.63
Mp	0.98	0.83	0.00	3.00	88	1.00	1.00	0.93	0.76
Intellect	0.53	0.56	0.00	2.00	120	0.50	0.00	0.44	−0.81
Zf	13.52	1.19	11.00	16.00	120	13.50	13.00	−0.19	−0.27
Zd	−0.13	2.32	−5.00	5.00	120	0.00	−3.00	0.22	−0.35
Blends	5.80	1.05	3.00	7.00	120	6.00	7.00	−0.39	−0.70
Col Shd Blend	0.42	[0.13]	0.00	1.00	22	0.00	0.00	7.65	57.43

Note: Standard Deviations shown in brackets indicate that the value is probably unreliable and/or misleading and should not be used to estimate expected ranges. Ordinarily, these variables should not be included in most parametric analyses.

Table 9. (Continued)

Variable	Mean	SD	Min	Max	Freq	Median	Mode	SK	KU
				10-Year-Olds ($N = 120$)					
Afr	0.63	0.09	0.50	0.85	120	0.58	0.58	0.94	−0.05
Popular	6.O7	0.84	3.00	7.00	120	6.00	6.00	−1.01	1.55s
X + %	0.76	0.08	0.45	0.88	120	0.79	0.75	−0.86	1.39
F + %	0.55	0.14	0.33	0.82	120	0.50	0.50	0.39	−1.03
X − %	0.08	0.06	0.00	0.25	104	0.07	0.05	1.46	5.42
Xu%	0.15	0.05	0.05	0.21	120	0.16	0.16	−0.44	−0.53
S − %	0.12	[0.14]	0.00	1.00	34	0.00	0.00	2.82	6.34
Isolate	0.19	0.03	0.14	0.26	120	0.19	0.16	0.67	−0.53
H	2.47	1.12	1.00	5.00	120	3.00	3.00	0.01	−0.83
(H)	1.48	0.74	0.00	2.00	102	2.00	2.00	−1.06	−0.37
Hd	0.25	0.47	0.00	2.00	28	0.00	0.00	1.65	1.80
(Hd)	0.85	0.36	0.00	1.00	102	1.00	1.00	−1.98	1.97
Hx	0.00	[0.00]	0.00	0.00	0	0.00	0.00	—	—
All H Cont	5.05	1.64	2.00	8.00	120	6.00	6.00	−0.59	−0.59
A	8.92	1.18	7.00	11.00	120	9.00	9.00	0.54	−0.43
(A)	1.20	[0.77]	0.00	3.00	96	1.00	1.00	−0.14	−0.88
Ad	1.35	[1.08]	0.00	3.00	76	2.00	2.00	−0.25	−1.49
(Ad)	0.07	[0.25]	0.00	1.00	8	0.00	0.00	3.52	10.56
An	0.67	[0.57]	0.00	2.00	74	1.00	1.00	0.14	−0.66
Art	0.53	0.56	0.00	2.00	60	0.50	0.00	0.44	−0.81
Ay	0.23	[0.41]	0.00	1.00	12	0.00	0.00	2.95	11.25
Bl	0.60	[0.59]	0.00	2.00	66	1.00	1.00	0.37	−0.70
Bt	2.17	0.74	1.00	4.00	120	2.00	2.00	0.49	0.33
Cg	1.48	1.03	0.00	3.00	102	1.00	1.00	0.33	−1.10
Cl	0.08	[0.28]	0.00	1.00	10	0.00	0.00	3.05	7.45
Ex	0.08	[0.28]	0.00	1.00	10	0.00	0.00	3.05	7.45
Fi	0.75	[0.44]	0.00	1.00	90	1.00	1.00	−1.17	−0.64
Fd	0.53	[0.50]	0.00	1.00	64	1.00	1.00	−0.14	−2.02
Ge	0.00	[0.00]	0.00	0.00	0	0.00	0.00	—	—
Hh	0.60	0.49	0.00	1.00	72	1.00	1.00	−0.41	−1.86
Ls	1.00	0.45	0.00	2.00	108	1.00	1.00	0.00	2.14
Na	0.30	[0.46]	0.00	1.00	36	0.00	0.00	0.88	−1.24
Sc	2.85	[0.40]	2.00	4.00	120	3.00	3.00	−1.17	1.62
Sx	0.00	[0.00]	0.00	0.00	0	0.00	0.00	—	—
Xy	0.00	[0.00]	0.00	0.00	0	0.00	0.00	—	—
Idio	0.08	0.28	0.00	1.00	10	0.00	0.00	3.05	7.45
DV	1.03	[0.61]	1.00	3.00	112	1.00	1.00	1.72	4.91
INCOM	1.35	[0.51]	1.00	3.00	103	1.00	1.00	1.01	−0.16
DR	0.18	[0.28]	0.00	1.00	30	0.00	0.00	3.05	7.45
FABCOM	0.65	[0.48]	0.00	1.00	82	0.00	0.00	0.64	−1.62
DV2	0.00	[0.00]	0.00	0.00	0	0.00	0.00	—	—
INC2	0.23	[0.43]	0.00	1.00	5	0.00	0.00	1.28	−0.38
DR2	0.02	[0.13]	0.00	1.00	2	0.00	0.00	7.65	57.43
FAB2	0.02	[0.09]	0.00	1.00	1	0.00	0.00	8.31	69.82
ALOG	0.47	[0.48]	0.00	1.00	49	0.00	0.00	0.56	−1.72
CONTAM	0.00	0.00	0.00	0.00	0	0.00	0.00	—	—
Sum6 Sp Sc	5.15	1.20	2.00	8.00	120	4.00	4.00	1.37	0.95
Sum6 Sp Sc2	0.09	[0.44]	0.00	1.00	10	0.00	0.00	1.17	−0.64
WSum6	10.22	3.79	3.00	17.00	120	7.00	7.00	1.08	0.65
AB	0.08	[0.28]	0.00	1.00	2	0.00	0.00	4.15	10.34
AG	1.57	0.62	1.00	3.00	120	1.50	1.00	0.61	−0.55
CFB	0.00	0.00	0.00	0.00	0	0.00	0.00	—	—
COP	1.73	0.84	1.00	4.00	120	2.00	2.00	1.41	1.94
CP	0.00	[0.00]	0.00	0.00	0	0.00	0.00	—	—
MOR	0.75	[0.62]	0.00	3.00	78	1.00	1.00	0.67	−0.50
PER	0.75	0.44	0.00	1.00	90	1.00	1.00	−1.17	−0.64
PSV	0.05	[0.22]	0.00	1.00	6	0.00	0.00	4.18	15.75

Table 9. (Continued)

Variable	Mean	SD	Min	Max	Freq	Median	Mode	SK	KU
				11-Year-Olds ($N = 135$)					
R	21.29	2.43	15.00	27.00	135	22.00	19.00	0.93	0.29
W	9.61	0.95	9.00	12.00	135	9.00	9.00	1.49	1.06
D	10.01	1.31	9.00	13.00	135	11.00	11.00	0.05	−1.09
Dd	1.67	[1.13]	0.00	4.00	128	0.00	0.00	2.12	3.75
S	1.75	[0.68]	1.00	3.00	135	2.00	2.00	0.36	−0.81
DQ+	8.07	1.22	6.00	10.00	135	8.00	7.00	0.10	−1.08
DQo	12.08	2.14	9.00	17.00	135	12.00	11.00	0.73	0.25
DQv	0.64	[0.88]	0.00	3.00	63	0.00	0.00	1.57	1.99
DQv/+	0.50	[0.69]	0.00	2.00	41	0.00	0.00	1.98	2.39
FQX+	0.21	0.38	0.00	1.00	9	0.00	0.00	3.08	11.42
FQXo	15.83	1.40	13.00	18.00	135	16.00	17.00	−0.29	−1.09
FQXu	3.18	1.26	1.00	6.00	135	3.00	3.00	0.52	0.49
FQX−	2.20	1.87	0.00	7.00	125	2.00	2.00	1.73	2.02
FQXNone	0.18	[0.27]	0.00	1.00	18	0.00	0.00	3.09	7.69
MQ+	0.11	0.45	0.00	1.00	3	0.00	0.00	4.24	13.85
MQo	3.59	1.38	1.00	6.00	135	4.00	3.00	−0.15	−0.69
MQu	0.33	0.47	0.00	1.00	44	0.00	0.00	0.75	−1.46
MQ−	0.20	[0.40]	0.00	1.00	27	0.00	0.00	1.52	0.30
MQNone	0.00	[0.00]	0.00	0.00	0	0.00	0.00	—	—
S−	0.31	[0.46]	0.00	1.00	52	0.00	0.00	0.82	−1.34
M	4.12	1.67	1.00	7.00	135	4.00	3.00	0.08	−0.56
FM	4.48	1.21	2.00	7.00	135	6.00	4.00	−0.51	−0.65
m	1.00	0.89	0.00	2.00	122	1.00	1.00	0.84	1.69
FM + m	5.48	1.21	4.00	8.00	135	7.00	7.00	−0.51	−0.65
FC	2.93	0.95	1.00	4.00	135	3.00	4.00	−0.19	−1.29
CF	3.43	1.13	2.00	6.00	135	4.00	4.00	0.10	−1.14
C	0.28	[0.27]	0.00	1.00	17	0.00	0.00	3.09	7.69
Cn	0.00	[0.00]	0.00	0.00	0	0.00	0.00	—	—
FC + CF + C + Cn	6.44	1.39	4.00	8.00	135	7.00	7.00	−0.57	−0.93
WGSum C	4.02	1.15	2.50	8.00	135	5.00	4.00	−0.36	−1.06
Sum C'	1.06	[0.71]	0.00	2.00	105	1.00	1.00	−0.09	−0.99
Sum T	0.94	[0.47]	0.00	2.00	116	1.00	1.00	−0.20	1.55
Sum V	0.00	[0.00]	0.00	0.00	0	0.00	0.00	—	—
Sum Y	0.85	[0.70]	0.00	2.00	91	1.00	1.00	0.21	−0.92
SumShd	2.85	1.10	1.00	4.00	135	3.00	4.00	−0.32	−1.31
Fr + rF	0.21	[0.41]	0.00	1.00	29	0.00	0.00	1.40	−0.03
FD	0.91	[0.84]	0.00	2.00	92	0.00	0.00	0.59	−1.34
F	6.70	2.37	4.00	12.00	135	6.00	5.00	1.12	0.09
PAIR	9.90	1.08	7.00	12.00	135	10.00	10.00	−0.31	0.86
3r(2)/R	0.53	0.04	0.35	0.75	135	0.58	0.50	0.44	0.38
LAMBDA	0.68	0.22	0.27	1.50	135	0.69	0.60	0.89	−0.62
EA	8.14	1.37	7.00	12.00	135	8.00	7.00	0.57	−0.53
es	8.33	1.72	4.00	12.00	135	9.00	7.00	−0.22	−1.08
D	−0.09	0.29	−1.00	0.00	135	0.00	0.00	−2.92	6.63
AdjD	−0.06	0.34	−1.00	1.00	135	0.00	0.00	−1.00	5.32
a (active)	7.89	1.42	6.00	11.00	135	8.00	7.00	0.67	−0.27
p (passive)	2.79	1.60	2.00	8.00	135	2.00	2.00	2.08	3.12
Ma	2.81	1.01	1.00	5.00	135	3.00	3.00	0.29	−0.01
Mp	1.38	1.33	0.00	5.00	104	1.00	1.00	1.26	0.76
Intellect	0.77	0.65	0.00	2.00	135	1.00	1.00	0.26	−0.67
Zf	13.70	1.22	11.00	16.00	135	14.00	15.00	−0.30	−0.72
Zd	0.60	2.74	−4.50	4.50	135	1.00	4.50	−0.07	−1.15
Blends	6.04	1.41	3.00	8.00	135	6.00	7.00	−0.28	−1.05
Col Shd Bl	0.00	[0.00]	0.00	0.00	0	0.00	0.00	—	—

Note: Standard Deviations shown in brackets indicate that the value is probably unreliable and/or misleading and should not be used to estimate expected ranges. Ordinarily, these variables should not be included in most parametric analyses.

Table 9. **(Continued)**

Variable	Mean	SD	Min	Max	Freq	Median	Mode	SK	KU
				11-Year-Olds ($N = 135$)					
Afr	0.62	0.09	0.47	0.80	135	0.58	0.58	0.33	−0.90
Popular	6.06	0.86	4.00	9.00	135	7.00	5.00	−0.76	−0.78
X + %	0.75	0.08	0.52	0.90	135	0.77	0.79	−1.65	2.46
F + %	0.54	0.16	0.27	1.00	135	0.50	0.60	0.75	0.92
X − %	0.10	0.07	0.00	0.26	125	0.09	0.09	1.42	1.41
Xu%	0.15	0.05	0.05	0.24	135	0.16	0.14	−0.35	−0.35
S − %	0.11	[0.19]	0.00	0.50	42	0.00	0.00	1.47	0.42
Isolate	0.20	0.05	0.14	0.37	135	0.18	0.17	2.07	4.31
H	2.80	1.27	1.00	5.00	131	3.00	3.00	0.23	−0.71
(H)	1.51	0.66	0.00	2.00	123	2.00	2.00	−1.01	−0.12
Hd	0.52	0.66	0.00	2.00	58	0.00	0.00	0.90	−0.30
(Hd)	0.87	0.33	0.00	1.00	118	1.00	1.00	−2.28	3.25
Hx	0.00	[0.00]	0.00	0.00	0	0.00	0.00	—	—
All H Cont	5.70	1.80	2.00	9.00	135	6.00	6.00	−0.22	0.04
A	8.58	1.25	7.00	11.00	135	8.00	8.00	0.83	−0.19
(A)	1.00	[0.83]	0.00	2.00	89	1.00	0.00	0.00	−1.54
Ad	1.54	[0.95]	0.00	3.00	101	2.00	2.00	−0.75	−0.78
(Ad)	0.16	[0.36]	0.00	1.00	21	0.00	0.00	1.92	1.72
An	0.73	[0.64]	0.00	2.00	85	1.00	1.00	0.30	−0.66
Art	0.56	0.50	0.00	1.00	76	1.00	1.00	−0.26	−1.96
Ay	0.21	[0.59]	0.00	2.00	17	0.00	0.00	2.62	5.19
Bl	0.44	[0.57]	0.00	2.00	54	0.00	0.00	0.87	−0.24
Bt	2.10	0.67	1.00	4.00	135	2.00	2.00	0.65	1.16
Cg	1.60	0.99	0.00	3.00	122	1.00	1.00	0.26	−1.15
Cl	0.16	[0.24]	0.00	1.00	18	0.00	0.00	3.77	12.44
Ex	0.23	[0.17]	0.00	2.00	14	0.00	0.00	3.61	9.92
Fi	0.85	[0.36]	0.00	1.00	72	1.00	1.00	−2.00	2.04
Fd	0.64	[0.48]	0.00	1.00	67	1.00	1.00	−0.61	−1.65
Ge	0.10	[0.27]	0.00	1.00	6	0.00	0.00	3.97	13.57
Hh	0.81	0.46	0.00	2.00	106	1.00	1.00	−0.65	0.55
Ls	1.28	0.61	0.00	2.00	124	1.00	1.00	−0.23	−0.58
Na	0.35	[0.48]	0.00	1.00	47	0.00	0.00	0.64	−1.61
Sc	2.96	[0.36]	2.00	4.00	135	3.00	3.00	−0.57	4.57
Sx	0.00	[0.00]	0.00	0.00	0	0.00	0.00	—	—
Xy	0.09	[0.29]	0.00	1.00	9	0.00	0.00	2.92	6.63
Idio	0.06	0.34	0.00	2.00	4	0.00	0.00	5.61	29.92
DV	1.21	[0.41]	1.00	2.00	135	1.00	1.00	1.46	0.13
INCOM	1.44	[0.63]	0.00	3.00	131	1.00	1.00	0.42	−0.06
DR	0.22	[0.32]	0.00	1.00	26	0.00	0.00	2.39	3.75
FABCOM	0.46	[0.48]	0.00	2.00	48	0.00	0.00	0.61	−1.65
DV2	0.00	[0.00]	0.00	0.00	0	0.00	0.00	—	—
INC2	0.12	[0.32]	0.00	1.00	16	0.00	0.00	2.39	3.75
DR2	0.03	[0.17]	0.00	1.00	4	0.00	0.00	5.61	29.92
FAB2	0.00	[0.00]	0.00	0.00	0	0.00	0.00	—	—
ALOG	0.28	[0.43]	0.00	1.00	39	0.00	0.00	1.20	−0.56
CONTAM	0.00	0.00	0.00	0.00	0	0.00	0.00	—	—
Sum6 Sp Sc	4.36	1.16	2.00	6.00	135	3.00	3.00	0.69	−0.54
Sum6 Sp Sc2	0.15	[0.36]	0.00	1.00	20	0.00	0.00	2.00	2.04
WSum6	8.93	3.04	3.00	16.00	135	8.00	7.00	0.78	1.10
AB	0.21	[0.39]	0.00	1.00	8	0.00	0.00	3.38	11.45
AG	1.42	0.57	1.00	4.00	135	1.00	1.00	0.94	−0.11
CFB	0.00	0.00	0.00	0.00	0	0.00	0.00	—	—
COP	1.56	0.50	1.00	4.00	135	2.00	2.00	−0.23	−1.98
CP	0.00	[0.00]	0.00	0.00	0	0.00	0.00	—	—
MOR	0.72	[0.57]	0.00	3.00	82	0.00	0.00	0.94	−0.11
PER	0.88	0.53	0.00	2.00	107	1.00	1.00	−0.11	0.38
PSV	0.09	[0.25]	0.00	1.00	8	0.00	0.00	4.47	18.26

Table 9. (Continued)

Variable	Mean	SD	Min	Max	Freq	Median	Mode	SK	KU
				12-Year-Olds ($N = 120$)					
R	21.40	2.05	14.00	23.00	120	20.00	22.00	−1.03	0.96
W	8.79	1.85	1.00	14.00	120	9.00	9.00	−1.94	7.05
D	10.85	1.96	1.00	13.00	120	11.00	12.00	−3.26	12.20
Dd	1.76	[1.11]	0.00	5.00	117	1.00	1.00	3.51	16.47
S	1.92	[0.76]	0.00	5.00	118	2.00	2.00	1.30	4.92
DQ+	8.16	1.90	2.00	10.00	120	8.00	10.00	−1.42	2.39
DQo	12.12	1.07	9.00	15.00	120	12.00	12.00	−0.13	1.90
DQv	1.03	[0.26]	0.00	2.00	72	1.00	1.00	0.65	2.43
DQv/+	0.38	[0.38]	0.00	2.00	16	0.00	0.00	3.62	13.45
FQX+	0.30	0.54	0.00	2.00	10	0.00	0.00	4.16	16.95
FQXo	15.34	2.32	5.00	17.00	120	16.00	17.00	−2.40	6.80
FQXu	3.77	0.89	1.00	5.00	120	4.00	3.00	−0.95	1.08
FQX−	1.95	1.04	1.00	7.00	120	2.00	2.00	3.71	16.47
FQXNone	0.43	[0.26]	0.00	2.00	42	0.00	0.00	2.65	7.43
MQ+	0.10	0.30	0.00	1.00	5	0.00	0.00	7.45	45.23
MQo	3.21	1.52	1.00	5.00	120	3.00	5.00	−0.33	−1.26
MQu	0.67	0.51	0.00	2.00	78	1.00	1.00	−0.32	−1.01
MQ−	0.22	[0.41]	0.00	1.00	26	0.00	0.00	1.39	−0.06
MQNone	0.02	[0.13]	0.00	1.00	2	0.00	0.00	7.65	57.43
S−	0.57	[0.62]	0.00	3.00	63	1.00	1.00	1.02	2.14
M	4.21	2.06	1.00	7.00	120	4.00	4.00	−0.22	−1.07
FM	5.02	1.66	0.00	9.00	118	6.00	4.00	−1.34	1.64
m	1.00	0.45	0.00	3.00	112	1.00	1.00	2.26	12.57
FM + m	6.02	1.70	1.00	9.00	120	7.00	7.00	−1.44	1.83
FC	2.87	1.17	0.00	4.00	106	3.00	3.00	−1.61	1.77
CF	3.14	1.40	0.00	5.00	112	3.00	3.00	−0.55	−0.30
C	0.39	[0.13]	0.00	1.00	38	0.00	0.00	1.65	7.43
Cn	0.00	[0.00]	0.00	0.00	0	0.00	0.00	—	—
FC + CF + C + Cn	6.03	2.29	0.00	8.00	119	7.00	7.00	−1.49	1.26
WGSum C	4.05	1.78	0.00	6.50	120	5.00	6.50	−1.17	0.69
Sum C'	1.08	[0.88]	0.00	3.00	99	1.00	1.00	0.38	−0.47
Sum T	0.88	[0.32]	0.00	1.00	106	1.00	1.00	−2.42	3.91
Sum V	0.07	[0.36]	0.00	2.00	4	0.00	0.00	5.27	26.16
Sum Y	1.01	[0.67]	0.00	2.00	108	2.00	2.00	−1.04	−0.13
SumShd	3.74	1.37	0.00	6.00	114	4.00	4.00	−0.98	1.25
Fr + rF	0.20	[0.13]	0.00	1.00	15	0.00	0.00	3.65	17.43
FD	1.48	[0.83]	0.00	2.00	94	2.00	2.00	−1.11	−0.61
F	5.84	1.65	5.00	13.00	120	5.00	5.00	2.75	7.47
PAIR	9.09	1.89	1.00	10.00	120	10.00	10.00	−2.89	9.00
3r(2)/R	0.54	0.08	0.10	0.50	120	0.55	0.50	−3.53	16.28
LAMBDA	0.66	0.58	0.29	4.25	120	0.70	0.50	5.18	30.28
EA	8.26	2.38	1.00	12.00	120	8.50	7.00	−1.38	1.99
es	8.97	2.59	1.00	13.00	120	8.00	6.00	−2.08	3.95
D	−0.21	0.53	−2.00	1.00	120	0.00	0.00	−1.17	2.25
AdjD	−0.11	0.67	−2.00	2.00	120	0.00	0.00	−0.04	1.74
a (active)	6.53	1.45	2.00	8.00	120	7.00	6.00	−1.34	2.04
p (passive)	4.00	2.01	0.00	8.00	118	3.00	2.00	0.50	−0.57
Ma	2.47	0.80	0.00	4.00	118	2.00	2.00	0.32	0.24
Mp	1.73	1.60	0.00	5.00	92	2.00	2.00	−0.06	−1.04
Intellect	1.05	0.59	0.00	4.00	120	1.00	1.00	2.96	12.69
Zf	13.14	1.96	5.00	16.00	120	14.00	14.00	−2.25	6.48
Zd	1.67	2.11	−4.50	5.00	120	1.50	1.50	−0.24	−0.26
Blends	6.67	2.29	0.00	9.00	118	7.00	8.00	−1.79	2.12
Col Shd Bl	0.05	[0.22]	0.00	1.00	6	0.00	0.00	4.18	15.75

Note: Standard Deviations shown in brackets indicate that the value is probably unreliable and/or misleading and should not be used to estimate expected ranges. Ordinarily, these variables should not be included in most parametric analyses.

Table 9. (Continued)

Variable	Mean	SD	Min	Max	Freq	Median	Mode	SK	KU
				12-Year-Olds ($N = 120$)					
Afr	0.65	0.11	0.21	0.67	120	0.69	0.67	−0.80	0.75
Popular	6.22	1.10	2.00	7.00	120	7.00	6.00	−1.53	2.56
X + %	0.75	0.09	0.29	0.88	120	0.77	0.77	−3.33	14.09
F + %	0.54	0.11	0.18	0.88	120	0.60	0.60	−0.10	1.95
X − %	0.10	0.05	0.05	0.41	120	0.09	0.09	4.05	19.33
Xu%	0.15	0.04	0.05	0.29	120	0.15	0.14	−0.27	2.29
S − %	0.27	[0.28]	0.00	1.00	63	0.33	0.00	0.42	−0.71
Isolate	0.15	0.04	0.00	0.33	120	0.16	0.18	0.19	5.42
H	3.38	1.64	1.00	5.00	120	3.00	5.00	−0.37	−1.42
(H)	1.24	0.84	0.00	4.00	97	1.00	1.00	0.38	0.53
Hd	0.59	0.69	0.00	3.00	61	1.00	0.00	1.37	2.75
(Hd)	0.78	0.41	0.00	1.00	94	1.00	1.00	−1.39	−0.06
Hx	0.13	[0.34]	0.00	1.00	2	0.00	0.00	7.57	46.38
All H Cont	6.00	2.56	2.00	11.00	120	5.00	5.00	−0.24	−1.18
A	7.70	1.29	4.00	13.00	120	8.00	7.00	0.65	4.48
(A)	0.47	[0.50]	0.00	1.00	57	0.00	0.00	0.10	−2.02
Ad	1.97	[0.45]	0.00	3.00	116	2.00	2.00	−2.44	11.96
(Ad)	0.36	[0.54]	0.00	2.00	20	0.00	0.00	3.10	5.86
An	1.14	[0.60]	0.00	2.00	106	1.00	1.00	−0.06	−0.27
Art	0.92	0.28	0.00	1.00	110	1.00	1.00	−3.05	7.45
Ay	0.03	[0.18]	0.00	1.00	4	0.00	0.00	5.27	26.16
Bl	0.26	[0.44]	0.00	1.00	31	0.00	0.00	1.12	−0.76
Bt	1.52	0.65	0.00	2.00	110	2.00	2.00	−1.04	−0.03
Cg	1.90	1.06	0.00	4.00	116	1.00	1.00	0.12	−1.63
Cl	0.22	[0.13]	0.00	1.00	12	0.00	0.00	7.65	57.43
Ex	0.47	[0.38]	0.00	2.00	40	0.00	0.00	3.16	4.84
Fi	0.57	[0.26]	0.00	2.00	81	1.00	1.00	−1.61	12.13
Fd	0.37	[0.34]	0.00	1.00	29	0.00	0.00	2.19	4.82
Ge	0.02	[0.13]	0.00	1.00	2	0.00	0.00	7.65	57.43
Hh	0.88	0.32	0.00	1.00	106	1.00	1.00	−2.42	3.91
Ls	1.36	0.60	0.00	2.00	112	1.00	1.00	−0.36	−0.65
Na	0.10	[0.35]	0.00	2.00	10	0.00	0.00	3.79	14.82
Sc	2.47	[0.87]	0.00	3.00	112	3.00	3.00	−1.72	2.12
Sx	0.02	[0.13]	0.00	1.00	2	0.00	0.00	7.65	57.43
Xy	0.06	[0.12]	0.00	1.00	7	0.00	0.00	4.95	21.11
Idio	0.15	0.51	0.00	3.00	12	0.00	0.00	4.02	17.31
DV	1.21	[0.55]	0.00	2.00	112	1.00	1.00	0.08	−0.13
INCOM	1.35	[0.57]	0.00	3.00	116	1.00	1.00	0.34	−0.10
DR	0.44	[0.43]	0.00	1.00	39	0.00	0.00	1.22	−0.51
FABCOM	0.46	[0.53]	0.00	2.00	36	0.00	0.00	1.95	2.99
DV2	0.02	[0.16]	0.00	1.00	3	0.00	0.00	6.16	36.58
INC2	0.17	[0.56]	0.00	3.00	13	0.00	0.00	3.54	12.65
DR2	0.02	[0.16]	0.00	1.00	3	0.00	0.00	6.16	36.58
FAB2	0.04	[0.20]	0.00	1.00	5	0.00	0.00	4.65	19.91
ALOG	0.41	[0.68]	0.00	2.00	27	0.00	0.00	1.94	3.61
CONTAM	0.00	0.00	0.00	0.00	0	0.00	0.00	—	—
Sum6 Sp Sc	4.06	0.95	1.00	6.00	120	3.00	4.00	−0.47	−1.06
Sum6 Sp Sc2	0.27	[0.68]	0.00	4.00	22	0.00	0.00	3.47	14.40
WSum6	8.86	3.85	2.00	19.00	120	8.00	4.00	2.33	9.04
AB	0.05	[0.22]	0.00	1.00	6	0.00	0.00	4.18	15.75
AG	1.08	0.66	0.00	2.00	99	1.00	1.00	−0.09	−0.65
CFB	0.00	0.00	0.00	0.00	0	0.00	0.00	—	—
COP	1.93	0.53	0.00	4.00	114	3.00	2.00	0.18	−0.19
CP	0.00	[0.00]	0.00	0.00	0	0.00	0.00	—	—
MOR	0.67	[0.37]	0.00	3.00	58	0.00	0.00	1.81	1.30
PER	0.93	0.36	0.00	2.00	108	1.00	1.00	−0.89	4.40
PSV	0.03	[0.18]	0.00	1.00	4	0.00	0.00	5.27	26.16

Table 9. (Continued)

Variable	Mean	SD	Min	Max	Freq	Median	Mode	SK	KU
				13-Year-Olds ($N = 110$)					
R	21.20	3.30	14.00	33.00	110	20.00	20.00	1.07	3.51
W	8.57	2.15	1.00	14.00	110	9.00	9.00	−1.07	3.04
D	11.15	3.09	1.00	21.00	110	11.00	12.00	−0.25	3.08
Dd	1.46	[1.66]	0.00	6.00	93	1.00	1.00	2.74	7.81
S	1.33	[1.16]	0.00	7.00	106	2.00	1.00	1.93	5.93
DQ+	7.70	2.54	2.00	15.00	110	8.00	8.00	0.24	1.27
DQo	12.40	2.02	8.00	20.00	110	12.00	12.00	0.73	2.74
DQv	0.45	[0.99]	0.00	4.00	24	0.00	0.00	2.31	4.70
DQv/+	0.24	[0.57]	0.00	2.00	18	0.00	0.00	2.33	4.18
FQX+	0.20	0.59	0.00	3.00	14	0.00	0.00	3.25	10.63
FQXo	15.24	3.04	5.00	23.00	110	15.00	17.00	−0.70	2.09
FQXu	3.27	1.53	0.00	8.00	106	3.00	3.00	0.42	1.24
FQX−	2.00	1.42	0.00	7.00	108	2.00	2.00	2.15	4.81
FQXNone	0.07	[0.32]	0.00	2.00	6	0.00	0.00	4.81	23.90
MQ+	0.13	0.43	0.00	2.00	10	0.00	0.00	3.52	11.76
MQo	3.23	1.66	1.00	8.00	110	3.00	5.00	0.34	−0.38
MQu	0.54	0.66	0.00	3.00	51	0.00	0.00	1.23	2.00
MQ−	0.14	[0.51]	0.00	2.00	12	0.00	0.00	2.08	3.61
MQNone	0.02	[0.13]	0.00	1.00	2	0.00	0.00	7.31	52.42
S−	0.52	[0.81]	0.00	4.00	43	0.00	0.00	2.16	5.84
M	4.14	2.24	1.00	11.00	110	4.00	4.00	0.50	−0.01
FM	4.42	1.94	0.00	8.00	108	4.00	6.00	−0.25	−0.89
m	1.25	0.94	0.00	5.00	98	1.00	1.00	1.88	4.46
FM + m	5.67	2.10	1.00	11.00	110	6.00	7.00	−0.28	−0.34
FC	2.95	1.72	0.00	9.00	96	3.00	3.00	0.42	1.72
CF	2.70	1.50	0.00	5.00	102	3.00	3.00	−0.07	−0.98
C	0.07	[0.26]	0.00	1.00	8	0.00	0.00	3.34	9.30
Cn	0.00	[0.00]	0.00	0.00	0	0.00	0.00	—	—
FC + CF + C + Cn	5.73	2.61	0.00	10.00	110	6.50	8.00	−0.71	−0.33
WGSum C	4.29	1.94	0.00	7.50	110	4.75	6.50	−0.61	−0.49
Sum C'	1.20	[0.89]	0.00	3.00	87	1.00	1.00	0.48	−0.37
Sum T	0.97	[0.51]	0.00	3.00	90	1.00	1.00	0.64	4.99
Sum V	0.14	[0.48]	0.00	2.00	10	0.00	0.00	3.31	9.70
Sum Y	1.02	[0.81]	0.00	2.00	80	1.00	2.00	−0.22	−1.44
SumShd	3.34	1.44	0.00	6.00	104	4.00	4.00	−0.55	−0.07
Fr + rF	0.45	[0.23]	0.00	1.00	32	0.00	0.00	2.98	4.08
FD	1.27	[0.87]	0.00	3.00	82	2.00	2.00	−0.39	−1.25
F	6.90	2.52	3.00	13.00	110	6.00	5.00	0.93	−0.20
PAIR	8.64	2.30	1.00	14.00	110	9.50	10.00	−1.18	2.59
3r(2)/R	0.49	0.10	0.20	0.66	110	0.48	0.50	−1.84	4.97
LAMBDA	0.67	0.61	0.20	4.33	110	0.38	0.33	4.44	24.00
EA	8.43	2.69	1.00	15.00	110	9.00	7.50	−0.60	0.64
es	9.01	3.01	1.00	14.00	110	10.00	8.00	−0.83	−0.02
D	−0.09	0.82	−2.00	3.00	110	0.00	0.00	0.78	3.45
AdjD	0.10	0.84	−2.00	3.00	110	0.00	0.00	0.74	2.06
a (active)	6.23	1.89	2.00	11.00	110	6.00	6.00	−0.34	0.13
p (passive)	3.61	2.11	0.00	8.00	104	3.00	3.00	0.45	−0.49
Ma	2.49	1.30	0.00	8.00	106	2.00	2.00	1.80	6.06
Mp	1.67	1.44	0.00	5.00	84	2.00	2.00	0.12	−0.80
Intellect	1.22	0.95	0.00	4.00	110	1.00	1.00	1.24	1.45
Zf	12.64	3.02	5.00	23.00	110	13.00	11.00	0.05	2.17
Zd	1.37	2.27	−4.50	5.00	110	1.50	−0.50	−0.35	−0.40
Blends	5.81	2.43	0.00	9.00	108	7.00	7.00	−0.90	−0.34
Col Shd Blend	0.16	[0.37]	0.00	1.00	18	0.00	0.00	1.84	1.42s

Note: Standard Deviations shown in brackets indicate that the value is probably unreliable and/or misleading and should not be used to estimate expected ranges. Ordinarily, these variables should not be included in most parametric analyses.

Table 9. (Continued)

| | | | | | | 13-Year-Olds ($N = 110$) | | | |
Variable	Mean	SD	Min	Max	Freq	Median	Mode	SK	KU
Afr	0.69	0.15	0.28	1.00	110	0.58	0.67	0.10	0.52
Popular	6.19	1.34	2.00	9.00	110	7.00	6.00	−0.59	0.79
X + %	0.76	0.11	0.30	1.00	110	0.77	0.77	−1.86	5.39
F + %	0.61	0.18	0.18	1.00	110	0.60	0.60	0.39	0.14
X − %	0.10	0.07	0.00	0.38	108	0.09	0.09	2.67	8.99
Xu%	0.16	0.07	0.00	0.33	106	0.15	0.14	−0.03	0.76
S − %	0.20	[0.28]	0.00	1.00	43	0.00	0.00	1.11	0.35
Isolate	0.16	0.06	0.00	0.33	110	0.16	0.18	0.59	1.30
H	3.09	1.72	1.00	8.00	110	3.00	5.00	0.42	−0.57
(H)	1.25	1.02	0.00	5.00	84	1.00	1.00	1.06	2.35
Hd	0.68	0.83	0.00	3.00	55	0.50	0.00	1.24	1.11
(Hd)	0.56	0.53	0.00	2.00	60	1.00	1.00	0.11	−1.21
Hx	0.00	[0.00]	0.00	0.00	0	0.00	0.00	—	—
All H Cont	5.59	2.46	2.00	11.00	110	5.00	5.00	0.13	−1.03
A	7.96	1.81	4.00	13.00	110	8.00	7.00	0.63	0.65
(A)	0.37	[0.49]	0.00	1.00	41	0.00	0.00	0.53	−1.75
Ad	2.00	[0.81]	0.00	4.00	106	2.00	2.00	0.42	1.71
(Ad)	0.00	[0.00]	0.00	0.00	0	0.00	0.00	—	—
An	0.84	[0.69]	0.00	2.00	74	1.00	1.00	0.22	−0.89
Art	0.85	0.48	0.00	2.00	88	1.00	1.00	−0.36	0.78
Ay	0.11	[0.31]	0.00	1.00	12	0.00	0.00	2.54	4.55
Bl	0.19	[0.39]	0.00	1.00	21	0.00	0.00	1.59	0.55
Bt	1.74	0.98	0.00	5.00	98	2.00	2.00	0.44	1.35
Cg	1.62	1.10	0.00	4.00	98	1.00	1.00	0.47	−0.93
Cl	0.05	[0.23]	0.00	1.00	6	0.00	0.00	3.98	14.08
Ex	0.09	[0.29]	0.00	1.00	10	0.00	0.00	2.89	6.44
Fi	0.76	[0.54]	0.00	2.00	78	1.00	1.00	−0.12	−0.23
Fd	0.42	[0.52]	0.00	2.00	46	1.00	0.00	−0.10	−1.15
Ge	0.04	[0.19]	0.00	1.00	4	0.00	0.00	5.02	23.65
Hh	1.07	0.81	0.00	4.00	90	1.00	1.00	1.35	2.87
Ls	1.10	0.97	0.00	6.00	84	1.00	1.00	2.28	10.32
Na	0.22	[0.50]	0.00	2.00	20	0.00	0.00	2.25	4.39
Sc	1.97	[1.14]	0.00	5.00	96	2.00	3.00	−0.18	−0.48
Sx	0.07	[0.42]	0.00	3.00	4	0.00	0.00	6.43	42.22
Xy	0.00	[0.00]	0.00	0.00	0	0.00	0.00	—	—
Idio	0.78	1.14	0.00	4.00	44	0.00	0.00	1.26	0.28
DV	1.01	[0.70]	0.00	3.00	86	1.00	1.00	0.32	0.05
INCOM	1.07	[0.79]	0.00	3.00	84	1.00	1.00	0.33	−0.33
DR	0.30	[0.66]	0.00	4.00	27	0.00	0.00	3.54	16.72
FABCOM	0.42	[0.71]	0.00	3.00	34	0.00	0.00	1.71	2.45
DV2	0.02	[0.13]	0.00	1.00	2	0.00	0.00	7.31	52.42
INC2	0.22	[0.60]	0.00	3.00	16	0.00	0.00	3.06	9.49
DR2	0.04	[0.19]	0.00	1.00	4	0.00	0.00	5.02	23.65
FAB2	0.07	[0.32]	0.00	2.00	3	0.00	0.00	4.81	23.90
ALOG	0.34	[0.19]	0.00	1.00	18	0.00	0.00	5.02	23.65
CONTAM	0.00	0.00	0.00	0.00	0	0.00	0.00	—	—
Sum6 Sp Sc	2.94	1.46	0.00	9.00	110	3.00	2.00	1.55	5.03
Sum6 Sp Sc2	0.34	[0.77]	0.00	4.00	24	0.00	0.00	2.73	8.42
WSum6	7.54	6.99	0.00	40.00	108	6.00	3.00	2.89	9.56
AB	0.13	[0.33]	0.00	1.00	14	0.00	0.00	2.27	3.20
AG	1.18	0.91	0.00	4.00	85	1.00	1.00	0.67	0.48
CFB	0.00	0.00	0.00	0.00	0	0.00	0.00	—	—
COP	1.84	1.22	0.00	6.00	101	2.00	1.00	1.59	3.11
CP	0.02	[0.13]	0.00	1.00	1	0.00	0.00	7.31	52.42
MOR	0.49	[0.74]	0.00	3.00	40	0.00	0.00	1.42	1.38
PER	1.05	0.89	0.00	5.00	90	1.00	1.00	2.31	7.82
PSV	0.04	[0.21]	0.00	1.00	5	0.00	0.00	3.68	14.48

Table 9. (Continued)

Variable	Mean	SD	Min	Max	Freq	Median	Mode	SK	KU
				14-Year-Olds ($N = 105$)					
R	21.72	3.36	14.00	33.00	105	20.00	20.00	1.11	3.43
W	8.92	2.19	4.00	14.00	105	9.00	9.00	−1.01	2.83
D	11.13	3.16	1.00	21.00	105	11.00	10.00	−0.23	2.82
Dd	1.67	[1.70]	0.00	6.00	98	2.00	1.00	2.67	7.31
S	1.32	[1.09]	0.00	7.00	101	2.00	2.00	1.89	5.56
DQ+	7.81	2.55	2.00	15.00	105	8.00	8.00	0.33	1.36
DQo	12.69	2.06	8.00	20.00	105	12.00	12.00	0.73	2.58
DQv	0.58	[1.01]	0.00	4.00	27	0.00	0.00	2.23	4.30
DQv/+	0.65	[0.58]	0.00	2.00	48	0.00	0.00	2.25	3.79
FQX+	0.14	0.50	0.00	2.00	11	0.00	0.00	3.16	9.97
FQXo	15.17	3.09	5.00	23.00	105	15.00	15.00	−0.64	1.93
FQXu	3.27	1.56	0.00	8.00	101	3.00	3.00	0.42	1.10
FQX−	1.84	1.25	0.00	5.00	103	2.00	2.00	2.10	4.46
FQXNone	0.02	[0.53]	0.00	1.00	4	0.00	0.00	4.69	22.65
MQ+	0.11	0.44	0.00	2.00	6	0.00	0.00	3.42	11.04
MQo	3.21	1.66	1.00	8.00	105	3.00	1.00	0.43	−0.26
MQu	0.51	0.67	0.00	3.00	46	0.00	0.00	1.34	2.18
MQ−	0.13	[0.50]	0.00	2.00	11	0.00	0.00	2.18	4.01
MQNone	0.00	[0.00]	0.00	0.00	0	0.00	0.00	—	—
S−	0.39	[0.82]	0.00	3.00	31	0.00	0.00	2.24	6.00
M	4.06	2.24	1.00	11.00	105	4.00	4.00	0.59	0.16
FM	4.35	1.96	0.00	8.00	103	4.00	6.00	−0.17	−0.92
m	1.27	0.96	0.00	5.00	93	1.00	1.00	1.81	4.08
FM + m	5.62	2.14	1.00	11.00	105	6.00	7.00	−0.21	−0.42
FC	2.93	1.76	0.00	9.00	91	3.00	3.00	0.45	1.59
CF	2.70	1.53	0.00	5.00	97	3.00	3.00	−0.08	−1.05
C	0.10	[0.27]	0.00	1.00	9	0.00	0.00	3.14	7.67
Cn	0.00	[0.00]	0.00	0.00	0	0.00	0.00	—	—
FC + CF + C + Cn	5.71	2.67	1.00	10.00	105	7.00	8.00	−0.69	−0.44
WGSum C	4.29	1.98	0.50	7.50	105	5.00	6.50	−0.60	−0.58
Sum C'	1.11	[0.91]	0.00	3.00	82	1.00	1.00	0.44	−0.50
Sum T	0.99	[0.52]	0.00	3.00	85	1.00	1.00	0.66	4.71
Sum V	0.13	[0.50]	0.00	2.00	8	0.00	0.00	3.21	9.06
Sum Y	0.88	[0.84]	0.00	2.00	75	1.00	2.00	−0.14	−1.44
SumShd	3.10	1.47	0.00	6.00	99	4.00	4.00	−0.49	−0.19
Fr + rF	0.38	[0.43]	0.00	1.00	15	0.00	0.00	3.97	10.25
FD	1.24	[0.87]	0.00	3.00	71	1.00	2.00	−0.31	−1.30
F	6.96	2.56	3.00	13.00	105	6.00	5.00	0.87	−0.35
PAIR	8.59	2.34	1.00	14.00	105	9.00	10.00	−1.12	2.38
3r(2)/R	0.47	0.10	0.05	0.56	105	0.45	0.50	−1.79	4.60
LAMBDA	0.67	0.62	0.20	4.33	105	0.38	0.33	4.34	22.96
EA	8.34	2.70	1.00	15.00	105	9.00	7.50	−0.55	0.60
es	8.92	3.06	1.00	13.00	105	9.00	9.00	−0.76	−0.15
D	−0.09	0.84	−2.00	3.00	105	0.00	0.00	0.78	3.19
AdjD	0.09	0.86	−2.00	3.00	105	0.00	0.00	0.74	1.95
a (active)	6.20	1.92	2.00	11.00	105	6.00	7.00	−0.32	0.06
p (passive)	3.49	2.07	0.00	8.00	99	3.00	3.00	0.52	−0.35
Ma	2.59	1.32	0.00	8.00	101	2.00	2.00	1.81	5.93
Mp	1.49	1.36	0.00	5.00	89	2.00	2.00	0.17	−0.74
Intellect	1.23	0.97	0.00	4.00	105	1.00	1.00	1.18	1.22
Zf	12.56	3.06	5.00	23.00	105	13.00	14.00	0.12	2.11
Zd	1.27	2.26	−4.50	5.00	105	1.50	−0.50	−0.30	−0.38
Blends	5.74	2.46	0.00	9.00	103	7.00	7.00	−0.84	−0.47
Col Shd Blend	0.17	[0.38]	0.00	1.00	18	0.00	0.00	1.77	1.15

Note: Standard Deviations shown in brackets indicate that the value is probably unreliable and/or misleading and should not be used to estimate expected ranges. Ordinarily, these variables should not be included in most parametric analyses.

Table 9. (Continued)

Variable	Mean	SD	Min	Max	Freq	Median	Mode	SK	KU
				14-Year-Olds (N = 105)					
Afr	0.69	0.16	0.31	0.89	105	0.68	0.67	0.03	0.47
Popular	6.02	1.17	3.00	9.00	105	7.00	6.00	−0.53	0.67
X + %	0.76	0.12	0.49	0.95	105	0.79	0.75	−1.81	5.01
F + %	0.69	0.18	0.38	1.00	105	0.60	0.60	0.34	0.03
X − %	0.09	0.07	0.00	0.27	105	0.09	0.05	2.60	8.43
Xu%	0.16	0.07	0.00	0.33	105	0.15	0.14	−0.03	0.61
S − %	0.19	[0.28]	0.00	1.00	38	0.00	0.00	1.27	0.76
Isolate	0.16	0.06	0.00	0.33	105	0.16	0.16	0.60	1.15
H	3.00	1.71	1.00	8.00	105	3.00	1.00	0.54	−0.35
(H)	1.23	1.03	0.00	5.00	79	1.00	1.00	1.14	2.44
Hd	0.67	0.85	0.00	3.00	52	0.00	0.00	1.28	1.07
(Hd)	0.56	0.54	0.00	2.00	57	1.00	1.00	0.13	−1.19
Hx	0.00	[0.00]	0.00	0.00	0	0.00	0.00	—	—
All H Cont	5.46	2.44	2.00	11.00	105	5.00	5.00	0.22	−0.91
A	7.97	1.85	4.00	13.00	105	8.00	7.00	0.60	0.49
(A)	0.39	[0.49]	0.00	1.00	41	0.00	0.00	0.46	−1.83
Ad	2.00	[0.83]	0.00	4.00	101	2.00	2.00	0.41	1.50
(Ad)	0.23	[0.41]	0.00	1.00	13	0.00	0.00	4.16	29.15
An	0.84	[0.71]	0.00	2.00	49	1.00	0.00	0.24	−0.97
Art	0.85	0.50	0.00	2.00	83	1.00	1.00	−0.32	0.62
Ay	0.15	[0.32]	0.00	1.00	14	0.00	0.00	2.46	4.13
Bl	0.20	[0.40]	0.00	1.00	20	0.00	0.00	1.52	0.32
Bt	1.73	1.00	0.00	5.00	91	2.00	2.00	0.44	1.22
Cg	1.55	1.08	0.00	4.00	94	1.00	1.00	0.60	−0.69
Cl	0.06	[0.23]	0.00	1.00	8	0.00	0.00	3.87	13.24
Ex	0.09	[0.29]	0.00	1.00	19	0.00	0.00	2.80	5.94
Fi	0.75	[0.55]	0.00	2.00	63	1.00	1.00	−0.06	−0.32
Fd	0.30	[0.53]	0.00	2.00	31	1.00	1.00	−0.02	−1.16
Ge	0.04	[0.19]	0.00	1.00	3	0.00	0.00	4.90	22.40
Hh	1.08	0.83	0.00	4.00	82	1.00	1.00	1.30	2.58
Ls	1.06	0.97	0.00	6.00	79	1.00	1.00	2.47	11.28
Na	0.23	[0.50]	0.00	2.00	24	0.00	0.00	2.18	4.01
Sc	1.93	[1.15]	0.00	5.00	96	2.00	3.00	−0.10	−0.48
Sx	0.08	[0.43]	0.00	1.00	3	0.00	0.00	6.27	40.17
Xy	0.04	[0.20]	0.00	1.00	5	0.00	0.00	5.18	31.60
Idio	0.82	1.16	0.00	4.00	44	0.00	0.00	1.19	0.10
DV	0.98	[0.69]	0.00	3.00	81	1.00	1.00	0.38	0.22
INCOM	1.05	[0.79]	0.00	3.00	79	1.00	1.00	0.39	−0.24
DR	0.29	[0.66]	0.00	4.00	25	0.00	0.00	3.61	16.99
FABCOM	0.44	[0.72]	0.00	3.00	34	0.00	0.00	1.64	2.18
DV2	0.02	[0.14]	0.00	1.00	2	0.00	0.00	7.14	49.92
INC2	0.12	[0.60]	0.00	3.00	6	0.00	0.00	3.06	9.40
DR2	0.03	[0.17]	0.00	1.00	2	0.00	0.00	5.74	31.57
FAB2	0.08	[0.33]	0.00	1.00	3	0.00	0.00	4.69	22.65
ALOG	0.11	[0.19]	0.00	1.00	10	0.00	0.00	4.90	22.40
CONTAM	0.00	0.00	0.00	0.00	0	0.00	0.00	—	—
Sum6 Sp Sc	2.89	1.38	0.00	8.00	103	3.00	2.00	1.61	5.11
Sum6 Sp Sc2	0.14	[0.38]	0.00	1.00	9	0.00	0.00	2.75	8.37
WSum6	7.42	7.14	0.00	20.00	105	6.00	3.00	2.85	9.12
AB	0.13	[0.34]	0.00	1.00	12	0.00	0.00	2.19	2.84
AG	1.30	0.92	0.00	4.00	89	1.00	1.00	0.63	0.36
CFB	0.00	0.00	0.00	0.00	0	0.00	0.00	—	—
COP	1.75	1.14	0.00	5.00	95	1.00	1.00	1.57	2.91
CP	0.00	[0.00]	0.00	0.00	0	0.00	0.00	—	—
MOR	0.61	[0.75]	0.00	3.00	48	0.00	0.00	1.35	1.17
PER	1.01	0.81	0.00	4.00	80	1.00	1.00	2.25	7.32
PSV	0.03	[0.12]	0.00	1.00	3	0.00	0.00	5.87	23.24

Table 9. (Continued)

Variable	Mean	SD	Min	Max	Freq	Median	Mode	SK	KU
				15-Year-Olds ($N = 110$)					
R	21.94	4.21	14.00	32.00	110	21.00	20.00	0.94	1.14
W	8.87	2.20	3.00	20.00	110	9.00	9.00	1.57	9.58
D	11.42	3.66	0.00	20.00	109	12.00	12.00	−0.31	1.91
Dd	1.65	[1.31]	0.00	7.00	91	1.00	1.00	1.31	3.76
S	1.44	[1.31]	0.00	5.00	104	2.00	1.00	2.66	12.86
DQ+	7.88	2.02	2.00	13.00	110	8.00	8.00	−0.33	0.15
DQo	12.67	3.62	5.00	29.00	110	12.00	12.00	1.49	5.43
DQv	0.75	[1.29]	0.00	4.00	40	0.00	0.00	1.84	2.46
DQv/+	0.14	[0.42]	0.00	2.00	12	0.00	0.00	3.22	10.13
FQX+	0.36	0.70	0.00	3.00	27	0.00	0.00	1.81	2.20
FQXo	16.35	3.34	7.00	29.00	110	16.00	15.00	0.60	2.79
FQXu	3.08	1.57	0.00	11.00	108	3.00	3.00	1.37	5.75
FQX−	1.60	0.91	0.00	6.00	99	2.00	2.00	0.81	3.89
FQXNone	0.04	[0.25]	0.00	2.00	4	0.00	0.00	6.07	39.81
MQ+	0.25	0.57	0.00	3.00	22	0.00	0.00	2.46	6.34
MQo	3.54	2.01	0.00	8.00	108	3.00	1.00	0.20	−0.91
MQu	0.44	0.52	0.00	2.00	48	0.00	0.00	0.43	−1.36
MQ−	0.12	[0.32]	0.00	1.00	13	0.00	0.00	2.40	3.82
MQNone	0.00	[0.00]	0.00	0.00	0	0.00	0.00	—	—
S−	0.38	[0.57]	0.00	2.00	37	0.00	0.00	1.22	0.52
M	4.35	2.17	1.00	9.00	110	4.00	4.00	0.06	−0.97
FM	4.82	1.73	1.00	9.00	110	5.00	6.00	−0.20	−0.80
m	1.17	0.78	0.00	4.00	97	1.00	1.00	1.49	3.79
FM + m	5.99	1.78	2.00	10.00	110	6.00	7.00	−0.14	−0.67
FC	3.14	1.14	0.00	6.00	107	3.00	3.00	−0.56	0.76
CF	2.85	1.53	0.00	6.00	101	3.00	2.00	−0.11	−0.73
C	0.03	[0.16]	0.00	1.00	3	0.00	0.00	5.88	33.24
Cn	0.02	[0.13]	0.00	1.00	2	0.00	0.00	7.31	52.42
FC + CF + C + Cn	6.04	2.01	1.00	10.00	110	7.00	8.00	−0.62	−0.37
WGSum C	4.47	1.68	0.50	8.00	110	4.50	3.50	−0.33	−0.64
Sum C'	1.63	[1.35]	0.00	10.00	94	1.00	1.00	2.49	12.61
Sum T	1.06	[0.51]	0.00	3.00	101	1.00	1.00	2.62	13.12
Sum V	0.18	[0.49]	0.00	2.00	12	0.00	0.00	2.75	6.73
Sum Y	1.30	[1.27]	0.00	10.00	83	1.00	2.00	3.35	20.69
SumShd	4.17	2.55	0.00	23.00	109	4.00	4.00	4.04	27.31
Fr + rF	0.50	[0.45]	0.00	2.00	26	0.00	0.00	6.67	53.57
FD	1.33	[0.97]	0.00	5.00	83	1.50	2.00	0.35	0.78
F	6.48	2.71	2.00	17.00	110	5.00	5.00	1.31	2.02
PAIR	9.10	2.00	1.00	14.00	110	10.00	10.00	−1.37	4.47
3r(2)/R	0.44	0.10	0.05	0.79	110	0.45	0.50	−0.58	4.63
LAMBDA	0.65	0.22	0.14	1.71	110	0.36	0.33	2.27	8.94
EA	8.82	2.34	2.00	13.50	110	9.50	9.50	−0.69	0.39
es	9.16	3.40	4.00	17.00	110	10.00	9.00	2.13	12.31
D	−0.45	1.39	−10.00	2.00	39	0.00	0.00	−3.73	20.85
AdjD	−0.25	1.07	−5.00	2.00	43	0.00	0.00	−1.71	5.14
a (active)	6.99	1.73	3.00	12.00	110	7.00	8.00	0.18	0.32
p (passive)	3.36	1.93	0.00	9.00	106	3.00	3.00	0.75	0.31
Ma	2.58	1.44	1.00	7.00	110	2.00	2.00	0.96	0.38
Mp	1.77	1.46	0.00	5.00	81	2.00	2.00	0.48	−0.51
Intellect	1.04	0.83	0.00	4.00	110	1.00	1.00	1.59	3.76
Zf	12.68	2.59	5.00	23.00	110	13.00	13.00	0.01	2.61
Zd	1.03	2.96	−6.50	9.00	110	0.50	−0.50	0.17	0.11
Blends	6.34	2.16	1.00	12.00	110	7.00	7.00	−0.63	0.03
Col Shd Blend	0.22	[0.51]	0.00	2.00	19	0.00	0.00	2.35	4.69

Note: Standard Deviations shown in brackets indicate that the value is probably unreliable and/or misleading and should not be used to estimate expected ranges. Ordinarily, these variables should not be included in most parametric analyses.

Table 9. **(Continued)**

Variable	Mean	SD	Min	Max	Freq	Median	Mode	SK	KU
				15-Year-Olds (*N* = 110)					
Afr	0.65	0.18	0.27	1.29	110	0.67	0.67	0.97	1.69
Popular	6.33	1.23	3.00	9.00	110	7.00	7.00	−0.59	0.22
X + %	0.78	0.07	0.50	0.90	110	0.77	0.75	−0.46	2.72
F + %	0.62	0.18	0.29	1.00	110	0.60	0.60	0.54	−0.44
X − %	0.07	0.05	0.00	0.43	99	0.09	0.05	3.29	23.26
Xu%	0.14	0.06	0.00	0.37	108	0.15	0.14	0.45	1.97
S − %	0.18	[0.27]	0.00	1.00	37	0.00	0.00	1.28	0.76
Isolate	0.15	0.07	0.00	0.47	110	0.15	0.16	1.76	8.18
H	3.42	1.96	0.00	8.00	109	3.00	5.00	0.49	−0.51
(H)	1.04	0.90	0.00	4.00	75	1.00	1.00	0.52	−0.15
Hd	0.57	0.82	0.00	4.00	48	0.00	0.00	1.97	5.02
(Hd)	0.54	0.50	0.00	1.00	59	1.00	1.00	−0.15	−2.01
Hx	0.00	[0.00]	0.00	0.00	0	0.00	0.00	—	—
All H Cont	5.57	2.28	1.00	9.00	110	5.00	5.00	−0.15	−0.95
A	7.98	1.96	3.00	15.00	110	8.00	7.00	0.55	1.91
(A)	0.36	[0.55]	0.00	3.00	37	0.00	0.00	1.55	3.35
Ad	2.08	[1.20]	0.00	9.00	102	2.00	2.00	2.26	11.70
(Ad)	0.05	[0.30]	0.00	2.00	4	0.00	0.00	5.80	34.15
An	0.43	[0.79]	0.00	3.00	43	1.00	0.00	0.24	−1.02
Art	0.85	0.63	0.00	4.00	82	1.00	1.00	1.01	4.67
Ay	0.14	[0.34]	0.00	1.00	15	0.00	0.00	2.15	2.66
Bl	0.22	[0.41]	0.00	1.00	24	0.00	0.00	1.38	−0.09
Bt	1.68	0.82	0.00	4.00	102	2.00	2.00	−0.05	−0.06
Cg	1.47	1.11	0.00	4.00	93	1.00	1.00	0.59	−0.80
Cl	0.09	[0.35]	0.00	2.00	8	0.00	0.00	4.12	17.53
Ex	0.12	[0.32]	0.00	1.00	13	0.00	0.00	2.40	3.82
Fi	0.69	[0.52]	0.00	2.00	73	1.00	1.00	−0.23	−0.72
Fd	0.30	[0.51]	0.00	2.00	25	1.00	1.00	−0.20	−1.47
Ge	0.01	[0.09]	0.00	1.00	1	0.00	0.00	10.49	110.00
Hh	0.89	0.60	0.00	4.00	88	1.00	1.00	1.36	7.28
Ls	1.12	0.71	0.00	2.00	88	1.00	1.00	−0.18	−1.00
Na	0.12	[0.35]	0.00	2.00	12	0.00	0.00	3.02	9.12
Sc	1.70	[1.34]	0.00	6.00	77	2.00	3.00	0.03	−0.83
Sx	0.11	[0.44]	0.00	3.00	8	0.00	0.00	4.64	23.43
Xy	0.04	[0.19]	0.00	1.00	4	0.00	0.00	5.02	23.65
Idio	1.09	1.47	0.00	7.00	52	0.00	0.00	1.49	2.28
DV	0.98	[0.70]	0.00	3.00	84	1.00	1.00	0.35	0.03
INCOM	0.88	[0.74]	0.00	4.00	76	1.00	1.00	0.75	1.58
DR	0.13	[0.33]	0.00	1.00	14	0.00	0.00	2.27	3.20
FABCOM	0.23	[0.46]	0.00	2.00	23	0.00	0.00	1.87	2.73
DV2	0.03	[0.16]	0.00	1.00	3	0.00	0.00	5.89	33.24
INC2	0.01	[0.09]	0.00	1.00	1	0.00	0.00	10.49	110.00
DR2	0.01	[0.09]	0.00	1.00	1	0.00	0.00	10.49	110.00
FAB2	0.04	[0.19]	0.00	1.00	4	0.00	0.00	5.02	23.65
ALOG	0.05	[0.26]	0.00	2.00	5	0.00	0.00	5.37	31.19
CONTAM	0.00	0.00	0.00	0.00	0	0.00	0.00	—	—
Sum6 Sp Sc	2.27	1.36	0.00	5.00	110	2.00	2.00	−0.11	−0.96
Sum6 Sp Sc2	0.08	[0.27]	0.00	1.00	9	0.00	0.00	3.09	7.71
WSum6	4.71	3.33	0.00	15.00	110	4.00	3.00	0.60	0.27
AB	0.03	[0.16]	0.00	1.00	3	0.00	0.00	5.89	33.24
AG	1.14	0.91	0.00	4.00	82	1.00	1.00	0.53	−0.05
CFB	0.00	0.00	0.00	0.00	0	0.00	0.00	—	—
COP	1.54	0.97	0.00	5.00	98	1.00	1.00	0.75	0.98
CP	0.00	[0.00]	0.00	0.00	0	0.00	0.00	—	—
MOR	0.54	[0.83]	0.00	4.00	41	0.00	0.00	1.74	3.06
PER	0.92	0.65	0.00	5.00	89	1.00	1.00	2.31	14.11
PSV	0.04	[0.19]	0.00	1.00	4	0.00	0.00	5.02	23.65

Table 9. (Continued)

Variable	Mean	SD	Min	Max	Freq	Median	Mode	SK	KU
				16-Year-Olds ($N = 140$)					
R	22.89	5.16	14.00	31.00	140	21.00	20.00	0.94	1.70
W	8.96	2.37	3.00	20.00	140	9.00	9.00	1.70	8.32
D	11.91	3.74	0.00	21.00	139	12.00	12.00	−0.23	1.41
Dd	2.02	[1.82]	0.00	7.00	121	2.00	1.00	3.49	15.11
S	1.24	[1.23]	0.00	5.00	132	2.00	2.00	2.70	14.04
DQ+	7.94	2.04	2.00	13.00	140	8.00	8.00	−0.28	−0.13
DQo	13.12	3.47	5.00	27.00	140	12.00	12.00	1.23	4.58
DQv	0.89	[1.35]	0.00	5.00	59	0.00	0.00	1.59	1.62
DQv/+	0.84	[0.53]	0.00	2.00	46	0.00	0.00	2.21	3.98
FQX+	0.54	0.83	0.00	3.00	48	0.00	0.00	1.26	0.31
FQXo	16.43	3.36	7.00	29.00	140	16.00	15.00	0.59	2.16
FQXu	3.19	1.56	0.00	11.00	138	3.00	3.00	1.18	4.32
FQX−	1.58	0.91	0.00	5.00	126	2.00	2.00	0.70	2.97
FQXNone	0.06	[0.26]	0.00	2.00	7	0.00	0.00	5.01	27.20
MQ+	0.35	0.64	0.00	3.00	38	0.00	0.00	1.96	3.75
MQo	3.50	2.01	0.00	8.00	138	3.00	1.00	0.29	−0.86
MQu	0.37	0.50	0.00	2.00	51	0.00	0.00	0.71	−1.07
MQ−	0.09	[0.29]	0.00	1.00	13	0.00	0.00	2.84	6.13
MQNone	0.00	[0.00]	0.00	0.00	0	0.00	0.00	—	—
S−	0.34	[0.55]	0.00	2.00	43	0.00	0.00	1.32	0.81
M	4.31	2.13	1.00	9.00	140	4.00	4.00	0.20	−0.88
FM	4.58	1.66	1.00	9.00	140	4.00	4.00	0.04	−0.73
m	1.14	0.80	0.00	4.00	117	1.00	1.00	1.10	2.43
FM + m	5.72	1.78	2.00	10.00	140	6.00	7.00	0.03	−0.73
FC	3.43	1.34	0.00	8.00	137	3.00	3.00	0.14	1.16
CF	2.78	1.45	0.00	6.00	130	3.00	3.00	−0.05	−0.59
C	0.04	[0.20]	0.00	1.00	6	0.00	0.00	4.56	19.10
Cn	0.01	[0.12]	0.00	1.00	2	0.00	0.00	8.27	67.44
FC + CF + C + Cn	6.26	2.08	1.00	11.00	140	7.00	8.00	−0.56	−0.16
WGSum C	4.56	1.66	0.50	8.00	140	5.00	3.50	−0.42	−0.49
Sum C'	1.15	[1.27]	0.00	6.00	118	1.00	1.00	2.48	13.59
Sum T	1.02	[0.48]	0.00	3.00	128	1.00	1.00	2.44	13.39
Sum V	0.19	[0.51]	0.00	2.00	20	0.00	0.00	2.64	6.03
Sum Y	1.04	[1.21]	0.00	5.00	95	2.00	1.00	3.25	20.79
SumShd	3.44	2.35	0.00	23.00	139	4.00	4.00	4.25	31.18
Fr + rF	0.48	[0.41]	0.00	3.00	32	0.00	0.00	6.27	48.14
FD	1.31	[0.93]	0.00	5.00	108	1.00	2.00	0.33	0.77
F	6.85	2.69	2.00	17.00	140	6.00	5.00	0.96	0.93
PAIR	9.04	2.00	1.00	14.00	140	9.00	10.00	−0.90	3.36
3r(2)/R	0.43	0.09	0.05	0.79	140	0.45	0.50	−0.32	3.89
LAMBDA	0.65	0.21	0.24	1.71	140	0.68	0.63	1.85	7.03
EA	8.87	2.23	2.00	13.50	140	9.00	8.50	−0.59	0.63
es	9.21	3.29	4.00	17.00	140	10.00	8.00	2.09	12.09
D	−0.31	1.31	−10.00	2.00	140	0.00	0.00	−3.70	22.64
AdjD	−0.11	1.04	−5.00	2.00	140	0.00	0.00	−1.56	5.47
a (active)	6.82	1.71	3.00	12.00	140	7.00	6.00	0.25	0.13
p (passive)	3.22	1.89	0.00	9.00	133	3.00	2.00	0.70	0.33
Ma	2.62	1.42	1.00	7.00	140	2.00	2.00	0.88	0.20
Mp	1.69	1.38	0.00	5.00	106	2.00	2.00	0.55	−0.32
Intellect	1.14	0.93	0.00	5.00	140	1.00	1.00	1.38	2.72
Zf	12.61	2.64	5.00	23.00	140	13.00	13.00	0.37	3.18
Zd	1.12	2.96	−6.50	9.00	140	0.75	−0.50	0.09	0.15
Blends	6.11	2.13	1.00	12.00	140	7.00	7.00	−0.44	−0.26
Col Shd Blends	0.24	[0.50]	0.00	2.00	28	0.00	0.00	2.08	3.56

Note: Standard Deviations shown in brackets indicate that the value is probably unreliable and/or misleading and should not be used to estimate expected ranges. Ordinarily, these variables should not be included in most parametric analyses.

Table 9. (Continued)

Variable	Mean	SD	Min	Max	Freq	Median	Mode	SK	KU
				16-Year-Olds ($N = 140$)					
Afr	0.65	0.17	0.27	1.29	140	0.67	0.67	0.80	1.61
Popular	6.46	1.27	3.00	10.00	140	7.00	7.00	−0.35	0.39
X + %	0.78	0.07	0.50	0.90	140	0.79	0.75	−0.42	2.27
F + %	0.74	0.18	0.29	1.00	140	0.70	0.67	0.36	−0.58
X − %	0.07	0.05	0.00	0.25	126	0.07	0.05	3.08	22.84
Xu%	0.14	0.06	0.00	0.37	138	0.15	0.15	0.45	1.42
S − %	0.16	[0.27]	0.00	1.00	43	0.00	0.00	1.48	1.38
Isolate	0.16	0.07	0.00	0.47	140	0.16	0.16	1.31	4.09
H	3.39	1.94	0.00	8.00	139	3.00	3.00	0.62	−0.28
(H)	1.07	0.89	0.00	4.00	97	1.00	1.00	0.36	−0.43
Hd	0.59	0.81	0.00	4.00	62	0.00	0.00	1.79	4.08
(Hd)	0.46	0.50	0.00	1.00	64	0.00	0.00	0.17	−2.00
Hx	0.00	[0.00]	0.00	0.00	0	0.00	0.00	—	—
All H Cont	5.51	2.12	1.00	9.00	140	5.00	5.00	−0.06	−0.76
A	8.04	1.97	3.00	15.00	140	8.00	7.00	0.46	1.18
(A)	0.32	[0.54]	0.00	3.00	41	0.00	0.00	1.73	3.69
Ad	2.11	[1.15]	0.00	9.00	131	2.00	2.00	1.98	10.34
(Ad)	0.07	[0.33]	0.00	2.00	7	0.00	0.00	4.94	24.56
An	0.41	[0.79]	0.00	4.00	32	1.00	0.00	0.45	−0.96
Art	0.83	0.68	0.00	4.00	97	1.00	1.00	0.79	2.33
Ay	0.19	[0.41]	0.00	2.00	25	0.00	0.00	1.95	2.75
Bl	0.21	[0.43]	0.00	2.00	29	0.00	0.00	1.68	1.61
Bt	1.87	1.03	0.00	6.00	130	2.00	2.00	0.62	1.27
Cg	1.39	1.06	0.00	4.00	116	1.00	1.00	0.65	−0.57
Cl	0.11	[0.36]	0.00	2.00	14	0.00	0.00	3.33	11.30
Ex	0.31	[0.32]	0.00	1.00	26	0.00	0.00	2.45	4.06
Fi	0.39	[0.57]	0.00	2.00	42	1.00	0.00	0.20	−0.76
Fd	0.31	[0.52]	0.00	2.00	31	0.50	0.00	0.13	−1.62
Ge	0.01	[0.12]	0.00	1.00	2	0.00	0.00	8.28	67.44
Hh	0.91	0.67	0.00	4.00	108	1.00	1.00	1.14	3.97
Ls	1.07	0.74	0.00	3.00	108	1.00	1.00	−0.00	−0.87
Na	0.17	[0.41]	0.00	2.00	22	0.00	0.00	2.36	5.05
Sc	1.51	[1.31]	0.00	6.00	93	2.00	0.00	0.23	−0.82
Sx	0.11	[0.41]	0.00	3.00	11	0.00	0.00	4.58	23.67
Xy	0.04	[0.19]	0.00	1.00	5	0.00	0.00	5.06	23.93
Idio	1.31	1.45	0.00	7.00	81	1.00	0.00	1.07	1.04
DV	0.99	[0.71]	0.00	3.00	107	1.00	1.00	0.39	0.11
INCOM	0.83	[0.75]	0.00	4.00	91	1.00	1.00	0.81	1.34
DR	0.14	[0.37]	0.00	2.00	19	0.00	0.00	2.48	5.51
FABCOM	0.21	[0.44]	0.00	2.00	28	0.00	0.00	1.89	2.75
DV2	0.02	[0.14]	0.00	1.00	3	0.00	0.00	6.68	43.26
INC2	0.01	[0.12]	0.00	1.00	2	0.00	0.00	8.28	67.44
DR2	0.01	[0.08]	0.00	1.00	1	0.00	0.00	11.83	140.00
FAB2	0.04	[0.19]	0.00	1.00	5	0.00	0.00	5.06	23.93
ALOG	0.05	[0.25]	0.00	2.00	6	0.00	0.00	5.49	32.88
CONTAM	0.00	0.00	0.00	0.00	0	0.00	0.00	—	—
Sum6 Sp Sc	2.22	1.34	0.00	8.00	124	3.00	2.00	0.03	−0.90
Sum6 Sp Sc2	0.08	[0.27]	0.00	1.00	11	0.00	0.00	3.17	8.14
WSum6	4.57	3.23	0.00	15.00	140	4.00	3.00	0.67	0.32
AB	0.06	[0.25]	0.00	1.00	9	0.00	0.00	3.59	11.06
AG	1.20	0.99	0.00	5.00	106	1.00	1.00	1.03	1.98
CFB	0.00	0.00	0.00	0.00	0	0.00	0.00	—	—
COP	1.60	1.10	0.00	5.00	120	1.00	1.00	0.69	0.45
CP	0.00	[0.00]	0.00	0.00	0	0.00	0.00	—	—
MOR	0.58	[0.81]	0.00	4.00	59	0.00	0.00	1.57	2.57
PER	0.96	0.72	0.00	5.00	110	1.00	1.00	1.60	7.12
PSV	0.04	[0.20]	0.00	1.00	4	0.00	0.00	4.56	29.10

Table 10. Frequencies for 33 Variables for 1,390 Nonpatient Children and Adolescents by Age

	Age 5 (N = 90)		Age 6 (N = 80)		Age 7 (N = 120)		Age 8 (N = 120)		Age 9 (N = 140)		Age 10 (N = 120)	
	Freq	%	Freq	%	Freq	%	Freq	%	Freq	%	Freq	%
EB Style												
Introversive	2	2%	1	1%	9	8%	16	13%	33	24%	26	22%
Pervasive	0	0%	0	0%	0	0%	0	0%	3	2%	0	0%
Ambitent	24	27%	20	25%	44	37%	48	40%	51	36%	38	32%
Extratensive	64	71%	59	74%	67	56%	56	47%	56	40%	56	47%
Pervasive	62	69%	46	58%	40	33%	32	27%	15	11%	26	22%
D Score & Adjusted D Score												
D Score > 0	0	0%	0	0%	0	0%	6	5%	7	5%	2	2%
D Score = 0	68	76%	51	64%	69	58%	90	75%	117	84%	100	83%
D Score < 0	22	24%	29	36%	51	43%	24	20%	16	11%	18	15%
D Score < −1	4	4%	4	5%	12	10%	8	7%	9	6%	2	2%
Adj D Score > 0	0	0%	0	0%	0	0%	6	5%	9	6%	6	5%
Adj D Score = 0	72	80%	63	79%	69	58%	98	82%	121	86%	96	80%
Adj D Score < 0	18	20%	17	21%	51	43%	16	13%	10	7%	18	15%
Adj D Score < −1	3	3%	4	5%	5	4%	8	7%	7	5%	2	2%
Zd > +3.0 (Overincorp)	3	3%	0	0%	0	0%	8	7%	28	20%	30	25%
Zd < −3.0 (Underincorp)	23	26%	27	34%	32	27%	19	16%	22	16%	19	16%
Form Quality Deviations												
X + % > .89	0	0%	0	0%	0	0%	0	0%	1	1%	0	0%
X + % < .70	51	57%	28	35%	22	18%	56	47%	48	34%	12	10%
X + % < .61	25	28%	13	16%	12	10%	16	13%	11	8%	13	11%
X + % < .50	4	4%	0	0%	0	0%	3	3%	3	2%	3	3%
F + % < .70	15	17%	27	34%	81	68%	68	57%	67	48%	92	77%
Xu% > .20	49	54%	59	74%	0	0%	32	27%	36	26%	22	18%
X − % > .15	9	10%	12	15%	12	10%	14	12%	21	15%	17	14%
X − % > .20	1	1%	1	1%	6	5%	2	2%	2	1%	8	7%
X − % > .30	0	0%	0	0%	0	0%	0	0%	0	0%	0	0%
FC:CF + C Ratio												
FC > (CF + C) + 2	0	0%	0	0%	9	8%	1	1%	0	0%	1	1%
FC > (CF + C) + 1	0	0%	0	0%	12	10%	9	8%	10	7%	14	12%

76

	N	%	N	%	N	%	N	%	N	%	N	%
(CF + C) > FC + 1	87	97%	71	89%	17	14%	48	40%	30	21%	60	50%
(CF + C) > FC + 2	43	48%	49	61%	11	9%	32	27%	19	14%	21	18%
Constellations & Indices												
HVI Positive	0	0%	0	0%	0	0%	0	0%	0	0%	0	0%
OBS Positive	0	0%	0	0%	0	0%	0	0%	0	0%	0	0%
SCZI = 6	0	0%	0	0%	0	0%	0	0%	0	0%	0	0%
SCZI = 5	0	0%	0	0%	0	0%	0	0%	0	0%	0	0%
SCZI = 4	0	0%	0	0%	0	0%	0	0%	0	0%	0	0%
DEPI = 7	0	0%	0	0%	0	0%	0	0%	0	0%	0	0%
DEPI = 6	0	0%	0	0%	0	0%	0	0%	0	0%	0	0%
DEPI = 5	0	0%	0	0%	0	0%	0	0%	0	0%	0	0%
CDI = 5	1	1%	2	2%	3	3%	3	3%	0	0%	0	0%
CDI = 4	11	12%	10	13%	13	11%	8	7%	9	6%	18	15%
Miscellaneous Variables												
Lambda > .99	12	12%	9	11%	14	12%	20	17%	20	14%	13	11%
S > 2	21	23%	4	5%	37	31%	9	8%	12	9%	14	12%
Sum T = 0	33	37%	11	14%	10	8%	8	7%	17	12%	14	12%
Sum T > 1	0	0%	0	0%	2	2%	8	7%	6	4%	8	7%
3r + (2)/R < .33	0	0%	4	5%	0	0%	1	1%	7	5%	4	3%
3r + (2)/R > .44	86	96%	68	85%	86	72%	82	68%	56	40%	110	92%
PureC > 1	14	16%	31	39%	9	8%	3	3%	9	6%	2	2%
Afr < .40	0	0%	12	15%	0	0%	1	1%	8	6%	2	2%
Afr < .50	13	14%	19	24%	9	8%	12	10%	16	11%	16	13%
(FM+m) < Sum Shading	0	0%	0	0%	2	2%	10	8%	14	10%	8	7%
Populars < 4	6	7%	8	10%	3	3%	4	3%	0	0%	4	3%
COP = 0	13	14%	13	16%	12	10%	6	5%	4	3%	6	5%
COP > 2	6	6%	5	6%	16	13%	30	25%	37	26%	21	18%
AG = 0	8	9%	40	50%	0	0%	24	20%	12	9%	3	3%
AG > 2	4	4%	4	5%	3	3%	13	11%	19	14%	18	15%
MOR > 2	3	3%	5	6%	6	5%	3	3%	11	8%	13	11%
Level 2 Sp.Sc. > 0	32	36%	16	20%	19	16%	13	11%	14	10%	10	8%
Sum 6 Sp. Sc. > 6	19	21%	22	27%	22	18%	32	27%	23	16%	21	18%
Pure H < 24	24	4%	63	30%	32	52%	31	27%	36	22%		30%
Pure H = 0	1	1%	8	10%	2	2%	4	3%	2	1%	4	3%
p > a + 1	7	8%	5	6%	16	13%	10	8%	19	14%	12	10%
Mp > Ma	9	10%	9	11%	11	9%	14	12%	17	12%	14	12%

Table 10. (Continued)

	Age 11 (N = 135)		Age 12 (N = 120)		Age 13 (N = 110)		Age 14 (N = 105)		Age 15 (N = 110)		Age 16 (N = 140)	
	Freq	%	Freq	%	Freq	%	Freq	%	Freq	%	Freq	%
EB Style												
Introversive	41	30%	38	32%	34	31%	36	34%	41	37%	52	37%
Super-Introversive	0	0%	8	7%	10	9%	10	10%	8	7%	12	9%
Ambitent	34	25%	39	33%	39	35%	26	25%	23	21%	27	19%
Extratensive	60	44%	43	36%	37	34%	43	41%	46	42%	61	44%
Super-Extratensive	14	10%	22	18%	18	16%	18	17%	18	16%	23	16%
EA − es Differences: D Scores												
D Score > 0	0	0%	4	3%	14	13%	10	10%	9	8%	14	10%
D Score = 0	123	91%	90	75%	70	64%	69	66%	71	65%	110	79%
D Score < 0	12	9%	26	22%	26	24%	26	25%	30	27%	16	11%
D Score < −1	5	4%	3	3%	4	4%	3	3%	10	9%	9	6%
Adj D Score > 0	4	3%	14	12%	25	23%	21	20%	16	15%	17	12%
Adj D Score = 0	119	88%	80	67%	65	59%	70	67%	67	61%	86	61%
Adj D Score < 0	11	8%	26	22%	20	18%	14	13%	27	25%	12	9%
Adj D Score < −1	4	3%	2	2%	2	2%	2	2%	6	5%	7	5%
Zd > +3.0 (Overincorp)	36	27%	34	28%	30	27%	21	20%	25	23%	30	21%
Zd < −3.0 (Underincorp)	14	10%	20	17%	15	14%	16	15%	16	15%	14	10%
Form Quality Deviations												
X + % > .89	2	1%	0	0%	2	2%	1	1%	7	6%	8	6%
X + % < .70	21	16%	18	15%	16	15%	16	15%	7	6%	12	9%
X + % < .61	14	10%	6	5%	8	7%	8	8%	3	3%	3	2%
X + % < .50	0	0%	4	3%	6	5%	4	4%	0	0%	0	0%
F + % < .70	117	87%	91	76%	82	75%	57	54%	77	70%	72	51%
Xu% > .20	26	19%	16	13%	16	15%	14	13%	9	8%	16	11%
X − % > .15	20	15%	6	5%	12	11%	10	10%	2	2%	2	1%
X − % > .20	18	13%	4	3%	6	5%	4	4%	2	2%	2	1%
X − % > .30	0	0%	2	2%	2	2%	0	0%	1	1%	0	0%
FC:CF+C Ratio												
FC > (CF + C) + 2	3	2%	8	7%	6	5%	4	4%	10	9%	18	13%
FC > (CF + C) + 1	17	13%	12	10%	12	11%	8	8%	20	18%	38	27%

	n	%	n	%	n	%	n	%	n	%	n	%
(CF + C) > FC + 1	45	33%	24	20%	19	17%	16	15%	23	21%	23	16%
(CF + C) > FC + 2	14	10%	0	0%	3	3%	3	3%	2	2%	2	1%
Constellations & Indices												
HVI Positive	3	2%	4	3%	3	3%	1	1%	0	0%	1	1%
OBS Positive	0	0%	0	0%	0	0%	0	0%	1	1%	1	1%
SCZI = 6	0	0%	0	0%	0	0%	0	0%	0	0%	0	0%
SCZI = 5	0	0%	0	0%	0	0%	0	0%	0	0%	0	0%
SCZI = 4	0	0%	0	0%	0	0%	0	0%	0	0%	0	0%
DEPI = 7	0	0%	0	0%	0	0%	0	0%	0	0%	0	0%
DEPI = 6	0	0%	0	0%	0	0%	0	0%	0	0%	0	0%
DEPI = 5	0	0%	1	1%	1	1%	0	0%	0	0%	0	0%
CDI = 5	0	0%	0	0%	0	0%	0	0%	1	1%	1	1%
CDI = 4	12	9%	29	24%	14	13%	13	12%	11	10%	12	9%
Miscellaneous Variables												
Lambda > .99	16	12%	10	8%	10	9%	7	7%	8	7%	9	6%
S > 2	18	13%	10	8%	16	15%	13	12%	17	15%	18	13%
Sum T = 0	19	14%	14	12%	20	18%	17	16%	6	5%	12	9%
Sum T > 1	11	8%	0	0%	4	4%	2	2%	9	8%	11	8%
3r + (2)/R < .33	0	0%	6	5%	18	16%	18	17%	7	6%	10	7%
3r + (2)/R > .44	123	91%	85	71%	62	56%	59	56%	49	45%	74	53%
PureC > 1	0	0%	0	0%	0	0%	0	0%	0	0%	0	0%
Afr < .40	0	0%	6	5%	8	7%	6	6%	5	5%	6	4%
Afr < .50	13	10%	45	38%	33	30%	24	23%	19	17%	21	15%
(FM+m) < Sum Shading	10	7%	12	10%	11	10%	9	9%	17	15%	20	14%
Populars < 4	0	0%	4	3%	4	4%	1	1%	3	3%	4	3%
COP = 0	6	4%	6	5%	10	9%	13	12%	12	11%	20	14%
COP > 2	13	10%	19	16%	16	15%	18	17%	15	14%	24	17%
AG = 0	5	4%	21	18%	25	23%	19	18%	28	25%	34	24%
AG > 2	10	7%	15	13%	8	7%	10	10%	8	7%	11	8%
MOR > 2	6	4%	6	5%	2	2%	5	5%	4	4%	5	4%
Level 2 Sp.Sc. > 0	20	15%	22	18%	13	12%	9	9%	9	8%	7	5%
Sum 6 Sp. Sc. > 6	22	16%	17	14%	16	15%	12	11%	9	8%	9	6%
Pure H < 2	27	20%	30	25%	28	25%	18	17%	23	21%	14	10%
Pure H = 0	4	3%	0	0%	0	0%	0	0%	1	1%	1	1%
p > a + 1	12	9%	10	8%	7	6%	13	12%	13	12%	15	11%
Mp > Ma	20	15%	18	15%	9	8%	8	8%	16	15%	17	12%

REFERENCES

Exner, J. E. (1988). Problems with brief Rorschach protocols. *Journal of Personality Assessment, 52,* 640–647.

Exner, J. E. (1991). *The Rorschach: A Comprehensive System: Vol. 2. Interpretation* (2nd ed.). New York: Wiley.

Exner, J. E. (1993). *The Rorschach: A Comprehensive System: Vol. 1. Basic foundations* (3rd ed.). New York: Wiley.

Exner, J. E., Thomas, E. E., & Mason, B. (1985). Children's Rorschachs: Description and prediction. *Journal of Personality Assessment, 49,* 13–20.

Ruiz, F., Panelos, M. L., Thomas, E. A., & Exner, J. E. (1980). *A comparison of 30 protocols from children in three Spanish speaking countries with normative data for the Comprehensive System* [Workshops Study No. 267 (unpublished)]. Rorschach Workshops.

Sendin, C. (1981). *Findings concerning Popular responses in a Spanish sample of nonpatient adults.* 10th International Rorschach Congress, Washington, DC.

CHAPTER 4

The Interpretive Process:
Some Nonpatient Records

It is often difficult to keep the somewhat elusive concept of normality in perspective when interpreting the Rorschach, or for that matter, when interpreting most psychological tests that focus on the issues of personality structure and/or behavior. Clinical training, including that concerning assessment, focuses mainly on the unusual, deviant, or pathological. The emphasis in training is to detect liabilities and to devise strategies that will eliminate them or at least minimize their collective impact on adjustment. The promises of training become reality in practice. Most psychological testing is administered to people with problems, or in the instance of younger clients, people who have been identified by others as having problems. In such a professional framework, it is easy to lose sight of the concept of normality or of the need to afford appropriate emphasis to the subject's psychological assets.

In part, normative data are at fault. They present guidelines against which troubled subjects often are compared, and the comparison only tends to emphasize perceived liabilities. Comments regarding the normative data from those who do clinical assessments routinely include statements such as, "But I don't see kids who look like this," or "I never get texture responses."

The failure of most youngsters who are subject to assessment to present data that are congruent with normative findings tends to create a set that usually is reinforced by the routines of the clinician. *Personal norms* are created, that is, the clinician has a marked tendency to judge each new subject or patient in light of subjects or patients who have been evaluated previously. As a consequence, an assessor may regard one subject as being markedly better or worse than previously evaluated subjects. It is an unfortunate situation that can affect all subjects of the Rorschach and especially younger clients. Thus, a seriously depressed 13-year-old may be perceived to be much "healthier" than an obstreperous 13-year-old conduct disorder or substance abuser even though that may not be the case. Similarly, a cooperative but withdrawn 9-year-old may appear to be much better adjusted than a 9-year-old conduct disorder who might be described as a psychological monster.

In some ways, personal norms contain elements of specific validity. A schizophrenic or substance abuser usually will be less well socially adjusted than a seriously depressed subject, and a withdrawn youngster may adapt much better to the demands of a classroom environment than will a conduct-disordered child. Those generalizations are not, however, among the critical objectives of personality assessment and certainly not among the major goals of Rorschach assessment.

The primary target of personality assessment is to understand people, that is, how they are organized as a unique entity and how they function. In the optimal assessment situation, findings concerning assets will be afforded as much weight as will the liabilities, and conclusions about the existence and/or potential for adjustment or maladjustment will be deferred until all facets of personality have been carefully reviewed. It is the weighing of findings that sometimes leads the interpreter astray. When a professional works almost exclusively with abnormality, it is difficult to maintain a proper perspective about people, especially youngsters, who are not necessarily abnormal even though they may have liabilities.

Three protocols have been selected for inclusion in this chapter to try to illustrate this point. Two of the three are from one male subject who participated in a longitudinal study that involved taking the Rorschach five times, once every 2 years beginning at age 8 (Exner, Thomas, & Mason, 1985). They provide an interesting picture of how youngsters change considerably during their developmental years. The remaining record is from a 10-year-old female, drawn randomly from the standardization project records. It was selected to illustrate a different age group from that represented by the two records from the male subject.

THE INTERPRETIVE PROCESS

In addressing each of these protocols, as well as those included in other chapters, the same process and principles of interpretation will be applied. In all instances, the seven basic

Table 11.   Interpretive Search Strategies Based on Positive Key Variables

SCZI > 3	IDEATION → MEDIATION → PROCESSING → CONTROLS → AFFECT → SELF PERCEPTION → INTERPERSONAL PERCEPTION
DEPI > 5	AFFECT → CONTROLS → SELF PERCEPTION → INTERPERSONAL PERCEPTION → PROCESSING → MEDIATION → IDEATION
D < ADJ D	CONTROLS → SITUATION STRESS → (The remaining search routine should be that identified for the next positive key variable or the list of tertiary variables)
CDI > 3	CONTROLS → AFFECT → SELF PERCEPTION → INTERPERSONAL PERCEPTION → PROCESSING → MEDIATION → IDEATION
ADJ D IS MINUS	CONTROLS → (The remaining search routine should be that identified for the next positive key variable or the list of tertiary variables)
LAMBDA > 0.99	PROCESSING → MEDIATION → IDEATION → CONTROLS → AFFECT → SELF PERCEPTION → INTERPERSONAL PERCEPTION
REFLECTION > 0	SELF PERCEPTION → INTERPERSONAL PERCEPTION → CONTROLS (The remaining search routine should be selected from that identified for the next positive key variable or the list of tertiary variables)
EB = INTROVERSIVE	IDEATION → PROCESSING → MEDIATION → CONTROLS → AFFECT → SELF PERCEPTION → INTERPERSONAL PERCEPTION
EB = EXTRATENSIVE	AFFECT → SELF PERCEPTION → INTERPERSONAL PERCEPTION → CONTROLS → PROCESSING → MEDIATION → IDEATION
p > a+1	IDEATION → PROCESSING → MEDIATION → CONTROLS → SELF PERCEPTION → INTERPERSONAL PERCEPTION → AFFECT
HVI POSITIVE	IDEATION → PROCESSING → MEDIATION → CONTROLS → SELF PERCEPTION → INTERPERSONAL PERCEPTION → AFFECT

clusters of data will be reviewed (controls, processing, mediation, ideation, affect, self-perception, interpersonal perception), and in some cases, the array of data concerning situationally related stress will be reviewed. The seven clusters, however, will not always be studied in the same order. Key variables will be used to select the interpretive routine. The basis for this procedure has been described elsewhere (Exner, 1991, 1993). The Key variables are shown in Table 11.

In the event that no positive Key variables exist in a record, the interpreter can use any of several Tertiary variables to determine the most appropriate strategy of addressing the cluster of data. The listing of Tertiary variables is shown in Table 12.

There are two important issues to consider before selecting the interpretative strategy: validity and Suicide Constellation (S-CON).

Interpretive Validity of the Record   The first issue concerns the interpretive validity of the record. This has been discussed earlier but may warrant added emphasis here. Younger clients, especially children, usually want to escape the assessment task as quickly as possible. They often are subtly irritated or openly hostile because of the demands of the task, and only reluctantly cooperative. Children who are threatened or annoyed by assessment procedures tend to approach the Rorschach with great reluctance. Typically, they deny the possibility of finding anything in a blot, or when pressed, they provide as few answers as possible. In many instances, they produce a

Table 12.   Interpretive Search Strategies Based on Positive Tertiary Variables

Positive Variable	Typical Cluster Search Routine
OBS POSITIVE	PROCESSING → MEDIATION → IDEATION → CONTROLS → AFFECT → SELF PERCEPTION → INTERPERSONAL PERCEPTION
DEPI = 5	AFFECT → CONTROLS → SELF PERCEPTION INTERPERSONAL PERCEPTION → PROCESSING → MEDIATION IDEATION
EA > 12	CONTROLS → IDEATION → PROCESSING → MEDIATION → AFFECT → SELF PERCEPTION → INTERPERSONAL PERCEPTION
M − > O, or Mp > Ma, or SUM6 SPEC SC > 5	IDEATION → MEDIATION → PROCESSING → CONTROLS → AFFECT → SELF PERCEPTION → INTERPERSONAL PERCEPTION
SUM SHAD > FM+m, or CF+C > FC+1, or Afr < 0.46	AFFECT → CONTROLS → SELF PERCEPTION → INTERPERSONAL PERCEPTION → PROCESSING → MEDIATION → IDEATION
X−% > 20%, or Zd > +3.0 or < −3.0	PROCESSING → MEDIATION → IDEATION → CONTROLS → AFFECT → SELF PERCEPTION → INTERPERSONAL PERCEPTION
3r+(2)/R < .33	PERSONAL PERCEPTION → INTERPERSONAL PERCEPTION → AFFECT → CONTROLS → PROCESSING → MEDIATION → IDEATION
MOR > 2, or AG > 2	PERSONAL PERCEPTION → INTERPERSONAL PERCEPTION CONTROLS → IDEATION → PROCESSING → MEDIATION → AFFECT
T = 0 or > 1	PERSONAL PERCEPTION → INTERPERSONAL PERCEPTION AFFECT → CONTROLS → PROCESSING → PROCESSING → IDEATION

record that is interpretively invalid. These are the very brief records, 13 or fewer answers. These records typically are quite barren; a majority of the answers are simple and articulated only for form features.

These protocols do not have much temporal consistency (Exner, 1988, 1993), and even if the record is temporally consistent for some variables, it is usually impossible to detect those that are psychometrically reliable from those that are not. As suggested earlier, the protocol should not be accepted and the subject should be asked, prior to the Inquiry, to repeat the test. Usually, this procedure will yield a valid protocol, but in some instances, examiners may be led to believe that acceptance of the brief record is the only possible alternative. If this is the case, the interpreter probably should not attempt to struggle through an interpretation of the scoring. In a few instances, variables such as the $X + \%$, the $a{:}p$ ratio, or the Egocentricity Index may be valid, but there is no way to know this. Thus, any interpretation of the brief record must be much more subjective and rely mainly on *very* conservative interpretations derived from highly unusual features of the protocol. There are exceptions to this general rule. In some cases, subjects with severe pathology may be resistant and offer only a limited number of responses. Even though the number of answers given is fewer than 14, their structural characteristics, that is form quality and special scores, indicate the presence of pathology beyond question, and these findings are unequivocally confirmed by other data. In these cases, the brief record probably is usable, but these are unusual instances, and many cases will raise questions about why the Rorschach was administered in light of other data. Nonetheless, the record may provide important information about the subject.

The Suicide Constellation   When interpreting the protocols administered to most younger clients, the S-CON is of little use. However, if a subject is age 15 or older, the interpretation should always begin by inspecting the value for the Suicide Constellation. The S-CON does not fall into any of the clusters of variables. This is probably because it is an array of variables from several clusters that, collectively, have an actuarial usefulness in detecting those who have features similar to individuals who have effected their own death. Some groupings of items in the S-CON have a conceptual similarity, but the entire listing does not.

The S-CON has no demonstrated usefulness for subjects who are age 14 or under, and earlier attempts to develop a similar constellation for younger subjects have not been successful. In fact, neither the original data set from which the S-CON was developed (Exner & Wiley, 1977) nor the cross-validation data set that was used to modify the constellation (Exner, Martin, & Mason, 1984) contain subjects under the age of 18. However, a study of the few available records of 15- and 16-year-old subjects who effected their own death within 60 days after having been administered the Rorschach indicates that about two thirds were correctly identified by the S-CON.

The early identification of the potential for self-destructive behavior is a persistent challenge for the clinician, especially when younger clients are involved. The classic works of Shneidman and Farberow (1957) and Farberow and Shneidman (1961) have demonstrated clear relationships between demographic and/or behavioral variables and effected suicide, and it is unlikely that any test data, taken alone, will provide a greater discrimination of suicidal risk. Nonetheless, those data often are not available; thus when test data can provide clues concerning this risk, they should be taken seriously as a warning to conduct a more extensive evaluation of the issue.

In that context, the actuarial finding of an S-CON value of 8 or more for a 15-, 16-, or 17-year-old should be regarded very seriously, as the subject is likely to have many of the features commonly found among those who effect their own death. The same data can probably be used more subjectively for younger adolescents, but caution should be exercised. Obviously, if a 12-, 13-, or 14-year-old has a high value on the S-CON, such as 9, 10, or 11, concern is warranted.

However, several of the variables in the S-CON overlap with the Depression Index, and younger clients who may be at risk for a self-destructive act do not always manifest the classic adult features of depression. In fact, many are more likely to have histories in which some form of acting out is common. For instance, if a younger adolescent has values of 6 or 7 on the S-CON, which consists of elevated scores for MOR and $S,$ and low values for the Egocentricity Index, $X + \%,$ and Pure $H,$ and a D Score of less than 0, the collective finding should warrant concern regardless of whether the DEPI is positive. If the DEPI is positive (5 or more), the concern should be warranted, and from a subjective perspective, if the value for AG is elevated the concern might be greater. Unfortunately, the complexity of features that promote self-destruction is such that no single variable (or small group of variables) can be expected to be accurate in identifying suicide potential.

Assuming that these first two cautions have been addressed, it is appropriate to interpret the record in the routine defined from the first positive Key or Tertiary variable.

CASE 1—AN 8-YEAR-OLD MALE

The first nonpatient protocol is of an 8-year 1-month-old male who was administered the Rorschach as part of a longitudinal study. The test was administered during the third week of school in the nurse's office. The parents had apparently prepared him well in accord with instructions and he was quite cooperative.

According to the second-grade teacher, he is an active youngster whom she had to discipline four or five times for his quarreling with other children, but she indicates that his second-grade deportment was generally good. She reports that his work habits are a bit sloppy but notes that he reads at an average pace and handles numbers relatively well. The third-grade teacher reports that he seems cooperative and gets along well with other children. She notes that the subject is somewhat smaller than most of the children in his class, but she attributes this to his also being the youngest in his class.

He is the oldest of two children. His father, age 30, is a coowner of a small auto repair and paint shop. He is a high school graduate. His mother is also age 30. She completed one year of junior college before her marriage. Shortly after her marriage, she worked part time as a sales clerk, but since the birth of the subject has maintained the role of a housewife. The subject's younger sibling is a female, currently age 5. She has recently entered kindergarten. The parents own their own home, and the children have separate bedrooms. According to the report of the mother, the subject is in good health and has no remarkable medical history. There is no psychiatric history in the immediate family, although the father does have a cousin who has been in a psychiatric hospital. The family belongs to a Methodist church but does not attend services regularly.

The subject says that he likes football and baseball, and that school is "OK, but it lasts too long." He also reports that he likes to read stories but does not like arithmetic. He has no definite aspirations for the future but says that he might like to be a truck driver of a "big 18-wheeler." He is interested in his father's CB radio but says that usually he is not permitted to talk on it. He reports that he usually plays with two neighbor boys after school, ages 8 and 9, and that they play baseball, ride their bicycles, or go sledding in the winter. He says that his sister is "OK, but she gets in my things a lot."

Case 1. An 8-Year-Old Male

Card	Response	Inquiry	Scoring
I	1. I thnk it's a black bird	E: (rpts Ss resp) S: Well sur, it's lik a black bird, it's got wings lik flying up, u kno thy hav big wings	Wo FMa.FC'o A 1.0
	E: I thk if u look some more u'll find sthg else too		
	2. Well mayb it cb an airplan too	E: (Rpts Ss resp) S: It just has wings & these (D1) cb the cannons in the front lik airplans have lik a fighting plane in the army or navy	Wo Fu Sc 1.0
II	3. Ther's some dogs there, thy got their noses touchg, thyr smelling e.o lik dogs do all the time	E: (Rpts Ss resp) S: I dk what kind, littl dogs I guess & thy got their noses touchg lik thyr smell e.o., c rite here (outlines) E: I'm not sur I c them rite, can you help me a littl S: Look, their noses & heads & littl legs	D + FMpo 2 A P 3.0
	4. That ll a thg w stingers on it	E: (Rpts Ss resp) S: Mayb a fish w stingers lik thy hav in the ocean E: A fish w stingers? S: I dk, some fish hav stingers, didn't u ever c a catfish, thyv got stingers, not lik ths but ths is mayb an ocean fish, lik the ones that float & the stingers hang down, thy call em squid fish or sthg	Do Fu A DV
III	5. That ll 2 guys wrestling or sthg	E: (Rpts Ss resp) S: Well mayb thr not wrestling, mayb thyr just fighting ovr ths thg, lik thyr pulling it apart, c thy got their arms down here & their pullg on ths thg lik thy each want to hav it & thyr pulling it apart, tht's dumb to do E: Dumb to do? S: Sur, if thy each want it but if thy pull it apart neither one will get anythg cuz thy ruin it, lik if u and sbody else want to play w smthg but u break it then nobody gets it. We learn tht in school, u hav to cooperate	D + Mao 2 H,Id P 3.0 PER.AG
	6. Tht part up there ll blood to me & there's som here too & mayb som here too	E: (Rpts Ss resp) S: Well there just red spots lik if u have a nosebleed & the blood drops out it makes a spot, all diff ways	Dv C 2 Bl PER

	E:	All diff ways?		
	S:	Just red spots, my sister gets them & she makes spots all ovr until thy stop it, u hav to use ice on u'r nose, I got one once when I fell off my bike but I was littl then & I didn't kno how to ride very good		
IV	7. Ugh, thts lik Bigfoot, lik ur laying down lookg up at his big feet	E: (Rpts Ss resp)	Wo FD.FTo (H) P 2.0	
		S: Didn't u ever see him in the cartoons, he's lik a big furry guy in the mts & he's real ugly but he does good things for people lik help them out of the snow & stuff		
		E: A big furry guy?		
		S: Yep, all covered w fur		
		E: I'm not sur what makes it ll fur		
		S: I dkno, it just does, c all ovr him (rubs card) & he's got these big feet, it ll u can c under them when u look up lik this (tilts head back)		
	S: vCan I look this way too			
	E: Sur, if u want to			
V	v8. Tht ll the head on a snail	E: (Rpts Ss resp)	Do Fu Ad	
		S: It just does ll one, c the littl feelers lik thy hav		
VI	9. Anothr black bird I don't c nothin else	E: (Rpts Ss resp)	Wo FC'.FMao A 1.0	
		S: Its got big wgs lik out here & here, mayb its a black bird, thy put their wgs tht r out lik ths when thy fly		
VI	10. Thts lik a cat but he's all mooshed	E: (Rpts Ss resp)	Wo Fo A P 2.5 MOR,DV	
		S: Yeah, u kno lik he's all flat, lik if he got mooshed by a truck or sthg		
		E: Help me to c it lik u r		
		S: Here's his head & his legs, he's all flat though, lik if a cat gets run ovr he winds up flat lik ths, ugh, he shoulda watched out crossg the street		
VII	11. Tht must be 2 Indian girls, thy wear one feather	E: (Rpts Ss resp)	D+ Fo 2 Hd.Cg P 1.0 ALOG	
		S: Just faces, 2 of em, here & here lik indian girls I wld say (outlines)		
		E: U said Indian girls?		
		S: Well if these r feathers then thyd b Indian girls cuz regular girls don't wear feathers in their hair & Indian men wear lots of feathers		

Case 1. (continued)

Card	Response		Inquiry	Scoring
VIII	12. Wow, what's tht . . . mayb it's lik sthg u put up at Xmas or smthg lik for a birthday	E:	(Rpts Ss resp)	Wv CFo Art
		S:	U kno lik a decoration for? the tree or tht u hang in the window lik thy do when u'r having a party	
		E:	I'm not sur I c it lik u do	
		S:	Well it's just a thing w a lot of colors, lik for a Xmas tree & up here is where u hang it, c the point	
	13. These ll tigers fr India	E:	(Rpts Ss resp)	Do FCo 2 A P ALOG
		S:	Thy do, pink one's lik from India, thyr pink there	
		E:	What makes them ll tigers?	
		S:	I dkno, thy just do, thy got legs & thy ll tigers	
IX	14. Tht ll a butterfly	E:	(Rpts Ss resp)	Wo CF – A 5.5
		S:	Well bf's hav diff colors, lik the orange & the green & the pink, ths one's got orange wgs	
X	15. These 2 guys ll crabs & thyr liftin up ths thg, lik a pole	E:	(Rpts Ss resp)	D + FMau 2 A,Id 4.0 FAB2,COP
		S:	Well thy ll crabs c all the legs & those thgs on their head & thyr pickin up ths pole, mayb thy want it for their house	
		E:	For their house?	
		S:	Sur mayb to hold up smthg lik the roof, if u got a house u gotta hav smthg to hold up the roof	
	16. Mayb some eggs here	E:	(Rpts Ss resp)	Do CF.YFo 2 Fd
		S:	When u fry em thy ll ths, yellow & the middle is more yellow & the other is a different yellow, thts how fried eggs r supposed to look when u eat em	
	17. Thes guys ll crabs too, brown ones	E:	(Rpts Ss resp)	Do FCo 2 A
		S:	Thy got alot of legs & thyr brown lik some crabs r	

88

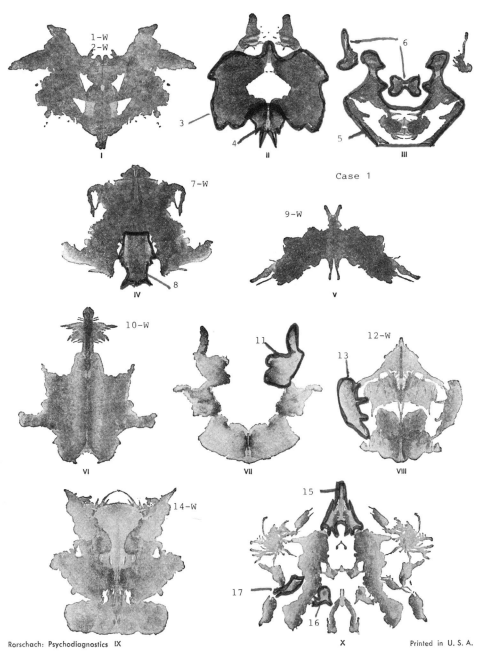

Case 1

Rorschach: Psychodiagnostics   IX   Printed in U. S. A.

Case 1

Case 1   **Sequence of Scores**

Card	No	Loc	#	Determinant(s)	(2)	Content(s)	Pop	Z	Special Scores
I	1	Wo	1	FMa.FC'o		A		1.0	
	2	Wo	1	Fu		Sc		1.0	
II	3	D+	1	FMpo	2	A	P	3.0	
	4	Do	3	Fu		A			DV
III	5	D+	1	Mao	2	H,Id	P	3.0	PER,AG
	6	Dv	2	C	2	Bl			PER
IV	7	Wo	1	FD.FTo		(H)	P	2.0	
	8	Do	1	Fu		Ad			
V	9	Wo	1	FC'.FMao		A		1.0	
VI	10	Wo	1	Fo		A	P	2.5	MOR,DV
VII	11	D+	1	Fo	2	Hd,Cg	P	1.0	ALOG
VIII	12	Wv	1	CFo		Art			
	13	Do	1	FCo	2	A	P		ALOG
IX	14	Wo	1	CF-		A		5.5	
X	15	D+	11	FMau	2	A,Id		4.0	FAB2,COP
	16	Do	2	CF.YFo	2	Fd			
	17	Do	7	FCo	2	A			

Case 1   **Structural Summary**

Location Features	Determinants		Contents	S-Constellation

Location Features	Blends	Single		S-Constellation
			H = 1, 0	. . FV+VF+V+FD>2
Zf = 10	FM.FC'	M = 1	(H) = 1, 0	. . Col−Shd Bl>0
ZSum = 24.0	FD.FT	FM = 2	Hd = 1, 0	. . Ego<.31,>.44
ZEst = 31.0	FC'.FM	m = 0	(Hd) = 0, 0	. . MOR > 3
	CF.YF	FC = 2	Hx = 0, 0	. . Zd > +− 3.5
		CF = 2	A = 9, 0	. . es > EA
W = 7		C = 1	(A) = 0, 0	. . CF+C > FC
(Wv = 1)		Cn = 0	Ad = 1, 0	. . X+% < .70
D = 10		FC' = 0	(Ad) = 0, 0	. . S > 3
Dd = 0		C'F = 0	An = 0, 0	. . P < 3 or > 8
S = 0		C' = 0	Art = 1, 0	. . Pure H < 2
		FT = 0	Ay = 0, 0	. . R < 17
DQ		TF = 0	Bl = 1, 0	x . . . . . TOTAL
. . . . . (FQ−)		T = 0	Bt = 0, 0	
+ = 4 (0)		FV = 0	Cg = 0, 1	Special Scorings
o = 11 (1)		VF = 0	Cl = 0, 0	Lv1 Lv2
v/+ = 0 (0)		V = 0	Ex = 0, 0	DV = 2x1 0x2
v = 2 (0)		FY = 0	Fd = 1, 0	INC = 0x2 0x4
		YF = 0	Fi = 0, 0	DR = 0x3 0x6
		Y = 0	Ge = 0, 0	FAB = 0x4 1x7
		Fr = 0	Hh = 0, 0	ALOG = 2x5
		rF = 0	Ls = 0, 0	CON = 0x7
Form Quality		FD = 0	Na = 0, 0	SUM6 = 5
		F = 5	Sc = 1, 0	WSUM6 = 19

	FQx	FQf	MQual	SQx			
+	= 0	0	0	0	Sx = 0, 0	AB = 0	CP = 0
o	= 11	2	1	0	Xy = 0, 0	AG = 1	MOR = 1
u	= 4	3	0	1	Id = 0, 2	CFB = 0	PER = 2
−	= 1	0	0	0		COP = 1	PSV = 0
none	= 1	—	0	0	(2) = 9		

Case 1   **Ratios, Percentages, and Derivations**

R = 17	L = 0.42		FC:CF+C = 2: 4	COP = 1 AG = 1
			Pure C = 1	Food = 1
EB = 1: 5.5	EA = 6.5	EBPer = 5.5	Afr = 0.55	Isolate/R = 0.00
eb = 4: 4	es = 8	D = 0	S = 0	H:(H)Hd(Hd) = 1:2
	Adj es = 8	Adj D = 0	Blends:R = 4:17	(HHd):(AAd) = 1:0
FM = 4 :	C' = 2 T = 1		CP = 0	H+A:Hd+Ad = 11:2
m = 0 :	V = 0 Y = 1			
		P = 6	Zf = 10	3r+(2) /R = 0.47
a:p = 4: 1	Sum6 = 5	X+% = 0.65	Zd = −7.0	Fr+rF = 0
Ma:Mp = 1: 0	Lv2 = 1	F+% = 0.40	W:D:Dd = 7:10: 0	FD = 1
2AB+Art+Ay=1	WSum6 = 19	X−% = 0.06	W:M = 7: 1	An+Xy = 0
M − = 0	Mnone = 0	S−% = 0.00	DQ+ = 4	MOR = 1
		Xu% = 0.24	DQv = 2	

SCZI = 1	DEPI = 2	CDI = 3	S-CON = N/A	HVI = No	OBS = No

INTERPRETIVE ROUTINE FOR CASE 1

The first positive Key variable is that the *EB* is Extratensive (1:5.5). This is not a surprising finding as nearly half of nonpatient 8-year-olds are extratensive. Thus, according to the Table 11 guidelines, the seven clusters of data available will be interpreted in the following order:

$$\text{AFFECT} \rightarrow \text{SELF-PERCEPTION} \rightarrow \text{INTERPERSONAL}$$
$$\text{PERCEPTION} \rightarrow \text{CONTROLS} \rightarrow \text{PROCESSING} \rightarrow \text{MEDIATION} \rightarrow \text{IDEATION}$$

Affect—Case 1   The data concerning affect for this record are shown in Table 13.

Table 13.   Affect Data for Case 1

DEPI = 2			BLENDS
EB = 1:5.5	*EBPer*	= 5.5	FM.FC'
eb = 4:4	*FC:CF* + *C*	= 2:4	FD.FT
	Pure *C*	= 1	FC'.FM
C' = 2 *T* = 1	*Afr*	= 0.55	CF.YF
V = 0 *Y* = 1	*S*	= 0	
	Blends/*R*	= 4:17	
	CP	= 0	

The DEPI value of 2 has no actuarial importance. The variables that have contributed to the DEPI will be reviewed elsewhere. The data for the *EB* (1:5.5) are quite important. They signal the presence of an extratensive style, indicating that this child tends to merge his feelings into his thinking much of the time when coping or decision making are required. In other words, his feelings are quite influential in his thinking. As noted earlier, this finding is not surprising for an 8-year-old. Most young children are impacted considerably by the way they feel, and to expect them to be able to put their feelings aside easily defies the fact that their neurological development remains limited.

The datum for *EBPer* (5.5) reveals that the extratensive style is quite marked; he is not very flexible about its use. Thus, even though some situations might be addressed more effectively if emotion were less involved, he usually will persist in this form of coping and decision making. Again, this is not uncommon for an 8-year-old. Nearly half of nonpatient 8's are extratensive, and more than half of those are pervasive in the use of that style. Longitudinal data indicate that this style may not persist as he continues to develop. Whereas most 8's are either extratensive or ambitents, they can be expected to alter styles as they progress chronologically and psychologically.

The value for the left side of the *eb* (4) is not remarkable. Values of 2, 3, or 4 are common. The more important issue is whether any of the values for the individual variables contributing to the left side *eb* value are unusual, and in this instance they are not. One *T* answer is expected as is one *Y* response. The two *C'* answers reflect a slight elevation from the expected value (1), but not one that is interpretively important. Thus, there is no reason to suspect the presence of unusual irritating internal stimulation with an affective basis.

The data for the *FC:CF* + *C* ratio (2:4) indicate that he does not modulate his emotional expressions very much. If this were the record of an adult or an older adolescent, this finding might be cause for concern, but it is a common finding for an 8-year-old. Children of this age do not worry much about how they express their feelings. They are exuberant and often even volatile. More than one fourth of the nonpatient sample have *FC:CF + C* ratios in which the right-side value is at least two points greater than the left-side value. Similarly, the presence of a Pure *C* response is not cause for concern, unless the content seems to have some pathognomic features. In this instance, it is blood (Card II), which again might be a troublesome finding in an older client, but about one third of all 8's give at least one blood answer.

The affective ratio (0.55) is a bit low for an 8-year-old. It may suggest that he is not as comfortable in processing emotionally toned stimuli as are most children of his age, but it is not very low and may simply indicate that he is less certain about how to deal with emotion than he might prefer. There are no space or color projection responses in the record, thus the values for both variables have no meaning.

There are four blends in the record, which is not unusual for an 8-year-old. All the blends involve two variables, the most common type for all subjects. None is especially striking, although both *C'* responses occur as blends and are combined with *FM* answers. In other words, they may have something to do with need states but that is not clear. One of the blends is a Color-Shading blend and contains a *Y* determinant. This suggests that he may have some confusion about his feelings, but this confusion is more than likely situationally related and could be a product of the test situation, especially in that he is extratensive.

Overall, the data do not suggest any significant affective liabilities. His pervasive expressive style will probably not be welcome to adults around him because it can be wearing on them, but that is the way of 8's. On a more positive note it is clear that, currently, he has a marked and predictable coping style and that he is not very concerned about modulating his affective displays. At times, he holds in his feelings, but not with any unusual frequency. He may be somewhat concerned about his emotionality, but this concern does not seem unusual or excessive, that is, he may be unsure about how best to express his feelings, but usually will give way to his pervasive affect style.

Self-Perception—Case 1   The data concerning the self-perception cluster are shown in Table 14. Much of the input regarding self-image and/or self-concept are derived subjectively, by searching carefully through the responses containing projected material. These are the minus and movement answers plus those that the verbiage embellishes in some way that goes well beyond a simple description of the blot characteristics.

There are no reflections in the record. If one or more did appear, it would not be unusual as about 25% of 8's give such answers, indicating an exquisite self-centeredness. The Egocentricity Index (0.47) is considerably lower than the average expected for this age (0.62). In fact, it is slightly more than one standard deviation (0.12) below the mean.

Table 14.   Self-Perception Data for Case 1

3r + (2)/R = 0.47	FD = 1	MOR = 1	Hx = 0	An + Xy = 0
Fr + rF = 0	Sum V = 0	H:(H) + Hd + (Hd) = 1: 2		Sx = 0

RESPONSES TO BE READ				
MOR Resp's	FQ- Resp's	M Resp's	FM Resp's	m Resp's
10	14	5	1,3,9,15	

This suggests that he does not regard himself as favorably as he does most of his significant others. Stated differently, his self-esteem is somewhat less than is expected for one of his age.

There is one *FD* answer in the record, which is not uncommon for an 8-year-old, and indicates that he is involved with the natural process of self-examining common to children. Fortunately, there are no vista responses in the protocol.

The record contains only one Pure *H* response, which is the expected value for an 8, suggesting, as is natural for a young child, that his self-image will be based much more on imagination than real experience. There is also one *MOR* response in the record, which is the expected frequency for 8's. It is Response 10, to Card VI, ". . . a cat but he's all mooshed (Inquiry) like if he got mooshed by a truck or something . . . like if a cat gets run over he winds up flat like this, ugh, he shoulda watched out crossing the street." This type of morbid answer to Card VI is very common among children and adults. Usually, it has no special interpretive importance, but in this instance, the subject offers some interesting embellishment (he shoulda watched out crossing the street). It hints at the possibility that he may regard the environment as potentially threatening, and that he may feel a need for caution in it because of his sense of vulnerability. This speculation is not inconsistent with his somewhat low Egocentricity Index.

The single minus answer, a butterfly to Card IX, does not offer any obvious projected material. However, the one *M* answer does include some interesting embellishment in the Inquiry. It is Response 5, to Card III, ". . . two guys wrestling or something (Inquiry) . . . maybe they're just fighting over this thing, like they're pulling it apart . . . like they each want to have it . . . that's dumb to do . . . but if they pull it apart neither will get anything cuz they ruin it, like if you and somebody else want to play with something but you break it then nobody gets it. We learn that in school, you have to cooperate." This is probably a direct representation of his concerns about socialization and impulse control.

The socialization issue seems less directly present in two of his four *FM* answers. Two of those answers (Nos. 1 and 9) consist of black birds in flight and do not appear to include easily interpreted projected material, but the remaining two are a bit more direct. The first, Response 3, to Card II is "dogs . . . they got their noses touching, they're smelling each other like dogs do all the time." The second, Response 15, to Card X, is ". . . crabs and they're lifting up this thing like a pole (Inquiry) . . . maybe they want it for their house . . . maybe to hold up something like the roof, if you've got a house you got to have something to hold up the roof."

It could be hypothesized that this composite of answers also tends to convey his own search for identity, that is, be careful and establish yourself firmly. This quest for identity seems evident in some of his other embellishments. For instance, in Response 6, to Card III, he describes a nosebleed and reveals, "I got one once when I fell off my bike, but I was little then and I didn't know how to ride very good." In Response 7, to Card IV (Bigfoot), he injects, ". . . he's real ugly but he does good things for people," and in Response 11, to Card VII, he offers, ". . . they'd be Indian girls cause regular girls don't wear feathers . . . Indian men wear lots of feathers."

None of the findings from the projected material are unusual for an 8-year-old. It is an age when issues of confidence in oneself and relations with others are quite important, yet often confusing. Probably the most important finding from this cluster is a tendency to value himself less than his significant others.

Interpersonal Perception—Case 1   The data for the interpersonal cluster are shown in Table 15.

Table 15.   Interpersonal Perception Data for Case 1

CDI = 3	$a{:}p$ = 4:1	T = 1	Human Cont = 3	Pure H = 1
HVI = Neg	Food = 1	PER = 2	COP = 1 AG = 1	Isolate/R = 0

RESPONSES TO BE READ

HUMAN MOVEMENT WITH PAIR	*HUMAN CONTENTS*
5	5,7,11

The CDI and HVI are both negative, and there are no useful data concerning interpersonal relations in the $a{:}p$ ratio. There is one Food answer in the record, indicating a marked dependency orientation. This is not an unusual finding for an 8-year-old. More than one third of the nonpatient 8's give at least one Food answer, probably signifying little more than the natural dependency needs of the young child. There is one T response, which is expected and suggests that he experiences his own needs for closeness much like others of his own age.

The number of human contents (3) is slightly lower than expected for his age. Although this could indicate less interest in others, that postulate does not coincide well with the findings from the self-perception data. Instead, it probably implies that he is less comfortable in interpersonal relationships. He does have two PER responses, which is slightly more than expected, and may suggest that he is a bit more defensive than most of his own age. There is one COP and one AG response, both of which are at the expected level for this age. Interestingly, the AG answer (guys wrestling) is criticized in the Inquiry (We learn that in school, you have to cooperate). The other movement answers containing a pair are the dogs smelling and the COP response of crabs trying to lift a pole. Although the data are limited, they imply an interest in developing interpersonal relations. The isolation Index is negative and the other human contents (Bigfoot, Indian girls) also tend to convey an interest in understanding people more fully.

In general, the data for the cluster are positive. Needs for closeness are evident and the natural need of the child to be somewhat dependent is present. It seems as though he is not very comfortable with his impressions of others, but is interested in learning more about people and his role in relation to them.

Controls—Case 1   The data relevant to issues of control and stress tolerance for this case are shown in Table 16.

Table 16.   Controls and Stress Tolerance Data for Case 1

EB = 1:5.5		EA = 6.5		D = 0	
eb = 4:4		es = 8	Adjes = 8	AdjD = 0	
FM = 4	C' = 2	T = 1		CDI = 3	
m = 0	V = 0	Y = 1			

The D and Adjusted D Scores are both zero, suggesting that his capacity for control and tolerance for stress is not much different than for most of his age. The *EA* of 6.5 is not very impressive if contrasted against that expected for older children or adults, but it is not unusual for an 8-year-old. In fact, the value of 6.5 is the mode for that age group. It merely signals that children of this age do not have much resource identified in ways that will make it readily available, and in that context, they are a bit more vulnerable to overload situations. Nonetheless, there is no evidence of overload in this youngster at this time. It may also be important to note that the data of the Four Square (*EA, EB, eb,* and *es*) offer no reason to question the validity of the Adjusted D Score. Thus, there is no reason to question the integrity of his capacity for control.

Processing—Case 1 The data for the cluster regarding information processing are presented in Table 17.

Table 17. Processing Data for Case 1

L = 0.42	$W:D:Dd$ = 7:10:0	Zd = −7.0	$DQ+$ = 4
Zf = 10	$W:M$ = 7:1	PSV = 0	$DQv/+$ = 0
HVI = No	OBS = No		DQv = 2

LOCATION SEQUENCING

I	W,W	IV	W,D	VII	D
II	D,D	V	W	VIII	W,D
III	D.D	VI	W	IX	W
				X	D,D,D

The value for Lambda is not remarkable, and the Obsessive Style (OBS) and Hypervigilance Indices (HVI) are negative. The *Zf* (10) is within the average range, but the *W:D:Dd* ratio (7:10:0) is a bit more conservative than is common for 8's. Usually, 8-year-olds give more *W* than *D,* and the reverse here suggests that he is somewhat more conservative in his processing efforts than most children his age. On the other hand, the *W:M* ratio (7:1) suggests that his aspirations are substantial. Possibly the most significant finding in this cluster is the *Zd* score (−7.0), which reveals a marked underincorporative style. Its presence indicates that he is a rather sloppy scanner and may often neglect important stimulus cues when attempting to deal with the stimuli of a field. Underincorporation is not uncommon among younger children. It appears among nearly 20% of 8-year-olds and probably should not become a focus for intervention unless considerable academic difficulty is present. However, it should be monitored; that is, if he has difficulty in either reading or math skills at the ages of 9 or 10, some correction for the problem would be in order.

The underincorporative style probably accounts for the limited number of synthesis answers (4) and the presence of the two *DQv* answers. Both of those values suggest that his overall processing activity is not yielding as much quality organization as might be expected. On the other hand, he does not perseverate, and the Location Sequencing indicates that he is reasonably consistent in his approach.

Overall, his processing activity is not unlike that of many of his age. His underincorporative style may be a handicap, but it is premature to suggest that this is the case. In general, his effort to process seems adequate, and further neurological growth may cause the underincorporative style to dissipate.

Mediation—Case 1   The data related to cognitive mediation, that is, how he translates stimulus inputs, are shown in Table 18.

Table 18.   **Cognitive Mediation Data for Case 1**

Lambda	= 0.42	OBS	= Neg	MINUS FEATURES
P	= 6	X+%	= .65	14
FQx+	= 0	F+%	= .40	
FQxo	= 11	Xu%	= .24	
FQxu	= 4	X−%	= .06	
FQx−	= 1	S−%	= .00	
FQxnone	= 0	CONFAB = 0		

The values for L and OBS are not relevant to the interpretation. There are six Popular answers, which is about average for an 8-year-old. Generally, they appear to the cards for which Popular answers occur frequently (II, III, IV, VI, VII, and VIII) and although Popular responses were not given to Card I and V, he did give winged object responses (birds). This finding suggests that, when afforded with obvious stimulus cues, he will probably give the more obvious or expected responses.

The $X + \%$ (.65) is slightly lower than average, but not remarkably so, and the finding is tempered by the fact that only one minus answer was given. Thus, it would be unreasonable to suggest that he has difficulties translating stimulus input, but the somewhat higher than average $Xu\%$ does indicate that some of his translations may be more individualistic. This is not an unexpected finding in light of the data concerning self and interpersonal perception implying that he is in a period of growth in which the issue of identifying social convention is ongoing. The single minus answer is not a serious distortion and offers no indication that he has problems defining what is real.

Ideation—Case 1   The data concerning ideation are shown in Table 19.

Table 19.   **Ideation Data for Case 1**

		M QUALITY	SPECIAL SCORES			
$EB = 1:5.5$	$EBPer = 5.5$					
$eb = 4:4$	$(FM = 4 \quad m = 0)$	+ = 0	DV	= 2	DV2	= 0
$a:p = 4:1$	$M^a:M^p = 1:0$	o = 1	INC	= 0	INC2	= 0
$2AB + Art + Ay = 1$		u = 0	DR	= 0	DR2	= 0
MOR = 1		− = 0	FAB	= 1	FAB2	= 0
			ALOG	= 2	SUM6	= 5
RESPONSES TO BE READ FOR QUALITY			CON	= 0	WSUM6	= 16
5						

The data for the EB have been reviewed earlier. This is a pervasively extratensive youngster who can be expected to merge his feelings into his thinking most of the time. In effect, he will not attempt to address decisions in the most logical way. The pervasiveness of this approach is common among youngsters of this age, and it will not be unusual to find that some of his logic may be flawed, not because he is extratensive, but more because his style is pervasive and he does not modulate his feelings very much. This is noted in two of his five answers that include special scores. His judgment is not very good. On Card VII he indicates that they must be Indian girls because regular girls don't wear feathers in their hair. Similarly, on Card VIII he argues that the tigers are from India because "they are pink there." This kind of flawed judgment is common-place among children of his age and is not cause for concern at this time.

The values for the *a:p* ratio (4:1) are quite disparate, indicating that he is not very flexible in the manner in which he thinks about issues. The data for the $M^a:M^p$ ratio, the Intellectualization Index, and the MOR value do not contribute to the interpretive yield. As noted earlier, there are five critical special scores in the record. This is about average for an 8-year-old and simply reflects that children of this age experience cognitive slips and/or faulty logic from time to time. None of the special scores reflect serious or bizarre form of thought. In addition to the two ALOG answers, there are two DV's, Response 4, in which he misuses the word "stringers" for stingers, and Response 10 in which he uses the word "mooshed." The single FABCOM is in Response 15, in which he has two crabs trying to lift a pole. The quality of the single *M* answer is about as sophisticated as might be expected from an 8-year-old.

In general, it seems reasonable to conclude that his thinking is immature, concrete, and often marked by poor judgment, but it is not unlike that found among most children of this age.

Summary—Case 1   This 8-year-old youngster presents a picture of a developing per-sonality that is probably not unlike most of his nonpatient peers. He has a marked coping style that relies mainly on feelings and much of his problem-solving behavior will involve trial-and-error activity. He does not modulate his emotional displays very much. Instead, it is likely that those around him will be well aware of his emotional expressions when they occur. He seems a bit uncomfortable about dealing with emotion and may avoid emo-tional stimulation more often than is typical for those of his age. His capacity for control seems adequate and there is no reason to suspect that he will become overly disorganized by stress. He is quite uncertain about his identity and tends to judge himself less favor-ably than he does other who are important to him. He is also very uncertain about his environment and perceives a need to be cautious about interacting with it. At the same time, he seems oriented toward becoming more adept at social interaction. Currently, he manifests a dependency orientation, which is not unusual for his age. He is a bit conserva-tive about processing new information and has a bad habit of scanning new stimulus fields hastily and sometimes incompletely. This probably causes him difficulties with some of his schoolwork, but it is not an uncommon finding for those of his age and should not become a focus for intervention unless his academic performance deteriorates consider-ably over the next year. He seems quite aware of conventionality, and although he some-times translates events in an overly idiographic manner, there are no significant problems with his reality testing. His thinking is somewhat immature and concrete, and his judg-ment is flawed at times, but this is typical for his age.

Overall, he seems to be a relatively healthy youngster who is progressing cautiously in search of a better understanding of himself and of the environment around him.

CASE 2—A 14-YEAR-OLD MALE

Case 2 represents the fourth testing of the Case 1 subject. He is now 14 years old and in the fifth month of the ninth grade, his first year in high school. The family constellation remains the same. His father is now 36 and is the sole owner of an auto repair shop. His mother is also now 36. She handles the billing and the bookkeeping for the business on a part time basis. His sister is 11 and in the seventh grade.

He attends a public school and was selected, because of his performance in eighth grade, to take an honors program in Spanish. All his other courses (algebra, English, basic science, and woodworking, physical education) are typical nonhonors courses. His grades in the fourth, fifth, and sixth grades were all average or slightly above. Most of his grades in the seventh and eighth grades were A's or B's. His midyear grades include three A's (Spanish, science, and algebra) and three B's (English, woodworking, and physical education). His teachers offer no explanation for his marked academic improvement except to note a change in schools beginning with the seventh grade. He reports that when he went to the junior high school he became more interested, "The teachers were really good." He says that he looks forward to going on to college and is considering the possibility of becoming a teacher.

He began taking trumpet lessons in the fourth grade and was in the school band in elementary and junior high schools, but he reports that he is not very interested in continuing with music. He tried out for the football team in high school but was not accepted, "I guess I'm too small." He looks forward to the spring when he intends to try out for the track team, "I run pretty well, and I think maybe I could pole vault." He has been selected as the class reporter for the school newspaper. His ninth-grade homeroom teacher reports that he is cooperative, dependable, and seemingly well liked by his peers. His science teacher has noted that he is easy to work with in the laboratory.

He reports that he has worked the past two summers helping his father paint cars. He also reports that he has several friends and attends school social functions, but emphasizes that he does not have a regular girlfriend.

Case 2. A 14-Year-Old Male

Card		Response		Inquiry	Scoring
I	1.	I thk I said a bat last time, yeah, a bat	E: S:	(Rpts Ss resp) Well it has a shape somethg lik a bat and it has the grey coloring to it like bats	Wo FC'o A P 1.0
	2.	It ll a person standg in the middle, mayb a guy gettg ready to hang glide cuz thes ll wgs	E: S: E: S:	(Rpts Ss resp) U can c a person's body in the center & if u thk of the wings too then it cb a guy whose gettg ready to push off Push off? Thts how thy hold em on, thy lik stand up the glider & then thy give a push off a hill or cliff, ths ll tht to me	W + Mao H,Sc 4.0 PER
II	3.	Oh yeah, it ll 2 clowns clowns doing an act I thk I said tht last time	E: S:	(Rpts Ss resp) Well thyr kinda hunched over and sorta slapping their hands together, lik a funny routine thyr doing. Thy have their red hats & red socks & shoes, its lik thyr doing some funny dance or smthg	W + Ma.FCo 2 (H),Cg 4.5 COP
	4.	Thes top thgs (D2) cb lungs	E: S: E: S:	(Rpts Ss resp) Thes 2 top thgs, thy are all red lik lungs bec of the bld in em & I thnk thyr tht shape too Bld in them? Yeah, the lungs hav a lotta littl bld vessels, ths r all red lik thy tht	Do CF − An,Bl
III	5.	Is this the same? I dnt rem ths one, it ll 2 guys doing a dance arnd ths drum a dance around a drum or sthg	E: S: E: S: E: S:	(Rpts Ss resp) Well it ll 2 guys who r doing a dance, kinda like natives or smthg, lik thyr dancg around this drum or table Help me to c it lik u r Here r the guys, c the legs & their arms & heads, lik thyr bending dwn ovr ths drum, lik dancg arnd it, mayb its more lik a table, I dk I just thot of a drum U said natives? Well thyr black, lik natives	D + Ma.FC'o 2 H,Sc P 3.0 COP
	6.	Tht cntr part ll a dumbell, lik in gym	E: S:	(Rpts Ss resp) It just has tht shape, u kno lik u use in the gym, u hold one in each hand	Do Fu Sc PER

IV	7.	I rem ths one, old Bigfoot sittg on a stump w his feet stretchd out	E: (Rpts Ss resp) S: He's sorta got his head tipped back, u can't c it very well, u c more of his big feet sticking out here in front & ths is what he's sittg on, a stump I guess	W + Mp.FDo (H),Bt P 4.0
	8.	Or, I guess it cb a frog lik he's just sittg hunchd lik thy do	E: (Rpts Ss resp) S: It cb one, w the big legs & the the littl head, just kinda hunched down lik thy sit E: Hunched dwn? S: Well, tht the way a frog looks when its sittg still	Wo FMpu A 2.0
V	9.	Ths ll a bird, mayb an eagle w its wgs stretchd out lik he's flyg around	E: (Rpts Ss resp) S: I guess the big wgs rem me of an eagle, thy'v got really big wgs, c thes wld be his . . . a . . . his feet but thy call em smthg else . . . talons I thk	Wo FMau A 1.0
VI	10.	Ths re me of a totem pole up on a mound or hill & thers a skin laid out in front of it	E: (Rpts Ss resp) S: Well the totem is up here, c the wgs r on either side & then this ll a bear skin laying out in fnt E: Out in front? S: Well, its bigger, it looks spread out lik for a ceremony or smthg E: U said a bear skin? S: Well some furry A, u can c all the markings lik the diff colorg of the fur	W + FD.FTo Ay,Ad P 2.5
	< 11.	Ths way it ll a fishing boat	E: (Rpts Ss resp) S: It rem me of a fishing boat, mayb a shrimp boat or one of thos kind, (outlines), here's the smokestack & the front, just lik it's chuggin along slow lik & ths wld b the water line (traces midline)	Do mao Sc.Na
VII	12.	I rem ths one, it ll 2 2 littl girls sittg on cushions lookg at e.o.	E: (Rpts Ss resp) S: Well, thy rem me of 2 littl girls cuz thy'v got their hair up & it's like thyr r sittg on thes big cushions facing e.o., c the nose & the chin is here	W + Mpo 2 H,Hh P 2.5
VIII	13.	Well, 1st it ll a couple of A's tht r climbg up ths tree	E: (Rpts Ss resp) S: One on either side, lik cats of or smthg, each one has one paw up on the top branch of the tree & anothr one dwn on this part here E: I'm not sur what makes it ll a tree S: Its pointed up here at the top & it has a tree shape to it	W + FMao 2 A,Bt P 4.5

101

Case 2. (continued)

Card	Response		Inquiry	Scoring
	14. There's 2 blue flags in the cntr	E: S:	(Rpts Ss resp) Thyr lik rectangles, lik a flag, thy just rem me of a cpl of blue flags	Do FCo 2 Art
IX	15. Ths ll the face of a clown	E: S:	(Rpts Ss resp) Well he's got a lot of orange hair & green cheeks & a pink collar, u almost can't c a face because it's all so painted, u can c his eyes out here tho (DdS29) & his nose	WSo CFu (Hd) 5.5
X	16. I guess these cb crabs up here	E: S:	(Rpts Ss resp) I dkno, thy just hav a lot of legs, I thk I've said tht every time	Do Fo 2 A P
	17. Up here it ll 2 more crabs r tryg to pick up ths post or push it over	E: S:	(Rpts Ss resp) Well, thy also have a lot of legs & the littl antennae & thyr pushg on ths post lik thyr trying to push it or pick it up, I guess push it down	D + FMau 2 A,Sc 4.0 COP,AG,FAB
	18. Down here thes thgs ll amoeba	E: S:	(Rpts Ss resp) Thy hav a kind of irreg shape & the middl part cb the nucleus, we've been studying thm in science	Do Fo 2 A PER
	v19. I don't thk I ever saw ths before but here ll 2 guys who r workg on a construction job	E: S:	(Rpts Ss resp) Well it looks lik thyr leaning out toward eo, lik hangg onto ths pink thg, lik part of a towr & it ll thyr holdg smthg or mayb one is handing smthg to the othr, lik on a construction job, or mayb its smthg thyr tryg to put into place between the 2 towers, c the arms & body & ths is what thyr holding onto	D + Mao 2 H,Sc 4.0 COP

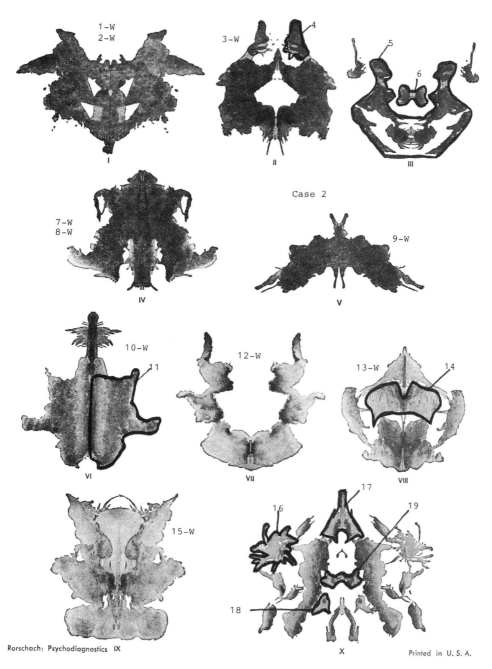

Case 2

Rorschach: Psychodiagnostics

Printed in U. S. A.

Case 2

Case 2   **Sequence of Scores**

Card	No	Loc	#	Determinant(s)	(2)	Content(s)	Pop	Z	Special Scores
I	1	Wo	1	FC'o		A	P	1.0	
	2	W+	1	Mao		H,Sc		4.0	PER
II	3	W+	1	Ma.Fco	2	(H),Cg		4.5	COP
	4	Do	2	CF-		An,Bl			
III	5	D+	5	Ma.FC'o	2	H,Sc	P	3.0	COP
	6	Do	3	Fu		Sc			PER
IV	7	W+	1	Mp.FDo		(H),Bt	P	4.0	
	8	Wo	1	FMpu		A		2.0	
V	9	Wo	1	FMau		A		1.0	
VI	10	W+	1	FD.FTo		Ay,Ad	P	2.5	
	11	Do	4	mao		Sc,Na			
VII	12	W+	2	Mpo	2	H,Hh	P	2.5	
VIII	13	W+	1	FMao	2	A,Bt	P	4.5	
	14	Do	4	FCo	2	Art			
IX	15	WSo	1	CFu		(Hd)		5.5	
X	16	Do	1	Fo	2	A	P		
	17	D+	11	FMau	2	A,Sc		4.0	COP,AG,FAB
	18	Do	2	Fo	2	A			PER
	19	D+	6	Mao	2	H,Sc		4.0	COP

Case 2   **Structural Summary**

Location	Determinants		Contents	S-Constellation
Features	Blends	Single		NO . . FV+VF+V+FD>2
			H = 4, 0	NO . . Col−Shd Bl>0
Zf = 13	M.FC	M = 3	(H) = 2, 0	YES . . Ego<.31,>.44
ZSum = 42.5	M.FC'	FM = 4	Hd = 0, 0	NO . . MOR > 3
ZEst = 41.5	M.FD	m = 1	(Hd) = 1, 0	NO . . Zd > +− 3.5
	FD.FT	FC = 1	Hx = 0, 0	NO . . es > EA
W = 10		CF = 2	A = 7, 0	NO . . CF+C > FC
(Wv = 0)		C = 0	(A) = 0, 0	YES . . X+% < .70
D = 9		Cn = 0	Ad = 0, 1	NO . . S > 3
Dd = 0		FC' = 1	(Ad) = 0, 0	NO . . P < 3 or > 8
S = 1		C'F = 0	An = 1, 0	NO . . Pure H < 2
		C' = 0	Art = 1, 0	NO . . R < 17
DQ		FT = 0	Ay = 1, 0	2 . . . . . TOTAL
. . . . . (FQ−)		TF = 0	Bl = 0, 1	
+ = 9 (0)		T = 0	Bt = 0, 2	Special Scorings
o = 10 (1)		FV = 0	Cg = 0, 1	Lv1 Lv2
v/+ = 0 (0)		VF = 0	Cl = 0, 0	DV = 0x1 0x2
v = 0 (0)		V = 0	Ex = 0, 0	INC = 0x2 0x4
		FY = 0	Fd = 0, 0	DR = 0x3 0x6
		YF = 0	Fi = 0, 0	FAB = 1x4 0x7
		Y = 0	Ge = 0, 0	ALOG = 0x5
Form Quality		Fr = 0	Hh = 0, 1	CON = 0x7
		rF = 0	Ls = 0, 0	SUM6 = 1
FQx FQf MQual SQx		FD = 0	Na = 0, 1	WSUM6 = 4
+ = 0 0 0 0		F = 3	Sc = 2, 4	
o = 13 2 6 0			Sx = 0, 0	AB = 0 CP = 0
u = 5 1 0 1			Xy = 0, 0	AG = 1 MOR = 0
− = 1 0 0 0			Id = 0, 0	CFB = 0 PER = 3
none = 0 — 0 0		(2) = 9		COP = 4 PSV = 0

Case 2   **Ratios, Percentages, and Derivations**

R = 19	L = 0.19		FC:CF+C = 2: 2	COP = 4 AG = 1
			Pure C = 0	Food = 0
EB = 6: 3.0	EA = 9.0	EBPer = 2.0	Afr = 0.58	Isolate/R = 0.21
eb = 5: 3	es = 8	D = 0	S = 1	H:(H)Hd(Hd) = 4:3
	Adj es = 8	Adj D = 0	Blends:R = 4:19	(HHd):(AAd) = 3:0
FM = 4 : C' = 2 T = 1			CP = 0	H+A:Hd+Ad = 13:2
m = 1 : V = 0 Y = 0				
		P = 7	Zf = 13	3r+(2) /R = 0.47
a:p = 8: 3	Sum6 = 1	X+% = 0.68	Zd = +1.0	Fr+rF = 0
Ma:Mp = 4: 2	Lv2 = 0	F+% = 0.67	W:D:Dd = 10:9: 0	FD = 2
2AB+Art+Ay=2	WSum6 = 4	X−% = 0.05	W:M = 10: 6	An+Xy = 1
M − = 0	Mnone = 0	S−% = 0.00	DQ+ = 9	MOR = 0
		Xu% = 0.26	DQv = 0	

SCZI = 0	DEPI = 0	CDI = 0	S-CON = 2	HVI = No	OBS = No

INTERPRETIVE ROUTINE FOR CASE 2

The first positive Key variable is, again, the *EB,* but now it is introversive (6:3.0). About one third of 14-year-olds are introversive. Thus, for this case, the order in which the data clusters will be reviewed is as follows:

IDEATION → PROCESSING → MEDIATION → CONTROLS → AFFECT
→ SELF-PERCEPTION → INTERPERSONAL PERCEPTION

Ideation—Case 2   The data related to the cluster regarding ideation are shown in Table 20.

Table 20.   Ideation Data for Case 2

EB = 6:3.0	EBPer = 2.0	M QUALITY		SPECIAL SCORES		
eb = 5:3	(FM = 4 m = 1)	+ = 0	DV = 0	DV2 = 0		
a:p = 8:3	$M^a:M^p$ = 4:2	o = 6	INC = 0	INC2 = 0		
2AB+Art+Ay = 2		u = 0	DR = 0	DR2 = 0		
MOR = 0		− = 0	FAB = 1	FAB2 = 0		
RESPONSES TO BE READ FOR QUALITY			ALOG = 0	SUM6 = 1		
2,3,5,7,12,19			CON = 0	WSUM6 = 4		

As noted earlier, an introversive style is not uncommon among 14-year-olds. Its presence signifies that, for whatever reason, the subject now prefers to push his feelings aside and try to mentally weigh possibilities before coming to a decision. Introversives are more cautious in decision making than are extratensives. They are attracted to clear logic systems and apparently are less prone to accept failure when they make decisions. Although he is introversive, the data for the *EBPer* suggest that the style is not pervasive. Therefore, it is likely that he is flexible and may choose a different method of coping when the circumstances do not favor a cautious, thoughtful approach.

The data for the left side of the *eb* (5) are not remarkable, consisting of 4 *FM* answers and 1 *m*. In other words, there is no unusual level of peripheral ideation that may interfere with his attention or concentration. The values in the *a:p* ratio (8:3) are slightly more disparate than expected, suggesting that he is not very flexible in his way of thinking about things, and his values probably are reasonably well fixed. The data for the $M^a:M^p$ ratio (4:2) are not meaningful. Similarly, the Intellectualization Index is not positive, and there are no MOR responses in the record.

There is one Critical Special Score, a FABCOM, that occurs in Response 17, to Card X. It involves crabs trying to pick up or push over a post. It is a childish response, but not necessarily one that indicates serious thinking problems. About one third of all nonpatient 14's give a FABCOM of this variety. Actually, his weighted Sum for Special Scores (4) is about average for those of his age. There are no *M−* responses. In fact, all six of his *M* answers have an ordinary Form Quality. When the six *M* answers are evaluated for quality, at least three are rather sophisticated (a guy ready to hang-glide, two clowns doing an act, and two guys working on a construction job). The remaining three *M* answers are very commonplace (guys dancing around a drum, Bigfoot sitting on a stump, and two girls looking at each other). In general, his thinking seems clear and reasonably sophisticated for one of his age, and in that context, his ideational style probably serves him well, especially in that it is not pervasive.

Processing—Case 2   The data concerning processing activity are shown in Table 21.

Table 21. Processing Data for Case 2

L = 0.19	$W{:}D{:}Dd$ = 10:9:0	Zd = +1.5	$DQ+$ = 9
Zf = 13	$W{:}M$ = 10:6	PSV = 0	$DQv/+$ = 0
HVI = No	OBS = No		DQv = 0

LOCATION SEQUENCING

I	W,W	IV	W,W	VII	W
II	W,D	V	W	VIII	W,D
III	D,D	VI	W,D	IX	W
				X	D,D,D,D

The OBS and HVI data are not positive. The Lambda is somewhat lower than might be expected for a 14-year-old, suggesting that he is quite involved in processing new stimuli. This could signal an inability to back away and be more economical, or it could result from an overincorporative style, but neither of those postulates seem relevant here. More likely, his involvement with new stimulus fields is probably the result of a healthy adolescent curiosity. If the data from his first Rorschach, taken at age 8, are considered, this less economical approach to process could be related to the uncertainty about his environment which was noted at that time. If the latter is true, data from the self-perception and interpersonal perception clusters will reveal a marked sense of insecurity and a tendency to be more isolated and reserved concerning his interpersonal relations.

For the moment, it seems reasonable to accept the adolescent curiosity hypothesis, mainly because of other data in this cluster. He does strive to organize (Zf = 13), but not more than most of his age. In fact, the $W{:}D{:}Dd$ (9:10:0) and $W{:}M$ (9:6) ratios are reasonably conservative. When he does organize, the results are quite good. There are nine $DQ+$ responses, no DQv answers, and no perseverations. The Zd score (+1.5) is well within expected limits, indicating that his scanning activity is not unlike others. This is a very positive finding in that he was an underincorporator at age 8.

Overall, his processing activity seems very positive for his age and, in fact, is commensurate with processing activity found in most interversive adults.

Mediation—Case 2   The data concerning mediation for Case 2 are presented in Table 22.

Table 22. Cognitive Mediation Data for Case 2

Lambda = 0.19		OBS	= Neg	MINUS FEATURES	
P = 7		$X+\%$	= .68	4	
$FQx+$ = 0		$F+\%$	= .67		
$FQxo$ = 13		$Xu\%$	= .26		
$FQxu$ = 5		$X-\%$	= .05		
$FQx-$ = 1		$S-\%$	= .00		
FQxnone = 0		CONFAB	= 0		

Neither Lambda nor OBS contribute data that are meaningful to the issue of mediation. There are 7 Popular answers in the record, which is about average for both nonpatient 14's and adults. Thus, it is reasonable to expect that he will make conventional responses whenever obvious stimuli are presented. The $X + \%$ (.68) is well within expected limits for one of his age. It also indicates that he tends to translate inputs in the reasonably conventional manner. The $Xu\%$ (.26) is slightly high for his age, but probably only signifies that he tends to translate events in a manner that is somewhat more individualistic than many of his peers. This might be a liability in some cases, but the fact that the $X + \%$ is within expected limits and there are seven Popular responses reduces that likelihood considerably here. In addition, the $X - \%$ (.05) is negligible, and the only minus answer in the record, which is the second response to Card II, ". . . lungs," is not a severe distortion. In effect, there is no reason to question his current functioning regarding the translation of new stimulus inputs.

Controls—Case 2   The data related to the capacity for control and tolerance for stress are shown in Table 23.

Table 23.   **Controls and Stress Tolerance Data for Case 2**

EB	= 6:3.0		EA = 9.0		D	= 0
eb	= 5:3		es = 8	Adjes = 8	AdjD	= 0
FM	= 4	C' = 2	T = 1		CDI	= 0
m	= 1	V = 0	Y = 0			

Both the Adjusted D and D Scores are zero, suggesting that his capacity for control and tolerance for stress are probably no different than for most nonpatients of his age. The data for the EA (9.0), EB (6:3.0), eb (5:3), and Adjusted es (8) indicate that there is no basis for questioning the validity of the D Scores. Therefore, it is reasonable to assume that, ordinarily, he is able to draw on accessible resources to formulate and implement decisions, and that most everyday stress situations do not throw him into undesirable overload states.

Affect—Case 2   The data related to affect for Case 2 are shown in Table 24.

Table 24.   **Affect Data for Case 2**

DEPI = 0				BLENDS
EB	= 6:3.0	$EBPer$	= 2.0	M.FC
eb	= 5:3	$FC:CF + C$ = 2:2		M.FC'
		Pure C	= 0	M.FD
C' = 2	T = 1	Afr	= 0.58	FD.FT
V = 0	Y = 0	S	= 1	
		Blends/R	= 4:19	
		CP	= 0	

The DEPI is not positive. As noted earlier, he is an introversive youngster, but the style is not pervasive. Thus, in most situations he prefers to push his feelings aside, but this is not an inflexible style, and at times, he will permit his feelings to play a more significant role in his decision making. The right side value of the *eb* (3) is in the expected range, and although the value for *C'* (2) is slightly higher than expected, it does not appear to have interpretive significance.

The *FC:CF* + *C* ratio (2:2) is also at the expected level for a 14-year-old. In some instances, his emotional displays will be somewhat intense and obvious, but in other instances they will be closely modulated. There are no Pure *C* responses. The *Afr* (.58) is also within expected limits for his age. There is one *S* answer, not unusual for his age, and four blend responses. The latter is slightly less than average for 14's, but he is introversive, and extrapolating from adult data, introversive subjects generally give fewer blends than extratensives who, in turn give fewer blends than ambitents. None of his blends involve more than two determinants, and none are color-shading blends or shading blends.

Overall, there is no cause for concern regarding his affective features. In fact, they are very similar to the affective operations of typical nonpatient 14's and not unlike those found among introversive subjects.

Self-Perception—Case 2   The structural data related to self-perception are shown in Table 25.

Table 25.   Self-Perception Data for Case 2

$3r+(2)/R = 0.47$	$FD = 2$	$MOR = 0$	$Hx = 0$	$An+Xy = 1$
$Fr+rF = 0$	Sum $V = 0$	$H:(H) + Hd + (Hd) = 4:3$		$Sx = 0$

RESPONSES TO BE READ				
MOR Resp's	*FQ* − Resp's	*M* Resp's	*FM* Resp's	*m* Resp's
	4	2,3,5,7,12,19	8,9,13,17	11

There are no reflection answers and the Egocentricity Index has a value of 0.47, which is average for a 14-year-old. Apparently, he regards himself as favorably as he does those who are significant to him. There are no vista answers in the protocol but there are two *FD* responses, which is not unusual for a child of this age. Fourteen-year-olds tend to be a bit more introspective, probably because they are experiencing many body changes and new interests, and are facing the challenges of assimilation into their peer group. It is a critical time for many, and self-inspection tends to increase. He has seven human contents, of which four are Pure *H*. This not only signals a marked interest in people, but more importantly, from a self-image perspective, suggests that his own self-concept is based more on experience than imagination. This is a very positive finding. There are no MOR contents and one anatomy response, which is his only minus answer.

The single minus answer is "lungs," as his second response to Card II. It has no obvious projected content, but on a very speculative level, it might relate to his interview comments about not being selected for the football team, "I guess I'm too small," and his intention to try out for the track team. The composite of six *M* answers provides an interesting picture. The first, Response 2 to Card I, is ". . . a guy getting ready to hang glide, . . . (Inquiry) . . . ready to push off." It implies a sense of daring, yet a willingness to test his capacities. The second, Response 3, to Card II is ". . . two clowns doing an act (Inquiry) . . . like a funny routine . . . they're doing some funny dance or something." It suggests a facade, funny on the outside but not specific about the inside. It could relate to a sense of uncertainty about himself and a need to present himself to others in a manner that is more false than true. Such an effort by a 14-year-old is not unusual. Fourteen's are insecure about their interpersonal role, and especially about their acceptance into their very important social role. His third *M* is his first answer to Card III, ". . . two guys doing a dance (Inquiry) . . . like natives or something, like they're dancing around this drum or table . . ." It is a COP answer, but also one in which he takes some distance from the activity (natives). He is not sure what they are dancing around (a drum or something), leading to the vague speculation that he is not really sure about what he is seeking but, nonetheless, understands that it should be sought. The fourth *M* is his first answer to Card IV, "old Bigfoot . . . (Inquiry) you can't see it very well . . . this is what he's sitting on, a stump I guess." It is very common response, but it may signal a sense of passiveness and uncertainty about his role. This speculation seems reinforced by his fifth *M* answer, the only response to Card VII, ". . . two little girls . . . looking at each other." Like the fourth *M,* it is also passive, suggesting some uncertainty about his role. The last *M* is his last answer, Response 19 to Card X, ". . . two guys working on a construction job (Inquiry) . . . holding something or one is handing something to the other . . ." It seems to reflect a desire to interact positively, and also may convey the same macholike desires suggested by the hang glider response.

The four *FM* answers seem to follow a similar pattern. The first, to Card IV, is a ". . . frog . . . sitting hunched like they do . . . ," whereas the next three are more active, ". . . an eagle . . . flying . . ." (Card V), ". . . a couple of animals that are climbing . . . " (Card VIII), and ". . . two . . . crabs are trying to . . ." (Card X). Collectively, they suggest a sense of uncertainty, yet a willingness to struggle for achievement and recognition as a person. This concept seems supported by his single *m* answer, to Card VI, " . . . a fishing boat . . . (Inquiry) . . . like it's chugging along slow . . ." It may convey his plodding but cautious search for identity. There are no markedly embellished answers among the remaining responses.

In general, the projected material seems to convey a strong sense of interest in feeling secure about himself and his role, yet a sense of cautiousness about how best to achieve that state. He is willing, but uncertain about himself. Nonetheless, his self-image, as now appears to be the case, is reasonably sturdy and not unlike that which might be expected in the nonpatient 14.

Interpersonal Perception—Case 2   The structural data concerning interpersonal perception and behavior for Case 2 are shown in Table 26.

Table 26.   Interpersonal Perception Data for Case 2

CDI = 0	*a:p* = 8:3	*T* = 1	Human Cont = 7	Pure *H* = 4
HVI = Neg	Food = 0	PER = 3	COP = 4 AG = 1	Isolate/R = .21

RESPONSES TO BE READ

HUMAN MOVEMENT WITH PAIR	*HUMAN CONTENTS*
3,5,12,19	2,3,5,7,12,15,19

The CDI and HVI are both negative. The *a:p* ratio is clearly in the active direction and thus is interpretively meaningless. There are no Food responses and there is one

Texture answer, suggesting that he experiences needs for closeness much like others of his age. As noted earlier, there are seven human contents, signaling a considerable interest in others. The fact that four of these seven human responses contain Pure *H* also suggests that his perceptions of others are based more on experience than imagination. The Isolation Index (.21) is negative, but there are three PER answers in the record. This indicates that he is often more defensive than is expected for one of his age, and that he tends to defend himself against the threats posed by others in a rather naive, authoritarian manner. This is not a serious problem but does tend to highlight a sense of peer insecurity that he may have about himself.

A much more positive finding is the four COP responses indicating that he tends to perceive interactions among people routinely as being positive, and that many of his own behaviors will be formulated in this context. Because of this attitude, it is likely that most of his peers will regard him positively and will seek him out for social exchange. The single AG response is not significant. His human movement answers that contain a pair include the clowns doing an act (Card II), natives dancing (Card III), little girls sitting on cushions looking at each other (Card VII), people who are shaking hands or something (Card X). In addition, there are two *FM* answers that contain a pair, a couple of animals climbing a tree (Card VIII), and crabs trying to pick up or push over a post (Card X). None are negative, and most all are positive, even though a hint of cautiousness seems evident in some.

Overall, the data for this cluster reveal a youngster who is quite interested in others and who probably presents a good facade with which he interacts with them. He is probably a likable fellow, but at a different level he may be less certain about his interpersonal role than he might prefer. However, this is no cause for concern as such a sense of uncertainty is very common for his age. He is not very certain about how best to deal with people, but his motives are healthy and his perception of people seems well founded in reality.

Summary—Case 2   When the findings from this protocol are compared with those for the same subject at age 8, substantial changes are noted. He now has a marked ideational style as contrasted with a more affectively dominated style at age 8. It is not an inflexible style and, as such, probably serves him well in decision making and problem solving. His thinking is reasonably clear and relatively sophisticated for one of his age, although he is probably not very flexible in his way of thinking about issues. His capacity for control and his tolerance stress are quite adequate, and he processes information diligently and effectively. When he translates new stimuli, he does tend to be somewhat idiographic, but not overly so. In fact, when afforded with obvious stimulus cues, he usually makes very expected translations. He seems to handle his feelings adequately. Like most 14's, there are times when they will be evident, but his exuberance is no different from that found among most of his age. In effect, he has no significant problems in dealing with his emotions or processing emotionally toned inputs from his environment. He appears to judge himself positively when evaluating his own worth. He engages in considerable self-examination, but probably no more so than most young adolescents. His self-image seems to be based mainly on experience. In other words, it has not developed as the result of fantasy. He probably remains somewhat uncertain about his self-concept, but seems quite willing to learn more about himself and overall, his self-image is rather sturdy for one of his age. He is interested in people and probably has learned to present a useful facade of interest and cooperativeness to others that serves him well in his interpersonal relations. He does seem vulnerable to threat by others and usually responds to these threats with a rather naive, somewhat authoritarian approach. This is not a significant liability for a 14 who is still struggling to find his place in the world, but it does denote his cautiousness about the environment, a feature that was also evident in the protocol taken when he was 8. He seems to perceive interactions among people as being positive, and it is likely that he follows that model in his own relations with others. In fact, it is probable that he is regarded by others as likable. Overall, he is a relatively solid and reasonably healthy youngster who has been able to cast off much of the immaturity that was present 6 years earlier. No significant liabilities are apparent in his current personality structure, and there is reason to believe he will continue to develop in a manner that portends well for his future.

CASE 3—A 9-YEAR-OLD FEMALE

This is a 9-year 8-month-old female whose Rorschach was taken as part of the nonpatient normative project. She is currently in the 6th month of her 4th year of school. Although her grades are generally satisfactory, the fourth-grade teacher reports that she is not a good reader and has had additional help concerning this problem from a teaching assistant. The teacher reports that generally, she seems accepted by her classmates and notes that she has at least two reasonably close friendships. She also notes, however, that at times her classmates become annoyed by her deportment, mainly by her being out-of-seat more often than most and being excessive when showing her likes or dislikes. The teacher indicates that she uses a time-out procedure as a part of her class management routine and that this subject has been timed-out more than most of the other students in the class. Reports from the third-grade teacher are more positive, indicating that the subject was very active but followed instructions faithfully and seemed well motivated for academic work. The third-grade teacher notes that the reading skills of the subject were lower than most in the class but indicates that the subject seemed well motivated to improve. She reports that during a parent conference, supplementary reading material was provided to her mother and during the next 3 months the subject seemed to improve in reading considerably.

The subject is the second of three children, having an older sister, age 13, and a younger brother, age 4. Her father, age 38, is a stonemason and bricklayer. The mother, age 31, works part-time (two days per week) selling tickets in a theater. The parents rent their house. The sisters share a bedroom and the brother has his own bedroom. According to the subject, she and her sister are "good friends," she likes school, and she has many friends with whom she plays after school. The examiner notes that the subject was reluctant about the test, noting, "My mom says I should do this."

Case 3. A 9-Year-Old Female

Card	Response	Inquiry	Scoring
I	1. It ll sk of a big bug, ugh!	E: (Rpts Ss resp) S: It just does ll tht E: I kno it does to u but rem, help me to c it too S: Well, its the kind tht flys, it has wgs, c here, mayb its a bird, but it cld b a bug, c the middl & the wgs E: U said it was a big one S: Well, mayb, but mayb its just a big picture of a littl one, I dkno, wht do u think?	Wo Fo A 1.0 ALOG
	S: I'll just say its a big one cause it ll tht E: tak ur time & look som mor & u'll prob find st else too S: Do I hav to? E: Please try, OK?	E: Whatevr it ll to u	
	2. Mayb its a mask, not a human but one u wear lik at a party	E: (Rpts Ss resp) S: Its lik thy giv out at parties, ths one ll a cat or st, c the big ears & thes r eyes & ths is the prt tht u talk thru, lik for your mouth, when u wear thm ppl dont kno who u r but when u talk thy can tell	WSo Fo (Ad) 3.5
II	3. Oh, thts 2 dogs, thyr noses are touching	E: (Rpts Ss resp) S: Yep, 1 & 1, c thy hav their noses togethr lik thy r smellg, dogs do tht, if 1 comes up to u he always sniffs around & u shd just stand still until thyr done cuz if u dont thy get scared & might bite u E: I c the noses but Im not sur I c the rest S: Well heres the ear & the nose & the neck, u cant c the rest	D + FMpo 2 Ad P 3.0
	4. These red thgs ll 2 muppet monsters	E: (Rpts Ss resp) S: Well if u watch the muppets thy hav all kinds of thes thgs, lik Kermit, hes a frog & Miss Piggy, shes a pig, & som r just monsters, lik these. These r red ones but thy hav ones tht r diff colors too E: Im not sur wht makes thm ll muppet monsters S: I dkno, thy just do, lik littl monsters, ths cld b the head & thyr tiny feet	Do FCo 2 (H) PER
III	5. Now tht ll a guy, som dude lookg in the mirror, mayb hes playg a bongo or a drum	E: (Rpts Ss resp) S: Well, ths is lik a drum & here he is, c the head & he has a big nose & here is the leg, u cant c the othr leg & heres the arm, dont count the red tho	D + Ma.Fro H,Sc P 3.0

113

Case 3. (continued)

114

Card	Response	Inquiry	Scoring
	6. Ths red ll a ribbon for ur hair	E: U said he was lookg in the mirror? S: Well its the same here, lik he was seeg himself, mayb hes practicg an act w the drum E: (Rpts Ss resp) S: Sometims girls wear thm, u tie thm in ur hair my sistr does tht all the time when she has cornrows, u kno? Thy hav all diff colors. I dnt lik em cuz kids pull em & untie em but my sistr wears em, she wears em alot cuz all the kids tht Doubl Dutch do. She has red lik ths, but she has blu ones & yellow too	Do FCo Cg PER
IV	7. Ugh, thts anothr bug	E: (Rpts Ss resp) S: It just looks all lik a bug, lik a squishd up bug lik sb steppd on it E: Lik sb steppd on it? S: It just goes in all directns lik if u squish a bug	Wo F – A 2.0 MOR,DV
V	8. Now thts lik a bird	E: (Rpts Ss resp) S: It has big wgs & a big body lik som birds, mayb lik an eagle, we hav pictrs of thm in school bc thy go w the flag, its lik a special bird tht lives in the mtns	Wo Fu A 1.0 PER
VI	9. Now tht one is really squishd up, lik a cat tht got run dwn by a car	E: (Rpts Ss resp) S: Well, u can c his head best, c his nose & these r whiskrs & his neck & the rest is just all thts left, his back & littl legs, c he has fur lik tabby cats E: Fur lik tabby cats? S: C its black & thn grey & thn black lik tabby cats fur, the lady in the next apt had one but it got loose & didnt come back	Wo F'To A P 2.5 MOR,PER
VII	10. Thts Chinese twins	E: (Rpts Ss resp) S: Its lik 2 girls, c thy hav their hair up high & their nose & their chin & their arms r out behind thm & here is where thy connect E: Connect? S: Well sometimes in China kids r born & thy r connectd & thy hav to get an operation to get thm apart, thy call em Chinese twins. somtimes thy get thm a job in the circus	W + Fo 2 H 2.5 DV2
VIII	11. It all ll ice cream	E: (Rpts Ss resp) S: Well if u evr get a carmel sundae it gets gooey lik ths, thyr really good thyr my favorite, we get em sometimes after church E: Im not sur I c it rite, help me S: Look, ths is the top, c its green lik peppermint & thrs pink sides & orange & blu, gosh, blu ice cream? Well mayb, but its lik a sundae with the diff kinds of ice cream & peppermint on top, cant u thk lik tht?	W + CF.YF– Fd 4.5 PER

E: I thk so, but u said gooey & Im not sur @ tht

S: It doesnt look gooey but it looks kinda melted dwn here, c the lines ths is pink but its orange too lik som had already melted, mayb the blu is som special stuff thy put on   Do Fo 2 A P

12. If u dont look at the othr prt, ths ll a cat

E: (Rpts Ss resp)

S: Just ths pink, it ll a cat & 1 ovr here too

E: Help me c it too

S: Look it has legs & the head & the tail, but cats arent pink, tht dont count, ok? (E: OK)   Do Fu Sc PER

13. Mayb ths is a spaceship too

E: (Rpts Ss resp)

S: Well it just does ll one, lik on the Empire, u kno, w Luke, he flies one lik ths, it has the big wgs & pointed nose for the guns

14. Ugh, thts just a bunch of paint or st

E: (Rpts Ss resp)   Wv C Art

S: Well, Id say sb cldnt paint very well & just put alot of colors togethr on the ppr, littl kids do tht in the 1st grade alot, thy dont kno much about paintg & so thy just use a lot of colors. It really ll a clown tho so mayb who paintd it wasnt a kid

IX

15. Wait, I kno, its a clown

E: (Rpts Ss resp)

S: Well if u go to the circus som of the clowns ll ths, thy paint their face w all diff colors just lik ths & thy all hav orange hair tht sticks up & heres his nose & big green cheeks & hes got a big pink bow around his neck   Wo CFu (Hd),Cg 5.5

X

S: Is ths the last 1?

E: Yes

S: Good I dont lik these

16. Well now, tht blu ll water

E: (Rpts Ss resp)

S: If u evr saw on the TV about cameras & thgs lik tht thy show how to take a pictur of a drop of water lik just when it hits & it ll ths, all blu & splashg up, one on each side   Dv CF.mpo 2 Na PER

S: Can I turn it ovr?

E: If u want to

E: Splashg up?

S: Well its not really comg up but it looks lik a splash, thy showd us in school & it look just lik ths kinda going out (demos w fingers)

v17. Ths ll a man, a really littl guy

E: (Rpts Ss resp)

S: Well look close now, c heres his legs & his arms & his head, c it? (E: yes)   Do Fo H ALOG

E: U said a littl guy?

S: He's so small, he must be a littl guy

18. U kno these guys up here ll 2 ants & thyr holdg up ths stick. There Im done

E: (Rpts Ss resp)

S: C 1 here & 1 here, thy hav littl tiny legs lik & thy hav thos littl feelrs on their heads & thyr holdin up ths stick here   D + FMao 2 A,Bt 4.0 FAB,COP

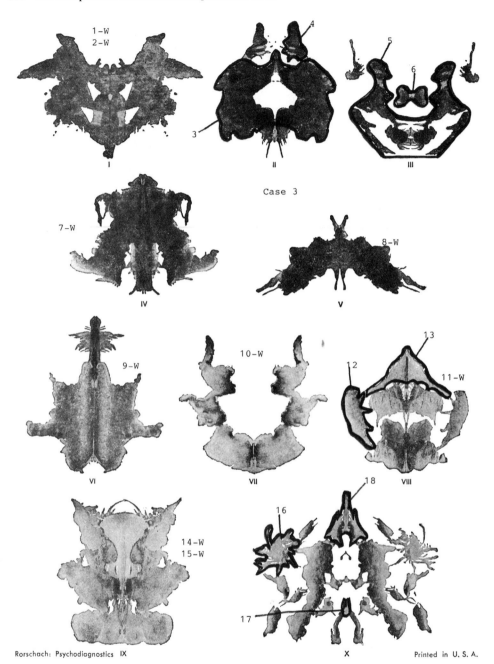

Case 3

Rorschach: Psychodiagnostics   IX

Printed in U. S. A.

Case 3

Case 3   **Sequence of Scores**

Card	No	Loc	#	Determinant(s)	(2)	Content(s)	Pop	Z	Special Scores
I	1	Wo	1	Fo		A		1.0	ALOG
	2	WSo	1	Fo		(Ad)		3.5	
II	3	D+	6	FMpo	2	Ad	P	3.0	
	4	Do	2	FCo	2	(H)			PER
III	5	D+	1	Ma.Fro		H,Sc	P	3.0	
	6	Do	3	FCo		Cg			PER
IV	7	Wo	1	F-		A		2.0	MOR,DV
V	8	Wo	1	Fu		A		1.0	PER
VI	9	Wo	1	FTo		A	P	2.5	MOR,PER
VII	10	W+	1	Fo	2	H		2.5	DV2
VIII	11	W+	1	CF.YF-		Fd		4.5	PER
	12	Do	1	Fo	2	A	P		
	13	Do	4	Fu		Sc			PER
IX	14	Wv	1	C		Art			
	15	Wo	1	CFu		(Hd),Cg		5.5	
X	16	Dv	1	CF.mpo	2	Na			PER
	17	Do	5	Fo		H			ALOG
	18	D+	11	FMao	2	A,Bt		4.0	FAB,COP

Case 3   **Structural Summary**

Location Features	Determinants — Blends	Determinants — Single	Contents	S-Constellation
			H = 3, 0	. . FV+VF+V+FD>2
Zf = 11	M.Fr	M = 0	(H) = 1, 0	. . Col−Shd Bl>0
ZSum = 32.5	CF.YF	FM = 2	Hd = 0, 0	. . Ego<.31,>.44
ZEst = 34.5	CF.m	m = 0	(Hd) = 1, 0	. . MOR > 3
		FC = 2	Hx = 0, 0	. . Zd > +− 3.5
W = 9		CF = 1	A = 6, 0	. . es > EA
(Wv = 1)		C = 1	(A) = 0, 0	. . CF+C > FC
D = 9		Cn = 0	Ad = 1, 0	. . X+% < .70
Dd = 0		FC' = 0	(Ad) = 1, 0	. . S > 3
S = 1		C'F = 0	An = 0, 0	. . P < 3 or > 8
		C' = 0	Art = 1, 0	. . Pure H < 2
		FT = 1	Ay = 0, 0	. . R < 17
DQ		TF = 0	Bl = 0, 0	x . . . . . TOTAL

DQ
	. . . . . (FQ−)
+ = 5	(1)
o = 11	(1)
v/+ = 0	(0)
v = 2	(0)

Determinants — Single (cont.)	Contents (cont.)
FV = 0	Cg = 1, 1
VF = 0	Cl = 0, 0
V = 0	Ex = 0, 0
FY = 0	Fd = 1, 0
YF = 0	Fi = 0, 0
Y = 0	Ge = 0, 0
Fr = 0	Hh = 0, 0
rF = 0	Ls = 0, 0
FD = 0	Na = 1, 0
F = 8	Sc = 1, 1
	Sx = 0, 0
	Xy = 0, 0
	Id = 0, 0

Special Scorings

	Lv1	Lv2
DV =	1x1	1x2
INC =	0x2	0x4
DR =	0x3	0x6
FAB =	1x4	0x7
ALOG =	2x5	
CON =	0x7	
SUM6	= 5	
WSUM6	= 17	

AB = 0		CP = 0	
AG = 0		MOR = 2	
CFB = 0		PER = 7	
COP = 1		PSV = 0	

(2) = 6

Form Quality

	FQx	FQf	MQual	SQx
+ =	0	0	0	0
o =	12	5	1	1
u =	3	2	0	0
− =	2	1	0	0
none =	1	—	0	0

Case 3   **Ratios, Percentages, and Derivations**

R = 18   L = 0.80

EB = 1: 5.5	EA = 6.5	EBPer = 5.5
eb = 3: 2	es = 5	D = 0
	Adj es = 5	Adj D = 0

FM = 2 :	C' = 0	T = 1	
m = 1 :	V = 0	Y = 1	

		P = 4
a:p = 2: 2	Sum6 = 5	X+% = 0.67
Ma:Mp = 1: 0	Lv2 = 1	F+% = 0.63
2AB+Art+Ay=1	WSum6 = 17	X−% = 0.11
M− = 0	Mnone = 0	S−% = 0.00
		Xu% = 0.17

FC:CF+C = 2: 4	COP = 1 AG = 0
Pure C = 1	Food = 1
Afr = 0.80	Isolate/R = 0.17
S = 1	H:(H)Hd(Hd) = 3:2
Blends:R = 3:18	(HHd):(AAd) = 2:1
CP = 0	H+A:Hd+Ad = 10:3

Zf = 11	3r+(2)/R = 0.50
Zd = −2.0	Fr+rF = 1
W:D:Dd = 9: 9: 0	FD = 0
W:M = 9: 1	An+Xy = 0
DQ+ = 5	MOR = 2
DQv = 2	

SCZI = 0   DEPI = 3   CDI = 2   S-CON = N/A   HVI = No   OBS = No

INTERPRETIVE ROUTINE FOR CASE 3

The first positive Key variable in this protocol is the presence of a reflection answer. This means that the first three clusters to be reviewed are self-perception, interpersonal perception, and controls; however, the remaining search order must be defined in accord with the next positive Key variable or Tertiary variable. In this case, the next positive Key variable is that the *EB* is extratensive. Thus, the complete order of cluster interpretation will be:

SELF-PERCEPTION → INTERPERSONAL PERCEPTION
→ CONTROLS → AFFECT → PROCESSING → MEDIATION → IDEATION

Self-Perception—Case 3   The structural data related to self-perception are shown in Table 27.

Table 27.   Self-Perception Data for Case 3

3r + (2)/R = 0.50	FD = 0	MOR = 2 Hx = 0	An+Xy = 0
Fr + rF = 1	Sum V = 0	H:(H) + Hd + (Hd) = 3:2	Sx = 0

RESPONSES TO BE READ				
MOR Resp's	FQ − Resp's	M Resp's	FM Resp's	m Resp's
7,9	7,11	5	3,18	16

The presence of the reflection answer indicates that she tends to overestimate her sense of self-worth considerably. This narcissisticlike feature is not unusual among younger children. It is found among 20% to 30% of 9- and 10-year-old nonpatients. Unfortunately, this element sometimes can inhibit development of self-concept and interpersonal relations because the person with this feature persists in a naive, fantasy-based conceptualization of self and must find ways to authenticate that unrealistic conceptualization. Usually, this involves an exaggeration of reinforcements or successes and a marked tendency to ignore or deny negative inputs or failures. When failures cannot be denied or ignored easily, the subject typically externalizes the cause. Rationalization becomes a prominent defensive tactic. In effect, the subject becomes self-deceptive and fails to profit developmentally from the natural cycle of success and failure that is a part of everyday life.

Consider, for instance, a speculation based on the academic history of this subject. She is having trouble reading and has been afforded special attention because of that difficulty. The issue is, how might she regard the problem and the special attention? First, she could, illogically, think that the attention shows she is a special person, while ignoring or denying that she has a problem; and/or second, that the problem exists because the reading tasks are too difficult, or unfair, or assigned by an uncaring person. If the latter is true, the fact that her peers are handling the assignments adequately will be put aside or denied, or attributed to the illogical notion that the teacher likes them better. If the former is true, it behooves her to continue having difficulty because of the attention it generates. In either instance, her overglorified self-image is sustained, at a cost of not facing the reality of herself or her situation.

This narcissisticlike feature is pervasive, intruding into thinking, causing a distorted sense of self, and typically, leading to interpersonal relations that lack depth and are based more on defensive exercises than real learning experiences. As noted earlier, however, this child is not yet 10, and this characteristic is not uncommon for those of her age. In fact, the data for the Egocentricity Index (.50) offer a more positive finding. It is in the average range for her age. Usually, people who are strongly committed to the reflection-related feature will have Egocentricity Indices that are well above average. Because that is not the case here, she may be going through the normal developmental process described by Piaget as decentration; that is, she is beginning to become aware she is not the very special person that she would prefer to believe, but instead, has no more or no less value than others. If this is true it portends well for her future. It seems likely that if this hypothesis is valid, the process is in the early stages as there are no *FD* or vista answers in the protocol. They are almost always present as the process evolves.

There are three Pure *H* responses in the record, which is also quite positive. It suggests that her self-concept is, or is becoming based more on experience than fantasy. Similarly, there are two MOR answers in the record, a bit more than expected for a 9-year-old. Their presence suggests that she may perceive some elements of her self-image as being more negative, or even undesirable. The contents of the two MOR responses are not very unusual for children, although they are somewhat homogeneous. The first, Response 7 to Card IV, "Ugh, that's another bug (Inquiry) . . . like a squished-up bug like somebody stepped on it." The second, Response 9 to Card VI is similar, "Now that one is really squished up, like a cat that got run down by a car." Both convey damage and a completely immobilized state. Quite possibly, she is more aware of her own limitations and her inability to respond to them than is implied by the reflection answer. This is both a positive and negative finding. It is positive because it defies the overglorification of the self. It is negative because it may represent the onset of bad feelings about herself. There are no anatomy or X-ray answers.

The projected material, derived from her minus answers, movement answers, and if there are any, her embellished responses will be important in attempting to flesh out more information about how she sees herself. There are two minus answers. One is the first of her two MOR responses, "Ugh, that's another bug . . . a squished-up bug like somebody stepped on it. The second is a Food answer, response 11 to Card VIII, "It all looks like ice cream (Inquiry) . . . a caramel sundae, it gets gooey like this . . . they are my favorite . . . but it looks kind of melted down here . . . maybe the blue is some special stuff they put on." The projected material from the first of the two minus answers seems obvious, but the second is more subtle. Is she suggesting that her need for dependency is becoming more difficult to gratify (melting) and/or is she suggesting that her own feelings about herself are more confused (color-shading blend)? Either or both of these propositions seem plausible.

Her single *M* answer, Response 5 to Card III, is more positive than either of the MOR answers even though it contains the reflection, ". . . a guy . . . looking in the mirror, maybe he's playing a bongo or a drum (Inquiry) . . . maybe he's practicing an act . . ." It does imply some self-inspecting and may suggest that she is developing an awareness of the necessity to present an acceptable picture of herself to others. The two *FM* answers seem to convey more of an interpersonal focus. The first, Response 3 to Card II, is quite interesting, ". . . two dogs, their noses are touching (Inquiry) . . . like they're smelling, dogs do that, if one comes up to you he always sniffs around and you should just stand still until they're done, cause if you don't they get scared and might bite you . . ."

It imparts a sense of interest but also a sense of caution and possible threat concerning interpersonal contacts, especially new ones. The second is more positive, even though marked by illogical thinking, ". . . look like two ants and they're holding up this stick (Inquiry) . . . they have little tiny legs and little feelers . . ." As her only COP answer it does convey a sense of sharing in a positive manner.

Her only *m* response, Number 16 to Card X, is simply ". . . water," which seems very loose and uncontrolled, however, in the Inquiry she injects considerable control, ". . . a picture of a drop of water like just when it hits . . . splashing up . . . not really coming up but it looks like a splash . . ." It may provide a glimpse about how she is attempting to exert more control over her feelings than has been the case in the past. The Inquiry material contains several interesting embellishments, many of which meet the criterion for some special score. For instance, in Response 1 she wavers about whether the bug is big or little. In Response 2 she notes that when you wear a mask people don't know who you are until you talk. In Response 4 she notes that there are specific muppets but that "these are just monsters." In Response 6 she reports that she doesn't like hair ribbons because "kids pull them and untie them." A phobiclike element seems apparent in Response 10, in which she says, ". . . they have to get an operation to get them apart . . . ," and in Response 14 she notes that ". . . little kids do that in the first grade a lot, they don't know much about painting . . ." Collectively, these embellishments impart a sense of childlike indecisiveness about herself and her role in the environment. Although this kind of indecisiveness is common among children, it is more typical among 7- and 8-year-olds. In that she is nearly 10, it suggests that her sense of self may be developing more slowly than might be expected for her age.

Overall, the data concerning self-perception seem to reveal an overly self-centered youngster who is probably struggling with her own identity. She seems less sure of herself than might be expected for one of her age and appears to evidence less maturity than most 9's who are approaching 10. She continues to deny and rationalize in self-defense but there is evidence to indicate that these mechanisms do not always work well for her. Although she overestimates her self-value, she does not appear to regard herself as being more important than her peers. She is quite cautious about her role with others and, at times, senses a threat from them. Nonetheless, it seems clear that she is working to develop new ways to interact with her environment.

Interpersonal Perception—Case 3   The structural data concerning her interpersonal perception and behaviors are shown in Table 28.

Table 28.   Interpersonal Perception Data for Case 3

CDI = 2	*a:p* = 2:2	*T* = 1	Human Cont = 5	Pure *H* = 3
HVI = Neg	Food = 1	PER = 7	COP = 1 AG = 0	Isolate/R = 0.17
		RESPONSES TO BE READ		
	HUMAN MOVEMENT WITH PAIR		*HUMAN CONTENTS*	
			4,5,10,15,17	

The CDI and HVI are both negative and the *a:p* ratio (2:2) includes no data that are interpretable in the context of interpersonal relations. There is a Food answer, which is not uncommon for younger children but unexpected for 9's. It suggests a marked need to be dependent and is not surprising in light of her struggles concerning her self-image. Children do feel more secure when they can rely on others for decisions and sustenance. The single texture answer indicates that she experiences needs for closeness in ways that probably are similar to most of her own age. The five human contents signify that she is about as interested in others as most of her age, and the three Pure *H* answers suggest that her perceptions of people are based more on experience than imagination.

A much more negative finding is the number of PER responses (7). It indicates that she is much more guarded and defensive in her interpersonal relations than should be the case. She apparently uses an authoritarian tactic to defend herself against the challenges of others. Its use probably is related quite directly to her tendency to overvalue her worth and can easily cause dislike for her. It is a "know it all" tactic that alienates others quickly. The fact that there is one COP and no AG answers is positive, but it should be noted that most of her age give more than one COP. In other words, she may not be as socially oriented as most of her peers. The Isolation Index (.17) is not positive, so there is no reason to believe that she might be withdrawn from interaction. There are only three movement answers containing pairs, the sniffing dogs, the water splashing, and the ants holding up a stick. The first is cautious, the second is more impulsive, and the last is cooperative. Collectively, the three probably reflect the confusion that she may have about she perceives people and how best to interact with them. Her human contents generally imply a sense of uncertainty about people as well as herself. The first is monster muppets, the second is a guy practicing an act, the reflection answer, the third is the Chinese twins that must be separated by an operation or possibly be sent to the circus, the fourth is a clown, and the last is a "really little guy." As might be expected for a young child, none are very certain and some are equivocal. This does not seem to be unusual for a 9-year-old, especially a 9-year-old who may be somewhat less mature than her peers.

Controls—Case 3   The data related to issues of control and tolerance for stress for Case 3 are shown in Table 29.

Table 29.   **Controls and Stress Tolerance Data for Case 3**

EB	= 1:5.5			EA	= 6.5		D	= 0
eb	= 3:2			es	= 5	Adj*es* = 5	AdjD	= 0
FM	= 2	C' = 0	T	= 1		CDI	= 2
m	= 1	V = 0	Y	= 1			

The D and Adjusted D Scores are both zero indicating that, ordinarily, she is able to draw on accessible resources to form and implement decisions and behaviors without much danger of being overwhelmed by stimulus demands. The values for the *EA* (6.5), *EB* (1:5.5), *eb* (3:2), and Adjusted *es* (5) provide no reason to challenge the validity of the D Scores; however, it may be important to consider the *EA* further. It is not very substantial. It falls near the lower end of the average range for 9-year-old nonpatients and is lower than the median value for the group (8). This suggests that her resources may be more limited than is the case for most of her age and that she may be a bit more vulnerable to overload than might be preferred. On the other hand, the modal *EA* value for 9-year-olds is 6.5. In other words, she may be like many 9's who are a bit slower to identify their potential resources and, as such, probably is somewhat more susceptible to disorganization under stress than many in her age group. Probably, this relates to the immaturity noted from the data concerning self and interpersonal perception. It is not a significant liability at this time but can become one if the pace of her growth does not accelerate during the next 12 to 18 months.

Affect—Case 3   The data related to her emotional structure and operations are shown in Table 30.

Table 30.   Affect Data for Case 3

DEPI = 3				BLENDS
EB = 1:5.5		*EBPer* = 5.5		M.Fr
eb = 3:2		*FC:CF* + *C* = 2:4		CF.YF
		Pure *C* = 1		CF.m
C' = 0	*T* = 1	*Afr* = 0.80		
V = 0	*Y* = 1	*S* = 1		
		Blends/*R* = 3:18		
		CP = 0		

The DEPI value of 3 is not interpretively significant. She is extratensive (*EB* = 1:5.5), and the style is pervasive (*EBPer* = 5.5). Thus, at the moment, she is oriented to merge her feelings into her thinking, and her decisions and behaviors will be largely based on a more intuitive approach. The problem, if there is one, is not with the style, but rather with its pervasiveness. About 40% of nonpatient 9's are extratensive, but only about one fifth of those are pervasive. They are the 9's who do not show much flexibility in their problem-solving or decision-making approaches and who often find themselves making errors be-cause they are not willing or able to work through decisions in ways that keep their feelings aside. It is a precarious way of going about life. Many decisions will be adaptive, but others will be ineffective and/or inappropriate for the situation.

The pervasive extratensive style in a 9- or 10-year-old child often produces unwanted behavior that is difficult to contain and sometimes may be quite irritating. The data for the *FC:F* + *C* ratio (2:4) seem to add potential to this problem issue. It includes a Pure *C* answer, Response 14 to Card IX, ". . . a bunch of paint . . ." which is a bit more childish than might be anticipated for one of her age. In effect, she does not modulate her emotional releases very much and, in fact, her feelings, or the product of them, will probably be evident to those around her. For instance, consider her high frequency of out-of-seat behavior. It probably relates directly to faulty judgment that is often created by her tendency to invest her somewhat intense, unmodulated feelings into her thinking. The same data were found in Case 1, who was also a pervasive extratensive subject, but his age was 8 years 1 month, and thus, it was not regarded as a liability. This subject is nearly 10 (9 years 8 months) and behavior that might have been tolerated 17 months earlier is now more likely to be judged as irritating and unacceptable. It is an unfortu-nate burden that children who develop more slowly must endure as they fall into a chronological spectrum of expected behaviors that are not necessarily commensurate with their development. A potential tragedy is that her parents, teachers, and peers have now become alerted that she is somewhat atypical.

The datum for the *Afr* (0.80) is typical for her age, signaling that she is quite involved with emotionally toned stimuli. There is only one Space response and only three blends in the record. The latter suggests that she is probably not as psychologically complex as might be expected for her age. In fact, two of the blends contain m and Y determinants, suggesting that her complexity may be considerably less than is characteristic for her age. Unfortunately, one of the blends is a color-shading blend, raising a question of whether she is confused by her own feelings. It could be a situational phenomenon (she may be confused about how best to handle her feelings in the test situation), but it might also reflect a more pervasive confusion about feelings that erupts whenever stress situations occur. If the latter is true, it is probably a positive sign that might portend well for her future: If confusion occurs under unexpected stress, a need exists to sort out feelings in ways that define the usefulness of feelings more precisely.

Overall, her feelings undoubtedly play an important role for her, possibly too much so in light of her age. She is an emotionally oriented youngster and it seems likely that, at times, her feelings may intrude on her decision-making and/or behavioral activities in ways that are ineffective and sometimes even detrimental. This pervasive affective style is likely to dissipate as she becomes more secure in her sense of self and discovers better ways of establishing and maintaining interpersonal relations. For the moment, however, it is somewhat of a handicap that does not serve her well in maintaining compatible relations with her peers and gaining the respect of those significant to her development.

Processing—Case 3   The data related to information-processing activity are shown in Table 31.

Table 31.   Processing Data for Case 3

L = 0.80	$W:D:Dd$ = 9:9:0	Zd = -2.0	$DQ+$ =
Zf = 11	$W:M$ = 9:1	PSV = 0	$DQv/+$ = 0
HVI = No	OBS = No		DQv = 2

		LOCATION SEQUENCING			
I	W,WS	IV	W	VII	W
II	D,D	V	W	VIII	W,D,D
III	D,D	VI	W	IX	W,W
				X	D,D,D

The values for Lambda, OBS, and HVI are not interpretively relevant. The Zf (11) is about average for her age and suggests a good motivation to process new information. The $W:D:Dd$ ratio (9:9:0) seems commensurate with this conclusion—she is no more or less economical in her approach to new stimulus fields than most of her peers. The $W:M$ ratio (9:1) indicates somewhat grandiose processing aspirations for her age, but this is not unusual for a younger child. The issue is whether she collects and handles new information adequately. The Zd score of -2.0 indicates that she probably scans new stimulus fields much like most of her peers. The developmental quality data are somewhat less reassuring. She has five $DQ+$ answers, which is slightly fewer than expected for one of her age. She also gives two DQv responses, which is more than expected for her age. These findings seem to indicate that, whereas her efforts at processing are appropriate, the end product sometimes falls short of what might be expected. Thus, although there are no serious processing problems, her processing activity does not yield as much as might be expected for her age. In general, it is somewhat less mature than might be expected, a finding that is not really surprising in light of other data regarding her level of development.

Mediation—Case 3   The data concerning mediational activities for Case 3 are shown in Table 32.

Table 32.   Cognitive Mediation Data for Case 3

Lambda	= 0.80	OBS	= Neg	MINUS FEATURES	
P	= 4	*X+%*	= .67	7,11	
FQx+	= 0	*F+%*	= .63		
FQxo	= 12	*Xu%*	= .17		
FQxu	= 3	*X−%*	= .11		
FQx−	= 2	*S−%*	= .00		
*FQx*none	= 1	CONFAB	= 0		

Neither the Lambda nor OBS values are interpretively significant. She has only four Popular responses, which is slightly less than expected from 9-year-olds and significantly less than found among nonpatient 10-year-olds. She does not translate new information in a very conventional manner, even in instances in which obvious clues to translation exist. Her Popular answers occur to the blots in which those cues are quite obvious, III, IV, VI, and VIII, but she does not translate into the most common responses on Cards I and V although she does note the presence of wings. This should not, however, be taken as serious cause for concern. The $X + \%$ (.67) is nearly average for her age as are the values for the $Xu\%$ (.15) and the $X - \%$ (.11). Actually, the $X + \%$ is suppressed by the presence of the Pure C answer. There is no homogeneity to her minus answers, and there is no obvious sequencing effect in which they occur. Neither are serious distortions. The first, Response 7 to Card IV is, ". . . a squished-up bug . . . ," and the second, Response 11 to Card VIII is ". . . ice cream . . ." Both have elements that are readily distinguished. In general then, there is no evidence to suggest that she has significant problems translating new stimuli, although at times, she does not follow the most obvious translation path.

Ideation—Case 3   The structural data concerning ideational activity are shown in Table 33.

Table 33.   Ideation Data for Case 3

		M QUALITY	SPECIAL SCORES			
EB = 1:5.5	*EBPer* = 5.5					
eb = 3:2	(*FM* = 2 *m* = 1)	+ = 0	DV	= 1	DV2	= 1
a:p = 2:2	*M*ᵃ:*M*ᵖ = 1:0	o = 1	INC	= 0	INC2	= 0
2AB + Art + Ay = 1		u = 0	DR	= 0	DR2	= 0
MOR = 2		− = 0	FAB	= 1	FAB2	= 0
RESPONSES TO BE READ FOR QUALITY			ALOG	= 2	SUM6	= 5
5			CON	= 0	WSUM6	= 17

It has already been noted that she is a pervasive extratensive subject whose feelings will usually merge into her thinking. This is not a significant problem for a child unless those feelings are overly intense and contribute to an excess of faulty judgment. This may be an important issue in this case because of earlier issues raised about her judgment. The value for the left side of the *eb* is quite modest (3), consisting of only two *FM* answers and one *m*. Although the single *m* answer is expected, the somewhat lower than expected value for *FM* (2) is a bit surprising. It might indicate that she has fewer need experiences than is common. That seems unlikely. The alternative interpretation is that she tends to act hastily on need experiences. In light of her rather pervasive extratensive style and her loose modulation of affect, it seems more likely that the latter is the case. In either event, it seems clear that she is not impinged on by much peripheral ideation.

The *a:p* and *M*ᵃ:*M*ᵖ ratios and the Intellectualization Index provide no interpretively useful information in that all are negative. The presence of the two MOR answers implies that some of her thinking may be a bit more pessimistic than is common for her age, but not markedly so. Similarly, the presence of five Critical Special Scores in the record is not unusual for a 9-year-old, but the presence of one Level 2 answer plus the fact that the Weighted Sum of the Special Scores is 17 raises a question about the clarity of her thinking. Very few nonpatient 9-year-olds give Level 2 Special Scores, and although many give at least one ALOG, very few give more than one. These are findings that are more common among 7's and 8's, and collectively, they indicate that her cognitive operations often are marked by more slippage than expected and that her logic often is more flawed than should be the case for her age. The issue of faulty judgment has been raised earlier regarding her self-centeredness, her affective style, and the more limited modulation of her emotional displays. The data concerning ideation suggest that these issues are relevant, and if the clarity of her thinking fails to become more like that expected for her age, a potential problem may exist. On a more positive note, her only *M* response, a guy looking in a mirror practicing an act with a drum, is rather sophisticated. It suggests that she is fairly inventive in her thinking, probably at least as much as might be expected for her age. This postulate seems supported by the fact that several of her answers are quite elaborate and hint at an above-average level of intelligence. Thus, while her reasoning may, at times, be less mature than expected for one who is nearly 10, the overall quality of her thinking seems to be reasonably good.

Overall, her naive judgment is cause for concern, and probably will not contribute positively to her immediate development. She is a very emotional youngster who tends to be persuaded much more by feelings than by logic. On the other hand, the general quality of her thinking is relatively good for her age, and although it may be a bit more pessimistic than expected at times, it is not usually intruded on by excessive peripheral ideation, or by unusual preoccupations.

Summary—Case 3   This youngster still maintains a marked tendency to overestimate her own worth, a narcissisticlike feature that may often contribute to flawed judgment and a tendency to rationalize her own failures. She prefers to maintain a more dependent relation with others, yet also prefers to think of herself as very important. These characteristics probably have inhibited her development to some extent. Nonetheless, she has developed a strong interest in others and does not overestimate her value in relation to them. This is a healthy developmental sign, suggesting that she may be nearing that developmental watershed in which many narcissistic features are relinquished. Unfortunately, her current coping style is based mainly in her feelings. Like many of her age, her feelings often become very intense and are not modulated well. She merges them into her thinking consistently, and they probably contribute to some of her faulty reasoning. Thus, even though she makes a respectable effort at processing new information, emotion impacts both her processing tactics and the way she translates new information. At times, these cognitive operations are less mature than might be expected for her age. Similarly, her thinking seems reasonably clear and quite sophisticated, but her judgments are sometimes less mature than expected. Overall, she seems less mature than most 9-year-olds, especially those who are approaching the age of 10. Her current liabilities are not major and certainly not pathological. Nonetheless, it is possible that more serious problems could evolve if any of three circumstances persist (a) her narcissistic self-involvement, (b) the pervasive extratensive style, and (c) the tendency to use faulty logic. Any or all of these features could lead to a further inhibition of her development and become especially harmful to her when she enters puberty. At this point in her life, her only evident problem involves her classroom behaviors, which, although sometimes irritating, are not major and do not appear to require intervention.

REFERENCES

Exner, J. E. (1988). Problems with brief Rorschach protocols. *Journal of Personality Assessment, 52,* 640–647.

Exner, J. E. (1991). *The Rorschach: A Comprehensive System: Vol. 2. Interpretation* (2nd ed.). New York: Wiley.

Exner, J. E. (1993). *The Rorschach: A Comprehensive System: Vol. 1. Basic Foundations* (3rd ed.). New York: Wiley.

Exner, J. E., Martin, L. S., & Mason, B. (1984). A review of the Suicide Constellation. 11th International Rorschach Congress, Barcelona.

Exner, J. E., Thomas, E. A., & Mason, B. (1985). Children's Rorschachs: Description and prediction. *Journal of Personality Assessment, 49,* 13–20.

Exner, J. E., & Wiley, J. (1977). Some Rorschach data concerning suicide. *Journal of Personality Assessment, 41,* 339–348.

Farberow, N. L., & Shneidman, E. S. (1961). (Eds.) *The cry for help.* New York: McGraw-Hill.

Shneidman, E. S., & Farberow, N. L. (1957). *Clues to suicide.* New York: McGraw-Hill.

PART II

Issues of Schizophrenia and Depression

CHAPTER 5

Issues of Schizophrenia

The frequency and severity of schizophrenic disturbance constitute a major mental health problem. Extensive epidemiological data collected by the National Institute of Mental Health indicate that from 1 to 2 people in every 100 are likely to suffer a schizophreniclike episode sometime during their lives and that, at any one point in time, 0.7% of the U.S. population over age 18 has a diagnosable schizophrenic or schizophreniform disorder (Regier et al., 1988). Schizophrenia is a disabling disturbance that frequently runs a chronic or recurrent course, especially when belated diagnosis or inadequate treatment delays recovery or minimizes improvement. Therefore, persistent schizophrenic impairment takes an enormous toll in wasted or diminished lives.

Rorschachers who work with young people should be aware that most forms of schizophrenia begin during or soon after the teenage years. Between 30% and 40% of schizophrenics experience their first psychotic episode before age 20, and over 70% of schizophrenic adults become seriously disturbed before age 25 (Keith, Reiger, Rae, & Matthews, 1992; Lewis, 1989). Research indicates that schizophrenia is diagnosed in 25% to 30% of adolescents admitted to public mental hospitals, and about 15% of those admitted to psychiatric units of general hospitals. Moreover, about 15% of schizophrenic patients being treated in private psychiatric hospitals are younger than 18 years (Rosenstein, Milazzo-Sayre, & Manderscheid, 1989; Tyrano & Apter, 1992; Weiner, 1992, Chap. 3). In addition to these instances of overt schizophrenia in young people, many adolescents who are destined to become schizophrenically disturbed adults are likely to show prodromal signs of the disorder during their teenage years.

Schizophrenia may also occur in preadolescent children as a form of childhood psychosis. Childhood psychosis is generally recognized as comprising two types of disorder that begin at different ages. Early-onset childhood psychosis begins before age 3 and is usually referred to as *infantile autism.* Infantile autism, which is a rare condition occurring in just 4 to 5 children per 10,000, bears little relationship to schizophrenia. The primary features of the disorder are lack of relatedness to people, the need to preserve sameness, and marked language abnormalities. Although autistic children are severely disturbed and rarely recover, they do not demonstrate typical signs of schizophrenic disturbance and they do not grow up to become schizophrenic adolescents or adults (Dawson & Castelloe, 1992; Gillberg, 1991; Green, 1988; Rutter & Schopler, 1987; Schreibman, 1988; Zahner & Pauls, 1987).

Late-onset childhood psychosis begins after children turn age 7 and is commonly called *schizophrenia in childhood.* This condition is also rare, perhaps no more frequent than infantile autism, but it shows an increasing incidence with each successive year as children approach adolescence. Although it is not unknown for childhood schizophrenia to begin before age 7, children who are first identified as psychotic between the ages of 3 and 6 are usually found to be autistic youngsters with previously overlooked psychological problems dating from infancy. Unlike the core features of autism, the clinical characteristics of late-onset childhood psychosis closely resemble those seen in older schizophrenics, and childhood schizophrenics unless successfully treated, become adolescent and adult schizophrenics (Cantor, 1988; Caplan & Sherman, 1990; Chambers, 1988; Howells & Guirguis, 1984; Tsiantis, Macri, & Maratos, 1986).

In assessing schizophrenia with the Rorschach, interpreters need to be attentive to emerging evidence of this disorder among late adolescents and must also be prepared to recognize its presence, albeit much less frequently, among early adolescents and even children age 7 or above. From age 7 through adolescence, however, with just a few adjustments related to age norms, Rorschach indications of schizophrenic impairment can be interpreted in similar fashion. The applicability of Rorschach indices of schizophrenia across age groups parallels clinical evidence (a) that child and adolescent schizophrenics show the same types of disturbed functioning as adult schizophrenics; (b) that standard diagnostic criteria for schizophrenia can be reliably applied with young people; and (c) that schizophrenic children and adolescents, as well as schizophrenic adults, can be differentiated from their nondisturbed peers on the basis of standard measures of such schizophrenic characteristics as formal thought disorder (Cantor, 1988; Caplan, Perdue, Tanguay, & Fish, 1990; Volkmar, 1991; Weiner, 1992, Chap. 3).

Nevertheless, the testing of latency-age children may, on occasion, be complicated by some overlapping features of childhood schizophrenia and infantile autism. Approximately 75% of autistic children are mentally retarded and earn IQ scores below 70 (Lincoln, Courchesne, Kilman, Elmasian, & Allen, 1988; Schreibman, 1988; Smalley, Asarnow, & Spence, 1988). These children usually are not appropriate for Rorschach testing, at least not with the Comprehensive System, because the normative base does not include retarded subjects. However, the 25% of relatively high-functioning autistics, some of whom demonstrate at least average intelligence, could be expected to provide a valid Rorschach protocol. As autism does involve some features of schizophrenia, such as withdrawal from people and poor reality testing, the Rorschach of a seriously disturbed 7- or 8-year-old may be equivocal with respect to distinguishing between recent-onset childhood schizophrenia and long-standing infantile autism.

In most cases, this distinction can be guided by the clinical history. Evidence of developmental difficulties from early in life will point to autism, whereas breakdown or regression in psychological functioning following some years of reasonably normal development will suggest schizophrenia. In some instances, however, clear schizophrenic disorder in latency-age children has been preceded by early childhood difficulties, including some autistic symptoms (Demb & Weintraub, 1989; Petty, Ornitz, Michelman, & Zimmerman, 1984; Watkins, Asarnow, & Tanguay, 1988). Accordingly, a retrospective clinical history may, at times, have to be supplemented by follow-up diagnostic study to differentiate infantile autism and schizophrenia in seriously disturbed children of apparently average intelligence.

Developmental issues aside, psychodiagnosticians should approach the assessment of schizophrenia with certain diagnostic criteria in mind. As discussed earlier, this conceptual approach to interpretation involves looking for relationships between the test data and aspects of personality functioning that have previously been identified as relevant to answering such referral questions as, "Does this person have a schizophrenic disorder?" Rorschachers may also have to acknowledge diagnostic criteria that have little to do with personality functioning but are regularly applied in the setting where they work. Most important in the latter regard are the diagnostic criteria promulgated in DSM-III-R (American Psychiatric Association, 1987), and anticipated for DSM-IV, which often must be utilized in reports prepared for agencies and health insurance providers. In summary form, the anticipated DSM-IV version of schizophrenia comprises the following five diagnostic criteria:

1. The presence of certain specific kinds of delusions or hallucinations, disorganized or incoherent speech, disorganized or catatonic behavior, and such negative symptoms as flattened affect, alogia, or avolition.
2. Decreased adequacy of work, social, and self-care functioning or, in cases of childhood or adolescent onset, failure to achieve an expected level of social development.
3. The absence of schizoaffective disorder and mood disorder with psychotic features.
4. A duration of disturbance of at least 6 months.
5. The absence of organic factors in the disturbance, such as direct effects of substance abuse or physical illness.

Some of these criteria call for inferences that are difficult or impossible to draw from psychological test data. Whether a disturbed person's present condition represents a decline from some previous level of functioning can be determined only with reference to the person's prior history. Likewise, the presence of delusions or hallucinations must be observed clinically and cannot be inferred with any certainty from a psychological test.

The criterion of 6 months' duration is impossible to apply from the Rorschach nor any other test. No test can indicate with precision how long a condition has lasted. Viewed in a more realistic perspective, the diagnosis of schizophrenia by duration is at best an arbitrary procedure. The DSM-III-R states explicitly that one and the same symptom picture should be labeled *schizophreniform disorder* if it has lasted less than 6 months and *schizophrenia* after 6 months of continuous disorder. Yet the development of DSM-III-R, as well as of its predecessor (DSM-III) and its successor (DSM-IV), is well known to have involved considerable uncertainty about how best to draw such time distinctions, which in the end were often determined by weight of conviction rather than solid empirical evidence (Keith & Matthews, 1991).

Those addressing Rorschach findings who must report in DSM-III-R or DSM-IV terms may have to consider their test findings not only in relation to the subject's previous level of functioning, which is always advisable to do, but also in terms of duration of disturbance, which is difficult to ascertain. With such considerations in mind, psychodiagnostic assessment should focus on evaluating the adaptiveness of psychological functions that exist as real phenomena, independent of administrative or arbitrary preferences concerning how they should be labeled. In this context, schizophrenia can be usefully conceptualized as a breakdown in certain cognitive, interpersonal, and integrative functions of the personality. Each of these personality impairments is reflected in certain kinds of Rorschach responses that help to identify the presence of a schizophrenic disorder. In addition, inferences can frequently be drawn from the Rorschach concerning features of chronicity and paranoid status in schizophrenia.

PERSONALITY IMPAIRMENT IN SCHIZOPHRENIA

Normally functioning individuals are generally able to think coherently, logically, and at appropriate levels of abstraction, to perceive themselves and their environment accurately, to establish and maintain rewarding relationships with other people, and to exert adaptive control over their thoughts, feelings, and impulses. In schizophrenia, these functions become impaired, so that schizophrenic individuals typically exhibit *disordered thinking, inaccurate perception, interpersonal ineptness,* and *inadequate controls.* As elaborated in an extensive literature, the clinical phenomena of schizophrenia derive in large part from these four impairments of psychological functioning (Andreasen & Flaum, 1991; Arieti, 1974; Bellak, Hurvich, & Gediman, 1973; Neale & Oltmanns, 1980; Strauss & Carpenter, 1981; Weiner, 1966). These impairments characterize schizophrenia among children and adolescents as well as among adults, although the age of schizophrenic persons can be expected to color the specific symptoms they show.

Disordered Thinking   The most prominent feature of schizophrenic disturbance is incoherent, illogical, or inappropriately abstract thinking. Incoherent thinking, or *dissociation,* involves a cognitive disruption in which thoughts do not flow continuously from one to another. People who are dissociated typically have difficulty keeping their minds focused on what they are saying in a conversation and what others are saying to them. Sometimes they lose their train of thought right in the middle of a sentence and become unable to continue, and at other times they may express a series of loosely related ideas that are difficult to follow. Asked "How are you?" one dissociated child replied, "I'm OK, but my father never takes me fishing do you like to bait hooks?"

Dissociation may also occur between a question asked and the answer given, as if the person were responding to a completely different question. Thus a dissociated child's response to "How are you?" may be "I'm around 10," or "I'm the same as my brother." Among mildly disturbed individuals who are just beginning to develop thought disorder, this type of dissociation is often very subtle. Answers to questions may be just slightly off the point, leaving it unclear whether the young person has responded strangely or has simply misheard or misunderstood the question.

Illogical thinking consists of reaching unreasonable conclusions on the basis of minimal or circumstantial evidence. Seeing several teachers in his school walking into the principal's officer, a boy concludes that they are meeting to talk about him and to devise a plan for punishing him. When he is told that they are in fact the teachers' program committee merely having their regular weekly meeting with the principal, he refuses to be "tricked" into feeling safe and relaxing his guard. What is faulty in such reasoning is not the boy's initial hypothesis that his welfare may be in jeopardy, especially if he has done something that warrants some punishment, but his unwillingness to consider other possibilities in the light of additional evidence.

These examples of subtle dissociation and circumstantial reasoning may appear to reflect childishness rather than psychopathology. However, such ways of thinking are normal only among very young children and seldom persist beyond age 7. Moreover, circumstantial thinking provides the basis on which people form delusions and develop ideas of reference, both of which are prominent symptoms of schizophrenia, and both of which constitute unrealistic beliefs derived from faulty reasoning.

Thinking at inappropriate levels of abstraction often causes schizophrenic people to form concepts and use words in an overly concrete or literal manner. As a consequence, the meaning of puns and figures of speech often escapes them. A schizophrenic youngster who is told, "Stop pulling my leg" may respond, "But I'm not even touching your leg." At other times, due to their being overly abstract, schizophrenics may become preoccupied with numbers, shapes, philosophical ideas, and other complex concepts at the expense of adequate attention to basic or ordinary ways of dealing with their experience (see Andreasen, 1979a; Harrow & Quinlan, 1985). One adolescent who was markedly estranged from ordinary peer group activities and interactions was fascinated with Amtrak and ardently devoted to studying train schedules. Another adolescent, asked in what way a cat and a mouse are alike, said, "They're both made by God."

Inaccurate Perception   Schizophrenics typically have difficulty perceiving their world and themselves accurately. Their perceptual distortions are reflected primarily in poor judgment and unusual sensory experiences. With respect to poor judgment, people who cannot assess themselves and external events realistically tend to act in odd or queer ways, to say things that are out of place, and to harbor far-fetched ideas about their own nature and about the world around them.

A schizophrenic boy, told that the psychologist would like to ask him a few questions, says, "How many days will it take?" Asked what you should do if you see smoke coming from the windows of your neighbor's house, he answers, "Blow it away." A slightly built, poorly coordinated high school student with no athletic background talks about playing football in college, not as a joke, but in the expectation that he will be able to finance his education on a football scholarship. A girl calls up her science teacher in the middle of the night to ask about the requirements for a routine daily assignment. Another girl, with no known musical talent, says she is going to earn money to buy Christmas presents by writing and selling some songs. The lives of schizophrenic persons are dotted with such instances of poor judgment, which stem from an unrealistic assessment of a situation, of themselves, or of the consequences of their actions.

Unusual sensory experiences, that is, breakdowns in perceptual accuracy in their most extreme form, provide the basis of hallucinations. The more people distort the reality of what they hear, see, smell, and feel, they more likely they are to experience auditory, visual, olfactory, and tactile impressions for which there are no external stimuli and to form distorted images of their own bodies (see Assad & Shapiro, 1986; Cutting & Dunne, 1989).

Interpersonal Ineptness   To establish and maintain comfortable and rewarding interpersonal relationships, people need to have good social skills and some interest in approaching and being close to others. Schizophrenic individuals frequently display both poor social skills and withdrawal from interpersonal contact. The disordered thinking and inaccurate perception of schizophrenic people often cause them to overlook or misjudge the feelings, motives, and actions of others. They are consequently likely to behave in ways that others find insensitive, inappropriate, embarrassing, contentious, presumptuous, or in some other way objectionable. These manifestations of their poor social skills make it difficult for schizophrenic people to make or keep friends, even when they try.

The withdrawal of schizophrenics may be either physical or emotional. Those who withdraw physically usually become reclusive individuals who prefer solitary activity in both their work and recreation and avoid situations that might bring them into close contact with others. Those who withdraw emotionally may actually seek out and enjoy crowds of people, particularly when they are all sharing some interests, as at a concert or an athletic event. Such public events sometimes help schizophrenics preserve the fiction that they are meaningfully involved with other people. In fact, however, they remain alone in the crowd. Their isolation from others is emotional rather than physical. Even when mingling with other people, they maintain a psychological distance by keeping their thoughts and feelings to themselves and interacting only on a formal, impersonal level (see Burnham, Gladstone, & Gibson, 1969; Erickson, Beiser, Iacono, Fleming, & Lin, 1989; Holzman, 1988; Wallace, 1984).

Inadequate Controls Schizophrenics are frequently unable to prevent anxiety-pro-voking and socially unacceptable ideas from occupying their thoughts. Uncontrollable aggressive and sexual fantasies, or constant concern about terrible events they might cause or suffer from are likely to make the schizophrenic's existence a waking night-mare. Schizophrenic individuals are consequently subject to severe bouts of anxiety and self-disgust, and they sometimes have difficulty distinguishing between their dreams and waking reality. Schizophrenics also commonly suffer from poor integration of their feelings and thoughts. As a result, they may show blunted affect, with little or no emo-tional response to any situation, or such inappropriate affect as giggling while relating to a violently aggressive fantasy or crying while describing how good they feel.

Finally, schizophrenic persons may, at times, be unable to prevent their aggressive and sexual ideas from being directly expressed in their behavior. They may erupt into sudden outbursts of violence against themselves or others, or into inappropriate or as-saultive sexual advances (see Tardiff & Sweillam, 1980).

Not all schizophrenics manifest all these personality impairments, nor is any of them unique to schizophrenia. Indices of disordered thinking are not uncommon in persons with an affective disorder. Similarly, poor reality testing characterizes many conditions in which people become psychotically incapacitated, including organic and drug-induced psychoses. Social withdrawal is common among shy, schizoid individu-als, and poor self-control and inappropriate emotionality are seen, respectively, in in-stances of impulsive or antisocial personality disorders and in depressive or histrionic disorders (see Andreasen, 1979a, b, 1988; Harrow, Grossman, Silverstein, & Meltzer, 1982; Millon, 1981; Oltmanns, Murphy, Berenbaum, & Dunlop, 1985).

Furthermore, each of the phenomena associated with schizophrenia can appear briefly in otherwise normal persons at times of stress, and no single characteristic of schizophrenia is by itself sufficient for conclusive identification of the disorder. How-ever, when several of the kinds of functioning impairments described in this section oc-cur together and persist for any length of time, especially when disordered thinking is prominent among them, the presence of schizophrenia is usually indicated.

RORSCHACH INDICES OF DISORDERED THINKING

Because disordered thinking embraces a broad range of schizophrenic personality impair-ments, several different Rorschach variables help to identify it. Probably, the most useful of these in making the diagnosis are *unusual verbalizations, inappropriate combinations, autistic logic,* and *abstract preoccupation.*

Unusual Verbalizations Disturbances of thought and language are closely related. Thus, many aspects of disordered thinking are reflected in unusual verbal productions. Two distinct types of unusual verbalization are scored in the Comprehensive System as Deviant Verbalization (DV) and Deviant Response (DR).

Deviant Verbalization (DV) DV answers are characterized by peculiar language that prevents the subject from communicating clearly and cannot be attributed to subcul-tural idiom or limited vocabulary skills. Some DV responses consist of stilted or redun-dant language, as in "a matched brace of stomachs with the food gullets attached, or "an X-ray of somebody's self," or "a male penis." More commonly, DV responses involve the use of neologisms or incorrect words in place of correct words that seem well within the subject's intellectual capacity: "something in a *biography lab,*" or "horses drinking out of a *stable* of water," or "two dogs with their *snoods* together," or "a crocodile with a *slithery* eye," or "It looks like a fire because of the *blaze*-colored part here."

When disordered thinking exists, such DV responses can be understood as instances of dissociation. Subjects giving DV answers are having difficulty maintaining the continuity of their thoughts and keeping their thoughts in proper relation to each other. Instead, thoughts that should be kept separate intrude on another: Thinking about a penis and a male sex organ results in the strange-sounding redundancy of "a male penis"; experiences in school with biology lab in science and biography in English class overlap to produce "something in a biography lab"; the fact that horses are kept in stables becomes mixed with a perception of them drinking to result in the malaprop of their "drinking out of a stable of water"; the idea that crocodiles slither leads to the peculiar description of part of their anatomy as "a slithery" eye; and the similar meanings of "fire" and "blaze" fuse to produce a "blaze-colored" fire.

Deviant Response (DR)   When dissociation takes the form of rambling, disjointed responses that jump from one idea to another, the appropriate score is a DR. A case in point is a child who gave the following response to Card V: "That's a bat, isn't it? Mr. Brown shot one up at our club. I think every family should belong to a club, don't you?"

This type of dissociation represents what Rapaport aptly described as taking too much distance from the Rorschach stimulus (Rapaport, Gill, & Schafer, 1968, pp. 424–463). The Rorschach task is to indicate what the blots might be and why, and subjects who take too much distance from this task display such off-task behavior as commenting on whether families should belong to clubs. These off-task ramblings in Rorschach responses constitute significant evidence that dissociation is occurring.

Subjects who take excessive distance from the Rorschach task often produce another type of DR response that Rapaport called "queer." The hallmark of a "queer" DR is an expression or statement that might be appropriate in some contexts but seems entirely out of place, irrelevant, or difficult to fathom in the context of the test situation. Such strange-sounding expressions result from subjects' failing to maintain an appropriate set in talking about what the blots might be, as in the following examples: "A crab, but I was hoping for a butterfly" (who in taking the Rorschach "hopes" to see anything in particular?); "That's like a monster that no one has ever seen" (if no one has ever seen it, how can the subject say that the blot looks like it?); "That reminds me of a bunch of garbage; that's what's wrong with a lot of people, they throw their garbage all over the place" (perhaps people do litter excessively, but what does this commentary on human nature have to do with saying what the blot might be and why?).

A final type of unusual Rorschach verbalization that reflects dissociation and thereby helps to identify thought disorder involves the subtle discontinuity between questions and answers noted earlier. When this type of discontinuity occurs on the Rorschach, the following type of exchange (in this example, to Card I) often complicates the examiner's task of taking the record:

> S: I see a lady here.
> E: (Inquiry) You said, "I see a lady here."
> S: Yes, right here.
> E: I'm not sure where you're seeing it.

    S: She's up a tree actually, actually it's a woman.
    E: A woman?
    S: Actually she looks like a witch, here's her broomstick.
    E: Could you show me the parts you're describing?
    S: What is it you'd like to know about it?

The inquiry in this example is more extensive than would ordinarily be the case. The examiner was concerned that the subject was using an unusual location and giving some distorted form in the original response and wanted to be careful not to assume that the response was the ordinary human percept of the center detail of Card I. As it turned out, neither the location nor the form level of this response was as unusual as the very confusing exchange, which suggests dissociation.

Inappropriate Combinations   Inappropriate combinations occur when subjects combine impressions and ideas into percepts that strain or violate realistic considerations. In one way or another, these unreasonable percepts imply unlikely, implausible, or impossible relations between images, blot qualities, objects, or activities attributed to objects. The three kinds of inappropriate combinations scored in the Comprehensive System are Incongruous Combination (INCOM), Fabulized Combination (FABCOM), and Contamination (CONTAM), each of which demonstrates illogical or circumstantial reasoning.

INCOM responses condense blot details or images into a single incongruous percept in which the parts or attributes do not belong together: "a person with the head of a chicken," or "tree branches with hands on them," or "red bears," or "a butterfly going tweet-tweet." FABCOM responses involve two or more discrete blot details between which some relationship is inferred that does not or cannot occur in nature: "a man with a dragon coming out between his legs," or "two insects hugging each other," or "a snake attacking a submarine," or "two bears giving each other a high five." CONTAM responses consist of the fusion of two or more impressions of one blot area into a single percept that cannot exist: "a butterflower," or "a heart bow," or "a pumpkin bat," or a "rainbow bullet."

Inappropriate combinations of these kinds always reflect circumstantial reasoning. Because certain blot details are adjacent or certain impressions arise at the same time, the subject arbitrarily concludes that there must be some relationship between them.

Autistic Logic   In INCOM, FABCOM, and CONTAM responses, illogical thinking is implied by the inappropriate combination that has occurred. Should the subject, instead or in addition, provide an explicit statement of circumstantial reasoning on which an unwarranted conclusion is based, the response is coded as Autistic Logic (ALOG). ALOG responses are typically justified by calling attention to stimulus characteristics of the blot or to the size, positioning, or number of objects included in the response, none of which constitutes a compelling explanation of what has been concluded: "The bat is black, so it must be night out"; "This is a pretty big bat, because it covers most of the card"; "This must be lettuce, because it's next to the rabbits and they eat lettuce"; "It's the North Pole because it's at the top"; "There are two big ones and a lot of little ones, so it's probably a family."

In Rapaport's terms, the essence of ALOG responses, as well as of inappropriate combinations in which faulty logic remains implicit, is loss of distance from the stimulus. Such responses stand in contrast to DR responses, in which subjects take too much distance from the task and elaborate their responses in ways that wander far afield from saying what the blots might be and answering the questions they are being asked. Instead, in *ALOG* and inappropriate combination responses, subjects take the blots too literally and lose distance from what is reasonable by inferring that whatever they see together in the blots must go together—even if one of two adjacent details looks like a snake and the other like a submarine, or if one looks like a rabbit and the other like nothing at all but is next to the rabbit.

Abstract Preoccupation   Normally functioning subjects, especially if they are intellectually oriented, sometimes attach symbolic meanings to Rorschach stimuli. About 14% of nonpatient adults give symbolic answers, scored *AB,* and adolescents ages 13 to 16 are only slightly less likely than this to give an AB response. However, consistent with the developmental expectation that formal operational thinking rarely begins to replace concrete operational thinking until adolescence, 10- to 12-year-olds hardly ever give *AB* responses, and the nonpatient frequency below age 10 is zero. Among nonpatients who do give them, *AB* responses constitute only a small percentage of the response total. When present, they usually occur as a second or third response to a card or are given as a fanciful elaboration of an already well-formulated response ("These are two people sort of leaning toward each other—let's say that the red in the middle stands for the love they feel for each other").

Hence, when *AB* responses become frequent, when they are offered as the initial or dominant response to a card, or when they are expressed with an air of certain reality ("This red in the middle *must* stand for some attraction between these two things on the side"), they begin to suggest a pathological preoccupation with abstraction. Formless *AB* responses, which consist only of an abstract impression without any other content at all ("I see happiness in this one"), are especially likely to identify such preoccupation. When difficulty in thinking at appropriate levels of abstraction shades from a normal range of intellectualization into a thought-disordered range of abstract preoccupation, the Rorschach frequently demonstrates *idiosyncratic symbolism,* and a suffusion of ordinary content occurs with *overly abstract elaborations.*

Idiosyncratic Symbolism   Conventional symbolism in Rorschach responses involves attaching culturally shared or stereotyped meanings to colors or concrete images. For example, common thinking associates blue with coldness, red with anger, green with envy, and black with evil. Similarly, conventional symbolic meanings are reflected in such responses as, "The bow makes it sort of ladylike, like in the olden days," or "There's a dove at the top, showing that all is peaceful."

By contrast, idiosyncratic symbolism is based on referents that are unique to the thinking of the subject: "The pink in there is a sign that things will turn out alright," or "The black shows that everything is confused," or "Two people with a cloud behind them, meaning that they are angry." Even one such response begins to raise a question of disordered thinking. The more frequently they appear, the more likely it is that the subject is abnormally preoccupied with abstract meanings at the expense of adequate attention to concrete and practical aspects of experience. In addition to being scored for *AB,* the idiosyncratic symbolism responses given by thought-disordered subjects often contain an ALOG as well, as in, "I know these people are confused, because they're black, and that's what black means."

Overly Abstract Elaborations   An inability to interpret experience at appropriate levels of abstraction often results in highly elaborated responses that describe abstract concepts and events as if they were real objects. The following examples of such responses, selected from the records of schizophrenic subjects, identify pathological preoccupation with abstractions:

> Card V: "Looks like a leg of something diving into something, diving into eternity, coming out of this world and going into nothing."
>
> Card VII: "Looks like a representation of the whole world closing in on you."
>
> Card IX: "It gives me a feeling of nature up here and of Hell down here, one against the other, beauty against evil, with a sense of really high ideals coming out of the whole thing."
>
> Card X: "In the center is something very desirable, and all these on the outside represent forces trying to get at what's in the middle, but the pink is a protective device, protecting the important thing."

As these examples indicate, many overly abstract elaborations will warrant scoring for DR or FABCOM as well as *AB*. Hence responses of this type, aside from their implications for abstract preoccupation, will enter into formal coding for disordered thinking as a result of the dissociation or circumstantial reasoning they frequently involve.

Considerations in Interpretation   These kinds of unusual verbalizations, inappropriate combinations, autistic logic, and abstract preoccupation all identify difficulties in thinking clearly and logically. Six of the formal scores to which they contribute—DV, INCOM, DR, FABCOM, ALOG, and CONTAM—constitute the Critical Special Scores of the Comprehensive System, and these Critical Special Scores provide the Rorschach's clearest window into possible thought disorder. Generally speaking, the more frequently subjects give such answers, the more likely they are to have a schizophrenic impairment of their thinking process. Beyond the general psychopathological significance of the Critical Special Scores, however, the implications of these categories of response will vary in four important respects.

First, some categories of thought-disordered response constitute more extreme deviations from coherence and logicality than others and thus identify more serious impairment. As indicated by the weights assigned in calculating the Weighted Sum of the Six Critical Special Scores (*WSum6*), DV (weight of 1) and INCOM (weight of 2) are relatively mild signs of disordered thinking; DR (weight of 3), FABCOM (weight of 4), and *ALOG* (weight of 5) are intermediate; and CONTAM (weight of 7) has the most serious implications for impairment. As an illustration of what this difference means qualitatively, one INCOM in a record is within normal limits, and even several of them, while suggesting cognitive slippage, will rarely be sufficient to document a schizophrenic degree of impairment. By contrast, just a single CONTAM leaves little doubt from age 7 on up that the subject has a serious thought disturbance.

Second, each kind of Critical Special Score occurs in a range of severity. One FABCOM may imply only a somewhat improbable relationship between objects, whereas another describes an impossibly absurd relationship. One DV may sound just a bit odd, whereas another makes the subject's meaning incomprehensible. With this in mind, all DV, INCOM, DR, and FABCOM responses are subcategorized either as Level 1 (indicating a mild extent of cognitive slippage that anyone might demonstrate occasionally) or Level 2 (indicating a severe manifestation of cognitive slippage, unlikely to appear in anyone whose thinking is not pathologically disturbed). As will be elaborated shortly, the Level 1/Level 2 distinction figures prominently in diagnostic decision making.

Third, subjects differ in the attitudes they express toward responses that contain critical special scores. Some subjects take any incoherent or illogical answers they deliver quite seriously ("Of course that's what it is"). Others may express reservations about them ("I guess that's not very good"), or disclaim responsibility for them ("I was just trying to be funny"), or try to take them back ("It can't really be that way, so I'll change it to something else"). The less able or willing subjects are to take some distance from their special score responses, and the more they assume or insist that these responses have been appropriately and precisely formulated, the more likely it is that these responses reflect disordered thinking.

Fourth, Critical Special Scores occur more frequently in records given by nonpatient children and adolescents than by nonpatient adults. This age difference derives from the fact that young people, because of their cognitive immaturity and their developmental need to make sense of many new and complex experiences, are normatively more prone than adults to display scattered ideation and strained reasoning. Age differences do not prevent Rorschach indices of disordered thinking from being used effectively with younger subjects, however. To the contrary, research findings have demonstrated that the Critical Special Scores discriminate disturbed from nonpatient subjects as clearly among young people as among adults (Weiner & Exner, 1978). Nonetheless, as the normative data indicate, higher scores for the sum and weighted sum of the Six Critical Special scores are necessary among children and adolescents than among adults before a pathological extent of incoherent or illogical thinking can be inferred. This is illustrated in Table 34.

Table 34.   Some Descriptive Statistics Concerning Critical Special Scores for Five Groups of Nonpatients

	Age 5		Age 8		Age 11		Age 14		Adult	
	M	*SD*	*M*	*SD*	*M*	*SD*	*M*	*SD*	*M*	*SD*
Sum6	6.88	2.01	6.15	1.96	4.36	1.16	2.89	1.38	1.59	1.25
WSum6	14.88	4.68	14.33	5.12	8.93	3.04	7.42	7.14	3.28	2.89

One issue, yet to be resolved, is whether intellectually gifted adolescents, without psychological disturbance, may give more Critical Special Scores than would normatively be expected at this age. Gallucci (1989) has presented data for a sample of 32 nonpatient 12- and 13-year-old gifted youngsters, with IQs in excess of 135. He concluded that gifted young people are much more likely than adolescents of average intelligence to have DV, INC, DR, and FABCOM responses in their records and consequently to have a considerably higher *WSum6*. This conclusion, however, may be seriously flawed. Gallucci reports a mean *WSum6* of 21.8 for his 17 gifted 12-year-olds and a mean of 27.3 for the 15 13-year-olds. The standard deviations for these groups are 25.5 and 36.7 respectively, but the modal values for the actual number of special scores are 4 for the 12-year-olds and 5 for the 13-year-olds. In other words, his small samples contain a few outliers who have given very large numbers of Critical Special Scores. For instance, one female subject whose record contains 35 answers gave 36 Critical Special Scores with a WSum6 of 106, and seven $M-$ answers were included. Whether the record illustrates seriously disturbed thinking or a more playful and creative attempt to malinger severe disturbance is not clear. In either event, the presence of such records in very small samples casts doubt on the validity of the findings. Obviously, the issue of special scores among gifted youngsters remains a subject for further investigation.

The Comprehensive System Schizophrenia Index (SCZI) includes two criteria involving the Critical Special Scores: (a) the presence of six or more Critical Special Scores or a weighted sum of the Critical Special Scores of more than 17; and (b) the presence of more than one Level 2 special score and at least one Level 2 FABCOM.

Criteria for the Schizophrenia Index (SCZI)

1. Either $X + \% < .61$ **and** $S - \% < .41$, **or** $x + \% < .50$.
2. $X - \% > .29$.
3. Either $FQ- \geqq FQu$ **or** $FQ- > (FQo + FQu)$.
4. Sum Level 2 *Critical Special Scores* > 1 **and** $FAB2 > 0$.
5. Either Raw Sum of *Critical Special Scores* > 6 **or** Weighted Sum of *Critical Special Scores* > 17.
6. Either $M- > 1$ **or** $X - \% > .40$.

Despite the higher frequency of Critical Special Scores among young people than adults, the cutting scores of the *SCZI* are applicable down to age 10. As shown in Table 34, the mean plus one standard deviation, which is a customary criterion for identifying the upper limit of normality, still falls below the SCZI criteria for the sum (*Sum6*) and weighted sum (*WSum6*) of the Critical Special Scores at age 11. Only at age 10 or younger does a score one standard deviation above the mean exceed the SCZI cutting score of more than six for *Sum6*, and only at age 9 or younger does a standard deviation above the mean exceed SCZI level for both *Sum 6* and *WSum6*. Table 34 shows, furthermore, that Level 2 special scores have a median and mode of zero at all ages. Hence in applying the SCZI with younger people, no adjustments need to be made after age 11. For subjects age 10 and younger, the normative tables should be used to determine whether *Sum6* and *WSum6* call for points on the SCZI, using as a criterion whether the obtained values exceed the mean by more than a standard deviation.

RORSCHACH INDICES OF INACCURATE PERCEPTION

The inaccurate perceptual functioning that characterizes schizophrenia is reflected on the Rorschach in poor form quality and, sometimes, by an insufficient number of Popular responses. With respect to form quality, the more closely Rorschach percepts correspond to the shape of the blots, the more strictly subjects are addressing their experience in a realistic fashion and the more likely they are to perceive objects and events the way most people do. Conversely, the more subjects deviate from commonly seen or easily visualized forms, the poorer grasp they have of reality and the more likely they are to perceive experience in an idiographic or distorted manner. The more frequently Popular answers are given, the more able and willing the subject is to recognize and endorse conventional modes of response. Conversely, an absence of Populars points to impaired perceptual accuracy and a disposition to showing bad judgment.

Poor Form Quality   Numerous research studies and considerable normative data have established the diagnostic significance of various levels of form quality. Generally speaking, a form level percentage that falls below 70% begins to raise questions of impaired translation in cognitive functioning, and a form level below 60% almost always identifies some pathologically inaccurate perception of reality.

These guidelines are equally applicable to children, adolescents, and adults. From age 5 to 16, nonpatient subjects show mean form levels ($X + \%$) ranging from 75% to 81%, and the average for adult nonpatients is 79%. Hence interpreters must avoid minimizing the significance of low form level in the younger client, as by saying, "But he's only a child." Hard evidence indicates that such allowances for developmental stage, while appropriate to a modest extent for some indices of scattered or illogical thinking, cannot be made for inaccurate perception. A form level below 70%, and especially below 60%, has the same implications for abnormal functioning in youthful as in adult subjects. Nevertheless, in using form level data to assess the possibility of schizophrenic disorder, examiners need to keep several additional considerations in mind.

First, $X + \%$ is usually a more reliable index of conventional reality testing than $F + \%$. The $X + \%$ includes all the responses in a record that have form demand, thus, it provides a larger and more reliable sample of a person's perceptual accuracy than the $F + \%$, which includes just the pure form responses. In psychometric terms, $X + \%$ is simply a longer test, and hence more reliable, than $F + \%$. Especially when Lambda is low, indicating that pure form answers constitute only a small percentage of the responses in a record, $F + \%$ can be misleading as an index of reality testing. For this reason, the SCZI does not include a criterion for $F + \%$, even though the relationship of $F + \%$ to $X + \%$ may, in some cases, have interpretive significance.

Second, it is important to distinguish between poor form answers that distort reality (minus responses) and those that are not commonly given but nevertheless conform to blot contours and can be quickly and readily seen by the examiner (unusual responses). Average form level runs in the 70% range, and subjects who give only good form responses ($X + \% = 90\%$ to 100%) tend to be either rigid, inflexible, overly perfectionistic individuals or people who are approaching the test-taking situation in an extremely guarded fashion. In well-adjusted subjects, the difference between perfect form level and the average of .75 to .81 is typically accounted for by unusual responses, in which the person shows some capacity for flexibility and individuality, rather than a dogged adherence to the obvious and commonplace. Too much individuality at the expense of adequate attention to conventional reality can also be a problem, however. Hence very low form level signifies a pathological lack of accurate perceptual functioning, whether the unconventional form responses are unusual or minus, but a preponderance of unusual responses may attenuate the implications of modestly low form level, at least to the extent of suggesting an unconventional rather than a distorted sense of reality. These considerations are reflected in the first three variables of the SCZI.

Third, the pathological implications of minus responses depend on the context in which they occur and the degree of distortion they include. In that context, the evaluation of form level should include scanning the sequence of scores to determine whether the minus responses in a record fall into any pattern. Sometimes minus responses cluster in the first few cards and become less frequent as the record proceeds. This pattern suggests that initial anxiety about the Rorschach situation temporarily impaired the subject's perceptual accuracy, and this circumstance tends to minimize the pathological implications of a high $X - \%$. On the other hand, a pattern in which minus form responses are scattered throughout a record or become more frequent as the test proceeds points to a generalized impairment of reality testing that becomes increasingly apparent the more a subject becomes involved in a situation.

Scanning the sequence of scores also reveals whether *minus* forms occur in any clusters that seem related to particular features of the subject's responses or of the blots themselves. The more such clusters become apparent, the more they suggest that the subject's perceptual inaccuracies are tied to specific concerns rather than to a pervasive inability to test reality. The most commonly observed clustering of this kind among children and adolescents involves minus form in responses that include white space (S) in the location. $S-$ responses identify perceptual distortion in the context of experiencing feelings of anger or resentment, and subjects who give numerous $S-$ responses are people of whom it can be said that anger frequently clouds their judgment. Hence a moderately poor form level in which a substantial percentage of the minus forms occurs in S responses has fewer implications for generally impaired reality testing than a moderately poor form level associated with a low $S-\%$. As shown in the list of criteria for the SCZI, this consideration in the evaluation of form level has been incorporated within the formal scoring of this index.

Another interpretively significant clustering of *minus* form responses in a record involves whether they appear primarily on Cards II and III (which might indicate special concerns about powerful or aggressive affects suggested by the red color); or primarily on the Cards IV–VII sequence of shaded achromatic stimuli (which might suggest depressive concerns); or on the multicolored VIII–X sequence (which might indicate particular difficulty in confronting complex emotional situations). Other possibilities to examine include whether poor forms occur primarily when the subject is using certain determinants, such as chromatic color or human movement, or is verbalizing particular content themes, such as aggression, dependency, or sex.

The personal significance of minus responses, as revealed by the context in which they occur, helps to generate hypotheses concerning the dynamics as well as the structure of a subject's personality functioning. In evaluating psychopathology, the frequency with which minus responses have obvious personal significance aids examiners in deciding whether perceptual accuracy is pathologically impaired. Extremely poor form level identifies poor reality testing, irrespective of contextual considerations. However, for subjects in whom marginally low $X+\%$ or marginally high $X-\%$ scores hover near the SCZI cutting scores, the extent to which bad form can be clearly tied to personal concerns points less toward pervasive pathology than toward circumscribed, situational susceptibility to inaccurate perception.

Finally, the degree of distortion in a poor form quality response is also important to evaluate. Examiners and interpreters need to determine whether the minus responses in a record bear at least some relationship to the contours of the blot. An estimated 80% to 90% of properly scored minus responses include some features that look something like some part of the stimulus, and the examiner/scorer can see some basis for the response. The popular animal detail on Card VIII can be used as an example. Responses such as "frog," "seal," and "turtle" are scored minus, but the resemblance of each of these percepts to a four-legged animal shows how these bad forms might have been suggested.

The remaining 10% to 20% of minus responses seem to have come out of nowhere and bear little or no relationship to the shape of the stimulus. Seeing the Card VIII side detail as a person or as a toilet bowl, for example, does not approximate in any way the actual appearance of the stimulus. Hence minus responses that bear little or no relationship to any blot contours involve a greater distortion level than minus responses that have at least some basis in realistic features of the blot stimuli.

The greater the distortion level of the minus responses in a record, the more likely the subject is to have pathologically impaired reality testing. Conversely, when form level is only moderately low and none of the minus responses is grossly distorted, the implications for schizophrenia may be attenuated. To put this consideration in further perspective, the minus responses given by reasonably well-adjusted subjects will fall exclusively among the 80% to 90% that have at least some basis in the stimulus, whereas the 10% to 20% that lack any such basis are very rarely given by other than seriously disturbed subjects.

Insufficient Populars   Normative data and research findings indicate that subjects who give fewer than four Popular (P) answers may be impaired in their ability and willingness to recognize and/or endorse conventional modes of response. This clue to inaccurate perception of one's world, which has direct implications for impaired judgment in life situations, must be applied in light of certain age and sequence considerations.

Younger people give somewhat fewer P responses than adults, although the median for P reaches seven at age 11 and remains at this level through adolescence and into adulthood. Children ages 7 to 10 have a median P of six, and the median falls to five at age 6 and to four at age 5. Accordingly, to fall within the nonpatient range, three P responses may be sufficient for 7- to 10-year-olds and just one or two for 5- and 6-year-olds. For subjects ages 11 and older, the expectation of at least four P holds as a criterion for normality.

The sequence is also important. The meaning of a certain number of P answers may influenced by where they occur in a record. Of the 13 P responses scored in the Comprehensive System, the four most common by far are the bat or butterfly on Card I, the human figures on Card III, the bat or butterfly on Card V, and the animal figures on Card VIII. Subjects who give four P responses will ordinarily not be considered to be deficient in recognizing conventional modes of response; however, should their four P answers not include any of the four most commonly given, question may still be raised concerning how fully they are in touch with reality. Similarly, the pathological significance of an adolescent's giving only three P answers is mitigated somewhat if all are among the most common four.

RORSCHACH INDICES OF INTERPERSONAL INEPTNESS

A person's current and past history of interpersonal relationships will typically provide the clearest indications of his or her social skills and interests. In addition, the way that people conduct themselves during an interview will usually say a great deal about their capacity to establish effective interpersonal contact. The Rorschach does not measure social functioning as directly as do historical data and interview observations. Rorschach responses can, however, provide clues to pathological social withdrawal and ineptness. Such clues appear primarily in the form of inadequate responses involving human content, particularly in the categories of human movement (M) and pure human content (Pure H).

Inadequate M   Among the several ways in which the M responses in a record may be inadequate, the most obvious is the low frequency of occurrence. M answers reflect in part an interest in human interaction, and subjects who give very few M are likely to be pathologically withdrawn from engaging in or even thinking about interactions with people. Failure to give at least one or two M is especially significant among adults, for whom the nonpatient mean M is 4.31 and the mode is three, and for youngsters age 11 and older, who

Table 35.   Data for *M* and Pure *H* Answers in Five Nonpatient Groups

	Age 5	Age 8	Age 11	Age 14	Adult
MEAN *M*	1.7	3.38	4.12	4.06	4.31
MODE *M*	1	2	3	4	3
% *M* = 0	0	0	0	0	0
% *M*− > 0	18.9	8.3	20.0	10.48	3.2
MEAN Pure *H*	2.19	1.87	2.8	3.0	3.4
% Pure *H* = 0	1	3	3	0	1
% Pure *H* < 2	4	27	20	17	10

have mean *M*'s above 4.00 and modes of three or more (see Table 35). Because *M* productivity among nonpatient children declines below age 11, down to a mean of just 1.70 and a mode of one at age 5, a small number of *M* must be interpreted more conservatively among younger children than among adolescents. Nevertheless, even at age 5, as at every other age, the percentage of nonpatients who give no *M* at all is zero.

Whereas an adequate number of *M*s in a record suggests social interest, their presence alone does not guarantee social skill. Just as some schizophrenic persons reach out for social contact but do so ineffectively, *M* responses in abundance may still be inadequate by virtue of their form level or their content. Subjects who give *M* responses with minus form level are showing interest in people but a propensity for inaccurate and unrealistic interpretations of interpersonal situations. Hence *M*− responses are as likely to be associated with deficient social skills and poor interpersonal relationships as the failure to produce any *M* at all. Young people are a bit more likely to give an *M*− response than adults. Nevertheless, among adolescents and even young children, the percentage of nonpatients giving *M*− is small enough to warrant viewing even a single distortion of this kind as evidence of an inclination to misperceive the implications of social situations and show poor judgment in interpersonal relationships. The SCZI includes this variable, but with a conservative criterion that requires at least two *M* − for scoring a point in the index.

The content of *M* responses is also important. Subjects whose interpersonal interests are associated with a fragmentary, depreciatory view of people or are focused on nonhuman objects rarely have sufficient social skill to maintain good interpersonal relationships. On the Rorschach, then, *M* responses limited to *(H), Hd, (Hd), A, (A), Ad,* and *(Ad)* contents are only slightly less indicative of difficulty in dealing comfortably with people than an inadequate number of *M*. Further implications of these kinds of inadequate *M* responses for borderline disorders are discussed in Chapter 7.

Inadequate Pure H   Because *Pure H* also reflects interest in people, it has the same pathological significance as *M* when it fails to appear or suggests distorted views of others *(H−)*. Like *M, H* shows a developmental trend, becoming gradually more frequent during childhood and beginning during adolescence to approach an adult level of frequency (see Table 35). Nevertheless, at all ages the absence of Pure *H* is extremely rare, and failure to give at least two Pure *H* warrants concern about maladaptive social distance.

The frequency of Pure *H* also provides a useful adjunct in interpreting lack of *M* in a record. *H* production requires less ideational activity and less perceptual differentiation than *M* production. Hence in some subjects who give few or no *M* because of a nonideational or poorly articulated approach to the task, the occurrence of good form Pure *H* responses can help to rule out interpersonal aversion. On the other hand, infrequent or poor quality Pure *H* together with inadequate *M* increases the likelihood of a pathological withdrawal from interpersonal interests and activities.

RORSCHACH INDICES OF INADEQUATE CONTROLS

The difficulty that schizophrenic people have in keeping anxiety provoking and socially unacceptable ideas out of their conscious awareness often leads to disturbed response content. Inadequate affective control, although often more apparent from inappropriate emotionality in subjects' test-taking behavior than in their test responses, can nevertheless contribute to diagnostically significant difficulties in modulating the color of the inkblots.

Disturbed Content   Schizophrenic individuals who are preoccupied with aggressive and sexual fantasies may produce Rorschach content themes of violent aggression and blatant sexuality that go well beyond minimum criteria for scoring aggression (AG), morbidity (MOR), or sex (Sx). Whereas "Two men fighting" is an AG response that falls within normal limits, "Two men tearing away at each other, ripping each other's guts out" suggests loss of control over aggressive thoughts and maladaptive preoccupation with being the perpetrator or victim of hostile acts. Likewise, "a dead cat" and "a person who looks sick," although MOR responses possibly related to depressive concerns, demonstrate far less ideational dyscontrol than "A squashed cat that someone ran over and squeezed all the juices out of" and "A person with some horrible disease, you can parts of him rotting away," both of which convey pathological preoccupation with terrible and destructive events.

Sometimes examiner reaction provides a good barometer for how disturbed such responses are. When examiners find themselves reacting with discomfort or distaste, especially if they become frightened or feel their skin crawl, they are probably listening to responses that reflect inadequate control over ideation. Schizophrenic subjects are especially likely to lack adaptive control over distressing imagery when many of their unusually aggressive or morbid responses involve minus form level.

These same considerations apply to *Sx* responses, which rarely appear in the records of nonpatients. Young children almost never give a sex response, and only about 5% of adolescents and adults give even one such response. The more frequently sex responses occur and the more often they involve minus form level, the more likely they are to indicate a pathological preoccupation with sexuality and a failure of ideational control. In addition, a pathological loss of control can often be separated from normal sexual anxieties by the degree to which *Sx* responses are elaborated. A young person who sees on Card IV "a man's thing, a big one" may be revealing some pressing developmental concerns. By contrast, one who reports "A man's part, all hard, slipping in and out of this woman's part, and there's blood and stuff all around" is likely to be suffering from some seriously disturbing preoccupations.

Poor Color Modulation   As already noted, Rorschachers are more likely to detect inappropriate affect from subjects' emotional responses to the testing situation than from specific features of their test responses. Nevertheless, because the manner in which people deal with chromatic color indicates how they are likely to deal with strong emotional stimulation, poorly modulated color responses may provide an important clue to inadequate emotional control. Most important in this regard is Pure C, a completely unmodulated use of color, which suggests a propensity for unrestrained emotionality with little or no effort to integrate one's feelings with the formal demands (i.e., inkblot contours) of their experience.

Studies of the temporal stability of Rorschach determinants have indicated that the presence of one Pure C in a record is not particularly reliable and should be interpreted as a situational event rather than as an indication of a persistent personality characteristic. However, the presence of two or more Pure C is fairly stable over time and can be taken as a probable indicator of inadequate emotional control (Exner, 1993). Although young people are slightly more inclined to give Pure C than adults, age makes very little difference in the clinical interpretation of this variable. The frequency among nonpatients of records with more than one Pure C is zero from age 11 through adolescence and into adulthood. From age 7 to 10, the nonpatient frequency of two or more Pure C ranges from 2% to 8%, and only at ages 5 (16%) and 6 (39%) does this finding approach normative expectation.

Accordingly, subjects age 7 or above who give more than a single Pure C response are likely to be having difficulty controlling their affects and integrating their feelings with other features of their experience. Pathologically impaired emotional control is especially indicated when Pure Cs break through in an otherwise unexpressive record (such as when the EB style is introversive) and are not balanced by demonstrations of more appropriate affective modulation (such as when FC and CF are absent or infrequent). Occasionally, a subject will give Pure C responses all of which involve abstraction, as in "The red in this one suggests happiness." Abstract Pure Cs of this type often suggest intellectualization of affect rather than emotional dyscontrol. Even so, an accumulation of abstract Pure Cs in the absence of well-modulated color use identifies impaired capacity for integration of affect.

DIAGNOSTIC DECISIONS

As the preceding material has indicated, many features of schizophrenic disturbance have correlates in Rorschach findings, most of which are captured by formal scoring categories and some of which appear in unscored verbal content of the record. However, this does not mean that all these findings will be present in the protocols of all schizophrenic subjects. In some cases of fairly clear schizophrenic disorder, some of these findings may not be positive. In other cases, especially among younger children, the findings may be technically positive but clinically equivocal. More often than not, a definitive opinion concerning the presence of a schizophrenic disorder must be based on a sophisticated integration of Rorschach findings with data from other psychodiagnostic instruments, observations on interview, and a detailed clinical history (see Weiner, 1987; 1992, Chap. 3).

Nevertheless, the SCZI as currently constituted, including age adjustments as necessary for children 10 years of age and younger, encompasses most of the Rorschach data relevant to identifying schizophrenic disorder and provides valid grounds for drawing diagnostic inferences. In actual practice, the use of the SCZI with children and adolescents must be guided by certain considerations in interpreting this index and in differentiating schizophrenia from other youthful conditions.

Considerations in Interpreting the SCZI   The SCZI should be interpreted with four considerations in mind. First, the SCZI has demonstrated approximately 80% accuracy in labeling patient groups as schizophrenic or nonschizophrenic, as measured against DSM-III-R criteria, and approximately 80% of the SCZI errors consist of false negative diagnoses (Exner, 1991, 1993). Hence, the customary cutoff score of four on the SCZI may fail to identify as many as one in five schizophrenic persons, but it rarely calls anyone schizophrenic who does not have a schizophreniclike disorder. Among nonpatient adults and young people at every age from 5 to 16, moreover, the percentage of subjects who show a SCZI index of 4 or more is zero. In other words, an elevated SCZI is extremely likely to identify schizophrenic features in a disorder, whereas a SCZI of less than four cannot be assumed with any confidence to rule out the possibility that schizophrenia is present.

Second, beyond the critical cutting score of 4 for SCZI, the implications of the findings vary with the actual number. A SCZI of 4 indicates that the subject is manifesting personality impairments found commonly among schizophrenic persons and infrequently among other subjects. This suggests the presence of schizophrenia but calls for close examination of the data to confirm this possibility. A SCZI of 5 indicates a strong probability of schizophrenia and calls for further examination of the data only to determine whether there is any mitigating evidence to raise doubts about this conclusion. A SCZI of 6 indicates a strong likelihood that schizophrenia is present, and only extremely compelling data to the contrary warrant altering this conclusion.

Third, those relatively few cases in which SCZI does produce a false positive occur almost exclusively with an index of 4 and hardly ever when SCZI is 5 or 6. Specifically, approximately 90% of false positive indications of schizophrenic disorder occur with a SCZI of 4. This empirical fact makes good sense in conceptual terms. Because of the manner in which the *SCZI* is constituted, subjects whose reality testing is very poor and who are having pronounced difficulty in managing interpersonal relationships, as reflected in very low form level and numerous $M-$, can receive a SCZI of 4 without demonstrating thinking disorder (without an elevation in *Sum6* or *WSum6*). As soon as SCZI reaches 5, however, the subject must, in addition to perceptual and interpersonal difficulties, have demonstrated sufficiently disordered thinking to elevate on the Critical Special Scores.

Although disordered thinking does not by itself demonstrate schizophrenia, thought disorder is the core ingredient of schizophrenia, and its presence is essential to diagnosis of the condition. Hence, when SCZI is 5, examiners need to look carefully at the six Critical Special Scores. If they are not sufficiently numerous or extreme to be contributing at least 1 point of the 4 present, then thought disorder is not being demonstrated and the subject's condition, although perhaps serious, is not likely to constitute schizophrenia. Generally speaking, impaired reality testing of sufficient proportion to elevate SCZI in the absence of thought disorder will identify psychotic functioning but point to a psychosis associated with some condition other than schizophrenia.

Fourth, in those instances of a false positive SCZI, other specific findings can frequently help the clinician to conclude that schizophrenia is not present. With respect to the Critical Special Scores, the implications of a *Sum6* greater then 6 and a *WSum6* greater than 17 are attenuated (a) when there is an accumulation of mild instances of slippage (DV and INCOM) but few if any of the more serious indications of slippage, (b) when there are no Level 2 special scores, and (c) when the more serious special scores do not include any FABCOMS, which seem to have special implications for schizophrenic thought disorder. As elaborated in the next chapter, those conditions other than schizophrenia in which some thinking disorder is commonly present are relatively unlikely to involve any accumulation of serious, Level 2, or FABCOM special scores.

Considerations in Differential Diagnosis   The problem of false positive diagnosis with SCZI is potentially greater among young people than adults. The task of the interpreter is to differentiate schizophrenia from three other conditions in which young people may show a positive SCZI: acute psychotic disorders, affective disorders, and developmental disorders.

Acute Psychotic Disorders   Patients at any age who are acutely psychotic, as defined by being out of touch with reality, confused and disoriented, unable to communicate sensibly, and preoccupied with distracting thoughts and distressing feelings, are almost certain to elevate on SCZI, often with indices of 5 or 6 as well as 4. Clinical experience indicates that reliable differential diagnosis can rarely be achieved among persons who are presently acutely psychotic by simply using the Rorschach. Acutely psychotic individuals of all kinds, whether schizophrenic, manic, intoxicated, or in the throes of a brief psychotic reaction, frequently display the same features—severely disordered thinking, seriously impaired reality testing, inept interpersonal relationships, and poor self-control. Only after their acute psychotic episode has subsided does it become possible to sort out the psychopathological origins of their psychotic breakdown.

Accordingly, acutely psychotic patients should not be tested, at least not with the expectation that the test findings will contribute to a differential diagnosis of schizophrenia. Testing should be deferred until the acute psychosis abates or has been alleviated by therapeutic intervention, at which time those patients who are schizophrenic will be much more likely to demonstrate persistent features of schizophrenic disorder, especially disordered thinking, than those who are not.

Some further qualification of this guideline is necessary, however, particularly with respect to drug-induced psychosis and bipolar affective disorder. Clinical and research findings have demonstrated that toxic amounts of alcohol and various other substances (including stimulants and hallucinogens) in the system can produce psychotic reactions that mimic schizophrenia clinically (with reports of delusions and hallucinations) and on the Rorschach (with indications of disordered thinking and inaccurate perception). With few exceptions, however, such clinical and test features of psychosis gradually disappear as people with drug-induced disorders become detoxified—unless they also happen to be schizophrenic. Persistence of schizophrenic features after detoxification identifies schizophrenic disorder; in such cases the drug abuse has apparently served not as the cause of the disorder, but as a stressor that has precipitated a psychotic episode in a person who, by virtue of being schizophrenic, was susceptible to psychotic breakdown. In this regard, schizophrenic persons with drug-induced psychotic reactions generally resemble drug-free schizophrenics in their patterns of premorbid adjustment, cognitive functioning, and course of disturbance (Hurt, Holzman, & Davis, 1983; Tien & Anthony, 1990; Turner & Tsuang, 1990; Vardy & Kay, 1983).

An important exception to this guideline involves cases of suspected amphetamine-induced psychosis. People vary widely in their sensitivity to amphetamines, and only a small dose can in some instances precipitate an apparent schizophrenic breakdown with paranoid features. Moreover, the lingering toxic effects of these drugs have been known to extend over many weeks or even months. Hence, if amphetamines have been used, the customary waiting period of 2 to 3 weeks of detoxification before evaluating a drug-abusing psychotic person may not be long enough to warrant inferring schizophrenia on the basis of persisting schizophrenic features in the Rorschach. For seriously disturbed young people who are known or suspected to have abused amphetamines, the differential diagnosis between schizophrenia and toxic psychosis may instead require long-term follow-up (see Krug, 1983; Leavitt, 1982, Chap. 5; Weiner, 1964).

Affective Disorders   Affective disorders, especially bipolar disorder with mania, often involve some elements of disordered thinking. Hypomanic individuals typically talk freely and invest considerable energy in producing long and complex Rorschach protocols. Their responsiveness provides ample opportunity for peculiarities in their thinking to become manifest. Hence, an elevated SCZI must sometimes be evaluated carefully to differentiate schizophrenic from hypomanic thought disorder, particularly with respect to the Critical Special Scores. As an aid in this evaluation, clinical and research findings indicate three respects in which disordered thinking in schizophrenia and affective disorder often differ.

First, disordered thinking tends to be more severe in schizophrenic than in depressed or manic individuals (Asarnow & MacCrimmon, 1981; Oltmanns et al., 1985). For the most part, SCZI as it stands takes this difference into account. Although affectively disordered patients who require hospitalization often receive points on SCZI for poor form level, they are much less likely than schizophrenic patients to demonstrate the severe extent of disordered thinking that is necessary to meet the SCZI criteria for *Sum6* and *WSum6*. As a result, persons with affective disorder show only an 8% to 10% frequency of false positive elevations on SCZI (Exner, 1991, 1993).

In a confirmation of Exner's data, Singer and Brabender (1993) found a SCZI of 4 or more in just 11% of 62 patients with affective disorder. However, some important differences emerged when they divided their subjects into more specific diagnostic groups. None of 29 unipolar depressed patients in their sample and only one of 15 bipolar depressed patients had a false positive elevation on SCZI, but one third of 18 bipolar manic subjects had a SCZI of 4 or more. By contrast, 82% of the 320 inpatient schizophrenics in the Comprehensive System reference data had a SCZI of 4 or more (Exner, 1991, p. 85). Nevertheless, if proved reliable in larger samples, the Singer and Brabender findings would suggest that as many as one in three manic patients might show a misleading elevation on SCZI.

Second, whatever its extent clinically or on the Rorschach, disordered thinking tends to be more persistent in schizophrenia than in affective disorder. Among schizophrenic patients, difficulties in thinking coherently and logically are likely to be revealed by psychological tests, even when treatment has markedly reduced such dramatic manifestations of thinking disorder as delusions and ideas of reference. For this reason, disordered thinking is often referred to as a *trait* component of schizophrenia. Among depressed and manic patients, by contrast, evidence of disordered thinking typically diminishes or disappears as their condition improves; for these affectively disturbed people, thinking disorder constitutes a *state* rather than a trait (Adair & Wagner, 1992; Docherty, Schnur, & Harvey, 1988; Gold & Hurt, 1990; Grossman, Harrow, & Sands, 1986; Grove & Andreasen, 1985; Harvey, Docherty, Serper, & Rasmussen, 1990; Jampala, Taylor, & Abrams, 1989; Pogue-Geile & Harrow, 1985). Hence, in those occasional instances of only marginally severe thinking disorder or of compelling reasons to suspect bipolar disorder despite a SCZI of even 5 or 6 (such as a strong family history of affective disorder), substantially reduced thinking disorder on retesting, following some period of clinical improvement, may be the final necessary step in ruling out schizophrenia.

Third, disordered thinking typically is displayed in qualitatively different ways by schizophrenic and manic individuals (Holzman, Shenton, & Solovay, 1986; Solovay, Shenton, & Holzman, 1987). Schizophrenic patients generally present manifestations of incoherent and illogical thinking earnestly and with expressed concern about keeping their ideas straight, finding correct answers, and being understood. They rarely enjoy themselves while giving Rorschach responses that involve special scores, and inquiry into these responses often becomes a tense affair in which subjects either become upset with themselves and apologetic for their confused answers, or become defensive about the quality of their ideation and resentful of the examiner's appearing to question their impressions.

Manic patients, by contrast, typically communicate in a playful, breezy fashion and rarely express concern about not responding clearly and effectively. Instead, they often seem to enjoy themselves while making plays on words and bouncing from one subject to another in ways that result in special scores on the Rorschach. Unlike the tension that often accompanies examining a schizophrenic person, testing of a manic individual tends to be a relaxed affair, in which the subject is more likely to be exuberant than distressed, self-confident than worried, and entertained rather than threatened by the Rorschach task.

Even these differential guidelines may, at times, fall short of supporting a clear distinction between schizophrenic and affective disorder in cases in which (a) there is clear evidence of severely disordered thinking, (b) there is equally clear evidence of a substantial affective component in the patient's disturbance, and (c) the indications of thinking disorder remain prominent after the patient's affective symptoms have moderated considerably. The most likely diagnostic possibility in these circumstances is schizoaffective disorder.

Developmental Disorders   Preadolescent children with developmental disorders may have psychological impairments that elevate SCZI and complicate differential diagnosis of schizophrenia. The most well-known such developmental disorder is infantile autism, discussed earlier in reference to discriminating between early- and late-onset childhood psychoses. As noted then, the most important consideration in differentiating early-onset schizophrenia in elementary school age children from persisting infantile autism may be a history of psychological peculiarities from early in life, which is more likely to characterize autism than schizophrenia.

When autistic subjects are not mentally retarded, however, examiners should be aware that relatively high-functioning autistic persons when tested as adults have been found to show many schizophrenic features on the Rorschach, including indications of disordered thinking. Among eleven 16- to 36-year-old autistic subjects with a mean *IQ* of 83, Dykens, Volkmar, and Glick (1991) obtained a mean *WSum6* of over 40. Three of these subjects had a SCZI of 4, and five had a SCZI of 5. Comparable Rorschach data on younger people with autism have not yet been published, and other research indicates that autistic children are no more likely than people in general to become schizophrenic as adolescents and adults (Volkmar & Cohen, 1991). Nevertheless, these findings emphasize the necessity of paying close attention to the developmental history in differentiating schizophrenia from high-functioning autism in elementary school children and adolescents as well.

Another developmental disorder that can arise independently of intellectual level and lead to misleading false positive elevations on SCZI is identified in DSM-III-R as expressive language disorder. Developmental expressive language disorder arises in the absence of autism, mental retardation, or any other pervasive developmental or neurological disorder and results in children of otherwise normal functioning demonstrating poor vocabulary skills (including inappropriate word usage), poor sentence structure (including omissions of critical parts of sentences), shortened sentences, simplified grammatical usage, unusual sequences of words, and tangential responses. Thus, children with expressive language disorder often give DV, INCOM, and DR responses on the Rorschach and consequently produce a *Sum6* and/or a *WSum6* suggestive of disordered thinking.

Clinicians examining elementary school age children must accordingly consider the possibility that apparent thinking disorder is a function of expressive language disorder rather than schizophrenia. Because expressive language disorder does not cause impaired reality testing, schizophrenia can often be ruled out in otherwise adequately functioning children with expressive language disorder who elevate on Critical Special Scores but do not show poor form level. In some cases, however, expressive language disorder may be associated with attention deficit disorder or learning disability, which does contribute to impaired reality testing. Acklin (1990) and Champion, Doughtie, Johnson, and McCreary (1984) have reported form levels well below normal expectation in learning-disabled children.

Hence when expressive language disorder is concurrent with learning disability, especially in young children, clear differentiation from early-onset schizophrenia may have to await retesting following some period of speech and language therapy. Although developmental language disorders may become persistent and lead to serious adjustment difficulties, many language-disordered children acquire improved communication skills in response to maturation or intervention during middle childhood (Cantwell, Baker, Rutter, & Mawhood, 1989; Paul, Cohen, & Caparulo, 1983). Language-disordered children with learning disability who acquire improved communication skills but continue to show signs of thought disorder on the Rorschach are thus likely to have an emerging schizophrenic disorder. This conclusion is buttressed by evidence that learning disability by itself rarely leads to incoherent or illogical thinking. Learning-disabled children are no more likely than their nondisabled peers to give responses with Critical Special Scores (Acklin, 1990).

These observations can be summarized as follows:

Young children who demonstrate apparent thought disorder (elevated *Sum6* and *WSum6*) but not impaired reality testing (adequate form level) should be studied further for developmental expressive language disorder.

Those who demonstrate both apparent thought disorder and impaired reality testing but do not seem schizophrenic should be examined further for the possible co-occurrence of developmental expressive language disorder and learning disability.

Those who demonstrate thought disorder and impaired reality testing in the absence of evidence for both language disorder and learning disability are likely to have a developing schizophrenic disorder, even if blatant clinical manifestations of schizophrenia are not yet present.

CHRONICITY

The more severely disabling a schizophrenic disturbance is and the longer it persists, the more likely it is to constitute a chronic disorder. Chronicity is also typically associated with an insidious onset involving slowly deteriorating functioning over a period of months or even years in the absence of clearly precipitating stressful events; with considerable symptom tolerance resulting in the disturbed person's displaying little concern about the schizophrenic features of his or her behavior and lacking awareness that his or her problems derive from psychological impairments; and with a history of prior maladjustment consisting of interpersonal and school or work difficulties that were evident even before an insidious onset began (Weiner, 1966, Chap. 13; Weiner, 1992, Chap. 3).

By contrast, acute schizophrenic disorder emerges rapidly and in relation to obviously distressing experiences. Acutely schizophrenic individuals tend to recognize and express concern about the unusual nature of their symptoms ("I don't know what's wrong with me, I just can't seem to think straight any more"). Typically, their prior behavior has been unremarkable, at least in the eyes of untrained observers, and those who know them well express surprise at their suddenly becoming so disturbed. Finally, as these differences between them imply, acute schizophrenic episodes respond more quickly to treatment than chronically persisting schizophrenic disorder.

Acute and chronic schizophrenia are not discrete conditions. Instead, they appear to constitute positions along a continuous dimension of chronicity. Psychopathologists differ concerning what chronicity entails in schizophrenia. Some regard the schizophrenic condition itself as a lifetime disturbance and argue that people who have had schizophrenic breakdowns remain schizophrenic even during periods of partial remission in which they are not psychotically impaired (Kety, 1980). Others contend that what persists in schizophrenia is not the schizophrenic condition itself, but rather a vulnerability to acute episodes of schizophrenic breakdown. From this perspective, inadequate treatment and excessive stress can lead to acute breakdowns remaining permanent, but favorable environmental circumstances can allow acutely disturbed schizophrenics to recover and not experience relapse (Zubin, 1986).

Both of these ways of viewing chronicity in schizophrenia can find support in research data. For example, Marengo and Harrow (1987) assessed a group of young adult schizophrenics (average age 23 years) 2 and 4 years following their discharge after a hospitalization averaging 4 months' duration. Of these patients, 40% showed persistent manifestations of disordered thinking at both reassessments, and another 37% demonstrated disordered thinking on either the first or the second follow-up evaluation. On the other hand, 23% of these patients did not display thought disorder at either the 2-year or 4-year follow-up. Similarly, McGlashan (1988, p. 257) concluded from a detailed review of long-term follow-up studies of schizophrenia, "Schizophrenia is a chronic disease, frequently disabling for a lifetime." However, each of the studies cited by McGlashan in support of this conclusion included subgroups of 20% to 25% of schizophrenics who did not show persistent impairment and were considered recovered.

Because degree of chronicity has important implications for the course and treatment of schizophrenia, every evaluation of possible schizophrenic disorder should address the person's status on this dimension. The more chronic the disorder, the less favorably it will respond to efforts at intervention and the more likely it will be to eventuate in long-term disability. Conversely, the less chronic it is, the better the prospects are for a positive treatment response and a good outcome. The indications of chronicity are best addressed by information concerning the nature of the onset of the disorder and the person's prior adjustment. The Rorschach can supplement this information by providing useful clues to the severity of the patient's disturbance and the extent to which he or she is accepting of it.

Severity of Disturbance   Severity of disturbance is directly reflected in the Rorschach in the extent to which features of the responses deviate from normative expectations. Generally speaking, the more deviant the indices of disordered thinking, inaccurate perception, interpersonal ineptness, and inadequate controls are in a schizophrenic person's record, the more chronic his or her condition is likely to be.

Degree of deviance in a Rorschach record can be assessed at several levels of specificity. Of the four general types of personality impairment in schizophrenia, is the subject showing difficulties in all or in just two or three? Of the Rorschach responses, what percentage show some kind of schizophrenic interference with good functioning? For each potentially pathological type of response, such as minus forms or excessively elaborated Sex contents, how many accumulate in the course of a record? The answers to these questions provide a fairly good basis for determining how severely disturbed schizophrenic subjects are and, accordingly, how chronic their disturbance is likely to be. Additionally, in some cases, a relatively mild degree of disturbance may help to identify an early or incipient stage of schizophrenic disorder (Weiner, 1966, Chap. 15). In these cases, the question of schizophrenia may be difficult to answer, and a conclusion may have to await retesting until the possible evidence for this condition will have either disappeared or become more clear.

One subtle exception to the general principle linking severity of disturbance with chronicity requires further consideration. Rorschach indices of schizophrenia and the personality processes they represent involve for the most part some withdrawal or failure to do something, such as the person's failure to keep thoughts together or emotions under control, withdrawal from interpersonal interaction, too little attention to the requirements of reality, and so forth. In contrast to this posture of retreat, one Rorschach manifestation of schizophrenia suggests an active effort to deal with the world and make better sense of it, namely, those efforts at complex reasoning that result in INCOM, FABCOM, and ALOG responses. For these Critical Special Scores, there may be reason to regard an elevated frequency as constituting increased severity in one sense but also, in another sense, as a sign of acute struggle with rather than chronic resignation to schizophrenic disorder.

This psychodiagnostic distinction is consistent with contemporary theory and research concerning positive and negative symptoms in schizophrenia. *Positive symptoms* involve the presence of behaviors or functions that do not ordinarily occur in normally functioning individuals; in schizophrenia, these consist of such dramatic and readily apparent manifestations of the disorder as markedly illogical thinking, bizarre actions, and prominent delusions or hallucinations. *Negative symptoms* involved the loss or absence of normal behaviors or functions, as reflected in impoverished thought, blunted affect, and social withdrawal. A predominance of negative symptoms in schizophrenic disorder correlates significantly with such features of chronicity as refractoriness to treatment and persistently serious incapacitation (Andreasen, 1985; Docherty, Schnur, & Harvey, 1988; Walker, Harvey, & Perlman, 1988).

Hence it may be that a dramatic frequency of INCOM, FABCOM, and ALOG responses in the Rorschach may reflect the kinds of positive schizophrenic symptomology that, although serious in degree, are associated with relatively acute rather than relatively chronic disorder. As noted in the next chapter, these positive symptoms of schizophrenic thought disorder are more likely to be shared with manic patients than is negative thought disorder, which is rarely observed in manic patients (Andreasen & Grove, 1986; Harrow & Marengo, 1986).

Acceptance of Disturbance   As previously noted, relatively acute and relatively chronic schizophrenics differ in how much they have accepted their psychological disorder. Acutely disturbed schizophrenics are typically confused and distressed by their inability to think effectively, relate to reality, and communicate with people. They are anxious about their mental state, threatened by situations that expose their abnormality, and actively engaged in efforts to resolve their condition.

Chronic schizophrenia, on the other hand, is characterized by considerable tolerance for what is an ingrained psychological disturbance. Chronic schizophrenics may be anxious about external circumstances, such as being admitted to or discharged from a hospital, but they display little concern about those features of their behavior that identify them as schizophrenic. These differences in self-awareness and symptom-related anxiety level are reflected in the Rorschach in the degree of critical distance people can take from disturbed responses and in the level of the D Score.

Critical Distance from Disturbed Responses   As noted earlier, the pathological implications of unusual verbalizations depend in part on whether the subject takes them seriously or instead expresses some reservations about them. Subjects who express reservations about their disturbed responses are demonstrating a capacity to take critical distance from them. Accordingly, self-critical reflections on responses that demonstrate schizophrenic impairments suggest nonacceptance of disturbance and a presently acute condition, as in the following examples: "I guess it doesn't make much sense, but that's the idea that came to me"; "Did I really say that? It doesn't look that way any more"; "That's probably not a very good answer, but it's the best I can do right now." The more frequently such comments accompany deviant answers, and the more spontaneously they emerge without prompting from the examiner, the more they help point toward relatively acute disturbance.

Conversely, disturbed subjects who show little awareness of how deviant their responses are and remain unconcerned about them even during Inquiry are failing to take critical distance from their impairments and thereby demonstrating acceptance of them as an appropriate and comfortable way to be. To sharpen their differential diagnosis of chronicity, examiners/interpreters need to take special pains to inquire deviant responses, even with some emphasis, to give subjects every possible chance to demonstrate some critical judgment (e.g., "And you say it looks like the two people are diving into *a puddle of oil?*"). The more that replies to such inquiry demonstrate bland acceptance of deviant responses rather than critical evaluation of them, the more likely it becomes that the subject's present condition is chronic in nature, as in the following comments: "Right, that's what it is"; "It just looks that way"; "Everybody's seen things like that, haven't you?"

The D Score   The D Score in the Comprehensive System provides a crude indication concerning the balance that is being struck between a person's resources that are accessible for formulating and implementing deliberate strategies for coping with demands that may be experienced (the *EA*), on the one hand, and the extent of the demands the person is in fact experiencing (the *es*). For the vast majority of people

(87% among nonpatient adults), the D Score is either zero or greater than zero, which reflects adequate capacity to manage their current level of stress and a general feeling of comfort and satisfaction with their current circumstances. A D Score in the minus range, on the other hand, identifies a stress overload in which people are being overwhelmed by more demands than they can find ways to meet, are feeling tense and anxious, are dissatisfied with the way things are in their lives, and are going through a relatively unstable stage in their lives.

Generally speaking, it is a minus D Score that identifies adjustment problems involving a troubling degree of anxiety and calling for evaluation and treatment. In a person who is already known to be seriously disturbed, the stability, sense of satisfaction, and freedom from subjectively felt distress associated with a D Score of zero, and especially D Scores in the range of +1 or greater, become negative indicators. They suggest that the individual may already be functioning about as well as he or she can and feels little need to change. Although D Scores of zero are difficult, if not impossible, to evaluate with regard to chronicity, a positive D Score in the record of schizophrenic subjects strongly suggests a relatively chronic disturbance. Conversely, a minus D Score reflects that type of subjectively felt distress and wish for change that characterizes relatively acute disturbance. This clue to chronicity is equally significant in the records of young people as adults.

PARANOID STATUS

Paranoia consists of a distinctive cognitive style and set of attitudes toward the environment. Paranoid individuals tend to be alert and vigilant people who scan their surroundings carefully. However, because they are rigid, inflexible, and narrow-minded, they fit new information into their previously held beliefs and rarely consider altering their views. Because they perceive their environment as hostile and potentially dangerous, they are exceedingly cautious and suspicious in their dealings with it. They mistrust the motives of others and fear being exploited or victimized. Hence, they maintain a formal distance in their social relationships and prefer to reflect on rather than share their thoughts and feelings with others. They sense a constant need to protect themselves and their self-esteem, and because of this, they tend also to be pompous and self-righteous individuals who criticize others freely and blame external circumstances for any problems they have (Akhtar, 1990; Magaro, 1980; Millon, 1981, Chap. 13; Shapiro, 1965, Chap. 3).

The combination of these paranoid styles and attitudes with schizophrenic impairments of thinking and perception produces such dramatic symptoms of paranoid schizophrenia as delusions of persecution ("I'm on a list to be killed"), delusions of grandeur ("I have the perfect body and mind"), and hallucinations with persecutory or grandiose overtones ("The voices keep telling me I'm going to be punished"; "I've been told I'll become a very important person"). Such symptoms appearing in a schizophrenic person point to active presence of a paranoid form of the disorder. Schizophrenic individuals who display the attitudes and orientations associated with paranoia but are not currently manifesting obvious paranoid symptoms can reasonably be expected to develop such symptoms if their condition persists or worsens.

Although exceptions occur, paranoia is much more often a potential rather than an already established feature of schizophrenic episodes in adolescence. Paranoid forms of schizophrenia have a later onset than nonparanoid forms and only infrequently become entrenched before age 20 (Lewine, 1980; Zigler & Levine, 1981). Nevertheless, the number of schizophrenic young people who show either active paranoia or a predilection to become paranoid is more than negligible, and clinicians need to be alert to paranoid features in the Rorschachs of the young. Rorschach indices identifying features of paranoid status may appear in either the structure of answers, the content of responses, the behavior in dealing with the inkblots, or in any two or all three of these Rorschach dimensions (Schafer, 1954, Chap. 9; Weiner, 1966, Chap 14).

Structural Variables The caution, suspiciousness, ideational orientation, and emotional control that characterize a paranoid way of dealing with the world translate directly into Rorschach signs of *unusual location choice, introversiveness,* and *constriction,* each of which increases the likelihood of paranoid status in a schizophrenic patient. In addition, the *Hypervigilance Index* (*HVI*) captures a variety of stylistic, affective, and interpersonal orientations that are associated with paranoid ways of viewing and dealing with the world.

Unusual Location Choice Unusual location choice includes the use of white space (*S*) and two kinds of *Dd* responses—rare, tiny details that are overelaborated into complex percepts and large arbitrary details that do violence to blot contours. Each of these three types of location choice is suited to paranoid individuals' exaggerated needs to examine their environment carefully and maintain autonomy in the face of perceived external threat.

More specifically, paranoid people are extremely sensitive to subtle nuances in their environment and prone to attach significance to inconsequential events. They are consequently more likely than nonparanoid schizophrenics to focus their attention on tiny details, and they are especially more likely to formulate elaborate, overgeneralized impressions of such *Dd*. Paranoid people distrust the obvious, hesitate to take anything at its face value, and tend to seek the "true" or "hidden" meanings in their experience. Hence, they are likely to ignore the contours of the large common details and instead to carve out their own boundaries for their percepts. Finally, in their struggle to protect their sense of separateness and integrity, paranoid people tend to exercise autonomy in part by rejecting the obvious figure-ground distinctions of the Rorschach blots in favor of attention to the white space. Told they are going to be shown inkblots and asked what these inkblots might be, they indicate instead what the white, noninkblot spaces might be.

Generally speaking, then, the more schizophrenic subjects focus their attention on *Dd* and *S* locations, the more likely they are to be paranoid. The major exception to this diagnostic guideline involves the relatively small percentage of paranoid persons who are primarily grandiose rather than suspicious. When taking the Rorschach, the performance of grandiose paranoid schizophrenics is radically different from that of suspicious paranoids. They are expansive where the suspicious paranoids hold back, blustery rather than constrained, and self-assured instead of worried about threats to their integrity.

Grandiose paranoids may consequently resemble manic subjects in many features of their Rorschach performance. Differential diagnosis between these two conditions is rarely of concern in work with children, because both are very infrequent in the early years. By adolescence, however, when neither is any longer unusual, distinguishing between them can be a difficult challenge. Further guidelines in making this distinction are discussed in Chapter 6.

Introversiveness   As already noted, a paranoid style of dealing with experience revolves around careful observations and orderly reflection on the significance of environmental events. Moreover, a major focus of paranoid individuals' attention is other people, whose actions they hope to anticipate and whose motives they are struggling to discern. This investment in ideational activity and attention to the motives of others typically combine to produce abundant *M* responses.

At the same time, the reluctance of paranoid individuals to reveal their thoughts and feelings leads them to shy away from spontaneous expression. Because they are concerned with keeping their affects and behavior under control, they tend to avoid giving color responses and to limit those they do give to *FC* determinants. These tendencies make an introversive *EB* an important clue to paranoid status. The more schizophrenic subjects emphasize human movement and the less affinity they show for chromatic color, the more likely they are to have a paranoid disturbance. Occasionally, numerous other indicators will point to paranoid status when the *EB* is extratensive, and there may even be more *CF* and *C* than *FC* responses. This circumstance often identifies a paranoid defensive style that is crumbling, and the subject should be considered at serious risk for personality disintegration and disturbing and potentially dangerous expressions of inadequately modulated emotions and actions.

Constriction   The characteristic guardedness of paranoid individuals results in their producing Rorschach protocols that are constricted in various ways. This guardedness may at times obscure schizophrenic impairments of perceptual accuracy, because some paranoid schizophrenics cautiously avoid reporting any impression that does not precisely fit the form characteristics of the blots. Then, especially in relatively brief records, form level may become unusually high, rather than low, and *P* responses may become numerous. Given other clear indices of schizophrenia, constriction as reflected in near-perfect form level and frequent *P* responses suggests paranoid status.

Among other indications of constriction having similar implications are reduced *R*, high Lambda, and an unusual frequency of usual detail and animal responses. Depending on how rigidly overcontrolled paranoid people are, they may even refrain from revealing themselves through *M* responses. For these subjects, as well as for other highly guarded subjects, the Rorschach data may become so limited as to preclude any firm differential diagnostic conclusions.

The Hypervigilance Index (HVI)   The criteria for HVI capture many features of a paranoid approach to the world. These include a distant interpersonal style in which there is little expectation of or reaching out for warm, trusting, and mutually supportive relationships with others (zero *T*); thorough scanning of the environment, close attention to relationships among events, and careful deliberation in coming to conclusions (high frequencies of *Z* and *Zd*); an unusual degree of underlying anger and resentment (many *S*); a great deal of attention to what other people are like or are doing (numerous human contents), much of it involving imagined rather than real figures (many parenthesized human and animal contents) and much of it involving a suspicious and hypercritical stance (elevation in human and animal details); and concerns about needing to shield oneself against danger (protective kinds of clothing) and/or being unable to discern exactly what other people are like or are up to (concealing kinds of clothing).

Criteria for the Hypervigilance Index (HVI)　　The first condition (zero T) and at least four of the remaining seven criteria must be true:

1. $FT + TF + T = 0$.
2. $Zf > 12$.
3. $Zd > 3.5$.
4. $S > 3$.
5. $H + (H) + Hd + (Hd) > 6$.
6. $(H) + (A) + (Hd) + (Ad) > 3$.
7. $H + A : Hd + Ad < 4:1$.
8. $Cg > 3$.

A positive finding for HVI is associated with an unusually alert, cautious, and suspicious approach to the world in general and constant concern about being exploited or victimized by other people in particular. Although this index does not provide sufficient basis by itself for inferring paranoia, people with a positive HVI typically display at least some paranoid personality features. When HVI is elevated in a subject who appears schizophrenic, there is good reason to believe that a paranoid form of schizophrenia is either present or emerging.

Content Themes　　Paranoid proclivities to see the world as a hostile and dangerous place usually contribute to two dramatic and closely related content themes. One of these themes involves response embellishments that suggest experienced external threat, and the other consists of responses that identify need for protection.

Experienced External Threat　　Paranoid people are prone to perceive aggressive intent in the actions of others, to consider themselves under the scrutiny of potential accusers and adversaries, and to anticipate being the helpless victim of various animate and inanimate forces that lie in wait for them. Each of these attitudes has distinctive manifestations in fantasy productions that point to paranoid tendencies.

In relation to perception of aggressive intent, paranoid people are likely to emphasize aggressive interactions between the animal and human figures they perceive on the Rorschach ("arguing," "fighting," "killing each other," "hate one another," and most other responses that warrant an AG score). In addition, they often display uneasy concern at not being privy to the mysterious and unfathomable motives of others, as in human percepts described as "cloaked," "hidden," or "covered up" and in such elaborations as "I can't make out what they're doing" or "It's not clear what kind of a person it is."

Subjects who are sensitive to being observed by potential malefactors often focus attention on scrutinizing organs and activities and on the trappings of accusation and indictment. Thus paranoid people are likely to stress eyes, ears, and faces in their percepts; to see figures as "looking," "peeping," "staring," and "spying"; and to report such uncommon images as "fingerprint," "footprint," "lie detector machine," and "wiretapping device" and such unique persons as "detective," "FBI man," and "judge." Responses such as these are particularly significant for paranoid concerns when they occur in dramatic or personalized combinations, such as "a pair of eyes peering out at me from behind a bush."

Fear of victimization is suggested on the Rorschach by the attribution of dangerous qualities to images ("evil man," "poisonous insect," "cloud of doom"); by perception of victimizing agents ("trap," "snare," "executioner," "jailer"); and by direct impressions of submission to overpowering forces ("a guy being beat up by two other guys"; "a squashed animal that's been run over by a car," "a tree being uprooted by the wind"). Victimization responses, like those involving scrutiny, most clearly indicate paranoid ideation when they are personalized, as in "a devil's face looking right at me," "a man with a gun coming toward me," or "a terrific windstorm blowing down my house."

Need for Protection   The needs of paranoid people to protect themselves against attack from the environment are also reflected in distinctive fantasy content. Relatively constricted paranoids erect barriers between themselves and others, and they are consequently likely to emphasize concealment, armor, masks, hard-shelled animals, and other categories of the Barrier score as defined many years ago by Fisher and Cleveland (1958). Those who tend toward grandiosity protect themselves by an inflated sense of competence and infallibility and correspondingly emphasize images of status ("emblem," "coat of arms"), power ("king," "crown," "idol"), and excellence of one kind or another (e.g., references to great historical, religious, or mythical figures).

Paranoid people also protect their sense of security and worth by depreciating the potency and significance of external objects and events. Hence, they may focus their imagery on depreciated as well as powerful figures, particularly in the form of human percepts that are dehumanized or otherwise belittled in their capacity to influence, injure, or oppose the perceiver. Significant in this regard are such (*H*) responses as, "A man raising a sword, but he's only a statue," and such (*Hd*) responses as, "A powerful looking guy who doesn't have any arms to do anything with." Also, descriptions such as "small," "weak," "stupid," "silly," and "deformed" tend to convey this characteristic, especially when it seems clear that these limitations are attributions to others and not projections of the subject's self-image. Such fantasies help subjects feel safe by establishing their superiority to other people, who can then be viewed as incapable of mounting any serious threat against them.

Behavioral Manifestations   The manner in which schizophrenic subjects approach and comment about the Rorschach and the test situation often provides clues that help to identify the unwarranted guardedness and suspicion that are common to the paranoid status. Behavioral manifestations of this type during a Rorschach examination usually consist of some combination of (a) *externalization of blame,* (b) *situational distrust,* and (c) *reluctance to make a commitment.* Although none of these behaviors is diagnostic of paranoid or unique to paranoid persons, their presence together with evidence of schizophrenia suggests a paranoid form of the disorder.

Externalization of Blame   Paranoid subjects tend to attribute any difficulty they are having in formulating responses to the nature of the examination. Externalizing comments are sometimes addressed to the stimuli ("These cards aren't made very well"), sometimes to the administration ("If you'd ask better questions, I could give better answers"), sometimes to the examiner ("I don't think you're doing a good job of giving these to me"), and sometimes to being examined ("I can't see how taking tests will serve any purpose"). Whatever direction they take, these comments allow subjects to justify any difficulties they are having in meeting the requirements of the testing situation.

Paranoid subjects may also feel a need to minimize the importance or accuracy of any unfavorable conclusions they fear the examiner might draw from their responses. Then they may criticize the examiner and the test: "I've heard these inkblots aren't any good for anything," or "Aren't there laws against people being tested this way?" or "Are you qualified to do this kind of work?" Like other efforts to protect themselves, these comments by paranoid individuals prepare for the blame to be placed elsewhere for any "bad" impressions they might convey.

Situational Distrust   Suspicious subjects are likely to express considerable concern about the nature, purpose, and implications of being tested and to show unusual interest in the examiner's behavior during the Rorschach administration. They may ask repetitively why the testing is needed, what it will reveal, how the results will be evaluated, and who will be told about them. They may ask why everything they say is being written down and why the examiner is asking them certain questions. They may inquire why the cards are made as they are, by whom and where they are made, and to what kinds of persons they are shown. They may also maintain the fiction that the blots have some specific meaning that is hidden from or intended to deceive them, and they may constantly ask, "What is it really supposed to be?" Taken singly, such behaviors are not necessarily pathological; however, their persistence in the face of reasonable, straightforward answers identifies the suspiciousness found in paranoid individuals.

Reluctance to Make a Commitment   "Better safe than sorry" is an overriding theme in the lives of paranoid people. On the Rorschach, correspondingly, such people protect themselves by familiarizing themselves as much as possible with the nature of the situation before responding to it. In addition to many questions about the nature and purpose of the test, they read the back of the cards, complain about not getting more detailed instructions, and continually ask for confirmation of the instructions they have received: "Just tell you what it looks like, that's what I'm supposed to do?" "Can I turn them?" "You want just the whole thing, or some of the parts too?" Such comments are often given by nonschizophrenic subjects with strong needs for support and direction from others. In the context of a schizophrenic disorder, their repetition points to paranoid caution.

SOME REFERENCE DATA

The data concerning Rorschach variables presented in Table 36 represents a composite of findings for 110 first admission adolescents, ages 12 to 17, who were ultimately diagnosed as schizophrenic using DSM-III-R criteria. The mean age for the group is 14.8 with a median and mode of 15. As a group, these subjects have completed an average of 9.36 years of education, with a median of 9 years and a mode of 10 years.

Table 37 provides some frequency data concerning critical variables, ratios, and percentages for the same group.

CASE 4—IMMATURITY AND UNDERACHIEVEMENT

The case selected for inclusion here illustrates how the onset of schizophrenia among children is often neglected or misunderstood. It is a fairly clear schizophrenic record, and at least in part, the challenge is to reconcile the test findings with information reported from teachers and from the subject's mother.

This is a 12-year 4-month-old female who is currently in the sixth grade. She has been referred for two reasons. First, she has consistently achieved less adequately than her

Table 36. Descriptive Statistics for 110 First Admission Adolescents Diagnosed as Schizophrenic from DSM-III-R Criteria

Variable	Mean	SD	Min	Max	Freq	Median	Mode	SK	KU
R	20.84	4.86	14.00	29.00	110	20.00	20.00	0.18	−1.37
W	6.12	3.06	1.00	12.00	110	6.00	6.00	0.58	−0.04
D	9.44	3.03	2.00	13.00	110	10.00	10.00	−1.57	1.23
Dd	5.28	[4.14]	0.00	12.00	102	3.00	3.00	0.37	−1.58
S	2.59	[1.44]	0.00	5.00	102	3.00	2.00	−0.01	−0.94
DQ+	5.23	2.36	1.00	8.00	110	6.00	6.00	−0.78	−0.63
DQo	12.90	3.02	6.00	18.00	110	14.00	14.00	−1.05	0.18
DQv	1.61	[1.17]	0.00	4.00	101	1.00	1.00	1.01	−0.08
DQv/+	1.10	[1.45]	0.00	4.00	48	0.00	0.00	0.97	−0.44
FQx+	0.01	0.10	0.00	1.00	1	0.00	0.00	10.48	110.00
FQxo	7.57	2.52	1.00	11.00	110	8.00	9.00	−1.51	1.16
FQxu	5.21	2.41	0.00	9.00	109	6.00	7.00	−0.27	−1.03
FQx−	7.86	1.83	4.00	11.00	110	8.00	9.00	−0.20	−1.10
FQxNone	0.18	[0.39]	0.00	1.00	20	0.00	0.00	1.67	0.81
MQ+	0.00	0.00	0.00	0.00	0	0.00	0.00	—	—
MQo	1.56	1.37	0.00	5.00	77	1.00	3.00	0.26	−1.39
MQu	1.09	1.10	0.00	3.00	64	1.00	0.00	0.48	−1.17
MQ−	1.92	[1.79]	0.00	6.00	91	1.00	1.00	1.24	0.57
MQNone	0.18	[0.39]	0.00	1.00	20	0.00	0.00	1.67	0.81
SQual−	2.16	[1.36]	0.00	4.00	102	2.00	1.00	0.27	−1.30
M	4.75	2.13	1.00	8.00	110	5.00	5.00	−0.40	−0.33
FM	1.34	0.97	0.00	5.00	94	1.00	1.00	1.24	2.44
m	2.11	2.24	0.00	5.00	68	1.00	0.00	0.42	−1.71
FC	1.25	1.11	0.00	4.00	84	1.00	1.00	1.05	0.52
CF	1.06	0.98	0.00	5.00	84	1.00	1.00	1.72	3.73
C	0.48	[0.75]	0.00	2.00	36	0.00	0.00	1.18	−0.17
Cn	0.00	[0.00]	0.00	0.00	0	0.00	0.00	—	—
Sum Color	3.17	1.77	0.00	9.00	108	3.00	2.50	0.95	1.20
WSumC	3.41	1.64	0.00	7.50	108	2.50	2.00	0.57	−0.63
Sum C'	1.15	[1.09]	0.00	5.00	66	1.00	0.00	0.48	−0.26
Sum T	0.52	[0.55]	0.00	2.00	54	0.00	0.00	0.42	−0.90
Sum V	0.07	[0.68]	0.00	1.00	4	0.00	0.00	2.16	5.19
Sum Y	1.32	[0.95]	0.00	5.00	84	1.00	2.00	0.37	1.02
Sum Shading	2.98	1.78	0.00	7.00	93	3.00	3.00	−0.30	−0.79
Fr + rF	0.40	[0.49]	0.00	1.00	31	0.00	0.00	0.41	−1.99
FD	0.00	[0.00]	0.00	0.00	0	0.00	0.00	—	—
F	9.43	3.46	3.00	15.00	110	10.00	5.00	−0.04	−1.23
(2)	7.89	1.50	5.00	11.00	110	7.00	7.00	1.10	0.11
3r + (2)/R	0.45	0.11	0.30	0.73	110	0.41	0.35	1.24	0.28
Lambda	1.31	1.97	0.27	13.00	110	0.69	0.45	4.52	23.00
FM + m	3.45	2.76	0.00	8.00	95	2.00	7.00	0.22	−1.68
EA	7.16	2.54	1.00	12.50	110	8.00	8.00	−0.82	−0.04
es	6.43	4.04	0.00	15.00	105	4.00	4.00	0.23	−1.43
D Score	0.24	0.93	−2.00	3.00	62	0.00	0.00	0.35	−0.05
AdjD	0.74	0.85	−2.00	3.00	57	1.00	0.00	0.51	−0.98
a (active)	3.56	2.15	0.00	8.00	93	4.00	4.00	−0.10	−0.49
p (passive)	4.64	3.03	1.00	10.00	110	3.00	8.00	0.28	−1.68
Ma	2.76	1.88	0.00	6.00	84	3.00	3.00	0.04	−0.44
Mp	1.99	0.61	1.00	4.00	110	2.00	2.00	0.49	1.40
Intellect	4.54	4.98	0.00	13.00	90	1.00	1.00	0.65	−1.34
Zf	9.61	3.24	3.00	14.00	110	10.00	10.00	−0.56	−0.68
Zd	3.52	3.21	−3.50	8.50	109	4.00	4.00	−0.76	−0.00
Blends	3.92	1.82	0.00	7.00	94	3.00	3.00	0.00	−0.87
Blends/R	0.13	0.07	0.00	0.28	94	0.14	0.10	−0.56	−0.16
Col-Shd Blends	0.27	[0.38]	0.00	2.00	29	0.00	0.00	1.75	1.10
Afr	0.56	0.09	0.27	0.73	110	0.56	0.67	−0.27	−0.63

Table 36. **(Continued)**

Variable	Mean	SD	Min	Max	Freq	Median	Mode	SK	KU
Populars	3.91	1.16	2.00	6.00	110	4.00	3.00	0.64	−0.66
X+%	0.36	0.12	0.07	0.57	110	0.36	0.33	−0.77	0.53
F+%	0.43	0.17	0.00	0.75	104	0.50	0.50	−0.84	0.21
X−%	0.39	0.13	0.25	0.71	110	0.36	0.30	1.48	1.06
Xu%	0.24	0.08	0.00	0.35	109	0.25	0.30	−1.15	0.66
S−%	0.30	[0.22]	0.00	0.80	102	0.22	0.22	0.85	−0.26
Isolate/R	0.21	0.19	0.00	0.54	102	0.10	0.06	0.59	−1.27
H	1.67	1.34	0.00	4.00	72	2.00	3.00	−0.21	−1.63
(H)	1.08	0.86	0.00	2.00	74	1.00	2.00	−0.15	−1.63
HD	2.96	1.47	0.00	6.00	109	3.00	2.00	0.43	−0.69
(Hd)	0.76	0.72	0.00	2.00	66	1.00	1.00	0.38	−0.97
Hx	0.00	[0.00]	0.00	0.00	0	0.00	0.00	—	—
H + (H) + Hd + (Hd)	6.47	2.89	0.00	11.00	109	7.00	8.00	−0.57	−0.29
A	4.91	2.34	1.00	9.00	110	4.00	6.00	0.29	−1.01
(A)	2.61	[3.66]	0.00	11.00	70	2.00	0.00	1.66	1.25
Ad	1.30	[1.15]	0.00	3.00	78	1.00	1.00	0.44	−1.25
(Ad)	0.00	[0.00]	0.00	0.00	0	0.00	0.00	—	—
An	0.21	[0.41]	0.00	1.00	23	0.00	0.00	1.45	0.11
Art	1.35	1.73	0.00	4.00	44	0.00	0.00	0.60	−1.51
Ay	0.79	[0.41]	0.00	1.00	87	1.00	1.00	−1.45	0.11
Bl	0.22	[0.42]	0.00	1.00	24	0.00	0.00	1.38	−0.09
Bt	1.81	0.91	0.00	3.00	102	2.00	2.00	−0.19	−0.88
Cg	1.37	1.36	0.00	4.00	73	1.00	0.00	0.80	−0.41
Cl	0.14	[0.35]	0.00	1.00	15	0.00	0.00	2.14	2.67
Ex	0.00	[0.00]	0.00	0.00	0	0.00	0.00	—	—
Fi	0.00	[0.00]	0.00	0.00	0	0.00	0.00	—	—
Food	0.15	[0.35]	0.00	1.00	16	0.00	0.00	2.03	2.20
Ge	0.00	[0.00]	0.00	0.00	0	0.00	0.00	—	—
Hh	0.40	0.49	0.00	1.00	44	0.00	0.00	0.41	−1.86
Ls	0.00	0.00	0.00	0.00	0	0.00	0.00	—	—
Na	1.55	[1.94]	0.00	4.00	45	0.00	0.00	0.47	−1.79
Sc	1.03	[0.86]	0.00	2.00	71	1.00	2.00	−0.05	−1.66
Sx	0.19	[0.40]	0.00	1.00	21	0.00	0.00	1.59	0.55
Xy	0.00	[0.00]	0.00	0.00	0	0.00	0.00	—	—
Idiographic	1.70	1.73	0.00	4.00	67	1.00	0.00	0.36	−1.67
DV	0.74	[0.55]	0.00	2.00	75	1.00	1.00	−0.03	−0.40
INCOM	0.21	[0.45]	0.00	2.00	21	0.00	0.00	2.04	3.51
DR	0.93	[0.94]	0.00	3.00	64	1.00	0.00	0.61	−0.72
FABCOM	0.05	[0.21]	0.00	1.00	5	0.00	0.00	4.42	17.90
DV2	0.26	[0.44]	0.00	1.00	29	0.00	0.00	1.08	−0.83
INC2	0.58	[0.50]	0.00	1.00	64	1.00	1.00	−0.33	−1.92
DR2	0.97	[0.98]	0.00	3.00	73	1.00	1.00	1.06	0.27
FAB2	0.65	[0.83]	0.00	3.00	47	0.00	0.00	0.84	−0.72
ALOG	0.65	[0.50]	0.00	2.00	70	1.00	1.00	−0.39	−1.31
CONTAM	0.00	0.00	0.00	0.00	0	0.00	0.00	—	—
Sum 6 Sp Sc	5.03	1.58	2.00	9.00	110	5.00	5.00	0.00	−0.75
Lvl 2 Sp Sc	2.46	[0.50]	2.00	3.00	110	2.00	2.00	0.14	−2.01
WSum6	20.55	4.37	11.00	30.00	110	22.00	24.00	−0.58	−0.43
AB	1.20	[1.59]	0.00	4.00	44	0.00	0.00	0.76	−1.14
AG	1.04	2.17	0.00	6.00	25	0.00	0.00	1.80	1.43
CFB	0.00	0.00	0.00	0.00	0	0.00	0.00	—	—
COP	0.55	0.87	0.00	3.00	49	0.00	0.00	1.87	1.80
CP	0.00	[0.00]	0.00	0.00	0	0.00	0.00	—	—
MOR	1.13	[0.97]	0.00	4.00	71	1.00	2.00	0.17	−0.95
PER	1.03	0.96	0.00	2.00	61	1.00	2.00	−0.05	−1.94
PSV	1.52	[3.07]	0.00	9.00	38	0.00	0.00	1.89	1.78

Table 37. Frequency Data for 110 First Admission Adolescents Diagnosed as Schizophrenic by DSM-III-R Criteria

EB STYLE			FORM QUALITY DEVIATIONS		
Introversive	57	52%	X + % > .89	0	0%
Super-Introversive	34	31%	X + % < .70	110	100%
Ambitent	32	29%	X + % < .61	110	100%
Extratensive	21	19%	X + % < .50	99	90%
Super-Extratensive	9	8%	F + % < .70	109	99%
			Xu% > .20	81	74%
EA - es DIFFERENCES: D-SCORES			X − % > .15	110	100%
D Score > 0	39	35%	X − % > .20	110	100%
D Score = 0	48	44%	X − % > .30	80	73%
D Score < 0	23	21%			
D Score < − 1	11	10%	FC:CF + C RATIO		
			FC > (CF + C) + 2	9	8%
Adj D Score > 0	36	33%	FC > (CF + C) + 1	12	11%
Adj D Score = 0	63	57%	(CF + C) > FC + 1	24	22%
Adj D Score < 0	11	10%	(CF + C) > FC + 2	3	3%
Adj D Score < −1	2	2%			
			S-Constellation Positive	0	0%
Zd > + 30 (Overincorp)	73	66%	HVI Positive	31	28%
Zd < − 30 (Underincorp)	10	9%	OBS Positive	0	0%

SCZI = 6	7	6%	DEPI = 7	0	0%	CDI = 5	0	0%
SCZI = 5	64	53%	DEPI = 6	1	1%	CDI = 4	32	29%
SCZI = 4	28	25%	DEPI = 5	12	11%			

MISCELLANEOUS VARIABLES

Lambda > .99	40	36%	(2AB + Art + Ay) > 5	34	31%
Dd > 3	44	40%	Populars < 4	51	46%
DQv + DQv/ + > 2	42	38%	Populars > 7	0	0%
S > 2	56	51%	COP = 0	91	83%
Sum T = 0	56	51%	COP > 2	4	4%
Sum T > 1	3	3%	AG = 0	55	50%
3r + (2)/R < .33	1	1%	AG > 2	28	25%
3r + (2)/R > .44	29	26%	MOR > 2	14	13%
Fr + rF > 0	31	28%	Level 2 Sp. Sc. > 0	110	100%
PureC > 0	36	33%	Sum 6 Sp. Sc. > 6	32	29%
PureC > 1	17	15%	Pure H < 2	44	40%
Afr < .40	1	1%	Pure H = 0	38	35%
Afr < .50	23	21%	p > a + 1	51	46%
(FM + m) < Sum Shading	37	34%	Mp > Ma	27	25%

peers in academic work in the fourth and fifth grades. She has not failed in any subjects but her work is marginal, and it seems clear that she is not a good reader. During the fifth grade, following a conference with her mother, an intelligence test (WISC-R) was administered by a school psychology trainee, yielding a Verbal IQ of 108, Performance IQ of 113, and a Full-Scale IQ of 110. The results were surprising to her teachers, who had suspected that she might be intellectually limited. Several additional tests were administered thereafter on the assumption that she might have an attention-deficit disorder. The results were mixed. The second reason for the referral concerns information provided by her sixth-grade teacher, who has asked for a second evaluation based on her observations that the subject seems very immature for her age, sometimes seems detached from the subject matter being studied, and often appears to be completely uninvolved with classroom activities. The sixth-grade teacher notes that, at times, the subject is verbally abusive to other students and that, generally, she is shunned by her peers.

She is the only child from a marriage that lasted less than 2 years, and her custody has been awarded to her mother, who is currently age 30. The mother states that she became pregnant during her last year of high school and married the father, who was also 18 at the time, shortly after her high school graduation. She reports that the marriage was stormy from the beginning. The father had a significant drug history and, after abandoning her and their daughter 15 months into the marriage, he "disappeared" and two years later was caught dispensing drugs; he was sentenced to a minimum of 15 years in prison. She has had no contact with him since their separation. During the subject's preschool years, the mother was on public assistance and lived "off and on" with her parents. When the subject was age 5, the mother, after receiving special training, obtained regular employment in a manufacturing firm and has continued in that employment. Her salary is supplemented by a public assistance stipend for dependent children. She and her daughter live in a small, three-room, apartment. The subject attends a day-care unit near her school after school hours until her mother collects her at about 5:30 P.M. The mother is quite firm in stating that she and her daughter are close and do many things together, especially on weekends. She cannot account for her daughter's marginal academic performance. She reports that there is no psychiatric history in her immediate family.

The subject confirms that she and her mother are close, and reports that she often visits her maternal grandparents on weekends. She says that she enjoys learning to sew and looks forward to completing a tablecloth that she and her grandmother have been making. She reports that school is boring and that she wishes that she had a different teacher because ". . . she makes us do too much work." She says that she likes her classmates and has several friends. She acknowledges that her academic performance has not been "very good" but says that the work is very hard.

Her fifth- and sixth-grade teachers indicate that she is rather isolated from her classmates and note that most do not select her when group activities are involved. Her sixth-grade teacher reports that her homework during the first two months of school has been badly prepared and often is difficult to grade because it is so "sloppy" (the mother reports that she assists with her daughter homework "almost every night"). The sixth-grade teacher admits that the subject is not a major disruptive influence, but she believes something is wrong because the subject appears to be so detached at times, or responds to questions in inappropriate ways that cause other children to "giggle." She states, "I get the impression that she is not with the rest of the class a lot of the time." She believes that the subject "might fare better" in a class for slow learners or possibly in a class for emotionally disturbed youngsters; "I think she may be depressed or something and she just cannot keep up with the other children."

A school counselor has interviewed the subject twice and finds no evidence of emotional problems, but does say that she seems less mature than most 12-year-olds that she has seen. The counselor reports that the mother is obviously irritated because of the attention focused on her daughter and has requested that she be transferred to another class, "with a more understanding teacher."

Case 4. A 12-Year-Old Female

Card		Response	Inquiry	Scoring
I	1.	It ll a little person with wings a little lady with 2 heads.	E: (Rpts S's resp) S: Her feet, dress, wings, hands, 2 little heads, kinda rem me of an angel.	W+ Fo (H),Cg 4.0 INC
	v2.	A hummingbird.	E: (Rpts S's resp) S: The wings & body & the beak is open gettg ready to eat this bell shaped thing, the other bird her is the same.	W+ FMpu 2 A,Id 4.0
	v3.	Oh, I c one more thing . . . a mt peak & a baby's head sticking up & this is a guy singg.	E: (Rpts S's resp) S: Arms, legs, he's hold-g onto ths peak & he's pull-g the mtn up, he's got one leg up here. E: U mentioned a baby's head? S: It's here, mayb its watching.	Dd+ Ma−p− H,Hd,Ls 4.0 FAB2
II	<4.	A rabbit.	E: (Rpts S's resp) S: Ears, nose & this is his tail, he has 2 tails, his body is here.	Do Fo A INC
	5.	I c a airplane, a jet really.	E: (Rpts S's resp) S: Fire comg out of the back, thes r the wings & this is the point. E: What makes that ll fire? S: The redness.	DS + ma.CFo Sc,Fi 4.5
III	6.	(laughs) I c a man.	E: (Rpts S's resp) S: Head, neck, bending over, he has fancy shoes on & he has his hands over this part lik making this heart here beat. E: I'm not sur about the heart S: Rite here (points to Dd31), it ll a heart & he's makg it beat.	Dd + Mp− H,An,Cg P 3.0 FAB2
	v7.	A bf too.	E: (Rpts S's resp) S: Its little wings & little body.	Do Fo A
IV	8.	A giant lookg thru his legs.	E: (Rpts S's resp) S: Boots here, he's bendg over & lookg thru his legs, his head is down here (D1).	W + Mp.FDu (H),Cg P 4.0
	>9.	I c a puppy too.	E: (Rpts S's resp) S: Head here & the tail, he's sitting on a weighing scale & barking. E: A weighing scale? S: It looks lik one to me, he just weighed himself & now he's barkg about it.	Dd + Ma− A,Sc 4.0 INC

167

Case 4. (Continued)

Card	Response		Inquiry	Scoring
V	10. It ll a big, big bat.	E:	(Rpts S's resp)	Wo Fo A P 1.0
		S:	Feet, wings & the head with big ears.	
		E:	U said a big, big bat?	
		S:	He's got big wings & big ears.	
VI	>11. Ah ha, I found me a boat.	E:	(Rpts S's resp)	W + ma.Fro Sc,Na 2.5 DV
		S:	Ths blows steam (Dd24), a wave is crashing in front of the boat, lik a fishg boat, here's the water & the reflectn dwn here & here's the pipe that blows smoke, but smoke is not comg out of it now.	
VII	12. 2 girls.	E:	(Rpts S's resp)	Do Mpo 2 H P
		S:	The nose & mouth & the ponytail is stickg up cuz they just jumped up & thyr coming down now.	
VIII	13. I c a monster.	E:	(Rpts S's resp)	Wo F− (H) 4.5
		S:	His hands, 2 big legs, shoulders & a head.	
	14. & I c a face.	E:	(Rpts S's resp)	D + Mp− 2 Hd,Bt 3.0 FAB2,INC
		S:	2 eyes, it has no mouth or nose its holdg ths 2 sticks with its ears here, its a man I thk.	
IX	15. A person riding a horse.	E:	(Rpts S's resp)	Dd+ Mp.FMa− H,A,Cg P 2.5
		S:	It ll a big lady riding a teeny weeny horse, her bonnet, mouth, her hands r holdg the reins, she's wearg a dress & sittg on the horse, his head is here & the 4 legs dwn here moving really fast.	
	v16. A bell hanging from a rope.	E:	(Rpts S's resp)	D+ mp.FCu Sc 2.5
		S:	A brown rope hooked onto the bell, here's the big part & gets skinny lik a bell, here's the top of it.	
X	17. It ll all pecs, bugs, I c 2 inchworms, spiders, 2 bad guys arguing.	E:	(Rpts S's resp)	D + Ma.FCo 2 A P 4.5 DV,FAB,AG
		S:	Here I saw bugs arguing, green inchworms here, the green curly tails & thes ll the spiders.	

168

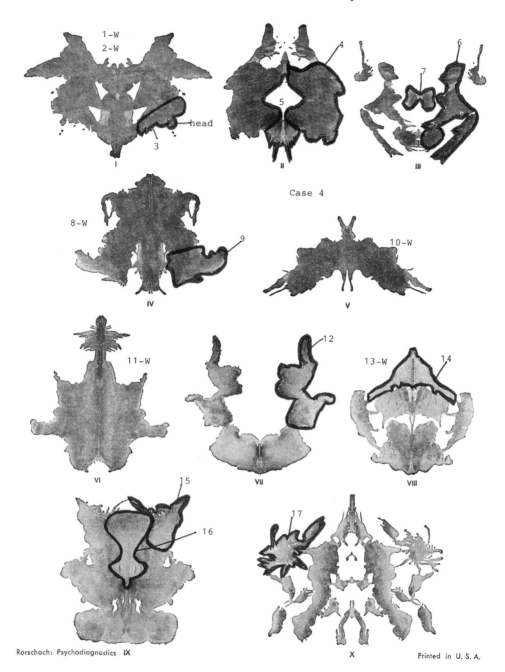

Case 4

Rorschach: Psychodiagnostics IX   Printed in U. S. A.

Case 4

Case 4   **Sequence of Scores**

Card	No	Loc	#	Determinant(s)	(2)	Content(s)	Pop	Z	Special Scores
I	1	W+	1	Fo		(H),Cg		4.0	INC
	2	W+	1	FMpu	2	A,Id		4.0	
	3	Dd+	99	Ma-p-		H,Hd,Ls		4.0	FAB2
II	4	Do	1	Fo		A			INC
	5	DS+	5	ma.CFo		Sc,Fi		4.5	
III	6	Dd+	31	Mp-		H,An,Cg	P	3.0	FAB2
	7	Do	3	Fo		A			
IV	8	W+	1	Mp.FDu		(H),Cg	P	4.0	
	9	Dd+	99	Ma-		A,Sc		4.0	INC
V	10	Wo	1	Fo		A	P	1.0	
VI	11	W+	1	ma.Fro		Sc,Na		2.5	DV
VII	12	Do	2	Mpo	2	H	P		
VIII	13	Wo	1	F-		(H)		4.5	
	14	D+	4	Mp-	2	Hd,Bt		3.0	FAB2,INC
IX	15	D+	3	Mp.FMa-		H,A,Cg	P	2.5	
	16	D+	8	mp.FCu		Sc		2.5	
X	17	D+	1	Ma.FCo	2	A	P	4.5	DV,FAB,AG

Copyright © 1976, 1985, 1990 by John E. Exner, Jr.

Case 4   **Structural Summary**

Location	Determinants	Contents	S-Constellation
Features	Blends Single		. . FV+VF+V+FD>2

Location Features	Determinants	Contents	S-Constellation
	Blends Single	H = 4, 0	. . Col−Shd Bl>0
Zf = 14	m.CF M = 5	(H) = 3, 0	. . Ego<.31,>.44
ZSum = 48.0	M.FD FM = 1	Hd = 1, 1	. . MOR > 3
ZEst = 45.5	m.Fr m = 0	(Hd) = 0, 0	. . Zd > +− 3.5
	M.FM FC = 0	Hx = 0, 0	. . es > EA
W = 6	m.FC CF = 0	A = 6, 1	. . CF+C > FC
(Wv = 0)	M.FC C = 0	(A) = 0, 0	. . X+% < .70
D = 8	Cn = 0	Ad = 0, 0	. . S > 3
Dd = 3	FC' = 0	(Ad) = 0, 0	. . P < 3 or > 8
S = 1	C'F = 0	An = 0, 1	. . Pure H < 2
	C' = 0	Art = 0, 0	. . R < 17
DQ	FT = 0	Ay = 0, 0	x . . . . . TOTAL

DQ

	(FQ−)		FT = 0	Ay = 0, 0
+ = 12	(5)		TF = 0	Bl = 0, 0
o = 5	(1)		T = 0	Bt = 0, 1
v/+ = 0	(0)		FV = 0	Cg = 0, 4
v = 0	(0)		VF = 0	Cl = 0, 0

Special Scorings

				Lv1	Lv2
			V = 0	Ex = 0, 0	DV = 2x1 0x2
			FY = 0	Fd = 0, 0	INC = 4x2 0x4
			YF = 0	Fi = 0, 1	DR = 0x3 0x6
			Y = 0	Ge = 0, 0	FAB = 1x4 3x7
Form Quality			Fr = 0	Hh = 0, 0	ALOG = 0x5
			rF = 0	Ls = 0, 1	CON = 0x7
	FQx FQf MQual SQx		FD = 0	Na = 0, 1	SUM6 = 10
+ = 0 0 0 0			F = 5	Sc = 3, 1	WSUM6 = 35
o = 8 4 2 1				Sx = 0, 0	AB = 0 CP = 0
u = 3 0 1 0				Xy = 0, 0	AG = 1 MOR = 0
− = 6 1 5 0				Id = 0, 1	CFB = 0 PER = 0
none = 0 — 0 0			(2) = 4		COP = 0 PSV = 0

Case 4   **Ratios, Percentages, and Derivations**

R = 17   L = 0.42

			FC:CF+C = 2: 1	COP = 0	AG = 1
			Pure C = 0	Food = 0	
EB = 8: 2.0	EA = 10.0	EBPer = 4.0	Afr = 0.42	Isolate/R = 0.24	
eb = 5: 0	es = 6	D = +1	S = 1	H:(H)Hd(Hd) = 4:5	
	Adj es = 3	Adj D = +2	Blends:R = 6:17	(HHd):(AAd) = 3:0	
			CP = 0	H+A:Hd+Ad = 14:2	
FM = 2 : C' = 0 T = 0					
m = 3 : V = 0 Y = 0					
		P = 6	Zf = 14	3r+(2)/R = 0.41	
a:p = 6: 8	Sum6 = 10	X+% = 0.47	Zd = +2.5	Fr+rF = 1	
Ma:Mp = 3: 6	Lv2 = 3	F+% = 0.80	W:D:Dd = 6: 8: 3	FD = 1	
2AB+Art+Ay=0	WSum6 = 35	X−% = 0.35	W:M = 6: 7	An+Xy = 1	
M − = 5	Mnone = 0	S−% = 0.00	DQ+ = 12	MOR = 0	
		Xu% = 0.18	DQv = 0		

SCZI = 6*   DEPI = 2   CDI = 3   S-CON = N/A   HVI = No   OBS = No

INTERPRETIVE ROUTINE FOR CASE 4

The first positive Key variable is the SCZI, which has a value of 6. Thus, the interpretive search routine will be:

$$\text{IDEATION} \to \text{MEDIATION} \to \text{PROCESSING} \to \text{CONTROLS} \to$$
$$\text{AFFECT} \to \text{SELF-PERCEPTION} \to \text{INTERPERSONAL PERCEPTION}$$

The fact that the SCZI has a value of 6 strongly suggests that a schizophrenic condition may be present, even though no major positive symptoms (delusions, hallucinations) seem to be present. In fact, like many young children, this child presents evidence of schizophrenia only through negative symptoms such as affective and intellectual detachment, social isolation and rejection by peers, and an academic performance that is inconsistent with her measured level of intelligence.

Ideation—Case 4   The data relevant to her ideational activities are shown in Table 38.

Table 38.   Ideation Data for Case 4

		M QUALITY	SPECIAL SCORES			
$EB = 8{:}2.0$	$EBPer = 4.0$					
$eb = 5{:}0$	$(FM = 2 \quad m = 3)$	$+ = 0$	DV	$= 2$	DV2	$= 0$
$a{:}p = 6{:}8$	$M^a{:}M^p = 3{:}6$	$o = 2$	INC	$= 4$	INC2	$= 0$
$2AB + Art + Ay = 0$		$u = 1$	DR	$= 0$	DR2	$= 0$
MOR $= 0$		$- = 4$	FAB	$= 1$	FAB2	$= 3$
			ALOG	$= 0$	SUM6	$= 10$
RESPONSES TO BE READ FOR QUALITY			CON	$= 0$	WSUM6	$= 35$
3, 6, 8, 9, 12, 14, 15, 17						

The *EB* (8:2.0) is introversive, and it is also a pervasive style (*EBPer* = 4.0). This is somewhat unusual for a 12. Although slightly more than 30% of nonpatient 12's are introversive, only 7% have a pervasive style. The presence of a pervasive introversive style indicates that she is markedly oriented to push her feelings aside and delay decisions and actions until she can think through their respective prospects. The introversive style poses no hazard at this age *provided that thinking usually is clear and logical;* however, her lack of flexibility in its applications can handicap her development to some extent. There is no doubt that problem-solving situations will arise in her young life for which a trial-and-error approach will prove much more useful, but the major handicap probably is that she fails to explore her feelings as they may be useful in decision making. Thus, not only is there an increase in the likelihood of decision errors, but she also misses opportunities to learn more about her feelings and their importance in her thinking.

The value for the left side *eb* (5) is not remarkable except that more than half of that value is composed of *m* answers. In other words, an increase in peripheral ideation is being created by situationally related stress. This is not necessarily unexpected in light of all the unwanted attention that she is receiving. The data for the *a:p* ratio (6:8) show that the values are not disparate. Although they will be important elsewhere, they offer no basis from which to suspect that her thinking and/or values are rigid or inflexible.

The M^a:M^p ratio (3:6) is a much different matter. It seems to indicate quite clearly that she invests herself in fantasy much of the time. This finding is incongruous with an introversive coping style and usually is highly detrimental to the effectiveness of that style, because reality is replaced with fantasy. As a result, nothing is accomplished. People, and especially children who have this Snow-white characteristic, tend to expect that others will resolve problems, and they proceed with their fantasy involvement until that happens. This seems to be particularly detrimental for this youngster. Although the Intellectualization Index is negative (0) and there are no MOR responses, she gives 10 Critical Special Scores, which is well beyond that expected for her age. They signify substantial cognitive slippage, a finding that is magnified by the WSum6 (35) and the fact that three of the Critical Special Scores are Level 2 Fabulized Combinations. They suggest that some of the slippage includes markedly disordered thinking, a hypothesis that seems supported when the characteristics of the responses containing those scores are examined.

The first occurs in her very first answer, ". . . a little lady with two heads." The second is the first of her Level 2 scores, ". . . a mountain peak and a baby's head sticking up and this is a guy singing . . . (Inquiry) . . . he's pulling the mountain up." The third is a rabbit with two tails. The fourth is the second Level 2 answer, ". . . a man (Inquiry) . . . his hands over this heart like making this heart here beat." The fifth and sixth also illustrate strained logic, but they are more like those given by young children, "a puppy (Inquiry) . . . he's just weighed himself and now he's barking about it" and ". . . here's the pipe that blows smoke . . ." The next two occur in Response 14 to Card VIII and include the third Level 2 score, ". . . a face (Inquiry) . . . it has no mouth or nose and it's holding these two sticks with its ears." It is a very unusual and bizarre answer. The last two appear in Response 17, which, although containing a strange word, is not necessarily unexpected for a young child, "It looks like all pecs, bugs . . . (Inquiry) . . . I saw bugs arguing . . ." The single Level 2 INCOM and the three Level 2 FABCOM responses are of greatest concern and appear to reflect very strained and/or strange logic.

In addition to the pathological findings illustrated by the Critical Special Scores, the record contains five $M-$ responses. Three of the five include the Level 2 FABCOM answers. The fourth, Response 9 to Card IV, involves the puppy who has weighed himself and is barking about it. The fifth, Response 15 to Card X, which involves a big lady (D3) riding a "teeny weeny" horse, might have been scored by some as a FABCOM, but regardless of whether a special score should have been coded, it is a serious distortion of the contours of the blot. In fact, at least three of the five $M-$ answers involve considerable blot distortion. Actually, in spite of the somewhat pathological content, the quality of her M answers is reasonably good and not at all inconsistent with her measured level of intelligence (a guy singing, a man bending over, a giant looking through his legs, a puppy who has weighed itself, two girls . . . they just jumped up and now they are coming down, a face holding two sticks with its ears, a person riding a horse, and bugs arguing).

Overall, this is apparently a reasonably bright and creative youngster. Unfortunately, her pervasive introversive style plus her marked tendency to rely greatly on fantasy to replace the harshness of reality does not serve her well. She disregards reality far too much and does not use her ideational style in a way that addresses real issues. She seems to live in another world much of the time. Consequently, her judgments often are ill formed, and currently, her thinking is much more strained and illogical than should be the case for her age. It seems to be commensurate with a schizophreniclike ideational activity.

Mediation—Case 4   The data concerning cognitive translation are critical to any decision about the presence of schizophrenia. This is especially true for Case 4. The data concerning mediation for Case 4 are shown in Table 39.

Table 39.   Cognitive Mediation Data for Case 4

Lambda	= 0.42	OBS	= Neg	MINUS FEATURES	
P	= 6	$X+\%$	= .47	3, 6, 9, 13, 14, 15	
FQx+	= 0	$F+\%$	= .80		
FQxo	= 8	$Xu\%$	= .18		
FQxu	= 3	$X-\%$	= .35		
FQx−	= 6	$S-\%$	= .00		
*FQx*none	= 0	CONFAB	= 0		

The findings for Lambda (0.42) and OBS (negative) are not significant. She gives six Popular responses, suggesting that when situations are obvious, she will usually give obvious or expected responses. She fails, however, to give the most common Popular answers to Cards I and VIII. The latter seems important because it is such an obvious answer that is given by almost all people, even those seriously disturbed. The failure to give a Popular answer to Card VIII may indicate some marked preoccupation that tends to nullify some aspects of reality testing.

The low $X+\%$ (.47) denotes that she is very unconventional in the way that she translates stimulus inputs, and the relatively high $X-\%$ (.35) signifies that many of her translations involve considerable distortion of the input. Actually, the $Xu\%$ (.18) is not atypical for her age, a finding that makes the $X-\%$ even more important. Stated differently, this is someone who ignores or distorts reality very often. There are no $S-$ answers. Thus, the distortions cannot be attributed to any abiding negativism or anger. Her minus answers occur to 5 of the 10 blots and occur when she delivers multiple responses. When she gives only one answer, such as to Cards V, VI, VII, and X, the form quality remains ordinary, but even in those instances, two of the four answers include Critical Special Scores.

Five of her six minus answers include human contents, and five of the six are $M-$ responses. This suggests that her mediational distortions often are provoked by her concerns with people and her strange thinking about them. Four of the six minus answers are given to cards that contain chromatic color. This may suggest that some of her proneness to distort is also provoked by affectively toned stimuli. This hypothesis seems especially viable in light of her pervasive introversive style. Although some of her minus answers contain features that can be detected by most examiners (Responses 6, 13, 15), at least two, Responses 3 and 9, and probably a third, Response 14, are defined in ways that make it difficult for even the most empathic person to perceive. In other words, some of her distortions are very severe and not unlike those found in the majority of records taken from schizophrenic subjects.

In effect, many of her perceptual activities appear to be sorely impaired, leading to the conclusion that she experiences considerable detachment from the real world when confronted with new stimuli. Although she usually can be expected to give conventional responses when circumstances are obvious, that expectation is sometimes tempered and distortions may occur. The composite of findings regarding mediation, considered in light of previously developed information concerning her thinking, points to a strong likelihood that schizophrenia is present.

Processing—Case 4   Data concerning her information-processing activities are shown in Table 40.

Table 40.   Processing Data for Case 4

L = 0.42	$W{:}D{:}Dd$ = 6:8:3	Zd = +2.5	$DQ+$ = 12
Zf = 14	$W{:}M$ = 6:7	PSV = 0	$DQv/+$ = 0
HVI = No	OBS = No		DQv = 0

LOCATION SEQUENCING

I	W,W,Dd	IV W,Dd	VII D
II	D,DS	V W	VIII W,D
III	Dd,D	VI W	IX D,D
			X D

The findings for Lambda (0.42) and the OBS and HVI (both negative) are not relevant. The data concerning motivation for processing are somewhat mixed. The Zf (14) is about average for a 12-year-old, suggesting that her organizational effort is at an expected level. However, the $W{:}D{:}Dd$ ratio (6:8:3) and $W{:}M$ ratio (6:7) both seem to indicate that she is somewhat conservative or economical in her processing approach. This is best illustrated by the fact that she tends to avoid W responses and uses slightly more Dd areas than is common. Three of her six W answers are to Cards I and V, for which W responses are easier to formulate than are D responses. On the other hand, she gives 12 $DQ+$ answers and no DQv responses. The Zd score (+2.5) is in the average range, and there are no perseverations. This composite of findings suggests that her processing activities are quite sophisticated, but apparently she tends to feel unsure of herself and prefers to deal with stimulus fields that seem more easily managed.

The location sequencing is generally consistent. Five of her six W answers are first or only responses and two of the three Dd responses are last answers. The single inconsistency occurs on Card III, to which she begins with a Dd response that includes a Popular D and became a Dd because of her strained reasoning (like making this heart here beat). All three Dd answers are minus, and all involve some sort of movement. This appears to indicate that her disturbed thinking not only impacts on her cognitive translations, but also tends to be quite influential in some of her processing activity. Thus, although there are no major concerns about her processing per se, there is little doubt that her processing activities will vary as the intensity of her disturbance varies.

Controls—Case 4   The data related to issues of control and stress tolerance are shown in Table 41.

Table 41.   Controls and Stress Tolerance Data for Case 4

EB = 8:2.0		EA = 10.0		D = +1	
eb = 5:0		es = 5	Adjes = 3	AdjD = +2	
FM = 2	C' = 0	T = 0		CDI = 3	
m = 3	V = 0	Y = 0			

Both D Scores are in the plus range, indicating that she has a solid capacity for control and apparently can tolerate new stress situations better than many of her peers. About 3% of nonpatient 12's have plus D Scores and about 12% have an Adjusted D Score in the plus range. The *EA* is substantial and both sides of the *EB* have values greater than zero. Therefore, there is no reason to question the validity of the Adjusted D score. It is important to note that the D Score is one point less than the Adjusted D Score, indicating the presence of situationally related stress. This is reflected by the presence of the three *m* answers, which are included among her six blend responses. Thus, there is an increase in her overall complexity because of the stress, and this appears to manifest primarily in an increase in peripheral mental activity. There are, however, no indications of potential overload or immediate threat to her capacity for control.

An important issue regarding her apparently sturdy capacity for control concerns its long-term stability. It seems clear that much of this sturdiness is related to the way in which she handles affect. There are no grey-black or shading answers in the record, a very unusual finding for a 12. Apparently, the nature of her disturbance has fomented some psychological tactics through which she is psychologically able to ignore or displace internally irritating feelings. As a result, she does not experience some of the more normal emotional demands that are common to most people, both children and adults. This avoidance of natural irritants increases her ability to form and direct behavior under various circumstances. For instance, had she given an average number of grey-black determinants for her age, about four, the *es* would increase to 9. In this hypothetical situation, the D score would be zero, but the Adjusted D score would continue to be in the plus range (+1). Thus, there is no compelling reason to suggest that her capacities for control are fragile. Although, her disturbed thinking and consequent distorted translation of events makes it likely that many of her decisions and behaviors will be inappropriate for the situation, they are, nonetheless, usually well-controlled activities.

Affect—Case 4   Data concerning her affective features are shown in Table 42.

Table 42.   Affect Data for Case 4

DEPI = 2			BLENDS
EB = 8:2.0	*EBPer* = 4.0		FM.FC'
eb = 5:0	*FC:CF* + *C* = 2:1		FD.FT
	Pure *C* = 0		FC'.FM
C' = 0	*T* = 0	*Afr* = 0.42	CF.YF
V = 0	*Y* = 0	*S* = 1	
		Blends/*R* = 6:17	
		CP = 0	

The DEPI value (2) is not significant. The fact that her pervasive introversive style orients her to push feelings aside in coping or decision-making situations has already been discussed. The right side *eb* value of zero also has been noted, but seems important to elaborate further in the context of two other variables. The *FC:CF* + *C* ratio is 2:1 (no Pure *C* answers) and the *Afr* (0.42) is quite low. These are unusual findings for a child. About 17% of nonpatient 12-year-olds give more *FC* than *CF* + *C,* and about a third of that sample has an *Afr* less than 0.50. Moreover, only 5% of the 120 nonpatient

12's included in the normative sample give records that contain no grey-black or shading answers.

The composite of validation data concerning these three variables argues that a mixture of findings, such as found in this record, strongly indicates some sort of emotional shutdown, or at least a remarkable avoidance of feelings. This is a very abnormal finding and forecasts a grim future for this youngster. Although the antecedents of this problem are not clear, it seems obvious that she is developing in an internal environment in which emotion plays little or no role. Apparently, she takes flight into her distorted and sometimes bizzare ideation to escape some perceived threat experienced when emotions are present. This probably relates to her strange classroom activity but also seems inconsistent with her report and that provided by her mother that they have a close relationship. If that is true, it must be a relationship in which little emotion is exchanged.

Although she gives an average number of blend answers for her age, half of them are created by m determinants. In other words, were it not for the presence of situational stress, she would manifest much less complexity than is typical for her age. Moreover, all of her color determinants appear in blends, two of the three containing inanimate movement ($m.CF$, $m.FC$, $M.FC$). On a speculative level, it may be that stress gives rise to feelings that otherwise may remain stringently controlled.

Overall, her emotional characteristics are unlike those of most 12-year-olds. She seems to work hard to contain her feelings and apparently has found some psychological tactic that permits her to ignore internally irritating feelings such as are common to most people. In general, these findings bode poorly for her developmental future, mainly because her constraint of feeling denies her access to the positive developmental yield that occurs when a child experiences and explores his or her emotions. In effect, her state of constraint only serves to contribute to an enhancement of her pervasive style and the disturbed and immature thinking that forms its core.

Self-Perception—Case 4   The structural data related to self-perception for this case are shown in Table 43.

Table 43.   Self-Perception Data for Case 4

$3r + (2)/R = 0.41$	$FD = 1$	$MOR = 0$ $Hx = 0$	$An + Xy = 1$
$Fr + rF = 1$	Sum $V = 0$	$H:(H) + Hd + (Hd) = 4:5$	$Sx = 0$
		RESPONSES TO BE READ	
MOR Resp's	$FQ -$ Resp's	M Resp's	FM Resp's m Resp's
	3,6,9,13,14,15	3,6,8,9,12,14,15,17	2,15 5,11,16

The presence of a reflection response is an important finding and could be related to the onset of her disturbance. The sort of exquisite self-involvement and overestimation of self-worth, represented by the reflection answer, is common among younger children and persists in more than 12% of nonpatient 12's. It is vitally important, however, for these children to be able to defend and reaffirm the belief that they are extremely valuable. In most instances, the defense of this belief occurs through forms of externalization or rationalization when things go wrong (the teacher isn't fair, the other children cheat, the work is too hard, etc.). Concurrently, some sourc must provide reassurance. Usually, it is parents or significant others who are willing to acknowledge the validity of the externalization as well as provide reinforcement to the naive beliefs concerning personal worth (you are beautiful, you are the most important thing in my life, don't worry about it, etc.).

Parents of developing children are continually faced with the problem of maintaining a closeness to their child while, at the same time, aiding the child to confront or test reality concerning himself or herself. At best, it is a difficult task because it is important to sustain the child's integrity. Sometimes, however, the best intentions go astray, mainly because the parents cannot keep the delicate balance between teaching the child and loving the child in correct perspective. When that happens, children become victimized by an excess of parental reassurance or left to fend for themselves. In this case, it is likely that the parent has been silently reassuring but also distant from the developmental task. Therefore, the subject has learned to rely on her fantasy world as the basic source from which she reaffirms her integrity.

At the same time, other factors appear to challenge her integrity. The Egocentricity Index (0.41) is lower than average for her age. This indicates that, when she compares herself with others, she concludes that she is not as valuable as they. That conclusion creates a conflict with her assumption that she is highly valuable and this creates confusion for her and probably contributes to her emotional constriction. The single *FD* response suggests that she does take some distance and attempt to self-examine, but the data concerning ideation and mediation do not indicate that the process will be very profitable. She has four Pure *H* contents, but three of the four are minus. Thus, although she may be developing a self-image that is based on experience, there is reason to suspect that she tends to distort that experience in ways that will not contribute meaningfully to her growth. Interestingly, there are no MOR responses in the protocol. This probably relates to the extent to which her distorted thinking has been successful in warding off reality-based estimates of her self-image and self-esteem.

Sorting through the projected material offers a picture of her distorted self-image. Five of her six minus answers involve the *M* determinant, and the sixth includes a human content. The first is one of her more bizarre answers, ". . . a mountain peak and a baby's head sticking up, and this is a guy singing (Inquiry) he's holding onto this peak and he's pulling the mountain up . . . maybe (the baby's head) is watching." It is a rambling response that is difficult to interpret when studied independently. The fact that there is a baby may suggest her own sense of insecurity. On the other hand, there is a "guy" singing who is also pulling up a mountain, indicating both happiness and strength. The answer may reflect on her sense of helplessness but her belief that she is, in some way, very powerful.

The implication of power is also present in the next minus response, ". . . his hands are over this part like making this heart here beat." The third minus also implies value of some sort, ". . . a puppy (Inquiry) . . . he's just weighed himself and now he's barking about it." The fourth minus answer is ". . . a monster," and if taken as a self-representation does not bode well concerning self-concept. The fifth is a face (Inquiry) ". . . it has no mouth or nose, it's holding these two sticks with its ears . . ." It does not appear to have any direct representation, but the fact that there is no mouth or nose does imply a sense of incompleteness. The last minus answer conveys a tenuous sense of self. It is ". . . a big lady riding a teeny weeny horse . . . hold the reins . . . the four legs down here moving really fast." It implies a sense of tenuous control. The teeny weeny horse is moving rapidly, and the big lady is simply holding the reins.

The remaining three *M* responses also have some strange elements. The first is a giant to Card IV, a common answer, but in this instance he is ". . . looking through his legs." It conveys a distorted picture of whatever he is seeing. The second, "two girls," is also very common, but the answer is made unique by the fact that they ". . . just jumped up and now they are coming down." It may signal something about a sense of potential control problems. The last involves ". . . two bad guys arguing" and might reflect her conflict about herself.

The two *FM* answers also are strange. The first involves a hummingbird, ". . . getting ready to eat this bell-shaped thing . . ." It seems like a dependency response, but that is not clear. The second involves the teeny weeny horse and the four legs moving "really" fast. The three *m* answers vary in uniqueness. The first is a commonplace answer, a jet airplane with fire coming from it. The second is less common, a boat with ". . . a wave crashing in front of the boat . . ." It implies a sense of threat, whereas the third is a more ominous response, "a bell hanging from a rope." Whether there is a sense of morbidity implied or whether the bell represents something else is not clear. It may be important to note that the hummingbird, given on Card I, was getting ready to eat "this bell-shaped thing." None of her other answers is embellished in a seemingly useful manner.

In general, the structural and content data do not convey the kind of relatively well established but still developing self-image that is common to 12-year-olds. To the contrary, her self-concept seems immature and muddled. She tends to overglorify herself, yet seems to judge herself as less worthy than those significant in her life. She does some self-examining, but it is unlikely that occurs in a useful, reality-based manner. There is evidence to suggest that she harbors some sense of grandiosity, but there other findings suggest that she feels very tenuous about her own sense of self. It is quite likely that she is conflicted about her self-image, and this sense of conflict only exacerbates her disturbance.

Interpersonal Perception—Case 4   The data related to interpersonal perception and behavior are shown Table 44.

Table 44.   Interpersonal Perception Data for Case 4

CDI = 3	*a:p* = 6:8	*T* = 0	Human Cont = 9		Pure *H* = 4
HVI = Neg	Food = 0	PER = 2	COP = 0	AG = 1	Isolate/R = 0.24

RESPONSES TO BE READ

HUMAN MOVEMENT WITH PAIR	*HUMAN CONTENTS*
12,14,17	1,3,6,8,12,13,14,15

The CDI and HVI are both negative. The *a:p* ratio (6:8) is quite important as it suggests she takes a passive role in her interpersonal relations, relying mainly on others to initiate activity or resolve problems. Although there are no Food responses, one may actually exist in her second response, ". . . getting ready to eat this bell-shaped thing." It implies more dependency than is evident in the structural data. At the same time, this is a *T*-less record. She does not appear to have the emotional experience of needs for closeness as do most children of her age. Instead, it is likely that she does not expect to be close to others and may even regard gestures of closeness with some dismay and/or distrust. Nonetheless, the nine human contents indicate that she is very interested in people.

Unfortunately, this strong interest may be based more on guardedness than a positive interest. She does not understand people very well. Even though there are four Pure H contents, two of the four involve Critical Special Scores and form distortion, and the remaining two have strange features. There are no COP answers and one AG response.

The Isolation Index (0.24) is not positive, but in light of the low Afr, there is no reason to believe that she is very involved in interpersonal activities. The movement answers containing pairs afford no reason to alter that hypothesis. The first is the hummingbird answer, the second involves the two girls who have jumped up and are now coming down, the third consists of two sticks being held by the ears of a man who has no mouth or nose, and the last is the two bugs arguing. None suggests social interest or social awareness. The nine human contents reflect a mishmash of immaturity and distorted reality (a little lady with two heads, a baby's head watching, a guy singing pulling up a mountain, a man making a heart beat, a giant looking through his legs, girls, a monster, a face with no nose or mouth, and a lady riding a teeny weeny horse).

Overall, there seems little doubt that this is an interpersonally impoverished youngster. She does not perceive people very realistically and has not developed the natural social skills commensurate with her age.

Summary—Case 4   This is a very disturbed child whose retreat into a fantasy-laden and distorted inner life has probably concealed the severity of her disturbance from those around her. Prior to the astute observations of her sixth-grade teacher, her other teachers have suspected a learning disability, and as might be expected, her mother expresses confusion about the current problems. She reports that she and her daughter are close and says that she assists her daughter almost every night with homework. It is a report that is difficult to believe in light of the rather extreme detachment from reality that seems to exist in this child. Her thinking is sometimes bizarre, and her perceptual inaccuracies are quite notable. Although some of this might be disregarded in a context of childish immaturity, even the most empathic person could not find that explanation suitable. Her emotional constriction is remarkable and extremely detrimental to her well-being, although from a different perspective, it provides a temporary defense from the threats posed by the real world. She has a naive and distorted tendency to overestimate her worth, but at the same time she is unsure of herself and easily threatened by her world when she is forced into confrontations with it. Her interpersonal world is impoverished and her conceptualizations of people seem distant from reality.

Some sort of residential care appears to be in order. She is currently experiencing some stress and supportive measures will be in order for the immediate future. Long-term treatment is likely to prove more difficult. She is in urgent need of an accepting and emotionally giving role model who can ultimately assist her in finding new ways to contend with reality, especially as she enters puberty. This will not be easy, however, because of her sturdy capacity for control and the apparent ease with which she is able to replace reality with fantasy. Possibly, her unsureness about herself will serve to help develop a therapeutic relationship, but the therapist must be made aware that she tends to mistrust others and does not expect closeness.

There is no reason to suspect that she has been actively psychotic and thus, the need for antipsychotic medication is not evident at this time. However, her ability to distinguish between fantasy and reality is little more than a delicate thread that may break at any time, and the likelihood of a subsequent need for a pharmacological adjunct to treatment is substantial.

REFERENCES

Acklin, M. W. (1990). Personality dimensions in two types of learning-disabled children: A Rorschach study. *Journal of Personality Assessment, 54,* 67–77.

Adair, H. E., & Wagner, E. E. (1992). Stability of unusual verbalizations on the Rorschach for outpatients with schizophrenia. *Journal of Clinical Psychology, 48,* 250–256.

Akhtar, S. (1990). Paranoid personality disorder: A synthesis of developmental, dynamic, and descriptive features. *American Journal of Psychotherapy, 44,* 5–25.

American Psychiatric Association. (1987). *Diagnostic and statistical manual of mental disorders* (Vol. 3, Rev.). Washington, DC: Author.

Andreasen, N. C. (1979a). Thought, language, and communication disorders: I. Clinical assessment, definition of terms, and evaluation of their reliability. *Archives of General Psychiatry, 36,* 1315–1321.

Andreasen, N. C. (1979b). Thought, language, and communication disorders: II. Diagnostic significance. *Archives of General Psychiatry, 36,* 1325–1330.

Andreasen, N. C. (1985). Positive vs. negative schizophrenia: A critical evaluation. *Schizophrenia Bulletin, 11,* 380–389.

Andreasen, N. C. (1988). Clinical phenomenology. *Schizophrenia Bulletin, 14,* 345–363.

Andreasen, N. C., & Flaum, M. (1991). Schizophrenia: The characteristic symptoms. *Schizophrenia Bulletin, 17,* 27–50.

Andreasen, N. C., & Grove, W. M. (1986). Thought, language, and communication in schizophrenia: Diagnosis and prognosis. *Schizophrenia Bulletin, 12,* 348–359.

Arieti, S. (1974). *Interpretation of schizophrenia* (2nd ed.). New York: Basic Books.

Asarnow, J. R., & MacCrimmon, D. J. (1981). Span of apprehension deficits during the postpsychotic stages of schizophrenia. *Archives of General Psychiatry, 38,* 1006–1011.

Assad, G., & Shapiro, B. (1986). Hallucinations: Theoretical and clinical overview. *American Journal of Psychiatry, 143,* 1088–1097.

Bellak, L., Hurvich, M., & Gediman, H. (1973). *Ego functions in schizophrenics, neurotics, and normals.* New York: Wiley.

Burnham, D. L., Gladstone, A. I., & Gibson, R. W. (1969). *Schizophrenia and the need-fear dilemma.* New York: International Universities Press.

Cantor, S. (1988). *Childhood schizophrenia.* New York: Guilford Press.

Cantwell, D. P., Baker, L., Rutter, M., & Mawhood, L. (1989). Infantile autism and developmental receptive dysphasia: A comparative follow-up into middle childhood. *Journal of Autism and Developmental Disorders, 19,* 19–31.

Caplan, R., & Sherman, T. (1990). Thought disorder in the childhood psychoses. In B. B. Lahey & A. E. Kazdin (Eds.), *Advances in clinical child psychology* (Vol. 13, pp. 175–206). New York: Plenum Press.

Caplan, R., Perdue, S., Tanguay, P. E., & Fish, B. (1990). Formal thought disorder in childhood onset schizophrenia and schizotypal personality disorder. *Journal of Child Psychology and Psychiatry, 31,* 1103–1114.

Chambers, W. J. (1988). Late onset psychoses of childhood and adolescence. In C. J. Kestenbaum & D. T. Williams (Eds.), *Handbook of clinical assessment of children and adolescents* (pp. 583–603). New York: New York University Press.

Champion, L., Doughtie, E. B., Johnson, P. J., & McCreary, J. M. (1984). *Journal of Clinical Psychology, 40,* 329–333.

Cutting, J., & Dunne, F. (1989). Subjective experience of schizophrenia. *Schizophrenia Bulletin, 15,* 217–231.

Dawson, G., & Castelloe, P. (1992). Autism. In C. E. Walker & M. C. Roberts (Eds.), *Handbook of clinical child psychology* (2nd ed., pp. 375–398). New York: Wiley.

Demb, H. B., & Weintraub, A. G. (1989). A five-year follow-up of preschool children diagnosed as having an atypical pervasive developmental disorder. *Journal of Developmental and Behavioral Pediatrics, 10,* 292–298.

Docherty, N., Schnur, M., & Harvey, P. D. (1988). Reference performance and positive and negative thought disorder: A follow-up study of manics and schizophrenics. *Journal of Abnormal Psychology, 97,* 437–442.

Dykens, E., Volkmar, F., & Glick, M. (1991). Thought disorder in high-functioning autistic adults. *Journal of Autism and Developmental Disorders, 21,* 291–301.

Erickson, D. H., Beiser, M., Iacono, W. G., Fleming, J. A., & Lin, T. (1989). The role of social relationships in the course of first-episode schizophrenia and affective psychosis. *American Journal of Psychiatry, 146,* 1456–1461.

Exner, J. E. (1991). *The Rorschach: A comprehensive system: Vol. 2. Interpretation.* New York: Wiley.

Exner, J. E. (1993). *The Rorschach: A Comprehensive System: Vol. 1. Basic foundations* (3rd ed.). New York: Wiley.

Fisher, S., & Cleveland, S. E. (1958). *Body image and personality* (2nd ed.). New York: Dover.

Gallucci, N. T. (1989). Personality assessment with children of superior intelligence: Divergence versus psychopathology. *Journal of Personality Assessment, 53,* 749–760.

Gillberg, C. (1991). Outcome in autism and autistic-like conditions. *Journal of the American Academy of Child and Adolescent Psychiatry, 30,* 375–382.

Gold, J. M., & Hurt, S. W. (1990). The effects of haloperidol on thought disorder and IQ in schizophrenia. *Journal of Personality Assessment, 54,* 390–400.

Green, W. H. (1988). Pervasive developmental disorders. In C. J. Kestenbaum & D. T. Williams (Eds.), *Handbook of clinical assessment of children and adolescents* (pp. 469–498). New York: New York University Press.

Grossman, L. S., Harrow, M., & Sands, J. R. (1986). Features associated with thought disorder in manic patients at 2–4 year follow-up. *American Journal of Psychiatry, 143,* 306–311.

Grove, W. M., & Andreasen, N. C. (1985). Language and thinking in psychosis. *Archives of General Psychiatry, 42,* 26–32.

Harrow, M., & Marengo, J. T. (1986). Schizophrenic thought disorder at followup: Its persistence and prognostic significance. *Schizophrenia Bulletin, 12,* 373–393.

Harrow, M., & Quinlan, D. M. (1985). *Disordered thinking and schizophrenic psychopathology.* New York: Gardner Press.

Harrow, M., Grossman, L. S., Silverstein, M. L., & Meltzer, H. Y. (1982). Thought pathology in manic and schizophrenic patients. *Archives of General Psychiatry, 43,* 781–785.

Harvey, P. D., Docherty, N. M., Serper, M. R., & Rasmussen, M. (1990). Cognitive deficits and thought disorder: II. An 8-month followup study. *Schizophrenia Bulletin, 16,* 147–156.

Holzman, P. S., Shenton, M. E., & Solovay, M. R. (1986). Quality of thought disorder in differential diagnosis. *Schizophrenia Bulletin, 12,* 360–371.

Holzman, P. S. (1988). Basic behavioral sciences. *Schizophrenia Bulletin, 14,* 413–426.

Howells, J. G., & Guirguis, W. R. (1984). Childhood schizophrenia 20 years later. *Archives of General Psychiatry, 41,* 123–128.

Hurt, S. W., Holzman, P. S., & Davis, J. M. (1983). Thought disorder: The measurement of its changes. *Archives of General Psychiatry, 40,* 1281–1285.

Jampala, V. C., Taylor, M. A., & Abrams, R. (1989). The diagnostic implications of formal thought disorder in mania and schizophrenia. *American Journal of Psychiatry, 146,* 459–463.

Keith, S. J., & Matthews, S. M. (1991). The diagnosis of schizophrenia: A review of onset and duration issues. *Schizophrenia Bulletin, 17,* 51–67.

Keith, S. J., Reiger, D., Rae, D., & Matthews, S. (1992). The prevelance of schizophrenia: Analysis of demographic features, symptom patterns, and course. In A. Z. Schwartzberg (Ed.), *International annals of adolescent psychiatry* (Vol. 2, pp. 260–284). Chicago: University of Chicago Press.

Kety, S. S. (1980). The syndrome of schizophrenia: Unresolved questions and opportunities for research. *British Journal of Psychiatry, 136,* 421–436.

Krug, R. S. (1983). Substance abuse. In C. E. Walker & M. C. Roberts (Eds.), *Handbook of clinical child psychology* (pp. 853–879). New York: Wiley.

Leavitt, F. (1982). *Drugs and behavior* (2nd ed.). New York: Wiley.

Lewine, R. (1980). Sex differences in age of symptom onset and first hospitalization in schizophrenia. *American Journal of Orthopsychiatry, 50,* 316–322.

Lewis, M. S. (1989). Age and incidence in schizophrenia. *Schizophrenia Bulletin, 15,* 75–80.

Lincoln, A. J., Courchesne, E., Kilman, B. A., Elmasian, R., & Allen, M. (1988). A study of intellectual abilities in high-functioning people with autism. *Journal of Autism and Developmental Disorders, 18,* 505–524.

Magaro, P. A. (1980). *Cognition in schizophrenia and paranoia.* Hillsdale, NJ: Erlbaum.

Marengo, J. J., & Harrow, M. (1987). Schizophrenic thought disorder at follow-up. *Archives of General Psychiatry, 44,* 651–659.

McGlashan, T. H. (1988). A selective review of recent North American long-term followup studies of schizophrenia. *Schizophrenia Bulletin, 14,* 515–542.

Millon, T. (1981). *Disorders of personality.* New York: Wiley.

Neale, J. M., & Oltmanns, T. F. (1980). *Schizophrenia.* New York: Wiley.

Oltmanns, T. F., Murphy, R., Berenbaum, H., & Dunlop, S. R. (1985). Rating verbal communication impairment in schizophrenia and affective disorders. *Schizophrenia Bulletin, 11,* 292–299.

Paul, R., Cohen, D., & Caparulo, B. K. (1983). A longitudinal study of patients with severe developmental disorders of language learning. *Journal of the American Academy of Child Psychiatry, 22,* 525–534.

Petty, L. K., Ornitz, E. M., Michelman, J. D., & Zimmerman, E. G. (1984). *Archives of General Psychiatry, 41,* 129–135.

Pogue-Geile, M. F., & Harrow, M. (1985). Negative and positive symptoms in schizophrenia and depression: A followup. *Schizophrenia Bulletin, 11,* 371–387.

Rapaport, D., Gill, M. M., & Schafer, R. (1968). *Diagnostic psychological testing* (Rev. edition edited by R. R. Holt). New York: International Universities Press (Original work published 1946).

Regier, D. A., Boyd, J. H., Burke, J. D., Rae, D. S., Myers, J. K., Kramer, M., Robins, L. N., George, L. K., Karno, M., & Locke, B. Z. (1988). One-month prevalence of mental disorders in the United States. *Archives of General Psychiatry, 45,* 977–986.

Rosenstein, M. J., Milazzo-Sayre, L. J., & Manderscheid, R. W. (1989). Care of persons with schizophrenia: A statistical profile. *Schizophrenia Bulletin, 15,* 45–58.

Rutter, M., & Schopler, E. (1987). Autism and pervasive developmental disorders: Concepts and diagnostic issues. *Journal of Autism and Developmental Disorders, 17,* 159–186.

Schafer, R. (1954). *Psychoanalytic interpretation in Rorschach testing.* New York: Grune & Stratton.

Schreibman, L. (1988). *Autism.* Newbury Park, CA: Sage.

Shapiro, D. (1965). *Neurotic styles.* New York: Basic Books.

Singer, H. K., & Brabender, V. (1993). The use of the Rorschach to differentiate unipolar and bipolar disorders. *Journal of Personality Assessment, 60,* 333–345.

Smalley, S. L., Asarnow, R. F., & Spence, A. (1988). Autism and genetics: A decade of research. *Archives of General Psychiatry, 45,* 953–961.

Solovay, M. R., Shenton, M. E., & Holzman, P. S. (1987). Comparative studies of thought disorders: I. Mania and schizophrenia. *Archives of General Psychiatry, 44,* 13–20.

Strauss, J. S., & Carpenter, W. T. (1981). *Schizophrenia.* New York: Plenum Press.

Tardiff, K., & Sweillam, A. (1980). Assault, suicide and mental illness. *Archives of General Psychiatry, 37,* 164–169.

Tien, A. Y., & Anthony, J. C. (1990). Epidemiological analysis of alcohol and drug use as risk factors for psychotic experiences. *Journal of Nervous and Mental Disease, 178,* 473–480.

Tsiantis, J., Macri, I., & Maratos, O. (1986). Schizophrenia in children: A review of European research. *Schizophrenia Bulletin, 12,* 101–119.

Turner, W. M., & Tsuang, M. T. (1990). Impact of substance abuse on the course and outcome of schizophrenia. *Schizophrenia Bulletin, 16,* 87–95.

Tyrano, S., & Apter, A. (1992). Adolescent psychosis: An eight-year follow up. In A. Z. Schwartzberg (Ed.), *International annals of adolescent psychiatry* (Vol. 2, pp. 317–324). Chicago: University of Chicago Press.

Vardy, M. M., & Kay, S. R. (1983). LSD psychosis of LSD-induced schizophrenia? *Archives of General Psychiatry, 40,* 877–883.

Volkmar, F. R. (1991). Childhood schizophrenia. In M. Lewis (Ed.), *Child and adolescent psychiatry* (pp. 621–628). Baltimore, MD: Williams & Wilkins.

Volkmar, F. R., & Cohen, D. J. (1991). Comorbid association of autism and schizophrenia. *American Journal of Psychiatry, 148,* 1705–1707.

Walker, E. F., Harvey, P. D., & Perlman, D. (1988). The positive/negative symptom distinction in psychoses: A replication and extensions of previous findings. *Journal of Nervous and Mental Disease, 176,* 359–363.

Wallace, C. J. (1984). Community and interpersonal functioning in the course of schizophrenic disorder. *Schizophrenia Bulletin, 10,* 233–257.

Watkins, J. M., Asarnow, R. F., & Tanguay, P. E. (1988). Symptom development in childhood onset schizophrenia. *Journal of Child Psychology and Psychiatry, 29,* 865–878.

Weiner, I. B. (1964). Differential diagnosis in amphetamine psychosis. *Psychiatric Quarterly, 38,* 707–716.

Weiner, I. B. (1966). *Psychodiagnosis in schizophrenia.* New York: Wiley.

Weiner, I. B. (1987). Identifying schizophrenia in adolescents. *Journal of Adolescent Health Care, 8,* 336–343.

Weiner, I. B. (1992). *Psychological disturbance in adolescence* (2nd ed.). New York: Wiley.

Weiner, I. B, & Exner, J. E. (1978). Rorschach indices of disordered thinking in nonpatient adolescents and adults. *Journal of Personality Assessment, 42,* 339–343.

Zahner, G. E. P., & Pauls, D. L. (1987). Epidemiological surveys of autism. In D. J. Cohen & A. M. Donnellan (Eds.), *Handbook of autism and pervasive developmental disorders* (pp. 199–207). New York: Wiley.

Zigler, E., & Levine, J. (1981). Age on first hospitalization of schizophrenics: A developmental approach. *Journal of Abnormal Psychology, 90,* 458–467.

Zubin, J. (1986). Implications of the vulnerability model for DSM-IV with special reference to schizophrenia. In T. Millon & G. L. Klerman (Eds.), *Contemporary directions in psychopathology* (pp. 473–494). New York: Guilford Press.

CHAPTER 6

Issues of Depression

Affective disorder is widely agreed to occur in two distinct forms: *unipolar affective disorder,* which consists of episodes of depression, and *bipolar affective disorder,* which involves episodes of mania as well as depression. Chronic disposition to recurrent but mild depressive episodes is commonly called *dysthymia,* and chronic disposition to alternating episodes of mild depression and hypomania is generally referred to as *cyclothymia.*

Despite the seeming clarity of these and their codification in DSM-III-R, the distinction between pathological and normal affective states often proves more difficult for diagnosticians than the identification of schizophrenia. Unlike schizophrenia, depression is a familiar psychological state that most people experience at times of disappointment and frustration. Such events as ending a close personal relationship, failing to achieve a desired goal, misplacing a valued possession, or becoming ill or incapacitated normally leave people feeling sad, discouraged, apathetic, or inadequate. Particularly distressing experiences, such as the death of a loved one, often produce the temporarily disabling depressive state referred to as *grief.* It is when normal episodes of depression or grief become more profound or prolonged than events would appear to justify that they constitute a pathological depressive condition.

Mania stands in sharp contrast to depression. Instead of sadness, discouragement, apathy, and malaise, its hallmarks are unflagging good spirits, unbounded optimism, enormous energy and enthusiasm, and a pervasive sense of well-being. Feeling more or less happy, like feeling sad, is a normal human experience as one's life turns for better or worse. Happy events may normally produce periods of elation, just as sad events cause moments of grief. It is when elation continues out of proportion to actual events that it identifies a pathological manic condition.

Using the Diagnostic Interview Schedule based on DSM-III-R criteria, the National Institute of Mental Health has collected extensive survey data concerning the frequency of depression and mania, as well as of other psychological disorders. According to these surveys, known as the Environmental Catchment Area (ECA) program, persons age 18 and older show a lifetime prevalence for major depressive episodes and dysthymic disorder combined of 9.1%. The incidence of depressive disorder over a 6-month period is 6.3%, and the frequency of cases within a 1-month period is 5.5%. For manic episodes, the lifetime prevalence in adults is 0.8% and the 6-month and 1-month incidence figures are 0.5% and 0.4%, respectively (Regier et al., 1988).

The apparent fact that almost 10% of persons will experience a diagnosable affective disorder sometime during their lives establishes the clinical importance of being able to recognize depression and mania, especially in its mild or early stages when intervention can have maximum impact. There has not yet been any large-scale epidemiological survey of young people akin to the ECA, and only sketchy information is available concerning the frequency of affective disorders in children and adolescents. Nevertheless, five recent studies employing diverse methods serve to document the emergence of these disorders during the developmental years.

Lefkowitz and Tesiny (1985) studied 3,020 elementary school students with the Peer Nomination Inventory of Depression and concluded that 5.6% of the girls and 4.8% of the boys were manifesting severe depression. In another study in which 550 early adolescents were given the Center for Epidemiological Studies Depression Scale on three occasions, in the seventh, eighth, and ninth grades, 8% to 10% received scores suggesting major depressive disorder each year, although young people giving depressive self-reports fluctuated considerably from one year to the next (Garrison, Jackson, Marsteller, McKeown, & Addy, 1990).

At the high school level, Kaplan, Hong, and Weinhold (1984) found a 13.5% frequency of mild depression and an additional 8.6% frequency of moderate or severe depression among 385 high school juniors and seniors given the Beck Depression Inventory. In a community study of 150 nonpatient 14- to 16-year-olds, clinical assessment identified an 8.0% point prevalence of major depression or dysthymic disorder (Kashani et al., 1987). Another clinical study of 356 nonpatient high school students indicated that 8.9% had already experienced a diagnosable depressive episode during their lifetime (Whitaker et al., 1990).

As these findings suggest, elementary school children are less likely to become clinically depressed than adolescents, whereas the frequency of depressive disorder in adolescents approaches or equals that of adults. Clinicians generally concur that puberty ushers in a substantial increase in the frequency with which young people become depressed. Estimates place the prepubertal incidence of depressive disorders at less than 3%, following which a growing susceptibility with each postpubertal year results in a threefold increase in this condition during adolescence (Fleming & Offord, 1990; Kashani, Rosenberg, & Reid, 1989; Weiner, 1992, Chap. 4).

The frequency with which depressive disorders occur among children and especially among adolescents means that whether and how seriously young people are depressed will often be among the questions that Rorschach clinicians are asked to examine. To give further weight to the importance of assessing youthful depression, long-term follow-up studies indicate that depressive syndromes in young people tend to persist through the adolescent years especially in the absence of professional intervention and that clinically depressed children and adolescents are much more likely than their nondepressed peers to experience disorder and psychiatric hospitalization as adults (Clarizio, 1989; Harrington, Fudge, Rutter, Pickles, & Hill, 1990).

As for manic episodes, neither their prevalence nor incidence has yet been examined systematically in persons under age 18. However, as testimony to the importance of assessing possible bipolar disorder in young people, there is evidence to indicate that this condition frequently has its beginnings during the developmental years. Specifically, Burke, Burke, Regier, and Rae (1990) concluded from the ECA data that bipolar disorder has a median age of onset of 19 years, which means that 50% of persons with this condition first become disturbed before they leave the teen years.

Questions concerning the preadolescent occurrence of manic episodes have been raised by Weller, Weller, Tucker, and Fristad (1986), who report an interesting study in which they reviewed 157 published case reports describing seriously disturbed 6- to 12-year-olds. Their assessment of these case reports identified possible or probable manic episodes in 33 of these 157 children, of whom only 17 had been diagnosed as having mania. There is accordingly reason to believe that mania will occur with some frequency among elementary school age children with serious psychological disorder, as well as among adolescents, and clinicians should accordingly guard against underdiagnosing this condition in young people.

Despite differences concerning origins, presentation, and issues of treatment, unipolar and bipolar affective disorders involve a similar dimension of disturbance. Assessment with the Rorschach usually can identify the presence of an affective disorder, but is less likely to provide a clear discrimination of the manic versus the depressed subject. This is true for adults, and possibly even more the case for younger clients. Findings concerning affective disturbance are reasonably clear in Rorschach data for adults, and to some extent, the same characteristics of affective disturbance will appear in children's data.

DIMENSIONS OF AFFECTIVE DISORDER

Affective disorder can usefully be conceived as comprising disturbances in *mood, attitudes, energy level,* and *physical status.* These disturbances constitute the basic dimensions of both depression and mania in people of all ages.

Disturbed Mood   Whereas schizophrenia is primarily a disorder of thinking, affective disorders are primarily disorders of mood, running from profound misery in the depths of depression to sheer ecstasy at the peak of mania. Pathologically depressed moods typically involve persistent feelings of sadness, spells of tearfulness, loss of interest in people and previously enjoyed pursuits, and diminished ability to experience pleasure. Pathologically elevated moods, by contrast, are reflected in unrelieved gaiety, constant smiling and laughing, infectious good humor, enthusiasm spreading in all directions, and pleasure experienced at every turn.

Depressed people tend to withdraw into themselves emotionally, are difficult if not impossible to cheer up, and usually have an unpleasant dampening effect on those around them. Manic individuals, on the other hand, actively reach out to other people and enliven social gatherings. However, because their ebullience persists even when the needs of others call for more subdued behavior, they can also make themselves socially disagreeable. In addition, both depressed and manic persons are likely to become episodically angry and irritable in ways that make it difficult for them and those around them to enjoy each other's company (see Coyne et al., 1987; Post et al., 1989; Riley, Treiber, & Woods, 1989).

Disturbed Attitudes   Affective disorder frequently involves very negative or very positive attitudes toward oneself, the world, and the future. Persons who are in the throes of depression tend to think poorly of themselves and to feel unable to control their destiny. They view themselves as inadequate, unattractive, and unlovable, and they often harbor a sense of guilt for having behaved improperly or sinfully. Their low self-esteem and self-depreciation may combine with deep reservoirs of pessimism and hopelessness to discourage them from even trying to improve their circumstances. Instead, regardless of their true potential and their actual accomplishments, depressed people compare themselves unfavorably with others, perceive painful discrepancies between their goals and their expectations, and evaluate their efforts and accomplishments negatively (see Clark & Nelson, 1990; Haage, Dyck, & Ernst, 1991; Kanfer & Zeiss, 1983; Prosen, Clark, Harrow, & Fawcett, 1983).

In just the opposite way, mania is characterized by an exaggerated sense of worth and importance, unrealistically high expectations, and an uncritical sense of optimism. No task is too difficult to achieve, no obstacle too great to surmount, and no shortcoming too serious to be overcome. Manic people expect to be loved and admired by all and to succeed in whatever they attempt. If they recognize failure when it occurs, they usually attribute it to the inadequacy or interference of others rather than to their own limitations. Whereas depressive attitudes discourage activity, the grandiosity that accompanies mania and the rose-colored glasses through which manic individuals view the world generate ambitious plans and considerable investment in carrying them out (see Carpenter & Stephens, 1980; Lerner, 1980; Van Valkenburg & Akiskal, 1985).

Whether very negative or very positive, the extreme attitudes of affectively disordered individuals distort reality to some extent. For this reason, both depression and mania can assume psychotic proportions should the person's present perceptions and future expectations begin to deviate markedly from what most people would consider realistic. Like schizophrenics, then, affectively disordered individuals may develop strange ideas about who they are and what they can or cannot do. They may even grossly misperceive the nature and implications of their experiences and show very poor judgment in how they conduct their daily lives. In such cases, the differential diagnosis between affective disorders of psychotic proportion and schizophrenia can be challenging.

Disturbed Energy Level   Depression often consists in part of diminished mental and physical energy that leads to lethargy and difficulty concentrating. Like a windup toy that is running down, depressed individuals move slowly, talk slowly, and think slowly. Because they cannot easily get their bodies to move and their minds to work, people who are depressed typically display psychomotor retardation and accomplish less than their capabilities would otherwise make possible. The deficits that depressed persons are show in processing information, in solving learning and reasoning problems, and in coordinating their attention and memory functions may at times seem to constitute a thinking disorder. However, these deficits can more parsimoniously be attributed to the depleted mental energy available to depressed persons for performing cognitive tasks than to any basic cognitive dysfunction (see Cohen, Weingartner, Smallberg, Pickar, & Murphy, 1982; Cornell, Suarez, & Berent, 1984; Silberman, Weingartner, & Post, 1983).

In mania, the tide flows in the other direction. Vast stores of energy appear to be available, frequently in greater supply than the person can harness effectively. This accounts for the characteristics of speech observed in manic individuals. Words often stumble over each other faster than they can be pronounced clearly. Thoughts seem to flow in quick succession, producing flights of ideas and causing the person to lose track of the point he or she was trying to make. The actions of manic persons appear to take many directions at once, making them seem driven, disorganized, and distractible and causing them to waste more effort than they use.

Disturbed Physical Status   The onset of affective disorder sometimes produces changes in physical status, usually referred to as the biological or vegetative features of these conditions. The most common physical changes associated with affective disorder involve disturbed patterns of sleeping and eating. Persons who are depressed tend to fall asleep slowly, sleep poorly, and wake easily. When they are successful in avoiding insomnia, fitfulness, and early morning awakening, they may still awake from long hours of sleep feeling fatigued and unrefreshed. Depressed people often experience a much smaller or much larger appetite than usual, and they may consequently lose or gain considerable weight. These disturbances in physical status more commonly accompany severe rather than mild depression, and they accordingly can provide an indication of how deeply depressed a person has become (Casper et al., 1985).

Even mild depression, without sleeping and eating problems, is likely to be reflected in a general sense of physical malaise and an exaggerated concern with health and bodily functions. As an aspect of such hypochondriasis, depressed persons frequently regard themselves as being in poorer physical condition than they used to be or would like to be, and they often experience an unusual number of aches, pains, and other somatic complaints that add to their worries about deteriorating health.

Manic individuals, by contrast, typically present a picture of robust health. They sleep soundly and require less sleep than usual to feel rested. They eat heartily, describe themselves as being in excellent condition, and rarely complain of any physical symptoms. In mania, this sense of well-being may persist despite actual physical ailments that should be causing the person concern. Manic individuals are in fact at risk for overlooking symptoms that herald the onset of illness and denying the existence of conditions for which they should receive medical treatment.

DIMENSIONS OF AFFECTIVE DISORDER IN CHILDREN AND ADOLESCENTS

Although the typical manifestations of depression and mania have been identified in studies concerning adult patients, the various dimensions of affective disorder have been demonstrated to characterize children and adolescents as well. Illustrative in this regard are the results of a study in which symptom formation was examined in 95 children (average age 9.6 years) and 92 adolescents (average age 14.7 years) who had been diagnosed as having major depressive disorder. With respect to mood, 97% of these young people displayed depressed mood, 88% demonstrated anhedonia, and 83% were notably angry or irritable. With regard to their attitudes, 78% had a negative self-image, 55% complained of hopelessness and helplessness, and 51% expressed guilt feelings. As for their energy level, 85% of the group had impaired concentration, 80% complained of fatigue, and 64% showed psychomotor retardation. Evaluations of their physical status revealed that 74% were insomniac and 73% had somatic complaints (Ryan et al., 1987).

Numerous other reports indicate that the disturbances in mood, attitudes, energy level, and physical status traditionally associated with affective disorder in adults can be readily observed and reliably measured in children and adolescents who demonstrate depression or mania (e.g., Carey, Finch, & Carey, 1991; Hops, Lewinsohn, Andrews, & Roberts, 1990; Kendall, Stark, & Adam, 1990). Clinicians and researchers have come to agree that only minor modifications of the criteria used with adults are necessary to identify these conditions in young persons (see Kendall, Cantwell, & Kazdin, 1989; Kovacs, 1989; Ryan, 1989; Strober, McCracken, & Hanna, 1989).

On the other hand, developmental changes do produce some variation with age in how affective disorders are likely to be manifested (see Weiner, 1982, Chap. 7; 1992, Chap. 4). For example, because elementary school children lack the capacities of older people to conceptualize and verbalize moods and attitudes, they tend to manifest affective disorder less along these dimensions than through disturbances in their energy level and physical status. For this reason uncharacteristic sluggishness, heightened activity, or distractibility in the absence of demonstrable attention deficit disorder, and various physical complaints, especially headache and abdominal pain, are often among the initial or most prominent indications of emerging affective disorder in young children. In the Ryan et al. (1987) study, for example, instances of depressed appearance and somatic complaints were significantly more frequent or more severe among the depressed children than the depressed adolescents.

As children approach puberty and become increasingly capable of evaluating themselves, those who become affectively disordered become more likely to show a deflated or inflated sense of their self-worth. Likewise, the emergence of formal operational thinking during adolescence and the continuing maturation of capacities for self-expression foster the formation of attitudes toward past and future events and the vivid description of emotional experience. Hence, with adolescence, the mood and attitudinal dimensions of affective disorder are likely to become relatively more prominent than they were earlier. Ryan et al. (1987) found significantly more frequent or more severe complaints of anhedonia and hopelessness or helplessness among their adolescent than their child subjects.

As adolescence proceeds, young people become very concerned with maintaining their self-esteem and sense of competence. Hence, they often find it difficult to admit depressive thoughts and feelings, especially of anhedonia and inadequacy, either to themselves or to others. Instead, they often deny any depressive concerns and seek to ward off depressive experiences through various kinds of oppositional, delinquent, or sensation-seeking behavior, including substance abuse (Weiner, 1992, Chap. 4).

THE DYNAMIC INTERPLAY OF DEPRESSION AND MANIA

Although developmental variations in the manifestations of affective disorder do not alter the basic dimensions of depression and mania, they do influence the Rorschach responses that subjects are likely to produce. Among subjects who harbor negative self-attitudes, for example, those who are able to formulate and express them clearly and are willing or even eager to do so will respond differently from those who cannot easily grasp their own attitudes or are attempting to deny having them. In addition, the Rorschach manifestations of affective disorder are likely to be influenced by a dynamic interplay between depression and mania.

Like most types of serious psychological disturbance, depression and mania both result from the pathological interaction of genetic dispositions and unfavorable life experiences. The genetic data in this regard demonstrate a close relationship between bipolar manic-depressive and unipolar depressive forms of affective disorder. The relatives of both adult and adolescent patients with bipolar affective disorder are significantly more likely than people in general to display or develop either bipolar or unipolar disorder (Andreasen et al., 1987; Kutcher & Marton, 1991).

The shared genetic origins of depression and mania are accompanied by some shared types of unpleasant experience as well. Depressed young people and adults who become depressed are much more likely than nondepressed individuals to have experienced disruptive life events signifying personal, interpersonal, or achievement-related losses. For those whose personality style is primarily socially oriented, these distressing events typically comprise interpersonal losses or disappointments; whereas the depression of people whose motivations center more around achievement than affiliation is more likely to involve unsuccessful striving than interpersonal difficulties (Barnett & Gotlib, 1988; Hammen & Goodman-Brown, 1990; Robins, 1990).

The events that contribute to mania have not yet been studied as extensively as those associated with depression. Nevertheless, some data suggest that stressful experiences of loss play an important role in precipitating manic as well as depressive episodes (Carpenter & Stephens, 1980; Dunner, Patrick, & Fieve, 1979; Neale, 1988). In addition, follow-up studies indicate that only 10% to 20% of persons with a major depressive disorder also develop episodes of mania, whereas individuals with mania almost always have a prior history of depression as well (Abrams & Taylor, 1974; Mendelwicz, 1980).

These findings support conceptualizing depression as the basic core of affective disorder and mania as an effort to ward off depression in the wake of stressful experiences of loss. People who become depressed are not destined to become manic, but people who display mania can be expected to slip into depression at times when they become unable to muster or sustain manic defenses against stress. Denial usually is the primary defensive ingredient in this dynamic interplay between depression and mania.

RORSCHACH INDICES OF DISTURBED MOOD

As affective disorders are primarily disorders of mood, Rorschach assessment of these conditions rests heavily on test indices of dejection. These indices of disturbed mood usually are drawn from structural features of Rorschach data, from the kinds of thematic imagery that appear, and from the manner in which subjects approach the test situation.

The key indices of the dejection or distress that characterizes a depressed mood are a greater frequency of shading responses (*SumSh*) than *FM* + *m* responses, which points to an unusual amount of experienced emotional distress; the presence of one or more Vista (*V*) answers that reflect painful internal feelings that result from rumination about oneself and which may often reflect a sense of guilt or remorse; frequent achromatic color (*C'*) responses, demonstrating an excess of unpleasant internalized affect with dysphoric overtones; and the presence of Color-Shading blends, which are usually associated with mixed or confused feelings that prevent people from enjoying themselves and render them anhedonic.

The difficulties that depressed individuals typically have in dealing comfortably with emotions often result in a low Affective Ratio, which signifies withdrawal from emotionally charged situations and a reluctance to become involved in exchanging feelings with others, and sometimes result in a high Intellectualization Index, which identifies defensive use of intellectualization as a way of taking distance from or diminishing the impact of emotional experience. Emotional withdrawal, particularly with respect to loss of interest in people and in social interactions, is reflected by an elevated Isolation Index and a limited number of cooperative movement (COP) responses. Finally, the feelings of anger and irritability that often accompany depression are indicated by frequent white space (*S*) responses. Each of these indices of depressed mood contributes to the Comprehensive System *Depression Index* (DEPI), which is listed in Table 45.

One additional structural variable that bears witness to extremely painful externalized affect is a shading-shading blend. Even a single response in a record that combines two or more elements of *C', Y, V,* or *T* suggests that the individual is experiencing considerable

Table 45.   Criteria for the Depression Index (DEPI)

1. $(FV + VF + V > 0)$ **or** $(FD > 2)$.
2. (Col-Shd Blends > 0) **or** (S > 2).
3. $(3r + (2)/R > .44$ and $Fr + rF = 0)$ **or** $(3r + (2)/R < .33)$.*
4. $(Afr < .46)$ **or** (Blends < 4).
5. $(SumShading > FM + m)$ **or** $(SumC' > 2)$.
6. (MOR > 2) **or** $(2AB + Art + Ay > 3)$.
7. (COP > 2) **or** $([Bt + 2Cl + Ge + Ls + 2Na]/R > .24)$.

*$3r + (2)/R$ should be adjusted to exceed plus or minus 1 SD
for younger clients.

dysphoria. Thematic imagery that includes the projection of feeling states into responses also helps to identify the disturbed moods of persons who are depressed. Prominent themes of sadness and disappointment, frequent images of people who are crying or mourning, and recurring impressions of bleak and dreary landscapes suggest dejection.

Finally with respect to assessing disturbed moods, dejected subjects will typically respond to the Rorschach task in ways that reflect how they are feeling. Depressed subjects often seem to be in poor spirits and find little enjoyment in looking at inkblots. Whether or not they overtly resist the task, they usually make it clear that being tested is a burden they would prefer to unshoulder ("Are we done yet?" "How many more are there?").

RORSCHACH INDICES OF DISTURBED ATTITUDES

The negative attitudes toward oneself, the world, and the future that accompany depression are measured structurally on the Rorschach by the presence of Vista responses (V) and/or Frequent Dimensionality (FD) responses, which identify painful introspection and harshly critical self-attitudes; by a low Egocentricity Ratio or a high Egocentricity Ratio in the absence of any reflections ($Fr + rF$), which, if low, indicates tendencies to compare oneself unfavorably with other people, or if high suggests an unusual preoccupation with the self; and by numerous morbid (MOR) responses, which suggests a generally pessimistic outlook on life. Each of these variables is included in the DEPI.

In addition, the helplessness that depressed individuals often experience with respect to controlling their destiny may be reflected in an elevated frequency of m and Y. As situational variables, however, m and Y are likely to fluctuate with daily changes in a depressed person's attitudes, rather than reflect a central feature of the disorder. Moreover, despite their implications for concerns about being helpless, m and Y are probably best interpreted as general signs of distress that are likely to become elevated in conjunction with anxiety as well as depression.

The thematic imagery indicators of negative self-attitudes involve projected images of oneself as a small, weak, insignificant, unattractive, and unworthy. Such projections occur most often in human and animal figures described in uncomplimentary terms ("a really ugly person"; "a stupid little worm") or seen as engaged in inept, unsuccessful or improper activity ("A guy on a motorcycle but he's not very good at it"; "Some animals sliding down a mountain they're trying to climb"; "These kids knocked over some paint, and they'll get caught"). In this regard, themes of guilt and punishment often flavor the responses of depressed subjects. In addition to actual descriptions of misbehavior, their records frequently include figures from whom bad behavior is expected ("devils," "gremlins," "skinhead") and surroundings commonly associated with retribution for one's transgressions ("Hades," "a crucifix," "things to torture people with"). As always, however, such imagery must be interpreted conservatively, in the context of the individual subject's frame of reference and with careful attention to alternative symbolic meanings, rather than as certain evidence of any specific attitude. Consider, for example, a boy who sees and thereby presumably identifies himself with "Damien." Perhaps he views himself as an evil person who deserves punishment; perhaps, however, he is identifying with Damien as a powerful person who can bend circumstances to his will, and accordingly views himself as a select individual entitled to get his way, whatever the cost to others.

In addition to self-denigrating themes, the Rorschach imagery of depressed subjects often reflects their negative views of the world and the future: "It's so dark, there must be a storm coming"; "It looks like what's left after a bomb fell"; "The ruins of an old castle, you can see where the walls have crumbled"; "It probably was pretty at one time, but the water has washed most of it away." Many responses of these kinds will be scored MOR and thereby counted in DEPI. At times, however, responses that do not meet requirements for scoring MOR will contain symbolic indications of negative forebodings, such as "a Doomsday machine" or "the Grim Reaper." What all such responses have in common is the reflected attitude that matters are not going very well right now, at least not as well as in the past, and that the worst is yet to come.

Subjects who are depressed tend to act as if they expect to perform poorly and be castigated for their ineptness. More often than not, they make extraneous comments that derogate themselves ("I'm not very good at this sort of thing"), belittle their responses ("That's probably not the kind of answer I'm supposed to give"), and indicate concern about a bad outcome ("What happens to me if these tests don't turn out right?").

RORSCHACH INDICES OF DISTURBED ENERGY LEVEL

The depleted energy level associated with states of depression typically diminishes the number and complexity of a subject's Rorschach responses. Lethargic individuals who are having difficulty keeping their psychological motors running rarely have much to say about what inkblots might be. Hence, their response total (R) is often lower than 20, and, even if their R is 20 or more, their individual answers frequently tend to be brief and unelaborated. When the lethargy element is substantial, depressed subjects are less likely than people in general to put much effort into organizing and synthesizing perceptual inputs and blending determinants. Hence, they may show a relatively low Zf, or a small number of $DQ+$ responses, or a small proportion of blends, the last of which is included among the DEPI criteria.

The thematic imagery expressed by depressed subjects sometimes projects their low energy level onto figures that are described as tired, bored, sleepy, listless, or stuck. Their movement responses often have a passive quality, with humans and animals perceived as "resting," "lying down," "just sitting there," "barely able to move," and the like, and the specific contents they select sometimes symbolize the inertia they are experiencing, as in "snail," "sloth," "Beetle Bailey,"or "a sailboat with no wind." The reduced energy level of some depressed subjects may carry over into their test-taking approach. They often take much time in responding and deliver their responses in a very deliberate fashion, and sometimes make the examiner's task difficult by mustering only limited enthusiasm for explaining their responses on Inquiry.

RORSCHACH INDICES OF DISTURBED PHYSICAL STATUS

For the most part, disturbances in physical status associated with an affective disorder appear in the clinical history and self-report inventories rather than on the Rorschach. Nevertheless, two structural variables often help to identify depressing somatic concerns. One of these consists of frequent morbid (MOR) responses, which is included in DEPI and signifies the subject's concern that his or her body is in some way weak, damaged, or deformed and is vulnerable to physical harm, illness, or deterioration. The other variable is the presence of more than two anatomy and X-ray $(An + Xy)$ responses, which is infrequent at all ages and indicates the subject has an unusual preoccupation with his or her body and how it is functioning.

DIAGNOSTIC DECISIONS

Rorschach indices of disturbances in mood, attitudes, energy level, and physical status can assist clinicians in making a variety of diagnostic decisions concerning the psychological status of young people with depression. These decisions should begin with interpretation of DEPI and continue with careful consideration of several specific diagnostic issues in differentiating the nature of affective disorder.

Considerations in Interpreting DEPI   As elaborated by Exner (1991, Chap. 1), a DEPI of 5 is likely to indicate the presence of depressive features in a subject's present condition, although not necessarily a diagnosable primary affective disorder, and a DEPI of 6 or 7 is likely to identify the presence of either a major depressive episode or a chronic disposition to becoming pathologically depressed. A DEPI of 4 or less may reflect some important individual components of depressive mood states or cognitions, such as numerous C' or a low Egocentricity Ratio; however, a DEPI less than 5 is meaningless as an actuarial index of depression and provides no information whatsoever concerning whether or not a subject is diagnosably depressed.

This empirically derived cutting score has significant clinical and research implications. Clinically, findings to date indicate that DEPI, like SCZI, contributes to psychodiagnosis by virtue of yielding very few false positives. Subjects with an elevated DEPI almost always turn out to be pathologically depressed, whereas nonpatients rarely show a DEPI of 5 or more, whatever their age. False negative findings with DEPI, on the other hand, are commonplace. In one group of 315 inpatient adults diagnosed as depressive disorder, just 75% had a DEPI of more than 4, which means that the index did not detect the diagnosed depression in the remaining one fourth of these patients (Exner, 1991, Chap. 2). Although comparable data for children and adolescents are sparse, they tend to confirm that the vast majority of young people with elevated DEPIs are clinically depressed, but that many children and adolescents who appear depressed are not identified as such by DEPI (Ball, Archer, Gordon, & French, 1991). Hence, clinicians are not only well advised to think seriously about the probable presence of an affective disorder when DEPI is elevated, but to avoid dismissing the possibility of affective disorder just because DEPI is less than 5.

This is illustrated quite well by the frequency data presented in Table 46 for a sample of 100 adolescents who were diagnosed as being seriously depressed using DSM-III-R criteria. They were randomly drawn from an available pool of 236 records. The subjects, 76 white, 15 black, and 9 Hispanic, range in age from 13 to 16, with a median age of 14.5. Forty-two of the subjects are outpatients, and 48 are first admission inpatients. Nineteen of the inpatients were admitted to public psychiatric hospitals, and 29 were admitted to private hospitals.

As will be noted in Table 46, only 69 of the 100 adolescent patients have a positive DEPI, that is, one with a value of 5 or greater. In fact, only 37 of the 100 have DEPI values greater than 5, that is, values sufficient from which to conclude that a serious affective problem exists. Some descriptive statistics for this sample are shown in Table 47.

Table 46. Frequency Data Concerning 100 Adolescents Diagnosed as Depressed Using DSM-III-R Criteria

RATIOS, PERCENTAGES AND SPECIAL INDICES					
EB STYLE			**FORM QUALITY DEVIATIONS**		
Introversive	34	34%	$X+\% > .89$	2	2%
Pervasive-Introversive	22	22%	$X+\% < .70$	79	79%
Ambitent	40	40%	$X+\% < .61$	54	54%
Extratensive	26	26%	$X+\% < .50$	32	32%
Pervasive-Extratensive	11	11%	$F+\% < .70$	68	68%
			$Xu\% > .20$	43	43%
EA - es DIFFERENCES: D-SCORES			$X-\% > .15$	71	71%
D Score > 0	12	12%	$X-\% > .20$	63	63%
D Score $= 0$	41	41%	$X-\% > .30$	12	12%
D Score < 0	47	47%			
D Score < -1	22	22%	**FC:CF + C RATIO**		
			$FC > (CF + C) + 2$	17	17%
Adj D Score > 0	26	26%	$FC > (CF + C) + 1$	29	29%
Adj D Score $= 0$	50	50%	$(CF + C) > FC + 1$	26	26%
Adj D Score < 0	24	24%	$(CF + C) > FC + 2$	16	16%
Adj D Score < -1	15	15%			
			S-Constellation Positive	13	13%
Zd $> +3.0$ (Overincorp)	41	41%	HVI Positive	18	18%
Zd < -3.0 (Underincorp)	21	21%	OBS Positive	0	0%

SCZI = 6	0	0%	DEPI = 7	8	8%	CDI = 5	19	19%
SCZI = 5	2	2%	DEPI = 6	29	29%	CDI = 4	22	22%
SCZI = 4	10	10%	DEPI = 5	32	32%			

MISCELLANEOUS VARIABLES					
Lambda $> .99$	19	19%	$(2AB + Art + Ay) > 5$	17	17%
Dd > 3	27	27%	Populars < 4	21	21%
DQv+DQv/+ > 2	16	16%	Populars > 7	11	11%
S > 2	76	76%	COP $= 0$	49	49%
Sum T $= 0$	53	53%	COP > 2	16	16%
Sum T > 1	14	14%	AG $= 0$	51	51%
3r + (2)/R $< .33$	43	43%	AG > 2	28	28%
3r + (2)/R $> .44$	31	31%	MOR > 2	46	46%
Fr + rF > 0	36	36%	Level 2 Sp.Sc. > 0	43	43%
PureC > 0	8	8%	Sum 6 Sp. Sc. > 6	25	25%
PureC > 1	2	2%	Pure H < 2	28	28%
Afr $< .40$	29	29%	Pure H $= 0$	2	2%
Afr $< .50$	46	46%	$p > a + 1$	51	51%
(FM + m) $<$ Sum Shading	59	59%	Mp $>$ Ma	61	61%

Table 47. Descriptive Statistics for 100 Adolescents Diagnosed as Depressed Using DSM-III-R Criteria

Variable	Mean	SD	Min	Max	Freq	Median	Mode	SK	KU
R	20.05	5.81	14.00	47.00	100	18.00	18.00	2.14	6.95
W	9.75	4.24	1.00	20.00	100	9.00	12.00	0.60	0.44
D	7.52	4.78	1.00	23.00	100	6.00	5.00	0.99	1.02
Dd	2.78	[2.86]	0.00	21.00	96	2.00	1.00	3.79	19.95
S	4.09	[2.09]	0.00	12.00	96	4.00	6.00	0.34	1.34
DQ+	6.96	3.59	1.00	16.00	100	7.00	7.00	0.93	0.89
DQo	11.70	6.14	6.00	40.00	100	10.00	9.00	2.23	5.79
DQv	0.96	[1.04]	0.00	4.00	55	1.00	0.00	0.84	0.18
DQv/+	0.43	[0.78]	0.00	3.00	27	0.00	0.00	1.66	1.62
FQx+	0.06	0.24	0.00	1.00	6	0.00	0.00	3.76	12.40
FQxo	11.17	3.49	5.00	22.00	100	11.00	11.00	0.45	0.34
FQxu	4.52	3.13	0.00	19.00	99	4.00	3.00	2.09	6.70
FQx−	4.14	2.57	0.00	11.00	92	4.00	4.00	0.25	−0.48
FQxNone	0.16	[0.60]	0.00	4.00	9	0.00	0.00	4.55	22.70
MQ+	0.01	0.10	0.00	1.00	1	0.00	0.00	10.00	100.00
MQo	2.89	1.81	0.00	8.00	90	3.00	4.00	0.13	−0.58
MQu	0.95	1.60	0.00	5.00	40	0.00	0.00	1.71	1.48
MQ−	1.12	[1.17]	0.00	4.00	68	1.00	1.00	1.25	0.81
MQNone	0.04	[0.20]	0.00	1.00	4	0.00	0.00	4.76	21.14
SQual−	1.59	[1.28]	0.00	6.00	73	2.00	2.00	0.48	0.15
M	5.01	3.11	1.00	13.00	100	5.00	2.00	0.72	−0.01
FM	3.18	1.62	1.00	6.00	100	3.00	2.00	−0.12	−0.66
m	2.05	2.52	0.00	9.00	70	1.00	1.00	1.62	1.90
FC	1.25	1.07	0.00	4.00	73	1.00	1.00	0.55	−0.72
CF	1.89	1.61	0.00	5.00	75	2.00	0.00	0.44	−1.03
C	0.13	[0.54]	0.00	4.00	8	0.00	0.00	5.46	33.10
Cn	0.00	[0.00]	0.00	0.00	0	0.00	0.00	—	—
Sum Color	3.37	2.25	0.00	8.00	98	3.00	6.00	0.46	−0.57
WSumC	2.71	1.98	0.00	9.00	91	2.00	1.50	0.73	0.02
Sum C'	2.14	[1.76]	0.00	8.00	77	2.00	0.00	0.48	−0.36
Sum T	0.81	[0.71]	0.00	3.00	47	0.00	1.00	1.93	1.89
Sum V	1.14	[1.58]	0.00	6.00	53	1.00	0.00	1.97	3.85
Sum Y	0.87	[1.35]	0.00	5.00	43	0.00	0.00	1.78	2.53
Sum Shading	5.46	3.31	0.00	14.00	88	4.00	5.00	1.40	2.70
Fr + rF	0.97	[1.01]	0.00	3.00	39	0.00	0.00	0.48	−1.13
FD	1.63	[1.69]	0.00	6.00	78	1.00	1.00	1.22	0.91
F	7.03	5.55	1.00	31.00	100	5.00	3.00	1.90	5.51
(2)	6.22	3.28	0.00	19.00	92	6.00	4.00	0.54	1.51
3r + (2)/R	0.47	0.18	0.00	0.89	99	0.43	0.56	0.51	0.27
Lambda	0.74	0.87	0.08	4.33	100	0.45	0.20	2.37	6.10
FM + m	5.23	3.01	1.00	11.00	100	5.00	5.00	0.77	−0.38
EA	7.72	4.43	1.00	18.50	100	8.25	9.50	0.72	0.23
es	9.69	5.61	1.00	25.00	100	10.00	10.00	1.15	1.65
D Score	−0.51	1.15	−3.00	3.00	59	0.00	0.00	0.61	1.09
AdjD	0.03	1.24	−2.00	3.00	50	0.00	0.00	0.23	0.18
a (active)	4.59	3.48	1.00	13.00	100	3.00	3.00	1.27	0.58
p (passive)	5.65	3.69	0.00	16.00	98	5.00	7.00	1.28	2.10
Ma	1.86	1.61	0.00	5.00	79	1.00	1.00	0.64	−0.72
Mp	3.15	2.39	0.00	10.00	92	3.00	4.00	1.13	1.05
Intellect	1.44	2.17	0.00	7.00	41	0.00	0.00	1.42	0.93
Zf	13.16	4.42	5.00	24.00	100	13.00	13.00	0.75	0.80
Zd	1.57	4.55	−6.50	12.00	98	1.25	3.50	0.54	−0.36
Blends	5.36	4.58	0.00	18.00	92	5.00	3.00	1.38	1.76
Blends/R	0.27	0.20	0.00	0.72	92	0.24	0.39	0.56	−0.56
Col-Shd Blends	0.66	[1.04]	0.00	4.00	45	0.00	0.00	2.27	5.10
Afr	0.50	0.16	0.21	0.88	100	0.53	0.64	0.00	−0.80

Table 47. (Continued)

Variable	Mean	SD	Min	Max	Freq	Median	Mode	SK	KU
Populars	5.48	2.11	2.00	10.00	100	5.00	5.00	0.42	−0.02
X+%	0.57	0.15	0.29	0.94	100	0.57	0.61	0.29	−0.70
F+%	0.64	0.22	0.18	1.00	100	0.67	0.67	−0.06	−0.55
X−%	0.21	0.11	0.00	0.47	92	0.22	0.22	−0.14	−0.34
Xu%	0.22	0.11	0.00	0.43	99	0.20	0.17	0.46	−0.37
S−%	0.38	[0.30]	0.00	1.00	73	0.43	0.00	0.36	−0.52
Isolate/R	0.29	0.21	0.00	0.80	95	0.22	0.22	0.99	0.55
H	2.56	1.60	0.00	8.00	98	2.00	2.00	1.03	0.68
(H)	1.98	1.45	0.00	5.00	81	2.00	2.00	0.44	−0.46
HD	1.42	1.26	0.00	9.00	84	1.00	1.00	2.73	12.92
(Hd)	0.89	1.01	0.00	3.00	51	1.00	1.00	0.69	−0.83
Hx	0.67	[0.74]	0.00	3.00	21	0.00	0.00	3.17	10.93
H + (H) + Hd + (Hd)	6.85	3.21	2.00	17.00	100	7.00	3.00	0.78	0.83
A	6.90	2.72	3.00	15.00	100	6.00	4.00	0.63	−0.45
(A)	0.44	[0.70]	0.00	3.00	33	0.00	0.00	1.47	1.40
Ad	2.30	[1.85]	0.00	8.00	85	2.00	1.00	0.79	0.12
(Ad)	0.29	[0.70]	0.00	2.00	15	0.00	0.00	2.04	2.28
An	0.44	[0.66]	0.00	4.00	39	0.00	0.00	2.30	9.03
Art	0.48	0.74	0.00	4.00	36	0.00	0.00	1.78	4.11
Ay	0.26	[0.61]	0.00	2.00	17	0.00	0.00	2.19	3.38
Bl	0.26	[0.44]	0.00	1.00	26	0.00	0.00	1.11	−0.78
Bt	1.29	1.33	0.00	6.00	68	1.00	1.00	1.19	1.12
Cg	1.70	1.39	0.00	4.00	79	1.00	1.00	0.46	−1.08
Cl	0.41	[0.65]	0.00	2.00	32	0.00	0.00	1.34	0.58
Ex	0.23	[0.57]	0.00	2.00	16	0.00	0.00	2.38	4.45
Fi	0.73	[0.84]	0.00	2.00	48	0.00	0.00	0.54	−1.36
Food	0.12	[0.41]	0.00	3.00	10	0.00	0.00	4.50	25.37
Ge	0.01	[0.10]	0.00	1.00	1	0.00	0.00	10.00	100.00
Hh	0.87	1.13	0.00	9.00	64	1.00	1.00	4.12	26.34
Ls	1.18	1.24	0.00	4.00	63	1.00	0.00	0.94	−0.06
Na	1.11	[1.17]	0.00	4.00	64	1.00	1.00	1.09	0.49
Sc	0.84	[1.06]	0.00	3.00	51	1.00	0.00	1.15	0.08
Sx	0.08	[0.37]	0.00	3.00	6	0.00	0.00	5.97	41.86
Xy	0.00	[0.00]	0.00	0.00	0	0.00	0.00	—	—
Idiographic	1.23	1.22	0.00	8.00	78	1.00	1.00	2.39	9.31
DV	1.31	[1.16]	0.00	3.00	70	1.00	1.00	0.39	−1.30
INCOM	1.30	[1.03]	0.00	3.00	71	1.00	2.00	0.10	−1.19
DR	0.23	[0.62]	0.00	3.00	14	0.00	0.00	2.70	6.52
FABCOM	0.39	[0.75]	0.00	2.00	23	0.00	0.00	1.55	0.63
DV2	0.08	[0.27]	0.00	1.00	8	0.00	0.00	3.14	8.04
INC2	0.44	[0.80]	0.00	3.00	29	0.00	0.00	1.85	2.74
DR2	0.02	[0.20]	0.00	2.00	1	0.00	0.00	10.00	100.00
FAB2	0.30	[0.67]	0.00	3.00	19	0.00	0.00	2.17	3.72
ALOG	0.41	[0.70]	0.00	2.00	29	0.00	0.00	1.42	0.57
CONTAM	0.00	0.00	0.00	0.00	0	0.00	0.00	—	—
Sum 6 Sp Sc	4.48	3.00	0.00	10.00	98	4.00	1.00	0.37	−1.07
Lvl 2 Sp Sc	0.84	[1.17]	0.00	5.00	43	0.00	0.00	1.36	1.31
WSum6	12.35	10.37	0.00	35.00	98	10.00	4.00	0.70	−0.73
AB	0.35	[0.63]	0.00	2.00	27	0.00	0.00	1.60	1.38
AG	1.15	1.38	0.00	4.00	49	0.00	0.00	0.75	−0.89
CFB	0.00	0.00	0.00	0.00	0	0.00	0.00	—	—
COP	0.91	1.12	0.00	4.00	51	1.00	0.00	1.01	−0.22
CP	0.07	[0.26]	0.00	1.00	7	0.00	0.00	3.42	9.91
MOR	1.98	[1.45]	0.00	7.00	83	2.00	3.00	0.45	−1.31
PER	1.17	1.48	0.00	5.00	48	0.00	0.00	0.98	−0.35
PSV	0.08	[0.31]	0.00	2.00	7	0.00	0.00	4.14	18.39

Large samples of Rorschach data concerning children under the age of 13 are not available, but it seems reasonable to suggest that if the protocols of at least 100 youngsters in the age range from 7 to 12 were available, the percentage having a positive DEPI (values of 5 or greater) would be smaller than is found among adolescents. This speculation is based on the fact that younger children usually do not manifest the features of depression as do adolescents or adults. This creates a considerable challenge for the Rorschach researcher, and that challenge is increased because DSM definitions of depression encompass a huge number of potential combinations of presenting symptoms. These problems often are compounded by the way in which research is designed and resulting data are analyzed or interpreted. For example, Lipovsky, Finch, and Belter (1989) reported on a study concerning the original DEPI and found that it did not distinguish between depressed and nondepressed adolescents, although the original DEPI correlated significantly with the MMPI Depression Scale among adolescents in this study. However, the depressed and nondepressed groups did not differ significantly in their mean DEPI value.

Examining mean differences for DEPI bears little relationship to how the index was developed. Whether a clinical index has criterion validity is a matter of whether it does what it is supposed to do, and what the original DEPI was supposed to do is distinguish between depressed and nondepressed subjects on the basis of their having a DEPI value of more than 4. The Lipovsky et al, study included 35 depressed and 25 nondepressed subjects, and although small samples are suitable for some kinds of research, these samples are too small to generate sufficiently powerful statistics to guard adequately against Type II error (i.e., accepting the null hypothesis when it is false and a meaningful relationship does in fact exist) (Acklin, McDowell, & Orndoff, 1992; Wampold & Freund, 1991). Nonetheless, the work of Lipovsky et al., seem to indicate quite clearly that the original DEPI was not very useful with younger clients, a finding that was already evident in data concerning false negatives with adults. It was because of studies such as Lipovsky et al. that the original DEPI was cast aside and the current version created. But that does not mean that the current DEPI has solved all problems concerning the diagnosis of depression, especially in younger clients.

Rorschach research concerning depression, whether with adults or children, must not only define criteria appropriately and employ samples of sufficient size but also select adequate validation criterion variables against which to compare whatever Rorschach indices are under study. If the criterion variable is an independently and carefully determined clinical diagnosis of depression, DEPI should be expected to rule in, although not necessarily rule out, depressive disorder accurately, but whether DEPI correlates with self-report and observational measures of depression may have less to do with its clinical validity than with similarities or differences between these various kinds of measures.

To amplify this point with respect to one of the DEPI components, a low Egocentricity Ratio has been found to correlate with a high Depression Scale on the MMPI but not with the Beck Depression Inventory, the Children's Depression Inventory, or the Piers-Harris Children's Self-Concept Scale (Belter, Lipovsky, & Finch, 1989; Caputo-Sacco & Lewis, 1991; Duricko, Norcross, & Buskirk, 1989). However, as noted in a discussion of multimethod assessment of depression by Shapiro, Leifer, Martone, and Kassem (1990), tests such as the Rorschach, self-report instruments such as the Children's Depression Inventory, and behavioral observation instruments such as the Child Behavior Checklist involve different types and levels of measurement. These various approaches may under some circumstances yield similar results, but they may also point in different directions, not because any lacks valid correlates, but because they assess depression from different perspectives and at different levels of awareness. In support of these observations, other research has demonstrated that parents' reports of depression in their children, whether during interviews or on parent report instruments, tend to underestimate the extent of depression that their children actually report or that is inferred from clinical evaluations (Angold, Weissman, Karen, & Merikangas, 1987; Fendrich, Weissman, & Warner, 1991).

Obviously, the Rorschach should not be regarded as inviolable when attempting to address the issue of depression or other affective problems. This is especially true when younger clients are involved, but good clinical judgment can often help. For instance, when clinically interpreting a record in which the DEPI is not positive, other features of the record may well provide a basis for inferring depressive features or diagnosing depressive disorder. A subject with two Morbids, an Affective Ratio of .40, and an Isolation Index of .23 could be just a whisker away from receiving three additional points on the DEPI; then suppose further that both of the Morbids produced by the subject point dramatically to extremely pessimistic thinking. An actuarial approach cannot make allowances for such near misses and unscored qualitative features, and indeed it should not in the context of research efforts to objectify Rorschach interpretation. Clinical sensitivity to these kinds of findings often leads interpreters to identify depression or depressive features that would otherwise go undetected by DEPI.

CASE 5—TRUANCY

This is a 9-year 10-month-old male referred by his school because he frequently runs away from school. He is currently in the 2nd month of the fifth grade in a private school to which he transferred this year because of behavior problems in the public school that have existed since his second-grade year. He is in good health and of normal height and weight for his age. His WISC-R performance yielded a Verbal IQ of 112, Performance IQ of 108, Full-Scale IQ of 111 (Info = 13, Sim = 15, Arith = 9, Voc = 12, Comp = 11, DigSp = 15, PC = 12, PA = 9, Blk = 12, OA = 10, Cdg = 10, Mz = 13).

His academic performance has been satisfactory although he did have some trouble with arithmetic for about half of the third grade. That problem has cleared, and at times he does above average work, but those intervals are generally brief and usually follow some punishment either by the school or the parents. He has a 3-year history of fighting with other children (usually 2 or 3 times per week) but claims that he gets along "OK" with most of his peers. He says that others provoke the fights, but he always gets blamed for them. He admits that he doesn't have any "really close" friends, and that he doesn't like the private school to which he has transferred because he has to ride the bus 40 minutes each way and none of his classmates live near him. He says that the new school is "extra, extra hard and extra extra long" (he does leave home for the bus at 7:30 A.M. and does not get home until 4:15 P.M.). Apparently when he leaves school, he wanders around the neighborhood, but occasionally will try to hitchhike home. He has been discovered a few times in a local store watching people play arcade games.

His father is 41 years old, has completed two years of college, and works as a computer technician. His mother is 39. She is a high school graduate and has not worked outside the home. He has an 8-year-old sister who apparently has to be coaxed into going to school and is often accompanied to school by mother. She is currently in the second grade. The family has moved three times since he was born and he has lived in the current residence for slightly less than 4 years. His parents claim to have a happy marriage and seem confused by their son's behavior. The father implies that the mother overprotected the subject during his early years, but when pressed on this, denies it. Apparently, the family does not do many things together although they do have an annual 2-week vacation at a nearby lake. The father belongs to a company bowling league that competes weekly except during the summer. He also usually plays golf with some friends on Sundays. The mother belongs to a women's rights organization that usually meets weekly and has been involved in "prochoice" activities during the past 2 years. The subject says that he gets along well with his parents and notes that his sister is "OK" He says that he does not fight with her "because she's a girl and you don't fight with girls." He says that he likes TV and computer games. He says that he likes to play computer games with his father. He does not like baseball but says he is "pretty good" playing soccer and football. He reports that if he does something wrong his father usually punishes him, sometimes by a spanking, but typically by restrictions. He states that he wants to be an airline pilot or an astronaut when he grows up.

The referral raises two basic issues. The first is a question raised by his teacher; namely, should he be in a special class for children with management problems? She argues that he is quite disruptive and is strongly disliked or avoided by others in his class. The school guidance counselor asks whether there is a psychiatric problem, such as some kind of school phobia that might require treatment.

Case 5. A 9-Year-Old Male

Card	Response		Inquiry	Scoring
I	1.	Ths ll st from the aliens, u kno, the movie	E: (Rpts S's resp) S: Yeah, did u c it (E: No). Well the alien was really lik disgusting, & it ll a guy's face that he mashd in	WSo Fu Hd 3.5 MOR,PER
	E:	Tak ur tim & look som more & I thk ull find st else	E: I'm not sur I'm seeg it rite, help me S: Well u had to c the movie, the alien hit ths guys face & mashd it up & it ll ths whn he did it, just lik som guy w a mashd face, c the eyes & whts left of his mouth, just mashd up, c his ears r spread out 2, I saw the movie twice	
	2.	A big giant bf	E: (Rpts S's resp) S: I don't thk it ll that. E: It did whn u lookd before, lets try & c it lik tht again S: I don't c it anymor E: Tak ur time & try, u saw it before S: Well, ths is parallel to tht (traces wgs) lik its got its wgs out, lik thy do whn thy fly E: U said it was a giant bf? S: Well it looks awful big here, lik a giant one	Wo FMao A P 1.0 DV2,ALOG
II	v3.	It ll a big explosion far away	E: (Rpts S's resp) S: U can c al th red stuff, lik an explosion, all going up outa ths hole, c its left a hole where all the stuff that got blown up used to b (traces D3 + DS5) E: U said it was far away? S: Yeah, its pretty small, lik I was far off lkg at it, all ths stuff tht used to b here is gettg blown up & its all burning & shootg all ovr the place, but its not near me	DS + ma.CF.FDo Ex,Ls 4.5 AG,MOR
	4.	Whn I look ths way it ll ths guy is fallg into ths big pit, its really deep.	E: (Rpts S's resp) S: Forget the red part, OK (E: OK) Ths (D4) ll som guy, lik som space guy cuz he's got a space helmet on him & sb just shot him or sthg & he's beging to fall ovr into ths big deep pit E: What makes it look deep? S: C th sides (traces) thy ll clifs, lik going dwn, c th colrs lik clifs so its prety deep dwn ther	DS + Mp.FVo (H),Ls,Cg 4.5 MOR

201

Case 5. (Continued)

Card	Response	Inquiry	Scoring
		E. And the space guy? He ll he's leang ovr, lik fallg lik ths (demos by movg his hands forward) lik sb shot him & he's fallg, c hre's his helmet (outlines)	
III	5. It ll a crab, thts all I c	E: (Rpts S's resp) S: Well, u can c the teeth thr & the eyes & c th claws r here & thes r the knuckles, u kno lik on a crab? E: I'm not sur I'm seeg it rite S: Lk (traces) eyes, teeth, claws, knuckles, OK? (E: OK.) Ths white is his back c (traces) OK? (E: OK.)	DdSo F– A 4.5 INC
IV	v6. A map	E: (Rpts S's resp) S: Doesn't it ll it c b a map? E: Show me how u c it S: I d k, it just cb a map, I cant explain it, it just does ll it cb a map to me. E: I'm not sur where ur lookg S: Oh, just all of it, it cb sk of map.	Wv Fu Ge
	7. Ths way it ll a monster, lik a snail monster or st	E: (Rpts S's resp) S: Well, it sorta ll tht, ths part at the bottom wb lik the snail tail & littl arms up here & thes r lik big flippers, lik a big monster outta the ocean or somplac, lik its pushg itself along w the big flippers	Wo FMao (A) 2.0 DV
V	8. Is it alrite if I say st I already said? (E: It's up to u) I'll say a bf, thts all	E: (Rpts S's resp) S: Lk, don't thy ll wgs? & ths wb the middl prt u kno & tht ll a tail, looks parallel to a bf	Wo Fo A P 1.0 DV
VI	9. It ll a wolf howling	E: (Rpts S's resp) S: Wel it just does, his head is up hre & u can c hs legs out hre, lik he was stretchg out lik thy do whn thy howl, thts y I said howlg, cuz thy stretch out to howl, lik blow up inside & let th air out & hs neck is out too lik whn thy howl	Wo FMau A 2.5
	10. Or mb a dead cat, lik it got flattend out by a car	E: (Rpts S's resp) S: Wel u kno whn a cat gets run ovr it gets al flt, I've seem em & it maks u wanta cry but I don't	Wo FYo A P 2.5 MOR

VII

11. 2 puppies lookg straight at eo

E: I'm not sur I'm seeg it rite, help me a littl
S: Lk, c th head here & th whiskers & th rest lks al flat if u look rite, thes r his legs & his back, whts left of it, it ll its got grease on it, c all the black marks on ther, its lik grease or tire marks

D + FMpo 2 A 3.0

E: (Rpts S's resp)
S: Thyr sitg ther & lkg at eo, lik staring
E: Can u tell me wht maks thm ll puppies
S: Sur can't u c em? Hre's the tail & th nose & the paw & thyr just lookg rite at eo

v12. Hah, ths way it ll 2 horses tht got stuck to a jellyfish

E: (Rpts S's resp)
S: Sur, thes parts ll 2 horses, c the nose & the head & th tail & up here is lik a jelyfsh, c its al round lik thy r & th 2 horses got stuck onto it & thyr just hangg there

W+ FMp– 2 A 2.5 FAB2

v13. Or its a very cloudy day & ther r 2 people standg ther under th cld

E: (Rpts S's resp)
S: Well u hav to thk of just this middl prt up hre (outlines) as lik a cloud, it must b realy low cuz it covers up som of the peoples head & thyr just standg ther, c thy hav a leg & arm & their heads r up in th clouds, thts wht our teacher says, don't get ur head in the clds.
E: I'm not sur whn u say th cld covrs som of their head, can u show me
S: C how it gets drkr here, lik the cld was comg ovr thm

W+ Mp.FVo 2 H,Cl 2.5 DR

VIII

14. Ths ll 2 moles fightg a big space blob

E: (Rpts S's resp)
S: Well thyr out here, c (points to D1) & thyr fitg w ths thg in the middl, I d k wht it is, its just a blob w a lotta colrs, lik st from space & thyr tryg to get it or keep it frm getg thm, thos blobs can really get u if u don't watch out, thy suck u rite in, I've seen em on th TV, did u evr c Jabba, he's a big blob

W+ FMa.CFu 2 A,(H),Sc P 4.5 AG,PER

IX

v15. A big giant cell monster

E: (Rpts S's resp)
S: Well, its lik all ovr the place, lik al spread out lik thos 1 cell monstrs, lik in a big blob & its got all diff colrs lik wht u c whn tht stuff runs thru the cell
E: Runs thru the cell?
S: Cells got stuff in em, diff colrd stuff & it keeps chng places, lik whn thy breath or stg, c th orange is go-g into th green prt & the pink up to the orange

Wv Mp.CF.YFu (H),Sc

203

Case 5. (Continued)

Card	Response	Inquiry	Scoring
		E: U said ths was a giant one?	
16.	Mb a rainbow too	S: Wel most cells r small, ths is a big 1, all spread out	Wv C Na
		E: (Rpts S's resp)	
		S: I didn't mean a real rainbow, it doesn't go in a curve lik a real rainbow	
		E: So wht did u mean?	
		S: Lik th colrs in a rainbow, jst th colrs, 3 or 4 lik r in a rainbow, lik if u just lkd at a prt of a rainbow lik th middle or sthg, not th whole thg, thn u'd c lik thes colrs, undrstnd? (E: Yes)	
X	17. It ll a spaceship is tryg to blast off & ther r othr spaceshps & space monsters tryg to catch it & destroy it	E: (Rpts S's resp)	W + ma.Ma.CFu 2 Sc,(H),Fi 5.5 AG,COP
		S: C ths is the spaceshp up here (D11) & all ths pink is th fire stootg out of it & thes blu thgs r space monsters tryg to catch it & thes othr thgs r lik star fightrs shoog at it	
		E: OK I understand th spaceship & th star fitrs but I'm not sur about the space monsters	
		S: Lk, 1 hre & hre, thyr big blu blobs lik a space monster mite b, lik sthg tryg to suck in the spceshp, lik monsters frm th dark side, u kno th drk side? (E: Yes) Wel thy cld hav thm, big blu space monsters tht can grab a ship if its smaller thn thy r, c thry tryg to capture th space ship by grabbing at it	

204

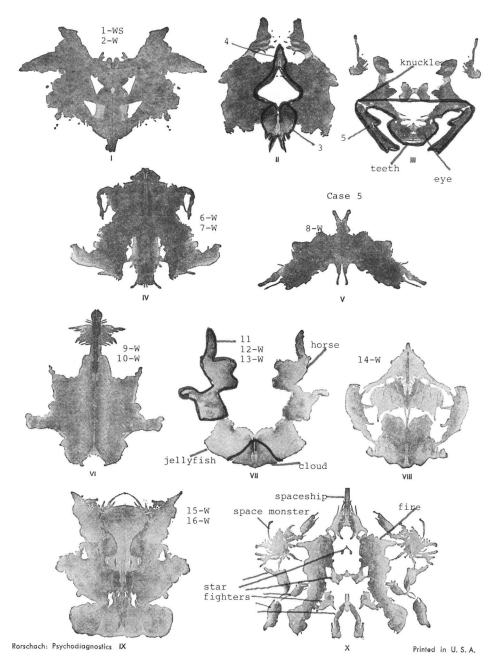

Case 5

Case 5   **Sequence of Scores**

Card	No	Loc	#	Determinant(s)	(2)	Content(s)	Pop	Z	Special Scores
I	1	WSo	1	Fu		Hd		3.5	MOR,PER
	2	Wo	1	FMao		A	P	1.0	DV2,ALOG
II	3	DS+	3	ma.CF.FDo		Ex,Ls		4.5	AG,MOR
	4	DS+	5	Mp.FVo		(H),Ls,Cg		4.5	MOR
III	5	DdSo	99	F-		A		4.5	INC
IV	6	Wv	1	Fu		Ge			
	7	Wo	1	FMao		(A)		2.0	DV
V	8	Wo	1	Fo		A	P	1.0	DV
VI	9	Wo	1	FMau		A		2.5	
	10	Wo	1	FYo		A	P	2.5	MOR
VII	11	D+	2	FMpo	2	A		3.0	
	12	W+	1	FMp-	2	A		2.5	FAB2
	13	W+	1	Mp.FVo	2	H,Cl		2.5	DR
VIII	14	W+	1	FMa.CFu	2	A,(H),Sc	P	4.5	AG,PER
IX	15	Wv	1	Mp.CF.YFu		(H),Sc			
	16	Wv	1	C		Na			
X	17	W+	1	ma.Ma.CFu	2	Sc,(H),Fi		5.5	AG,COP

Case 5   **Structural Summary**

Location Features	Determinants		Contents	S-Constellation

Location   Determinants   Contents   S-Constellation
Features   Blends   Single

			H = 1, 0	. . FV+VF+V+FD>2
Zf = 14	m.CF.FD	M = 0	(H) = 2, 2	. . Col−Shd Bl>0
ZSum = 44.0	M.FV	FM = 5	Hd = 1, 0	. . Ego<.31,>.44
ZEst = 45.5	M.FV	m = 0	(Hd) = 0, 0	. . MOR > 3
	FM.CF	FC = 0	Hx = 0, 0	. . Zd > +− 3.5
W = 13	M.CF.YF	CF = 0	A = 8, 0	. . es > EA
(Wv = 3)	m.M.CF	C = 1	(A) = 1, 0	. . CF+C > FC
D = 3		Cn = 0	Ad = 0, 0	. . X+% < .70
Dd = 1		FC' = 0	(Ad) = 0, 0	. . S > 3
S = 4		C'F = 0	An = 0, 0	. . P < 3 or > 8
		C' = 0	Art = 0, 0	. . Pure H < 2
		FT = 0	Ay = 0, 0	. . R < 17
DQ		TF = 0	Bl = 0, 0	x . . . . . TOTAL
. . . . . (FQ−)		T = 0	Bt = 0, 0	
+ = 7 (1)		FV = 0	Cg = 0, 1	Special Scorings
o = 7 (1)		VF = 0	Cl = 0, 1	Lv1 Lv2
v/+ = 0 (0)		V = 0	Ex = 1, 0	DV = 2x1 1x2
v = 3 (0)		FY = 1	Fd = 0, 0	INC = 1x2 0x4
		YF = 0	Fi = 0, 1	DR = 1x3 0x6
		Y = 0	Ge = 1, 0	FAB = 0x4 1x7
		Fr = 0	Hh = 0, 0	ALOG = 1x5
Form Quality		rF = 0	Ls = 0, 2	CON = 0x7
		FD = 0	Na = 1, 0	SUM6 = 7
FQx FQf MQual SQx		F = 4	Sc = 1, 2	WSUM6 = 21
+ = 0 0 0 0			Sx = 0, 0	AB = 0 CP = 0
o = 8 1 2 2			Xy = 0, 0	AG = 3 MOR = 4
u = 6 2 2 1			Id = 0, 0	CFB = 0 PER = 2
− = 2 1 0 1				COP = 1 PSV = 0
none = 1 — 0 0		(2) = 5		

Case 5   **Ratios, Percentages, and Derivations**

R = 17   L = 0.31   FC:CF+C = 0: 5   COP = 1   AG = 3
                                           Pure C   = 1   Food   = 0
EB = 4: 5.5   EA = 9.5   EBPer = N/A   Afr   = 0.31   Isolate/R   = 0.41
eb = 8: 4   es = 12   D =   0   S   = 4   H:(H)Hd(Hd) = 1:5
               Adj es = 10   Adj D = 0   Blends:R = 6:17   (HHd):(AAd) = 4:1
                                           CP   = 0   H+A:Hd+Ad = 14:1
FM = 6 :   C' = 0   T = 0
m = 2 :   V = 2   Y = 2
                         P   = 4   Zf   = 14   3r+(2) /R = 0.29
a:p   = 7: 5   Sum6 = 7   X+% = 0.47   Zd   = −1.5   Fr+rF   = 0
Ma:Mp = 1: 3   Lv2   = 2   F+% = 0.25   W:D:Dd = 13: 3: 1   FD   = 1
2AB+Art+Ay=0   WSum6 = 21   X−% = 0.12   W:M = 13: 4   An+Xy   = 0
M −   = 0   Mnone = 0   S−% = 0.50   DQ+ = 7   MOR   = 4
                             Xu% = 0.35   DQv = 3

    SCZI = 3   DEPI = 6*   CDI = 3   S-CON = N/A   HVI = No   OBS = No

INTERPRETIVE ROUTINE FOR CASE 5

The *DEPI* (6) is the first positive Key variable, indicating that the interpretive routine should address the various clusters in the following order:

AFFECT → CONTROLS → SELF-PERCEPTION → INTERPERSONAL
PERCEPTION → PROCESSING → MEDIATION → IDEATION

Affect Case 5—   The structural data concerning affect for Case 5 are shown in Table 48.

Table 48.   Affect Data for Case 5

DEPI = 6				BLENDS
EB = 4:5.5		*EBPer* = N/A		M.FV
eb = 8:4		*FC:CF* + *C* = 0:5		M.FV
		Pure *C* = 1		M.CF.YF
C' = 0	*T* = 0	*Afr* = 0.31		FM.CF
V = 2	*Y* = 2	*S* = 4		m.M.CF
		Blends/*R* = 6:17		m.CF.FD
		CP = 0		

The fact that the DEPI has a value of six provides a strong basis from which to hypothesize that a major affective disturbance is present. When the DEPI is positive, it is always important to review the variables in it to determine if the positive variables are related more to affective or cognitive features. The DEPI includes 13 variables. Six of the DEPI variables appear directly related to affective experience (vista, color-shading blends, *S*, number of blends, the sum of shading, and the *C'* variable). Five others are related more to cognitive activities or attitudes (*FD*, Egocentricity Index, Affective Ratio, MOR responses, and the Intellectualization Index). The remaining two variables concern interpersonal features. In some instances, a positive DEPI will occur because all variables related to affective experience are positive. In other cases, a positive DEPI will be created because all variables related to cognitive activity are positive. In most records having positive DEPI a combination of positive affective and cognitive variables will be found, but it is always important to review the positive variables because if a notable trend exists among the variables contributing to the positive DEPI it can have a significant input to treatment planning. In this case, three positive variables that relate directly to affect (vista, color-shading blends, *S*); three positive variables that relate to cognitive activity (Egocentricity Index, *Afr*, MOR); and both variables related to interpersonal activity (COP < 1, Isolation Index > .24) are positive. This suggests that the origins and the impact of the affective problem are broad based and tend to intrude on almost all the major psychological operations of the subject.

The data in the cluster related to affect reveal some important findings. First, the *EB* (4:5.5) indicates that he is an ambitent. This is not surprising as about a third of 9- and 10-year-old nonpatient records yield similar findings. However, it is important in this case because it suggests that he is very inconsistent in his coping and problem-solving behaviors. In some instances, he will employ the more expressive, trial-and-error tactics of the extratensive, but in other instances he may be more prone to use the delay, ideational tactics of the introversive. This tendency to vacillate in coping and problem-solving behaviors increases the likelihood of errors and the probability that some errors will be repeated. In effect, ambients have a more difficult time contending with everyday challenges, and while this is a natural experience for children at one time or another during their developmental years, the extra effort required to get by often exacerbates problems that may exist. Stated differently, his lack of coping and problem-solving consistency tends to make it more difficult for him to deal with his affective problems.

Interestingly, the right-side value of the *eb* (4) is not excessive for a 9, and the fact that it is lower than the left side value (8) gives no indication of felt distress. On the other hand, the variables contributing to the right-side value ($V = 2$; $Y = 2$) suggest that when internal experiences of irritating emotion do occur, they are intense and include a marked feeling of paralysis or helplessness.

The most dramatic findings in this cluster are threefold. First, the $FC:CF + C$ ratio (0:5) is inordinately lopsided for a 9. It suggests that when he does release emotion, it is fairly intense and not well modulated for his age. It will be obvious to those around him, and sometimes it is likely to be inappropriate for the situation. One of the five chromatic color answers is a Pure *C* response, which by itself is not very important, but when taken in relation to the $FC:CF + C$ ratio and the content, which in this instance is a vague Nature answer, (a rainbow—Response 16), implies that he is not very concerned about attempting to modulate his emotional displays and that they become overly intense at times.

The second important datum in the cluster is the low *Afr* (0.31). It is well below that expected for a 9, and signals a marked tendency to avoid emotionally toned stimuli whenever possible. It is impossible to determine from the Rorschach data precisely why he is avoidant of emotion, but it is reasonable to speculate that he has some awareness of the difficulty he has in controlling his own emotional displays and may be trying to avoid situations in which those emotional blunders occur. It is equally reasonable to argue that he does not want to contend with his own negative or disruptive feelings and an avoidant orientation aids him in denying or ignoring those feelings.

The third important finding from this cluster is the large number of *S* responses (4). They suggest that he is a very negative, somewhat angry youngster. Their presence is not unexpected in light of his history of aggressiveness, but it is important to note that all his *S* responses occur in the first five answers that he gives in the test. This suggests that his anger tends to be more situationally provoked, probably as a challenge to his integrity. It seems likely that it is a reaction related to the low *Afr,* that is, when forced into coping situations with which he feels uncomfortable, he is quick to anger. This probably accounts for some of his past aggressiveness and his current pattern of running away from school, which is an indirect form of aggressiveness.

The number of blends (6) is not unusually high for a 9-year-old. At first glance, it seems that none are situationally related, that is, none would be eliminated if an *m* or *Y* determinant were not present. However, two of the blends contain Vista, and although Vista is usually considered to be a very stable variable, there is some evidence to suggest that it may appear situationally in relation to guilt or remorse (Exner, 1993b). Therefore, it may be that he is psychologically more complex than has appeared to be the case. In either instance, the presence of a color-shading blend signals that he is confused about his feelings, a feature that tends to increase the vacillation in decision making caused by his being an ambient.

Overall, there are numerous liabilities in the affective structure and operations of this youngster, the foremost of which is that he is apparently quite depressed. The presence of the depression is complicated by the fact that he does not modulate the release of his emotions very well and much of the time, his emotional displays will be overly intense and possibly inappropriate for the situation. He probably has an awareness of this problem and works hard to avoid emotionally toned situations, but that avoidant orientation is not successful; manifestations of rather intense negativism or anger are often included in his early responses. He seems confused by his feelings, and that confusion only serves to exacerbate his other affective problems. Information concerning his stress tolerance and capacity for control will be important in understanding how these affective liabilities impact on his overall psychological makeup.

Controls—Case 5   The Case 5 data concerning capacity for control and tolerance for stress are shown in Table 49.

Table 49.   Controls and Stress Tolerance Data for Case 5

$EB = 4:5.5$		$EA = 9.5$		$D\ \ \ \ = 0$
$eb\ \ = 8:4$		$es\ \ = 12$	$Adjes = 10$	$AdjD\ = 0$
$FM = 6$	$C' = 2$	$T\ \ \ = 0$		$CDI\ \ = 3$
$m\ \ \ = 2$	$V\ = 2$	$Y\ \ \ = 2$		

The Adjusted D Score is zero, suggesting that his capacity for control and tolerance for stress are similar to others of his age. There is no reason to question the validity of the Adjusted D Score as the value for EA (9.5) is well into the average range for 9-year-olds and indicates that he does have considerable resource readily accessible from which to form and implement behaviors. Similarly, there is no reason to question the validity of the EA as there are substantial values in each side of the EB (4:5.5). In effect, this suggests that although some of his actions may seem impulsivelike, most, including his rather intense affective displays are deliberately formulated and implemented, probably because he believes that is the best course of action to relieve demands on himself and to resolve the situation in which he finds himself. However, it is important to note that the es (12) is somewhat higher than expected; in fact, if the es were only one point greater, the D Score would fall into the minus range.

Thus, although his current capacity for control seems adequate, he is vulnerable to being pushed into a stimulus overload state if there is any notable increase in peripheral mental activity or subjectively felt distress. Should that occur, the likelihood of impulsiveness, either in thinking or behavior, increases substantially and the consequences of his affective liabilities could become even more pronounced than is now the case.

Self-Perception—Case 5   The data pertaining to self-perception for Case 5 are shown in Table 50.

Table 50.   Self-Perception Data for Case 5

$3r + (2)/R = 0.29$	$FD = 1$	$MOR = 4$ $\ \ \ Hx = 0$		$An + Xy = 0$
$Fr + rF = 0$	$Sum\ V = 2$	$H:(H) + Hd + (Hd) = 1:5$		$Sx = 0$
		RESPONSES TO BE READ		
MOR Resp's	$FQ-$ Resp's	*M* Resp's	*FM* Resp's	*m* Resp's
1,3,4	5,12	4,13,15,17	2,7,9,11,12,14	3,17

The Egocentricity Index is extraordinarily low for a 9-year-old. It indicates that his self-esteem, based on a comparison of himself with those significant to him, is quite low. Children tend to regard themselves quite favorably, whether that is true or not. When they fail to do so, the resulting sense of inadequacy often causes them to withdraw or, as is probably the case here, to establish complex patterns of behavior to try to defend against revelations of their ineptness. The history of this boy includes a lengthy period of aggressiveness in school, actions that he probably felt necessary to defend himself. Now his behaviors have changed from direct aggression to a form of withdrawal from competition with his peers. Running away from school provides a temporary respite from his anguish.

He is very down on himself. The record contains two Vista answers plus an *FD* response. Collectively, they denote a great deal of self-rumination, much of which results in painful internal experiences. As noted earlier, the Vista answers could relate to a situationally invoked sense of guilt or remorse, but in light of the low Egocentricity Index plus the lengthy history of using aggression to ward off challenges to his integrity, it seems likely that this ruminative process has existed for quite some time.

The presence of six human contents is typical for his age, but the fact that only one is a Pure *H* answer indicates that he has a limited understanding of people, which in turn, generalizes to his own self-image. The four MOR responses tend to reaffirm the notion that his self-image is quite negative. The substance of these four answers conveys something about how he feels about himself. The first, Response 1, is ". . . something from the aliens (Inquiry) ". . . it looks like a guy's face that he mashed in . . ." First answers often convey a direct sort of projection. If that is the case here, a strong sense of damage is implied. The second, Response 3 to Card II is " . . . a big explosion (Inquiry) . . . it's left a hole where all the stuff that got blown up used to be . . . but it's not near me," also implies a sense of damage, and an attempt to retreat from the insult. The third, Response 4 to Card III, ". . . this guy is falling into this big pit, its really deep (Inquiry) . . . somebody just shot him or something and he's beginning to fall over into this big deep pit . . ." also conveys damage plus a sense of hopelessness concerning his plight. The last, Response 10 to Card VI, is equally devastating, ". . . a dead cat, like it got flattened out by a car (Inquiry) . . . it makes you want to cry-but I don't." In effect, he is saying that he is not able to convey the suffering that he experiences.

The contents of the two minus answers also do not portend well for his self-concept. The first, Response 5 to Card III, is ". . . a crab (Inquiry) . . . eyes, teeth, claws, knuckles . . ." It is a very defensive and aggressivelike response. The second, Response 12 to Card VII, is a more helpless answer, ". . . two horses that got stuck to a jellyfish . . . (Inquiry) . . . they are just hanging there."

The thematic imagery in the four human movement answers is also quite negative. Response 4 is ". . . a guy falling into this really big pit . . ." Response 13 to Card VII, ". . . it's a very cloudy day and there are two people standing under this cloud (Inquiry) . . . their heads are up in the clouds, that's what our teacher says, don't get your head in the clouds . . ." implies a sense of resignation to his current state and also a sense of impending doom. Response 15, to Card IX, seems to illustrate the diffuseness and/or confusion that exists concerning his self-image and possibly his feelings, "A big giant cell monster (Inquiry) ". . . cells got stuff in them, different colored stuff and it keeps changing places." The last *M* answer is his exit answer, Response 17. It seems to intimate something about how he feels about his relationship to his world, ". . . a spaceship trying to blast off and there are other spaceships and space monsters trying to catch it and destroy it."

The six *FM* answers do not provide any sense of reassurance concerning his negative self-concept. Most are naive, unrealistically grandiose, or reflect a strong defensive orientation. The first, Response 2 to Card I, is a ". . . big giant butterfly (Inquiry) . . . like when they do when they fly." The second, Response 7 to Card IV, is a ". . . snail monster (Inquiry) . . . pushing itself along with the big flippers. The third, Response 9 to Card VI, is ". . . a wolf howling." The fourth, Response 11 to Card VII, is ". . . two puppies looking straight at each other (Inquiry) . . . staring." The fifth, two horses stuck to a jellyfish has been noted previously. The last, Response 14 to Card VIII, is ". . . two moles fighting a big space blob (Inquiry) . . . if you don't watch out, they suck you right in . . ." This last *FM* answer suggests a strong sense of threat from the environment and an almost paranoidlike defensive orientation. This sense of threat is also revealed in the two *m* answers, an explosion in which stuff that used to be is blown up (Response 3) and a spaceship trying to blast off and other spaceships or space monsters are trying to catch it (Response 17).

The composite of structural variables and the thematic content creates a picture of his self-concept that is extremely negative, especially for a child. He perceives his own worth to be considerably less than the value he places on significant others. He apparently ruminates a great deal about flaws that he sees in himself and probably experiences some guilt or remorse about them. He views himself as battered or damaged, having many unwanted features. He seems to feel out of place and/or bewildered by his environment and apparently senses that he is quite vulnerable to the attack of others.

Interpersonal Perception—Case 5   Table 51 contains the data related to his perceptions of others.

Table 51. Interpersonal Perception Data for Case 5

CDI = 3	*a:p* = 8:4	*T* = 0	Human Cont = 6		Pure *H* = 1
HVI = Neg	Food = 1	PER = 2	COP = 1	AG = 3	Isolate/R = 0.41

RESPONSES TO BE READ

HUMAN MOVEMENT WITH PAIR	*HUMAN CONTENTS*
13,17	1,4,13,14,15,17

Neither the CDI nor the *a:p* ratio offers data that are interpretable. Likewise, the HVI is not positive, but it seems worth noting that the HVI would be positive if he had given one more human content response (*T* = 0, *Zf* > 12, *S* > 3, parenthesized contents > 3, but all human contents are not greater than 6). Although he does not meet the actuarial criteria for hypervigilance, the composite of positive structural variables, plus the clear sense of environmental threat noted in some of the thematic contents of his responses when reviewing the self-perception data, suggest that he is much more guarded and mistrusting of his environment than is common for a youngster.

The cornerstone, and probable precursor, of hypervigilance is the absence of *T* responses, which equates very directly to interpersonal attitudes and perceptions. About 88% of nonpatient 9-year-olds give a texture response. Thus, the absence of *T,* as with adult records, usually is quite meaningful. However, when interpreting the *T*-less record of a younger child, it is always important to raise two issues in attempting to determine if the absence of *T* is a valid finding. First, does the record contain any achromatic (*C'*) or other shading (*Y* or *V*) determinants? This is important because some younger children do have problems in articulating shading, and if there are no achromatic or shading answers in a T-less record, the absence of T should be approached very cautiously. Second, did the subject give the Popular answer to Card VI, or another answer such as a monster response to Card IV in which texture might easily have been present? If the answers to either of these questions are positive, it is likely that the T-less finding is valid and interpretable, and that proposition becomes strengthened considerably if the answers to both questions are positive.

In this case, the answers to both questions are positive. He gave four shading answers ($V = 2$; $Y = 2$), so there is no reason to attribute the absence of T to a failure of articulation, and he did give the Popular response to Card VI and, in fact, used shading (Y) in the answer. Therefore, the T-less finding seems valid, and suggests that he does not expect to be close to others, and probably does not experience his own needs for closeness as do others of his age. It also suggests that he is more preoccupied with issues of personal space than is common for those of his age. At the same time, it is intriguing to note that he does give a Food response, which correlates rather directly with a dependency need or orientation. Food responses are not uncommon in preadolescent children, and probably relate to the fact that younger children still feel insecure about themselves and often prefer the support and decision making of significant others. Thus, although this boy does not expect to be close to others, he seems to harbor the desire to be dependently close, if not emotionally close.

The six human contents signal a substantial, and expected interest in others. It is unfortunate that only one of the six is a Pure H answer, indicating that his conceptions of people are probably based more on imagination than real experience. In light of the T-less finding, and the possibility that he is becoming hypervigilant, his interest in others actually may be more defensive than one indicating a desire for interaction. The presence of two PER responses is not interpretable, but the data concerning COP and AG responses are quite important. COP responses usually are regarded favorably, even if only one occurs, but in this instance, the cooperative movement involves aggression (space monsters trying to catch and destroy a spaceship). In fact, three of his answers include the AG special score, indicating that he has identified aggression as being a natural component in interpersonal relationships and has incorporated that element into his orientation toward the environment. This finding coincides neatly with his history of being aggressive to his peers since the second grade and raises a question about how this traitlike feature evolved.

The Isolation Index is positive, which is not surprising in light of the history and in light of the low Afr. People who do not like to be around emotional give-and-take often find themselves unable to create close relationships with others. There are only two human movement responses that contain a pair (two people standing under a cloud; monsters from the dark side trying to capture a spaceship by grabbing it). There are also three animal movement answers involving a pair (puppies staring at each other; horses stuck to a jellyfish; moles fighting a big space blob). Three of the five answers are aggressive. One of the five (staring) is almost paranoidlike, and the last (standing under a cloud) has an ominous, almost depressive quality. The human contents are equally disappointing (a guy's face mashed in; guy falling into a pit; people standing under a cloud; a big space blob; a giant cell monster; space monsters).

A summary of this youngster's interpersonal perceptions and behaviors is as negative as the findings concerning his self-image or concept. He regards people as being threatening. He apparently does not expect to be close to anyone, and is probably mistrusting of any gestures of closeness. Although he is quite interested in people, that interest seems to be based on a perceived need to defend himself rather than an interest in developing deep or enduring contacts with others. He also perceives aggressiveness as a natural phenomenon in relations with others, a perception that is probably strengthened by the fact that he really does not understand people very well. An important question is whether these negative impressions of himself and others are based on real experience or whether they have evolved because of some strangeness in his thinking. The data for the cognitive triad may answer this important question.

Processing—Case 5   The data concerning the information-processing activity for Case 5 are shown in Table 52.

Table 52.   Processing Data for Case 5

L = 0.31	$W{:}D{:}Dd$ = 13:3:1	Zd = −1.5	$DQ+$ = 7
Zf = 14	$W{:}M$ = 13:4	PSV = 0	$DQv/+$ = 0
HVI = No	OBS = No		DQv = 3

LOCATION SEQUENCING

I	W,W	IV	W,W	VII	D,W,W
II	D,D	V	W	VIII	W
III	Dd	VI	W,W	IX	W,W
				X	W

The value for Lambda (0.31) is lower than expected for a 9-year-old, suggesting that he becomes more involved in the complexity of a stimulus situation than is common for most of this age. This could be a consequence of his near-hypervigilant situation, or it could simply be a product of his depression. In either event, it suggests that he devotes considerable energy to processing. This proposition seems supported by the data for the Zf (14), $W{:}D{:}Dd$ ratio (13:3:1), and the $W{:}M$ ratio (13:4). The first indicates that he attempts to organize a field more than most of his age. The second reveals that he usually tries to take on the whole field rather than take a more economical approach, and the third indicates that he often sets objectives for himself that go well beyond his functional capabilities. This pattern of motivation to process is not unusual for a youngster and simply implies that, like other children, he does not want to miss anything. However, in this case, that motive may be stronger than usually is the case because of his guardedness. He does synthesize several of his answers ($DQ+$ = 7), which is about average for his age. On the other hand, he gives three DQv answers, which is considerably more than are given by most 9's, and some of his processing is rather sloppy, in spite of his age. The Zd score (−1.5) is in the average range. There are no perseverations, and the location sequencing is reasonably consistent. Taken as a whole, the data suggest that his processing activities are not very different from most of his age, except that some of his processing is more primitive or sloppy than expected for his age.

Mediation—Case 5   The data related to cognitive mediation activities for Case 5 are shown in Table 53.

The number of Popular answers (4) is slightly lower than expected for his age. Similarly, the $X + \%$ (0.47) is also lower than anticipated. Collectively, they suggest that he

Table 53.   Cognitive Mediation Data for Case 5

					MINUS FEATURES
Lambda	= 0.31	OBS	= Neg		5,12
P	= 4	*X*+%	= .47		
FQx+	= 0	*F*+%	= .25		
FQxo	= 8	*Xu*%	= .35		
FQxu	= 6	*X*−%	= .12		
FQx−	= 2	*S*−%	= .50		
*FQx*none	= 1	CONFAB = 0			

does not translate new information very conventionally, and even when obvious stimulus cues are provided, he may not make the most conventional response. This is not because he distorts new inputs considerably. The $X - \%$ (.12) is modest and well within the average range for his age. The key to the problem is revealed by the $Xu\%$ (.35), which indicates that he tends to personalize the translation of many inputs. The two minus response have no distinct similarities, although both are marked by special scores, and neither could be judged to be a severe distortion. Overall, his reality testing, although not distorted, is marked by many personal biases and/or preoccupations, most of which probably are influenced by his perception of himself and his perception of others.

Ideation—Case 5   The data concerning ideational activity for Case 5 are shown in Table 54.

Table 54.   Ideation Data for Case 5

		M QUALITY	SPECIAL SCORES			
EB = 4:5.5	*EBPer* = N/A					
eb = 8:4	(*FM* = 6 *m* = 2)	+ = 0	DV	= 2	DV2	= 1
a:p = 7:5	$M^a{:}M^p$ = 1:3	o = 2	INC	= 1	INC2	= 0
2AB + Art + Ay = 0		u = 2	DR	= 1	DR2	= 0
MOR = 4		− = 0	FAB	= 0	FAB2	= 1
			ALOG	= 1	SUM6	= 7
RESPONSES TO BE READ FOR QUALITY			CON	= 0	WSUM6	= 21
5						

The data concerning ideation are interesting and important in fleshing out the psychology of this youngster. The *EB* (4:5.5) has already been reviewed, and it has been noted that, at times, he will adopt the strategy of the introversive and try to delay and think through his decisions. However, this is not a well-developed tactic and he probably will flounder in its use as often as he will find it successful. More errors than are common for the true introversive will be likely to occur and he is also prone to repeat more of those errors, but this is not uncommon among 9-year-olds as more than one third are ambitents still trying to find the most effective approach to decision making.

A more important datum is the value for the left side of the *eb* (8). The value would be rather high for almost any subject and signals the presence of considerable peripheral ideation. In this instance, the bulk of the value is created by six *FM* responses, a number that is higher than expected for either adults or children meaning that much of the peripheral ideational activity is being created by experienced need states. The two *m* answers simply indicate that the peripheral thinking is being enhanced by situationally created stresses. The end result is much nondirected thinking that often intrudes into conscious awareness and detracts from deliberate thinking. These intrusions frequently interfere with attention and concentration, and for a child, tend to disrupt work activity, that is, daily educational performance. More importantly, the presence of excessive need state activity often leads to a reduction in the clarity of thought and an overall discomfort because of this.

Interestingly, the $a:p$ ratio (7:5) offers no evidence that he is unusually narrow or rigid in the way he approaches issues or in his value system. On the other hand, the $M^a:M^p$ ratio (1:3) suggests that he often takes flight into fantasy to avoid confrontations with reality. He drifts away from the real world and substitutes his own fantasies for it. All people do this from time to time, but he does this as a defense. His expressed interests in television and computer games probably are good representations of how he used this tactic to avoid reality. There is no evidence that he intellectualizes, but the presence of the four MOR responses does signal that much of his thinking is marked by a strong sense of pessimism. He does not expect things to go well, and when evaluating various situations or problems, this attitude will be strongly influential in his thinking.

The number of Critical Special Scores (7) is not unusual for a 9-year-old, but the WSum6 (21) is higher than average. It is increased beyond the expected by the presence of two Level 2 answers: the DV2 in Response 2, ". . . a big giant butterfly," and the FABCOM2 in Response 12, ". . . horses that got stuck to a jellyfish." They are not necessarily pathological, but both do reflect a sort of immature cognitive slippage that is more common for a 6- or 7-year-old than a 9-year-old. His M answers are complex and reflect some intellectual sophistication even though their contents are sometimes also less mature.

In summary, his ideational activity, although potentially sophisticated, is marked by several liabilities. Possibly, the most important of these are his excessive use of fantasy and his pessimistic orientation. These seem to have created a rather immature kind of thinking in which reasonable logic or good judgment is often cast aside. In addition, unusually frequent or intense need states probably interfere with his attention and/or concentration and this can contribute to some of his flawed reasoning or the onset of cognitive slippage from time to time.

Summary—Case 5   This is a very depressed youngster whose self-image is quite negative. He perceives himself as having many unwanted features and judges himself to be less worthy than his significant others. He does not have a very good understanding of himself or others and seems confused about his world and those in it who are important to him. He appears to have reasonably strong dependency needs, not unlike those common to young children, but at the same time, he appears to have abandoned expectations of being emotionally close to people. In fact, he looks on his world with a sense of fear, bewilderment, and anger, and he has become guarded and mistrusting of others. As a consequence, he has become quite isolated from others, a factor that only serves to perpetuate his lack of understanding of them.

He does not understand or handle his emotions very well, and when they are released, they often are overly intense and sometimes inappropriate for the situation. He seems to have some awareness of this problem and has become oriented to avoid emotional situations whenever possible. On the other hand, he has come to perceive aggressiveness as a natural part of interpersonal activity, and frequently vents his confusion and anger in aggressive behaviors. This only serves to isolate him further from his peers. His recourse to this isolation has been to rely heavily on his fantasy world for respite, a tactic that probably offers transient relief from the problems of everyday living, but which also reinforces a less mature way of thinking and thwarts the development of much needed social skills. Actually, as revealed by intelligence test data and the quality of his Rorschach performance, he is not intellectually handicapped. On the contrary, the seeds of sophisticated thinking appear to exist, but they have not been exploited to his advantage. His processing activities are not very inconsistent for his age, although at times, some of his processing actions are negligent and immature. Similarly, his translations of new stimuli do not lead to distortions, but they are less conventional, apparently because of his preoccupations with himself and his world.

In effect, he is a youngster who is well on the road to disaster. His parents seem unaware of his troubling feelings, and it appears likely that they have, possibly inadvertently, offered models for feelings and behavior that are inconsistent with the needs of a child. Similarly, his teachers have focused on issues of deportment, and in doing so, have failed to consider him as a frightened and bewildered child. His current teacher suggests that he might do better if placed in a special class for management problems. This would probably prove disastrous as it would only reaffirm his negative image of himself and exacerbate his depression. The guidance counselor raises a question about school phobia or other psychiatric disturbance. There is no school phobia as such. It is more like a world phobia! He does need treatment for depression but the characteristics of that treatment should be planned carefully, and in the context of a more thorough history from the parents. Either they are very naive about their son, or withholding information that could be very important to the course of treatment. In fact, the possibility of family treatment should not be overlooked, as there may well be more than one patient in the total family unit.

OTHER CONSIDERATIONS IN DIFFERENTIAL DIAGNOSIS

When Rorschach findings suggest the presence of an affective disorder, several questions of differential diagnosis become important to address. These include distinguishing between unipolar and bipolar disorder, identifying schizoaffective disorder, separating reactive from endogenous disorder, and recognizing apparent depression that is rooted in helplessness.

Unipolar and Bipolar Disorder   Unipolar affective disorder, whether consisting in DSM-III-R terms of major depressive disorder or dysthymia, should be inferred from an elevated DEPI especially when numerous other structural, thematic, and test-taking variables discussed earlier as Rorschach indices of depression also occur. Moreover, in light of how frequently false negatives can occur with DEPI especially among young people, prominent indications of dejected mood, negative cognitions, depleted energy, and poor physical status that are not included among the DEPI variables should also alert Rorschach clinicians to possible depressive features even when the DEPI value is below 5.

Correct identification of bipolar disorder, whether involving manic-depressive disorder or cyclothymia, is a much more difficult issue. Empirical findings are, at best, sparse. It is true that sometimes, the bipolar or cyclothymic subject can be identified on the Rorschach by the co-occurrence of prominent depressive features, *including an elevated DEPI,* with Rorschach indices of unusually elevated mood, unrealistically positive cognitions, excess energy, and an exaggerated sense of physical well-being. Should bipolar individuals be examined while in the depths of a depressive episode, their manic tendencies may be submerged by the depressive features of their Rorschach records. At such times, neither the Rorschach nor any other personality assessment instrument will help very much to discriminate between unipolar and bipolar affective disorder, and the differential diagnosis must usually be referred to the subject's clinical history. The stronger the evidence of past episodes of manic behavior, the more likely it is that a present episode of depression is a manifestation of bipolar rather than unipolar disorder.

The clinical history, however, is less reliable in distinguishing bipolar from unipolar depression in young people than in adults. People who develop recurrent manic-depressive episodes typically pass through a period of depression prior to becoming manic for the first time. Among adults who have experienced many such cycles, the developmental depression-to-mania sequence no longer has any bearing on the diagnostic utilization of the clinical history. But for young people in whom a bipolar disorder is just beginning to emerge, there may not yet be any prior history of manic episodes even when a present state of depression does in fact herald the inception of a manic-depressive or cyclothymic disorder (see Weiner, 1992, Chap. 4).

One way in which the Rorschach may prove helpful in addressing this diagnostic problem is suggested by the findings of Singer and Brabender (1993), who studied unipolar depressed, bipolar depressed, and bipolar manic adults in an inpatient setting. They found that adult manic patients often are positive on the SCZI, mainly because they display some disordered thinking in the form of Critical Special Scores, especially INCOM, DR, and FABCOM. The mean values Singer and Brabender obtained for Sum6 and WSum6 were significantly higher in their 33 bipolar than in their 29 unipolar subjects, and significantly higher in their 18 manic than in their 44 depressed subjects. Among the depressed subjects, the Critical Special Scores were significantly more frequent in the 15 bipolars than the 29 unipolars. These results suggest that evidence of disordered thinking in a depressed Rorschach without indications of manic tendencies may hold a clue to bipolar rather than unipolar depression. Exner (1993a) has reviewed the protocols of 16 adolescents, ages 15 to 17, who were ultimately diagnosed as having a bipolar disorder. The DEPI was positive for 13 of the 16 cases, but the more striking data occur for the Critical Special Scores DR1 and DR2. The mean for DR1 + DR2 for this group is 3.4, which a median and mode of 4. All three values are considerably higher than is common among adolescents who are diagnosed as having a unipolar depression or dysthymia.

In sorting out the complexities of unipolar and bipolar affective disorder, as in wrestling with the differential diagnosis of schizophrenia, clinicians need to keep in mind that Rorschach findings constitute only one piece of any diagnostic puzzle. Positive diagnostic indices provide a reasonable basis for inferring that a particular condition is present, but negative or inconclusive indices rarely justify ruling out the possibility that a condition is present. In either case, conclusions are best drawn when they represent an integration of Rorschach findings with data from numerous other sources.

Schizoaffective Disorder   The issue of bipolarity is complicated by the possibility that a seeming bipolar record may, in fact, reflect a schizoaffective disturbance. This has been a controversial diagnostic category that, in general, is not applicable for younger clients. However, in some protocols, the evidence of disturbed mood, attitudes, energy level, and physical status may also be accompanied by indications of inaccurate perception and disordered thinking. Rorschach indices of inaccurate perception identify difficulties in reality testing that prevent people from meeting the demands of everyday living and that accordingly suggest a psychoticlike disturbance. In like fashion, perceptual inaccuracy in the Rorschachs of subjects with demonstrable affective disorder suggests that their disorder is of psychotic proportions.

In addition, persons with affective disorder, especially with bipolar disorder and most especially during episodes of mania, are likely to display some of the same Rorschach indications of tangential and circumstantial reasoning as do persons with schizophrenia. However, thought disorder in mania tends to be less severe, less persistent, and less distressing than among schizophrenic individuals. Thus, it probably can be inferred that when unequivocal Rorschach manifestations of affective disorder are accompanied by equally clear evidence of disordered thinking that is severe, persistent, and distressing, a distinct possibility is the presence of a schizoaffective disorder. Schizoaffective disorder has received very little attention in the Rorschach literature, and only two extended discussions of how it might be manifested on psychological tests (Hurt, Reznikoff, & Clarkin, 1991, pp. 137–182; Weiner, 1966, Chap. 17). Moreover, clinicians have sometimes questioned whether schizoaffective disorder exists as a condition independently of either schizophrenia with pronounced affective overtones or affective disorder with pronounced cognitive components (see Coryell, Keller, Lavori, & Endicott, 1990; Tsuang, 1979).

Nevertheless, schizoaffective disorder is classified in DSM-III-R as a psychotic disorder in its own right, and there is a body of research concerning its familial incidence, premorbid patterns, course, and outcome (Baron, Gruen, Asnis, & Kane, 1982; Coryell, Endicott, & Keller, 1990; Grossman, Harrow, Fudala, & Meltzer, 1984). These studies have consistently placed schizoaffective disorder at some midpoint between schizophrenia and affective disorder. For example, people with schizoaffective disorder are more likely to have a remitting course with good outcome and familial incidence of affective disorder than schizophrenic patients, while they are more likely than patients with an affective disorder to have a persistent course with poor outcome and a low familial incidence of affective disorder.

In whatever way individual preferences influence the classification of schizoaffective disorder, there is some consensus that it combines core features of schizophrenia and affective disorder. Accordingly, the Rorschach protocols produced by schizoaffective subjects can be expected to demonstrate both schizophrenic and affective functioning impairments. Records from older adolescents in which SCZI is 4 or more (especially when it is more than 4) and DEPI is 5 or more (especially when it is more than 5) can be strongly suggestive of schizoaffective disorder.

Reactive and Endogenous Depression   Although depressive conditions always arise in part as reactions to stressful life events, clinical and research findings have demonstrated numerous advantages of distinguishing between relatively reactive and relatively endogenous depression. When depression is primarily reactive, precipitating life events are prominently in evidence, the depressed state tends to be brief and self-remitting, and treatment produces comparatively good results in comparatively short order. The more endogenous a depression is, on the other hand, the more likely it is to involve a chronic disposition to becoming depressed in response to minimal stress and in the absence of dramatic precipitating events; the greater the likelihood of prolonged and recurrent depressive episodes; and the more time and effort will be required to implement successful therapy (see Robins, Block, & Peselow, 1990; Zimmerman, Coryell, & Pfohl, 1986).

The DEPI as currently constituted is sensitive primarily to endogenous depression and should not be expected to identify depressive reactions that are not sufficiently severe, prolonged, or recurrent to warrant a diagnosis of major depressive disorder or dysthymia.

Accordingly, clinicians should take the general caution against ruling out depressive disorder on the basis of a low DEPI especially with respect to reactive or situational depressive states. In this regard, false negative cases in research studies of DEPI may well include many subjects who report feeling depressed or have been described clinically as being depressed but whose condition is mild and reactive.

Nevertheless, there are two ways in which the Rorschach may be sensitive to reactive depressive episodes, especially when painful object loss has precipitated depression in an otherwise well-functioning person. One of these involves the Texture (T) response which is not included in DEPI but which is exquisitely sensitive to how people feel about possibilities for engaging in close, intimate, and mutually supportive relationships with others. Research findings indicate that an increase in T often accompanies the rupture of previously enjoyed interpersonal relationships. For example, elevations in T have been observed among married adults subsequent to their becoming divorced or separated and among children placed in foster homes subsequent to the loss of one or both parents (Exner, 1991, pp. 338–339).

The vast majority of subjects at all ages give one T in responding to the Rorschach. Just 11% of adult nonpatients give more than one T, and records with multiple Ts are even less frequent among nonpatient young people—3.6% in 5- to 10-year-olds and 5.1% in 11- to 16-year-olds. Hence, there is reason to believe that adults and young people alike with elevated T, defined as having two or more such responses, are experiencing unmet needs for intimacy and nurturance. A small percentage of subjects with elevated T may turn out to be chronically disposed to feeling emotionally deprived, such that no amount of love and care from others suffices to fill their cup. Most often, subjects with more than one T, whatever their age, will be found to have experienced some painful object loss in their recent past. Commonly in this regard, such people readily indicate in interviews and on self-report measures that they feel lonely or needier than usual of people to take care of them.

Second, in addition to utilizing elevated T as a clue to reactive depression, examiners may also be able to distinguish relatively situational from relatively persistent depression by examining the stability of whatever DEPI variables are positive. As indicated by their retest correlations, V, the Egocentricity Index, and the Affective Ratio are more stable over time than C', which in turn is more stable than Y. These differences in stability characterize the Rorschach records of children and adolescents as well as adults, even though the time frame in which these differences are meaningful is shorter in younger people.

If DEPI is elevated, then the examiner should determine whether the indicators present are likely to be persistent or ephemeral. In light of the stability data, subjects whose elevated DEPI is heavily weighted with several V and a very low Egocentricity Index and Affective Ratio are unlikely to have become the way they are as result of yesterday's events, and they are equally unlikely to become free of these indices of self-derogation, low self-worth, and emotional withdrawal as a result of tomorrow's events. However, if one or two of these very stable negative variables were replaced in an elevated DEPI by an elevated C', which is only modestly stable, then the subject's possibilities for having a less entrenched, less persistent depressive disorder would improve.

The implications of DEPI for persistent depression are attenuated even further when Y and Color-Shading blends involving Y are prominent. As a highly unstable and situational variable, Y can disappear overnight in response to changing circumstances. When Y disappears, its contribution to the DEPI through SumSh and Color-Shading blends disappears along with it. Hence, in instances in which elimination of Y from a record would have the effect of reducing an elevated DEPI to less than 5, serious consideration should be given to the presence of a relatively reactive depression.

Helplessness Depression   As summarized in Volume 2 of the *Comprehensive System* (Exner, 1991, pp. 23–29), three different kinds of people tend be diagnosed as depressed or as having a depressive disorder: some who are emotionally distraught; some who are cognitively pessimistic, lethargic, and self-defeating; and some who are helpless in the face of contending with the demands of their daily existence. Although being emotionally depressed, being cognitively depressed, and being unable to cope effectively with life typically overlap in depressive disorder, one or the other usually constitutes the primary psychological difficulty of a person with this type of disturbance.

The Rorschach variables scored in DEPI reflect emotional and cognitive variables that, for the most part, do not measure the impaired coping capacities of people with helplessness depression. People who complain of feeling lonely and unfulfilled, of having only limited involvements with other people, of lacking initiative to do something about their situation, and of not being able to find ways of dealing effectively with demands they are facing at home, in school, and on the job are frequently diagnosed as being depressed if they seek or are brought for professional help. Often, however, such people present with bland or dull rather than depressed affect, and with noncommittal rather than negative cognitions, and they consequently tend not to elevate on DEPI.

As elaborated in Volume 2, this observation led to the formulation of the *Coping Deficit Index* (CDI). Records that contain any four or all of the five CDI variables will usually identify helplessness depression. Whether clinicians choose to consider this indication of deficient coping as diagnostic of depression is, at this point in time, a matter of individual preference rather than any well-established diagnostic guideline.

With respect to research, however, it should be noted that many false negative outcomes in validity studies of DEPI are likely to involve diagnosed depressive patients who have coping deficits. In the original studies from which CDI emerged, 79% of subjects diagnosed with affective disorder who were not positive on DEPI obtained values of 4 or 5 on the CDI. The basic reference data on 315 adult inpatient depressives published in Volume 2 provide some further perspectives on the relationship between these two indices: 25% of these depressed patients are positive on both DEPI and CDI, 50% are positive on DEPI but not CDI, and 18% are positive on CDI but not DEPI. Taken together, then, the two indices identify 93% of the group.

Although similar data are not available for young people, deficient coping as measured by the CDI is not simply a matter of immaturity. Nonpatient children and adolescents are slightly more likely than adults to show an elevated CDI, but values of 4 or 5 on this index are infrequent at all ages among nonpatients. Specifically, the frequency of elevated CDI among nonpatient adults is 3%; among the 1,390 nonpatient 5- to 16-year-olds in the normative sample, the frequency is 12%, and the frequency at age 5 (13%) is barely different from the frequency at age 16 (10%). Whatever the age of the young person, then, an elevated CDI should be interpreted as evidence of coping difficulties, particularly with respect to impoverished or unrewarding social relationships.

As noted, some clinicians may with good reason prefer to interpret an elevated CDI as indicating helplessness depression. Among young people, however, clinical experience suggests that most children and adolescents who elevate on CDI but not DEPI can be more sensitively described in terms of their difficulties in coping, especially with respect to social relatedness, than in terms of their being depressed. Accordingly, a treatment plan focused primarily on enhancing social skills may well prove more effective for such young people than a plan focused on alleviating depression.

SUICIDAL BEHAVIOR

The tragedy of suicide is a problem primarily of adulthood rather than the developmental years. Among the 30,407 known deaths by suicide in the United States in 1988, only 6 involved children less than 10 years old, 237 were ages 10 to 14, and 2,059 were 15 to 19 years old. Young persons committed 7.6% of the suicides reported nationwide that year, whereas young adults (ages 20–29) accounted for 22.9% and persons over 60 for 26.5% of the known suicides (National Center for Health Statistics [NCHS], 1991). As these data indicate, however, the suicide rate increases sharply during the adolescent years. From 1.4% per 100,000 among 10- to 14-year-olds, it increases eightfold to 11.3% per 100,000 among 15- to 19-year-olds (NCHS, 1991).

Three additional facts indicate that suicidal behavior, while extremely unlikely among children, must be a central concern to clinicians evaluating troubled adolescents. First, youthful suicide has increased at an alarming rate during the past quarter century. Between 1960 and 1986 the rate of suicide in the total United States population grew by approximately 20%, whereas among 15- to 19-year-olds it tripled during the same period. Second, self-inflicted harm is a more frequent cause of death among 15- to 19-year-olds than among any other age group. The three leading causes of death among 15- to 19-year-olds are not diseases or illnesses of any kind, but preventable mishaps classified, in order, as accidents, suicide, and homicide. Third, along with dying from suicide in disproportionate numbers, adolescents are as likely as adults to think about suicide and to make suicide attempts, and actual suicide in young people is almost always preceded by suicidal thoughts and attempts. An estimated 65% to 75% of young people contemplate suicide at least once during their adolescence, and 25% have thoughts about suicide even as preadolescents (Berman & Jobes, 1991; Bolger, Downey, Walker, & Steininger, 1989; Weiner, 1992, Chap. 9).

Extensive clinical and research studies have demonstrated that suicidal behavior in young people emerges as the end result of a gradually unfolding process involving long-standing instability, mounting distress, dissolving social relationships, and repeated failures to find nonsuicidal solutions to persistent problems. For the most part, these disposing circumstances to self-destructive acts must be assessed primarily from a young person's clinical history rather than from psychological test data. Indeed, earlier research established fairly clearly that psychodiagnostic data, including Rorschach findings, can be expected to account for only a small portion of the variance in predicting suicidal behavior (Goldfried, Stricker, & Weiner, 1971, Chap. 8; Neuringer, 1974).

On the other hand, clinical and research studies leave little doubt that suicidal behavior goes hand-in-hand with affective disorder. Although people who harm themselves or take their own lives may display a wide range of personality styles and patterns of psychopathology, the most common psychological concomitant of suicidal behavior is a depressive constellation of dejection, discouragement, hopelessness, and self-loathing, in adolescents as well as adults (Brent, Kolko, Allan, & Brown, 1990; Brown, Overholser, Spirito, & Fritz, 1991; Myers, McCauley, Calderon, & Treder, 1991). In addition, it seems reasonable to expect that suicidal risk in depressed young people will be increased among those who feel overwhelmed by stress, who lack restraint in expressing themselves, who have difficulty solving problems in an efficient manner, and who are inclined to exercise poor judgment.

Many of these personality characteristics are captured by the variables in the Comprehensive System Suicide Constellation (S-CON). Although the S-CON was developed from data on subjects age 18 or older, the reasonable stability of Rorschach variables from midadolescence on indicates that this index may provide reliable information beginning at about age 15.

As noted in Chapter 4, the S-CON is an empirically derived index, and as indicated by the actuarial data summarized in Volume 1 of the *Comprehensive System* (Exner, 1993a), its most efficient cutting score is 8. If any 8 of the variables are positive, any adolescent age 15 or older should be identified as being at risk for suicidal behavior. Identifying young people as being at risk for suicide on this basis should never be construed as a *prediction,* however, but only as a *warning.* This warning should nevertheless be stated with sufficient emphasis to leave little doubt in the minds of referral sources that active steps should be taken to explore further the likelihood of self-destructive behavior and to alleviate circumstances that may be conducive to it.

On the other hand, an S-CON below 8 should not be interpreted as ruling out the possibility of suicidal behavior. As the case of DEPI the strength of the S-CON index lies in its low rate of false positives, not in a minimal frequency of false negatives. The distinct possibility that false negatives will occur, that is, that truly suicidal young people may not elevate on the S-CON is a trade-off for the certainty with which an elevated S-CON identifies the likelihood of suicidal risk. In clinical practice, the utilization of a comprehensive test battery along with observational and historical data, each piece of which may include false negatives but contributes some portion of true positives, represents the most effective way to assess suicidal potential accurately.

With children under age 15, the S-CON cannot be expected to contribute to the assessment of suicidal risk. Some of the variables in this index are normatively elevated in young people to an extent that may substantially increase the rate of false positives. Efforts to validate a revised S-CON for children have thus far proved unsuccessful, primarily because the very low frequency of suicide prior to age 15 and especially age 10 make it difficult to obtain adequate samples for developing such indices. Clinically, there is probably good reason to expect that children who take their own lives suffer from the same kinds of hopelessness, self-derogation, poor judgment, and interpersonal alienation that typically precede self-destructive behavior in older people. For the present, however, there is no validated way of quantifying such suicidal dispositions in the Rorschach protocols of children and early adolescents.

REFERENCES

Abrams, R., & Taylor, M. A. (1974). Unipolar mania. *Archives of General Psychiatry, 30,* 441–443.

Acklin, M. W., McDowell, C. J., & Orndoff, S. (1992). Statistical power and the Rorschach: 1975–1991. *Journal of Personality Assessment, 59,* 366–379.

Andreasen, N. C., Rice, J., Endicott, J., Coryell, W., Grove, W. M., & Reich, T. (1987). Familial rates of affective disorder. *Archives of General Psychiatry, 44,* 461–469.

Angold, A., Weissman, M. M., Karen, J., & Merikangas, K. R. (1987). Parent and child reports of depressive symptoms in children at low and high risk of depression. *Journal of Child Psychology & Psychiatry, 28,* 901–915.

Ball, J. D., Archer, R. P., Gordon, R. A., & French, J. (1991). Rorschach depression indices with children and adolescents: Concurrent validity findings. *Journal of Personality Assessment, 57,* 465–476.

Barnett, P. A., & Gotlib, I. H. (1988). Psychosocial functioning and depression: Distinguishing among antecedents, concomitants, and consequences. *Psychological Bulletin, 104,* 97–126.

Baron, M., Gruen, R., Asnis, L., & Kane, J. (1982). Schizo-affective and affective disorders: Morbidity risk and genetic transmission. *Acta Psychiatrica Scandinavica, 65,* 253–262.

Belter, R. W., Lipovsky, J. A., & Finch, A. J. (1989). Rorschach egocentricity index and self-concept in children and adolescents. *Journal of Personality Assessment, 53,* 783–789.

Berman, A. L., & Jobes, D. A. (1991). *Adolescent suicide: Assessment and intervention.* Washington, DC: American Psychological Association.

Bolger, N., Downey, G., Walker, E., & Steininger, P. (1989). The onset of suicidal ideation in childhood and adolescence. *Journal of Youth and Adolescence, 18,* 175–190.

Brent, D. A., Kolko, D. J., Allan, M. J., & Brown, R. V. (1990). Suicidality in affectively disordered adolescent inpatients. *Journal of the American Academy of Child and Adolescent Psychiatry, 29,* 586–593.

Brown, L. K., Overholser, J., Spirito, A., & Fritz, G. K. (1991). The correlates of planning in adolescent suicide attempts. *Journal of the American Academy of Child and Adolescent Psychiatry, 30,* 95–99.

Burke, K. C., Burke, J. D., Regier, D. A., & Rae, D. S. (1990). Age at onset of selected mental disorders in five community populations. *Archives of General Psychiatry, 47,* 511–518.

Caputo-Sacco, L., & Lewis, R. J. (1991). MMPI correlates of Exner's Egocentricity Index in an adolescent psychiatric population. *Journal of Personality Assessment, 56,* 29–34.

Carpenter, W. T., & Stephens, J. H. (1980). The diagnosis of mania. In R. H. Belmaker & H. M. van Praage (Eds.), *Mania: An evolving concept* (pp. 7–24). New York: Spectrum.

Carey, T. C., Finch, A. J., & Carey, M. P. (1991). Relation between differential emotions and depression in emotionally disturbed children and adolescents. *Journal of Consulting and Clinical Psychology, 59,* 594–597.

Casper, R. C., Redmond, E., Katz, M. M., Schaffer, C. B., David, J. M., & Koslow, S. H. (1985). Somatic symptoms in primary affective disorder. *Archives of General Psychiatry, 42,* 1098–1104.

Clarizio, H. F. (1989). Continuity in childhood depression. *Adolescence, 24,* 253–276.

Clark, V. F., & Nelson, W. M. (1990). Negative expectations and self-evaluations in dysphoria. *Journal of Youth and Adolescence, 19,* 57–62.

Cohen, R. M., Weingartner, H., Smallberg, S. A., Pickar, D., & Murphy, D. L. (1982). Effort and cognition in depression. *Archives of General Psychiatry, 39,* 593–597.

Cornell, D. G., Suarez, R., & Berent, S. (1984). Psychomotor retardation in melancholic and non-melancholic depression: Cognitive and motor components. *Journal of Abnormal Psychology, 93,* 150–157.

Coryell, W., Endicott, J., & Keller, M. (1990). Outcome of patients with chronic affective disorder: A five-year follow-up. *American Journal of Psychiatry, 147,* 1627–1633.

Coryell, W., Keller, M., Lavori, P., & Endicott, J. (1990). Affective syndromes, psychotic features, and prognosis: I. Depression. II. Mania. *Archives of General Psychiatry, 47,* 651–662.

Coyne, J. C., Kessler, R. C., Tal, M., Turnbull, J., Wortman, C. B., & Greden, J. F. (1987). Living with a depressed person. *Journal of Consulting and Clinical Psychology, 55,* 347–352.

Dunner, D. L., Patrick, V., & Fieve R. R. (1979). Life events at the onset of bipolar affective illness. *American Journal of Psychiatry, 136,* 508–511.

Duricko, A. J., Norcross, J. C., & Buskirk, R. D. (1989). Correlates of the Egocentricity Index in child and adolescent outpatients. *Journal of Personality Assessment, 53,* 184–187.

Exner, J. E., Jr. (1991). *The Rorschach: A comprehensive system:* Vol. 2. *Interpretation* (2nd ed.). New York: Wiley.

Exner, J. E., Jr. (1993a). *The Rorschach: A comprehensive system:* Vol. 1. *Basic foundations* (3rd ed.). New York: Wiley.

Exner, J. E., Jr. (1993b). Vista and guilt or remorse. *Alumni Newsletter.* Asheville, NC: Rorschach Workshops.

Fendrich, M., Weissman, M. M., & Warner, V. (1991). Longitudinal assessment of major depression and anxiety disorders in children. *Journal of the American Academy of Child and Adolescent Psychiatry, 30,* 38–42.

Fleming, J. E., & Offord, D. R. (1990). Epidemiology of childhood depressive disorders: A critical review. *Journal of the American Academy of Child and Adolescent Psychiatry, 29,* 571–580.

Garrison, C. Z., Jackson, K. L., Marsteller, F., McKeown, R., & Addy, C. (1990). A longitudinal study of depressive symptomatology in young adolescents. *Journal of the American Academy of Child and Adolescent Psychiatry, 29,* 581–585.

Goldfried, M. R., Stricker, G., & Weiner, I. B. (1971). *Rorschach handbook of clinical and research applications.* Englewood Cliffs, NJ: Prentice-Hall.

Grossman, L. S., Harrow, M., Fudala, J. L., & Meltzer, H. Y. (1984). The longitudinal course of schizo-affective disorders. *Journal of Nervous and Mental Disease, 172,* 140–149.

Haage, D. A., Dyck, M. J., & Ernst, D. (1991). Empirical status of cognitive theory of depression. *Psychological Bulletin, 110,* 215–236.

Hammen, C., & Goodman-Brown, T. (1990). Self-schemas and vulnerability to specific life stress in children at risk for depression. *Cognitive Therapy and Research, 14,* 215–227.

Harrington, R., Fudge, H., Rutter, M., Pickles, A., & Hill, J. (1990). Adult outcomes of childhood and adolescent depression. *Archives of General Psychiatry, 47,* 465–473.

Hops, H., Lewinsohn, P. M., Andrews, J. A., & Roberts, R. E. (1990). Psychosocial correlates of depressive symptomatology among high school students. *Journal of Clinical Child Psychology, 19,* 211–220.

Hurt, S. W., Reznikoff, M., & Clarkin, J. F. (1991). *Psychological assessment, psychiatric diagnosis, and treatment planning.* New York: Brunner/Mazel.

Kanfer, R., & Zeiss, A. M. (1983). Depression, interpersonal standard setting, and judgments of self-efficacy. *Journal of Abnormal Psychology, 92,* 319–329.

Kaplan, S. L., Hong, G. K., & Weinhold, C. (1984). Epidemiology of depressive symptomatology in adolescents. *Journal of the American Academy of Child Psychiatry, 23,* 91–98.

Kashani, J. H., Rosenberg, T. K., & Reid, J. C. (1989). Developmental perspectives in child and adolescent depressive symptoms in a community sample. *American Journal of Psychiatry, 146,* 871–875.

Kashani, J. H., Carlson, G. A., Beck, N. C., Hoeper, E. W., Corcoran, C. M., McAllister, J. A., Fallahi, C., Rosenberg, T. K., & Reid, J. C. (1987). Depression, depressive symptoms, and depressed mood among a community sample of adolescents. *American Journal of Psychiatry, 144,* 931–934.

Kendall, P. C., Cantwell, D. P., & Kazdin, A. E. (1989). Depression in children and adolescents: Assessment issues and recommendations. *Cognitive Therapy and Research, 13,* 109–146.

Kendall, P. C., Stark, K. D., & Adam, T. (1990). Cognitive deficit or cognitive distortion in childhood depression. *Journal of Abnormal Child Psychology, 18,* 255–270.

Kovacs, M. (1989). Affective disorders in children and adolescents. *American Psychologist, 44,* 209–215.

Kutcher, S., & Marton, R. (1991). Affective disorders in first-degree relatives of adolescent onset bipolars, unipolars, and normal controls. *Journal of the American Academy of Child and Adolescent Psychiatry, 30,* 75–78.

Lefkowitz, M. M., & Tesiny, E. P. (1985). Depression in children: Prevalence and correlates. *Journal of Consulting and Clinical Psychology, 53,* 647–656.

Lerner, Y. (1980). The subjective experience of mania. In R. H. Belmaker & H. M. van Praag (Eds.), *Mania: An evolving concept* (pp. 77–88). New York: Spectrum.

Lipovsky, J. A., Finch, A. J., & Belter, R. W. (1989). Assessment of depression in adolescents: Objective and projective measures. *Journal of Personality Assessment, 53,* 449–458.

Mendlewicz, J. (1980). X-linkage of bipolar illness and the question of schizoaffective illness. In R. H. Belmaker & H. M. van Praag (Eds.), *Mania: An evolving concept* (pp. 89–96). New York: Spectrum.

Myers, K., McCauley, E., Calderon, R., & Treder, R. (1991). The 3-year longitudinal course of suicidality and predictive factors for subsequent suicidality in youths with major depressive disorder. *Journal of the American Academy of Child and Adolescent Psychiatry, 30,* 804–810.

National Center for Health Statistics. (1991). *Vital statistics of the United States, 1986: Vol. 2. Mortality.* Hyattsville, MD: Author.

Neale, J. M. (1988). Defensive functions of manic episodes. In T. F. Oltmanns & B. A. Maher (Eds.), *Delusional beliefs* (pp. 138–156). New York: Wiley.

Neuringer, C. (Ed.). (1974). *Psychological assessment of suicidal risk.* Springfield, IL: Charles C. Thomas.

Post, R. M., Runbinow, D. R., Uhde, T. W., Roy-Byrne, P. P., Linnoila, M., Rosoff, A., & Cowdry, R. (1989). Dysphoric mania. *Archives of General Psychiatry, 46,* 353–358.

Prosen, M., Clark, D. C., Harrow, M., & Fawcett, J. (1983). Guilt and conscience in major depressive disorders. *American Journal of Psychiatry, 140,* 839–844.

Regier, C. A., Boyd, J. H., Burke, J. D., Rae, D. S., Myers, J. K., Kramer, M., Robins, L. N., George, L. K., Karno, M., & Locke, B. Z. (1988). One-month prevalence of mental disorders in the United States. *Archives of General Psychiatry, 45,* 977–986.

Riley, W. T., Treiber, F. A., & Woods, M. G. (1989). Anger and hostility in depression. *Journal of Nervous and Mental Disease, 177,* 668–674.

Robins, C. J. (1990). Congruence of personality and life events in depression. *Journal of Abnormal Psychology, 99,* 393–397.

Robins, C. J., Block, P., & Peselow, E. R. (1990). Endogenous and non-endogenous depressions: Relations to life events, dysfunctional attitudes and event perceptions. *British Journal of Clinical Psychology, 29,* 201–207.

Ryan, N. D., Puig-Antich, J., Ambrosini, P., Rabinovich, H., Robinson, D., Nelson, B., Iyengar, S., & Twomey, J. (1987). The clinical picture of major depression in children and adolescents. *Archives of General Psychiatry, 44,* 854–861.

Ryan, N. D. (1989). Major depression. In C. G. Last & M. Hersen (Eds.), *Handbook of child psychiatric diagnosis* (pp. 317–329). New York: Wiley.

Shapiro, J. P., Leifer, M., Martone, M. W., & Kassem, L. (1990). Multimethod assessment of depression in sexually abused girls. *Journal of Personality Assessment, 55,* 234–248.

Silberman, E. K., Weingartner, H., & Post, R. M. (1983). Thinking disorders in depression. *Archives of General Psychiatry, 40,* 775–780.

Singer, H. K., & Brabender, V. (1993). The use of the Rorschach to differentiate unipolar and bipolar disorders. *Journal of Personality Assessment, 60,* 333–345.

Strober, M., McCracken, J., & Hanna, G. (1989). Affective disorders. In L. K. G. Hsu & M. Hersen (Eds.), *Recent developments in adolescent psychiatry* (pp. 201–232). New York: Wiley.

Tsuang, M. T. (1979). "Schizoaffective disorder" dead or alive? *Archives of General Psychiatry, 36,* 633–634.

Van Valkenburg, C., & Akiskal, H. S. (1985). Affective disorders. In M. Hersen & S. M. Turner (Eds.), *Diagnostic interviewing* (pp. 79–110). New York: Plenum Press.

Wampold, B. E., & Freund, R. D. (1991). Statistical issues in clinical research. In M. Hersen, A. E. Kazdin, & A. S. Bellack (Eds.), *The clinical psychology handbook* (2nd ed.; pp. 313–328). New York: Pergamon Press.

Weiner, I. B. (1966). *Psychodiagnosis in schizophrenia.* New York: Wiley.

Weiner, I. B. (1982). *Child and adolescent psychopathology.* New York: Wiley.

Weiner, I. B. (1992). *Psychological disturbance in adolescence* (2nd ed.). New York: Wiley.

Weller, R. A., Weller, E. B., Tucker, S. G., & Fristad, M. A. (1986). Mania in prepubertal children: Has it been underdiagnosed? *Journal of Affective Disorders, 11,* 151–154.

Whitaker, A., Johnson, J., Shaffer, D., Rapoport, J. L., Kalikow, K., Walsh, B. T., Davies, M., Braiman, S., & Dolinsky, A. (1990). Uncommon troubles in young people. *Archives of General Psychiatry, 47,* 487–496.

Zimmerman, M., Coryell, W., & Pfohl, B. (1986). The validity of the dexamethasone suppression test as a marker for endogenous depression. *Archives of General Psychiatry, 43,* 347–355.

PART III

Other Issues

CHAPTER 7

Faltering Personality Development

The preceding two chapters have focused on serious pathological states in children that might be best described as symptomatic disorders because the underlying impairments of personality functioning by which they are defined produce symptoms that wax and wane. Schizophrenic patients have their good days and bad days. They alternate between lucidity and incoherence and between being relatively realistic and relatively inappropriate, and at any point in time, they can be described as being more or less overtly schizophrenic. Likewise, affectively disordered youngsters suffer from a cyclical disorder marked in its natural course by episodes of remission and relapse and dramatic alternations in prevailing mood state.

By contrast, most young people who are subjected to personality assessment do not fall neatly into these categories and, as such, cannot be defined by symptoms that come and go. Instead, they are usually identified because their persistent ways of viewing and coping with experience seem out of step with their peers and often cause them to falter markedly in some of their everyday experiences. For one reason or another, their personality development has left them wanting when issues of effective academic and/or social functioning are used as a gauge of adequacy. In some circles, these youngsters are often identified as having a borderline disorder, and some are characterized by the hallmarks that have been defined as constituting a borderline disorder, such as being emotionally unstable and having a vulnerability to brief psychoticlike episodes. However, these symptomatic manifestations do not reflect stable and enduring characteristics of the child. Having a temper tantrum or a psychoticlike episode does not make a youngster a borderline disorder. Similarly, the passing of episodes of detachment or unwieldy emotional outbursts does not signal recovery from the borderline condition.

It is feasible that all youngsters whose behaviors are marked by emotionally lability or some form of detachment from reality may have some homogeneous features, but that seems unlikely unless homogeneity is defined very broadly such as has been done by Spitzer and Endicott (1979), whose work provided the basis for the DSM-III-R distinction between schizotypal and borderline personality disorders. The notion of a borderline core linking these two conditions derives from Meissner's (1984) approach to conceptualizing a "borderline spectrum" of disorders. Both of these formulations are consistent with research demonstrating (a) that borderline disorders can be reliably distinguished from other forms of psychopathology; (b) that most patients with borderline disorder will show a clearly differentiable emphasis on either cognitive or affective manifestations; (c) that the remaining patients will show a mixture of these features and function at some intermediate point on the borderline spectrum at which schizotypal and borderline personality disorder overlap; and (d) that these distinctions can be as readily drawn among adolescents as adults (Barrash, Kroll, Carey, & Sines, 1983; Esman, 1989; Hurt, Clarkin, Koenigsberg, Frances, & Nurnberg, 1986; Ludolph et al., 1990; McManus, Lerner, Robbins, & Barbour, 1984).

The problem with this approach is that it tends to push all youngsters whose personality development has been limited for one reason or another into one or two categories and assumes that there are common features to all who fall into these categories. Somewhere in this theoretical model an appreciation for individual differences has been lost or disregarded. It may be appropriate to create this pseudohomogenization for purposes of bookkeeping, but it tends to defy reality. At the very least, youngsters who have trouble coping with the demands made on them and in forming responses to their world can be differentiated into more than two groups.

Some longitudinal data reported by Lofgren, Bemporad, King, Lindem, and O'Driscoll (1991) are of considerable interest in this regard. They conducted follow-up diagnostic interviews with 19 subjects 10 to 20 years after they had been diagnosed as "borderline children" when 6 to 10 years old. Sixteen of these former borderline children demonstrated an array of personality disorders as adults, including antisocial, avoidant, narcissistic, paranoid, and schizotypal as well as borderline disorder; three were free of diagnosable disorder, and there were no instances of schizophrenia or affective disorder.

Obviously, one small sample study must be judged cautiously, but logic, based on findings from other studies of individual differences, suggests that these findings should not be surprising. The search for some kind of diagnostic specificity and continuity will continue, but it is doubtful that Rorschach findings will be of any particular assistance to that end. Fortunately, the Rorschach goes well beyond group categorization. Rorschach data focus on the individual and the complex features that are unique to the person. Some findings may, in fact, illustrate patterns closely resembling the characteristic manifestations of schizotypal or borderline personality disorders. However, other findings from subjects whose overt symptoms might cause them to be categorized as "borderline" may simply be manifestations of other flaws in personality development that cause them to act in ways that will neatly place them into some category on the so-called borderline spectrum. Clinicians should be quite reluctant to diagnose a young person as a borderline disorder, especially when there is no clear developmental history of the symptom patterns associated with the childhood borderline syndrome. In fact, it is probably more beneficial to the child if the diagnostic label is reserved and the description of the psychological functioning is offered.

During the adolescent years, when personality patterns become increasingly stable, some problems in personality structure also start to become fully established. It is probably for this reason that most authors who write about borderline disorders in adolescents have traditionally described them in the same way (see Kernberg, 1978; Masterson, 1980).

Accordingly, troubled children and adolescents should be more reasonably viewed as having problems in personality development more than as symptomatic conditions. Like other disorders, these are conditions that tend to originate early in life and produce prodromal manifestations during childhood. In middle and late adolescence, when individual personality style begins to crystallize, these disorders tend to become more fully established. Although many of these disordered children and adolescents share several core features, they also comprise some distinctive varieties of adjustment difficulty.

CATEGORIES OF FLAWED OR FALTERING PERSONALITY

Generally, for purposes of understanding and treatment planning, many disordered youngsters can be conceptualized as having any of a variety of personality impairments. These impairments include disruptions in cognitive, and/or affective, and/or interpersonal functioning that characterize the young person who has difficulty contending with his or her world. Variations in which of these impairments are most prominent and how they are manifested may aid to categorize the troubled young person, but again, categorization is far less important than understanding. Those youngsters whose persistent dysfunctions are mainly cognitive in nature may be developing some form of *obsessive* disorder, and if the cognitive dysfunction is accompanied by interpersonal isolation they may be well along in developing a *schizoid or even a schizotypal problem.* Those whose dysfunctions are primarily affective in nature and who display interpersonal overinvolvement may be developing a *hysteroid problem or even meet the criteria for borderline condition.* Others may settle into a more compliant or deferential mode of overt behavior and could be developing a *passive-dependent or passive-aggressive problem.* In effect, all manifest some elements of flawed or faltering personality development, which, if they continue unrectified, will ultimately evolve into marked personality disorder.

At times, it has been suggested that the characteristic unpredictability, instability, and ambivalence that accompany faltering personality development closely resemble the manner in which adolescents normally go about their lives during the difficult transition years between childhood and adulthood. However, contrary to any such impressions, abundant data demonstrate (a) that nonpatient adolescents do not display maladaptive symptomatology, (b) that the behaviors of the troubled child do not comprise maladaptive exaggerations of normal adolescent behavior patterns, and (c) that careful clinical evaluation can distinguish the behaviors of the troubled child or adolescent from the normal range of variability readily and reliably in adolescents (Weiner, 1992, Chaps. 1, 5).

CORE PROBLEMS

The flawed or faltering personality has at various times been held responsible for a range of dysfunctional thoughts, feelings, and actions. Grinker (1977, p. 162) covered most of the bases by noting early on that borderline disorder can be described as a form of psychopathology that combines features of psychotic, neurotic, and characterological disturbance with elements of normality as well. Despite the range and complexity of these phenomena, the following five characteristics have traditionally been considered to constitute the core of the developing personality destined for trouble (see Dahl, 1990; Gunderson & Singer, 1975; Perry & Klerman, 1980; Weiner, 1992, Chap. 5).

1. *Overly Intense Emotions.*   Some young people are prone to becoming extremely angry, anxious, and depressed. The intensity of their affect often makes other people uncomfortable, especially when they bristle with rage or become racked with worry or despair. Their sometimes seething fury may result in outbursts of temper and violence, but more often it seeps out in the form of persistent irritability, impatience, petulance, argumentativeness, sarcasm, and devaluation of other people and what they are doing. Their sometimes incapacitating depression typically involves a sense of emptiness or loneliness and the feeling that life is not worth living.

Along with their prevailing affects of anger, anxiety, and depression, young people whose developing personality is flawed or inhibited are also likely to cycle through periods of self-satisfaction and elation. The quality of their affect is always less distinctive than its quantity, and at various points in time, they become very anxious, very mad, very happy, or very sad but will rarely display any of these affects in mild or muted form.

2. *Poor Self-Control.* The actions of all young people are frequently poorly planned and/or poorly controlled. This feature occurs more often among those who have problems in Personality development. Their characteristic impulsivity and intolerance for frustration place them at high risk for antisocial and self-destructive behavior. Because of their poor self-control, they often have brushes with authority, and some have a likelihood of truancy, running away, and other delinquent conduct.

As for self-destructive behavior, persons with a flawed or faltering personality are more likely than other youngsters in general to abuse alcohol and other drugs, to become sexually promiscuous, to engage in acts of self-mutilation, and to make suicide attempts. If they become preoccupied with self-destruction, their behavior is often blatantly manipulative, with threats or some minor but very dramatic self-injury being used in an effort to influence the attitudes or actions of others.

3. *Illusory Social Adaptation.* Often, young people who have flaws in their personality development appear to be functioning adequately, especially when they have been able to confine themselves to situations that do not tax their coping capacities. They may show a conventional face to the world, seem appropriately engaged with other people, and present an apparently good record of effort and accomplishment in school or in part-time jobs. However, close scrutiny typically reveals that this apparently good adaptation has been maintained in undemanding social, academic, and work environments in which their abilities were far more than adequate to guarantee success.

More typically, young people with flawed personality cannot cope effectively with challenge and uncertainty, nor can they easily tolerate stress or ambiguity. When unsure of what is expected or faced with changing demands that strain their capacities, they are likely to function poorly until they can get themselves back into a comfortable, predictable, and easily manageable situation. Hence, most of these young people will either show a history of apparently successful adaptation that in fact represents marked underachievement in relation to their abilities, or they will show a spotty record in which periods of accomplishment have alternated with social and school or occupational failure.

4. *Strained Interpersonal Relationships.* Although capable of managing superficial relationships with other people, the youngster whose personality development is faltering cannot deal effectively with close or intimate interpersonal involvements. They consequently tend to vacillate between transient, distant acquaintanceships and intensely dependent and demanding attachments to other people. Frequently, when they are functioning in social isolation, they suspect the motives of others and fear being exploited or rejected. Such fears prevent them from reaching out for intimacy, no matter how lonely they feel. Their social isolation is sometimes compounded by a tendency to misperceive or ignore various characteristics of other people and to form whatever inaccurate or incomplete image fits their needs at the moment.

When, instead of being isolated, they become overinvolved with others, they tend to form intense, clinging, dependent relationships. Like social isolation, such overinvolvement is governed by self-serving rather than altruistic motives. In effect, some of these youngsters are interpersonal takers, not givers, and their egocentric demandingness places a heavy burden on those who befriend or attempt to love them.

5. *Persistence of Problems.* As already noted, the dysfunctions that occur among those with flawed, faltering personalities constitute characteristic ways of dealing with

experience and present a persistent rather than an episodic pattern of psychopathology. These are conditions that usually originate in early life experiences and gradually take shape by formative experiences during the developmental years. Once the flaws become consolidated in the basic personality structure, they are unlikely to change except in response to extraordinary life events or therapeutic intervention.

There often is a paradox in the behavior of youngsters who are suffering from flawed personality development. It is that their affective, social, and interpersonal lives are dramatically marked by shifting sands. How they think, feel, and act one day may bear little relationship to how they will be or how they will behave the next day. What is most predictable in their lives is their unpredictability. Grinker (1977) captured this fact by identifying "stable instability" as an overriding characteristic when describing the borderline disorder. What persists in many troubled young people is a chronic disposition to dramatic variations in affective tone, self-control, social adaptation, personal relatedness, and cognitive functioning.

An unfortunate and somewhat chronic feature of the youngster who has a flawed personality development is the considerable tolerance that he or she has for the condition. Unlike persons with symptomatic disorders, who regard their psychopathology as ego-alien, youngsters with faltering personality typically maintain an ego-syntonic stance; that is, they view the problems that they have as perfectly natural and they are comfortable with their ways, except when challenged by failure or social rejection. For instance, when they are depressed, they long to escape painful feelings of dysphoria and discouragement, but they will not see anything unusual in the emotional intensity and lability that make them vulnerable to episodes of depression. Angry youngsters often lash out at a friend or therapist they feel has let them down, but they will not regard their anger as unjustified or the interpersonal uncertainties that led to it as inappropriate.

These flawed personalities in children and adolescents do not always portend poorly for their future. Some of these young people are confronted with life experiences that promote change, but unfortunately, others are destined to carry the flaws that have marked their development into adulthood, and their difficulties in getting along in the world intensify.

As noted earlier, flawed or faltering personality problems are neither symptomatic nor cyclical conditions but, instead, comprise persistent ways of viewing and coping with experience. Researchers generally concur that these disorders can best be understood as variants of psychopathology rather than as specific or transient reactions to stressful situations (Perry, 1988; Widiger, 1989). They tend to share three basic features that are generally considered to constitute personality disorders:

1. These conditions usually begin early in life and are shaped by dispositions and experiences that, during their preschool years, start to influence how people characteristically think, feel, and relate to others.
2. They gradually become identifiable during the developmental years, as young persons mature and take on increasingly stable personality characteristics, and they become more or less crystallized during late adolescence and early adulthood, when adult identities and orientations typically become established.
3. They are ego-syntonic, in that their identifying characteristics are viewed by the disordered individuals as how they naturally happen to be, and not as aberrations or alterations in personality functioning that are bothersome, unwelcome, or in need of modification.

In light of these features of a potential for pathology, children who are destined to manifest full-blown personality disorders by the time they pass from adolescence into adulthood can be expected to display forerunners of the condition long before it becomes fully established. Even though these disorders probably originate in events of early childhood, prodromal symptoms are unlikely to emerge during the preschool years. Basic personality structures are normally still too amorphous at this early age for children to show indications of developing personality disorder.

During the elementary school years, children become much more capable of focusing their thoughts and harnessing their feelings effectively, and they also begin to take on consistently distinctive ways of managing social interactions. Such maturation makes it increasingly possible to distinguish normal development from the kinds of cognitive, affective, and interpersonal incapacities that characterize the faltering personality. With this in mind, some developmental psychopathologists argue that the elementary school age is when an emerging personality problem begins to become identifiable (Pine, 1983). Although the possible childhood forerunners of these disorders are many and varied, children having personalities that are flawed exhibit many behaviors that are considerably less than effective (see Petti & Vela, 1990; Vela, Gottlieb, & Gottlieb, 1983; Wenning, 1990). These include disturbed interpersonal relationships, marked by extremely ambivalent feelings toward other people; a disturbed sense of reality, marked by extreme withdrawal into grandiose fantasies; difficulty distinguishing pretend play from real life; paranoid ideation and magical thinking; frequent bouts of anxiety, sometimes marked by panic states; excessive impulsivity and emotionality.

The appropriate diagnosis for school-age children who display some critical number of these symptom patterns is a matter of debate. Can they properly be regarded as having a personality disorder when they have not reached the level of maturity at which personality is sufficiently formed to be considered disordered? Some clinicians prefer to call these youngsters "borderline children" and to formulate assessment and treatment strategies for working with them as if they have a discrete and specific condition (Chethik, 1986; Kernberg, 1983; Leichtman & Nathan, 1983; Nagy & Szatmari, 1986). Others question whether any discrete picture exists in children and worry that this label may be overused, without providing any real assistance in treatment planning for children whose problems are difficult to understand (Greenman, Gunderson, Cane, & Saltzman, 1986; Gualtieri, Koriath, & Van Bourgondien, 1983; Shapiro, 1983).

SOME RORSCHACH CLUES TO A FALTERING PERSONALITY

As any competent Rorschacher knows, there are no well-established profiles or clusters of data that equate neatly with the presence of a personality disorder in adult subjects. This is even more the case with younger subjects, as they are in an almost continuous state of physical and psychological development until their late adolescent years, at the very least. Thus, potentials for trouble that may exist in one year may dissipate considerably in the next year. However, it is also important to note that some unwanted or undesirable features of personality often become quite persistent, especially if they develop in the early phases of childhood and/or if they remain present into adolescence. These unwanted or negative features typically form the basis from which personality structure and the psychological operations that follow from it falter and result in less effective functioning.

The age of the youngster is critically important in determining whether a feature might be regarded as representing a negative finding. For instance, the presence of two

Pure *C* answers in the record of a 7-year-old probably would not be regarded as a negative finding, whereas the presence of the same two answers in the record of a 15-year-old might be regarded as being extremely negative. However, as always is the case in Rorschach interpretation, no single clue or negative finding concerning personality structure should be overinterpreted; that is, when studied by itself, it probably means very little. There are some exceptions to this general rule, but even they must be viewed with caution when dealing with the record of a youngster. Generally, Rorschach clues that suggest the possibility of flawed or faltering personality development will derive from any of the basic clusters of structural data, and it is the accumulation of several such clues that ultimately signals cause for concern.

Clues Regarding Problems in Coping Styles and Stress Tolerance   Usually, the data of the *EB* or the value for Lambda provide no hints about whether the basic coping style of a young subject is a hazard to adjustment. Almost all children between the ages of 5 and 12 will manifest a High *Lambda* Style during one year or another, regardless of whether or not it is the best approach to adaptation. On the other hand, if the High *Lambda* Style persists into adolescence, it should be cause for concern, as it may signal the sort of backing away from complexity that will decrease growth experiences.

Similarly, almost all developing youngsters will have an ambient *EB* at one time or another during their growth years. The chances are substantial that the ambient status will change to a more definitive style by the time the subject reaches the age of 15 or 16, but if this does not occur, it is a clear warning about the potential for future difficulties. But, being an ambient does not necessarily equate with having a flawed personality. Many ambients go through life effectively and successfully. Probably, their success is facilitated by the availability of considerable resource, as reflected by the Rorschach value of *EA*.

The *EA* value is often extremely important in identifying the personality that is faltering during development. Children between the ages of 5 and 9 are not expected to have a substantial *EA*. Values of 5.0, 6.0, or 7.0 are commonplace for those in this age range. Accordingly, youngsters in this age range are commonly vulnerable to overload situations when stress demands occur, especially when the stress is unexpected or very complex. It is the way of the young child. Conversely, low *EA* values are less common among children who are between the ages of 10 and 12, and far less frequent among those age 13 or greater. When the *EA* value is less than 7.0 in a youngster who is age 10 or older, some concern is warranted. Available resources may be less than required, and the potential for an overload state and a potential for impulsivity and unpredictability may exist.

Obviously, the Adjusted D score provides some information about that potential, but it must be applied very cautiously when working with the record of a young person. An Adjusted D score of less than zero usually is regarded as a negative finding in an adult record; however, this score may appear frequently in the records of nonpatient children. A cursory review of the frequency data for nonpatient children indicates that, at almost every year between the ages of 8 and 15, at least 15% have Adjusted D scores of less than zero, and for some years the frequency exceeds more than 20%. On the other hand, very few nonpatient youngsters have Adjusted D scores that are less than -1. Thus, Adjusted D scores of -2 or lower, especially in records in which *EA* values are also low, probably signal a lag in personality development that ultimately can be costly to the person's functioning. Such a finding becomes even more important when the subject appears to accept his or her condition without being distressed by it. If they seem to feel comfortable with their test responses, it is probably not a good sign. They may be anxious or angry about being examined, but they rarely express any concern about how they are responding. Unlike subjects with a more acute problem, who frequently take critical distance from their disturbed responses ("That's not very good, is it?"; "Let me take that one back and give another one instead"; "I didn't really mean to say it that way"; "It doesn't look like that"; "I can't find it now"), subjects with a faltering personality development tend to deliver even bizarre responses with bland self-assurance.

Clues to Cognitive Difficulties   Cognitive difficulties are not always present in the flawed or faltering personality. If they are, they usually will appear in the protocols of young people whose faulty development is orienting them toward an obsessive or schizoid way of life, or even a schizotypal disorder. At times, serious cognitive difficulties are reflected in indices of disordered thinking and impaired reality testing, such as a substantial $Sum6$ or $WSum6$ or a low $X + \%$ and high $X - \%$. In fact, some of these young people are positive on the SCZI, but typically, these will be judged to be false positive cases when the record is examined thoroughly. Nonetheless, when the values for any combination of these four variables are substantial in a subject older than age 9, it is reasonable to conclude that cognitive difficulties do, indeed, exist. This is especially true when the number of Popular answers falls well below the expected range.

Possibly an even more important warning about potential cognitive problems in children under the age of 9 or 10 is the presence of an introversive style. Younger children usually do not have the neurophysiological development that is necessary to engage in formal or conceptual operations. Typically, their thinking is more primitive and concrete. Thus, if they begin to rely extensively on a system of delaying responses until they have ideationally weighed the potential of each, the likelihood of concreteness, or even synchretistic thinking is considerable.

This also can be a problem into the early adolescent years. Thus, an introversive style prior to the age of 13 may create some hazards to growth, and, prior to the age of 10, almost always signals a potential cognitive problem. The presence of such a problem will most always be confirmed when the data also indicate an inclination to withdraw excessively into fantasy. These are the youngsters who tend to replace constructive problem solving with fantasy or magical thinking. This is reflected in a considerably higher frequency of passive versus active human movement responses $(Mp > Ma)$. Whenever Mp exceeds Ma by more than one, it indicates a defensive abuse of fantasy in which reality is replaced by controlled ideation, and usually the subject will ignore reality demands. In a young person, this defensive tactic only serves to thwart development.

Clues to Affective Difficulties   Affective difficulties often are found in young people whose personality development is faltering. They are reflected on the Rorschach in indices of intense anger, excessive emotional intensity, or an unusual withdrawal from emotional stimuli. In adolescents, evidence of a failure to be developing as much modulation of emotional expressions as their peers can also provide a clue to affective difficulties.

Some evidence of oppositionality, negativism, or hostility will manifest in the protocols of most youngsters, usually in the form of one, two, or even three S responses. These responses probably reflect some of the frustration that young people experience because their lives are dominated by others. However, this negativism or hostility can become more generalized and overly intense in some who feel particularly burdened by the intrusions and manipulations of others, or who feel abandoned by those around them. When this occurs, the natural experience of negativism takes on the traitlike feature of intense anger. Usually, it will be manifest in the Rorschach by more than four S answers, and some of those may be combined with the special scores AG or MOR. Anger of this magnitude is rarely situational and typically indicates that the emotions of the subject frequently will be marked by, or even directed by, these intense feelings. The resulting behaviors often will be incongruous with healthy growth experiences and can cause the overall personality development to suffer. If the anger is not expressed directly, it may become a precursor for a passive-aggressive kind of personality problem.

Another clue to affective difficulties in the young person will be evidence of excessive emotionality. Persistence of this characteristic will contribute often to the development of a hysteroidlike problem, or if carried to an extreme, can predispose a classic borderline picture. Excessive emotionality is, at best, difficult to detect in the Rorschach in subjects under the age of 10, but there are some instances in which it is detectable in the 8- or 9-year-old. Typically, young subjects will give at least one Pure C response, and because Pure C is not a very reliable variable, it is usually not afforded much concern. Some very young children, ages 5, 6, or 7, give multiple Pure C responses, but usually no more than two. Whenever more than two Pure C answers appear in the protocol of a young person, especially those who are older than 8, it should be some cause for concern. However, this finding tends to vary with age, and studied alone does not necessarily mean that emotions are excessively intense.

The content and quality of the Pure C answers become critically important when addressing this issue, and if the answers are more primitive and chaotic, it seems reasonable to assume that the affects are overly intense and less well controlled and may produce behaviors that run contrary to a useful development of personality features. Sometimes, excessive emotionality will be evidenced by the presence of many more $CF + C$ answers than FC responses. Anyone familiar with the literature of developmental psychology is aware that, as the young person enters into adolescence, some sort of learning occurs through which youngsters begin to modulate the expression of their feelings more so than may have been the case in their past years. This is probably because socialization has become important, and peers no longer accept the casual and seemingly random casual outbursts as much as was the case earlier.

Similarly, adults also tend to expect less emotional chaos than they might have been willing to accept in the behaviors of a younger child. In the Rorschach, this means that more FC responses can be expected. It does not mean that the frequency of FC answers will be greater than CF and Pure C responses, as that would require more modulation of emotional expression than can be expected of the growing youngster. Nonetheless, Rorschach pictures in which the composite of $CF + C$ is inordinately greater than the frequency of FC are not expected among young people, age 14 or older. When this occurs, the finding suggests that there is some sort of developmental lag concerning the use of, or expression of, feeling and may indicate the sort of flaw that can ultimately lead to problems.

Sometimes, young people who have a faltering personality have found it more convenient to avoid emotional situations. They tend to feel more secure when emotional stimuli are not present. This sort of problem can become a forerunner of an obsessive, or schizoidish personality problem. Ordinarily, this tendency will manifest in the Rorschach by a very low Afr. This does not mean an Afr that simply falls lower than the average range. Many children, and especially adolescents who are developing an introversive style, may have values for the Afr that fall into an area lower than expected. Instead, a marked and potentially pathological withdrawal from affect will be indicated by an Afr that is well below .45. In most instances, these are Afr's that fall into the .30's range or lower and often coincide with a low very low *WSumC*. In some more serious instances, not only are the *Afr* and *WSumC* low, but a substantial number of *C'* answers also exist in the record, frequently reflecting a larger value than the *WSumC*. Avoidance of emotion can be a disaster for developing young people because it breeds a tendency to avoid their own feelings and detracts seriously from the growth experiences that follow from a sharing of feelings with others.

Clues to Problems in Self-Concept   Most all developing youngsters struggle, at times, with the issues of who they are and what they are. Younger children in particular will often base self-image more on fantasy or imagination than real experience and, as a result, their notions of self-image are not very realistic. In light of this natural phenomenon, it is difficult to detect serious self-concept problems in children under the age of 12 unless they are blatant. Typically, self-concept problems in the younger child will manifest in the Rorschach by depressive features. The most prominent of these is a low Egocentricity Index, which, in most instances, will be accompanied by evidence of a ruminative preoccupation with perceived negative features of the self, as indicated by the presence of Vista answers, and the presence of more than one Color-Shading blend, indicating a marked confusion about feelings.

The collection of these features often can detect the young person who is well on the road to withdrawal, but more important they connote a developing self-image that may lead to form of social timidity, or even withdrawal, especially if combined with some of the features of affective problems indicating withdrawal from direct affective experience. On the other hand, negative findings about self-image that coincide with problems of excessive emotional intensity may signal a form of personality development in which elaborate defenses are being developed to ward off acknowledgment of the negative sense of self. In this situation, overt behaviors may be marked by extremes in emotional expressions that only serve to cause peers to turn away and, in effect, validate some of the child's conceptions of the self.

Quite often, problems in self-concept are reflected in the characteristics assigned to responses that include Pure *H* content. It is common for young people to give parenthesized human contents. Their world is filled with an emphasis on monsters or other fantasy objects. But, developing youngsters also gain some appreciation about real humans. When they give answers involving real humans, the descriptive features should be positive. When this is not the case, that is, when they are notably passive or negative, this sheds some light on the conceptions that the youngster holds about himself or herself.

Sometimes the ambivalent and fluctuating attitudes that typify problems in self-concept, which can become sources of interpersonal difficulty, are reflected in thematic imagery that is similarly uncertain, unstable, or inconsistent. One 14-year-old girl said the following about the center detail on Card I: "It's like a woman here, a nice person—or maybe not such a nice person, maybe on the mean side—but now it looks nice again; are they supposed to change back and forth like that?"

Ambivalently held attitudes about the self are also likely to be illustrated in pairs of figures that are perceived as different in some way: "There are two animals, on each side, climbing up a mountain; one is smiling and the other is frowning"; "I see a flying dinosaur here, like Puff the Magic Dragon; if I turn it, I see another one on this side, but it's not quite the same; this one looks friendly and smarter than the other one, and this one looks sort of mean." Responses of this kind often identify the processes that are at work in object splitting. That is, no single object (person) can be seen as combining desirable and undesirable features in some indefinite mix; the object is either smart or dumb, or friendly or mean, and, in order to attribute both characteristics, two objects are necessary.

A different kind of problem regarding self-image sometimes is noted among adolescents older than age 13. It is the presence of reflection answers. Reflection responses are common among most developing young people, but usually, the narcissticlike feature that they illustrate dissipates by the age of 12 or 13. Between the ages of 10 and 13, most youngsters, who have harbored the naive belief that they are more important or valuable than others, learn through experience and their ability to conceptualize in a more sophisticated way than had been the case earlier in their life, that this may not be true. They come to acknowledge that they are like others in some ways, different from others in some ways, and overall, that they are neither more nor less valuable than most of their peers. This process of giving up some focus on the self and extending their focus of concern to the environment generally is considered to be a healthy developmental sign.

When this transition of focus on the self to the external world occurs, it typically will breed more effective social relationships. Unfortunately, some adolescents do not go through this transitional stage and continue to harbor a naive belief regarding their own self-value. If this persists into midadolescence, development is likely to suffer, as the individual must seek out ways to defend this naive belief. Externalization of responsibility for errors becomes routine, and the need to cross-validate beliefs about the self become increasingly frequent. This pattern often is a precursor to a narcissistic disorder in which interpersonal relations usually are transient and rarely gain depth. These indications of inflated self-esteem, a narcissistic sense of entitlement, and tendencies to externalize blame are particularly likely to accompany the faltering personality that, ultimately, will be characterized as a hysteroid or borderline disorder. More than a third of adult persons diagnosed as having a borderline personality disorder are likely to have reflections in their records, compared with 10% or less of schizophrenics, schizotypal personalities, and nonpatient adults (Exner, 1986).

Clues to Other Interpersonal Difficulties   The interpersonal difficulties that characterize young people with a flawed or faltering personality are often manifested on the Rorschach in indications of excessively close or distant ways of relating to others, distorted impressions of what people are like and how they interact, and markedly ambivalent or fluctuating attitudes toward other people. Young people who become interpersonally distant can develop any of several personality problems, ranging from a mild form of obsessive isolation, to the more serious manifestations of paranoid style, a schizoid condition, or even a schizotypal disorder.

Manifestations of social interaction in Rorschach findings may include poor quality M and H responses or can be reflected by an extreme loneliness in reactive depression, as reflected in elevated T. In many instances, social ineptness is represented in Rorschach findings by an elevated CDI. In some cases, problems in social interaction constitute a young person's primary adjustment difficulty and are causing rather than resulting from other kinds of difficulty. Often, these are young people who appear depressed but who do not show a Rorschach elevation on DEPI, but are positive on the CDI. Such subjects probably should be described more in terms of difficulties in social relatedness than in terms of being depressed. They are likely to benefit more from a treatment plan focused on enhancing their coping skills than from therapy addressed to alleviating depression. Usually, these are the shy, withdrawn, avoidant, socially inept youngsters who are not seriously disturbed, not misbehaving or doing poorly in school, and may not be diagnostically anxious or depressed. Nevertheless, they are unhappy, unfulfilled, in need of treatment, and at risk for disordered and problematic behavior in later years if treatment is not forthcoming. The key Rorschach finding in identifying such children and adolescents is an elevated CDI in the absence of indices of serious maladjustment elsewhere in the record.

A CDI of 4 does occur somewhat frequently in younger nonpatient subjects, ages 5 through 13. The percentages of subjects having a CDI value of 4 range from 6% at age 9 to 24% at age 12. These percentages probably reflect those who are struggling with social skills and who, at a given time, do not function in social situations very well. Conversely, CDI values of 5 are very infrequent from age 5 through adolescence. A value of 5 appears in only 3% of 7- and 8-year-old nonpatient subjects, does not appear at all among subjects who are between the age of 9 and 14, and occurs only among 1% of the 15- and 16-year-old groups. Thus, while CDI values of 4 in the protocols of younger people must be interpreted very cautiously, CDI values of 5 should be interpreted as evidence of marked coping difficulties, particularly with respect to impoverished or unrewarding social relationships. Reviewing the implications of the individual components of this index will provide a further sense of what it may mean for a youngster to have a CDI value of 5.

A person with a CDI of 5 would be expected to have a limited capacity to formulate and implement deliberate strategies for coping with life situations; a withdrawal from involvement in interactions with other people; a limited ability to recognize and deal with feelings comfortably or a discomfort with emotional interchanges and a preference to avoid or withdraw from situations in which strong feelings are being expressed; an inclination to take a passive role in interpersonal relationships, shunning initiative and deferring to the wishes of others, or a disinterest in what other people are really like; and feelings of unmet needs for closeness and intimacy and a sense of object loss or loneliness, or an isolated existence in which few other people play an important part.

Any person, young or old, whose adjustment is handicapped by these characteristics is extremely likely to be experiencing social interaction problems. Occasionally, young people who are positive on the CDI may present the deceptive appearance of normal development. Typically, they are bright, talented, and/or attractive to adults. They may do well in the classroom, be admired for their appearance, or earn praise for their artistic or academic prowess, but they are suffering from an arrest in social development and are unlikely to be enjoying rewarding peer relationships or to be feeling good about themselves.

In similar fashion, as noted earlier, proper interpretation of a positive CDI often will aid in avoiding erroneous interpretation of an Adjusted D of zero as evidence of adequate coping resource, especially if *EA* is lower than expected. Not infrequently, young people with limited coping resources will find ways to maintain their psychological equilibrium and avoid subjectively felt distress by minimizing the demands they are likely to encounter. They limit their daily lives as much as possible to familiar and predictable situations in which they will be able to do what is required of them, they ask little of themselves, and they try to deal with problems in the simplest possible way. Young people who are adapting in this manner often have an Adjusted D of zero that is based on a low *EA* but also a low *es*. These are youngsters who, when confronted with new and unfamiliar situations, unexpected and challenging demands, or with problems requiring complex solutions, can quickly be precipitated into a stress overload.

Another feature of the flawed or faltering personality that is being created by social problems is interpersonal distance. Some young people tend to isolate themselves from others, whereas some tend to become overinvolved with others and even are dependent on them. One of the key Rorschach variables concerning either of these tendencies is the frequency of Texture responses. Many who are prone to social isolation are likely to give no T at all, which bears witness to their very limited sense of attachment to other people, their minimal expectation of being able to form close, intimate relationships with others, and their disinclination to reach out or make themselves available for such mutually involved relationships.

Caution should be exercised when interpreting the absence of T answers in the protocols of children under the age of 9. Children between the ages of 5 and 9 do show lower frequencies of T answers than do children in the older age groups. This is probably a function of more limited articulation skills. However, beginning at age 10, the frequency of T-less protocols is very similar to that found among adults and should be interpreted accordingly. Typically, the more withdrawn youngster will give a protocol in which there is no T, and the finding should be interpreted appropriately, especially if a Popular answer is given to Card VI. In fact, if the Popular answer to Card VI is given by children under the age of 10, but contains no Texture, the proposition concerning the absence of T may be warranted.

On the other hand, records in which more than one T answer appears are quite uncommon for almost any age. Usually, such an elevation in the T frequency signals a recent and serious emotional loss, although in some instances it may reflect a more chronic neediness that is often manifested by more reaching out and dependency gestures than are common among children. When there has been no immediate severe emotional loss, the multiple T finding typically will represent intense, unmet needs for closeness and a propensity for clinging, dependent, and demanding relationships with others.

The concerns of individuals with problems of interpersonal distance typically influences the thematic content as well as the structure of their Rorschach responses. Among withdrawn or isolated subjects who worry about or are determined to maintain their isolation there may be themes of loneliness or abandonment ("This is an island"; "It looks like a boy there, or maybe an animal, and he's by himself"; "It's like a party in there, and these out here are people who are looking in"), or there may be compensatory themes of self-sufficiency and self-satisfaction ("Two people dancing, but they're each doing it their own way"; "There's an animal climbing up a mountain, and no one's helping him, but he's going to make it anyway"). Rarely in the records of withdrawn or isolated individuals will there be movement responses in which people or animals are perceived as being mutually involved in joint activities or perceived as helping or depending on each other in any way.

By contrast, those who are overinvolved with others frequently produce thematic imagery that reflects their concerns about maintaining attachments and avoiding separations. At times, a brief response suffices to indicate anxiety about problems of attachment and separation, such as "Siamese twins." At other times, more elaborate descriptions of people engaged in coming together or pulling apart suggests that the subject tends to become similarly enmeshed in strained and sticky interpersonal relationships: "Two people holding tight to each other"; "This one is hard to figure—down here they look stuck together, but up here they seem to be leaning away from each other"; "It looks like they're trying to get closer to each other, but they're still far apart"; "These are people kneeling down to pray, and they're joined at the knees."

Usually, an unfavorable balance in the $H:(H) + Hd + (Hd)$ ratio, with Pure H being less numerous than the total of these other content categories, speaks to the social discomfort often experienced by people who have difficulties in dealing with real human beings in their entirety. Whereas $M-$ responses identify outright social misperceptions, dehumanized contents suggest more subtle tendencies to use fantasy and imagination to make people into what one would like them to be, instead of what they are, which is what borderline individuals do when they form idealized or depreciated images of others. Focusing on partial human contents resembles paying attention to just those aspects of other people one chooses to recognize.

Ambivalence and fluctuation are similarly indicated by responses in which the nature of interactions between figures is ambiguous or volatile: "A couple of animals, but I can't tell if they're fighting or playing"; "These are two girls who used to be best friends but now they're yelling at each other"; "It's like a Star Wars, with all these different creatures taking sides against each other—it's hard to tell who are the good guys and who are the bad guys, but in the next war they could all be on different sides anyway."

THE PASSIVE STYLE AND INTERPERSONAL PROBLEMS

One of the most devastating problems that contributes to a flawed or faltering personality is *passivity*. A young person can manifest the development of a passive style in several ways. It can affect school learning, a pattern of disturbance that has often been labeled *passive-aggressive underachievement* (see Weiner, 1992, Chap. 7). Passive-aggressive underachievement typically involves (a) considerable anger toward parents that cannot be expressed directly; (b) concerns about rivalry that generate fears of failing or fear of being successful; and (c) a preference for passive-aggressive modes of coping with stressful situations.

None of these patterns is unique to psychologically conflicted underachieving children and adolescents. When they occur together, however, especially in families that value education, the stage is often set for passive-aggressive underachievement to occur (Heavey, Adelman, Nelson, & Smith, 1989; Mandel & Marcus, 1988). Other studies of underachieving students have traced their anger specifically to resentment of parental authority that they perceive as restrictive and unjust (Dornbusch, Ritter, Leiderman, & Roberts, 1987; Grolnick, Ryan, & Deci, 1991; Steinberg, Elmen, & Mounts, 1989).

Passivity is not always a product of anger or a strategy the child uses to punish parents. Most passive styles that develop in younger people emerge because of other factors such as concerns about rivalry. This often leads children to avoid competition. Through inaction or by a variety of self-defeating maneuvers, individuals who are made anxious by rivalry refrain from their best effort and fail to accomplish as much as they could. This does not necessarily breed a poor academic performance. On the contrary, passive youngsters often flourish academically because they follow directions faithfully and try hard to please those significant to them. Sometimes, especially in grades 1 through 6, they become highly favored by teachers because of their effort and cooperation. But, when they become older, teachers often find them to be overly dependent and seeking direction or assistance too often.

In effect, their passive orientation becomes merged with a dependency orientation and a *passive-dependent* style evolves. Frequently, these are failure-fearing children who are reluctant to set goals realistically and who, for one reason or another, rarely take risks. They seldom chance doing or saying anything that might be wrong. Sometimes they fear success, and even though they often feel very capable, they have become concerned that doing well independently will bring them unhappiness. Conversely, if their success can be attributed to the incentives provided by others, a sense of security is experienced.

Passive youngsters often make light of their abilities, even when they are considerable ("I'm not very good in math"); they set limited goals that are easily within their grasp ("I'll be happy if I can get Cs; that's all I'm working for"); and they exert themselves just enough to reach these minimal goals, after which they stop making an effort and disclaim any further aspirations ("I was lucky to do as well as I did, and you couldn't expect me to do any better"). By such attitudes toward their schoolwork, these insecure students avoid accomplishments or even any appearance of being talented that might threaten their loved ones or diminish whatever support they receive from them.

Rorschach Clues to Passivity   A passive style usually will manifest in the data of the $a{:}p$ ratio. Whenever p is greater than $a + 1$, it reflects a passive orientation in social relationships, and the influence or pervasiveness of the style probably is illustrated by the extent to which the value for p is greater than $a + 1$. For instance, as many as 14% of nonpatient 9-year-olds and 13% of nonpatient 7-year-olds have an $a{:}p$ ratio in which $p > a + 1$ as do 12% of 14- and 15-year-old nonpatient adolescents. However, a closer inspection of the data reveal that nearly two thirds of those subjects in each of the four age groups have $a{:}p$ ratios in which p exceeds $a + 1$ by only 1 point, such as 3:5; 4:6, and so forth. Conversely, an examination of data for children and adolescents who are described clinically as being passive-aggressive or passive-dependent reveals that more than 65% have $a{:}p$ ratios in which p is greater than $a + 1$ by 2 points or more, such as 3:6; 4:8, 2:7, etc. Thus, it may be reasonable to conclude that when p exceeds $a + 1$ by only 1 point, it reflects a less assertive, more submissive role in social activities, but when p exceeds $a + 1$ by 2 points or more, a marked passive style is present.

Usually, the presence of a passive style is confirmed by data in the $M^a{:}M^p$ ratio that will suggest, at the very least, a tendency to use fantasy or imagination more frequently than most as a tactic of escaping from reality. This will be represented by more M^p responses, and usually by ratios in which M^p exceeds M^a by more than 1 point. Positive findings for both ratios leave little doubt about a marked passive orientation or style. Evidence concerning how a passive style influences decisions and behaviors typically will be reflected in other Rorschach data concerning self and interpersonal perception.

For instance, a tendency toward passive-aggressive behavior is likely to be manifest in an elevated S. From age 8 to age 16 the percentage of nonpatients who give more than two S responses ranges from 8% to 15%, and the presence of four or more S can accordingly be taken as indicative of an unusual extent of anger and resentment and probably of proclivities for stubborn and oppositional behavior as well. This tendency is often reaffirmed by the presence of several AG responses, signaling that the subject regards aggressiveness as a natural phenomenon in social relations. Passive-aggressive youngsters also often display Rorschach features commensurate with low energy or lethargy such as numerous unelaborated responses, a High *Lambda* Style, and not many $DQ+$ answers. Often these young people are bright and have remained enthused about activities outside the classroom, but give a dismal academic performance.

Often, passive-aggressive youngsters will manifest their problems by the way that they approach the test. Their intentional inaction, by which they frustrate others, frequently is reflected by the manner in which they approach the Rorschach task. Sometimes they adopt a sulky, irritable demeanor and snipe (indirect aggression) throughout, at the test and the examiner ("Who invented these silly things?" "Do I *really* have to go through them again?" "Is this *all* you do with your time"). They may also respond very slowly, forcing the examiner to sit and wait, and they may answer questions with the minimum possible answer short of refusing to cooperate, causing the examiner to experience the inquiry as a seemingly endless pulling of teeth.

Those who have a more passive-dependent style usually will not have a substantial number of S answers. Similarly, they do not give many, if any, AG responses. Instead, their dependency is represented structurally by *Food* answers and thematically by the kinds of movement responses that typify their dependency orientation ("Little birds hiding under a tree," "People bowing to each other," "Baby geese in a nest waiting for their mother to feed them," "Dogs or wolves looking for something to eat," "Bugs eating a leaf"). Passive-dependent youngsters also often seek direction from the examiner while taking the test, "Do you see it too?" "How many do you want me to give?" "Am I doing OK?"

CASE ILLUSTRATIONS

It is impractical to present the large number of case illustrations that would be necessary to reflect the broad range of faltering or flawed personalities found among children who are having trouble or who are destined for future problems. Thus, two cases have been selected to illustrate the wide variations that exist among these young people. Both are school referrals provoked by academic or social problems.

CASE 6—SOCIAL ISOLATION

This is an 11-year 4-month-old female who was referred by the school because of both academic problems and issues of social inappropriateness. She is currently in the fifth grade, but her general progress is marginal and her teacher reports that she often seems detached during classroom discussions. This detachment appears in the form of asking questions that are irrelevant to the topic at hand, or making comments during a class discussion that are either repetitions of previous comments or inappropriate to the discussion. The teacher notes that her peers do not seem to like her and avoid her during play activities or in the school lunchroom. The evaluation is being conducted with the cooperation of the mother.

According to the teacher, the subject sometimes becomes involved in petty disputes with other children, and this seems to add to their avoidance of her by them. In addition, the teacher notes that when she corrects the subject, she cries easily and promises to try harder, but the renewed effort lasts for only a brief period. Similar behaviors were noted during the fourth grade, but her overall performance was considered adequate enough to warrant promotion to the fifth grade. The fourth-grade teacher noted that she often would interrupt other children with seemingly extraneous or sometimes verbally hostile comments, and that most of the other children seemed to dislike her.

The fifth-grade teacher emphasizes that the dislike of other children for the subject is due mainly to her interrupting others, including the teacher. According to the teacher, these interruptions are seemingly impulsive and, at times, are completely irrelevant to whatever is going on in the classroom. She stresses that the subject does not have any close relationships and tends to stay by herself during play periods unless there is some organized activity. She also notes that, during organized activities, others selected in the subject's group tend to ignore her or make fun of her.

The subject lives with her mother, age 33, who is an X-ray technician. The mother reports having married at age 20, following her technical training, to a man 5 years older than herself who was a sergeant in the army. He was discharged shortly thereafter and took a position as an electronics technician for a manufacturing firm. During the fourth year of their marriage (shortly after she became pregnant), the husband stated that he had been seeing another woman and wanted a divorce. The subject's mother did not object, as she felt that their relationship had grown more distant during the preceding 2 years. She was granted custody of the child, and the father continues to pay monthly support, even though he has moved to a distant state.

The mother works in a special X-ray unit in a general medical center and has regular hours from 8:00 A.M. to 4:00 P.M. She did not work for the first 6 months following the birth of her daughter, and when she returned to work, employed a baby-sitter for her daughter until she was 4 years old. At that time, she was entered in a day-care center and continues in an after-school relationship to it. During her kindergarten year (she was an afternoon student), she would attend the day-care program in the mornings and then return there after school until her mother retrieved her. The mother has taken her daughter to school in the mornings since she entered first grade; after school, she is transported to the day-care center, where she stays until her mother picks her up at approximately 5:00 P.M.

According to the mother, she and her daughter have a very close relationship and there are no problems at home. The mother admits that she dates, usually on weekends, but points out that she has used the same baby-sitter for several years.

The subject says that she does not like school. She does not like the teachers. She does not like the other children. She complains that the days are too long and that there is not enough time to play. She says that sometimes the work that is assigned is too difficult for her, but that at other times she is just not interested.

The results of a WISC-R yield a Full-Scale IQ of 111; Verbal IQ = 108, Performance IQ = 113. There is no significant scatter among the scaled scores for the subtests. Those scores range from 9 (Arithmetic, Digit Span) to 13 (Comprehension, Block Design). After having tentatively ruled out the possibility of a learning disorder, the notion of attention deficit hyperactivity disorder is being entertained. The assessment is focusing on psychological and/or personality factors that may be contributing to her poor performance and disruptive behavior. The main assessment questions are (a) whether the results are commensurate with an ADHD diagnosis, (b) what personality factors appear to be contributing to the problem, and (c) whether there are any specific intervention recommendations.

Case 6. An 11-Year-Old Female

Card	Response	Inquiry	Scoring
I	1. An insect I guess	E: (Rpts Ss resp) S: Up here w wgs & stuff E: And stuff? S: Its got littl hands & a littl body & big wgs, lik some kind of insect	Ddo Fu A INC
	2. Ths part ll a dress	E: (Rpts Ss resp) S: Just ths prt down here (outlines), it's lik a skirt, I hav one lik it E: I'm not sur wht maks it ll a skirt S: It just does, it has the shape of a skirt	Ddo Fu Cg PER
	3. Mayb its a person with wgs u kno, lik an angel, standg w her wgs spread out	E: (Rpts Ss resp) S: Tht ll wings, big wgs & it cb a person in the middl, not a real person, but lik an angel, thy hav the wgs, I kno abt angels, I c thm when I go the church	Wo Mpo (H) 1.0
II	4. Two dogs, thyr sniffing e.o.	E: (Rpts Ss resp) S: It's just their heads, c the noses, thyr touchg, lik dogs sniff eo, here's the ear over here, dogs sniff lik ths when thyr not sur of eo	D+ FMpo 2 Ad P 3.0
	5. Two fishes too, red fishes	E: (Rpts Ss resp) S: These 2 parts (D2) thy ll red fishes E: I'm not sur I c thm rite S: I dk, tht just hav tht shape, c ths cb their tails (lower part of D2)	Do FC− 2 A
III	6. Thts 2 people leaning on a table	E: (Rpts Ss resp) S: These are the people & that's the table (D7) E: Help me to see it too S: See the way thy're bent down, these ll hands, thyr lik on the table, here's their legs & their heads & noses & thy hav hi heel shoes	D+ Mp+ 2 H,Hh,Cg P 3.0
	7. It cb 2 people fightg about smthg	E: (Rpts Ss resp) S: The people r the same but it cb tht thyr fiting ovr this thg in the middl, lik each wants it & thyr pullg on it, lik thy r havg a fite & each one is tryg to push the othr one away E: I'm not sur abt the thg in the middl S: I dkno wht it is but thy each want to hav it	D+ Mao 2 H,Id P 3.0 AG

248

| IV | 8. | An ugly doll | | W+ mp.FT+ (H),Id P 4.0 PER |

E: (Rpts Ss resp)
S: It's got the feet & the body & arms & head, it just ll a doll on a stand, when u buy a doll thy giv u a stand to hold it up lik ths, (D1), I hav 2 of thm but thyr not ugly lik ths one
E: Ugly?
S: Ths one's all furry, dolls aren't furry, thy'r supposed to hav pretty clothes on
E: I'm not sur why it looks furry
S: All those lines in there, it just ll fur to me

| | 9. | Or it cb a creature too | | W+ Mpo (H),Bt P 4.0 |

E: (Rpts Ss resp)
S: His legs & arms & head, lik he's sittg dwn on a tree stump or a log, lik som creature on TV, ugh!

| V | 10. | A bird, a black one | | Wo FC'.FMao A 1.0 |

E: (Rpts Ss resp)
S: It's the wgs & head, lik his wgs r out lik he's soaring, mayb an eagle or a hawk

| | 11. | It cb a bf too | | Wo Fo A P 1.0 INC |

E: (Rpts Ss resp)
S: The wgs & the little hands, it cb a bird but it cb a bf too

| VI | 12. | A roadkill, sm A tht got run ovr, prob a cat | | Wo FTo A P 2.5 MOR |

E: (Rpts Ss resp)
S: It's lik whn u c thm all flat lik ths, thy call'em roadkills, any kind of A tht got run ovr
E: U said prob a cat?
S: It ll a cat, furry sorta, c the diff lines, it cb fur, anyhow, there's the head & legs out here & thes cb the whiskers

| | 13. | The top cb an airplane a sleaky one | | Do Fu Sc DV |

E: (Rpts Ss resp)
S: The one's u can't c on radar, thy call'em sleaky the wgs & the body of it

| VII | 14. | Two bunnys, thyr sittg on a rock | | W+ FMpo 2 A,Ls 2.5 INC |

E: (Rpts Ss resp)
S: Thy hav big ears & their face & arms r out back
E: U said thyr sittg on a rock
S: Yep, rite dwn here (D4)

| | 15. | Or it cb two Indians too, theyr yelling at e.o. | | D+ Ma+ 2 H P 3.0 AG |

E: (Rpts Ss resp)
S: Theyv got feathers in their hair, thy ll thyr in a big argument, yellg abt which way to go, c one here & one here & here (D2), c the nose & mouth & feather & arm, & thyr body, thyr really mad, lik a big fite

249

Case 6. (Continued)

Card	Response	Inquiry	Scoring
VIII	16. Two dogs climbg up a tree	E: (Rpts Ss resp) S: It ll thyr climbg up ths tree E: Show me so I can c it too S: Thes r the dogs (D1) c their legs & their heads & tails & their bodies, thy ll dogs & the rest is the tree, it has a trunk & blue leaves, & a pointed top, but none of ths dwn here (D2) counts	D+ FMa.FC+ A,Bt P 3.0 INC,FAB
IX	17. A ghost, it's white so it must b one	E: (Rpts Ss resp) S: The white part, it ll a ghost E: I'm not sur wht makes it ll a ghost? S: Ghosts ll tht, thy hav tht curvy shape & thyr white, lik ths, it's just a ghost	DSo FC'o (H)
	18. A deer too	E: (Rpts Ss resp) S: The face of one, these r its horns (D3) & nose (D8) & its mouth, its a face w horns so it must b a deer	Do F− Ad ALOG
X	19. Insects up here, thyr eating smthg	E: (Rpts Ss resp) S: These (D8) ll insects & thyr eating on ths thg, it's lik a piece of wood, mayb thyr termites eating this piece of wood E: I'm not sur I c it rite S: Look, c thes (D8) r littl bugs, lik termites, thy hav a big body, littl legs, thes r their antennae or feelers, & thyr up on ths piece of wood, lik thyr eatg it, lik thyr havg dinner or breakfast	D+ FMa+ 2 A,Bt,Fd 4.0
	20. These r insects too	E: (Rpts Ss resp) S: Thyr just round lik insects, one on each side, I dk wht kind, sk of brown ones	Do FCu 2 A

250

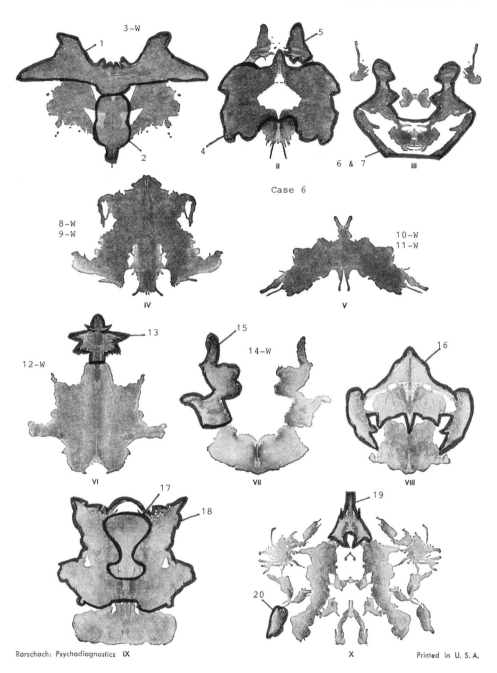

Case 6

Rorschach: Psychodiagnostics   IX

Printed in U. S. A.

Case 6

Case 6   **Sequence of Scores**

Card	No	Loc	#	Determinant(s)	(2)	Content(s)	Pop	Z	Special Scores
I	1	Ddo	99	Fu		A			INC
	2	Ddo	24	Fu		Cg			PER
	3	Wo	1	Mpo		(H)		1.0	PER
II	4	D+	1	FMpo	2	Ad	P	3.0	
	5	Do	2	FC-	2	A			
III	6	D+	1	Mp+	2	H,Hh,Cg	P	3.0	
	7	D+	1	Mao	2	H,Id	P	3.0	AG
IV	8	W+	1	mp.FT+		(H),Sc	P	4.0	PER
	9	W+	1	Mpo		(H),Bt	P	4.0	
V	10	Wo	1	FC'.FMao		A		1.0	
	11	Wo	1	Fo		A	P	1.0	INC
VI	12	Wo	1	FTo		A	P	2.5	MOR
	13	Do	3	Fu		Sc			DV
VII	14	W+	1	FMpo	2	A,Ls		2.5	INC
	15	D+	1	Ma+	2	H,Cg	P	3.0	AG
VIII	16	D+	1	FMa.FC+	2	A,Bt	P	3.0	INC,FAB
IX	17	DSo	8	FC'o		(H)			
	18	Do	2	F-		Ad			ALOG
X	19	D+	11	Fma+	2	A,Bt,Fd		4.0	
	20	Do	13	FCu	2	A			

Case 6   **Structural Summary**

Location Features	Determinants		Contents	S-Constellation

Location Features	Determinants Blends	Determinants Single	Contents	S-Constellation
			H = 3, 0	. . FV+VF+V+FD>2
Zf = 13	m.FT	M = 5	(H) = 4, 0	. . Col−Shd Bl>0
ZSum = 35.0	FC'.FM	FM = 3	Hd = 0, 0	. . Ego<.31,>.44
ZEst = 41.5	FM.FC	m = 0	(Hd) = 0, 0	. . MOR > 3
		FC = 2	Hx = 0, 0	. . Zd > +− 3.5
W = 7		CF = 0	A = 9, 0	. . es > EA
(Wv = 0)		C = 0	(A) = 0, 0	. . CF+C > FC
D = 11		Cn = 0	Ad = 2, 0	. . X+% < .70
Dd = 2		FC' = 1	(Ad) = 0, 0	. . S > 3
S = 1		C'F = 0	An = 0, 0	. . P < 3 or > 8
		C' = 0	Art = 0, 0	. . Pure H < 2
DQ		FT = 1	Ay = 0, 0	. . R < 17
. . . . . (FQ−)		TF = 0	Bl = 0, 0	x . . . . . TOTAL
+ = 9 (0)		T = 0	Bt = 0, 3	
o = 11 (2)		FV = 0	Cg = 1, 2	Special Scorings
v/+ = 0 (0)		VF = 0	Cl = 0, 0	Lv1 Lv2
v = 0 (0)		V = 0	Ex = 0, 0	DV = 1x1 0x2
		FY = 0	Fd = 0, 1	INC = 4x2 0x4
		YF = 0	Fi = 0, 0	DR = 0x3 0x6
		Y = 0	Ge = 0, 0	FAB = 1x4 0x7
		Fr = 0	Hh = 0, 1	ALOG = 1x5
Form Quality		rF = 0	Ls = 0, 1	CON = 0x7
		FD = 0	Na = 0, 0	SUM6 = 7
FQx FQf MQual SQx		F = 5	Sc = 1, 1	WSUM6 = 18
+ = 5 0 2 0			Sx = 0, 0	
o = 9 1 3 1			Xy = 0, 0	AB = 0 CP = 0
u = 4 3 0 0			Id = 0, 1	AG = 2 MOR = 1
− = 2 1 0 0				CFB = 0 PER = 3
none = 0 — 0 0		(2) = 5		COP = 0 PSV = 0

Case 6   **Ratios, Percentages, and Derivations**

R = 20	L = 0.33		FC:CF+C = 3: 0	COP = 0 AG = 2
			Pure C = 0	Food = 1
EB = 5: 1.5	EA = 6.5	EBPer = 3.3	Afr = 0.33	Isolate/R = 0.20
eb = 6: 4	es = 10	D = −1	S = 1	H:(H)Hd(Hd) = 3:4
	Adj es = 10	Adj D = −1	Blends:R = 3:20	(HHd):(AAd) = 4:0
			CP = 0	H+A:Hd+Ad = 16:2
FM = 5 : C' = 2 T = 2				
m = 1 : V = 0 Y = 0				
		P = 9	Zf = 13	3r+(2) /R = 0.45
a:p = 5: 6	Sum6 = 7	X+% = 0.70	Zd = −6.5	Fr+rF = 0
Ma:Mp = 2: 3	Lv2 = 0	F+% = 0.20	W:D:Dd = 7:11: 2	FD = 0
2AB+Art+Ay=0	WSum6 = 18	X−% = 0.10	W:M = 7: 5	An+Xy = 0
M − = 0	Mnone = 0	S−% = 0.00	DQ+ = 9	MOR = 1
		Xu% = 0.20	DQv = 0	

SCZI = 1	DEPI = 3	CDI = 3	S-CON = N/A	HVI = No	OBS = Yes

INTERPRETIVE ROUTINE FOR CASE 6

The first positive Key variable is that the Adjusted D Score is less than zero. Thus, according to the table concerning cluster review order, the interpretive routine will begin with a study of data concerning controls. However, the table also indicates that this positive Key variable does not predict the complete order in which the data clusters should be reviewed, and the next positive Key or Tertiary variable must be used to identify the remaining interpretive strategy. In this case, the next positive Key variable is an introversive *EB*. Thus, the full interpretive routine is as follows:

CONTROLS → IDEATION → PROCESSING → MEDIATION →
AFFECT → SELF-PERCEPTION → INTERPERSONAL PERCEPTION

Controls—Case 6   The data concerning capacity for controls and issues of stress tolerance for Case 6 are shown in Table 55.

Table 55.   **Controls and Stress Tolerance Data for Case 6**

EB = 5:1.5			EA = 6.5		D = −1
eb = 6:4			es = 10	Adjes = 10	AdjD = −1
FM = 5	C' = 2		T = 2		CDI = 3
m = 1	V = 0		Y = 1		

The Adjusted D Score is −1, suggesting that she is in a chronic overload state that reduces her capacity for control and her tolerance for stress. In effect, the stimulus overload makes her vulnerable to impulsiveness in thinking, emotional organization, and behavior. A challenge to the validity of the Adjusted D Score proves negative. The *EA* has a value of 6.5, which is slightly lower than expected for an 11-year-old, and there is no reason to question the validity of the *EA* as the *EB* does not contain a zero on either side of the ratio. In effect, she simply does not have enough resource readily available for use to contend with all the internal stimulus demands that she experiences. As a consequence, some of her behaviors will not be well planned and/or well implemented and she may, at times, manifest behaviors that seem impulsive.

In this case, the overload that is creating a potential for problems is the slightly higher than average *es*. Usually, children of this age will have an Adjusted *es* of 7 or 8, or even 9. Typically, the *es* consists of 3 or 4 *FM* answers, a *C'* response, and a *T* response. In this instance, each of these three variables is a bit higher than expected, especially the number of *T* answers. For instance, if the value for *T* were only 1, as is expected, the Adjusted D Score would be zero, or if the value for *FM* were 4 instead of 5, the Adjusted D would be zero. Thus, some sort of unfulfilled needs for closeness appear to have produced the overload and increased her vulnerability to impulsiveness.

Young people like this usually are able to function adequately in well-structured situations, but when their circumstances become more complex or ambiguous, they tend to falter and emit behaviors that are not always appropriate to the situation at hand. This may account for some of the complaints of the teacher that she tends to be inappropriate and/or impulsive during class discussions.

Ideation—Case 6   The data regarding ideation for Case 6 are shown in Table 56.

Table 56.   Ideation Data for Case 6

		M QUALITY	SPECIAL SCORES			
$EB = 5{:}1.5$	$EBPer = 3.3$					
$eb = 6{:}4$	$(FM = 5 \quad m = 1)$	$+ = 2$	DV $= 1$	DV2	$= 0$	
$a{:}p = 5{:}6$	$M^a{:}M^p = 2{:}3$	o $= 3$	INC $= 4$	INC2	$= 0$	
$2AB + Art + Ay = 0$		u $= 0$	DR $= 0$	DR2	$= 0$	
MOR $= 1$		$- = 0$	FAB $= 1$	FAB2	$= 0$	
			ALOG $= 1$	SUM6	$= 7$	
RESPONSES TO BE READ FOR QUALITY			CON $= 0$	WSUM6	$= 18$	
3,6,7,9,15						

The *EB* (5:1.5) and the *EBPer* (3.3) reveal that she is a markedly introversive youngster. She has learned to give preference to the tactic of delay, during which she attempts to weigh the respective value of various possible responses and then selects one that seems most appropriate to the situation. Nearly one third of nonpatient 11-year-olds manifest this style, but none show a pervasive style, as is the case here. Pervasiveness usually means that there is little flexibility concerning the use of the style. It will be applied even though the situation may be more appropriate for a trial-and-error approach.

The presence of this pervasive style seems incongruous with the reported impulsive-like behaviors in class, and it is. However, information developed earlier concerning her vulnerability to impulsiveness appears to explain these behaviors. Even though the style is well in place, she is unable to contain herself. The inappropriateness of her behaviors is not necessarily a function of the pervasive style. Instead, it probably reflects difficulties in her logic or, stated differently, reflects more cognitive slippage than is common for those of her age. This is not uncommon among youngsters who develop an introversive style prematurely, and the pervasive style here suggests that may have occurred.

The left-side value of the *eb* (6) is not unusual for an 11-year-old. Similarly, the *a:p* ratio (5:6) offers no hint of inflexibility in her ideational approach to issues. The intellectualization Index (0) is negative, and there is only one MOR response in the record. Thus, there is no reason to assume that her thinking is markedly gloomy or pessimistic. However, the $M^a{:}M^p$ ratio (2:3) is in an unexpected direction, and signifies that she uses fantasy as a tactic of defense more often than is common for those of her age. This tactic or defense apparently is confounded by the presence of more cognitive slippage than should be the case for her age. There are seven Critical Special Scores in the record, yielding a *WSum6* of 18. Although this is not uncommon for a 7- or 8-year-old, it represents more flawed logic or thinking than should be the case for an 11-year-old and takes on even more importance because of her pervasive introversive style and her limited controls.

None of the Critical Special Scores convey bizarreness, that is, none are of a Level 2 variety. Nonetheless, collectively, they reflect more immature thinking or strained logic than should be evident in a child of this age whose intelligence is at least average, as is the case here. A review of the Critical Special Scores illustrates this point quite well. The single DV occurs in Response 13 to Card VI, ". . . they call'em sleaky . . ." This word sleaky probably means stealth and does have a similar connotation. The INCOM answers occur in Response 1 (an insect with hands), Response 11 (a butterfly with hands), Response 14 (bunnies with their arms out), and Response 16 (blue leaves on a tree). They are very similar to answers given by younger children. The FABCOM in Response 16, to Card VIII, indicates strained reasoning (two dogs climbing a tree), and the ALOG answer illustrates even more flawed logic (it's a face with horns so it must be a deer).

None of these answers could be viewed as pathological, but collectively, they indicate that her thinking is less sophisticated than expected for an 11-year-old, and these frequent cognitive slips warn of difficulty for an introversive youngster who relies so heavily on thinking as a tactic for decision making and problem solving. Fortunately, there are no $M-$ answers in the record; thus, notions of peculiar thinking probably are not appropriate. She simply has a style of coping that requires a higher level of ideation than is present and, as a result, she often conveys ideation that is not really well thought through or that is not commensurate for the levels of thinking expected for her age. When this problem is considered in light of her control problems, some of her unwanted behaviors become easier to understand.

Processing—Case 6   The data concerning processing activity for Case 6 are shown in Table 57.

Table 57.   Processing Data for Case 6

L = 0.33	$W:D:Dd$ = 7:11:2	Zd = −6.5	$DQ+$ = 9
Zf = 13	$W:M$ = 7:5	PSV = 0	$DQv/+$ = 0
HVI = No	OBS = Yes		DQv = 0

LOCATION SEQUENCING

I Dd,Dd,W	IV W,W	VII W,D	
II D,D	V W,W	VIII D	
III D,D	VI W,D	IX DS,D	
		X D,D	

The findings for two variables in the processing cluster make matters worse. First, the value for Lambda (0.33) is lower than expected for most people and especially for a child. She tends to become overly involved with stimuli and, in doing so, runs a risk of sacrificing the natural tendency to economize at times. Second, and much more important, is the fact that she is positive on the Obsessive Index. This is a rather frightening finding for a child, especially a pervasively introversive child. It suggests that she becomes overly involved with the details of a field and can often lose sight of the forest for the trees.

Fortunately, the evidence of obsessiveness is not all negative. The positive OBS evolves from her having an unusually high number of Popular answers (9), more than 12 Zf (13), and five answers scored as form quality *plus* because of her overelaboration of form. This pattern is quite different from what is often found in the pathologically obsessed person who rambles in responses, giving many DR1 and/or DR2 answers, or the obsessive who simply cannot manage a semiambiguous field and must re-create the field with numerous Dd answers. This is not to suggest that the overelaborative obsessivelike finding is unimportant. That is not true. But, it does suggest that an obsessive style is not so strongly embedded in the developing personality structure that it cannot be changed. In fact, the manifestations of her developing obsessive style can be used to her advantage provided they do not become exaggerated.

Her obsessiveness probably does not serve her well because of the pervasiveness of her introversive style and her immature thinking or strained logic. For instance, several of the features of her processing behavior are positive. She invests considerable effort in processing, but not excessively so. The Zf (13) is more than expected, but the $W:D:Dd$ ratio (7:11:2) reflects an economized approach, and the $W:M$ ratio (7:5) does not indicate any striving for goals that exceed her functional capacities. In fact, the $DQ+$ value (9) suggests that she synthesizes new information quite well, especially when viewed in the absence of DQv answers, which are not uncommon among children of her age.

On the other hand, the Zd score of -6.5 signals that she is an underincorporator. She does not scan a new field very well. Instead, her scanning activities are likely to be haphazard, and stored information may often be incomplete, neglecting critical stimulus cues. This habit of underincorporation probably is contributing substantially to some of the strange or inappropriate ideas that she expresses in class, and underincorporation and a potential for impulsiveness in a person whose thinking tends to be immature can only lead to behavioral disasters.

Interestingly, her approach to processing, as indicated by the sequence of location selections, is reasonably consistent once she gets beyond the first blot. In responding to the first blot, she begins with her only two Dd responses and then proceeds to a W answer. Subsequently, she is much more consistent. This may indicate that she is able to be much more routine in processing once she becomes familiar and/or comfortable with a task.

Overall, the data regarding processing indicate the presence of a significant problem (underincorporation) and a marked potential for another problem (obsessiveness). The former should be correctable quite easily, and the latter might be useful to plans for aiding her to reorganize her development and functioning levels.

Mediation—Case 6   The data regarding mediational operations for Case 6 are shown in Table 58.

Table 58.   Cognitive Mediation Data for Case 6

Lambda	= 0.33	OBS	= Yes	MINUS FEATURES	
P	= 9	$X+\%$	= .70	5,18	
$FQx+$	= 5	$F+\%$	= .20		
$FQxo$	= 9	$Xu\%$	= .20		
$FQxu$	= 4	$X-\%$	= .10		
$FQx-$	= 2	$S-\%$	= .00		
FQxnone	= 0	CONFAB	= 0		

A tendency toward obsessiveness, in the absence of severe pathology, usually will produce an $X+\%$ that is at least average, as is the case here (.70). Thus, at first glance, it seems reasonable to conclude that there are no significant problems in the way that she translates stimuli, or more positively, that she seems to translate stimuli about as conventionally as do most 11-year-olds. However, either of those conclusions may be too simplistic and fail to identify a potential problem.

She gives nine Popular answers, more than typically are found in most nonpatient records, either from children or adults. In reality, two of the nine have some perseverative qualities, even though they do not meet the scoring criteria for PSV. These are the second responses to Cards III and IV and, although the content and/or descriptions are different, the basic substance of the answers is very similar to the previous answer. Her second response to Card III simply changes the activity of the people from passive to active, and on Card IV the doll on a post is revised to be a creature on a stump or log. Although there is no question about the conventionality of these responses, they hint at a failure in cognitive shifting. This is not a major problem, especially in the record of a child, but it creates structural data that are easily misleading.

For instance, if the record is reviewed more carefully, it will be noted that 9 of the 14 conventional answers ($FQ+$ or FQo) are the Popular responses. In effect, if the 11 answers that are not Popular are studied, less than half (5) are conventional. In other words, when she is afforded obvious stimulus cues, she translates in a conventional or expected manner, but when the cues are not so obvious, her translations become more individualistic and sometimes are even distorted. This is a very important finding if some sort of intervention is to be planned. The fact that three of her seven Critical Special Scores occur in the context of Popular answers also is quite important, as it conveys that her sometimes immature and illogical thinking becomes intrusive when the conceptualization of obvious stimulus cues occurs.

That she gives unusual answers ($Xu\% = .20$) seems to be a positive finding because it indicates she has not become a slave to her obsessive tendencies. Even the presence of two minus answers ($X - \% = .10$) does not warrant concern. The minus responses are scattered, one on Card II (fishes) and one on Card IX (a deer). Both involve considerable distortion and both are second answers, following ordinary responses. Similarly, two of the unusual responses are second answers that follow ordinary responses. Thus, when she attempts to extend herself beyond the obvious translations of stimuli, her obsessive orientation toward doing the right thing may be prone to falter.

Overall, there seem to be no major problems with her mediational activities, but some potential problems exist. She seems to function most conventionally when cues for responses are distinct; when those distinct cues are absent or ignored, the responses may become far less conventional. It seems easy to hypothesize that there may be a relation between her underincorporativeness and this finding. The underincorporation might account for the first two answers to Card I, but it seems unlikely to have a relation to the other less than ordinary responses as all are second answers. Regardless of whether the underincorporative style impacts on mediation, some of the findings concerning mediation have important implications for treatment planning.

Affect—Case 6   The data concerning affect for Case 6 are shown in Table 59.

Table 59.   Affect Data for Case 6

DEPI = 2				BLENDS
EB	= 5:1.5	$EBPer$	= 3.3	FM.FC
eb	= 6:4	$FC:CF + C$ = 3:0		m.FT
		Pure C	= 0	FC'.FC
$C' = 2$	$T = 2$	Afr	= 0.33	
$V = 0$	$Y = 0$	S	= 1	
		Blends/R	= 3:20	
		CP	= 0	

The datum for DEPI (2) does not appear to have importance. However, other data in this cluster seem very important. It has already been established that she is a pervasive introversive youngster. This means that, in almost all her problem-solving and decision-making activities, she tries to keep her feelings at a more peripheral level so that they will not influence her thinking. Introversive people tend to do this, but those who are not pervasive also are aware that, at times, a merging of feelings into thinking and the use of a more trial-and-error approach to working through a situation may be useful.

This type of flexibility appears to exist in most nonpatient children and adults who have an introversive style. On the other hand, the inflexibility of the pervasive introversive appears to predispose trouble, and that predisposition is even greater in children whose thinking is not always clear or logical. In effect, it suggests that such persons have not come to appreciate and use their feelings to their advantage, and as a result, probably do not deal with any emotions very well. That seems to be the case here.

The right-side *eb* value (4) is slightly higher than expected, but the substance of the value is more important. Of the 4 points, 2 consist of Texture responses. She is lonely and apparently cannot contend with that loneliness easily. It is creating unwanted irritating emotions. In addition, she gives two *C'* responses, which would not be unusual except that the total is greater than the *WSümC* (1.5). Any time that the Sum of *C'* answers exceeds the *WSumC* a hypothesis concerning emotional avoidance and/or constriction is warranted. In this case, such a hypothesis seems supported by the low *Afr* (0.33) and the constricted *FC:CF + C* ratio (3:0). This composite of data leaves little doubt that she has considerable trouble with her feelings and seems fearful about expressing them or even contending with them very directly.

This finding seems relevant to her seemingly extraneous or inappropriate classroom behaviors. They may allow her to reach out for some emotional contact or simply to express some of her feelings in a less obvious way, but her actions do not serve her well. On the contrary, they only push her peers further from her and alienate her teacher. The presence of only one Space response is surprising because children who are emotionally isolated often experience a great deal of anger. This does not seem to be the case here. Similarly, children troubled by feelings will often give many blend answers, indicating the psychological complexity that is being created by the emotional confusion. That is not the case here. Often, Color-Shading blends will occur, signaling the confusion of the subject about feeling, but again, that is not the case here. There are only three blend responses, and none seem especially unusual. Often, when the proportion of blend responses is low, the value for Lambda is high, but that is not the case with this subject.

Overall, this appears to be a youngster whose feelings have been contained for quite some time. For one reason or another, she has learned to rely on her thinking and avoid emotional confrontations. Because her thinking is not sufficiently clear or logical to be an advantage to her much of the time, her emotions have become more of a nemesis to her. She is fearful of them, tries to avoid processing them, and apparently does not know how to express them directly. Thus, she will often internalize feelings that she would prefer to express, and harbors a chronic feeling of loneliness.

Self-Perception—Case 6   The data regarding self-perception for Case 6 are shown in Table 60.

There are no reflection responses, and the Egocentricity Index (0.45) is lower than expected for an 11-year-old. It indicates that she does not value herself very positively when

Table 60.   Self-Perception Data for Case 6

3r + (2)/R = 0.45	FD = 0	MOR = 1	Hx = 0	An + Xy = 0
Fr + rF = 0	Sum V = 0	H:(H) + Hd + (Hd) = 3:4		Sx = 0

RESPONSES TO BE READ

MOR Resp's	FQ − Resp's	M Resp's	FM Resp's	m Resp's
12	5,18	3,6,7,9,15	4,10,14,16,19	8

she compares her own worth with the worth she attributes to significant others. Surprisingly, there are no Vista or *FD* responses in the record. Usually, people who do not value themselves as favorably as others engage in sorts of self-inspection, trying to detect their flaws with an object of improving themselves. That does not seem to be the case here and creates some concern that she may have accepted some lesser role for herself.

A more positive finding is the presence of the three Pure *H* answers, even though they make up less than half of her human content responses. At least there are three, suggesting that some of her self-concept will be based on experience rather than imagination. However, it should be noted that two of the three Pure *H* answers include aggressive movement, which probably does not portend well for her self-image or her interpersonal relationships.

There is only one MOR answer, so there is no reason to suspect that her self-concept is marked by very negative features or a strong sense of damage. It is a Popular answer to Card VI (a roadkill, some animal that got run over) and, although it has dramatic content, it must be approached cautiously when considering issues of self-concept. The two minus answers possibly are more important, but their contents are difficult to interpret in the context of self-image. The first is two red fishes and the second is a deer face, identified as such because of the horns.

The five human movement answers are a bit easier to work with in a self-image framework. The first, Response 3 to Card I, is a "person with wings, like an angel, standing with her wings spread out." It is a special but different person, not really doing anything except displaying herself. Angels are sometimes considered as symbolic of purity and goodness, and some might interpret this response as being related to the present (if you look carefully at me, you will find that I am special). Others might interpret this as a wish for the future that may include a morbid element (someday I will become an angel). The next two human movement answers appear to Card III, two people leaning on a table and two people fighting about something. The reversal in action, from extreme passivity (leaning) to extreme aggressiveness (fighting) is interesting and probably indicates her confusion about her social role. It is also interesting that neither answer includes a sex identification. Both are "people."

The fourth *M* answer appears on Card IV, "a creature . . . sitting down on a tree stump or a log." It reverts to the passivity evidenced in Responses 3 and 6 and although defined as a male, offers no distinctly positive or negative connotations. It is simply a creature. The last *M* is Response 15 to Card VII, articulated as "two Indians . . . yelling about which way to go . . . they are really mad, like a big fight." The conflict is obvious and the issue of "which way to go" may have implications about her developing sense of self and the confusion that she has about it. In fact, when studied collectively, none of the five convey the impression of a little girl. They are more ambiguous, distant, and noncommittal.

Most of the five *FM* answers are also rather impoverished for information regarding self-image. The first, Response 4 to Card II, is dogs sniffing, ". . . when they are not sure of each other." The second, Response 10 to Card V, is a bird, ". . . he's soaring, maybe an eagle or a hawk." It conveys a sense of strength and independence. The third, Response 14 to Card VII, reverts to passivity again, "bunnies sitting on a rock." The fourth, Response 16 to Card VIII, is less distinctive, "dogs climbing up a tree." The last *FM,* Response 19 to Card X, may be the most revealing. It is insects eating something, ". . . maybe they are termites eating this piece of wood . . . like they are having dinner or breakfast." It implies the seeking of nutrients (food), but the identity of the insects, termites, conveys a very negative implication for self-image. Termites are not desirable because they are destructive, and people go to great lengths to rid themselves of the threat that termites pose.

The single *m* response may be the most telling of all of the movement answers. It is an ugly doll (Card IV, Response 8) that should not be furry but instead, should have pretty clothes. The key words seem to be ugly, furry, and "supposed to have pretty clothes." The negative sense of self seems clear. There is also a marked implication that her needs for closeness make her ugly.

None of the other answers are embellished in unusual ways that might aid in fleshing out more information about her self-image. The sleaky airplane (Card VI) that you cannot see on radar and the ghost (Card IX) might suggest her feeling of being ignored, but that is a more speculative postulate.

Generally, this appears to be a youngster who does not think well of herself and may be accepting of a less important role in life than she would prefer. There is little doubt that she is confused about her role in life, and it seems likely that she is not developing some of the features of self-identity that are common among young females. Although she is very needy, she tends to regard that neediness quite negatively and apparently presumes it makes her unattractive to those around her. This has obvious implications for her social relationships, especially when considered in light of her immature and naive thinking, her obsessivelike struggle to be correct or conventional, and her fearfulness about feelings and her marked attempts to contain and/or avoid them.

Interpersonal Perception—Case 6   The data concerning interpersonal perception and behaviors are shown in Table 61.

Table 61. Interpersonal Perception Data for Case 6

CDI = 3	*a:p* = 5:6	*T* = 2	Human Cont = 7		Pure *H* = 3
HVI = Neg	Food = 1	PER = 3	COP = 0	AG = 2	Isolate/R = 0.20
		RESPONSES TO BE READ			
	HUMAN MOVEMENT WITH PAIR		*HUMAN CONTENTS*		
	6,7,15		3,6,7,8,9,15,17		

The CDI and HVI are not positive and the *a:p* ratio offers no firm evidence to suggest that she has developed a passive style. However, other variables in this cluster are quite revealing and very important. She has the two Texture answers and the Food response. She has very strong needs for closeness, and there is no reason to suspect that they are situationally related. Instead, she has probably been a needy, lonely child for quite some time. It is also likely that her needs for closeness have prompted many of the unwanted academic and social behaviors that have led to her referral. She wants to have some sort of dependency relationship. This is important for two reasons. First, most children have some sort of dependency relation with either or both parents. Apparently she does not. Second, girls of this age typically are becoming more peer oriented and prone to reduce or even minimize their dependency on parents. It seems clear that she is not, at least with regard to her emotional needs.

Although she is interested in people, as illustrated by the seven human contents, only three of the seven are Pure H and all of the remainder are parenthesized, indicating that her conceptions of people probably are based mainly in imaginary ideas rather than in real experience. This interpersonal confusion appears to be confounded more by her development of a rather authoritarian, know-it-all, approach in her interpersonal relationships (PER = 3). Moreover, there are no COP answers and two AG responses. Although two AG answers should not be overinterpreted, their presence, in the context of other findings, suggests that she perceives relations between people as being naturally marked by sorts of aggressiveness. This probably accounts for some of the unwanted classroom behaviors.

The Isolation Index (.20) is not significant, but probably is a false negative as it seems unlikely, from the history and the test data, that she has any close relationships. This postulate appears supported by a casual review of the activities in her seven movement answers that contain pairs. They include sniffing, leaning, fighting, sitting, yelling, climbing, and eating. None are very positive. Instead, five of the seven are passive or aggressive. Similarly, the human contents do not convey very realistic ideas about people. They include an angel, people leaning, people fighting, an ugly doll, a creature, Indians, and a ghost. In effect, her interpersonal world seems barren and confused, and it is doubtful that she can relate to others easily or effectively.

CASE 6—SUMMARY

This seems to be a youngster who has been psychologically and/or emotionally abandoned. She is a very lonely and needy child who appears to have been seriously neglected during her earlier developmental years. As a result, she has developed an overideational style of coping that does not serve her well because her thinking is very immature and naive. She often is illogical when forming cause-and-effect relationships and is quite confused about her feelings and how to respond adequately to emotional stimuli in her world. Her response to this emotional confusion has been one involving considerable avoidance and/or withdrawal from emotional situations, including those within her. As a consequence, she is not able to express her feelings very directly, and often suffers the irritating results of holding her feelings inside herself.

Her inability to handle and express emotions easily, when combined with her strained and immature thinking, has thwarted the natural development of healthy interpersonal relations and has contributed significantly to the formation of a confused and threatened sense of self. She really does not understand who she is, or how to display herself to others. She has adopted an obsessivelike tactic that she uses to interpret the ongoings in her world and tries hard to make conventional and/or acceptable responses to it. In spite of this worthy motive, her immature thinking plus her misunderstandings about people often produce unwanted behaviors that result in her being isolated from her peers.

Although this youngster should have some form of treatment, she probably is not the key player in any intervention strategy. It is true that she processes hastily and haphazardly and that can be an immediate target for intervention. It is also true that her thinking often is naive and illogical, and that can be another intervention target. Similarly, she is fearful of emotion and does not know how to handle it. That problem constitutes a third major treatment objective. And, she is confused about her self-image and about people and how to relate to them. These are other major treatment objectives that may be achieved with a well-thought-through treatment plan, but it will be difficult to achieve success unless a more major element in the life of this child is confronted.

The mother appears to be psychologically and possibly physically absent from the life of this child. The history indicates that, essentially, the father has had no significant contact with the child. The mother was prepared occupationally to provide for her daughter at the time of her birth and has done so financially. But, since this subject was approximately 6 months old, the mother has worked regularly, depending on a baby-sitter until the youngster was 4 years old, then using a day-care center as a full-time custodian for a year until the child entered school. Even after her daughter's entry into school, the mother has used the day-care center to fill in after-school hours until she retrieves her child.

The mother states that she and her daughter have a very close relationship and that there are no problems at home. Knowing the psychology of this child makes it difficult to accept the mother's report. There is no close relationship, at least in the experience of the daughter. There probably are not problems at home reported by the mother because she is absent as much as she is present. It may well be that the most significant person in the life of this child has been a baby-sitter, who cared for her during most of her first four years and apparently cares for her on weekends when the mother pursues her own interests. There is no information about the baby-sitter, but if the psychology of the child is used as a source from which to speculate, the sitter has not provided much emotional reassurance or much of a model from which the child can develop.

Treatment must involve the mother, and it will be the response of the mother to treatment that will be most important to any treatment of the child. If the mother is uncooperative in this venture, then some other role model should be substituted. In either case, the possibility of group treatment, with other children who do not have stable or emotionally satisfying homes, might be warranted, but the optimal intervention will involve both the mother and child, each separately and together in a family model. This form of treatment probably will require more sacrifice by the mother than the child. If that occurs, the awareness of the mother of the child's needs will superimpose itself on the mother's behaviors, and ultimately, the child will profit, ideationally, emotionally, and with regard to the development of a more well-defined and secure sense of herself.

CASE 7—DISRUPTIVE BEHAVIOR

This 15-year-old female was evaluated at the request of her parents on the advice of a high school guidance counselor. She has completed 5 months of her first year of high school, and has been reported by three different teachers to be disruptive, uncooperative, and argumentative. They note that she challenges and ridicules other students, sometimes ridicules the teachers, and often is unresponsive to their efforts to correct her deportment.

The counselor has interviewed her four times concerning various classroom incidents and reports that she is quite hostile about being singled out, usually blaming others for the episodes. During two of those interviews, the subject spoke openly about being intrigued with death as an escape from the harshness of the world. The mother also reports that, in at least one instance during an argument, the subject stated, "You'd feel differently if I were dead."

The subject is the youngest of three children. Both parents are high school graduates and have been married for 24 years. Her father, age 48 is an electrician and coowner of a small business. Her mother, age 46, has worked for the past 4 years as a department store clerk. Her only other work experience was during the two years preceding her marriage when she worked in a drugstore. She reports that her daughter had a normal developmental history and feels that they have been reasonably close. She admits that she and her daughter became more distant after the daughter entered the seventh grade and began devoting more time to peer relationships. The mother feels that neither she nor her husband are overly strict but admits that her husband is often quite critical of the friendships that the daughter has created.

The older siblings are both male, ages 21 and 19. The oldest brother is in the Navy, a Second Class Petty Officer on a destroyer. The second brother is a freshman at a state university and lives in residence there. Both parents report no problems with either of the male siblings, citing that the oldest was a basketball star in high school and entered the Navy shortly after his graduation, and the second son graduated in the top 10% of his high school class and has a state scholarship that partially supports his current education. He is a preengineering student.

The guidance counselor reports that the subject appears to have two or three close friendships with female students who are generally considered as "outsiders" and whose grades are substandard but not failing. He has no firm reason to suspect that the subject or her friends are drug involved but concedes that drug abuse is a matter of concern in the school. The subject's grades in elementary school were usually above-average and remained at an average to above-average level through the seventh and eighth grades. There is no indication of disciplinary action in the school records for earlier school years.

The subject looks somewhat older than her age and could easily be taken for 17 or 18 years old. She is 5 feet 6 inches, 120 pounds and was described as quite attractive by the female interviewer. She was admittedly hostile about the evaluation, but her cooperation was generally good. She admits to having discussed death with the guidance counselor but claims he brought up the subject and that she was willing to discuss it because it had been a topic of conversation among her peers after two recent suicides of students in the school district. She disclaims her mother's report and says that she has never seriously thought about suicide.

She concedes a strong dislike for school and most of her peers: "They all seem so stupid and they cheat." She states that she is quite interested in two male students, one a junior and one a senior, and she says that she spends some time with them during lunch or after school. She feels that they are "more grown up" and easier to talk to. She admits to drinking beer and wine with them but denies drug use. She also denies any sexual activity. She reports that menstruation began when she was 12 and that her periods are regular and not usually a problem. She states that the only "really good" things about school are the athletic events, which she attends with her two female friends, and "the end of the day when you can go home."

She says that her teachers are not very stimulating and often are boring. She finds the work reasonably easy to do and that her troubles in class occur because she asks questions that teachers do not want to answer. Her performance on the WISC-R yielded a full-scale IQ of 123 (Verbal IQ = 125; Performance IQ = 119), and there is no substantial scatter among the subtests.

In a second interview, following the testing, the subject expressed interest in learning of the results and also expressed a willingness to "try to find ways" to get along better in school. She revealed that she spends a great deal of time keeping a diary. She described her father as being cold and strict and "not understanding" and her mother as "OK." She feels that if she were in a different school the problems for which she is being evaluated would not have occurred.

The referral raises questions about any evidence of a suicidal preoccupation or concern; asks whether there is a serious psychological problem for which treatment is appropriate; requests recommendations to the guidance counselor and teachers; and asks about recommendations concerning treatment in or away from the school.

Case 7. A 15-Year-Old Female

Card	Response		Inquiry	Scoring
I	1. How should I kno, mayb a bird	E: S:	(Rpts Ss resp) Just sk of weird bird, it's all black, thes r wgs & ths is the body, it's got white spots on its wgs, I dk wht kind I never saw one lik it	WSo FC'o A 3.5
	(E: Take ur tim & look sm more & I thk u'll find smthg else too)			
	2. Mayb a face, ugly, not a real one, did u c *Pet Semetary*, it's lik from tht	E: S:	(Rpts Ss resp) Yeah, it's lik the face of sm dog or cat, a cat I guess, not real, more lik a ghost face, lik a dead cat, c the white is the mouth & eyes & thes r the ears, it's really ugly, lik fr the movie, I thot it was neat	Wso Fo (Ad) 3.5 MOR,PER
II	3. Another face, lik really weird, it's got red ears & white eyes, his mouth is open lik he's been hit, lik he's been hurt bad	E: S: E: S:	(Rpts Ss resp) It's lik fr *Friday the 13th* or smthg weird, c his ears up here (D2) r all red & his eyes r here (space betw D1 & D2) & ths is his mouth (DS5), its open lik he's hurt U said he's been hurt? Yeah, he's got his mouth open lik in pain & ths red (D3) is lik bld on his chin, lik he's hurt bad	WS+ Mp.CF− Hd,Bl 4.5 MOR
III	4. Tht ll 2 wm, lik thyr fiting about ths thg dwn here	E: S: E: S:	(Rpts Ss resp) It ll thyr pullg on ths thg, each one wants it I dk wht it is tho I'm not sur how u r seeg thm Thy just do ll tht, c the head & legs & arms & ths (D7) is wht thyr fiting abt	D+ Mao 2 H,Id P 3.0 AG
	v5. If I look ths way it's a lot diff, ths part ll a monster face, som A monster	E: S:	(Rpts Ss resp) It has big black eyes & weird teeth, thyr not really teeth, fangs, yeah lik big fangs, really neat, he's got 'em coming out of his head too, lik fr som monster movie	Do FC'− (Ad)
IV	6. Tht ll som creature, lik he's laying down, lik I'm lookg down at him	E: S: E: S:	(Rpts Ss resp) Som monster thg, lik Bigfoot, he's got big feet & a tail & these thing-a-jigs r lik arms or claws U said lik u'r lookg dwn at him? Lik fr an angle, lik I'm closer to his feet	Wo Mp.FDo (H) P 2.0 DV
	v7. Ths way its smoke fr a fire	E: S:	(Rpts Ss resp) Lik when thy burn tires or oil, the smoke gets really black lik ths, it ll it's floatg up lik smoke does, I've seen tht lots of times, thy burn tires alot out at the dump & u can c the smoke fr a long way off, it really smells bad too if u get too close	Wv mp.C'Fu Fi PER

266

	No.	Response	Inquiry	Score
V	8.	Hey, tht ll Dracula, he's got his big cape on	E: (Rpts Ss resp) S: It looks a lot lik him w his black cape, he's standg w his arms out, here r his legs, but thyr too small & he's got horns too, c up here, real spooky lik, I've seen tht movie two or three times, it's really, really funny	W+ Mp.FC'o (H),Cg 2.5 INC,PER
VI	9.	Tht's lik a cat tht got smooshed by a car	E: (Rpts Ss resp) S: It's just all flattened out, c the legs & the back & the head up here & thes wb whiskers E: I'm not sur wht maks it ll a cat S: It just does, mayb the whiskers, dogs don't hav whiskers, at least not tht big	Wo Fo A P 2.5 MOR,DV
VII	10.	Tht ll a girl dancing or practicing a cheer in front of a mirror	E: (Rpts Ss resp) S: Well, she's lik jumping up & dwn & her hair is bouncg up, its lik in a pony tail, c her nose & chin & she's lik lookg at herself while she's doing it, ths (Dd23) is her skirt & she's got her arm behind her, c it's all the same over on ths side too, lik a mirror image	W+ Ma.Fr.mpu H 2.5
	11.	Or it cb 2 rabbits sittg on a rock lookg at e.o.	E: (Rpts Ss resp) S: If u thk of it tht way, there's one on each side E: I'm not sur I c them lik u do S: Oh yeah, well one's here & here, c this wb the ear & the nose & the tail & theyr sittg on ths thg, it's prob a rock or smthg	W+ FMpo 2 A,Ls 2.5
VIII	12.	Mayb a mask, lik a weird Halloween mask, it looks w all the diff colors	E: (Rpts Ss resp) S: Lik some mask tht costs alot, it's shaped lik a face but its got all the diff colors lik a mask has & thos white slits r for the eyes & mouth, it's kinda lik a mask tht's made to ll the face of so from space, u kno, lik a Martian or smbody w a pointd head & big round cheeks, u see ones lik ths smtimes on TV or in stores at Halloween, but thy cost alot of money cuz thyr so involved E: U said it's got big round cheeks? S: Yeah, the pink parts, c how thy stick out	WSo CFu (Hd) 5.5 PER
	< 13.	If I turn it ths way it ll a pink A jumpg across som rock or thgs by a lake	E: (Rpts Ss resp) S: Ths (D1) is lik an A & he's kinda, stretched out lik jumpg across thes thgs dwn here & u can c it all reflected in the water E: Mayb u can help me c it better S: Ok, here's the A, lik a dog, c his head & legs & body & I guess ths mite be his tail & the blue is the water & thes r colored rocks & bushes & it's all the sam dwn here lik its all being reflected u know?	W+ FMa.Fr.CF+ A,Na P 4.5 INC

Case 7. (Continued)

Card	Response		Inquiry	Scoring
IX	14. Ths one ll a face of som creature	E:	(Rpts Ss resp)	WSo CFu (Hd) 5.5 DV
		S:	It's all diff colors, orange ears & big green cheeks & the white is littl slitty eyes & a big pink mouth, it's really weird, lik som creature fr space, pretty cool, I don't thk I evr saw one lik ths but I'd lik to, I don't mean for real but lik in a movie	
	15. Just the pink part re me of muscle lik in the science book	E:	(Rpts Ss resp)	Dv CF.FV− An PER
		S:	We're studying the body & thy always mak muscles pink colored lik this, sort of twisty lookg lik a muscle is supposd to b	
		E:	Twisty lookg?	
		S:	The lines in there make some parts ll thy bulge out more, lik when muscles twist some parts go out & som parts go in	
X	16. Up here ll 2 littl ants tryg to push dwn ths stick or smthg	E:	(Rpts Ss resp)	D+ FMao 2 A,Bt 4.0 AG,COP
		S:	Thy just ll ants w their little legs & those littl feeler thgs, thyr lik crawlg up ths stick lik thyr to tryg & push it ovr so thy can take it away	
	17. Thes dwn here ll 2 dogs, lik thyr sittg dwn barkg at smthg, thyr prob watchdogs	E:	(Rpts Ss resp)	Do FMao 2 A AG,ALOG
		S:	Well, thy ll dogs, c the frnt foot is here (points) & the head & thy got their mouths open lik thyr barkg at smthg	
		E:	U said thyr prob watchdogs	
		S:	Yeah, thy bark a lot	
	18. Thes blue thgs cb sapphire earrings	E:	(Rpts Ss resp)	Do CFu 2 Art PER
		S:	Thyr all blue, lik sapphires, & thy hav a star-burst shape, really nice lookg earrings, I'v seen som lik them in a catelog	
	v19. Ths way it's lik a face, lik the face of a goat	E:	(Rpts Ss resp)	
		S:	Thy hav littl beards lik ths (D11) & the eyes (D2), the nose the mouth, a littl mouth (D3), it ll a goat's face to me	

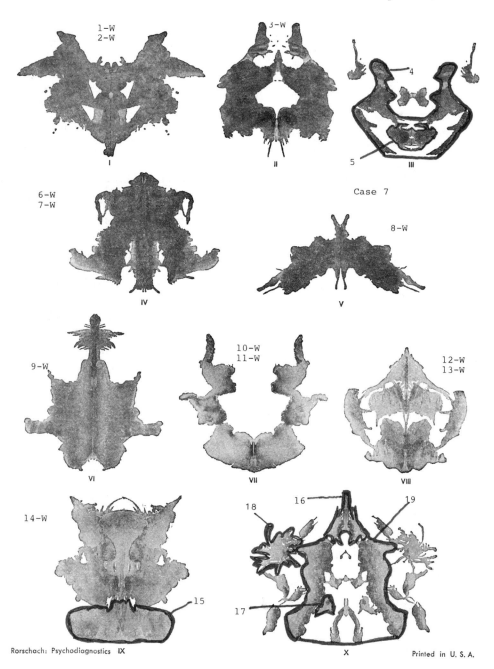

Case 7

Case 7   **Sequence of Scores**

Card	No	Loc	#	Determinant(s)	(2)	Content(s)	Pop	Z	Special Scores
I	1	WSo	1	FC'o		A		3.5	
	2	WSo	1	Fo		(Ad)		3.5	MOR
II	3	WS+	1	Mp.CF-		Hd,Bl		4.5	MOR
III	4	D+	1	Mao	2	H,Id	P	3.0	AG
	5	Do	7	FC'-		(Ad)			
IV	6	Wo	1	Mp.FDo		(H)	P	2.0	DV
	7	Wv	1	mp.C'Fu		Fi			PER
V	8	W+	1	Mp.C'Fo		(H),Cg		2.5	INC,PER
VI	9	Wo	1	Fo		A	P	2.5	MOR,DV
VII	10	W+	1	Ma.Fr.mpu		H,Cg		2.5	
	11	W+	1	FMpo	2	A,Ls		2.5	
VIII	12	WSo	1	FCu		(Hd)		4.5	PER
	13	W+	1	FMa.Fr.CF+		A,Na	P	4.5	INC
IX	14	WSo	1	CFu		(Hd)		5.5	DV
	15	Dv	6	CF.FV-		An			PER
X	16	D+	11	FMao	2	A,Bt		4.0	AG,COP
	17	Do	2	FMao	2	A			AG,ALOG
	18	Do	1	CFu	2	Art			PER
	19	DdSo	21	F-		Ad			

Case 7   **Structural Summary**

Location	Determinants		Contents	S-Constellation
Features	Blends	Single		NO . . FV+VF+V+FD>2
			H = 2, 0	YES . . Col−Shd Bl>0
Zf = 13	M.CF	M = 1	(H) = 2, 0	YES . . Ego<.31,>.44
ZSum = 45.0	M.FD	FM = 3	Hd = 1, 0	NO . . MOR > 3
ZEst = 41.5	m.C'F	m = 0	(Hd) = 2, 0	NO . . Zd > + − 3.5
	M.C'F	FC = 1	Hx = 0, 0	YES . . es > EA
W = 12	M.Fr.m	CF = 2	A = 6, 0	YES . . CF+C > FC
(Wv = 1)	FM.Fr.CF	C = 0	(A) = 0, 0	YES . . X+% < .70
D = 6	CF.FV	Cn = 0	Ad = 1, 0	YES . . S > 3
Dd = 1		FC' = 2	(Ad) = 2, 0	NO . . P < 3 or > 8
S = 6		C'F = 0	An = 1, 0	NO . . Pure H < 2
		C' = 0	Art = 1, 0	NO . . R < 17
DQ		FT = 0	Ay = 0, 0	6 . . . . . TOTAL
. . . . . (FQ−)		TF = 0	Bl = 0, 1	
+ = 7 (1)		T = 0	Bt = 0, 1	Special Scorings
o = 10 (2)		FV = 0	Cg = 0, 2	Lv1 Lv2
v/+ = 0 (0)		VF = 0	Cl = 0, 0	DV = 3x1 0x2
v = 2 (1)		V = 0	Ex = 0, 0	INC = 2x2 0x4
		FY = 0	Fd = 0, 0	DR = 0x3 0x6
		YF = 0	Fi = 1, 0	FAB = 0x4 0x7
		Y = 0	Ge = 0, 0	ALOG = 1x5
Form Quality		Fr = 0	Hh = 0, 0	CON = 0x7
		rF = 0	Ls = 0, 1	SUM6 = 6
	FQx FQf MQual SQx	FD = 0	Na = 0, 1	WSUM6 = 12
+ = 1 0 0 0	F = 3	Sc = 0, 0	
o = 9 2 3 2		Sx = 0, 0	AB = 0 CP = 0
u = 5 0 1 2		Xy = 0, 0	AG = 3 MOR = 3
− = 4 1 1 2		Id = 0, 1	CFB = 0 PER = 5
none = 0 — 0 0	(2) = 5		COP = 1 PSV = 0

Case 7   **Ratios, Percentages, and Derivations**

R = 19		L = 0.19		FC:CF+C = 1: 5	COP = 1 AG = 3
				Pure C = 0	Food = 0
EB = 5: 5.5	EA = 10.5	EBPer = N/A		Afr = 0.73	Isolate/R = 0.21
eb = 6: 5	es = 11	D = 0		S = 6	H:(H)Hd(Hd) = 2:5
	Adj es = 10	Adj D = 0		Blends:R = 7:19	(HHd):(AAd) = 4:2
				CP = 0	H+A:Hd+Ad = 10:6
FM = 4 : C' = 4 T = 0					
m = 2 : V = 1 Y = 0					
			P = 4	Zf = 13	3r+(2) /R = 0.58
a:p = 5: 6	Sum6 = 6	X+% = 0.53	Zd = +3.5	Fr+rF = 2
Ma:Mp = 2: 3	Lv2 = 0	F+% = 0.67	W:D:Dd = 12: 6: 1	FD = 1
2AB+Art+Ay=1	WSum6 = 12	X−% = 0.21	W:M = 12: 5	An+Xy = 1
M − = 1	Mnone = 0	S−% = 0.50	DQ+ = 7	MOR = 3
		Xu% = 0.26	DQv = 2	

SCZI = 0   DEPI = 5*   CDI = 0   S-CON = 6   HVI = Yes   OBS = No

INTERPRETIVE ROUTINE FOR CASE 7

The first positive Key variable is that the number of reflection answers is greater than zero. Thus, according to the table regarding the order of cluster search, the interpretation will begin with a review of the data concerning self-perception.

When the presence of one or more reflection answers is the first Key variable, the entire interpretive strategy is not defined. Instead, only the first three clusters (self-perception, interpersonal perception, controls) are identified, and the next positive Key variable is used to define the remaining order of search. In this case, there are no other positive Key variables; therefore, the table of Tertiary variables must be used to determine the order in which the remaining four clusters should be reviewed. In this case, the first positive Tertiary variable is DEPI = 5, and as such, indicates that the data concerning affect should be reviewed after the interpretation of the controls data is complete. Thus, the complete order by which the record will be addressed is:

$$\text{SELF-PERCEPTION} \to \text{INTERPERSONAL PERCEPTION} \to$$
$$\text{CONTROLS} \to \text{AFFECT} \to \text{PROCESSING} \to \text{MEDIATION} \to \text{IDEATION}$$

Self-Perception—Case 7   The data concerning self-perception for Case 7 are shown in Table 62.

Table 62. Self-Perception Data for Case 7

3r + (2)/R = 0.58	FD = 1	MOR = 3	Hx = 0	An + Xy = 1
Fr + rF = 2	Sum V = 1	H:(H) + Hd + (Hd) = 2:5		Sx = 0
		RESPONSES TO BE READ		
MOR Resp's	FQ − Resp's	M Resp's	FM Resp's	m Resp's
2,3,9	3,5,15,19	3,4,6,8,10	11,13,16,17	7,10

The presence of one or more reflection answers in the protocol of a 15-year-old is some cause for concern. Although they are commonplace in the records of younger children, they are less common in the records of older adolescents and may signal potential trouble. As has been noted earlier, one or more reflection answers indicate the presence of a narcissisticlike self-centeredness. People with this feature tend to regard their own worth as being much greater than those around them, and they often go to great lengths to defend or protect this conceptualization of themselves, usually by externalizing the cause of any faults.

Sometimes, adolescents who manifest this characteristic will have an average or even lower than average Egocentricity Index, indicating a struggle with the extreme self-centeredness as contrasted with a more realistic view of their place in the world. However, that does not appear to be the case here. The Egocentricity Index (.58) is above average, suggesting that she does not really appreciate that she may not be as important as she has believed. There is one V response and one FD response in the record, which might signal some backing away and review of her estimates of her self-worth. On the other hand, the Vista answer could be situational, and as such, could represent more a sense of guilt or remorse that has been provoked by her disruptive and uncooperative classroom behaviors. Possibly some other data in the protocol will resolve this question.

If the Vista answer is not situational, it could represent a healthy reevaluation of the self. Conversely, if it is situational, the growth benefits from it will be minimal concerning self-concept.

There are seven human contents in the protocols, indicating a strong interest in people, but only two of the seven are Pure *H* responses. This suggests that her conception of people and her perception of herself is based much more on imagination or fantasy than on real experience. Ideally, people, and especially young people, will think of themselves in the framework of their experience. When this does not occur, the resulting self-concept will be distorted and/or detached from reality. Although there is one *An* response, it affords no structural importance to the interpretation, although the content of the answer may be important later in the interpretation of these data. There are three MOR responses. Their presence indicates that she perceives some of the features of herself to be negative and/or damaged. The presence of these MOR responses suggests that the Vista answer may reflect a more chronic preoccupation with one or more negative characteristics that she perceives in herself. If this is true, it may be a positive growth sign, but it also reflects the presence of much conflict concerning her self-image at the moment.

The contents of the MOR answers are quite interesting with regard to this issue. The first, Response 2 to Card I, is "Maybe a face, ugly, not a real one . . . a dead cat." It is a response in which she takes some distance from the object (not a real one), and in the Inquiry she appears to deny the negative implications, "like from the movie, I thought it was neat." The second, Response 3 to Card II, is, "Another face, like really weird, . . . like he's been hurt bad." She also appears to neutralize the negative features of this answer by associating it with a movie, "like from *Friday the 13th* or something weird," but the denial is not as marked as in the previous MOR answer. In fact, she emphasizes that "he's been hurt bad" twice, once in the answer and again in the Inquiry. The third is a more typical MOR answer, Response 9 to Card VI, ". . . a cat that got smooshed by a car . . . just all flattened out."

Her five *M* answers are also interesting. The first is the Card II answer, the face that has been hit and "hurt bad." The second, Response 4 to Card III, is "two women fighting about this thing . . . each one wants it, I don't know what it is though . . ." This is not necessarily an unusual response except that she is not able to identify what they are fighting about, which may suggest some confusion about her identity. The third, Response 6 to Card IV, is a creature laying down, ". . . I'm looking down at him." Again it is a common answer except for the fact that she is looking down at him, "I'm closer to his feet," which probably has implications but they are not easily translated. The fourth, Response 8 to Card V, is a bit more obvious. It is Dracula, described as "real spooky like," but then neutralized by her comment, "I've seen that movie two or three times, it's really, really funny." The last *M* is one of her reflection answers, Response 10 to Card VII, "a girl dancing or practicing a cheer . . . looking at herself while she's doing it." Even though it is a reflection, it implies some self-examining. Collectively, the *M*'s are more negative than positive; although they tend to convey an unwillingness to accept the negative features, they also convey a curiosity about them.

The four *FM* answers are somewhat less consistent for substance and also less negative. The first, Response 11 to Card VII, is two rabbits sitting, looking at each other. The second, Response 13 to Card VIII, is a pink animal jumping across some rock or things. It is her second reflection answer. The third, Response 16 to Card X, is two ants trying to push down a stick, so they can take it away, and the fourth, Response 17 to Card X, is two dogs barking, probably watchdogs. It is the most unique of the four and includes the only evidence of scorably flawed logic in the record—watchdogs bark a lot. It may convey something about her cautiousness regarding the environment.

The first of the two *m* answers, Response 7 to Card IV, smoke from a fire, is a less common response, it is "floating up . . . I've seen that lots of times . . . it really smells bad too if you get too close." It suggests that she has experienced a sense of helplessness often, and it also implies that if people "get too close" to her, they will not like what they experience. This projection may coincide with the negative self-implications suggested in the MOR answers. The second *m* is more common. It is in Response 10 to Card VII, hair bouncing up. It conveys a sense of reacting to the actions of others and a sense of being out of control, but this conclusion is somewhat speculative.

She does embellish several other answers in ways that may relate to her self-image. For instance, Response 1 is a weird bird. Response 5 is a monster face, "really neat . . . like from some monster movie." Response 12 is a weird Halloween mask, like the face of someone from space, "you see ones like this sometimes on TV." Response 14 is the face of some creature, "I don't think I ever saw one like this but I'd like to, I don't mean for real but like in a movie." Response 15 is her single Vista answer, a muscle, "twisty looking," and her last answer, Response 19, is the face of a goat. Collectively, these represent a sense of strangeness and even distortion. None are positive and, like two of the MOR answers, she neutralizes the negative impact of several by identifying them as being from movies or television. As a group, they seem to indicate a sense of strangeness about herself, but also an unwillingness to confront her own negative features.

Overall, the data concerning self-perception seem to suggest quite strongly that she is struggling with her notions about her self-image. Even though the reflection answers imply a tendency to overglorify her sense of self, the presence of the vista response, the MOR answers, and the contents of the movement and embellished answers imply a marked awareness that all is not well. At the same time, there is a tendency to take distance and/or neutralize these negative features of the self. This struggle to define herself may contribute significantly to the onset of many of her unwanted or unacceptable behaviors. In other words, her disruptive and argumentative behaviors are efforts to defend her integrity, but at the same time they can be a call for attention and even a plea for assistance for her attempts to understand herself more realistically. The data concerning interpersonal perception and affect should serve to clarify this postulate.

Interpersonal Perception—Case 7   The data concerning interpersonal perception and behaviors are shown in Table 63.

Table 63. Interpersonal Perception Data for Case 7

CDI = 0	$a:p$ = 5:6	T = 0	Human Cont = 7	Pure H = 2
HVI = Pos	Food = 0	PER = 5	COP = 1 AG = 3	Isolate/R = .21

RESPONSES TO BE READ

HUMAN MOVEMENT WITH PAIR	*HUMAN CONTENTS*
4	3,4,6,8,10,12,14

The most important finding in this cluster is the positive Hypervigilance Index. She is very guarded about people. She does not trust them and does not expect to be close to them. In fact, she is prone to regard gestures of closeness with considerable suspiciousness and this will usually lead to the anticipation that others are attempting to intrude on her own personal space. Hypervigilant people devote a great deal of energy to a state of preparedness, that is, they believe that they must be alert to danger and/or confrontation. This hyperalert state causes them to challenge the motives of others and usually results in an interpersonal world in which they are avoided by others because of their excessive guardedness and/or seeming hostility.

Hypervigilant people typically have a firm, although usually distorted sense of themselves. The previously reviewed data concerning self-concept suggest that may not be the case here, and lead to the speculation that the hypervigilant state is less well fixed than is common for an older person. The implication is that some form of intervention that includes the creation of a close therapeutic relation might fragment the hypervigilance before it becomes well embedded in her personality structure and functioning. However, at the moment, it tends to clarify the cause of some of her argumentative and disruptive behaviors.

The *a:p* ratio is not positive for passivity but does tend in that direction. Should she become more passive, any prognosis for change would be more gloomy in light of her hypervigilant state. The substantial number of human contents (7) usually would be regarded positively and taken as a strong interest in others. In this instance, the strong interest is there but not for favorable reasons. Instead, it is generated more by guardedness than by an interest in creating relations with others.

In a related context, there is a strong likelihood that she will alienate those around her. This is evidenced by the five PER answers. One or two PER answers are not uncommon among young people who feel a need to defend themselves against the intellectual challenges of others. However, when the number of PER is considerably greater, as is the case here, it signifies an authoritarian form of defensiveness in which the subjects convey the message, "I know what I am talking about and anything you say is irrelevant because of my personal knowledge." People like this try to dominate others with their pseudoexpertise, and this irritating, know-it-all feature usually causes others to back away from them.

There is one COP response, but it is combined with an aggressive feature. Overall, there are three AG responses, indicating that she perceives interpersonal relations as being naturally marked by aggressiveness. This also contributes to her disruptive and aggressive classroom behavior. Surprisingly, the Isolation Index (0.21) is not positive. This could be a false negative but could also reflect that she maintains a few friendships and expresses a sincere interest in older boys at her school. Conversely, the movement responses that contain pairs are not very positive. They include women fighting, rabbits looking, ants pushing over a stick, and watchdogs barking. None really convey a sense of smooth or deep social relations. Similarly, most of her human contents are much more negative than positive: a face, hurt, from *Friday the 13th,* two women fighting, a monster face, a creature laying down, Dracula, a girl dancing in front of the mirror, a weird Halloween mask, and the face of a creature. Only two, the women fighting and the girl dancing are real, and neither of those is a very desirable answer. In other words, her perceptions of people seem to be more distorted than real.

Overall, this is a very guarded, mistrusting youngster, who regards others more as threatening than as sources of friendship or emotional closeness. Her conceptions of people are not well founded, and her misunderstandings of them probably contribute significantly to her guarded and mistrusting attitude. She defends herself arduously against their intrusions and apparently prohibits herself from the possibility of closeness. She is often very authoritarian, and this know-it-all form of defense probably makes her less likable or attractive to others. In addition, she tends to perceive aggressiveness as a basic feature in interpersonal relations and thus can be expected to be more aggressive in her behaviors, which also serves to reduce the likelihood of developing close relations. Her hypervigilant state may be in its early stages of development and this possibility could bode favorably for intervention efforts.

Controls—Case 7   The data concerning capacity for control and tolerance for stress are shown in Table 64.

Table 64.   Controls and Stress Tolerance Data for Case 7

EB = 5:5.5		EA = 10.5		D = 0	
eb = 6:5		es = 11	Adjes = 10	AdjD = 0	
FM = 4	C' = 4	T = 1		CDI = 0	
m = 2	V = 1	Y = 0			

The Adjusted D Score is zero, and there is little reason to question its validity. The *EA* (10.5) is well into the average range for 15's, and the *EB* (5:5.5) has substantial values on both sides of the ratio. The Adjusted *es* (10) is also in the expected range for a subject of this age and neither side of the *eb* is unusually high. Thus, it seems reasonable to conclude that her capacity for control and her tolerance for stress is not unlike those of her age. Ordinarily, she has enough resource available to formulate and implement decisions and, in most instances, will be not become disorganized in stress situations. There are two pieces of data in this cluster that warrant concern, but neither appears to have a significant potential for disrupting her overall capacity for control. They are the ambitent *EB* and the large number of *C'* answers. Both will be studied more specifically in the next cluster.

Affect—Case 7   The data relating to affect for Case 7 are shown in Table 65.

Table 65.   Affect Data for Case 7

DEPI = 5				BLENDS
EB = 5:5.5		*EBPer* = N/A		M.CF
eb = 6:5		*FC:CF* + *C* = 1:5		M.FD
		Pure *C* = 0		M.C'F
C' = 4	T = 1	*Afr* = 0.73		M.Fr.m
V = 1	Y = 0	S = 6		FM.Fr.CF
		Blends/*R* = 7:19		CF.FV
		CP = 0		m.C'F

The DEPI (5) is positive and represents a very important finding. It indicates that her psychological structure is marked by many of the features that give rise to frequent episodes of emotional disruption. These episodes may be experienced as frequent bouts of sadness or depression, but could take other forms of emotional discomfort, such as anxiety, tension, or even feelings of uneasiness or irritation. Sadness or depression seem most likely because, when the 14 variables that compose the DEPI are reviewed, the 4 of the 6 that are positive (Vista > 0; Color-Shading blends > 0; *S* > 2; *Sum C'* > 2) relate directly to negative or confused feelings. If the majority of positive DEPI variables had been related to cognitive activities, it would be less likely that sadness or depression might manifest directly.

As noted earlier, the data for the *EB* are a cause for concern. She is an ambitent, that is, neither of the more basic coping styles, introversive or extratensive, is present. This is less common among 15-year-olds than younger children and signifies that she is not consistent in the use of her feelings in coping or decision-making situations. Instead, she vacillates in her approach to these issues. At times, she may delay decisions, attempt to push feelings aside, and try to think things through. In other instances, she will merge her feelings into her thinking and they will become quite important in her decisions. In that neither of these approaches is well formed, she is less likely to use either efficiently. As a result, she is prone to make more errors in her coping behaviors, profit less from them, and become prone to repeat them.

This is not necessarily a disastrous situation, as about one fifth of older nonpatient adolescents and adults do not have a distinctive coping style. However, it can make life more difficult, especially with regard to the profitable use of feelings. Ambitents are often confused by their feelings, giving way to them at times and attempting to curtail their influence at other times, but not necessarily in ways that are logical or profitable to their objectives. Thus, it will be difficult to predict her emotional reactions to any of a variety of situations.

As also noted earlier, the right-side value of the *eb,* though not unusually high for someone of this age, contains four *C'* answers. The value is not greater than the WSumC and therefore does not signal some form of constriction, but it is much higher than expected for any age group. It indicates that, more often than most people, she internalizes feelings that she would prefer to express overtly. This results in discomfort, as the internalized emotions do not become dormant. Instead, they persist and create irritation that ultimately may provoke other emotionally related manifestations. Some people who do this to excess develop somatic difficulties. Many others, as is probably the case here, find ways of expressing their contained emotions in less direct ways. For instance, some of her irritating behaviors that are not really directed at any one person could be displacements of these internalized feelings.

The Affective Ratio (0.73) is average for her age and indicates that she is as willing to process emotional stimulation about as much as most of her age. Usually, this is a good prognostic sign, but in this instance, the presence of her hypervigilant style plus her tendency to internalize feelings excessively suggests that it only contributes to some of her problems. Processing emotional stimulation often requires some sort of exchange. If the person is unwilling or uncertain about being involved in such an exchange, the emotional input simply exacerbates the tendency to internalize and can increase the already present mistrust or suspicions about others or about exhibiting feelings.

The *FC:CF + C* (1:5) ratio identifies another problem. She does not modulate her emotional expressions as much as do most of her age. Instead, when she expresses feelings, she does so in an overly intense or less well-controlled manner. In other words, when she is emotional, those around her will be very aware of the expression of her feelings. Sometimes, this may be regarded by others as exuberance, but even when the release of intense feelings involve positive emotions, they can be wearing on others. If the feelings released are not positive, the interpersonal impact can be much more trying, and people who are emotionally intense in the release of negative affect usually cause others to become annoyed with them. This is probably the case here as she gives six *S* responses signaling the presence of considerable anger. Thus, if many or most of her emotional displays are indirect manifestations to suppressed feeling and exhibited as forms of anger, she will be likely to irritate most of those around her.

The ratio of blends to *R* (7:19) represents more than a third of her answers. This is not surprising for an ambient and illustrates the sort of psychological complexity that ambitents often experience. One of the blends is a Color-Shading blend, signaling the confusion that she often feels regarding her emotions.

In general, the data concerning affect reveal numerous problems. First, she does not deal with feelings very consistently. Second, she often holds in feelings that she would prefer to express and this leads to feelings of discomfort. Third, when she does express herself, it is likely to be in ways that are overly intense or less well controlled for her age. Fourth, she is a very angry person and apparently is not able to deal with this anger in effective ways. Fifth, she often is confused about her feelings, and finally, she has many features that will provoke emotional disruption, often leading to experiences of depression or, at least, instances of considerable irritation and discomfort. Emotion is a major problem for her and made even more of a problem because she is hypervigilant.

Processing—Case 7   The data regarding processing activities for Case 7 are shown in Table 66.

Table 66.   Processing Data for Case 7

L = 0.19	$W:D:Dd$ = 12:6:1	Zd = +3.5	$DQ+$ = 7
Zf = 13	$W:M$ = 12:5	PSV = 0	$DQv/+$ = 0
HVI = Yes	OBS = No		DQv = 2

LOCATION SEQUENCING

I	WS,WS	IV	W,W	VII	W,W
II	WS	V	W	VIII	WS,W
III	D,D	VI	W	IX	WS,D
				X	D,D,D,DdS

The low value for Lambda (0.19) suggests that she becomes overly involved with stimuli. She does not back way from complexity from time to time as do most people. Instead, she tends to immerse herself in a stimulus field. Sometimes people do this because they are interested and challenged by their world but, in this case, the excessive involvement is apparently created by her hypervigilant style. She does not want to miss anything for fear that she may be unexpectedly overwhelmed by it. As noted earlier, the hypervigilant style requires the investment of considerable energy, as is reflected in her processing effort.

The *Zf* (13) is above average. The *W:D:Dd* ratio (12:6:1) indicates that she is not very economical, and the *W:M* ratio (12:5) suggests that she sets considerable goals for herself. The *Zd* (+3.5) signals an overincorporative style that involves a considerable scanning effort. Surprisingly, the product of this considerable effort is not always good quality. She gives an average number of synthesized answers (7), but there are also two *DQv* responses, which is considerably more than expected of a 15-year-old, especially those who make strong efforts to process. It suggests that some of her processing activities may be less mature than she would desire, or that some sort of preoccupation may be interfering with her processing objectives. Her approach to processing seems reasonably consistent as illustrated by the location selections. She tends to W most of the time, but selects D answers when the field is more broken and complex as in Cards III and X.

In general, she works hard to process new information and is not very concerned with being economical about the use of her energy. Usually, the effort is beneficial to her, but in some instances, personal elements interfere with her desired goals and the processing effort is less desirable that she prefers. These elements may have to do with mediational or conceptual activities.

Mediation—Case 7   The data concerning mediation for Case 7 are shown in Table 67.

Table 67.   Cognitive Mediation Data for Case 7

Lambda	= 0.19	OBS	= Neg	MINUS FEATURES		
P	= 4	*X+%*	= .53	3,5,15,19		
FQx+	= 1	*F+%*	= .67			
FQxo	= 9	*Xu%*	= .26			
FQxu	= 5	*X−%*	= .21			
FQx−	= 4	*S−%*	= .50			
*FQx*none	= 0	CONFAB	= 0			

She gives fewer Popular answers (4), than do most of her age. The average P for 15's is more than six and the median and mode for that age are both seven. This suggests that, even when the cues to conventionality are obvious, she does not give the obvious response. However, this is not because of mediational difficulties. Instead, this is probably a good illustration of the collective impact of the low Lambda tendency to become overly involved with stimuli and the hypervigilant style. For instance, she does not give a Popular answer to Card I, yet her first answer includes the basic features of the Popular. Similarly, in Response 10 to Card VII, the Popular head or face is included in her answer but not scored, because she uses the entire blot as two people. In effect, she has disregarded the Popular for a more detailed response that incorporates more features of the field.

This is a positive finding because it signals an awareness of the obvious cues. On the other hand, it also signifies that she translates stimuli in less common ways, and this probably accounts for the lower than average $X + \%$ (.53). The $Xu\%$ is higher than average and she gives four minus answers, yielding an $X - \%$ of .21. If considered in the context of intervention, the fact that most of her nonconventional answers are Unusual rather than minus suggests that a cognitive approach, designed to orient her toward more conventional behaviors, should have some reasonable chance of success.

However, there are affective features that suggest such an approach might not be as successful. The $S - \%$ (.50) is high, and four of her six S responses are either minus or unusual. Thus, her rather intense anger and her hypervigilant style will continue to interfere with the effectiveness of her mediational efforts. For instance, three of the four minus responses are faces and tend to signify her paranoid-like suspiciousness of others. Interestingly, three of the four minus answers are last responses and the fourth is the only response given to Card II. It is almost as if she works to distort the field in the framework of her suspiciousness. In addition, all the minus answers occur to blots in which chromatic color is present, again suggesting that her problems with emotion are contributing to her set in translating stimuli. Fortunately, none of the four minus answers involves a complete disregard for the stimulus field.

Overall, the data suggest that she often is too idiosyncratic in her mediational activities. Some of this individualism results from her hypervigilant style, but some also results from her problems in dealing effectively with her feelings, especially her anger.

Ideation—Case 7   The data regarding ideational activities for Case 7 are shown in Table 68.

Table 68.   Ideation Data for Case 7

				M QUALITY			SPECIAL SCORES		
EB	= 5:5.5	*EBPer* = N/A		+ = 0		DV = 3		DV2	= 0
eb	= 6:5	(*FM* = 4 *m* = 1)		o = 3		INC = 2		INC2	= 0
a:p	= 5:6	$M^a:M^p$ = 2:3		u = 1		DR = 0		DR2	= 0
$2AB + Art + Ay$ = 1				− = 1		FAB = 0		FAB2	= 0
MOR	= 3					ALOG = 1		SUM6	= 6
RESPONSES TO BE READ FOR QUALITY						CON = 0		WSUM6	= 12
3,4,6,8,10									

The vacillation in coping and decision-making activities indicated by ambient status has been discussed earlier with regard to affect. Similar concerns are warranted concerning ideation; that is, at times she will delay and attempt to mentally weigh alternative decisions and/or behaviors. However, as is the case with the use of her feelings in problem solving, her use of delay and thinking things through cannot be very efficient. She is prone to make ideational errors and repeat those errors more than should be the case, simply because this is not a tactic with which she has learned to be comfortable and efficient.

There is no reason to believe that her thinking is intruded on by peripheral ideation more than most of her age. The left-side *eb* value is well within the expected range. There also is no reason to suspect that she is inflexible in the way that she mentally approaches issues or values as the *a:p* ratio is 5:6. There is, however, reason to believe that she drifts into fantasy more than should be the case. The $M^a:M^p$ ratio is 2:3, indicating that she tends to use fantasy more defensively than do most of her age. This is not necessarily a major problem, but one that can tie together with her excessive guardedness about others and should be considered carefully when and if intervention is planned. The negative finding for the Intellectualization Index (1) is positive. In many instances, hypervigilant subjects who have trouble handling their emotions begin to rely more and more on intellectualization as a way of neutralizing the impact of their feelings. That is not the case here.

The three MOR contents indicate that her thinking will be marked by more pessimism than should be the case. The tendency for pessimism to influence thinking often causes people to view their own decisions as being unrelated to outcomes, that is, "it does not matter what I do, the results are beyond my control." This attitude can be especially devastating when a hypervigilant state is presence as it tends to reaffirm the sense of vulnerability that underpins the state. The number of Critical Special Scores (6) is somewhat higher than occurs among nonpatient 15's but is not an inordinately high number, especially when considered in light of the *WSum6* (12). Five of the six are Level 1 DV and INCOM answers, and probably, only the ALOG response reflects serious cognitive slippage.

The three DV responses all seem to involve adolescent jargon, with words such as "thing-a-jig," "smooshed," and "slitty." The two INCOM answers also reflect a more juvenile characterization of features. Dracula has horns (Card V), and the dog (Card VIII) is inappropriately identified as being pink. The ALOG (Card X) is somewhat more concrete and illogical for a 15-year-old. She argues that the dogs are watchdogs because they bark a lot.

As speculated earlier, none of the Critical Special Scores is evidence of serious problems in thinking. Similarly, the single $M-$ response is the weird face that has been "hurt bad" on Card II. It seems to convey the influence of her own damaged sense of self on her thinking and there is no reason to assume that this influence is markedly pervasive in her ideational activities. Actually, if the form quality and special score issues are ignored, the quality of her M answers is reasonably good and in some instances is more sophisticated than might be expected (the hurt face, women fighting, a creature laying down, Dracula with a big cape on, and a girl dancing or practicing a cheer).

In general, the problems with her thinking are not major, except the extent to which her ideation is influenced by her hypervigilant style. Her ideational activity is marked by a series of relatively minor problems, none of which taken alone will cause problems. However, the composite does present some obstacles to a more effective functioning. First, she does not use the ideational tactic of delay very consistently in decision making, and thus, it is not always very efficient. Second, she tends to use fantasy as an escape more often than most of her peers. This is not a major defense, but at times, it interferes with the way she deals with issues. Third, her thinking often is more pessimistic than should be the case and this can orient her toward giving up on reality-oriented solutions to problems and reinforce her hypervigilant attitude toward her environment. Overall, her thinking is not unsophisticated, but many of the conclusions that she draws will not be well couched in a realistic assessment of her situation.

CASE 7—SUMMARY

This is a very complex youngster who is alienated from her world. She is struggling with her self-image, apparently vacillating between her childlike narcissism and an awareness that she has some undesirable features. This struggle probably contributes significantly to her erratic pattern of unwanted behaviors. Unfortunately, she is becoming more and more mistrustful of others. In part, this mistrust evolves from her abandonment of her own expectations for emotional closeness and her misconceptions about people. This mistrust is developing a state of insecurity and hypervigilance that causes her to be extremely guarded and apprehensive about her environment. She defends herself by attempts to conceal her feelings or express them only indirectly. When she does express her emotions, it is likely to be in ways that are overly intense and less well controlled than should be the case. In part, the intensity of her emotional expressions is prompted by her intense anger that she does not understand well or handle effectively.

She has developed a very authoritarian manner of dealing with people, and she perceives aggressiveness as a necessary and routine phenomenon in everyday relations. Thus, her tendency to be more aggressive socially becomes a sort of defense that permits her to keep others at a distance. Although some of her behaviors appear to be impulsive, they are not. Her capacity for control and tolerance for stress is not dissimilar to that of others of her age. Instead, her disruptive behaviors simply reflect her naivety about how to express emotions, and her anger and defensiveness often become overriding factors.

Generally, she processes new information very thoroughly, but sometimes her own preoccupations interfere with her processing activity and produce a less sophisticated effort than she would prefer. Similarly, her mediation or translation of stimulus inputs is too idiosyncratic; that is, she tends to perceive things through her own special sets. Thus, her reality testing, though not seriously impaired, will be marked by her own strong orientation to be individualistic. Her thinking is adequate but inconsistent. She apparently invests too much effort into fantasy, and much of her thinking is conspicuous for the pessimistic attitudes that she harbors. Thus, many of the conclusions that she draws are not well framed in reality, but rather in the framework of her struggling, defensive sense of self and her misconceptions of the environment.

The referral asks if there is a suicidal preoccupation; whether a psychological problem is evident; for advice to teachers and counselors; and if treatment is needed, whether it should occur in the school or away from the school.

There is no significant evidence of a suicidal preoccupation, but that does not rule out the possibility. She is confused about herself, emotionally isolated from her world, and very angry, and these are features that often cause young people to consider self-destruction. She has serious psychological problems that will become much more serious if not treated. It is difficult to offer advice to her teachers and counselors except to help them to understand her plight. She should be treated away from the school, and it should be emphasized that this is not an easy treatment case and rapid improvement cannot be expected. The parents may be an important aspect of any treatment plan, but that is difficult to ascertain without additional assessment information. Generally, the prognosis for this case will be contingent on how firmly in place the hypervigilant style has become. Some data suggest that it is still developing, and if that proves true, prognosis should be favorable. Conversely, if it is more well fixed, the prognosis will be much more modest, or even poor concerning her responsiveness to treatment. She is a person who seems to have many potential assets, but they are being thwarted by the several psychological liabilities present in her current personality structure. If they can be brought to the forefront in her psychological operations, she may well flourish in herself and in her environment, but if they remain suppressed, her future will be much more bleak.

REFERENCES

Barrash, J., Kroll, J., Carey K., & Sines, L. (1983). Discriminating borderline disorder from other personality disorders. *Archives of General Psychiatry, 40,* 1297–1302.

Chethik, M. (1986). Levels of borderline functioning in children: Etiological and treatment considerations. *American Journal of Orthopsychiatry, 56,* 109–119.

Dahl, A. A. (1990). Empirical evidence for a core borderline syndrome. *Journal of Personality Disorders, 4,* 192–202.

Dornbusch, S. M., Ritter, P. L., Leiderman, P. H., & Roberts, D. F. (1987). The relation of parenting style to adolescent school performance. *Child Development, 58,* 1244–1257.

Esman, A. H. (1989). Borderline personality disorder in adolescents: Current concepts. In S. C. Feinstein (Ed.), *Adolescent psychiatry* (Vol. 16, pp. 319–336). Chicago: University of Chicago Press.

Exner, J. E. (1986). Some Rorschach data comparing schizophrenics with borderline and schizotypal personality disorders. *Journal of Personality Assessment, 50,* 455–471.

Greenman, D. A., Gunderson, J. G., Cane, M., & Saltzman, P. R. (1986). An examination of the borderline diagnosis in children. *American Journal of Psychiatry, 143,* 998–1003.

Grinker, R. R. (1977). The borderline syndrome: A phenomenological view. In P. Hartocollis (Ed.), *Borderline personality disorders* (pp. 159–172). New York: International Universities Press.

Grolnick, W. S., Ryan, R. M., & Deci, E. L. (1991). Self-perceptions, motivation, and adjustment in children with learning disabilities: A multiple group comparison study. *Journal of Learning Disabilities, 23,* 177–184.

Gualtieri, C. T., Koriath, U., & Van Bourgondien, M. E. (1983). "Borderline" children. *Journal of Autism and Developmental Disorders, 13,* 67–71.

Gunderson, J. G., & Singer, M. T. (1975). Defining borderline patients: An overview. *American Journal of Psychiatry, 132,* 1–10.

Heavey, C. L., Adelman, H. S., Nelson, P., & Smith, D. C. (1989). Learning problems, anger, perceived control, and misbehavior. *Journal of Learning Disabilities, 22,* 46–50.

Hurt, S. W., Clarkin, J. F., Koenigsberg, H. W., Frances, A., & Nurnberg, H. G. (1986). Psychometric properties and validity. *Journal of Consulting and Clinical Psychology, 54,* 256–260.

Kernberg, O. (1978). The diagnosis of borderline conditions in adolescence. In S. C. Feinstein & P. L. Giovacchini (Eds.), *Adolescent psychiatry* (Vol. 6, pp. 298–320). Chicago: University of Chicago Press.

Kernberg, P. F. (1983). Borderline conditions: Childhood and adolescent aspects. In K. S. Robson (Ed.), *The borderline child* (pp. 224–234). New York: McGraw-Hill.

Leichtman, M., & Nathan, S. (1983). A clinical approach to the psychological testing of borderline children. In K. S. Robson (Ed.), *The borderline child* (pp. 121–170). New York: McGraw-Hill.

Lofgren, D. P., Bemporad, J., King, J., Lindem, K., & O'Driscoll, G. (1991). A prospective follow-up study of so-called borderline children. *American Journal of Psychiatry, 148,* 1541–1547.

Ludolph, P. S., Westen, D., Misle, B., Jackson, A., Wixom, J., & Wiss, C. A. (1990). The borderline diagnosis in adolescents: Symptoms and developmental history. *American Journal of Psychiatry, 147,* 470–476.

Mandel, H. P., & Marcus, S. I. (1988). *The psychology of underachievement.* New York: Wiley.

Masterson, J. F. (1980). *From borderline adolescent to functioning adult.* New York: Brunner/Mazel.

McManus, M., Lerner, H., Robbins, D., & Barbour, C. (1984). Assessment of borderline symptomatology in hospitalized adolescents. *Journal of the American Academy of Child Psychiatry, 23,* 685–694.

Meissner, W. W. (1984). *The borderline spectrum.* New York: Aronson.

Nagy, J., & Szatmari, P. (1986). A chart review of schizotypal personality disorders in children. *Journal of Autism and Developmental Disorders, 16,* 351–368.

Perry, J. C. (1988). A prospective study of life stress, defenses, psychotic symptoms, and depression in borderline and antisocial personality disorders and Type II affective disorder. *Journal of Personality Disorders, 2,* 49–59.

Perry, J. C., & Klerman, G. L. (1980). Clinical features of the borderline personality. *American Journal of Psychiatry, 137,* 165–173.

Petti, T. A., & Vela, R. M. (1990). Borderline disorders of childhood: An overview. *Journal of the American Academy of Child and Adolescent Psychiatry, 29,* 327–337.

Pine, F. (1983). Borderline syndromes in childhood. In K. S. Robson (Ed.), *The borderline child* (pp. 83–100). New York: McGraw-Hill.

Shapiro, T. (1983). The borderline syndrome in children: A critique. In K. S. Robson (Ed.), *The borderline child* (pp. 11–29). New York: McGraw-Hill.

Spitzer, R. L., & Endicott, J. (1979). Justification for separating schizotypal and borderline personality disorders. *Schizophrenia Bulletin, 5,* 95–104.

Steinberg, L., Elmen, J. D., & Mounts, N. S. (1989). Authoritative parenting, psychosocial maturity, and academic success among adolescents. *Child Development, 60,* 1424–1436.

Vela, R. M., Gottlieb, E. H., & Gottlieb, H. P. (1983). Borderline syndromes in childhood: A critical review. In K. S. Robson (Ed.), *The borderline child* (pp. 32–48). New York: McGraw-Hill.

Weiner, I. B. (1992). *Psychological disturbance in adolescence* (2nd ed.). New York: Wiley.

Wenning, K. (1990). Borderline children: A closer look at diagnosis and treatment. *American Journal of Orthopsychiatry, 60,* 225–232.

Widiger, T. A., (1989). The categorical distinction between personality and affective disorders. *Journal of Personality Disorders, 3,* 77–91.

CHAPTER 8

Problems in Behavior

Problems in behavior consist of persistent misconduct that violates established rules and regulations and is disruptive to the environment. In some instances, problem behavior occurs only in a specific environment, such as in school or at home. More commonly, misconduct in one area of the environment generalizes to other areas as well. Consequently, young people referred for evaluation of behavior problems typically have a history of misconduct in school, conflict at home, and troublemaking in a variety of other settings or activities.

Children and adolescents who persistently misbehave are not homogeneous with respect to their personality structure or the origins of their adjustment difficulties. Instead, clinical and research studies suggest a fourfold classification of youthful behavior problems including (a) *socialized* misconduct, in which misbehaving youth show little psychological disturbance but engage in antisocial acts as members of a delinquent subculture; (b) *characterological* misconduct, in which antisocial acts derive from a chronically self-centered, exploitative, and inconsiderate personality style; (c) *neurotic* misconduct, in which young people misbehave as a symptomatic expression of underlying needs and concerns; and (d) *psychotic* or *neuropsychological* misconduct, in which young people behave badly as a result of substantial impairments of judgment, impulse control, and other integrative functions of the personality (see Weiner, 1992, Chap. 8).

Misbehavior that disrupts the environment and violates the rights of others, taken together with delinquent acts that break the law, regularly confronts clinicians who work with young people. More children and adolescents are referred to mental health professionals for misconduct than for any other reason, and between one third and one half of all young people seen in outpatient clinics have been in difficulty because of antisocial behavior (Kazdin, 1987; Quay, 1986a, b; Tolan, Ryan, & Jaffe, 1988).

SOCIALIZED MISCONDUCT

Socialized misconduct involves problem behavior associated with membership in a subculture that endorses antisocial standards of conduct. The members of antisocial subcultures collaborate in disturbing and illegal activities as a regular feature of their daily lives that they regard as entirely appropriate and acceptable. This pattern of misbehavior is commonly referred to as being "subculturally deviant" and is categorized in DSM-III-R as "group type" delinquency (American Psychiatric Association, 1987; Quay, 1987). These groups often are not well defined, and in some instances may involve as few as two or three youngsters who feel alienated from their peer environment.

Consistent with this description, socialized misconduct is characterized by adaptive rather than maladaptive behavior and by social rather than solitary acts. The adaptive nature of socialized misconduct was first described by Jenkins (1955), who did some of the early research on differentiating juvenile delinquents according to their personality style. As Jenkins and other writers have elaborated, socialized delinquents engage in planned, easily understandable behavior that breaks the law as an expression of their group's needs and attitudes. Socialized delinquents have not been found to differ behaviorally from nondelinquents in any major way, aside from their lawbreaking. They do, however, account for an estimated one third of young people incarcerated by the criminal justice system (Quay, 1987). Moffitt (1993) has suggested that most of these young people are "adolescence-limited" in their antisocial behavior, and that later in life, the incidence of antisocial behavior among them will be far less than is the case during adolescence.

Subcultures that foster misconduct respect the successful lawbreakers in their midst and reject those who decline to participate in antisocial activities. In such circumstances, misbehaving youths experience a sense of belongingness and well-being, whereas well-behaved youngsters feel outcast and unworthy. Socialized delinquents identify with and feel close to their peers; they are well-integrated members of a social group that they value and to which they feel loyal; and they are no more likely than young people in general to demonstrate adjustment difficulties (see Arbuthnot, Gordon, & Jurkovic, 1987; Quay, Routh, & Shapiro, 1987).

The social nature of this form of misconduct refers to the fact that it typically involves group rather than individual behavior. Socialized misbehavers rarely misbehave by themselves, except perhaps to impress their friends or as required by the group, and they are unlikely to keep any solitary misbehavior a secret from their peers. By contrast, a preference for solitary misconduct usually indicates a psychological problem related to individual disturbance rather than a manifestation of group influence. This does not rule out the possibility that some members of an antisocial gang may be psychologically disturbed. Typically, in such instances, the group itself recognizes which of its members are relatively unstable and unreliable, and hence not to be put in positions of trust or leadership, and which are relatively lacking in realistic regard for their own safety and the welfare of others, and hence are good candidates for particularly dangerous or foolhardy assignments on behalf of the group.

CHARACTEROLOGICAL MISCONDUCT

Characterological misconduct comprises behavior problems that reflect a primarily asocial personality orientation. Unlike socialized young people who misbehave, children and adolescents with characterological behavior problems are usually loners who have no group membership or loyalties. They get into or cause trouble either by themselves or in temporary alliance with other troublemakers whom they seldom consider friends. They trust no one and are loyal only to themselves. They may pretend trust and loyalty when it serves their purpose to do so, but their collaboration is a matter of convenience rather than of mutual support or self-sacrifice. They keep their misconduct to themselves, unless they decide to mention their exploits as a way of impressing or intimidating others.

The troublesome conduct of youngsters with characterological behavior problems occurs as a consequence of their disregard for the rights and feelings of other people and their inability or unwillingness to refrain from doing them harm. They quickly translate aggressive, acquisitive, and pleasure-seeking impulses into self-gratifying action, with scant concern for how others may suffer in the process. These young people misbehave not in response to group influence or needs for peer acceptance, but merely to express anger, satisfy a whim, or obtain something they want. Their characterological problems begin by some form of stunting of psychological growth that occurs early in their development. They persist in manifesting the "I want" features common to preschool children and tend to be concerned only with the immediate gratification of needs with little regard for the rationality of their acts or for the long-term consequences of them.

For these reasons, characterological misconduct has typically been classified as "undersocialized" or "solitary type" delinquency (Adam, Kashani, & Schulte, 1991; American Psychiatric Association, 1987). The interpersonal orientation and behavioral style of children and adolescents who display characterological problem behavior closely approximate expectation in young people classified as conduct disordered in DSM-III-R, and this pattern of deviance constitutes in budding form the adult condition usually diagnosed as psychopathic or antisocial personality disorder.

Psychopathic personality disorder revolves primarily around an underdeveloped conscience and a disinclination to identify with other people. Lacking conscience, psychopaths are guiltless individuals who rarely regret trampling on the rights and feelings of others. Lacking identification, they are loveless individuals who avoid interpersonal intimacy and seldom form deep or enduring relationships with others. Psychopathic individuals keep interpersonally distant from others, and only rarely give or expect sympathy, support, or nurturance. For them, other people exist to be used and manipulated, not to be cared about or depended on. Psychopaths are self-centered individuals who blame other people or circumstances for whatever difficulties they cause or encounter and who feel fully justified in doing just as they please (see Meloy, 1988; Quay, 1987; Schalling, 1978).

Asocial attitudes and a lack of concern for the welfare of others make young people with psychopathic tendencies highly prone to misconduct. Usually they are deterred from antisocial acts only by fears of being caught and punished; internalized standards of decency and propriety seldom govern their behavior. Not surprisingly, then, the majority of young people who are placed in detention for misconduct demonstrate this kind of emerging characterological pathology. Not all psychopathic youngsters become lawbreaking delinquents, however. Some, despite being selfish and self-aggrandizing and heartlessly exploiting people and circumstances to their own ends, may carefully avoid overt criminal acts. Clinicians should accordingly avoid being too restrictive in diagnosing emerging psychopathic personality disorder. Aside from not being synonymous with criminality, psychopathy, like schizophrenia and depression, occurs in degrees of severity. The fact that a youngster has made a friend or two, or has shown kindness now and then, or displays some other appealing personality qualities does not rule out this condition. Psychopathy implies the presence of at least some of its defining characteristics, but its diagnosis does not require extreme, unrelieved manifestations of all the personality warps associated with it.

As noted earlier, psychopathy is a chronic disorder that begins early in life, crystallizes in late adolescence, and usually persists throughout the adult years. The antisocial conduct that accompanies this condition accordingly shows considerable continuity from childhood into adolescence and beyond. Overly aggressive children tend to become assaultive adolescents and violent adults; children who steal tend to become adolescent thieves and adults who commit crimes against property (Kupersmidt & Coie, 1990; Loeber, Lahey, & Thomas, 1991; Loeber & Stouthamer-Loeber, 1987; Stattin & Magnusson, 1989).

Conduct-disordered children who are future psychopaths begin in elementary school to lie, cheat, steal, and behave cruelly toward others. They bully children younger or smaller than themselves, they mistreat animals as well as people, and, early on, they display a demanding and self-centered lifestyle.

In adolescence, the persistence of these childhood characteristics brings budding psychopaths increasingly into conflict with their peers, parents, teachers, and community. They are more likely than other young people to lack friendships and to be argumentative and disobedient at home. In school, they are much more likely than their classmates to miss classes and to be suspended or expelled for aggressive or disruptive conduct, especially fighting and defiance. Unless they are sufficiently intelligent to succeed academically without conscientious effort, they often get held back one grade or more.

The predictability of such progressive adjustment difficulty varies in the individual case with several features of a young person's misconduct. The more frequently children misbehave and the more harmful their actions are to other people and their property, the more likely they will be to show persistent and serious antisocial behavior in adolescence and become what has been called "life-course persistent" in their antisocial activities (Moffitt, 1993). The earlier the onset of their misconduct, the more varied it is, (e.g., both stealing and fighting), and the more settings in which it occurs (e.g., both at home and in school), the more likely it is to persist and the more serious it will become. Conversely, relatively late onset of minor, infrequent, and situation-specific antisocial conduct minimizes the likelihood of persistent and increasingly severe offenses (Kelso & Stewart, 1986; Loeber, 1990; Tremblay et al., 1991).

These findings identify a stepping-stone effect that assists in the clinical identification of characterological misconduct. Misbehaving children are generally at risk for subsequent antisocial behavior, but not all childhood conduct problems eventuate in adolescent delinquency or adult antisocial personalities. On the other hand, adolescents rarely become conduct disordered without previously having been misbehaving children. Characterological misconduct in adolescence will, with few exceptions, have been preceded by childhood misconduct, and most chronic delinquents will have been recognizable in elementary school from such behavior (Loeber, 1988). These findings are sufficiently reliable to contraindicate the diagnosis of psychopathy or antisocial personality disorder in the absence of such early developmental difficulties.

NEUROTIC MISCONDUCT

In neurotic misconduct, young persons misbehave neither as well-integrated members of an antisocial subculture nor as a reflection of an asocial characterological orientation. Instead, the troubles that these young people cause and get into are individual and personally meaningful attempts to communicate unmet psychological needs. In common with many other neurotic behaviors, this kind of misconduct is thus symptomatic of underlying concerns that it serves indirectly to express.

Whereas socialized and characterological misconduct often involves recurrent misbehavior that becomes a way of life, neurotic misconduct typically consists of occasional, situationally determined episodes of problem behavior. These episodes usually begin following the emergence or exacerbation of some personal difficulty that generates feelings of tension, remorse, or discouragement, and they tend to cease soon after this difficulty has been resolved. Accordingly, this pattern of problems in behavior has often been described as "acute, "accidental," "situationally provoked," or "anxious-withdrawn-dysphoric" (Genshaft, 1980; Quay, 1987). Although young people who fall into this category do not fit usual stereotypes of being a "juvenile delinquent," anxious-withdrawn-dysphoric youths account for one fourth of institutionalized delinquents (Quay, 1987).

Instead of demonstrating the antisocial attitudes seen in socialized problem youngsters or the childhood aggressiveness and selfishness associated with characterological misconduct, young people who begin to misbehave for neurotic reasons have typically been cordial and conforming individuals in the past. Their present misconduct contrasts sharply with a previous pattern of propriety, and people who know them express surprise at their sudden unpleasantness and loss of respect for law and order. As a general principle, the more a misbehaving youngster's problem behavior diverges from a past history of good conduct, the more likely he or she is to be neurotically disturbed.

Of the particular unmet needs that foster indirect communication through neurotic misconduct, those most commonly found are needs to be recognized and respected and needs to receive help. Needs for recognition and respect can on occasion motivate children and adolescents who feel unnoticed and unappreciated to misbehave in some dramatic fashion. A detected delinquent act can command the attention of teachers, police, and other important adults; it can require otherwise unavailable parents to become engaged in court, school, or clinical deliberations; and it can promote visibility among otherwise disinterested peers. The use of public antisocial behavior to gain recognition and peer status, especially in young persons suffering from low self-esteem, has been observed in numerous clinical and research studies (see Berndt & Zinn, 1984; Bynner, O'Malley, & Bachman, 1981).

Regarding needs for help, troubled young persons who are afraid or embarrassed to confide their concerns to others, or whose efforts to confide have been falling on deaf or disinterested ears, may resort to misconduct as an indirect way of communicating their concerns. Their problem behavior compels others to recognize at last that they are having psychological difficulties and to do something about it. The single most frequent problem underlying communication of psychological neediness through misconduct is previously undetected depression. For example, uncharacteristic recalcitrance and the sudden onset of stealing can often be traced to events in a young person's life that have left him or her feeling lonely or discouraged. As mentioned earlier, such symptomatic neurotic behavior frequently appears soon after the loss of some important person in a youngster's life, as when a parent dies or an unfriendly divorce is finalized (see Chiles, Miller, & Cox, 1980; Cole & Carpentieri, 1990; Weiner, 1992, Chap. 4).

PSYCHOTIC AND NEUROLOGICALLY RELATED MISCONDUCT

Emerging psychopathy and neurotic symptom formation account for most instances of misconduct associated with psychological disturbance. However, clinicians must also be alert to occasions when antisocial behavior derives from psychotic or neuropsychological disorder. Studying 285 adolescents referred to a juvenile court clinic, Lewis and Balla (1976, Chap. 7) found that one third showed signs of psychosis, central nervous system impairment, or both. Although delinquent young people in general are not as likely to demonstrate such serious disorders as did the Lewis and Balla sample of adjudicated lawbreakers referred for mental health care, these findings indicate the advisability of considering the possibility of these disorders in the individual case.

Psychotic misconduct emerges primarily in schizophrenic young people whose faulty logic, impaired judgment, and shaky self-control lead them into antisocial behavior (see

Chap. 5). In one study of psychiatrically hospitalized adolescents, schizophrenia was the most common discharge diagnosis among those who had been admitted with a diagnosis of conduct disorder (Lewis, Lewis, Unger, & Goldman, 1984). Evidence that antipsychotic medication reduces violence associated with schizophrenia demonstrates the importance of accurate differential diagnosis in planning treatment for aggressive, psychotic adolescents (Cavanaugh, Rogers, & Wasyliw, 1981).

Neuropsychologically related misconduct occurs most often in connection with attention-deficit hyperactivity disorder (ADHD) and temporal lobe epilepsy (TLE). The susceptibility of ADHD children to problematic interpersonal relationships and antisocial conduct, as well as to school learning difficulties, is noted in Chapter 9. Among adolescents, social and conduct problems are the most prominent manifestations of persisting ADHD (Brier, 1989; Lambert, 1988). In one study, hyperactive boys at age 14, compared with non-ADHD boys, were seven times more likely to have been suspended from school on one or more occasions and six times more likely to have had trouble with the law (Lambert, Sassone, Hartsough, & Sandoval, 1987).

For preexisting ADHD, as in the case of psychotic disorder, accurate differential diagnosis in misbehaving young people has important implications for specialized treatment planning. In some cases, apparent ADHD with prominent behavior problems may in fact constitute a conduct disorder that represents an early manifestation of emerging psychopathy (see Lillienfeld & Waldman, 1990). However, among truly ADHD young people with persistent hyperactivity and distractibility, stimulant medication is a demonstrably effective means of promoting improved behavior, and cognitive and perceptual-motor skill training can boost the low self-esteem that often contributes to misconduct in neuropsychologically impaired young people (Henker & Whalen, 1989; McDaniel, 1986).

Explosive outbursts of angry, assaultive, antisocial behavior that resemble manifestations of psychopathy can occur with certain kinds of epileptic disorders. Sometimes they constitute psychomotor seizures, also referred to as TLE because of the usual temporal focus of the abnormal brain activity associated with this condition (Bear, Freeman, & Greenberg, 1984; Blumer, 1982). Psychomotor seizures occurring independently or in combination with other types of epileptic attack are characterized by a sudden onset of strange body movements that serve no apparent purpose. These actions persist in an automatic, stereotyped fashion for anywhere from a minute to several hours, and efforts to stop the person or change his or her behavior during the attack often provoke combative rage. Subsequently, the person usually has little or no memory for what he or she has done and, unlike psychopathic individuals following an aggressive outburst, sincerely regrets any damage or offense to others that may have occurred.

Accordingly, episodic aggressive outbursts followed by amnesia and remorse should be investigated for their possible origin in TLE. When this explosive behavior disorder is positively identified, moreover, beneficial effects are likely to result from including anticonvulsant medication in the treatment plan (O'Donnell, 1985; Stewart, Myers, Burket, & Lyles, 1990).

RORSCHACH ASSESSMENT OF PROBLEM BEHAVIOR

Rorschachers need always to keep in mind that their test data can rarely be translated directly into conclusions about behavior. There are no discrete indices or configurations on the Rorschach that can reliably identify an acting-out child or discriminate between delinquent and nondelinquent young people. To formulate a useful differential diagnosis and treatment plan, clinicians using the Rorschach in a behavior-problem case will require a detailed case history and precise information concerning the problem behaviors. Psychological test data in these cases contribute to diagnostic and treatment planning by identifying dimensions of personality associated with the problem behaviors that have led to a referral.

Rorschach data in cases of socialized misconduct data will have little to contribute to differential diagnosis. Young people showing socialized misconduct will be heterogeneous in their personality style and level of adjustment. Variations among them may have implications for interventions that would be beneficial, as when Rorschach findings reveal that a young person has limited tolerance for frustration or feels uncomfortable dealing with affect. However, socialized misconduct is a behavior problem that, by definition, arises independently of such personality characteristics. It is diagnosed on the basis of the group context in which it occurs, not the individual personality style of group members. Youngsters involved in group misconduct are therefore likely to produce many different kinds of Rorschach protocols, none of which would identify them as being socialized delinquents.

On the other hand, psychotic and neuropsychological misconduct do constitute problem behavior rooted in individual disturbance. With respect to psychotic misconduct, the Rorschach can be extremely valuable in detecting the presence of schizophrenic disorder. Neuropsychological impairments contributing to problem behavior can best be identified by appropriate neuropsychological and neurological examination. In addition, however, Rorschach information concerning underlying thoughts and feelings and personality strengths and weaknesses can be useful in treatment planning for young people whose primary handicaps are neuropsychological in nature.

Rorschach findings can be used to discriminate between characterological and neurotic origins of problem behavior. However, the most critical diagnostic information in such cases *will come from the history,* particularly with respect to how persistent and typical a young person's problem behavior has become, as opposed to being episodic and uncharacteristic. Nevertheless, the psychopathic personality features associated with characterological misconduct and the anxious-withdrawn-depressed personality features associated with neurotic misconduct are delineated much more clearly among Rorschach findings.

SOME RORSCHACH FEATURES OF CHARACTER-DISORDERED YOUNGSTERS

The characteristic attitudes, feeling state, and coping style of characterologically antisocial individuals has several Rorschach corollaries that can help to identify the presence or emergence of this personality style. Usually, the selfish, self-centered attitudes and tendencies to externalize blame and responsibility in adolescent psychopaths are illustrated by reflection responses and an elevated Egocentricity Index in the Rorschach. In a study by Gacono, Meloy, and Heaven (1990), 48% of a group of adults with DSM-III-R diagnosed antisocial personality disorder who scored relatively high on Hare's Psychopathy Checklist gave reflections and had an above-average Egocentricity Index.

However, some adjustments must be made when interpreting these indices of maladaptive self-centeredness and self-aggrandizement in the protocols of young people.

First of all, children and adolescents normatively give more reflection responses and have a higher Egocentricity Index than adults; at all ages from 5 to 16, for example, nonpatients are more likely to give reflections than were Gacono et al.'s adult psychopathic subjects. Second, even the usual criterion of identifying as abnormal values that exceed normative expectation by one standard deviation, or that exceed the median or modal value considerably for such nonparametric variables as reflections, may not necessarily identify a pathological degree of self-centeredness in young people.

To be sure, children and adolescents who give an unusually large number of reflections and an Egocentricity Index substantially above age expectation are displaying the type of selfishness, inflated sense of self-worth, and tendency to externalize blame that characterize the emergence of an antisocial or psychopathic orientation. However, it may well be that these features of self-centeredness do not always crystallize sufficiently in adolescence to establish an antisocial personality disorder and hence may not distinguish between psychopathic and nonpsychopathic individuals until the adult years. Three conclusions seem reasonable to draw in light of current knowledge:

1. Most young people who are developing an antisocial personality orientation are likely to show reflection responses and an elevated Egocentricity Index.
2. Among misbehaving young people, those who do not demonstrate reflection responses and an elevated Egocentricity Index are less likely to be emerging psychopaths than those who do.
3. Among young people with numerous reflections and an elevated Egocentricity Index, some will be progressing toward antisocial personality disorder whereas others will still be working their way through developmental self-centeredness that will pass in time.

Negative attitudes toward themselves are also important in differentiating characterologically antisocial or psychopathy prone adolescents from those who are struggling with various kinds of developmental issues. Characterologically antisocial youngsters tend to shun introspection and to experience little in the way of guilt, remorse, or negative self-attitudes, which makes them relatively unlikely to produce *FD, V,* or MOR answers. The absence of *FD, V,* or *MOR* can characterize many different kinds of psychological status, including functioning in the normal range, and is in no way diagnostic of an antisocial or psychopathy-oriented feature. On the other hand, should Rorschach indices of introspectiveness and self-critical attitudes accumulate, there is good reason to question, if not rule out, an antisocial personality disorder.

However, as in the case of self-centeredness, the diagnostic implications of self-critical attitudes must be interpreted cautiously. Although psychopathic individuals are less likely than most people to experience object loss, they are just as capable of becoming depressed or discouraged when ill fortune comes their way. Moreover, even if they maintain an inflated sense of their own worth and entitlement, they may at times berate themselves for having made mistakes or done something they regard as stupid or disadvantageous—such as ill-advised actions that have led to their getting caught or arrested for breaking the law. Accordingly, in misbehaving young people who are presenting substantial evidence of depressive features, the presence of *V* and *MOR* may not suffice to rule out the possibility of emerging antisocial personality disorder.

The attitudes of characterologically antisocial youngsters toward other people typically include a preference to keep themselves interpersonally distant, to avoid intimacy, to manipulate and exploit rather than collaborate mutually with others, and to preserve self-determination by avoiding dependency. These features are likely to be evidenced by such Rorschach findings as T, a low frequency of human contents and of Pure H, and the occurrence of $p > a + 1$.

For instance, the absence of T often is a critical Rorschach finding in differentiating characterological from neurotic misconduct, especially if the total number of human contents is lower than average, *and/or* the frequency of Pure H is less than 2. The absence of T, taken alone, is not necessarily unusual among young people, either patients or nonpatients. Between 10% and 20% of nonpatient youngsters give no T. In younger children, ages 5 through 9, this finding may simply reflect an articulation problem, but for young people ages 10 through 16, the T-less finding probably is more valid, and indicative of early life deprivations that have prevented the development of a basic sense of attachment and bonding to other people. Nonetheless, the absence of T must be approached intelligently and considered in light of other data. Thus, issues of the number of human contents, representing interests in others, plus the number of Pure H answers, representing how reality based the child's conceptions of people may be, become quite important.

Subjects of all ages who produce no T on the Rorschach sometimes long for close interpersonal relationships, but they almost never anticipate being able to form intimate and mutually supportive emotional relationships with others. This is more true for subjects who are age 10 or older, when the absence of T cannot simply be disregarded as a result of limited articulation skills. Legitimately T-less youngsters rarely reach out to others to give solace and comfort, except as insincere gestures to serve their own ends, nor do they expect solace and comfort from others. They prefer to keep people at a distance, and they dislike having other people draw near and intrude on their physical and psychological privacy. The low frequencies of human content and/or the low frequency of Pure H answers tends to confirm this feature. Youngsters such as this may even go out of their way, giving offense if necessary, to discourage people from becoming friendly or close to them. Taken together, the combination of a record without T, the presence of reflections and a high Egocentricity Index, and the low frequency of human contents or a very low frequency of Pure H captures the essence the youngster prone to antisocial activity in which putting his or her own needs ahead of the rights and welfare of others and exploiting other people without remorse become common orientations.

The interpersonal distance that antisocial or psychopathic youngsters prefer is also likely to be reflected on the Rorschach in an $a{:}p$ ratio in which p does not exceed a by more than one point, an elevated Isolation Index, little or no Cooperative Movement, and the absence of Food responses.

As in the case of $T = 0$, neither a low frequency of human content, a low frequency of Pure H, an elevated Isolation Index, $COP = 0$, or $Fd = 0$ should be considered specific to or diagnostic of antisocial or psychopathy proneness. However, such findings lend support to an impression of pending disregard for the environment and even psychopathy proneness, and evidence to the contrary, that is, an individual who seems actively involved with people (low Isolation Index), who anticipates collaborative interactions with them ($COP > 1$), and who is experiencing unmet dependency needs ($Fd > 0$), makes characterologically antisocial and/or psychopathic behavior less likely.

In each of these respects, the thematic imagery that subjects produce can help to demonstrate antisocial or asocial attitudes toward themselves and others. These may include indications of narcissistic focusing on self-attributes and invulnerability ("This looks like a really powerful guy who no one would mess with"); blandly reported fantasies of violence and destruction that the subject views without sympathy from the perspective of a perpetrator rather than a victim ("It's a hole in a wall that I just put my fist through"; "That's that stupid wolf in the cartoon that just got flattened by the coyote who outsmarted him"; "Like when you step on some fat bug and it gets squished flat like this, and this here is the juice that came out of it"); and themes of surviving in a difficult world without expecting or needing to depend on anyone ("These are some animals climbing up something, and they're sort of stuck in this junk down here, but they'll find a way to make it"). Regarding this last illustrative response, a cooperative version in which two animals climbing on Card VIII are being aided by "two hands up here, reaching down to help them up" would seriously call into question a psychopathic frame of reference.

The feeling state of characterologically antisocial or psychopathy-prone youngsters tends to be illustrated by the anger and sometimes cruel views that they have concerning their world, and this manifests in the Rorschach by the production of a substantial number of S responses and numerous responses in which the figures perceived are criticized and demeaned. Giving more than three S responses is unusual at any age and more than four S signals the kinds of resentment, bitterness, and oppositionality that often dominate the affective life of antisocial youngsters.

Angry feelings toward people and toward a seemingly hostile world, populated with potential obstacles to getting what they want, may lead characterologically antisocial subjects to be highly critical and derogatory in describing what they see in the inkblots. Like the "stupid wolf" in the preceding example, human and animal figures may be labeled in various pejorative ways, and even inanimate objects may come in for their share of spleen ("A dumb painting, by one of those kooky artists"; "It looks like a sunset, but it's not drawn very well"). Such thematic indications of hostility and cynicism in the records of characterologically antisocial subjects must be differentiated from depressive themes of inadequacy or morbidity. When depressed subjects see depreciated or damaged objects (e.g., "an odd-looking person"; "a cat that's in really bad shape"), they appear to be identifying with these objects as a manifestation of their poor self-image. When character disorders verbalize demeaned percepts, on the other hand, their identification tends to be with the critic rather than with what is being criticized. Thus a "dumb painting" has nothing to do with themselves in the mind of characterologically antisocial people; it is what those "kooky artists" do, and that's their problem. Likewise, the "stupid wolf" has been "outsmarted by the coyote"; the identification in this response is with the smarter of the two animals, who triumphs over the dumb one.

A further structural clue to the feeling states of characterologically antisocial or psychopathic individuals is their typically shallow affect and the ways in which they deal with their own emotionality. These are likely to influence how they use chromatic color in the Rorschach. Persons who are prone to antisocial behavior often show intense emotion, especially when their wellsprings of anger are tapped. They rarely form stable and enduring feelings about anything. In parallel with their superficial interpersonal relatedness, their emotional reactions flare suddenly and subside just as quickly, and they make little effort to restrain or modulate these reactions. Thus, becoming angry for an antisocial youngster is much more likely to constitute a precipitous outburst of temper, soon forgotten, than a slow burn, long remembered. In using chromatic color, then, these individuals are particularly likely to show an excess of $CF + C$ over FC and to give multiple Pure C answers.

A predominance of color-form over form-color responses and the presence of Pure *C* answers occur more commonly in young people than in adults, especially before age 12. However, these developmental differences do not preclude being able to interpret deviant scores on these variables as indicative of an affective style commonly associated with conduct disorder and/or psychopathy. The tables of data for nonpatients indicate that youngsters age 12 or older hardly ever have a *CF* + *C* that exceeds their *FC* by more than two, and none of the 11- to 16-year-olds in the normative group gave more than one Pure *C*. Accordingly, an unusual frequency poorly modulated chromatic color responses given by a misbehaving adolescent can be interpreted as indicative of the kinds of feeling states often found among psychopathy-prone youngsters. However, similar patterns of color use may occur among adolescents who are not conduct disordered at all but have other forms of disturbance, especially affective disorders; these patterns are common among both patient and nonpatient groups in the 5- to 10-year age group.

In addition to being associated with poorly modulated affective expression, characterologically based misconduct may be reflected in a high Lambda and infrequent *FM* responses. A Lambda of 1.00 or more at any age suggests a single-minded pursuit of simple solutions with little sensitivity to nuances and little patience with complications. High Lambda records are often predictive of problem behavior resulting from an unwillingness to exercise restraint, which is characteristic of youngsters whose actions ignore the conventions of the environment. For similar reasons, *FM* answers, which are associated with ideational promptings evoked by need states, may occur infrequently in the records of antisocial or psychopathic individuals. This is because of their inclination to gratify needs immediately rather than allowing them to intrude into conscious awareness as irritants.

As characterologically antisocial youngsters tend to be nonconformists who prefer doing things their own way, they may also give fewer Popular responses and more Unusual responses than would normatively be expected. From age 10 through adolescence, records with fewer than four *P* and an *Xu%* greater than 25% are rarely given by nonpatients and are suggestive of disregard for conventionality.

In a similar context, youngsters who have a marked antisocial or an emerging psychopathic orientation usually are not burdened by a stimulus overload or trouble with aspects of stress tolerance. If they are misbehaving simply because of an antisocial orientation, they are unlikely to show Adjusted D scores indicative of markedly limited capacities to manage stress. Like other people who feel comfortable with themselves as they are, even if they are getting into trouble or causing trouble for others, most antisocial youngsters, especially those who are emerging psychopaths, show an Adjusted D Score that is at least zero, and often will be greater than zero.

Typically, if they become enmeshed in situations over which they have little control, such as being institutionalized or adjudicated, characterological misbehavers may accumulate *m* and *y* responses that generate a minus *D* score. Even in these situations, however, their *Adjusted D* is likely to equal or exceed zero, as an indication of their generally having a stable and comfortable coping style and feeling little need to change.

At times, the persistent personality problems of young people with characterological misconduct may become apparent in how they relate to the examiner or comply with the requirements of being examined. In particular, such young people may approach the Rorschach situation in a disobedient, defiant, impertinent, uncooperative, argumentative, or profane manner. One boy whose first words to Card I were, "This looks like a piece of shit, and you can't make me say anything more about it," did not leave much to the examiner's imagination concerning his personality style. More often, such hostile and self-centered oppositionality appears in more subtle fashion, as shown by one girl who took each Rorschach card when it was handed to her but then flung it scornfully on the table before beginning to say what it might be.

On the other hand, some budding psychopaths, even as children, possess excellent social skills for manipulating other people to suit their purposes. As described by Weiner (1992, Chap. 8), these so-called "charming" or "superior" psychopaths may treat the examiner with good grace and go out of their way to be cooperative and even complimentary ("I think this is very important work that you are doing"). The infrequency with which most young people enjoy being examined or concern themselves with making the examiner feel good provides some guidance in being able to identify too much good grace and too many compliments as manipulative rather than sincere behavior. Clever, socially skillful, and well-integrated antisocial or psychopathic youngsters may also take pains to eliminate any angry or aggressive themes from their Rorschach responses. However, unless they have been carefully briefed, they cannot prevent their records from demonstrating the self-centeredness, self-satisfaction, superficiality, and underlying interpersonal frigidity that characterizes this personality disorder.

RORSCHACH FEATURES OF ANXIOUS/DYSPHORIC ANTISOCIAL YOUNGSTERS

More often than not in differential diagnostic assessment with the Rorschach, important distinctions rest with subtle differences between somewhat overlapping variables. Distinguishing between manifestations of thought disorder in schizophrenic and affectively disordered young people is a case in point. Rorschach differentiation between characterologically determined and neurotically determined misconduct proves a welcome exception to this challenge. In many respects, the Rorschach protocols of neurotically disturbed young people differ sharply from the records of characterologically antisocial or psychopathic adolescents, and these differences often provide valuable clues to the basic nature of the problem in misbehaving youth.

Beyond calling attention to specific symptoms, such as phobias or compulsions, definitions of neurotic disorder in young people typically suffer from lack of precision (see Beiser, 1990; Sperling, 1974; Weiner, 1992, Chap. 6). Rorschach assessment of neurotic difficulties has been facilitated by the work of Quay (1986a, 1986b), who utilized empirically derived dimensions of developmental psychopathology to identify an anxious-withdrawn-dysphoric pattern in which young people show the following four characteristics: They are likely to be anxious, fearful, and tense, to worry a lot, and to cry frequently; they tend to be shy, timid, bashful, and interpersonally aloof; they report feeling sad, depressed, self-conscious, and easily embarrassed; and they suffer from feelings of inferiority, worthlessness, low self-esteem, and a propensity to become flustered and confused. The co-occurrence of these symptoms of anxiety, withdrawal, and dysphoria in many neurotically disturbed children and adolescents has been widely demonstrated in diagnostic and treatment studies (See King, Ollendick, & Gullone, 1991).

As a manifestation of these personality features, misbehaving young people who are neurotically disturbed will give far different Rorschachs from their characterologically antisocial peers. Most significantly, they are likely to display an elevated Depression Index in which the positive variables will reflect a dysphoric mood and pessimistic thinking. Their dysphoria usually will be reflected by numerous C' and V responses, and Color-Shading or Shading-Shading blends, which identify painful and ambivalent internalized affects and difficulty experiencing pleasure. Their negative thinking will be reflected in a low Egocentricity Index and numerous Morbid responses, signifying low self-esteem, critical self-attitudes, and general feelings of psychological and physical inadequacy and unworthiness. Typically, these youngsters also harbor considerable anger, as is typified by a significant number of S responses. Usually, the anger that they experience leads to the disregard for convention and the resulting behaviors that are asocial or antisocial.

In addition, neurotically disturbed young people are likely to present substantial evidence of tension and anxiety. Many subjects may show situational distress reflected in elevated m and Y and a $D < 0$. However, only persons who have persistently suffered from tension and anxiety related to being unable to muster sufficient resources to cope with the demands they are experiencing are likely to show an Adjusted $D < 0$. An Adjusted $D < 0$ is strongly suggestive of persistent susceptibility to unmanageable subjective distress and accompanying states of tension, irritability, and low frustration tolerance. The self-satisfaction and sense of sufficiency that are common to the character disorder, although sometimes dented by situations that threaten the individual's self-determination, rarely allow for the kinds of persisting sense of coping inadequacy that characterizes neurotic individuals and produces a minus Adjusted D.

Finally, the interpersonal anxieties of misbehaving young people who are neurotically disturbed tend to be manifested in indices of reluctance to engage in emotional interchange with others, hesitancy to initiate social interactions, and a loss of interest in being with or thinking about other people. These personality features are likely to be reflected in the Rorschach by a low Affective Ratio, a small number of human contents, a predominance of passive over active movement responses, and an elevated Isolation Index.

In addition, the characteristic absence of T in the records of character disorders is much less likely to occur in the Rorschachs of young people who are misbehaving for neurotic reasons that include needs for attention and recognition. To the contrary, the psychological neediness of neurotic young people is often reflected in an elevation of T and in frequent FM responses as well, which contrasts with the usual $T = 0$ and often low FM found in characterologically antisocial youngsters.

These clues to differentiating neurotic from characterological misconduct with the Rorschach derive primarily from ways of conceptualizing these conditions and the test findings likely to be associated with them, and empirical confirmation of these relationships has only recently been undertaken. As one example of current research, however, Weber, Meloy, and Gacono (1992) examined the Rorschach records of 13- to 16-year-old adolescents hospitalized with DSM-III-R diagnoses of conduct disorders or dysthymia. Their 30 dysthymic subjects were significantly more likely to have Texture in their records than their 48 conduct-disordered subjects, indicative of attachment to others (63% versus 29%), and significantly more likely to have Y responses, indicative of distress (83% versus 52%).

Also of interest are some previously unpublished data from the Rorschach protocols of 140 adolescents age 12 to 16 who had been diagnosed by DSM-III criteria as demonstrating aggressive conduct disorder. These adolescents were evaluated in several different clinical settings, where on the basis of staff conferences they had been diagnosed as "undersocialized aggressive" in 80 cases and as "socialized aggressive" in 60 cases. The total group, whose Rorschach data are presented in Tables 69 and 70, are likely to include some mixture of young people who would be considered either socialized or characterological delinquents according to contemporary terminology. However, because all of them had acted aggressively toward others, the group is unlikely to include any youngsters of the anxious/dysphoric antisocial type, that is, those with neurotic delinquency. Neurotic delinquents are much less likely than either socialized or characterological delinquents to display aggressive misconduct; their misbehavior is typically directed against property (stealing, vandalism) rather than against people (assault, rape, robbery).

Inspection of Tables 69 and 70 confirms, in preliminary fashion, many of the expectations suggested in the preceding discussion of personality characteristics associated with emerging antisocial personality disorder and their Rorschach indices. This is particularly the case with respect to Rorschach indications of distant, uncomfortable interpersonal relationships. Compared with normative expectations for their age group, these 140 aggressive conduct disorders were much more likely to have no T in their records, no COP, and fewer than 2 Pure H. They were also unusually likely to elevate on HVI and on the Isolation Index.

Similarly expected findings occur with respect to aspects of these conduct-disordered youngsters' affective expression, mediation of perceptual input, and coping style. They were much more likely than normative adolescents to show an excess of $CF + C$ over FC responses, more than one Pure C, and more than two S. They were much more likely to have a high X-%, an Xu% greater than 20, and fewer than four P. They were much more likely to have a high Lambda, they gave an unusually small number of FM responses, they were much less likely to give FD responses, and they were more likely than the normative group to have an Adjusted D greater than 0.

There are two surprises in Tables 69 and 70, although both were anticipated in the preceding discussion. First, with respect to the issue of self-centeredness, these 140 aggressive conduct-disordered adolescents did not differ from normative expectation in their frequency of reflection responses or their Egocentricity Index. This finding supports the conjecture that, although unusually numerous reflections and an unusually high Egocentricity Index may help to identify antisocial personality tendencies among conduct-disordered adolescents, the absence of these indices may not be helpful in ruling out this possibility.

The second surprise involves the apparent fact that this group of misbehaving adolescents, although unlikely to include many neurotic delinquents, nevertheless had a high frequency of depressive features. Over half (52%) had a DEPI of five or more, which meant that such indices of distress as C', Color-Shading blends, MOR, and V, instead of being uncommon, occurred more frequently than normative expectation. Hence, as in the case of self-centeredness, experienced distress must be interpreted cautiously in the differential diagnosis of youthful misconduct. Misbehavior in the absence of signs of negative self-attitudes and painful internalized affect is very likely to identify a characterological pattern of misconduct rooted in antisocial tendencies rather than a neurotic pattern rooted in anxiety and depression. On the other hand, the presence of distressing attitudes and feelings does not rule out emerging psychopathy in conduct-disordered young people, but may instead identify some depressive aspects of their current status.

Some further preliminary analysis of the Rorschach records of these adolescents revealed several interesting and statistically significant ($p < .02$) differences between the

Table 69.   Frequency Data Concerning 140 Adolescents Diagnosed as Conduct Disorder Using DSM-III-R Criteria

RATIOS, PERCENTAGES AND SPECIAL INDICES

EB STYLE			FORM QUALITY DEVIATIONS		
Introversive	36	26%	$X+\% > .89$	2	1%
Super-Introversive	24	17%	$X+\% < .70$	126	90%
Ambitent	34	24%	$X+\% < .61$	110	79%
Extratensive	70	50%	$X+\% < .50$	22	16%
Super-Extratensive	6	4%	$F+\% < .70$	124	89%
			$Xu\% > .20$	80	57%
EA - es DIFFERENCES: D-SCORES			$X-\% > .15$	72	51%
D Score > 0	46	33%	$X-\% > .20$	58	41%
D Score $= 0$	58	41%	$X-\% > .30$	20	14%
D Score < 0	36	26%			
D Score < -1	6	4%	FC:CF + C RATIO		
			$FC > (CF + C) + 2$	0	0%
Adj D Score > 0	52	37%	$FC > (CF + C) + 1$	4	3%
Adj D Score $= 0$	70	50%	$(CF + C) > FC + 1$	44	31%
Adj D Score < 0	18	13%	$(CF + C) > FC + 2$	38	27%
Adj D Score < -1	0	0%			
			S-Constellation Positive	2	1%
Zd $> +3.0$ (Overincorp)	36	26%	HVI Positive	20	14%
Zd < -3.0 (Underincorp)	6	4%	OBS Positive	0	0%

SCZI = 6	0	0%	DEPI = 7	2	1%	CDI = 5	6	4%
SCZI = 5	2	1%	DEPI = 6	0	0%	CDI = 4	18	13%
SCZI = 4	18	13%	DEPI = 5	52	37%			

MISCELLANEOUS VARIABLES

Lambda $> .99$	44	31%	$(2AB + Art + Ay) > 5$	10	7%
Dd > 3	40	29%	Populars < 4	14	10%
DQv + DQv/ + > 2	42	30%	Populars > 7	8	6%
S > 2	114	81%	COP = 0	70	50%
Sum T = 0	86	61%	COP > 2	10	7%
Sum T > 1	16	11%	AG = 0	68	49%
3r + (2)/R $< .33$	26	19%	AG > 2	26	19%
3r + (2)/R $> .44$	44	31%	MOR > 2	42	30%
Fr + rF > 0	32	23%	Level 2 Sp.Sc. > 0	74	53%
PureC > 0	48	34%	Sum 6 Sp. Sc. > 6	28	20%
PureC > 1	28	20%	Pure H < 2	48	34%
Afr $< .40$	44	31%	Pure H = 0	4	3%
Afr $< .50$	58	41%	$p > a + 1$	26	19%
(FM + m) $<$ Sum Shading	56	40%	Mp $>$ Ma	56	40%

undersocialized and socialized groups. Consistent with the conceptual notions presented earlier, the undersocialized group displayed much more interpersonal distance than the socialized group, whereas the socialized group was much more likely to display indications of distress. Regarding interpersonal distance, the undersocialized adolescents were twice as likely as the socialized adolescents to show $T = 0$ and more than three times as likely to show COP $= 0$, a positive HVI, and Pure $H < 2$. Regarding distress, the undersocialized adolescents were markedly less likely than the socialized adolescents to show DEPI > 4, C', V, Color-Shading blends, MOR > 2, and ($FM + m <$ SumSh); in this same

Table 70. Descriptive Statistics Concerning 140 Adolescents Diagnosed as Conduct Disorder Using DSM-III-R Criteria

Variable	Mean	SD	Min	Max	Freq	Median	Mode	SK	KU
AGE	14.27	1.15	12.00	16.00	140	14.00	15.00	−0.14	−0.89
Years Education	8.91	2.40	6.00	11.00	132	9.00	9.00	−2.30	5.88
R	24.19	6.56	14.00	47.00	140	27.00	28.00	0.44	0.66
W	6.53	3.66	1.00	17.00	140	4.50	4.00	1.06	−0.10
D	14.69	7.98	1.00	23.00	140	16.00	23.00	−0.32	−1.50
Dd	2.97	[3.70]	0.00	21.00	132	1.00	1.00	2.43	7.21
S	3.60	[2.05]	0.00	12.00	136	3.00	3.00	1.47	3.75
DQ+	5.96	2.67	1.00	12.00	140	6.00	4.00	0.52	0.01
DQo	16.43	6.06	6.00	40.00	140	20.00	20.00	0.48	1.55
DQv	1.51	[1.48]	0.00	4.00	98	1.00	1.00	0.69	−0.96
DQv/+	0.29	[0.68]	0.00	3.00	26	0.00	0.00	2.61	6.47
FQx+	0.03	0.17	0.00	1.00	4	0.00	0.00	5.72	31.17
FQxo	13.20	3.50	5.00	22.00	140	14.00	14.00	−0.40	−0.30
FQxu	6.21	3.55	0.00	19.00	138	5.50	5.00	0.54	0.71
FQx−	4.09	2.36	0.00	11.00	138	4.00	2.00	0.60	−0.25
FQxNone	0.66	[1.14]	0.00	4.00	42	0.00	0.00	1.48	0.70
MQ+	0.01	0.12	0.00	1.00	2	0.00	0.00	8.27	67.44
MQo	2.51	1.39	0.00	8.00	134	2.00	2.00	1.12	2.68
MQu	0.99	1.08	0.00	5.00	84	1.00	0.00	1.49	3.35
MQ−	0.77	[0.90]	0.00	4.00	76	1.00	0.00	1.30	1.74
MQNone	0.04	[0.20]	0.00	1.00	6	0.00	0.00	4.56	19.10
SQual−	0.93	[1.26]	0.00	6.00	64	0.00	0.00	1.53	2.62
M	4.33	2.10	1.00	13.00	140	4.00	4.00	1.06	3.55
FM	3.03	1.48	0.00	6.00	132	3.00	4.00	−0.21	−0.69
m	1.30	1.09	0.00	6.00	116	1.00	1.00	1.60	3.86
FC	2.16	1.96	0.00	5.00	106	1.00	1.00	0.43	−1.45
CF	2.94	2.01	0.00	7.00	116	4.00	5.00	−0.17	−1.41
C	0.70	[1.13]	0.00	4.00	48	0.00	0.00	1.40	0.56
Cn	0.00	[0.00]	0.00	0.00	0	0.00	0.00	—	—
Sum Color	5.80	3.91	0.00	11.00	126	7.00	10.00	−0.15	−1.54
WSumC	5.07	3.45	0.00	10.00	126	6.00	7.50	−0.15	−1.60
Sum C'	2.37	[2.31]	0.00	8.00	92	2.00	0.00	0.47	−1.18
Sum T	0.50	[0.69]	0.00	2.00	54	0.00	0.00	1.04	−0.20
Sum V	0.39	[0.62]	0.00	2.00	44	0.00	0.00	1.37	0.78
Sum Y	0.81	[1.01]	0.00	5.00	68	0.00	0.00	1.32	2.46
Sum Shading	4.07	3.42	0.00	10.00	106	4.00	0.00	0.35	−1.16
Fr + rF	0.27	[0.53]	0.00	2.00	32	0.00	0.00	1.86	2.60
FD	0.51	[0.97]	0.00	4.00	40	0.00	0.00	1.97	2.98
F	9.61	4.83	1.00	31.00	140	8.00	8.00	1.36	4.00
(2)	9.06	3.70	0.00	15.00	138	10.00	11.00	−0.22	−0.97
3r + (2)/R	0.41	0.12	0.00	0.71	138	0.41	0.39	−0.61	1.16
Lambda	0.91	0.90	0.08	4.33	140	0.78	1.00	2.37	5.58
FM + m	4.33	1.95	1.00	11.00	140	4.00	3.00	0.71	0.66
EA	9.40	4.22	1.00	14.50	140	11.00	13.00	−0.75	−0.86
es	8.40	4.92	1.00	16.00	140	7.50	3.00	0.29	−1.39
D Score	0.36	1.38	−2.00	3.00	82	0.00	0.00	0.73	−0.20
AdjD	0.63	1.27	−1.00	3.00	70	0.00	0.00	0.85	−0.43
a (active)	4.86	2.64	1.00	13.00	140	4.00	3.00	0.68	−0.28
p (passive)	3.80	2.72	0.00	11.00	138	3.00	2.00	1.14	0.24
Ma	2.11	1.47	0.00	5.00	120	2.00	1.00	0.21	−1.12
Mp	2.21	1.85	0.00	10.00	126	2.00	1.00	1.63	3.97
Intellect	0.86	1.44	0.00	6.00	56	0.00	0.00	2.06	3.89
Zf	10.49	3.51	5.00	20.00	140	9.00	7.00	0.56	−0.37
Zd	1.84	3.76	−5.00	12.00	128	1.00	0.50	1.05	0.86
Blends	4.11	2.94	0.00	11.00	126	4.00	1.00	0.12	−1.24
Blends/R	0.17	0.12	0.00	0.48	126	0.18	0.04	0.27	−0.68
Col-Shd Blends	0.37	[0.72]	0.00	3.00	36	0.00	0.00	2.08	3.88

Table 70. (Continued)

Variable	Mean	SD	Min	Max	Freq	Median	Mode	SK	KU
Afr	0.57	0.21	0.21	0.88	140	0.64	0.75	−0.27	−1.57
Populars	5.24	1.50	2.00	10.00	140	5.00	5.00	1.07	2.62
X+%	0.56	0.11	0.29	0.94	140	0.55	0.50	0.88	2.24
F+%	0.52	0.19	0.18	1.00	140	0.50	0.50	0.49	0.32
X−%	0.18	0.11	0.00	0.47	138	0.16	0.07	0.96	0.33
Xu%	0.24	0.10	0.00	0.43	138	0.27	0.18	−0.28	−0.89
S−%	0.21	[0.29]	0.00	1.00	64	0.00	0.00	1.22	0.53
Isolate/R	0.26	0.13	0.00	0.50	134	0.29	0.43	−0.17	−0.79
H	2.44	1.77	0.00	8.00	136	2.00	2.00	1.26	0.79
(H)	1.80	1.09	0.00	5.00	118	2.00	2.00	0.13	0.25
HD	1.81	1.22	0.00	5.00	124	2.00	2.00	0.60	−0.20
(Hd)	0.27	0.59	0.00	3.00	30	0.00	0.00	2.48	6.76
Hx	0.00	[0.00]	0.00	0.00	0	0.00	0.00	—	—
H + (H) + Hd + (Hd)	6.33	2.64	2.00	17.00	140	6.00	5.00	1.32	2.71
A	8.43	2.31	3.00	15.00	140	9.00	9.00	−0.27	0.14
(A)	0.41	[0.62]	0.00	3.00	50	0.00	0.00	1.59	3.04
Ad	4.21	[2.40]	0.00	7.00	130	5.00	6.00	−0.40	−1.33
(Ad)	0.06	[0.33]	0.00	2.00	4	0.00	0.00	5.72	31.17
An	0.23	[0.51]	0.00	3.00	28	0.00	0.00	2.86	10.68
Art	0.41	0.71	0.00	4.00	46	0.00	0.00	2.39	8.07
Ay	0.16	[0.44]	0.00	2.00	18	0.00	0.00	2.88	7.91
Bl	0.19	[0.39]	0.00	1.00	26	0.00	0.00	1.63	0.68
Bt	0.57	0.97	0.00	6.00	54	0.00	0.00	2.98	12.90
Cg	2.00	1.21	0.00	4.00	128	2.00	1.00	0.14	−1.10
Cl	0.67	[0.77]	0.00	2.00	68	0.00	0.00	0.64	−1.03
Ex	0.04	[0.20]	0.00	1.00	6	0.00	0.00	4.56	19.10
Fi	0.27	[0.59]	0.00	2.00	28	0.00	0.00	2.04	3.00
Food	0.74	[1.12]	0.00	3.00	54	0.00	0.00	1.27	0.04
Ge	0.01	[0.12]	0.00	1.00	2	0.00	0.00	8.27	67.44
Hh	0.57	1.23	0.00	9.00	48	0.00	0.00	4.82	30.32
Ls	1.29	0.95	0.00	4.00	100	2.00	2.00	−0.08	−0.70
Na	1.63	[1.09]	0.00	3.00	108	2.00	2.00	−0.30	−1.19
Sc	0.51	[0.73]	0.00	3.00	58	0.00	0.00	1.71	3.32
Sx	0.06	[0.38]	0.00	3.00	4	0.00	0.00	7.28	54.54
Xy	0.00	[0.00]	0.00	0.00	0	0.00	0.00	—	—
Idiographic	1.59	1.46	0.00	8.00	122	1.00	1.00	1.83	4.15
DV	0.71	[1.06]	0.00	3.00	56	0.00	0.00	1.32	0.36
INCOM	1.59	[1.12]	0.00	5.00	108	2.00	2.00	0.12	−0.27
DR	0.31	[0.60]	0.00	3.00	36	0.00	0.00	2.16	5.24
FABCOM	0.51	[0.69]	0.00	2.00	56	0.00	0.00	0.99	−0.28
DV2	0.01	[0.12]	0.00	1.00	2	0.00	0.00	8.27	67.44
INC2	0.91	[1.29]	0.00	6.00	70	0.50	0.00	1.87	3.67
DR2	0.10	[0.35]	0.00	2.00	12	0.00	0.00	3.69	14.12
FAB2	0.23	[0.66]	0.00	3.00	18	0.00	0.00	3.05	8.69
ALOG	0.10	[0.35]	0.00	2.00	12	0.00	0.00	3.69	14.12
CONTAM	0.00	0.00	0.00	0.00	0	0.00	0.00	—	—
Sum 6 Sp Sc	4.49	3.30	0.00	15.00	136	3.00	3.00	1.39	1.20
Lvl 2 Sp Sc	1.26	[1.91]	0.00	10.00	74	1.00	0.00	2.31	6.22
WSum6	13.27	12.02	0.00	61.00	136	8.00	8.00	1.77	3.05
AB	0.14	[0.39]	0.00	2.00	18	0.00	0.00	2.77	7.48
AG	1.13	1.23	0.00	4.00	72	1.00	0.00	0.49	−1.25
CFB	0.00	0.00	0.00	0.00	0	0.00	0.00	—	—
COP	0.89	1.04	0.00	4.00	70	0.50	0.00	0.85	−0.23
CP	0.00	[0.00]	0.00	0.00	0	0.00	0.00	—	—
MOR	1.97	[2.02]	0.00	7.00	106	1.00	1.00	1.38	1.30
PER	1.63	1.56	0.00	5.00	98	1.00	0.00	0.61	−1.04
PSV	0.34	[0.51]	0.00	2.00	46	0.00	0.00	1.00	−0.24

vein, the undersocialized group was significantly more likely to have AdjD > 0, whereas the socialized group was significantly more likely to have D < 0.

Among some additional differences between these two groups, the adolescents with undersocialized conduct disorder were significantly more likely than the socialized group to have an excess of *CF + C* over *FC* responses, a Lambda of 1.00 or more, and a high *X-%*. On the other hand, the socialized group had a significantly greater frequency of *Xu%* > 20. These differences in adequacy of mediation raise the possibility that, among misbehaving adolescents who come to professional attention, those who are "socialized" in DSM-III terms are inclined to be unconventional in their views and judgments, whereas those who are "undersocialized" are inclined to be inaccurate and unrealistic in the impressions they form.

CASE 8—AN UNDERSOCIALIZED CONDUCT DISORDER

This 15-year-old male had been in juvenile detention for 11 days at the time of this evaluation. He is 5 feet 10 inches, weighs 165 pounds, and looks older than his age. He had completed 2 months of the 10th grade at the time of incarceration.

He is the third of five children (sister, age 19, is a high school graduate who works in office; sister, age 17, is in the third year of high school; sister, age 13, is in the seventh grade; brother, age 10, is in fifth grade). All siblings have, or are doing average or better in school and none have exhibited any conduct problems. His father is 38 and works as a housepainter. His mother is age 37 and is a housewife. There is no reported psychiatric history in immediate family other than problems with the subject. The family attends church, and the younger children also attend Sunday school regularly, although the subject often refuses.

The subject has been a behavior problem in school since the sixth grade. Most of the reported problems concern fighting with peers. He became noted as the "class bully" in the sixth grade and was disciplined in both seventh and eighth grades for fighting (both instances involved other boys and occurred during gym classes). He was placed on probation in ninth grade for stealing pens from a teacher's desk and was suspected for breaking into student lockers, a suspicion that was not proven. His grades were above average through the eighth grade, although marginal in ninth grade.

He apparently began using marijuana in the seventh or eighth grade, but claims he has never used other drugs, a claim that is regarded as being very questionable by his teachers and the school counselor. He is also reported to have been a source of drugs for students during eighth and ninth grades but was never caught. Shortly after beginning the tenth grade, he was apprehended in the girls' gym locker room in possession of three purses plus a plastic bag filled with underwear. He claimed it was to be a joke and that he was going to send the underwear to the girls in the mail. He was placed on probation again and had to report to a detention room for 1 hour each day after school. Shortly thereafter, he began to be truant, often missing 2 or 3 days per week.

His parents have been cooperative with school authorities, but the mother says the boy lies to them and is difficult to manage. When he began to be overly aggressive in seventh grade, the parents arranged for him to attend a 4-week camp during the summers following the seventh and eighth grades. Since being placed on probation in ninth grade, he has seen a church counselor weekly who reports that he has been cooperative and contrite because of his problems. However, the counselor also feels that subject has a very "distorted sense of values."

The current incarceration occurred after he was apprehended in a neighbor's house during the day. He had a bag filled with valuables and a second bag with some underwear of two young females, sisters, who live in the house.

The developmental history reported by mother is unremarkable; apparently, he walked at 1 year, talked in sentences between the ages of 2 and 3, and has had no serious illness or injuries. The mother notes that he and his oldest sister have argued frequently, but she reports that he gets along well with his other siblings. She reports that the subject and his father played baseball and football during his early developmental years and often went fishing together. She also notes that the father sometimes took the subject on painting jobs during summer and paid him as a helper. The mother insists that the subject and his father were very close until about age 12, at which time the subject became more interested in peers. He played one year on the junior high baseball team and liked to ride his bicycle with others.

Beginning in seventh grade, he exhibited much more aggression than usual. The mother reports that he began to talk a lot about unfair teachers and enemies at school. His older sisters complain that he is often in their room without permission, and the 19-year-old has accused him of stealing money from her purse although this has never been verified. According to his teachers, he "hangs around" with a group of two or three boys who are suspected of being involved with drugs. He shows little apparent interest in girls, but in an interview, he says that two or three write notes to him in school and that he has been thinking about "taking one out." He denies, but then admits to regular masturbation. He became quite upset when asked about homosexuality, vigorously denying any incidents and speaking very negatively about homosexuals, claiming to know of one at school. He says that he would like to have intercourse but is afraid of getting AIDS.

He says that he was robbing the house for money to buy a guitar and says that the theft of the underwear was "just to scare them." He denies hallucinations or strange thoughts. He would like to be placed on probation, but would also like to attend another school "where they have better teachers." He feels that he has a good family and regrets the problems that he has caused for them.

A neurological examination (including CT scan and stress EEG) are negative. The results of the WISC-R reveal Verbal IQ = 113, Performance IQ = 111 (Information = 10; Comprehension = 10; Arithmetic = 15; Similarities = 14; Vocabulary = 14; Digit Span = 15; Picture Completion = 16; Picture Arrangement = 10; Block Design = 11; Object Assembly = 13; Coding = 15). On neuropsychological screening, he achieved a WMS MQ = 109; Recall 100% for both semantic and figures; TPT rt 2'41; lft 2'09; both 1'52; remembered = 7; localized = 5; Aphasia 0 errors; Trails A = 46" (no errors); Trails B = 63" (no errors).

The assessment questions include (a) Is there a psychiatric disability present that would mitigate the juvenile court decision; (b) how does the theft of underwear relate to the problem; and (c) what are the recommendations concerning residential center placement versus special school placement versus probation with outpatient treatment?

Case 8. A 15-Year-Old Male

Card	Response		Inquiry	Scoring
I	1. Nothin I evr saw, just a dumb looking face, lik a cat thts gettin ready to bite sb	E:	(Rpts Ss resp)	WSo FMao (AD) 3.5 AG
		S:	Its got big teeth & crooked eyes lik som cat frm some othr world, lik anothr planet, its not really a cat but a cat monstr, its got its mouth open lik its ready to bite & its ears r all stickg out lik its realy mad	
		E:	Look som mor, I thk u'll find smthg else too	
	2. Mayb its a thng lik the Ninjas throw	E:	(Rpts Ss resp)	Wo F- Sc 1.0 DV,PER
		S:	Whaddaucallem, thm thngs l w dagers on em, all th way around, c l thse dager thgs (Dd34) & thy whip them around & thy r really sharp & thyr better thn a knife, I thk its a starrip, yeah a starrip I'v seen em in lots of Ninja movies	
II	3. Thts a mess, lik sb got shot in th stomach u can c th hole & th bld all ovr	E:	(Rpts Ss resp)	WSv/+ CF- An,Bl 4.5 MOR
		S:	Sb shot him hes got a big hole in the stomach & thers bld up hre & down here	
		E:	I'm not sur I c it th way u do	
	S: Can I just look at a part?	S:	Lk all th red is bld u cant c any legs or arms or head its j sb's stomach tht got shot & heres the hole	
	E: Whatever u want			
	4. Just the blk ll 2 dogs but thr noses r glued togethr	E:	(Rpts Ss resp)	D+ mpo 2 Ad P 2.0 FAB2
		S:	Its not the whol dogs just their heads & necks & sb wanted to hang thm up on th wall, no wait, scratch tht out, mayb its just a pict tht sb painted & thy used too much paint where the noses r thyr not really glued togethr	
III	5. Two guys fightn ovr st	E:	(Rpts Ss resp)	D+ Mao 2 H,Sx P 3.0 AG,PER
		S:	Idk wht thyr fightg abt especially w/o any clothes on, but thyr both pullg hard on ths thg in th middl lik pullg it aprt	
		E:	U said thy dont hav clothes on	
		S:	Yep, u can c thr dongs, realy weird man, mayb thyr som k o naked wrestlrs or st & whoevr gets th most of ths middl thg is th winner thy do tht kinda thg ovr in China & Japan I saw em on TV but thy mak em covr thr dongs whn thyr on TV	

	#	Response		Inquiry	Scoring
	6.	Thse thgs up here ll guitars	E: S: E: S:	(Rpts Ss resp) Yeah, lik fancy electric guitars Fancy Well thy don't hav a regulr shape, thyr a special made kind lik th heavy metal guys use, neat	Do Fu 2 Sc
IV	7.	Man thts mean lookin, som big frog whos got an awful big tongue or st (laughs) he's prob the jumpin winner	E: S: E: S: E: S:	(Rpts Ss resp) Well he's sur got big feet & his head is up here & he's got ths big thg stickin out, mayb his tongue, but mayb somthg else (laughs) Somthg else? Don't ask me its just pretty big for a tongue U said he is prob the jumpin winner He's so big thre he cld jump mor thn any of thos othr frogs lik in contests so he must b the winner bec tht's why his tongue is out so far out, he's all jumpd out	Wo Fu A 2.0 ALOG
V	8.	Tht ll a rabit tht got slicd rite dwn the middl	E: S: E: S:	(Rpts Ss resp) Its l split dwn th middl & half is laid out on ea side, lik som huntr did it aftr he shot him Can u sho me how ur cg it Lik th head & ear & th body & th leg	W+ Fu 2 Ad 2.5 MOR
VI	9.	Tht ll som cat tht got run ovr	E: S: E: S:	(Rpts Ss resp) It just lks all flatend, lik a truck ran ovr it, c th head & whiskrs & th legs stickin out I'm not sur why it ll a cat I gues th whiskrs cats got whiskrs lik tht	Wo Fo A P 2.5 MOR
	10.	U kno up here it ll a face	E: S: E: S:	(Rpts Ss resp) Sorta l a face of a man, its not clear tho so u can't c it very well but u can almost c th eyes & the nose prt, just a face, sorta weird lkg Weird looking? U just cant c it too well, it ll som guy fr *Star Wars* or smthg lik tht	Ddo F− (Hd)
VII	v11.	Tht ll ur hip bones	E: S:	(Rpts Ss resp) Well thyr shapd l tht, whaddaucallem, pelvis bones, l whre ur legs & hips come to join up c ths prt up here is for the hip joint & dwn here is for the leg joint	Wo F− An 2.5

Case 8. (Continued)

Card	Response	Inquiry	Scoring
VIII	12. Tht ll a couple lions or tigers tearg up som A tht thy caught	E: (Rpts Ss resp) S: U kno lik thy show on TV whn the lions run aftr som A & catch it, thy kil it & thy tear chnks off E: Show me how ur seeg it S: Look, heres the lions (D1) & the rest is som A tht thy killd & thyr tearg it up c th bones hre (D3) & ths dwn hre (D2) is lik bloody meat E: Bloody meat S: Sur man, its all red & orange lik meat & up here (D4) is whts left of the head	W+ FMa.CF− 2 A,Ad,Bl P 4.5 AG,MOR
	13. Just ths prt is sorta ll a mask, lik th guy in *Star Wars* had	E: (Rpts Ss resp) S: Its pointd on top & thse white parts r r where u look out out & th rest protects u & nobody can tell who u r, neat huh E: I'm not sur I kno where ur looking S: Look hre (outlines D8)	DSo Fu (Hd),Sc 4.0
IX	14. Thts lik som guy w paint all ovr his face	E: (Rpts Ss resp) S: I've seen guys who paint up lik ths to go to concerts so thy can really get into it, ths guys got orange hair & green on him & pink around his neck, really neat E: Is it just th face & neck S: Yeah, his hair is stickg up, wow, he just painted his whole face	Wo CFu (Hd) 5.5 PER
X	15. Thes r far out, thres anothr guys face all paintd diff colors, he's got pink hair & he's wearg a helmet	E: (Rpts Ss resp) S: C his hair is all pink & hes got got som funny metal helmet on & a green mustache, ths stuff dont count E: A metal helmet S: Its all grey, lik metal helmets, but I dk wht ths is out here (outside D9)	DdS+ CF.FC'− Hd,Cg 4.0
	16. Ths ll a spider grabg a bug, one here too	E: (Rpts Ss resp) S: Ths blu thg ll a spidr c all th legs & it caught ths litl bug & its gonna eat it or smthg or whtevr thy do to em in thr web, thy both got one	D+ FMao 2 A P 4.0 AG

17.	Ths prt ll an ant tht got steppd on & a lotta yellow mush is comg outa his head	E:	(Rpts Ss resp)	D+ ma.CF− A,Id 4.0 FAB,MOR
		S:	If u step on an ant a lotta yellow stuff comes out lik ths, c ths is whts left of him (D7) & ths yellow stuff is ozing outa his head, bad man	
18.	Thes thgs r lik a cpl bugs	E:	(Rpts Ss resp)	Do Fo 2 A
		S:	Just littl bugs, thy just ll tht, I dk wht kind tho	
19.	Hey, tht ll a rabbits head	E:	(Rpts Ss resp)	Do Fo Ad
		S:	Just here (D5), c th eyes & the ears, just a rabbits face	
20.	And ths litl part ll a bullet, thts all man	E:	(Rpts Ss resp)	Ddo F− Sc PER
		S:	Its just lik a bullet, lik thos special bullets thy hav tht can go thru anythg, thy hav thm u kno & thy ll ths, I've seen em in pictures	

307

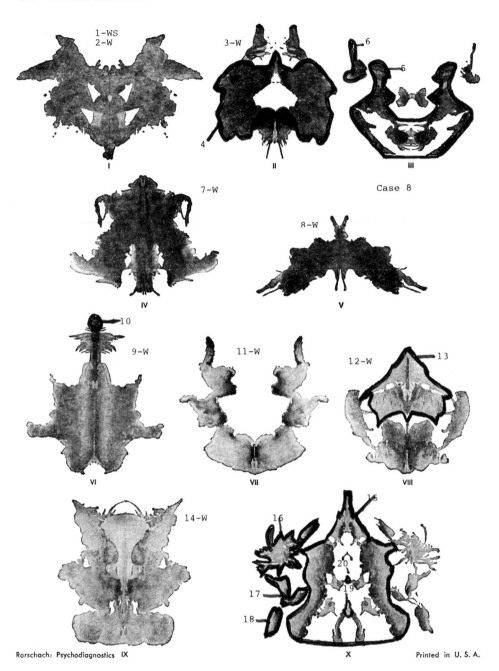

Case 8

Rorschach: Psychodiagnostics

Printed in U. S. A.

Case 8

Case 8   **Sequence of Scores**

Card	No	Loc	#	Determinant(s)	(2)	Content(s)	Pop	Z	Special Scores
I	1	WSo	1	FMao		(Ad)		3.5	AG
	2	Wo	1	F-		Sc		1.0	DV,PER
II	3	WS/	1	CF-		An,Bl		4.5	MOR
	4	D+	1	mpo	2	Ad	P	3.0	FAB2
III	5	D+	1	Mao	2	H,Sx	P	3.0	AG,PER
	6	Do	2	Fu	2	Sc			
IV	7	Wo	1	Fu		A		2.0	ALOG
V	8	W+	1	Fu	2	Ad		2.5	MOR
VI	9	Wo	1	Fo		A	P	2.5	MOR
	10	Ddo	23	F-		(Hd)			
VII	11	Wo	1	F-		An		2.5	
VIII	12	W+	1	FMa.CF-	2	A,Ad,Bl	P	4.5	AG,MOR
	13	DSo	8	Fu		(Hd),Sc		4.0	
IX	14	Wo	1	CFu		(Hd)		5.5	PER
X	15	DdS+	22	CF.FC'-		Hd,Cg		4.0	
	16	D+	1	FMao	2	A	P	4.0	AG
	17	D+	7	ma.CF-		A,Id		4.0	FAB,MOR
	18	Do	13	Fo	2	A			
	19	Do	5	Fo		Ad			
	20	Ddo		F-		Sc			PER

Case 8   **Structural Summary**

Location Features	Determinants Blends · Single	Contents	S-Constellation

| | | | | H = 1, 0 | NO . . FV+VF+V+FD>2 |

Location
Features

Zf   = 15
ZSum = 50.5
ZEst = 49.0

W = 9
  (Wv = 0)
D = 8
Dd = 3
S = 4

DQ
. . . . . (FQ−)
+ = 7 (3)
o = 12 (4)
v/+ = 1 (1)
v = 0 (0)

Form Quality

	FQx	FQf	MQual	SQx
+	= 0	0	0	0
o	= 7	3	1	1
u	= 5	4	0	1
−	= 8	4	0	2
none	= 0	—	0	0

Determinants
Blends
FM.CF
FC.FC'
m.CF

Single
M	= 1
FM	= 2
m	= 1
FC	= 0
CF	= 2
C	= 0
Cn	= 0
FC'	= 0
C'F	= 0
C'	= 0
FT	= 0
TF	= 0
T	= 0
FV	= 0
VF	= 0
V	= 0
FY	= 0
YF	= 0
Y	= 0
Fr	= 0
rF	= 0
FD	= 0
F	= 11

(2) = 7

Contents
H	= 1, 0
(H)	= 0, 0
Hd	= 1, 0
(Hd)	= 3, 0
Hx	= 0, 0
A	= 6, 0
(A)	= 0, 0
Ad	= 3, 1
(Ad)	= 1, 0
An	= 2, 0
Art	= 0, 0
Ay	= 0, 0
Bl	= 0, 2
Bt	= 0, 0
Cg	= 0, 1
Cl	= 0, 0
Ex	= 0, 0
Fd	= 0, 0
Fi	= 0, 0
Ge	= 0, 0
Hh	= 0, 0
Ls	= 0, 0
Na	= 0, 0
Sc	= 3, 1
Sx	= 0, 1
Xy	= 0, 0
Id	= 0, 1

S-Constellation
NO . .	FV+VF+V+FD>2
YES . .	Col−Shd Bl>0
NO . .	Ego<.31,>.44
YES . .	MOR > 3
NO . .	Zd > +− 3.5
YES . .	es > EA
YES . .	CF+C > FC
YES . .	X+% < .70
YES . .	S > 3
NO . .	P < 3 or > 8
YES . .	Pure H < 2
NO . .	R < 17
7	TOTAL

Special Scorings

		Lv1	Lv2
DV	=	1x1	0x2
INC	=	0x2	0x4
DR	=	0x3	0x6
FAB	=	1x4	1x7
ALOG	=	1x5	
CON	=	0x7	
	SUM6	= 4	
	WSUM6	= 17	

AB	= 0	CP	= 0
AG	= 4	MOR	= 5
CFB	= 0	PER	= 4
COP	= 0	PSV	= 0

Case 8   **Ratios, Percentages, and Derivations**

R = 20   L = 1.22

EB = 1: 5.0	EA = 6.0	EBPer = 5.0
eb = 5: 1	es = 6	D = 0
	Adj es = 5	Adj D = 0

FM = 3 : C' = 1   T = 0
m = 2 : V = 0   Y = 0

a:p	= 5: 1	Sum6	= 4
Ma:Mp	= 1: 0	Lv2	= 1
2AB+Art+Ay=0		WSum6	= 17
M −	= 0	Mnone	= 0

P	= 5
X+%	= 0.35
F+%	= 0.27
X−%	= 0.40
S−%	= 0.25
Xu%	= 0.25

| FC:CF+C = 0: 5 |
Pure C	= 0
Afr	= 0.82
S	= 4
Blends:R	= 3:20
CP	= 0

COP = 0	AG = 4
Food	= 0
Isolate/R	= 0.00
H:(H)Hd(Hd)	= 1:4
(HHd):(AAd)	= 3:1
H+A:Hd+Ad	= 7:9

Zf	= 15
Zd	= +1.5
W:D:Dd	= 9: 8: 3
W:M	= 9: 1
DQ+	= 7
DQv	= 0

3r+(2)/R	= 0.35
Fr+rF	= 0
FD	= 0
An+Xy	= 2
MOR	= 5

SCZI = 3   DEPI = 4   CDI = 2   S-CON = 7   HVI = Yes   OBS = No

INTERPRETIVE ROUTINE FOR CASE 8

The structural data reveal the first positive Key variable is that the value for Lambda is greater than 0.99. This finding suggests that the appropriate strategy for reviewing the clusters of data will be:

PROCESSING → MEDIATION → IDEATION → CONTROLS →
AFFECT → SELF-PERCEPTION → INTERPERSONAL PERCEPTION

Processing—Case 8   The data related to information processing for Case 8 are shown in Table 71.

Table 71.   Processing Data for Case 8

L = 1.22	$W:D:Dd$ = 9:8:3	Zd = +1.5	$DQ+$ = 7
Zf = 15	$W:M$ = 9:1	PSV = 0	$DQv/+$ = 1
HVI = No	OBS = No		DQv = 0

LOCATION SEQUENCING

I	W,W	IV	W	VII	W
II	WS,D	V	W	VIII	W,DS
III	D,D	VI	W,DdS	IX	W
				X	DdS,D,D,D,D,Dd

The presence of the High *Lambda* Style indicates that he usually is oriented to simplify a stimulus field in ways that will make it easier to manage. When a High *Lambda* Style influences processing activities to limit outputs or make them easier to deal with, the number of *W* answers is usually lower than average, as is the frequency of synthesized responses. Such a pattern does not exist in this case, probably because a Hypervigilant style is also present. Nearly half of his answers are *W* responses and he gives seven *DQ+* responses. In fact, there are more *W* than *D* responses, and the *W:M* ratio is 9:1, suggesting that he will often set processing goals that may exceed his functional capacities. The *Zd* score (+1.5) indicates that his scanning activity probably is no more or less efficient than found for most of his peers. It is likely that the greater than expected effort is the product of the Hypervigilant style.

Thus, even though a High *Lambda* Style exists, there is no evidence to suggest that he is negligent or haphazard in dealing with new information. This is probably because he is also hypervigilant. In this circumstance, the hypervigilance tends to supersede the orientation to oversimplify or neglect complex fields and prompts a substantial effort to process new information more thoroughly than might be the case otherwise.

Mediation—Case 8   The data regarding the cognitive mediation activities for Case 8 are shown in Table 72.

The consequences of the composite High *Lambda* Style and Hypervigilant style appear to have a significant impact on the way that he translates stimulus inputs. He gives only five Popular answers, which is somewhat lower than expected for his age. This suggests that even when obvious cues concerning a translation exists, he does not give the obvious response. Instead, he is more prone to distort inputs, as indicated by the substantial $X\text{-}\%$ (.40), or translate them in a more personalized manner ($Xu\% = .25$). In some

Table 72.   **Cognitive Mediation Data for Case 8**

Lambda	= 1.22	OBS	= Neg	MINUS FEATURES	
P	= 5	$X + \%$	= .35	2,3,10,11,12,15,17,20	
FQx+	= 0	$F + \%$	= .27		
FQxo	= 7	$Xu\%$	= .25		
FQxu	= 5	$X - \%$	= .40		
FQx−	= 8	$S - \%$	= .25		
FQxnone	= 0	CONFAB	= 0		

instances, a High *Lambda* Style will produce a more conventional approach to reality, which will be manifested by an $F + \%$ that is substantially higher than the $X + \%$. That is not the case here. The $F + \%$ is quite low (.27); eight of his 11 Pure F answers are either Unusual or minus.

A neurologically related problem could be a possible explanation for this, but there is no evidence in the intelligence test data or the neuropsychological screening to support that contention. Thus, it seems most likely that his translations of events are markedly influenced by his sets about the world that are created by his hypervigilance. He tends to see what he wants or expects to see and ignores things in his environment that do not coincide with those expectations or wants.

In some cases, the presence of considerable anger will lead to distortions of reality, but that does not appear to be the true for this case. Only two of his eight minus answers involve the use of space. Similarly, in some cases, the $X + \%$ will be lowered significantly because of the failure to use form in developing an answer, but again, that is not the case here. All his answers include some use of form. Actually, his minus answers are spread through out the record, having been given to Cards I, II, VI, VII, VIII, and X.

Two focus on anatomy and two others have a science content; at first glance, there is no homogeneity among the eight, but that may not be true. Three of the eight, Responses 3, 12, and 17, include MOR content, somebody shot in the stomach, lions or tigers tearing up some animal, and an ant that got stepped on. Two others, Responses 2 and 20 have a science content, but both involve destructive weapons (a Ninja "starrip" and a special bullet), and two of the remaining three are strange faces. Collectively, seven of the eight seem to relate to issues of threat, damage, or the potential for damage, and at least three, (somebody shot in the stomach on Card II; a face of a man, some guy from *Star Wars* on Card VI; and an ant that got stepped on and a lot of yellow mush is coming out of his head on Card X) deviate substantially from an appropriate use of form. Collectively, the eight minus responses seem related to a set or preoccupation about frailty, guardedness, and a failure of defenses.

Overall, his mediational operations are quite different than expected for a young adolescent. He tends to disregard reality far too much, and seems to distort reality when it meets his own expectations or sets. The result is a considerable detachment from the real world and a substitution for it by an inner world that emphasizes potential threat and/or damage. Stated simply, the composite of his High *Lambda* Style and his Hypervigilant style cause him to ignore, bend, or distort reality much more than should be the case, and this will lead often to inappropriate behaviors.

Ideation—Case 8   The data concerning ideation for Case 8 are shown in Table 73.

The data for the *EB* (1:5:0) and *EBPer* (5.0) indicate that, ordinarily, he is not a person who will stop and consider various solutions to a problem. On the contrary, he

Table 73.   Ideation Data for Case 8

EB	= 1:5.0	EBPer = 5.0	M QUALITY		SPECIAL SCORES			
eb	= 5:1	(FM = 3 m = 2)	+ = 0	DV	= 1	DV2	= 0
a:p	= 5:1	$M^a:M^p$ = 1:0	o = 1	INC	= 0	INC2	= 0
2AB + Art + Ay = 0			u = 0	DR	= 0	DR2	= 0
MOR	= 5		− = 0	FAB	= 1	FAB2	= 1
				ALOG	= 1	SUM6	= 4
RESPONSES TO BE READ FOR QUALITY				CON	= 0	WSUM6	= 17
	5						

is influenced strongly by feelings and, invariably, will adopt a more intuitive, trial-and-error approach to decision making. In many circumstances, this tactic will not be a major liability, but, in this case, where there is also a High *Lambda* Style and a Hypervigilant style, the result can be disastrous. The tendency to oversimplify tends to negate some of the feedback from trial-and-error behavior, but more importantly, the hypervigilant set often causes some of the feedback from the trial-and-error behavior to be misinterpreted in light of the set. The result is a proclivity for strange thinking. Actually, his thinking is not as markedly distorted or strange as might be predicted, but it is cause for concern when examined closely.

There is no reason to suspect that his attention or concentration are impaired by an excess of peripheral ideation. The left-side value of the *eb* (5), is well within the expected range. On the other hand, the values for the *a:p* ratio (5:1) are more disparate than desired. The broad difference suggests that his thinking is not very flexible and his values are well set. Again, this might not be a liability except for the Hypervigilant style, which includes a very marked and somewhat negative orientation about the world. The data for the $M^a:M^p$ ratio and the Intellectualization Index are negative, but the frequency of MOR responses (5) is very important. The substantial value for MOR indicates that much of his thinking will be marked by pessimistic sets that cause him to view the world negatively, and assume that few events will be favorable for him.

His inflexibility and negative or pessimistic thinking become compounded much more by episodes of strangeness that mark his thinking. He has only four Critical Special Scores, a value that is within acceptable limits for adolescents, but, the *WSum6* value of 17 is much greater than expected. It signals much more cognitive slippage than should be the case for a 15-year-old. Actually, all four of his Critical Special Scores have serious implications. The DV answer (starrip) is much more deviant than most DV answers. The two FABCOM answers are also much more bizarre than expected from a 15-year-old (dogs, but their noses are glued together; an ant that got stepped on and lot of yellow mush is coming out of his head). The ALOG answer may illustrate his most distorted form of logic (some big frog whose got an awful big tongue, he's probably the jumping winner . . . he must be the winner because that's why his tongue is so far out).

Collectively, these four answers signal very strained and illogical judgment, and support the notion that his thinking often deviates markedly from reality. Even his single *M* response conveys this sort of strangeness or preoccupation in his thinking (two guys fighting over something . . . they don't have any clothes on . . . you can see their dongs, really weird man).

Overall, his thinking is cause for concern because he is not very flexible in the way that he thinks about things and is prone to distort and/or ignore the results of feedback. His thinking is not really pathological if compared with that of psychotic people, but it involves much strained logic and detachment from reality. It is likely the product of the combination of the High *Lambda* and Hypervigilant styles.

Controls—Case 8   The data regarding capacity for control and tolerance for stress are shown in Table 74.

Table 74.   Controls and Stress Tolerance Data for Case 8

EB = 1:5.0		EA = 6.0			D = 0	
eb = 5:1		es = 6	Adjes = 5		AdjD = 0	
FM = 3	C' = 1	T = 0			CDI = 2	
m = 2	V = 0	Y = 0				

The D Scores are both zero, implying that his capacity for control and tolerance for stress is not unlike that of most of his peers. However, that conclusion is probably misleading. Although the Adjusted D Score is zero, the value for the *EA* is only 6.0, which is lower than average for one of his age. As has been noted earlier, low *EA* values must be interpreted as signifying limited resource, and as such, constitute a vulnerability for stimulus overload. Currently, the values for *es* and the Adjusted *es* of 6 and 5 are not high and thus, no overload exists. This is mainly because the experience of need states (*FM* = 3) is modest and there is a very low right-side *eb* (1) value. If experienced need states increase slightly, and/or if internal experiences of internally felt distress increase to levels that are more typical for his age, the *es* or Adjusted *es* could easily reach a value of 9. In that condition, the D or Adjusted D scores would fall into the minus range and create a tendency to impulsiveness in both thinking and behavior.

In general, he should be regarded as being fragile with regard to his capacity for control or tolerance for stress. It seems obvious that his High *Lambda* Style forms a tenuous defense on which he relies heavily, but its effectiveness is impeded by his limited resources plus the presence of his hypervigilant state. Hypervigilance requires the commitment of considerable resource to maintain the required state of alertness, and he simply does not have enough resource to do so over a lengthy period. In effect, he is a youngster who is vulnerable to a loss of control quite easily, and it seems likely that some of his rather bizarre behaviors reflect instances in which such a situation has occurred.

Affect—Case 8   The data concerning affect for Case 8 are shown in Table 75.

Table 75.   Affect Data for Case 8

DEPI = 4				BLENDS
EB = 1:5.0		$EBPer$ = 5.0		FM.CF
eb = 5:1		$FC:CF + C$ = 0:5		FM.FC'
		Pure C = 0		m.CF
C' = 1	T = 0	Afr = 0.82		
V = 0	Y = 0	S = 4		
		Blends/R = 3:20		
		CP = 0		

Some of the data concerning affect are not unexpected for a pervasive extratensive youngster. He is an intuitive person who merges his feelings into his thinking in most decision-making situations; and he is oriented toward trial-and-error behaviors. The *WSumC* is greater than the *SUMC'* (5:1) and the *Afr* (0.82) is well into the expected range for a person with this pervasive style. In other words, there is no evidence of affective constriction, and there is evidence that he is quite willing to process and be involved with emotional stimuli.

There are, however, important findings among these data. First, the right-side value for *eb* (1) is quite low. Second, the *FC:CF + C* ratio (0:5) is unusual for one of his age. Third, there are a substantial number of *S* responses (4), and, finally, the number of blends (3) is modest.

The low right-side *eb* value has been noted earlier. It consists of only one *C'* response and indicates that he does not experience as much internalized negative affective stimulation as do most people. The implication is that, unlike most people, he is not prone to empathy and is not sensitive about feelings. The absence of *T* and the hypervigilant state apparently have caused him to become somewhat detached about feelings. The *FC:CF + C* finding (0:5) indicates that he does not modulate his feelings very much when expressing them. This is quite unexpected for his age. He is an intense person who, when expressing affect, will usually leave no doubt about his feelings. This lack of modulation is very important in light of the elevation in *S*. It signifies the presence of considerable negativism and hostility. When considered in light of his hypervigilance, it seems likely that he is a hateful person, and his hate probably influences many of his decisions and behaviors. When hate or hostility merge in a person who does not modulate emotional expression very much, the consequence is often ominous. That probability is increased in this case because four of his five chromatic color answers have a minus form quality, and the fifth is Unusual. The implication is that when he releases emotion, he will often do so in ways that disregard convention or reality. The low proportion of blends is probably a product of his High *Lambda* Style, that is, he simply will not become involved very much with complexity when feelings are involved. Unfortunately, his way of handling emotion involves distortion.

Overall, he might be regarded as a potentially volatile person when his emotions are inspected closely. He uses his feelings much of the time when reaching decisions, but apparently, he does not allow his feelings to manifest directly in most situations. He is very hostile but probably conceals that hostility and releases it only in indirect ways. He has also adopted a defensive pattern through which emotions do not cost him in the sense that he holds them in or ruminates about failures to express them. On the contrary, he uses them in ways that are designed to fend off perceived threats from others. It would be foolish to disregard his destructive potential.

Self Perception—Case 8   The data concerning self-perception for Case 8 are shown in Table 76.

The data concerning self-perception add to concerns about his potential for destructiveness. His Egocentricity Index (0.35) falls at the lower end of the average range for his age. This leads to the speculation that he does not regard himself very favorably when he compares himself with significant others. There are no *FD* or Vista responses. Thus, there is no reason to believe that he is involved with self-examining, a process that often is quite important for the developing adolescent. Only one of his five human contents is a Pure *H* answer, indicating that his conception of people and his conception of

Table 76.   Self-Perception Data for Case 8

3r + (2)/R = 0.35	FD = 0	MOR = 5	Hx = 0	An + Xy = 2
Fr + rF = 0	Sum V = 0	H:(H) + Hd + (Hd) = 1:4		Sx = 1

RESPONSES TO BE READ

MOR Resp's	FQ − Resp's	M Resp's	FM Resp's	m Resp's
3,8,9,12,17	2,3,10,11,12,15,17,20	5	1,12,16	4,17

himself are based far less on reality than imagination. In addition, he has two Anatomy answers, indicating more body concern than should be the case for his age.

One of the most important findings among these data are the five MOR answers. They reflect a marked sense of damage or injury and suggest that his self-image is conceived as having many more negative features than he would prefer. In effect, when he compares his perceived self to his notions of what he should be, the result is unacceptable to him. All five of these answers are rather dramatic, (Card II, Response 3, ". . . a mess, like somebody got shot in the stomach"; Card V, Response 8, ". . . a rabbit that got sliced right down the middle . . . like some hunter did it after he shot him"; Card VI, Response 9, ". . . some cat that got run over"; Card VIII, Response 12, ". . . some animal that they killed and they are tearing it up"; and Card X, Response 17, "an ant that got stepped on and a lot of yellow mush is coming out of his head"). All are the result of aggression, suggesting that he perceives his negative features as having been created by the actions of others.

Three of the five MOR answers are minus (Responses 3, 8, and 17), and the remaining five minus answers add to the proposition that he feels damaged and/or extremely threatened by others. They include two weapons (Card I, Response 2, ". . . a thing like the Ninjas throw"; Card X, Response 20, ". . . a bullet . . . like those special bullets . . . that can go through anything"); a second anatomy response (Card VII, Response 11, ". . . hip bones . . . where your legs and hips come to join up"); and two face responses (Card VI, Response 10, ". . . a face . . . you cannot see it too well, it looks like some guy from *Star Wars,*" and Card X, Response 15, ". . . another guy's face all painted different colors").

The single M response (Card III, ". . . two guys fighting over something . . . you can see their dongs, really weird man") highlights a sexual preoccupation and hints at a vulnerability that he senses about his masculinity. All three of his FM responses are aggressive (a cat getting ready to bite, lions or tigers tearing up some animal, a spider grabbing a bug). They suggest an apparent belief that aggression is a way of life through which a person is able to defend against being damaged or exploited. Conversely, the two m answers seem to convey a sense of helplessness or futility, (the heads of dogs with their noses glued together, and mush coming out of the head of an ant).

Seven of his 20 answers are faces or heads. This is a disproportionate number, which often occurs in the records of people who are hypervigilant or paranoid. His hypervigilance seems to be imparted in several of his answers that emphasize his need to protect and/or reassure himself. The Response 1 cat is really mad and ready to bite; the Response 2 "starrip" is really sharp, better than a knife; the Response 6 guitars are a special made kind; the Response 7 frog is the jumping winner; the Response 13 mask has white parts where you look out and the rest protects you; the Response 14 face has paint so you can really get into it [the concerts]; the Response

15 face is wearing a helmet; and the Response 20 bullet is a special bullet that can go through anything.

Overall, there are major self-perception problems. He seems to be struggling to maintain his self-esteem, but at another level he perceives himself as a damaged or battered person and apparently blames the world for his plight. He has obvious sexual concerns that are not necessarily unusual for his age, but which are marked by more strained reasoning than should be the case for a reasonably bright 15-year-old. It appears certain that his self-concept is unreal and that many of his perceptions concerning his negative features have been exaggerated. He seems to feel that he is a psychologically battered person, and to some extent there probably have been a series of events in his life that validate that notion for him, even though the history, provided mainly by his mother, offers no supporting evidence. Whatever the cause, his self-concept problems have contributed significantly to the development of his hypervigilant state.

Interpersonal Perception—Case 8   The data regarding interpersonal perception and behaviors are shown in Table 77.

Table 77.   Interpersonal Perception Data for Case 8

CDI = 2	a:p = 5:1	T = 0	Human Cont = 5	Pure H = 1
HVI = Yes	Food = 0	PER = 4	COP = 0 AG = 4	Isolate/R = 0

RESPONSES TO BE READ

HUMAN MOVEMENT WITH PAIR	HUMAN CONTENTS
5	5,10,13,14,15

As emphasized earlier, the positive HVI is probably the most important finding in this cluster of data. It signifies that he is a guarded, distant person, who regards others with an undue suspiciousness. He does not expect to be close to people and tends to mistrust them and/or their motives. He is quite preoccupied with issues of personal space and devotes considerable energy to the maintenance of a state of hyperalertness, so as to be prepared to contend with threats by others even though he has no notion about the nature of, or circumstances under which such threats may occur.

The a:p ratio offers no useful information in the context of interpersonal perception, and as expected, there are no Food answers. The presence of five human contents signals a substantial interest in others, but in this instance, it reflects more guardedness than interest in developing social relationships. The value for PER (4) illustrates a common defense that he uses with others. It is an authoritarianlike "know-it-all" tactic that permits a defense of his integrity and, at the same time, tends to keep others at a distance.

As might be expected for a hypervigilant person, there are no COP responses, suggesting that he does not or cannot perceive relations among people as having positive features. On the other hand, there are four AG responses, which, as noted earlier, indicates that he perceives aggression as a normal phenomenon in interpersonal relationships. He expects people to be aggressive toward him, and in turn, he expects to be aggressive toward others. His only human movement answer with a pair is two guys fighting over something. Surprisingly, the Isolation Index (0) is negative, but this is probably a false negative, possibly created because of his considerable Afr (0.82). His five human contents probably illustrate his perceptions of people quite well (guys fighting, a face of a man from *Star*

Wars, a mask like the guy in *Star Wars,* a guy with paint all over his face, and another guy's face all painted different colors).

He is not a social person. On the contrary, he has developed a set about people that has caused him to become detached from others and very guarded about them. Apparently, he has abandoned notions of closeness to others and replaced those typical expectations with ones that view people as being potentially harmful.

CASE 8—SUMMARY

It is difficult to describe this young fellow without experiencing a sense of sadness, for at some time in his early life, he was probably little different than other youngsters struggling to develop. Unfortunately, his development has become seriously flawed, and he now poses a threat to himself and his world. He is a very angry person who regards others quite negatively. In part, his regard for them reflects his regard for himself. He sees himself as having been treated unfairly and expects that unfair treatment to continue. His self-concept is commensurate with that of the battered child, and yet there are no data in the history to support that conclusion. Nonetheless, it is his perception of himself.

His perception of the world is that it is a place in which aggression is commonplace, and as a result, he has become aggressive. The history suggests that his aggressiveness has been both direct and indirect. He fights with peers and steals money, pens, and underwear. Yet, the potential for more direct violence cannot be ignored. He has become accustomed to relying extensively on his feelings to make decisions and formulating his behaviors, but he has not learned to modulate his emotional expressions very well. Instead, when his feelings are released, they tend to be unbridled and more childlike. Obviously, this alienates those around him, and that alienation is exacerbated by his authoritarian, know-it-all stance.

The intensity of his hostility toward people has caused him to become more and more defensive and mistrusting, and apparently he perceives his world as a battleground on which he is continuously at odds with others. He distorts reality at will, usually in the context of his warped sets about people, and often views things through an oversimplified view of the world.

Although he can usually maintain adequate controls, they are fragile and he is vulnerable to an overload state in which some of his actions could become more impulsive. This fragility, plus his proneness to considerable distortion of reality, plus his disregard for modulating affect, plus his extreme sense of vulnerability and guardedness toward others makes for a very bad psychological mixture. It must be considered in light of the fact that aggressiveness seems to have become a way of life for him. Given this composite, it seem likely that his acts of aggression can become more and more direct unless some marked changes in his personality structure occur.

The referral asks whether there are psychological problems that might mitigate a court ruling or sentence. Obviously, there are serious psychological problems, but it is unlikely that they can be used as a basis to mitigate a ruling or sentence as many might regard him as a budding psychopathic personality. The referral also asks about the stealing of underwear. In effect, it is an aggressive act, designed to provide him with a sense of control over others: "If I can threaten you, you cannot threaten me." It also has obvious sexual implications. The final question in the referral asks for a recommendation concerning residential or special school placement versus a probationary status with outpatient treatment. It is a most difficult question to address. Under ideal circumstances, a residential treatment facility should be the selection, but, residential treatment centers are often little more than custodial housing centers in which inmates learn to abide by the rules of the center. Nonetheless, probationary status with outpatient care voids any guarantees the he will not become involved in more antisocial and/or aggressive acts in the immediate future.

Optimally, a residential setting can be found in which reasonably intense, uncovering psychotherapy might occur. It should be designed to explore the antecedents for his distorted sense of self and probably should be supplemented by some sort of family intervention, as it is difficult to believe that the sense of damage that he perceives about himself was not facilitated in the home in some way. The issue of a controlled environment is very important in light of his anger, his failure to control his emotional displays, and his unreasonable mistrust of people. A controlled environment might also reduce his sense of threat from others, but only if it truly is a therapeutic community. Unfortunately, this is the type of youngster who, if not treated aggressively in a controlled environment, will mark time until his release and spew forth his anger and frustration on the world when his release occurs.

CASE 9—SOCIALIZED AGGRESSION IN A CONDUCT DISORDER

This 14-year-old male was referred for evaluation by the assistant principal of the junior high school that he attends. The subject has a high frequency of truancy, he is suspected to be part of a group of boys alleged to have set a fire in the girls' gymnasium locker room, and most recently he challenged two teachers while in the lunchroom with a switchblade knife. In that altercation, the teachers, who were serving as monitors, reported that he was taking food (fruit and/or milk) from other children and he drew the knife when they ordered him to desist and be seated. He was subdued by another teacher, but only after he had made a seemingly serious attempt to cut one of the monitors.

According to the assistant principal, police were notified of the incident and the subject was removed from school to a juvenile detention center from which he was released the next day to the custody of his mother. Two days later, the mother appeared with the subject in the principal's office indicating that she had a long discussion with her son about his aggressive act and, that he had promised not to get into trouble again. The principal has tentatively agreed to his readmission pending psychological evaluation.

The assistant principal reports the school records show there to be no father in the home. The mother, age 30, is a high school graduate and currently works part-time in the housekeeping department of a local hospital. She has one other child, a female, age 10, who apparently does not have the same genetic father as this subject. The assistant principal also alleges that the subject is a member of a gang that has been identified as being involved in terrorizing activities in a local park (wilding) and has a notoriously bad reputation among local merchants. On a more positive note, the assistant principal reports that the youngster is able to do academic work which is at least average and that his academic history shows no significant problems prior to the seventh grade. Apparently, the mother has been called to the school once or twice concerning his aggressive conduct and in each instance claims to have disciplined the subject at home. There is no indication that the younger sibling is having any difficulty in school.

The subject is smaller than his stated age and, according to the examiner, would probably be judged as no older than 10 or 11. He is described as a handsome youngster, neatly dressed, and quietly cooperative during the examination. The results of a WISC-R yield a Verbal IQ of 103; Performance IQ of 107; Full-Scale IQ of 105, with no significant scatter among scale scores, which ranged from 9 through 12.

The subject denies any gang involvement or drug/alcohol involvement. He states that teachers tend to single him out more often than other students for doing the same behaviors that they do. He denies that he was taking food from other students and says that he drew his knife when "I just lost my temper, I didn't really mean to do it." He said that he did not like being in juvenile detention, that he was treated badly and that he was threatened by older youngsters in the detention center. He says that he has several close friends, likes to play basketball and baseball, and is not interested in seeing a school counselor.

He states that he and his sister and mother get along well. He acknowledges that his mother has had difficulty finding a full-time job and he is embarrassed by visits from the welfare social worker. He states that when he is old enough he plans to quit school and get a job to support his mother and sister.

The assessment issues are twofold: (a) Is there sufficient evidence of emotional disturbance to warrant special class placement, and (b) is there any reason to be concerned about the subject's potential for future violence?

Case 9. A 14-Year-Old Male

Card	Response	Inquiry		Scoring
I	1. Kinda ll a bf, do u hold it just ths way (E: Any way u lik)	E: S:	(Rpts Ss resp) The body, the wgs, & the head	Wo Fo A P 1.0
	v2. Kinda ll the spaceship voyager	E: S: E: S:	(Rpts Ss resp) These r wgs, the body rite in the middl,it ll ur seeg it fr on top, lik lookg dwn on it u can c the windows Windows? Thyr white, lik it's lit up, lik at nite u can c the white windows	WSo FD.FC'u Sc 3.5
II	3. Kinda ll 2 A's, bears fightg w eo	E: S: E: S:	(Rpts Ss resp) Rite here kinda ll their heads (D2) feet r dwn here U said thyr fightg? It kinda ll tht, thyv got bld all ovr thm, thr heads & feet r all red, thyr really fierce	W+ FMa.CFo 2 A,Bl 4.5 AG
	v4. Sorta ll lungs in a way	E: S:	(Rpts Ss resp) Dwn here (D2) its how thy go out lik ths, the shape, thy ll lungs	Do F– An
	5. Ths kinda ll ths wld b lake rite here, ths mtns back here, land arnd here mb the woods	E: S:	(Rpts Ss resp) The lake here (DS5) & the mtns around here (D4), this is all around it, the lake, the woods, its all lik ur lookg at it far away, on an angle, lik fr a plane, th mts r furthest away, dont count any of th red prts tho	DS+ FDu Na 4.5
III	v6. Kinda ll a bug w a bow	E: S:	(Rpts Ss resp) There wld b its arms, body, eyes, head, kinda ll a red bow on it, it has tht shape it goes out at the side & its got claws on the arms, lik thyr really sharp, I dk, its got the bow, mayb its just som red mark on its back, on the white part, his back	DdS+ FC.FC'– A,Cg 4.5 INC,FAB
	7. Or it cld ll 2 ppl holdg the ends of a basket	E: S:	(Rpts Ss resp) Their body, legs, feet, here's where thyr holdg on to this basket in th middl, lik thyr pullg on it, each wants it & wont let th othr one hav it, lik a tug of war	D+ Mao 2 H,Hh P 3.0 AG
IV	8. Kinda ll a big tree	E: S:	(Rpts Ss resp) The trunk, out here r the leaves & branches	Wo Fo Bt 2.0

321

Case 9. (Continued)

Card	Response	Inquiry	Scoring
< 9.	Or ths here ll a cliff, yeah, & its all the same here, kinda lik a reflectn in a river	E: (Rpts Ss resp) S: Its just a cliff w an old dead tree on the edge & it all lks the sam dwn here, lik its all reflectd in ths rivr (points to midlin) at nite E: At nite? S: Its all dark, black lik at nite	W + rF.C'Fo Na 4.0 MOR
10.	Or lik a big creature lik Bigfoot	E: (Rpts Ss resp) S: His head, arms, pointed hands, & really big feet don't count this (D1) tho	Do Fo (H) P
V	11. Looks kinda lik bf	E: (Rpts Ss resp) S: The wgs here, the head w the antennae, & the legs back here	Wo Fo A P 1.0
	12. Or a bat	E: (Rpts Ss resp) S: Bat's r kinda scary lik ths, the wgs & head E: Scary lik ths? S: Its the shape of wgs, its got thgs at end lik claws, thy can grab u	Wo Fo A P 1.0 INC,PSV
VI	13. Kinda lik one of those furs thy use for rugs w an A head, prob a bear	E: (Rpts Ss resp) S: U can c th arms & legs stretchd out, the head is up here, just lik th skin of an A tht smbdy made into a rug E: U said its fur? S: Yeah, kinda the coloring there maks it ll fur on the back	Wo FTo Ad P 2.5
	14. It cld all be a plane	E: (Rpts Ss resp) S: 1 of thos jazzy nite fightrs, w a big cannon in th front, lik thy can't c at nite E: I'm not sur I c it rite S: The cannon, the wgs, its all black so u cant c it w th radar, lik thy hav thos spec ones now, lik thy used in th dessert	Wo FC'u Sc 2.5 DR
VII	15. Kinda ll 2 ppl staring at eo lik thyr gettg ready to fite	E: (Rpts Ss resp) S: Thres 2 faces, mayb hair up here & their body, its lik thyv got a skirt, prob 2 girls gettg ready to fite caus one said smthg th othr one didnt lik so thyll fite it out E: U said thyv got a skirt? S: Dwn hre (Dd23), thyv got lik an apron on too, ths (Dd21) is whre it ties in th back	W + Mau 2 H,Cg 2.5 AG

322

	v16.	Kinda ll a frog, a smushd frog	E: (Rpts Ss resp) S: Ths (D4) ll head but ll got pushd dwn on back, thse (D2) ll legs, th way its curvd shapd around lik frogs legs, but its all smushd & its got a big hole in th centr	WSo F− Ad 4.0 MOR,DV
VIII	17.	A's climbg on som rocks theyr tearg up smthg	E: (Rpts Ss resp) S: Thyr standg on thse rocks (D2), u can c thr legs & heads & bodies & thyr gettg ready to tear up ths thg at th top, thyv got their legs on it lik to eat it or tear it apart, kinda lik smthg thy caught to eat	W+ FMao 2 A,Id,Ls P 4.5 AG
	v18.	Mayb a vampire bat	E: (Rpts Ss resp) S: In the blue, thyr blue smtimes I thk, it has huge big wgs l thy do & just a littl body but thy can really can do damage if thy bite smbody	Do FCu A DV,INC
IX	<19.	Kinda ll an A thts sittg dwn, w his arms folded	E: (Rpts Ss resp) S: An elephant, it has big ears l an elephant but he's got his arms in, folded, l he's crouching or sittg dwn, u dont c th feet vry well	Do FMp− A INC
	20.	Ths way it kinda ll fire w coals under a pot & flames comg out	E: (Rpts Ss resp) S: These (D6) r hot coals, all pink lik thy get & ths green & white is lik a pot, I guess it gets white whn it gets really hot & ths orange up hre is lik th flames going up around th pot, smthgs gettin boiled	WS+ CF.ma.FC'u Fi,Hh 5.5
X	21.	Kinda ll a lotta thgs fightg, lik a war of creatures	E: (Rpts Ss resp) S: Th pink r l giant creatures, & th blu thngs r diff knds of creaturs tht r fightg, th pink ones & th littl ls r helpg E: I don't thk I c it rite S: Th pink ls r th giants, lik giant worms or smthg lik tht & th blue ls r th good guys & thyr leadg all thes littl guys to defeat th worms, l th invasion of space worms, c th worms already ate st at th top & its just bones left	W+ Ma.FCu 2 (A),(H),An 5.5 AG,MOR
	v22.	A fire bombing	E: (Rpts Ss resp) S: Its just blowg up & all th pieces of whtevr its bombg r kinda blowg out all ovr th place E: U say it's just blowg up? S: Yeah, lik it hit hre (D11) & its shootg all ths red fire out (D9) & all th rest is pieces of wht its blowg up	Wv/+ ma.CFu Ex,Fi 5.5 AG,MOR

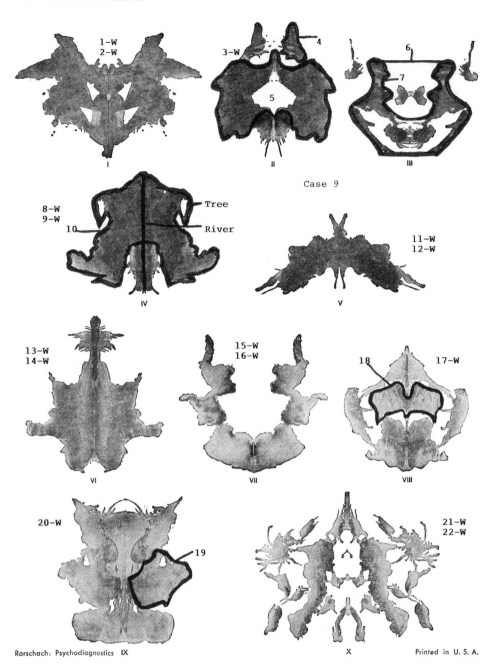

Case 9

Rorschach: Psychodiagnostics   Printed in U. S. A.

Case 9

Case 9   **Sequence of Scores**

Card	No	Loc	#	Determinant(s)	(2)	Content(s)	Pop	Z	Special Scores
I	1	Wo	1	Fo		A	P	1.0	
	2	WSo	1	FD.FC'u		Sc		3.5	
II	3	W+	1	FMa.CFo	2	A,Bl		4.5	AG
	4	Do	2	F-		An		4.5	
	5	DS+	6	FDu		Na			
III	6	DdS+	99	FC.FC'-		A,CG		4.5	INC,FAB
	7	D+	1	Mao	2	H,Hh	P	3.0	AG
IV	8	Wo	1	Fo		Bt		2.0	
	9	W+	1	rF.C'Fo		Na		4.0	MOR
	10	Do	7	Fo		(H)	P		
V	11	Wo	1	Fo		A	P	1.0	
	12	Wo	1	Fo		A	P	1.0	INC,PSV
VI	13	Wo	1	FTo		Ad	P	2.5	
	14	Wo	1	FC'u		Sc		2.5	DR
VII	15	W+	1	Mau	2	H,Cg		2.5	AG
	16	WSo	1	F-		Ad		4.0	MOR,DV
VIII	17	W+	1	FMao	2	A,Id,Ls	P	4.5	AG
	18	Do	5	FCu		A			DR,INC
IX	19	Do	1	FMp-		A			INC
	20	WS+	1	CF.ma.FC'u		Fi,Hh		5.5	
X	21	W+	1	Ma.FCu	2	(A),(H),An		5.5	AG,MOR
	22	W/	1	ma.CFu		Ex,Fi		5.5	AG,MOR

Case 9   **Structural Summary**

Location Features	Determinants Blends	Single	Contents	S-Constellation

Location Features

Zf   = 18
ZSum = 61.5
ZEst = 59.5

W = 15
 (Wv = 0)
D = 6
Dd = 1
S = 5

DQ
. . . . . (FQ−)
+ = 9 (1)
o = 12 (3)
v/+ = 1 (0)
v = 0 (0)

Form Quality

	FQx	FQf	MQual	SQx
+	= 0	0	0	0
o	= 10	5	1	0
u	= 8	0	2	3
−	= 4	2	0	2
none	= 0	—	0	0

Determinants

Blends
FD.FC'
FM.CF
FC.FC'
rF.C'F
CF.m.FC'
M.FC
m.CF

Single
M = 2
FM = 2
m = 0
FC = 1
CF = 0
C = 0
Cn = 0
FC' = 1
C'F = 0
C' = 0
FT = 1
TF = 0
T = 0
FV = 0
VF = 0
V = 0
FY = 0
YF = 0
Y = 0
Fr = 0
rF = 0
FD = 1
F = 7

(2) = 5

Contents

H   = 2, 0
(H) = 1, 1
Hd = 0, 0
(Hd) = 0, 0
Hx = 0, 0
A   = 8, 0
(A) = 1, 0
Ad = 2, 0
(Ad) = 0, 0
An = 1, 1
Art = 0, 0
Ay = 0, 0
Bl = 0, 1
Bt = 1, 0
Cg = 0, 2
Cl = 0, 0
Ex = 1, 0
Fd = 0, 0
Fi = 1, 1
Ge = 0, 0
Hh = 0, 2
Ls = 0, 1
Na = 2, 0
Sc = 2, 0
Sx = 0, 0
Xy = 0, 0
Id = 0, 1

S-Constellation
NO . . FV+VF+V+FD>2
YES . . Col−Shd Bl>0
NO . . Ego<.31,>.44
YES . . MOR > 3
NO . . Zd > +− 3.5
YES . . es > EA
NO . . CF+C > FC
YES . . X+% < .70
YES . . S > 3
NO . . P < 3 or > 8
NO . . Pure H < 2
NO . . R < 17
  5 . . . . . TOTAL

Special Scorings

		Lv1	Lv2
DV	=	1x1	0x2
INC	=	4x2	0x4
DR	=	2x3	0x6
FAB	=	1x4	0x7
ALOG	=	0x5	
CON	=	0x7	
	SUM6	= 8	
	WSUM6	= 19	

AB	= 0	CP	= 0
AG	= 6	MOR	= 4
CFB	= 0	PER	= 0
COP	= 0	PSV	= 1

Case 9   **Ratios, Percentages, and Derivations**

R = 22   L = 0.47

EB = 3: 4.5   EA = 7.5   EBPer = N/A
eb = 5: 6   es = 11   D = −1
                  Adj es = 10   Adj D = 0

FM = 3 : C' = 5   T = 1
m = 2 : V = 0   Y = 0

a:p   = 7: 1   Sum6 = 8
Ma:Mp = 3: 0   Lv2 = 0
2AB+Art+Ay=0   WSum6 = 19
M −   = 0   Mnone = 0

P   = 7
X+% = 0.45
F+% = 0.71
X−% = 0.18
S−% = 0.50
Xu% = 0.36

FC:CF+C = 3: 3
Pure C   = 0
Afr   = 0.38
S   = 5
Blends:R = 7:22
CP   = 0

Zf   = 18
Zd   = +2.0
W:D:Dd = 15: 6: 1
W:M = 15: 3
DQ+ = 9
DQv = 0

COP = 0   AG = 6
Food   = 0
Isolate/R   = 0.27
H:(H)Hd(Hd) = 2:2
(HHd):(AAd) = 2:1
H+A:Hd+Ad = 13:2

3r+(2)/R = 0.36
Fr+rF   = 1
FD   = 2
An+Xy   = 2
MOR   = 4

SCZI = 2   DEPI = 5*   CDI = 2   S-CON = 5   HVI = No   OBS = No

INTERPRETIVE ROUTINE FOR CASE 9

An examination of the structural data reveals that the first positive Key variable is that the D Score is less than the Adjusted D Score. This indicates that the cluster of data concerning Controls should be reviewed first, and that findings from the array of variables related to Situational Stress should be added to those findings. But, this Key variable finding does not dictate the entire interpretive strategy, and thus, the next Key variable should be used to determine the order in which the other clusters of data should be reviewed. In this case, the value for reflection answers is greater than zero. Thus, the interpretive routine will continue with the clusters concerning self-perception and interpersonal perception. However, as with the first positive Key variable, the complete order of cluster search is not defined by the reflection variable and the next positive Key variable or Tertiary variable defines the remainder of the interpretive routine. In this instance, no other Key variables are positive and the first positive Tertiary variable is DEPI = 5. Thus, the clusters should be reviewed in the following order:

$$\text{CONTROLS} \rightarrow \text{SITUATIONAL STRESS} \rightarrow$$
$$\text{SELF-PERCEPTION} \rightarrow \text{INTERPERSONAL PERCEPTION} \rightarrow$$
$$\text{AFFECT} \rightarrow \text{PROCESSING} \rightarrow \text{MEDIATION} \rightarrow \text{IDEATION}$$

Controls—Case 9   The data concerning capacity for control and tolerance for stress for Case 9 are shown in Table 78.

Table 78.   **Controls and Stress Tolerance Data for Case 9**

EB = 3:4.5		EA = 7.5		D = -1	
eb = 5:6		es = 11	Adjes = 10	AdjD = 0	
FM = 3	C' = 5	T = 1		CDI = 2	
m = 2	V = 0	Y = 0			

The Adjusted D score is zero, implying that, ordinarily, his capacity for control and tolerance for stress are no different than for most of his peers. There is no reason to challenge the validity of the Adjusted D Score as the value for EA (7.5) is in the average range for his age, and values greater than zero appear in both sides of the EB (3:4.5) and eb (5:5). However, it seems the value for the Adjusted es (10) is somewhat higher than expected. This is caused primarily by a substantial right-side eb value (6), which includes five C' responses.

Thus, whereas his capacity for control usually seems adequate, the possibility for an overload state does exist. If additional situationally related stresses occur, as appears to be the case here, a D Score in the minus range results. Similarly, if need states increase only slightly, and/or if internally felt distress experiences increase modestly, the Adjusted D Score could fall into the minus range. In either of these circumstances, he becomes much more vulnerable to episodes of impulsiveness. This now appears to be the case, and in light of his aggressive orientation, the resulting behaviors do not seem difficult to predict.

Situationally Related Stress—Case 9   The data from the array of variables related to situationally related stress are shown in Table 79.

Table 79.   Situational Stress Data for Case 9

					ANALYSIS OF DETERMINANT BLENDS	
D	= −1	EA	= 7.5		Total Blends	= 7
Adj D	= 0	Pure C	= 0		Blends created by m, Y, T	= 1
Sum T	= 1				Blends created by m or Y	= 1
Sum m	= 2	M Q−	= 0		Color-Shading Blends created by Y = 0	
Sum Y	= 0	M Qnone	= 0			

As previously noted, the current state of overload renders him vulnerable to impulsiveness in his thinking and in his behaviors. This overload appears to have been created by an increase in peripheral ideation that has been generated by a sense of helplessness, a finding that is not unexpected when considered in light of his current plight. Interestingly, the impact of the stress has not created substantially more complexity as the number of blends have increased by only one. Similarly, the overload itself is modest and would not exist if one fewer m answer had been given. However, the fact that only a slight increase in stress-related experiences has created this potential for impulsiveness should be considered carefully if some treatment plan is to be devised. In other words, his vulnerability to overload is probably less important than the causes for that vulnerability. Data from the other clusters should clarify this issue.

Self-Perception—Case 9   The data related to self-perception for Case 9 are shown in Table 80.

Table 80.   Self-Perception Data for Case 9

3r + (2)/R = 0.36	FD = 2	MOR = 4	Hx = 0	An + Xy = 2
Fr + rF = 1	Sum V = 0	H:(H) + Hd + (Hd) = 2:2		Sx = 0
		RESPONSES TO BE READ		
MOR Resp's	FQ − Resp's	M Resp's	FM Resp's	m Resp's
9,16,21,22	4,6,16,19	7,15,21	3,17,19	20,22

The presence of the reflection answer signifies that this young man continues to harbor a childlike self-centeredness in which he overestimates his own worth and defends that premise by externalizing blame for noxious experiences. There is evidence, however, that this narcissiticlike feature may be faltering, or, at least, is subject to challenge in his thinking. The Egocentricity Index (0.36) is lower than average for his age. It suggests that he no longer perceives himself to be more important or valuable than those significant to him. In addition there are two FD responses, indicating that he is much more involved in self-examining behavior than is customary for the self-centered, narcissistic person. In effect, he may be undergoing the natural transition from a state of exquisite self-centeredness to one that estimates self-worth in the context of a more social world. This transition usually occurs between the ages of 11 and 14 among nonpatient children. In this instance, however, the result may be a tendency to weigh his own self-worth as being less important than that of his significant others.

Half of his human content responses are Pure H, indicating that he may be recasting his self-concept in light of experience rather than imaginary events. Usually, this is a healthy sign, suggesting that he no longer externalizes blame for his own faults and is willing to evaluate himself in the hard light of reality. However, in this instance, his reevaluation may produce results that are less than desirable for the developing adolescent. The two *An* answers suggest the presence of an unusual body preoccupation, and the four MOR responses can be used to argue that his current perceptions of himself include many more negative features than is common for one of his age. They convey a sense of damage or inadequacy that only serves to lower estimates of self-worth, and may account for the lower than average Egocentricity Index.

The projected substance of the MOR responses appears to support this contention and conveys a sense of helplessness and/or despair: Card IV, Response 9 (his reflection answer) "an old dead tree"; Card VII, Response 16, "a smushed frog"; Card X, Response 21, "a war of creatures . . . the worms already ate something at the top and it's just bones left"; and, Card X, Response 22, "a fire bombing . . . all the pieces of whatever it's bombing are kind of blowing out all over." Collectively, they reflect a marked sense of vulnerability and/or helplessness, neither of which make for a solid or secure self-concept. His minus responses also convey an insecure and/or damaged self of self (Card II, Response 4, "lungs"; Card III, Response 6, " a bug with a bow"; Card VII, Response 16, "a smushed frog"; and Card IX, Response 19, "an animal sitting down with his arms folded . . . an elephant . . . crouching or sitting down . . .").

The three *M* answers also are much more negative than positive and suggest that he may feel quite embattled in his world (Card III, Response 7, "people holding the ends of a basket . . . each wants it and won't let the other have it"; Card VII, Response 15, "two people staring at each other like they are getting ready to fight"; Card X, Response 21, "a lot of things fighting, like a war of creatures").

The three *FM* responses also are negative when considered in the context of self-image. Two of the three are aggressive (Card II, Response 3, "bears fighting with each other . . . they've got blood all over them"; Card VIII, Response 17, "Animals climbing on some rocks, they are tearing up something"). The third *FM* answer is the Response 19 animal, sitting with his arms folded, like he's crouching or sitting down. Similarly, neither of the two *m* responses contain positive features. The first, to Card IX, Response 20, is a "fire with coals under a pot . . . it gets white when it gets really hot . . . something is getting boiled." The second, to Card X, Response 22, is "A fire bombing . . . all the rest is pieces of what it's blowing up." Both convey a sense of being victimized by aggression, and being helpless to prevent it from happening. At least two of his other answers are embellished in ways that imply a defensively aggressive notion of self. They are Responses 12 and 18, both of which involve bats. The first being "scary" with claws at the end of the wings, "they can grab you," and the second a "vampire bat" that can "do damage if they bite you."

Overall, this seems to be a youngster who is struggling to establish some sense of identity, and unfortunately, tends to see the world as a place in which aggression must be a feature in anyone who is to contend effectively with the potential devastation that exists.

Interpersonal Perception—Case 9   The data related to interpersonal perception and behavior are shown in Table 81.

Neither the CDI or HVI are positive, and the *a:p* ratio provides no evidence to suggest a passive interpersonal role. Similarly, there are no Food responses, but there is a Texture answer. It suggests that he experiences needs for closeness and, in spite of findings concerning his self-concept, is amenable to emotional contacts with others. The four human

Table 81. **Interpersonal Perception Data for Case 9**

CDI = 2	a:p = 7:1	T = 1	Human Cont = 4	Pure H = 2
HVI = Neg	Food = 0	PER = 0	COP = 0 AG = 6	Isolate/R = 0.27

RESPONSES TO BE READ

HUMAN MOVEMENT WITH PAIR	*HUMAN CONTENTS*
7,15,21	7,10,15,21

contents are slightly less than might be desired, but, nonetheless, do signal an interest in others. Two of the four human responses are Pure *H*, another positive sign, implying that his conceptions of people are probably based at least as much in real experience as on imaginary experience. There are no PER responses, which is a positive finding, but there are no COP answers, which is a very negative finding. Apparently, he does not expect social relations to be positive.

One of the most negative findings in this cluster of data is the value for AG (6). It is much greater than desired, and indicates that he perceives aggressiveness as a natural phenomenon in social relations. Undoubtedly, this distorted set about aggression is very influential in his interpersonal behaviors and probably relates to the fact that his Isolation Index is positive (0.27). Most people usually do not want to be close to those whose behaviors frequently are marked by aggressiveness, regardless of whether it is social or asocial, verbal or nonverbal. His orientation to perceive the world as aggressive, and to be aggressive himself, apparently is quite pervasive. All three of his *M* answers and two of his three *FM* responses contain aggressive content. They represent all his answers in which a pair is reported and include three of his four human content responses.

In general, this seems to be a young person who would like to have close relationships, but whose sets about relationships tend to merge with his own sense of damage and/or inadequacy to create behaviors toward others that are defensive and aggressive. As a result, he has become isolated socially and is probably regarded negatively by most of his peers and significant others.

Affect—Case 9   Data concerning affect for Case 9 are shown in Table 82.

Table 82. **Affect Data for Case 9**

DEPI = 5				BLENDS
EB	= 3:4.5		EBPer	= N/A	M.FC
eb	= 5:6		FC:CF + C	= 3:3	FM.CF
			Pure C	= 0	m.CF
C' = 5		T = 1	Afr	= 0.38	CF.m.C'F
V = 0		Y = 0	S	= 5	rF.C'F
			Blends/R	= 6:22	FD.FC'
			CP	= 0	

The DEPI value is 5, suggesting that he has many characteristics that give rise to frequent experiences of emotional disruption. It is likely that most of these events will involve sadness or depression, but they could manifest in other ways, such as acting-out behaviors. The *EB* (3:4.5) reveals that he is not consistent concerning the use of his feelings when in coping or decision-making situations. He is an ambitent, prone to be inconsistent about his feelings and how to use them. The substantial right-side *eb* value (6) has been noted earlier and signals the presence of considerable distress. That it consists mostly of *C'* answers indicates he is prone to internalize feelings that he would prefer to release directly. The value for *C'* exceeds the *WSumC*, signaling some form of emotional constriction; this seems to coincide directly with the very low *Afr* (0.38), which suggests that he does not like to process emotionally toned stimuli.

The fact that he tends to avoid and/or internalize emotions excessively signals a confusion and possibly even a fearfulness about affect. This might be easy to understand if he has difficulty modulating his emotional expressions, but that does not seem to be the case. The *FC:CF* + *C* ratio (3:3), which includes no Pure *C* answers, suggests that when he releases his feelings, he tends to modulate them about as much as do most of his age. The confusion probably derives from two elements. First, he gives five space responses, indicating a great deal of hostility and/or anger. Second, he is a youngster who believes that aggression is a natural way of life. This composite probably causes many more of his emotional responses to be less than appropriate for the situation, and apparently, he has learned that it is better to avoid emotional confrontations than respond to them.

It seems clear that his hostility/anger causes him to bend or distort reality at times. Three of the five *S* answers have an unusual form quality and the other two are minus. Interestingly, none of the *S* answers involve aggressive movement. Thus, it may be that the hostility/anger is being contained to some extent, but the set concerning aggression still dictates many of his behaviors and emotion will often manifest in them. For instance, only one of his six chromatic color responses has ordinary form quality. The remaining five include four that are coded Unusual, and one that is minus. However, three of the six chromatic color answers also involve aggression and two of the remaining three include Critical Special Scores. This suggests that when his feelings are released, it is likely that they will manifest in ways that convey his aggressiveness and/or in ways that will involve some disregard for reality.

There are seven blends in the record, approximating more than 30% of his answers. This is not unusual for an ambitent and illustrates considerable psychological complexity. Much of the complexity seems related to emotions that he internalizes. Four of the seven blends include *C'* answers and two of the four are Color-Shading blends, indicating his confusion about feelings.

Overall, emotions are a significant problem for him. He is prone to frequent episodes of emotional disruption that probably occur as depression; he is inconsistent in the way that he uses emotion in his decision making; and he tries hard to avoid emotionally provocative stimuli and often holds feelings in that he would prefer to release. He is a very hostile or angry youngster, and this feature often manifests in the way that he expresses his feelings. There is no doubt that his set concerning aggressiveness only adds to impressions that he is a volatile person. He seems to be a young person who flounders when feelings are involved and has little notion about how best to deal with them.

Processing—Case 9   The data concerning information-processing activities for Case 9 are shown in Table 83.

The findings concerning Lambda, OBS, and HVI offer no significant information concerning his processing activity. In general, the data suggest that he works hard to process new information. The *Zf* of 18 is well above average and the *W:D:Dd* ratio (15:6:1) indicates that he is quite willing to tackle a complex stimulus field with little

Table 83.   Processing Data for Case 9

L = 0.47	$W:D:Dd$ = 15:6:1	Zd = +2.0	$DQ+$ = 9
Zf = 18	$W:M$ = 15:3	PSV = 1	$DQv/+$ = 1
HVI = No	OBS = No		DQv = 0

LOCATION SEQUENCING

I	W,W	IV	W,W,D	VII	W,WS
II	W,D,DS	V	W,W	VIII	W,D
III	DdS,D	VI	W,W	IX	D,WS
				X	W,W

regard for the effort that will be required. In fact, the *W:M* ratio (15:3) suggests that he often takes on processing tasks in ways that exceed his functional capabilities. Nonetheless, the product seems commendable. He generates nine *DQ +* answers and only one *DQv/+* response, and the *Zd* score (+2.0) is well within expected parameters. If there are any liabilities concerning his processing activities it could be that he works a bit too hard, but when considered in light of the processing product, this extra effort tends to serve him well.

Mediation—Case 9   Structural data related to the mediation activities for Case 9 are shown in Table 84.

Table 84.   Cognitive Mediation Data for Case 9

Lambda = 0.47	OBS = Neg		MINUS FEATURES	
P = 7	X+% = .45		4,6,16,19	
FQx+ = 0	F+% = .71			
FQxo = 10	Xu% = .36			
FQxu = 8	X−% = .18			
FQx− = 4	S−% = .50			
*FQx*none = 0	CONFAB = 0			

Although his processing activities are more than adequate, the way in which he translates information is less appropriate. He does give seven Popular answers, indicating that when cues are obvious, he will generate obvious, conventional responses. However, the $X + \%$ is low (.45), suggesting that, overall, his translations are much less conventional than should be expected for his age. This is not because his distorts a great deal. The X-% (.18) is slightly higher than expected and includes only four minus answers. Instead, his tendency to be unconventional occurs mainly because he tends to personalize many of his translations as illustrated by the *Xu%* of .36. It implies that he is not very aware of convention, or if he is, he disregards it in favor of his own needs, sets, or feelings.

His difficulties with feelings appear to have a significant impact on how he mediates or translates stimuli. Six of his eight Unusual Form Quality responses include the use of chromatic and/or achromatic color and all five of his *S* responses are coded as *u* or minus. In fact, when he disregards the complexity of blots and formulates responses based *only* on form, his answers are much more conventional ($F + \% = .71$). Five of his seven Pure *F* answers have an ordinary Form Quality and include four of his seven Popular responses.

Overall, it would be foolish to suggest that there are no significant problems concerning the manner in which he translates stimuli. However, it is important to emphasize that the problems that exist, orienting him toward less conventional mediation, seem to be affect related. Whenever his feelings become involved, the likelihood of mediational distortions or translations of stimuli in unconventional ways increase significantly. In effect, his emotions tend to dictate how he sees the world, and in turn, how he sees the world usually dictates how he will respond to it.

Ideation—Case 9   Data concerning ideational activities for Case 9 are shown in Table 85.

Table 85.   Ideation Data for Case 9

EB	= 3:4.5	EBPer = N/A	*M* QUALITY		SPECIAL SCORES			
eb	= 5:6	(FM = 3 m = 2)	+ = 0	DV	= 1	DV2	= 0
a:p	= 7:1	M^a:M^p = 3:0	o = 1	INC	= 4	INC2	= 0
2AB + Art + Ay = 0			u = 2	DR	= 2	DR2	= 0
MOR	= 4		− = 0	FAB	= 1	FAB2	= 0
RESPONSES TO BE READ FOR QUALITY				ALOG	= 0	SUM6	= 8
	7,15,21			CON	= 0	WSUM6	= 19

The findings concerning ideation are, in one sense, not terribly remarkable, but in another sense they are important. The *EB* (3:4.5) indicates that he is not very consistent about how he uses his thinking in coping or problem solving. Sometimes, he may push his feelings aside and attempt a logical approach to issues. In other instances, his feelings with merge with his thoughts and assume a priority in his decisions. This type of ambitent vacillation is not uncommon among 14-year-olds but makes for potential difficulties. If the thinking of the ambitent is reasonably clear, few problems are likely to occur, but if the thinking of the ambitent is also marked by faulty logic, the result can be disastrous.

In this case, his thinking falls short of the optimal. There is no reason to suspect that his thoughts are intruded on excessively by peripheral ideation as the left-side *eb* value is within expected limits (5). However, the *a:p* ratio (7:1) is quite disparate, suggesting that he is not very flexible in the way that he thinks about issues and probably has a well-fixed value system. There is no evidence that he intellectualizes (2AB + Art + Ay) = 0, but the presence of the four MOR answers indicates that much of his thinking will be marked by a significantly pessimistic attitude. Usually, when he thinks about things that are important to him, he does not expect favorable results. In light of his apprehensiveness about feelings, this pessimistic attitude bodes poorly for emotional relationships.

Probably, the most important data in this cluster concern cognitive slippage. His record includes eight Critical Special Scores that have a *WSum6* of 19. This is well beyond the expected for his age and indicates much more faulty thinking than should be the case. To his credit, he occasionally seems aware of his flawed thinking. For instance, two of his seven Critical Special Scores appear in his sixth response, given to Card III, "a bug with a bow," which, in the Inquiry, he suggests might be, "some red mark on its back." He wants to take back the INCOM. But, in most instances, he does not seem aware of his faulty associations and in some instances tends to exaggerate them, apparently because of his emotional associations.

For example, in Response 14, to Card VI, he argues that the plane is a "jazzy night fighter . . . like they can't see at night." In Response 18, to Card VIII, he argues that vampire bats have blue wings, "they are blue sometimes," and goes on to elaborate inappropriately that "they can really do damage if they bite somebody." Neither of these examples reflect serious thinking problems, and the composite of the seven Special Scores responses does not raise major questions about the integrity of his thinking (arm on a bug; claws on the wings of a bat; a smushed frog). Most are child- or adolescentlike; however, the frequency is sufficient to warrant concern in light of his age and especially in light of his other problems. Fortunately, there are no $M-$ answers and all of his M answers are of reasonably good quality even though the contents may be less than desirable.

Findings concerning his thinking might best be summarized as illustrating more unsophisticated ideation than might be expected for one of his age, but there is no evidence of a serious problem in thinking. He is not very flexible in the way that he thinks about things and probably is somewhat rigid in his values. The most important finding is his markedly pessimistic attitude toward the world and the fact that this pessimism will influence many of his ideas and judgments.

SUMMARY—CASE 9

This is a youngster who appears to have lost his way on the path to adolescence. It seems clear that, at one time, he regarded himself very highly, as is often the case with younger children, but more recently he has been confronted with the harshness of reality and the fact that he may not be as important as he once believed. His self-image tends to be much more negative than positive. It is a situation that he does not want to accept, and for which he tends to blame the world.

This conflict has created havoc with his emotions. He seems bewildered by his feelings and very uncertain about how best to deal with them. The confusion that they create for him tends to intrude into most of his psychological operations. His thinking is influenced by a considerably pessimistic attitude, and his reality testing is overly influenced by his own preoccupations. He apparently is fearful about his feelings, and this seems to have formed the basis from which frequent episodes of sadness and/or depression occur.

His emotions include considerably more anger or hostility than should be the case for one of his age, and this adds to his problems by sometimes clouding over his perceptions of reality. It seems likely that much of his anger is related to his struggles with self-image as he tries to maintain a high sense of self-esteem while being confronted with evidence to the contrary. Apparently, he goes to great lengths to internalize and thereby contain much of his anger, but the situation is confounded by his perception of aggressiveness as a natural part of the everyday social routine; as confirmed by the history data, he has learned to be quite aggressive.

Interestingly, he does not seem to associate his aggressiveness directly with his anger, that is, aggressiveness is a way of life, whereas anger is something to be contained or expressed only in indirect ways. He would like to be close to others, but does not conceptualize them very accurately. Gradually, he has become isolated from his peers and significant others because of his aggressiveness and his misunderstandings about people, and the threats to his integrity that they seem to pose for him.

Usually, he has sufficient capacity for control and tolerance for stress, but this has become more marginal because he holds many of his feelings inside. Currently, he is under some situational stress, and this has impaired his controls and made him more vulnerable to impulsiveness and has increased his potential for disorganization.

He works hard to process new information, and does so with reasonable effectiveness. However, his feelings influence the manner in which he translates this information, and unless the cues for translation are quite obvious, he tends to become overly personalized or individualistic in his view of reality. This leads him into behaviors that are less conventional and influenced mainly by his feelings and his insecure sense of self. His thinking is not seriously warped or distorted but tends to be less mature than might be expected and, as noted earlier, is marked by considerable pessimism about himself and his future.

He poses an interesting and difficult treatment challenge. Obviously, his aggressive behaviors will be a major focus of attention, but his depressive features cannot be overlooked and without attention to them, his behavioral patterns are unlikely to change.

Exner and Weiner (1982) reported on an aborted study involving adolescents, from nine school districts, all of whom had been identified as school behavior problems, not sufficient to provoke expulsion, but serious enough to warrant parent conferences and referral to school counseling services or community mental health units, and all became involved with a behavioral management form of intervention.

All subjects were administered some testing, usually cognitive, as a part of the regular referral routine. Once a potential subject was identified for the project, a Rorschach was administered if it had not already been collected as a part of the referral routine, and a Peterson and Quay Behavior Problem Checklist was completed concerning the prospective subject by someone from the school who was familiar with the case. Usually this was done by someone from the guidance service.

A positive response to at least 12 of 20 critical items in the Checklist concerning unwanted behaviors was set as a criterion for inclusion in the study. These items all dealt with disruptive, asocial, antisocial, inattentive, impertinent, negative, and temper kinds of behavior. Unfortunately, the scheme for follow-up became unwieldy and the project was terminated after approximately one year; however, during that interval, data were collected concerning the basic intervention format, and it was possible to have the Behavior Problem Checklist repeated for the subjects. In all 91 cases, the basic format for intervention was management oriented, typically using a behavioral model. The data for these 91 cases were reviewed retrospectively and the Rorschach data were reviewed with the objective of creating two groups: (a) Depressed, identified by a positive finding on the original DEPI, and (b) Nondepressed, identified by a negative finding for the original DEPI.

This procedure led to the classification of 24 of the subjects (26%) as depressed and 67 of the subjects as not depressed (74%). The working hypothesis for the study was that significantly more change would occur in the ratings of behavior problems for the not-depressed subjects than for the depressed group after approximately one year. The rationale for this hypothesis is that management-oriented forms of intervention usually do not focus extensively on emotional problems. Thus, if depression exists at the onset of intervention, it should persist over time; and if it is manifest in socially unwanted behaviors, those behaviors should also tend to persist more over time. Thus, a significant change in the mean score derived from the 20 critical items of the Peterson and Quay Behavior Problem Checklist related to asocial or antisocial behaviors was predicted for the not-depressed group, but not for the depressed group.

The findings were quite significant, indicating a significant reduction in unwanted behavior among the not-depressed subjects, but only a slight reduction (not statistically significant), for the depressed group. They can be interpreted to suggest that if a core problem, in this instance depressive features, is not dealt with effectively in intervention, the presenting problems are likely to persist.

These findings have a direct bearing on intervention planning for Case 9. His aggressiveness behaviors will obviously be a focal issue in treatment planning, and some form of behavioral management seems appropriate. However, his very confused and disruptive emotions must also be an important treatment target, and, of course, they stem from his conflicted self-image. Thus, while some form of behavioral management form of intervention may be appropriate for immediate purposes, a much different form of intervention should parallel that program. It should focus on his conceptions of himself and his feelings about himself and about others, and ultimately, how to use his emotions to his advantage. If this individual, dynamic form of treatment is not included in the overall intervention package, more direct forms of intervention aimed at altering his aggressive behaviors are unlikely to succeed, and his unwanted behaviors are likely to persist.

REFERENCES

Adam, B. S., Kashani, J. H., & Schulte, E. J. (1991). The classification of conduct disorders. *Child Psychiatry and Human Development, 22,* 3–16.

American Psychiatric Association. (1987). *Diagnostic and statistical manual of mental disorders* (3rd ed.). Washington, DC: American Psychiatric Association.

Arbuthnot, J., Gordon, D. A., & Jurkovic, G. J. (1987). Personality. In H. C. Quay (Ed.), *Handbook of juvenile delinquency* (pp. 139–183). New York: Wiley.

Bear, D., Freeman, R., & Greenberg (1984). Behavioral alterations in patients with temporal lobe epilepsy. In D. Blumer (Ed.), *Psychiatric aspects of epilepsy* (pp. 197–225). Washington, DC: American Psychiatric Press.

Beiser, H. R. (1990). Symptomatic disturbances and clinical manifestations of neurosis in children and adolescents. In M. H. Etezady (Ed.), *The neurotic child and adolescent* (pp. 25–39). Northvale, NJ: Aronson.

Berndt, D. J., & Zinn, D. (1984). Prominent features of depression in affective- and conduct-disordered inpatients. In D. Offer, E. Ostrov, & K. I. Howard (Eds.), *Patterns of adolescent self-image* (pp. 45–56). San Francisco: Jossey-Bass.

Blumer, D. (1982). Specific psychiatric complications in certain forms of epilepsy and their treatment. In H. Sands (Ed.), *Epilepsy* (pp. 97–110). New York: Brunner/Mazel.

Brier, N. (1989). The relationship between learning disability and delinquency: A review and reappraisal. *Journal of Learning Disabilities, 22,* 546–553.

Bynner, J. M., O'Malley, P. M., & Bachman, J. G. (1981). Self-esteem and delinquency revisited. *Journal of Youth and Adolescence, 10,* 407–441.

Cavanaugh, J. L., Rogers, R., & Wasyliw, O. E. (1981). Mental illness and antisocial behavior. In W. H. Reid (Ed.), *The treatment of antisocial syndromes* (pp. 3–19). New York: Van Nostrand Reinhold.

Chiles, J. A., Miller, M. L., & Cox, G. B. (1980). Depression in an adolescent delinquent population. *Archives of General Psychiatry, 37,* 1179–1184.

Cole, D. A., & Carpentieri, S. (1990). Social status and the comorbidity of child depression and conduct disorder. *Journal of Consulting and Clinical Psychology, 58,* 748–757.

Exner, J. E., & Weiner, I. B. (1982). *The Rorschach: A Comprehensive System: Vol. 3. Assessment of children and adolescents.* New York: Wiley.

Gacono, C. B., Meloy, J. R., & Heaven, T. R. (1990). A Rorschach investigation of narcissism and hysteria in antisocial personality. *Journal of Personality Assessment, 55,* 270–279.

Genshaft, J. L. (1980). Personality correlates of delinquent subtypes. *Journal of Abnormal Child Psychology, 8,* 279–283.

Henker, B., & Whalen, C. K. (1989). Hyperactivity and attention deficits. *American Psychologist, 44,* 216–223.

Jenkins, R. L. (1955). Adaptive and maladaptive delinquency. *Nervous Child, 11,* 9–11.

Kazdin, A. E. (1987). Treatment of antisocial behavior in children: Current status and future directions. *Psychological Bulletin, 102,* 187–203.

Kelso, J., & Stewart, M. A. (1986). Factors which predict the persistence of aggressive conduct disorder. *Journal of Child Psychology and Psychiatry, 27,* 77–86.

King, N. J., Ollendick, T. H., & Gullone, E. (1991). Negative affectivity in children and adolescents: Relations between anxiety and depression. *Clinical Psychology Review, 11,* 441–460.

Kupersmidt, J. B., & Coie, J. D. (1990). Preadolescent peer status, aggression, and school adjustment as predictors of externalizing problems in adolescence. *Child Development, 61,* 1350–1362.

Lambert, N. M. (1988). Adolescent outcomes for hyperactive children. *American Psychologist, 43,* 786–799.

Lambert, N. M., Sassone, D., Hartsough, C. S., & Sandoval, J. (1987). Persistence of hyperactivity symptoms from childhood to adolescence and associated outcomes. *American Journal of Orthopsychiatry, 57,* 22–32.

Lewis, D. O., & Balla, D. (1976). *Delinquency and psychopathology.* New York: Grune & Stratton.

Lewis, D. O., Lewis, M., Unger, L., & Goldman, C. (1984). Conduct disorder and its synonyms: Diagnoses of dubious validity and usefulness. *American Journal of Psychiatry, 141,* 514–519.

Lillienfeld, S. O., & Waldman, I. D. (1990). The relation between childhood attention-deficit hyperactivity disorder and adult antisocial behavior reexamined: The problem of heterogeneity. *Clinical Psychology Review, 10,* 699–725.

Loeber, R. (1988). Natural histories of conduct problems, delinquency, and associated substance use. In B. B. Lahey & A. E. Kazdin (Eds.), *Advances in clinical child psychology* (Vol. 11, pp. 73–124). New York: Plenum Press.

Loeber, R. (1990). Development and risk factors of juvenile antisocial behavior and delinquency. *Clinical Psychology Review, 10,* 1–41.

Loeber, R., & Stouthamer-Loeber, M. (1987). Prediction. In H. C. Quay (Ed.), *Handbook of juvenile delinquency* (pp. 325–382). New York: Wiley.

Loeber, R., Lahey, B. B., & Thomas, C. (1991). Diagnostic conundrum of oppositional defiant disorder and conduct disorder. *Journal of Abnormal Psychology, 100,* 379–390.

McDaniel, K. D. (1986). Pharmacologic treatment of psychiatric and neurodevelopmental disorders in children and adolescents. *Clinical Pediatrics, 25,* 65–71.

Meloy, J. R. (1988). *The psychopathic mind.* Northvale, NJ: Aronson.

Moffitt, T. E. (1993). Adolescence-Limited and Life-Course-Persistent antisocial behavior: A taxonomy. *Psychological Review, 100,* 674–701.

O'Donnell, D. J. (1985). Conduct disorders. In J. M. Wiener (Ed.), *Diagnosis and psychopharmacology of childhood and adolescent disorders* (pp. 251–287). New York: Wiley.

Quay, H. C. (1986a). Conduct disorders. In H. C. Quay & J. S. Werry (Eds.), *Psychopathological disorders of childhood* (3rd ed.; pp. 35–72). New York: Wiley.

Quay, H. C. (1986b). Classification. In H. C. Quay & J. S. Werry (Eds.), *Psychopathological disorders of childhood* (3rd ed.; pp. 1–34). New York: Wiley.

Quay, H. C. (1987). Patterns of delinquent behavior. In H. C. Quay (Ed.), *Handbook of juvenile delinquency* (pp. 118–138). New York: Wiley.

Quay, H. C., Routh, D. K., & Shapiro, S. K. (1987). Psychopathology of childhood. *Annual Review of Psychology, 38,* 491–532.

Schalling, D. (1978). Psychopathy-related variables and the psychophysiology of socialization. In R. D. Hare & D. Schalling (Eds.), *Psychopathic behaviour* (pp. 85–106). Chichester, England: Wiley.

Sperling, M. (1974). *The major neuroses and behavior disorders in children.* New York: Aronson.

Stattin, H., & Magnusson, D. (1989). The role of early aggressive behavior in the frequency, seriousness, and types of later crime. *Journal of Consulting and Clinical Psychology, 57,* 710–718.

Stewart, J. T., Myers, W. C., Burket, R. C., & Lyles, W. B. (1990). A review of psychopharmacotherapy of aggression in children and adolescents. *Journal of the American Academy of Child and Adolescent Psychiatry, 29,* 269–277.

Tolan, P., Ryan, K., & Jaffe, C. (1988). Adolescents' mental health service use and provider, process, and recipient characteristics. *Journal of Clinical Child Psychology, 17,* 229–236.

Tremblay, R. E., Loeber, R., Gagnon, C., Charlebois, P., Larivee, S., & LeBlanc, M. (1991). Disruptive boys with stable and unstable high fighting behavior patterns during junior elementary school. *Journal of Abnormal Child Psychology, 19,* 285–300.

Weber, C. A., Meloy, J. R., & Gacono, C. B. (1992). Rorschach study of attachment and anxiety in inpatient conduct-disordered and dysthyic adolescents. *Journal of Personality Assessment, 58,* 16–26.

Weiner, I. B. (1992). *Psychological disturbance in adolescence* (2nd ed.). New York: Wiley.

CHAPTER 9

School Learning Problems

School learning problems commonly result in young people being referred to mental health professionals. Poor school performance is among the most frequent difficulties that psychologists who work with children and adolescents are asked to evaluate. Evaluation of school learning problems requires comprehensive consideration of developmental, intellectual, psychological, interpersonal, and environmental factors that can contribute to poor performance in the classroom. Rorschach findings bear directly on some of these factors, whereas in other respects, personality test data have little relevance to the problem.

The usefulness of personality assessment in the clinical management of school learning problems depends on the reasons a youngster is doing poorly in school or less well than would be expected on the basis of his or her grades in the past or scores on tests of intelligence or achievement. In some instances, serious psychological disorder is impairing the youngster's ability to study and learn. Young people who have difficulty thinking clearly, exercising good judgment, mustering productive energy, sustaining a reasonable level of concentration, and feeling comfortable in interpersonal situations are prone to problems in achieving grades commensurate with their ability. Accordingly, school learning problems may arise as a secondary consequence of schizophrenia, affective or borderline disorders, or other psychopathological conditions that compromise effective mental functioning and task performance.

To the extent that the Rorschach helps to identify such pathological conditions, it may provide a telling explanation of why a young person is doing poorly in school and point to recommendations to alleviate the school learning problem through treatment of the major psychopathological condition. The contribution of the Rorschach in such instances is indirect, however, in that it relates to personality and psychopathology in general rather than to any specific parameters of the school learning process.

Motivational determinants unrelated to psychopathology can also play a prominent role in school learning problems. Research findings indicate that young people who do well in school tend to be interested in learning, enjoy getting good grades, and see a clear relationship between achieving in school and realizing other goals that are important to them. By contrast, young people who lack commitment to intellectual values or academic goals see little reason to work hard in school. They are rarely inclined to exert themselves in the classroom, except perhaps just enough to avoid the inconvenience of outright failure. They typically dislike school and do not anticipate that doing well academically will yield either inner satisfaction or external rewards (Carr, Borkowski, & Maxwell, 1991; Gottfried, 1985; Pintrich & de Groot, 1990; Wentzel, Weinberger, Ford, & Feldman, 1990).

Low academic motivation is shaped by a variety of negative family, peer group, and sex-role influences (see Weiner, 1992, Chap. 7). Parents who place little value on the educational process and doubt whether formal education helps people get ahead in life often instill unenthusiastic attitudes toward school learning in their offspring. Young people who are striving for acceptance within a social group that endorses nonintellectual values and belittles academic achievement may be tempted to turn away from academic pursuits. Prevailing attitudes either at home or among peers concerning what constitutes appropriate male and female behavior can also detract from motivation to achieve in school, if they cause boys to anticipate that good students will be perceived as feminine and girls to anticipate that good students will be perceived as masculine.

The hallmark of low motivation as a determinant of academic underachievement is its ready acknowledgment. Unmotivated underachievers will openly admit that they dislike school and see no reason to become well educated. In such circumstances, personality assessment rarely helps to understand how a school learning problem originated and what can be done about it.

Often, however, school learning problems arise neither as secondary consequences of psychological disturbance nor as sociocultural phenomena unrelated to disturbance, but instead constitute primary manifestations of an intellectual, neuropsychological, or psychological condition. Some young people earn low grades in school because of limited intelligence, and others perform poorly relative to their abilities because of specific learning disabilities or disorders of attention or because of family interaction difficulties that produce a syndrome of primary psychological underachievement.

LIMITED INTELLIGENCE

Referral questions involving learning problems always call for careful evaluation of a young person's overall intelligence, as indicated by an IQ score, and of his or her intellectual strengths and weaknesses, as reflected in varying scores on measures of specific kinds of intellectual function. This evaluation may indicate that a young person's poor school grades are commensurate with his or her abilities and simply reflect limited intelligence. The school learning difficulty in such cases is a cognitive problem that requires educational planning, not a personality problem that requires psychological intervention. Differential diagnosis and treatment planning will accordingly proceed on the basis of an intellectual evaluation in which the Rorschach plays little part.

However, even though primary school learning problems can be meaningfully differentiated with respect to intellectual, neuropsychological, or psychological causation, these causes are far from being mutually exclusive. They may overlap in individual children who have the misfortune of being both intellectually limited and learning disabled. In addition, most young people who develop school learning problems demonstrate behavioral difficulties as well. Thompson, Lampron, Johnson, and Eckstein (1990) assessed behavioral disturbance in four groups of students ages 6 to 17 who had been referred to an evaluation center because of poor school performance. Of these subjects, 34 had learning disabilities, 14 subjects were mentally retarded (IQ < 70), 14 demonstrated borderline intelligence (IQ 70–84), and 17 subjects showed neither learning disabilities nor cognitive impairment. Of these poorly performing students, 71% met criteria for a DSM-III Axis I disorder, and 92% showed behavioral disturbance on the Missouri Children's Behavior Checklist. The types and rates of behavioral disturbance differed only slightly among the four groups, and the overall rate of disturbance approximated that seen among young people referred to psychiatric clinics.

As these findings indicate, even poor learners whose academic difficulties derive primarily from limited intelligence may often have adjustment difficulties. How do these young people view themselves, and how are they coping psychologically with the handicap of limited intellectual endowment? What capacities do they have for tolerating frustration and controlling their behavior? Do they harbor fears or resentments of other people that are complicating their school learning problems by making them excessively withdrawn or aggressive in social relationships? Because questions of this type concern aspects of personality functioning, the Rorschach can often provide information that helps to answer them. Accordingly, when treatment planning for young people of limited intelligence involves such considerations, Rorschach findings can make important contributions to whatever plans are made.

In using the Rorschach to describe personality functioning in young people with limited intelligence, clinicians must proceed cautiously in working with protocols of young people whose measured IQ falls below 80. The age-related normative data were collected from students in regular class placements. These subjects do not adequately represent young people with IQs of less than 80, who often are placed in some special class or program, and they are especially unlikely to represent retarded youngsters with IQs less than 70, who ordinarily are placed outside a regular school setting.

The absence of intellectually borderline or retarded young people from the normative data does not mean that the Rorschach is inapplicable to children and adolescents with IQs in the 70s or low 80s. Interpreters need to recognize the lack of standardization data on this population and to communicate this fact in reporting their evaluations of borderline retarded subjects; conclusions should not be based on reference data that do not exist. On the other hand, an obtained Full-Scale IQ in the 70s may not be representative of the true functioning of the subject, any more than does a Full-Scale IQ in the 80s. Both are an average that comprises specific kinds of ability that, for some abilities, may range well into the below-average level or beyond. All clinicians who work with children appreciate that a young person who receives an IQ score in the 70s may be someone of at least below-average intelligence whose test performance in specific areas is being suppressed by some specific psychological or neuropsychological difficulties.

Hence, young people with borderline intelligence may frequently produce Rorschach records of adequate length that are just as informative and interpretable as those given by youngsters with IQs in the 80s and 90s. In such cases, clinicians should feel comfortable in interpreting and basing conclusions and recommendations on the data obtained, as long as they keep sight of the fact that they are extrapolating from age-level reference data rather than working from adequate standardization. At the same time, interpreters need to expect that a substantial proportion of borderline retarded youngsters will produce brief or unelaborated records that provide little information about their personality functioning. In other words, their Rorschachs tend to coincide quite directly with what might be expected in light of the intelligence test findings.

As intellectual limitations become more severe, the Rorschach becomes increasingly impoverished. When IQ falls below the mid-70s or lower, and intelligence tests show little variability in performance, Rorschach findings may no longer support any useful conclusions. These young people have limited capacities for differentiating discrete thoughts and feelings, forming complex concepts, and expressing themselves verbally, and they also lack life experiences on which to draw in formulating responses to unfamiliar situations. Consequently, they tend to give brief Rorschachs with a preponderance of *Pure F* responses. Movement responses rarely appear in their records, and they seldom respond to the subtleties of shading or achromatic color. Use of chromatic color, should it occur, tends to be primitive and poorly modulated and to include a greater than usual frequency of Color Naming. Their developmental quality shows few if any $DQ+$ responses, and their form quality is often poor, with a low $X + \%$ and numerous Unusual and minus answers. The range of contents is narrow and rarely extends beyond animal, botany, and landscape percepts, and the number of Popular answers is typically lower than average.

These Rorschach expectations in mental retardation have been demonstrated in what there is of a very sparse literature. Two important sources of information in this regard remain contributions by Rorschach and Beck from over 60 years ago. Rorschach (1921/1942) included 12 "feeble-minded" individuals among the 405 subjects he examined in preparing his original monograph. He provides several tables comparing these retarded subjects to other diagnostic groups on such characteristics as their location choice, color use, and form level, and he includes a case example of an "Imbecile, age 17" (p. 132). Beck (1930) describes his research with retarded children at the New York City Children's School on Randall's Island, in what was the very first paper on the Rorschach to appear in an American journal.

Despite this auspicious beginning, very little Rorschach work with retarded young people has been published. Good examples of Rorschach and other test performance appear in case studies of intellectually limited children (Siegel, 1987, Chap. 14) and of adolescents (Hirsch, 1970, Chap. 2). Like the earlier research, these examples confirm that the restricted protocols of mentally retarded subjects usually provide little basis for drawing diagnostic inferences or suggesting treatment approaches. For example, whether a moderately retarded youngster is psychotic or depressed will rarely be answerable from a Rorschach test. On the other hand, Rorschachs taken from the intellectually impaired usually do provide a fairly accurate picture of their personality structure which, unfortunately, typically appears as being quite impoverished.

On occasion, the Rorschach of a young person with apparent intellectual limitations, as reflected in poor grades and a measured IQ in the borderline range, will be surprisingly rich rather than impoverished. This is especially likely to occur when a child or adolescent has capacities for complex concept formation and integrative thinking that may not be tapped by standard tests of intelligence. For example, Developmental Quality and $DQ+$ responses in particular are known to correlate with intelligence, and some children with relatively low IQs (70–89) have been found to show higher perceptual integration scores than other children with similar IQs (Acklin & Fechner-Bates, 1989; Gerstein, Brodzinsky, & Reiskind, 1976; Ridley & Bayton 1983). In these circumstances obtained IQ scores may, for one reason or another, not be truly representative of a youngster's talents, and further cognitive studies are needed to determine whether he or she is intellectually handicapped. The same proposition might be put forth should a Rorschach include several good quality Ms, adequate $X + \%,$ a rich and varied number of contents, and a wide range of determinants. These features are usually not present in the records of persons whose Full-Scale IQs fall in the 70–79 range or lower.

Returning to the subject of school learning problems, Rorschach findings can often contribute to treatment planning for young people who are intellectually limited but not retarded and have IQs in the 80s. The more such youngsters are showing behavioral difficulties along with their poor grades, the greater the Rorschach's contribution is likely to be in determining their treatment needs. Sometimes the problem with the below-average or borderline intelligence student is not simply poor school performance, but rather how the parents react to that performance. Case 10 provides an illustration of this type of problem.

CASE 10—AN ISSUE OF INTELLECTUAL LIMITATIONS

This is a 10-year, 3-month-old male who was evaluated at the request of his parents and with mutual agreement from the school guidance counselor. He is currently in the 3rd month of repeating the fourth grade and has been assigned to a resource room for 1 hour each day to work on problems in reading and arithmetic. His overall academic progress has not been very good since the second grade, and in each subsequent year he appears to fall lower than the expected acceptable level of performance. His second-, third-, and fourth-grade teachers all acknowledge that his effort is usually adequate but note that his motivation tends to wane when his efforts do not yield a satisfactory performance. His current fourth-grade teacher, different than the one he had in the fourth grade last year, describes him as usually easygoing and usually not upset by failure, but she also notes that occasionally he does become quite emotional when he does not do well. She says that during those times when he becomes overly emotional he becomes angry, tearful, and generally avoidant of those around him. In general, his response to failure seems less mature than that of others in her class. However, she does not perceive this as a major problem. She identifies the major problem to be that he does not retain information well, and even though he is repeating previous learning experiences, he does not do as well as might be expected, and his overall performance is substandard. She has made the referral for the additional help in the resource room.

Prior to his acceptance to the resource room, he was administered a variety of cognitive tests, including the administration of the WISC-R. The results of the latter yield a Verbal IQ of 82 (scaled scores of 6 on Information and Arithmetic, 9 on Vocabulary, 8 on Similarities, and 10 on Digit Span), and a Performance IQ of 84 (scaled scores of 7 on Coding, 9 on Block Design and Mazes). His WRAT performance places him at a grade level of between 2.5 and 2.7 for all three sections of the test. He had 13 errors on the speech sounds test of the Halstead-Reitan; 39 errors on the Categories Test; completed the six-figure Tactual Performance Test in 4 minutes 7 seconds with his right hand and 2 minutes 35 seconds with his left hand and was able to localize only three figures and remembered only three figures; and completed Trails A in 84 seconds and Trails B in 2 minutes 12 seconds while making three errors. In effect, all the cognitive test data can be used to argue in favor of the conclusion that this is an intellectually disadvantaged youngster who probably cannot keep up with his peers easily in an intellectually dominated atmosphere.

His parents have objected strenuously to this conclusion and have sought the advice of an independent psychologist who has administered the WISCR-R again and the K-ABC. The psychologist has interpreted her findings to suggest that, while the WISC-R findings are not very different than those obtained by the school, some of the test results suggest that the subject is experiencing slower than common intellectual growth, and she has suggested that the subject can be expected to do better as he gets older. She has recommended that the amount of resource room time be reduced by 50% with the objective of no resource room help by the end of the year. She has also recommended private tutoring in selected material. Her recommendations are based on her belief that (a) the subject will increase his intellectual capacities as he grows, and (b) that excessive time in the resource room tends to inhibit social development and is causing the subject to develop a negative self-image. The parents translate this recommendation into the notion that, if he continues with as much resource room involvement as is now the case, it will lead to more psychological problems. They are considering a private school placement but are reluctant to make such a change because many of his peers from grades 3, 4, and 5 live in the immediate neighborhood.

The subject is slightly taller and heavier than most of the children in the fourth grade, but the fourth-grade teacher does not believe that this difference is substantial. She points out that at least three boys in the class are taller and four are heavier. The parents report nothing remarkable in the medical history. He is the second of three children. His older brother, age 12, is in the sixth grade and doing above-average work. His sister, age 7, is in the second grade and doing satisfactory work. His father, age 34, is a pharmacist and own half interest in the drugstore in which he works. The mother is a college graduate who works part-time (10–15 hours per week) in the drugstore. She reports a normal birth and says that the subject walked at about the age of 18 months and spoke sentences before the age of 3 years. She says that he gets along well with his siblings and takes an active interest in household-related matters. She notes that he is involved with a Little League baseball team, but admits that he does not play much. She also notes that he looks forward to playing soccer at school.

The subject commented freely about his trouble with arithmetic, but said that he likes to read, play baseball, and soccer. He also reports that the family has a small computer on which he often plays games with his brother but admits that he doesn't win most of the time. He says that when he grows up he would like to drive a race car.

Case 10. A 9-Year-Old Male

Card	Response	Inquiry		Scoring
I	1. Mayb a bird or	E:	(Rpts S's resp)	Wo Fo A 1.0
		S:	Well it cb one, thes r wgs & its got a tail dwn hre lik a bird wld hav	
	2. A bf	E:	(Rpts S's resp)	Wo Fo A P 1.0 DV,PSV
		S:	Wel bfs got wgs 2 jst l thes & thr's th tail 2 & bfs hav thes litl feely thngs on thr heads it realy cb a bf	
II	3. Tht ll blood up thre	E:	(Rpts S's resp)	Dv C 2 Bl
		S:	I guess it just does	
		E:	I kno it does to u but help me to c it 2	
		S:	Lk its al red j lik bld lik 2 spts bld spts	
	4. Thr's a hole in it	E:	(Rpts S's resp)	DSv Fo Id MOR
		S:	Its jst a hol in th papr c it used to b colrd l th rst but it got punchd out & its j a hol	
		E:	Wht makes it ll a hol	
		S:	Thrs nothin thre thre ain't nothin in holes	
III	5. Two people	E:	(Rpts S's resp)	Do Fo 2 H P
		S:	One here & one here	
		E:	Wht is thr tht makes thm ll people	
		S:	Each one has a head & legs lik 2 people	
	6. Ths is lik blood spots 2	E:	(Rpts S's resp)	Dv C 2 Bl
		S:	Its red lik th othr ones 2 spots	
IV	7. Nothin except a pile of dirt	E:	(Rpts S's resp)	Wv CFu Ls
		S:	If u make a pile of dirt it ll ths	
		E:	I d thnk I c it lik u do help me o.k.	
		S:	Dirts all blck & ths is all blk & if u make a pil of it thn it ll ths lks	
V	8. A fly	E:	(Rpts S's resp)	Wo Fu A 1.0 INC
		S:	Its got wgs & th stingrs on thm & litl hands out hre	
		E:	Show me the stingers	
		S:	Out here (D10)	
VI	9. A dead cat	E:	(Rpts S's resp)	Wo FTo A P 2.5 MOR
		S:	Its al flat it prob got hit by a car & its all flat	
		E:	Wht makes it ll a cat	
		S:	Its got a nose & whiskers & its legs r out hre & its fuzzy too lik a cat	
		E:	Fuzzy	
		S:	Sure (rubs blot)	

Case 10. (Continued)

Card	Response	Inquiry	Scoring
VII	10. Smoke & fire, no wait	E: (Rpts S's resp)	Wv mpu Fi
		S: It doesnt ll tht now	
		E: Well lets try to find how it lookd	
		S: Jst al I gues its smok but no fir I dont c fr	
		E: How does it ll smoke	
		S: IDK its just going up lik smoke smoke can ll anythng its really 2 rabbits	
	11. Its realy 2 rabits	E: (Rpts S's resp)	Do Fo 2 A
		S: 1 hre & here c thy hav long ears lik rabits & thy have a tail	
VIII	12. Lions	E: (Rpts S's resp)	Do Fo 2 A P
		S: One here & here thy hav legs & a tail	
	13. A skeleton too	E: (Rpts S's resp)	DSo Fu An
		S: Just som bones lik a skeleton (outlines DS3) c right in here	
IX	14. A flower	E: (Rpts S's resp)	W+ CFo Bt 5.5 PER
		S: It ll a flowr its pretty w orange flowrs & its got green leaves 2 not ths stuf tho thts not prt of it thts a pot lik u hav th flowr in my mothr has 1 lik ths 1	
X	15. A lot of lites flashing	E: (Rpts S's resp)	Wv ma.C Sc
		S: Its lik whn thy flash lites w all th diff colrs thy go off & on ths is lik thyr on	
	16. These r lik blue crabs	E: (Rpts S's resp)	Do FCo 2 A P
		S: Lik u get at th shor blu crabs thyr realy good to eat & thyr hard to get somtimes	
		E: Im not sur why thy ll blu crabs	
		S: Thyv got all th legs & thyr blue	

346

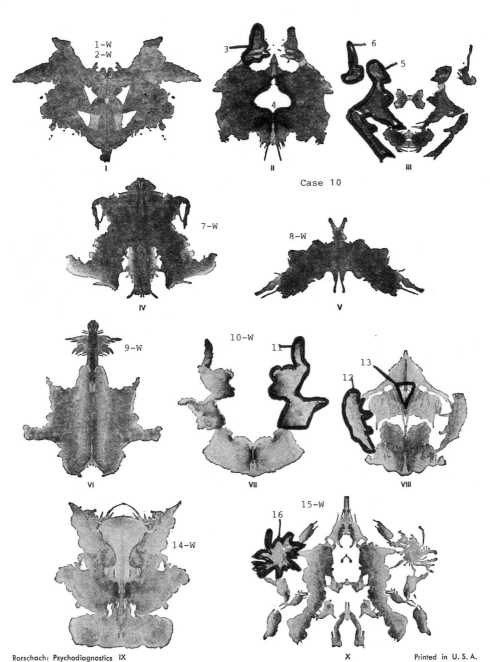

Case 10

Case 10   **Sequence of Scores**

Card	No	Loc	#	Determinant(s)	(2)	Content(s)	Pop	Z	Special Scores
I	1	Wo	1	Fo		A		1.0	
	2	Wo	1	Fo		A	P	1.0	DV,PSV
II	3	Dv	2	C	2	Bl			
	4	DSv	5	Fo		Id			MOR
III	5	Do	9	Fo	2	H	P		
	6	Dv	2	C	2	Bl			
IV	7	Wv	1	C'Fu		Ls			
V	8	Wo	1	Fu		A		1.0	INC
VI	9	Wo	1	FTo		A	P	2.5	MOR
VII	10	Wv	1	mpu		Fi			
	11	Do	2	Fo	2	A			
VIII	12	Do	1	Fo	2	A	P		
	13	DSo	3	Fu		An			
IX	14	W+	1	CFo		Bt		5.5	PER
X	15	Wv	1	ma.C		Sc			
	16	Do	1	FCo	2	A	P		

Copyright © 1976, 1985, 1990 by John E. Exner, Jr.

Case 10   **Structural Summary**

Location	Determinants		Contents	S-Constellation
Features	Blends	Single		. . FV+VF+V+FD>2
			H = 1, 0	. . Col−Shd Bl>0
Zf = 5	m.C	M = 0	(H) = 0, 0	. . Ego<.31,>.44
ZSum = 11.0		FM = 0	Hd = 0, 0	. . MOR > 3
ZEst = 13.5		m = 1	(Hd) = 0, 0	. . Zd > +− 3.5
		FC = 1	Hx = 0, 0	. . es > EA
W = 8		CF = 1	A = 7, 0	. . CF+C > FC
(Wv = 3)		C = 2	(A) = 0, 0	. . X+% < .70
D = 8		Cn = 0	Ad = 0, 0	. . S > 3
Dd = 0		FC' = 0	(Ad) = 0, 0	. . P < 3 or > 8
S = 2		C'F = 1	An = 1, 0	. . Pure H < 2
		C' = 0	Art = 0, 0	. . R < 17
DQ		FT = 1	Ay = 0, 0	x . . . . . TOTAL
. . . . . (FQ−)		TF = 0	Bl = 2, 0	
+ = 1 (0)		T = 0	Bt = 1, 0	Special Scorings
o = 9 (0)		FV = 0	Cg = 0, 0	Lv1 Lv2
v/+ = 0 (0)		VF = 0	Cl = 0, 0	DV = 1x1 0x2
v = 6 (0)		V = 0	Ex = 0, 0	INC = 1x2 0x4
		FY = 0	Fd = 0, 0	DR = 0x3 0x6
		YF = 0	Fi = 1, 0	FAB = 0x4 0x7
		Y = 0	Ge = 0, 0	ALOG = 0x5
Form Quality		Fr = 0	Hh = 0, 0	CON = 0x7
		rF = 0	Ls = 1, 0	SUM6 = 2
FQx FQf MQual SQx		FD = 0	Na = 0, 0	WSUM6 = 3
+ = 0 0 0 0		F = 8	Sc = 1, 0	
o = 9 6 0 1			Sx = 0, 0	AB = 0 CP = 0
u = 4 2 0 1			Xy = 0, 0	AG = 0 MOR = 2
− = 0 0 0 0			Id = 1, 0	CFB = 0 PER = 1
none = 3 — 0 0		(2) = 6		COP = 0 PSV = 1

Case 10   **Ratios, Percentages, and Derivations**

R = 16	L = 1.00		FC:CF+C = 1: 4	COP = 0 AG = 0
			Pure C = 3	Food = 0
EB = 0: 6.0	EA = 6.0	EBPer = 6.0	Afr = 0.45	Isolate/R = 0.13
eb = 2: 2	es = 4	D = 0	S = 2	H:(H)Hd(Hd) = 1:0
	Adj es = 3	Adj D = +1	Blends:R = 1:16	(HHd):(AAd) = 0:0
			CP = 0	H+A:Hd+Ad = 8:0
FM = 0 : C' = 1 T = 1				
m = 2 : V = 0 Y = 0				
		P = 5	Zf = 5	3r+(2)/R = 0.38
a:p = 1: 1	Sum6 = 2	X+% = 0.56	Zd = −2.5	Fr+rF = 0
Ma:Mp = 0: 0	Lv2 = 0	F+% = 0.75	W:D:Dd = 8: 8: 0	FD = 0
2AB+Art+Ay=0	WSum6 = 3	X−% = 0.00	W:M = 8: 0	An+Xy = 1
M− = 0	Mnone = 0	S−% = 0.00	DQ+ = 1	MOR = 2
		Xu% = 0.25	DQv = 6	
SCZI = 1	DEPI = 4	CDI = 3	S-CON = N/A HVI = No	OBS = No

INTERPRETIVE ROUTINE FOR CASE 10

The first positive Key variable is that the D Score is lower than the Adjusted D Score. When this occurs, the interpretation must always begin with a review of the cluster concerning controls, adding to that review any added information developed from the array of variables related to situational stress. However, the remainder of the interpretive strategy must be defined on the basis of the next positive Key or Tertiary variable. In this case, the next positive Key variable is the value for Lambda (1.00), which is greater than 0.99 and, as such, defines the rest of the interpretive routine. Therefore, the interpretation will review the data in the various clusters in the following order:

CONTROLS → SITUATIONAL STRESS → PROCESSING → MEDIATION →
IDEATION → AFFECT → SELF-PERCEPTION →
INTERPERSONAL PERCEPTION

Controls—Case 10   The data concerning issues of capacity for control and tolerance for stress for Case 10 are shown in Table 86.

Table 86.   Controls and Stress Tolerance Data for Case 10

EB = 0:6.0		EA = 6.0	D = 0
eb = 2:2		es = 4 Adjes = 3	AdjD = +1
FM = 0	C' = 1	T = 1	CDI = 3
m = 2	V = 0	Y = 0	

The Adjusted D Score of +1 is probably misleading, though not completely so. It must be challenged because the EA (6.0) is made up only of the left-side value for the EB. The absence of M responses is quite unusual, and likely a product of affective flooding, that is, a situation in which the emotions are so strong and influential in the psychological operations of a person that they impair the ability to delay. Thus, attention and concentration often falter, and thinking is less consistent and more haphazard. Under different circumstances in which the flooding does not occur, the EA may be higher, but it is equally plausible to postulate that EA may remain the same or even be lower because more control might be exerted over affective discharges. Therefore, under other circumstances, the Adjusted D might remain greater than zero or might be zero.

In either event, it is more important to focus on the low es and Adjusted es. Whereas es values of 6, 7, or 8 are expected for youngsters of this age, the obtained value is only 4, and includes no FM answers. This could mean that he keeps his experienced needs at a very low level by acting on them quickly, or for one reason or another, he does not experience his own needs as do most of his age. The low level of internally irritating stimuli indicated affords greater relative strength to the rather modest level of available resource as reflected in the EA of 6.0. Obviously, if the level of experienced stimulation increases slightly, the D Scores will fall, and should the es or Adjusted es increase by more than 4 points to an expected range, both D Scores would fall into the minus range. In other words, he is quite vulnerable to an overload state even though, at the moment, that possibility seems remote and he does have sufficient available resources to contend with his experienced demands. Obviously, the data concerning affect will be quite important to any useful understanding of this youngster.

Situationally Related Stress—Case 10   The data related to situational stress for Case 10 are shown in Table 87.

Table 87.   Situational Stress Data for Case 10

					ANALYSIS OF DETERMINANT BLENDS	
D	= 0	*EA*	= 6.0		Total Blends	= 1
Adj D	= +1	Pure *C*	= 3		Blends created by *m,Y,T*	= 1
Sum *T*	= 1				Blends created by *m* or *Y*	= 1
Sum *m*	= 2	*M*Q−	= 0			
Sum *Y*	= 0	*M*Qnone	= 0		Color-Shading Blends created by *Y* = 0	

Ordinarily, the 1-point difference between the D Scores would suggest that current stresses have reduced the capacity for control and the tolerance for stress. In this case, as the validity of the Adjusted D Score is questionable, that may not be the case. As noted earlier, the *EA* value is quite low and indicates some vulnerability to overload. That vulnerability is probably well illustrated by the fact that one *M* response creates a difference between the D Scores. Nonetheless, the presence of situational stress is incontrovertible. It manifests in the two *m* answers, indicating that his level of peripheral thought is being increased by the stress and this will result in a reduction in attention and concentration abilities. It also manifests in the fact that his only blend answer is created by an *m* determinant, implying that his overall psychology is being made more complex than is usual by the stress situation. It is also important to note that there are three pure *C* responses, raising a question about whether they would persist in a retest or whether they are the product of the current stress.

Processing—Case 10   The data related to his information-processing activities are shown in Table 88.

Table 88.   Processing Data for Case 10

L	= 1.00	*W:D:Dd*	= 8:8:0	*Zd*	= −2.5	*DQ*+	= 1
Zf	= 5	*W:M*	= 8:0	PSV	= 1	*DQv/+*	= 0
HVI	= No	OBS	= No			*DQv*	= 6

<table>
<tr><td colspan="6" align="center">LOCATION SEQUENCING</td></tr>
<tr><td>I</td><td>W,W</td><td>IV</td><td>W</td><td>VII</td><td>W,D</td></tr>
<tr><td>II</td><td>D,D</td><td>V</td><td>W</td><td>VIII</td><td>D,D</td></tr>
<tr><td>III</td><td>D,D</td><td>VI</td><td>W</td><td>IX</td><td>W</td></tr>
<tr><td></td><td></td><td></td><td></td><td>X</td><td>W,D</td></tr>
</table>

The positive value for Lambda reveals that he is oriented to avoid complexity and deal with new situations in a simplistic or narrow manner. This is not surprising in light of his limited intellect, but it is a stylistic orientation that invariably causes problems. People who routinely tend to oversimplify, whether young or old, often neglect critical stimulus cues. Thus, when they formulate responses, many are likely to be ineffective or even inappropriate because of the disregard for some of the more important aspects of a situation. When this neglect of important inputs occurs routinely in a learning situation, such as an elementary or secondary school, it is inevitable that the resulting performance will fall short of what is required. Even if the motivation for learning seems adequate, the basic High *Lambda* Style will interfere with the learning objectives.

A High *Lambda* Style is not uncommon among those who are intellectually limited as it often provides immediate relief from the unwanted complexities of life that they may experience as being potentially overwhelming. The immediate relief tends to be quite reinforcing for the moment, and longer term objectives are put aside in favor of the immediately experienced sense of well-being. Usually, no single instance of simplification yields a sharply negative result. Instead, the products of the style are cumulative and ultimately lead to some imposed penalty such as school or occupational failure.

The other data in the cluster are consistent with a finding of intellectual or neurologically related deficit. The *Zf* is very low (5) for a 10-year-old, suggesting that he is not very prone to try to organize new stimulus fields. The data for the *W:D:Dd* (8:8:0) and *W:M* ratios (8:0) imply somewhat more motivation for processing than the *Zf* datum, and the sequence by which he selects locations is consistent. However, the *W:M* seems to indicate that he sets processing objectives that are well beyond his functional capacities and he does have one within card PSV. Thus, he probably has the desire, but his limited capabilities are highlighted by the rather devastating findings concerning the quality of his processing activity. There is only one *DQ+* response as contrasted with six *DQv* answers, three of which are *W* answers, and four of which are first responses. The latter suggests that he does not store information quickly in ways that are easily translated. These findings lead directly to the implication of an intellectual or neurological deficit unless other evidence of severe pathology exists. Interestingly, the *Zd* score of −2.5 is in the average range, a finding that might not be expected in light of other processing data. It indicates that his scanning activity is probably not very different than for most of his age.

In effect, the composite of data can be used to argue that, although his motivation and scanning activity are typical for his age, the actual procedures of gathering new inputs are much more primitive than should be the case. In many instances, he oversimplifies new fields to the extent that they do not become very meaningful and, as a result, are stored in ways that make them of little use in the future.

Mediation—Case 10   The data concerning cognitive mediation for Case 10 are shown in Table 89.

Table 89.   Cognitive Mediation Data for Case 10

Lambda	= 1.00	OBS	= Neg	MINUS FEATURES	
P	= 5	*X+%*	= .56		
FQx+	= 0	*F+%*	= .75		
FQxo	= 9	*Xu%*	= .25		
FQxu	= 4	*X−%*	= .00		
FQx−	= 0	*S−%*	= .00		
*FQx*none	= 3	CONFAB	= 0		

When reviewing the data for this cluster, the High *Lambda* Style becomes a focal issue again. People, especially younger people, who have this style are prone to translate new information somewhat haphazardly, that is, they identify or translate stimuli more quickly than should be the case. They do so in accord with their orientation to deal with the stimulus field in an easy and simple manner. This often results in a distortion of the field or a translation of it in a simplistic and unconventional way. Thus, for many high Lambda subjects, and especially children, the $X - \%$ and/or the $Xu\%$ are atypically high, and the frequency of Popular answers is unusually low.

In Case 10, the number of Popular answers (5), is slightly lower than expected for a 10-year-old and the $X + \%$ (.56) is considerably lower than expected. Interestingly, there are no minus responses and the $Xu\%$ (.25) is only slightly greater than might be expected for this age, leading to an expectation that the $X + \%$ should be at least 70% However, the $X + \%$ is pushed down because of three no-form answers, all of which are pure C responses. This seems to indicate that his reality testing is being interfered with by affective elements, or that the no-form responses could be a product of faulty processing. Two of the three pure C responses *are* first answers which could equate with a processing problem, but the third is a second response, which tends to defy the processing postulate. Thus, it is likely that a composite of processing and affective problems are contributing to a general reduction in the manner in which he deals with the reality of situations.

Ideation—Case 10   The data related to ideational activity for Case 10 are shown in Table 90.

Table 90.   Ideation Data for Case 10

			M QUALITY		SPECIAL SCORES			
EB	$= 0{:}6.0$	*EBPer* = 6.0						
eb	$= 2{:}2$	(*FM* = 0 *m* = 2)	+ = 0	DV	= 1	DV2	= 0
a:p	$= 1{:}1$	$M^a{:}M^p = 0{:}0$	o = 0	INC	= 1	INC2	= 0
2AB + Art + Ay = 0			u = 0	DR	= 0	DR2	= 0
MOR	= 1		− = 0	FAB	= 0	FAB2	= 0
				ALOG	= 0	SUM6	= 2
RESPONSES TO BE READ FOR QUALITY				CON	= 0	WSUM6	= 3

The data for the *EB* (0:6) are striking and important. As noted earlier, the zero value on the left side of the ratio indicates that he is emotionally *flooded*. His emotions are so intense that they impede his ability to delay and think things through when a new decision-making situation occurs. Flooding breeds impulsiveness in thinking, and decisions are often made too hastily and without regard for the reality of the situation. This impulsiveness often is manifested in behaviors, especially those that are inappropriate for the situation, and probably accounts for some of the deficits noted concerning his processing and mediational activity. The data for the *EB* also note that he is markedly extratensive, a finding confirmed by the datum for the *EBPer* (6.0). He is a youngster whose feelings dominate his thinking when he responds to new situations, and, as a result, he is markedly prone to a trial-and-error approach to problem solving, regardless of whether or not it may be the best way to address the situation.

The data for the *a:p* (1:1), $M^a{:}M^p$ (0:0) ratios and the Intellectualization Index (0) offer no interpretable findings but there are two MOR responses in this relatively brief record. They probably denote for pessimism to be prevalent in much of his thinking, that is, a gloomy outlook when he ponders about things. There are only two Critical Special Scores, one DV and one INCOM, which is considerably less than expected from a 10-year-old. Thus, there is no reason to believe that his thinking is unclear, or marked by pathological features. In general, his thinking appears to be at least as clear as most of his own age, but many of his decisions seem to be much more influenced by his feelings than should be the case.

Affect—Case 10   The data concerning affect for Case 10 are shown in Table 91.

Table 91.   Affect Data for Case 10

DEPI = 4				BLENDS
EB = 0:6.0		$EBPer$ = 6.0		m.C
eb = 2:2		$FC:CF + C$ = 1:4		
		Pure C = 3		
C' = 1	T = 1	Afr = 0.45		
V = 0	Y = 0	S = 2		
		Blends/R = 0:16		
		CP = 0		

The DEPI value (4) is not interpretively significant, but the data for the EB (0:6.0), as noted earlier, are quite important. The flooding phenomenon signals that feelings play a dominant role in most every decision that he makes, and often, those feelings can lead him into behaviors that are inappropriate and even unwanted. The EB conveys an extratensive style, but it is difficult to ascertain whether this is a transient result of the flooding. If the flooding did not exist, he might remain extratensive, but he also might be an ambitent. In either event, the pervasiveness of the current extratensive style limits his flexibility and means that most of his attempts at problem solving will involve trial-and-error actions that sometimes may often ignore the realities of a situation. The matter is made somewhat worse by the findings of the $FCF + C$ ratio (1:4). Most children, by the time they reach their 10th year, learn that sometimes it is best to modulate the expression of feelings. Typically, 10-year-olds are better controlled than 6-year-olds. This boy is not, and the excess of feeling that is conveyed in his behaviors probably will be regarded by his elders and his peers as a manifestation of immaturity. Three of his five color answers are pure C, increasing this likelihood and also the probability that many of his displays will be in the form of unbridled affect, which can only serve to alienate those around him. The content of the three pure C responses offers little to temper this postulate. Two of the three are blood and the third is lights. Although these answers may have been situationally prompted, there is no reason to assume that, under other conditions, he would exhibit much greater control.

At the same time, the Afr (0.45) is considerably lower than expected for a 10-year-old. It hints that he may have some awareness of his problems in dealing with emotion and tries to avoid emotionally loaded situations when possible. Unfortunately, as a 10-year-old child, his world frequently is laden with such stimuli. Interestingly, the right-side value of the eb (2), which is not atypical for a 10, contains a single C' response that also may hint at an effort to contain the release of feelings. The number of S answers (2) is not unusual for his age, and the single blend answer is not unexpected. It may signal something about his apparent quick reaction to need states, but more likely, it simply reflects the rather limited cognitive structure that exists.

Overall, there is no question that emotion poses a major problem for this young boy. He seems confused and overwhelmed by it and often is directed by its impact. It clouds his thinking and may be at least partially responsible for some of his processing and mediation difficulties. When he releases his feelings, they are not well modulated and frequently will manifest in ways that are overly intense and inappropriate for the situation. He seems fearful and avoidant of feelings and, as a result, is prone to avoid situations in which they are prominent. This avoidance only serves to add to his cognitive limitations and reduce the possibility of effective functioning.

Self-Perception—Case 10   Data concerning self-perception for Case 10 are shown in Table 92.

Table 92.   Self-Perception Data for Case 10

$3r + (2)/R = 0.38$	$FD = 0$	$MOR = 1$ $Hx = 0$		$An + Xy = 1$
$Fr + rF = 0$	Sum $V = 0$	$H:(H) + Hd + (Hd) = 1:0$		$Sx = 0$
		RESPONSES TO BE READ		
MOR Resp's	$FQ -$ Resp's	*M* Resp's	*FM* Resp's	*m* Resp's
9				10

The Egocentricity Index (0.38) is quite low for his age, indicating that he estimates his own worth to be much lower than that of those important to him. The absence of Vista or *FD* answers is not very surprising. There is only one human content in the record and it is a pure *H* response (Card III, Response 5), "Two people (Inquiry) Each one has a head and legs." If it is a self-representation, it is very nondescript and almost diffuse. The presence of even one *An* answer is somewhat unusual for a 10-year-old and could hint at body concern. Conversely, the presence of a single MOR answer is commonplace for most age groups. The content of the MOR (Card VI, response 9) "A dead cat (Inquiry) It's all flat, it probably got hit by a car . . . ," is the most common MOR answer given by children and does not offer much interpretive substance when studied alone.

Unfortunately, the record lacks the rich direct projections that often are important in fleshing out information concerning self-image. There are no minus answers and only two movement answers, both of which are *m*'s given to Card VII in Response 10, and Card X in Response 15. They may simply reflect a sort of situational helplessness and ideational confusion. The first is, "Smoke and fire" which he attempts to deny, and the second is, "A lot of lights flashing (Inquiry) . . . they go off and on . . ." Flashing lights usually provide a warning or at least call attention to something. In this instance, he (they) may be calling attention to his sense of discomfort with the test situation.

On the other hand, although the protocol may seem bland and even impoverished, parts of it do convey something about how this youngster perceives himself and his world, and a few answers are embellished in ways that are quite important. At least half of the responses can be considered as having a negative tone or feature; blood, a hole, blood spots, a pile of dirt, a fly, a dead cat, smoke and fire, and a skeleton. Most of these eight answers are diffuse and three, Response 4 (a hole), Response 7 (a pile of dirt), and Response 10 (smoke and fire) are described in ways that convey a sense of desolation. The first, Response 4, is elaborated in the Inquiry as, ". . . it used to be colored . . . but it got punched out and it's just a hole." The second, Response 7, is described as "Nothing except a pile of dirt (Inquiry) Dirt's all black and this is all black and if you make a pile of it then it looks like this." The third, Response 10, is an answer that he wanted to reject ("no wait . . . [Inquiry] It doesn't look like that now, . . . it's smoke but no fire, I don't see fire . . . smoke can look like anything . . ."). Collectively, these three answers impart a negative, strained, and diffuse sense of the self that probably haunts him in his everyday living. They suggest an awareness of his limitations and a feeling of helplessness in light of them.

Interpersonal Perception—Case 10   The data concerning interpersonal perception and behaviors for Case 10 are shown in Table 93.

Table 93.   Interpersonal Perception Data for Case 10

CDI = 3	$a{:}p$ = 1:1	T = 1	Human Cont = 1	Pure H = 1
HVI = Neg	Food = 0	PER = 1	COP = 0 AG = 0	Isolate/R = 0.13

RESPONSES TO BE READ

HUMAN MOVEMENT WITH PAIR	*HUMAN CONTENTS*
	5

As might be expected, the data concerning interpersonal relations and behaviors are sparse. The CDI and HVI are both negative, the $a{:}p$ ratio offers nothing of interpretive substance, and there are no Food answers. The most positive finding is the one Texture response, indicating that he does experience needs for closeness, but even that finding is tarnished by the fact that the answer is morbid (dead cat). As noted earlier, there is only one human content in the record and, thus, no reason to believe that he is very interested in people. The single PER answer is of little interpretive significance except for the fact that he identifies the object (flower) with his mother. There are no COP or AG answers, and the Isolation Index is not positive. There are no movement answers containing a pair and the single human content response is bland.

Overall, there are no data from which to suggest that this young boy's interpersonal life is rich and/or profitable for him. On the contrary, these data imply that his interpersonal life is sparse and unrewarding.

SUMMARY—CASE 10

This is, as might be predicted from the cognitive test data, a very impoverished youngster who is currently struggling desperately with his intense feelings. He does not have much capacity for control, and that which does exist is now impaired by situational stress that impairs his abilities to attend to and concentrate on new stimulus fields. But even if the stress did not exist, his emotions tend to run rampant throughout his psychological operations. They dictate many of his thoughts and dominate many of his behaviors. The matter is made more complex because he perceives himself quite negatively and has only a crude and unsophisticated sense of himself and others. He would like to be close to others but apparently has never developed the social skills that could make close relationships possible.

His poor performance in school is only a symptom of a much more extensive developmental problem. He has not learned how to contain his feelings, or how to delay and reprocess a field before attempting to translate it. Moreover, he probably doesn't even understand his feelings, much less how to delay their manifestations. He is not necessarily doomed because of his intellectual limitations, but they pose a major problem for his continuing growth. A question has been raised about whether he might do better academically in some sort of special class. The answer is "probably not," and in fact, additional special placement may only serve to enhance his already impoverished sense of self. At the same time, a continuation of his present academic circumstances will not be useful unless two important things change. First, the resource room time is being used to assist in reading and arithmetic. The subject matter may be appropriate, but the specific tactics employed should focus on the much broader goal of training him to delay and rescan the stimulus field before reaching conclusions and/or making a response. It is very important that his processing activity be altered with the hope that such an alteration will also eliminate the High *Lambda* Style on which he appears to rely too much at the present time. This alteration not only is critical to his academic troubles but also relates to several other psychological operations. It is especially important concerning the manner in which he processes and responds to affect and extends as well to his perceptions of himself and of people in relation to himself.

If he can become more comfortable about processing complex stimulus fields, it seems reasonable to predict that he will deal with his feelings more directly and less haphazardly and, hopefully, gain greater confidence in his abilities even though he is intellectually disadvantaged. Abandonment of the High *Lambda* Style also creates a better potential for perceiving his social environment differently and creates a greater likelihood that his interpersonal relations will develop in a more favorable manner.

A major task in this intervention process concerns the perception that his parents have of him. They seem quite unwilling to accept his intellectual limitations and are seeking alternatives. The conclusions of the consulting psychologist have been detrimental in this context as they have been afforded some hope that he might ultimately develop a more complex neurological structure that will permit him to function at a higher level. It is very important for them to understand that this is unlikely, and the pressures that they now exert on him only serve to exacerbate his difficulties. If they can accept him as he is, and gradually come to aid in his perceptual retraining, all involved will benefit. Their active participation in the retraining may also contribute significantly to needed changes in his self-image and in the development of social skills that currently are in disarray. Their support for this intervention plan can be crucial; without it, the plan can be easily undermined creating the potential for more disaster in the future.

SPECIFIC LEARNING DISABILITIES AND ATTENTION DEFICIT DISORDER

Specific learning disabilities (SLD) consist of deficits in essential learning processes that cause young people to achieve below expectation in the absence of any primary emotional disorder, lack of motivation, or inadequate opportunity to learn. Although these specific disabilities are not attributable to demonstrable neurological disorder, they are widely believed to result from dysfunctions in the central nervous system that impair spatial perception, visual-motor coordination, memory, capacity for abstraction, and ability to understand or use written or spoken language. In the classroom, such impairments take their toll primarily on the acquisition and utilization of skills in listening, speaking, reading, writing, reasoning, and mathematics, and SLD youngsters will perform in one or more of these areas at levels substantially below what would be expected on the basis of their overall intellectual ability as measured by a Full-Scale IQ (see Hammill, Leigh, McNutt, & Larsen, 1987; Obrzut & Hynd, 1983; Ysseldyke & Stevens, 1986).

Perceptual cognitive deficits that are causing learning difficulties often occur in conjunction with the condition categorized in DSM-III-R as Attention Deficit Hyperactivity Disorder (ADHD). There is currently widespread opinion that ADHD begins in early childhood and is characterized primarily by an age-inappropriate extent of inattentiveness, impulsivity, and hyperactivity (American Psychiatric Association, 1987; Goldstein & Goldstein, 1990, Chap. 1; Hunt, 1988; Loney, 1987). An estimated 50% to 80% of children with ADHD also have specific learning disabilities. However, despite considerable overlap between ADHD and SLD, the remaining 20% to 50% of ADHD children, while at risk for performing poorly in school, do not give evidence of any specific learning disability. Likewise, many children who are handicapped by one or more types of SLD do not demonstrate an ADHD syndrome (Cantwell & Baker, 1991; Routh, 1986; Silver, 1990).

The primary characteristics of ADHD typically produce dramatic behavioral and learning problems from the time children enter elementary school. Because ADHD children are restless and distractible, they have difficulty focusing attention on their teachers and assignments. They absorb less than other students from group discussions, they benefit less from individual study, they are slow to complete their homework and test papers, and they often fail to remember and follow directions. Because they are impulsive and excitable, ADHD children frequently make themselves unpopular. Their aggressive and disruptive ways lead classmates and teachers to dislike and reject them. Frustrating experiences of academic ineptness and social isolation contribute to their forming low opinions of themselves and being drawn into various kinds of antisocial behavior (Anastopolous & Barkley, 1992; Brown, Borden, Clingerman, & Jenkins, 1988; Ross & Ross, 1982, Chap. 8; Whalen & Henker, 1985). In one study of 182 ADHD youngsters using the Diagnostic Interview for Children and Adolescents, over half met criteria for additional diagnoses, with oppositional disorder and anxiety/mood disorders being the most frequent (Livingston, Dykman, & Ackerman, 1990).

Even in the absence of an ADHD syndrome, school failures caused by specific learning disabilities are found to lead to contentious interpersonal relationships, a deflated self-image, and an inclination to misbehave. Research studies of SLD children consistently demonstrate that they are less well-liked by their classmates than children without learning disabilities, less satisfied with their level of competence, less able to tolerate frustration, more likely to be involved in classroom behavior problems, and generally more likely to show signs of emotional maladjustment (Bender & Smith, 1990; Grolnick & Ryan, 1990; Salyer, Holmstrom, & Noshpitz, 1991; Stone & la Greca, 1990; Toro, Weissberg, Guare, & Liebenstein, 1990).

Perceptual-cognitive deficits and the learning disabilities they spawn run a different developmental course from the primary behavioral manifestations of ADHD. Youngsters with ADHD are likely to remain more restless, distractible, and impulsive than other children, but they gain increased self-control as they mature and become less different from their classmates in these respects. In contrast to this diminution of ADHD behaviors during adolescence, perceptual-cognitive deficits and basic skill deficits in reading, spelling, and arithmetic tend to persist. In the absence of adequate intervention, learning difficulties in these children typically worsen over time and are reflected not only in poor grades but also in an elevated frequency of grade retentions, suspensions and expulsions, and dropping out of school (Brown & Borden, 1986; Cantwell, 1986; Fischer, Barkley, Edelbrock, & Smallish, 1990; Lambert, 1988; Wallender & Hubert, 1985).

The cumulative nature of learning difficulties is important in this regard. As subject matter becomes more difficult during high school and builds on previous learning, students with deficient skills and spotty prior learning find it increasingly hard to keep up. Mildly learning-disabled children who have managed to struggle through junior high school science and mathematics, for example, may fall by the wayside in algebra and chemistry, and those who read well enough to cope with seventh-and eighth-grade assignments may not be able to maintain the reading pace required in high school English and social science courses.

Maladaptive secondary reactions to school learning difficulties are also likely to outlast the primary manifestations of ADHD and worsen over time if allowed to run their natural course. Repeated experiences of failure and rejection during middle childhood frequently propel ADHD and SLD youngsters toward increasing unhappiness, withdrawal, and self-depreciation as adolescents. Episodes of feeling sad, discouraged, incompetent, and apathetic mar their lives. Socially, they tend either to have few friends or to seek the company of younger children, who pose less threat to their fragile sense of adequacy than do peers their own age (Dollinger, Horn, & Boarini, 1988; Pihl & McLarnon, 1984; Waddell, 1984).

In a similar way, the mounting frustrations and needs for attention that cause some ADHD children to engage in antisocial behavior often lead to increasingly serious conduct problems during adolescence. Sometimes, delinquent behavior obscures all the other difficulties these youngsters have as teenagers. In some cases, adolescents with learning problems that have never been detected come to professional attention for the first time because of fighting, stealing, vandalism, and other kinds of blatant disregard for authority and the law. Various follow-up studies indicate that as many as 60% of ADHD children are likely to display diagnosable conduct disorder or oppositional defiant disorder as adolescents, and 25% to 35% engage in antisocial acts that frequently lead to contact with the police (Barkley, Fischer, Edelbrock, & Smallish, 1990; Klein & Mannuzza, 1991; Mannuzza, Klein, & Addalli, 1991; Weiss & Hechtman, 1986, Chap. 4).

These features of ADHD and SLD point to some special considerations in the evaluation of underachieving youngsters who have reached adolescence. First, although ADHD can be at the root of unexpectedly poor performance in a junior or senior high school student, it seldom raises a new diagnostic question at this age. ADHD emerges in childhood, not adolescence, and there is widespread professional and general public awareness of its manifestations. The sensitivity of school personnel to age-inappropriate inattentiveness, impulsivity, and hyperactivity, supported by sophisticated methods available for neuropsychological assessment of children, makes it unlikely for instances of ADHD to pass unnoticed during the elementary school years (see Franzen & Berg, 1989; Goldstein & Goldstein, 1990; Hynd, Snow, & Becker, 1986; Taylor & Fletcher, 1990).

Second, in contrast to the relative ease with which they can usually identify long-standing ADHD, clinicians working with adolescents who are underachieving must be alert to the possibility of specific learning disabilities that either have gone undetected or have only recently become manifest in underachievement. There are distinctive and discriminable behavior patterns among (a) learning-disabled elementary school children who do not have ADHD, (b) ADHD children who are not learning disabled, and (c) children with both ADHD and SLD. Whereas all three groups may be underachieving as adolescents, it is the SLD youngsters without ADHD whose basic problem is most likely to have escaped notice. Typically, these youngsters will have displayed age-appropriate behavior developmentally, without restlessness, distractibility, or impulsivity; they will not begin to show any untoward social or emotional reactions unless or until they have suffered repeated school failures; and, especially if they are highly intelligent or have developed good compensatory skills, they may have underachieved without failing or may even have received good grades prior to the current academic problems that have led to their being referred for evaluation.

Given what is known about the defining characteristics of SLD and ADHD, Rorschach assessment may often be useful in describing the particular personality features of a young person with such disorders. However, Rorschach findings cannot serve to diagnose the presence of these conditions. The Rorschach measures personality processes, and neither SLD nor ADHD is primarily a disorder of personality functioning. The diagnosis of SLD must be referred to appropriate measures of intellectual functioning and academic skills; the diagnosis of ADHD proceeds best from an informed combination of information derived from parent interviews, behavior rating scales by parents and teachers, direct observations of behavior, and neuropsychological and neurological evaluations (see DuPaul, Guevremont, & Barkley, 1991; Hunt, 1988).

Very little Rorschach research has in fact been conducted with SLD and ADHD children. The most notable study to date is reported by Acklin (1990), who compared 41 nine to twelve-year-old learning-disabled children with 143 similarly aged nonclinical children. Based on their WISC performance, Acklin divided his learning-disabled subjects into two groups, one demonstrating primarily auditory-linguistic impairments and the other showing primarily visual-perceptual difficulties. As would be expected from the fact that neither type of learning disability derives from personality characteristics, these two groups of learning-disabled children did not differ substantially from each other in their patterns of responding to the Rorschach. Taken together, however, these learning-disabled children did differ from the nondisabled youngsters in several notable ways.

With respect to corollaries of basic cognitive deficits that contribute to learning disability, the LD children in Acklin's study were significantly more likely than his comparison group to demonstrate poor perceptual accuracy (low form level), a hasty and careless style of processing information (underincorporation), and a problem-solving approach characterized by rigidity, poor frustration tolerance, and impulsivity (high Lambda and a minus Adjusted D). With respect to some of the maladaptive secondary consequences of being learning disabled, his LD group showed a relatively high level of emotional distress ($SumSh > FM + m$) and relatively poor self-esteem (low Egocentricity Ratio).

Findings of this kind make sense in understanding some of the reasons why SLD children do poorly in their schoolwork and feel badly about themselves. However, none of these Rorschach findings is specific to learning disability, nor can these or any other configuration of Rorschach findings be expected to distinguish SLD or ADHD children from young people with various other kinds of adjustment difficulties.

In the individual case, on the other hand, identifying that a particular underachieving youngster is underincorporative or self-denigrating helps not only to understand the problem but also to establish treatment targets that can point the way to effective intervention. The underachieving SLD or ADHD child who is underincorporating will benefit considerably from an intervention plan that includes guided instruction in how to approach problem-solving situations in a more careful and deliberate fashion. Likewise, the underachiever whose psychological adjustment is being compromised by low self-esteem will feel better and probably come to perform better if he or she can be helped to form a more positive self-image. The data for Case 11 illustrate the SLD subject.

CASE 11—AN ISSUE OF LEARNING DISABILITY

This is a 8-year 9-month-old female, described as an attractive petite youngster. She was referred by mutual agreement of her parents and school authorities on the recommendation of her third-grade teacher and a consulting school psychologist. Her teacher describes her as an unhappy, oppositional, manipulative child who is doing very poorly in the third grade, and who is often quite aggressive to other children. The teacher notes that her episodes of aggressiveness are not consistent and seemingly spontaneous without any specific provocation. Her mother describes her as being easily frustrated, doing many things to get attention, and critical of herself and others. The teacher says that during the 6 months the subject has been in the third grade, her performance generally has been substandard and indicates that it is highly likely that she will have to repeat the third grade unless placed in a special class. She notes that the subject does not take direction well but is not sure if this is a product of laziness, oppositionality, or some handicap. A WISC-R, administered by the school psychologist yielded a Full-Scale IQ of 98 (Verbal IQ = 97; Performance IQ = 100) but also showed considerable scatter among the subtests (Info = 9; Comp = 12; Arith = 6; Simil = 12; DigSp = 8; Vocab = 9; DigSym = 12; PicCom = 11; Blk = 9; ObjAsm = 9; PicArr = 9).

Neuropsychological testing, using the Halstead-Reitan battery yielded similar results for the WISC, a Wechsler Memory Scale MQ of 59; 77 errors on the Categories Test; an Aphasia Screening Test score of 13 errors; Completion times of 54" and 136" respectively for Trails A and B; a Seashore Rhythm rank of 10; and Sensory Perceptual test scores yielding right-side errors of 5 and 7 respectively for visual and fingertip number writing. Overall, the results of the Halstead-Reitan present an impairment index of .69 (moderate), suggesting considerably more cognitive limitation than is common for this age.

Following the neuropsychological assessment, the subject was included in a "child study team" part-time special class that meets for 2 hours, 3 times per week. She has attended these special classes for approximately 2 months, but no significant progress has been noted. The subject complains that she gets headaches when required to read and objects to any tests that might be required. She has recently had a complete ocular examination and reading glasses have been prescribed, which she has been wearing for about 3 weeks.

The subject says that she has fewer friends now than she had before "everybody started to try to get in my head." She claims that she likes most of the other children at school but admits that, sometimes, they do not want to play with her and "it makes me mad." She says that she is sorry when she gets angry at her peers, but "they don't always play fair." She says that she likes to play the piano, watch TV, and enjoys coloring and watercolor painting. She says that her parents are "really nice," but that her brother (age 7) is a "real pain a lot of the time." She also notes that she doesn't like the special class ("the other kids all know") and describes her teacher as "always picking on me."

The father, age 45, is a mechanical engineer who has worked for the same firm for 18 years. The mother, age 32, is a housewife. She is a college graduate. The parents have been married for 11 years. The mother states that she usually is responsible for any punishment of either child and that it usually involves the withdrawal of privileges. She describes her daughter as being difficult to manage because she refuses to obey much of the time. The mother notes that the subject seems very remorseful when she gets into trouble but persists in the same behavior even though punished for it. The mother describes her son as a precocious, overachieving youngster whose successes often lead his sister to fight with him. The mother notes that the developmental history of the subject was different than for her son, "he was no trouble, she had all kinds of problems." She describes the problems as including diaper rash, multiple urinary infections, bronchitis at age 3, ear infections at ages 3 and 4, nail biting between the ages of 3 and 5, and the development of irregular teeth and cavities during her preschool years that required numerous traumatic visits to a dentist. The subject was placed in a nursery school at age 3 but was withdrawn at the request of the school because of temper tantrums and problems of fighting with other children.

The referral asks about current personality structure and questions how much of the problem behavior may be attributed to psychological versus neurological factors. Specific recommendations concerning intervention are also requested.

Case 11. A 8-Year-Old Female

Card	Response	Inquiry	Scoring
I	1. Pumpkin	E: (Rpts S's resp) S: Bec rite hre it has shapes lik eys & the mouth (points to spaces) & its k o round lik a pumpkin, it ll a pumpkin, sur it does	Wo Fu (Hd) 3.5
	2. A person standg in middl w a big black coat on, she is holdg her arms out	E: (Rpts S's resp) S: Hre in the middl, c her legs & body E: And the coat? S: The drk on the sides, lik its one of thos big coats lik a cape & she's holdg her arms out, lik the coat is open	WS+ MP.FC'o 2 H,Cg 4.0
II	3. Two witches w red hats & red shoes	E: (Rpts S's resp) S: C the hats r here (D2) & their hands r touchg & thy hav black coats on & their red shows r dwn here (D3), witches wear pointy hats lik ths	W+ FC'.Mp.FC'o 2 (H),Cg 4.5
	4. A clown's face	E: (Rpts S's resp) S: It lks weird bec tht wld b th nose, (DS5) its white & the othr E: makeup S: Othr makeup Its black on th face & the red eyes & chin	WSo FC'.FC- (Hd) 4.5
III	5. S o is practicing bowling	E: (Rpts S's resp) S: Ths guy is holdg a ball & standg lik hes ready to throw it, lik he's lookg in th mirror to mak sur he's standg rite, lik he's practicing how to stand when u bowl, c the ball dwn here	Dd+ Mp.Fro H,Sc P 4.0
IV	6. A monster, he's layg dwn	E: (Rpts S's resp) S: He has big feet, it ll thyr comg out toward u & he has a littl head back up here, lik a giant tht went to sleep on his back	Wo Mp.FDo (H) P 2.0
	7. Or a big bird, thts dead	E: (Rpts S's resp) S: I don't c it now it dsnt ll tht E: Try hard, u found it befor S: Oh yeah, c the head up here & the arms out here but the legs r cut off lik its dead, its weird	Ddo F- Ad MOR, INC
V	8. Mayb a bf	E: (Rpts S's resp) S: All of it, th wgs r big lik a bf	Wo Fo A P 1.0

Card	Response	Inquiry	Scoring
	v9. Ths way it ll a crow	E: (Rpts S's resp) S: The wgs & th body in th middle & its black lik crows r blk	Wo FC'u A 1.0
	10. U kno thos thgs thy hav in hauntd houses, vampires lik thy turn into thos thgs tht fly	E: (Rpts S's resp) S: It all ll tht if u cut off thse thgs on the top & bottm, then it wld ll a vampire w the big black wgs	Ddo FC'u (H)
VI	11. A behind	E: (Rpts S's resp) S: Rite thr & thr it wld ll a behind & I kno wht else, but I cant tell I'm too embarrassed to say (lafs) E: Too embarrassed? S: Yeah, at the bottm, its lik where u go to the bathroom but I'm not gonna say it	Do F- Hd,Sx DR
	12. Wait, mayb its a fly	E: (Rpts S's resp) S: Rite up hre wb his head & ths r the big wgs, lik he's flyg	Wo Fma- A 2.5
	13. Or wait mayb its a cat crawling along	E: (Rpts S's resp) S: The head is rite thr (D3) & ths is all of his body & legs, it has thos lines lik on the back of a cat (rubs) it ll he's crawlg along lik he's ready to catch a bird, u kno how thy do? I'v seen them lik their ready to jump & catch a bird	W+ FMa.FTu A 2.5
VII	14. Land surrounded w islands	E: (Rpts S's resp) S: No, I didn't mean tht its water all surrounded w islands, no wait, islands surrounded by water, c thyr connectd to eo, it not real, its lik on a map u mite c in school, a map of islands & all ths (space) in the middl is around the islands	Wv/+ Fo Ge 2.5 DR2
	15. Or a "U" cld b the lettr "U"	E: (Rpts S's resp) S: Oh yeah it cld b a "U" if u don't mak it very well, it really shldn't hav thes littl thgs (Dd21) stickg out but mayb who made it didn't tak her time	Wo Fu Id 2.5
	16. Or it cb clouds w a helicopter thr in the middl	E: (Rpts S's resp) S: Its lik lookg dwn fr way up, th helicopter is ths littl thg (points to D6) & all arnd here is clds, its flyg ovr the clds E: I'm not sur why it ll clds S: Thyr just shaped lik em	W+ ma.FDu Sc,Cl 2.5

			E/S	Score
			E: & why does tht ll a helicopter?	
			S: It's just a littl thg, I thot of a helicopter, lik flying over the clds, it doesn't want to get dwn into them or it cld get lost	Do CF- A
VIII	17.	Bfs, diff colord bfs	E: (Rpts S's resp)	
			S: 1,2,3 bfs, thy all hav thos colors lik a bf, c 1 here (D4) & here (D5) & here (D2), each one is shaped diff than the othr two, bfs r lik tht, all diff colors but thy all hav wgs lik these & thyr all colord diff	
	18.	Bears I mean lions mayb climbg up mtns or rocks	E: (Rpts S's resp)	W+ FMa 2 A,Ls P 4.5
			S: Thse r th lions & thse r rocks or a mt	
			E: Help me to it lik u r	
			S: C the head & legs & ths shaps r all diff lik thy cb rocks or mayb its a big mt	
IX	19.	Animals fightg mayb	E: (Rpts S's resp)	W+ Ma- 2 A 5.5 AG, FAB2
			S: Ths ll reindeer, ths ll a hipopotamus, thes r snails, thyr all on top of eo lik thyr fightg or squishg eo, its lik a bunch of thgs in a fite	
	v20.	A merry-go-round	E: (Rpts S's resp)	W+ CF.Mp- 2 Sc.A 5.5 FAB2, MOR
			S: Its all th merry-go-round & w all the colors & mayb thr r som A's holdg on to it, but its not going around bec its broken so thy just sit on it	
			E: Wht maks it look broken?	
			S: It dsnt go up & dwn or anythg	
			E: & ther r A's on it?	
			S: Yep, lik ants here (D1) & othr insects just sittg waitg for a ride	
			E: U mentioned all the colors	
			S: Its got a pink top & some orange sides	
X	21.	A lot of spiders & othr bugs tht r fiting w eo	E: (Rpts S's resp)	W+ FMao 2 A P 5.5 AG
			S: Thy all ll bugs, thes spidrs (D1) r attackg & squishg eo & som hre (D7) ll ants & the rest is othr bugs	
			E: I'm not sur I c it rite	
			S: Thr shapes, evrythg is shapes rite, thy all hav bug shapes, I'm tired of sayg th same thngs ovr again	
			E: We'r finished now	
			S: Well its about time, ths is a dumb thg	

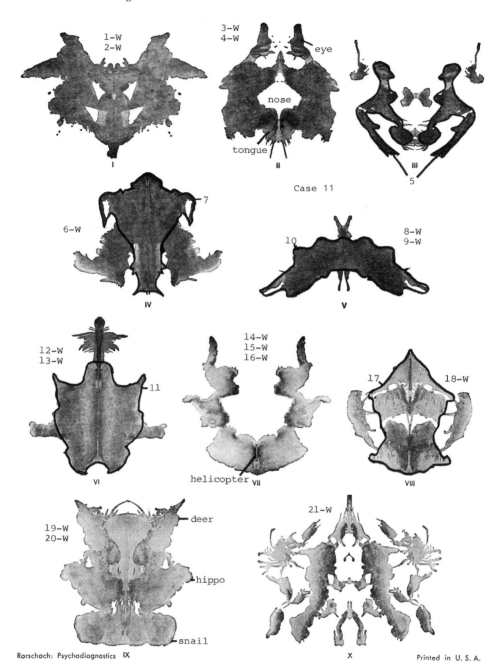

Case 11

Rorschach: Psychodiagnostics IX

Printed in U. S. A.

Case 11

Case 11   **Sequence of Scores**

Card	No	Loc	#	Determinant(s)	(2)	Content(s)	Pop	Z	Special Scores
I	1	WSo	1	Fu		(Hd)		3.5	
	2	WS+	1	Mp.FC'o		H,Cg		4.0	
II	3	W+	1	FC.Mp.FC'o	2	(H),Cg		4.5	
	4	WSo	1	FC'.FC-		(Hd)		4.5	
III	5	Dd+	31	Mp.Fro		H,Sc	P	4.0	
IV	6	Wo	1	Mp.FDo		(H)	P	2.0	
	7	Ddo	99	F-		Ad			MOR,INC
V	8	Wo	1	Fo		A	P	1.0	
	9	Wo	1	FC'u		A		1.0	
	10	Ddo	99	FC'u		(H)			
VI	11	Do	1	F-		Hd,Sx			DR
	12	Wo	1	FMa-		A		2.5	
	13	W+	1	FMa.FTu		A	P	2.5	AG,PER
VII	14	W/	1	Fo		Ge		2.5	DR2
	15	Wo	1	Fu		Id		2.5	
	16	W+	1	ma.FDu		Sc,Cl		2.5	
VIII	17	Do	6	CF-		A			
	18	W+	1	FMao	2	A,Ls	P	4.5	
IX	19	W+	1	Ma-	2	A		5.5	AG,FAB2
	20	W+	1	CF.Mp-	2	Sc,A		5.5	FAB2,MOR
X	21	W+	1	FMao	2	A	P	5.5	AG

Case 11   **Structural Summary**

Location	Determinants		Contents	S-Constellation
Features	Blends	Single		. . FV+VF+V+FD>2
			H = 2, 0	. . Col−Shd Bl>0
Zf = 17	M.FC'	M = 1	(H) = 3, 0	. Ego<.31,>.44
ZSum = 58.0	FC.M.FC'	FM = 3	Hd = 1, 0	. . MOR > 3
ZEst = 56.0	FC'.FC	m = 0	(Hd) = 2, 0	. . Zd > +− 3.5
	M.Fr	FC = 0	Hx = 0, 0	. . es > EA
W = 16	M.FD	CF = 1	A = 8, 1	. . CF+C > FC
(Wv = 0)	FM.FT	C = 0	(A) = 0, 0	. . X+% < .70
D = 2	m.FD	Cn = 0	Ad = 1, 0	. . S > 3
Dd = 3	CF.M	FC' = 2	(Ad) = 0, 0	. . P < 3 or > 8
S = 3		C'F = 0	An = 0, 0	. . Pure H < 2
		C' = 0	Art = 0, 0	. . R < 17
DQ		FT = 0	Ay = 0, 0	x . . . . . TOTAL
. . . . . (FQ−)		TF = 0	Bl = 0, 0	
+ = 9 (2)		T = 0	Bt = 0, 0	Special Scorings
o = 11 (5)		FV = 0	Cg = 0, 2	Lv1 Lv2
v/+ = 1 (0)		VF = 0	Cl = 0, 1	DV = 0x1 0x2
v = 0 (0)		V = 0	Ex = 0, 0	INC = 1x2 0x4
		FY = 0	Fd = 0, 0	DR = 1x3 1x6
		YF = 0	Fi = 0, 0	FAB = 0x4 2x7
		Y = 0	Ge = 1, 0	ALOG = 0x5
		Fr = 0	Hh = 0, 0	CON = 0x7
Form Quality		rF = 0	Ls = 0, 1	SUM6 = 5
		FD = 0	Na = 0, 0	WSUM6 = 25
FQx FQf MQual SQx		F = 6	Sc = 2, 1	
+ = 0 0 0 0			Sx = 0, 1	AB = 0 CP = 0
o = 8 2 4 1			Xy = 0, 0	AG = 3 MOR = 2
u = 6 2 0 1			Id = 1, 0	CFB = 0 PER = 1
− = 7 2 2 1				COP = 0 PSV = 0
none = 0 — 0 0		(2) = 5		

Case 11   **Ratios, Percentages, and Derivations**

R = 21	L = 0.40		FC:CF+C = 2: 2	COP = 0 AG = 3
			Pure C = 0	Food = 0
EB = 6: 3.0	EA = 9.0	EBPer = 2.0	Afr = 0.31	Isolate/R = 0.19
eb = 5: 6	es = 11	D = 0	S = 3	H:(H)Hd(Hd) = 2:6
	Adj es = 11	Adj D = 0	Blends:R = 8:21	(HHd):(AAd) = 5:0
			CP = 0	H+A:Hd+Ad = 14:4
FM = 4 : C' = 5 T = 1				
m = 1 : V = 0 Y = 0				
		P = 6	Zf = 17	3r+(2) /R = 0.38
a:p = 6: 5	Sum6 = 5	X+% = 0.38	Zd = +2.0	Fr+rF = 1
Ma:Mp = 0: 0	Lv2 = 3	F+% = 0.33	W:D:Dd = 16: 2: 3	FD = 2
2AB+Art+Ay=0	WSum6 = 25	X−% = 0.33	W:M = 16: 6	An+Xy = 0
M − = 2	Mnone = 0	S−% = 0.14	DQ+ = 9	MOR = 2
		Xu% = 0.29	DQv = 0	

SCZI = 6*	DEPI = 5*	CDI = 1	S-CON = N/A	HVI = No	OBS = No

INTERPRETIVE ROUTINE FOR CASE 11

The first positive Key variable is the SCZI which has a value of 6. It suggests the likelihood of a schizophrenic disorder. The demography and history tend to argue against this postulate. Her age is not consistent with the typical onset of a schizophreniclike disturbance and her general history, although somewhat chaotic, does not reflect marked autisticlike features. Nonetheless, the demography and history do not rule out the possibility of schizophrenia and the issue must be considered carefully. The interpretive strategy will address the data clusters in the following order:

IDEATION → MEDIATION → PROCESSING → CONTROLS → AFFECT →
SELF-PERCEPTION → INTERPERSONAL PERCEPTION

Ideation—Case 11   The data relevant to an evaluation of thinking for Case 11 are shown in Table 94.

Table 94.   Ideation Data for Case 11

			M QUALITY		SPECIAL SCORES			
EB	= 6:3.0	*EBPer* = 2.0						
eb	= 5:6	(*FM* = 4 *m* = 1)	+ = 0	DV	= 0	DV2	= 0	
a:p	= 6:5	M^a:M^p = 1:5	o = 4	INC	= 1	INC2	= 0	
2AB + Art + Ay = 0			u = 0	DR	= 1	DR2	= 1	
MOR	= 2		− = 2	FAB	= 1	FAB2	= 2	
				ALOG	= 0	SUM6	= 5	
RESPONSES TO BE READ FOR QUALITY				CON	= 0	WSUM6	= 25	
	2,3,5,6,20							

The *EB* (6:3.0) indicates an introversive style, which is very unusual for an 8-year-old. In the sample of nonpatient 8's, only 13% have an introversive style. As noted in Chapter 2, if this approach, which relies extensively on delay and thinking things through, evolves early in the developmental span, it is likely to persist creating some obvious hazards. Young children do not have enough cortical development to conceptualize issues very well, and a risk exists for some of the ideational tactics associated with the style to become overly concrete and potentially counterproductive in complex problem solving or decision-making situations. The introversive style is very common among the majority of adults and adolescents who are diagnosed as being schizophrenic.

The value for the *EBPer* (2.0) is somewhat reassuring because the style does not appear to be pervasive. Therefore, it seems likely that, at times, she will use more intuitively oriented tactics to achieve decisions or address problems. The left-side value for the *eb* (5) is not unusual for an 8-year-old. There is considerable but not excessive peripheral ideation present. Similarly, the value for the *a:p* ratio (6:5) is not unexpected and offers no interpretive input; however, the M^a:M^p ratio (1:5) is significant. It indicates that she has developed an extensive fantasy life that she uses in an abusive manner to escape from reality and replace it with a more manageable world. It also suggests that she prefers to avoid decision making and relies mainly on others to resolve problem situations. The latter tendency is not unusual for an 8-year-old, but when done to excess, as is the case here, it tends to reduce the number of direct problem-solving experiences and gives rise to strange thinking or faulty logic. Consequently, experiences that contribute to development fail to occur and development is thwarted.

The datum for the Intellectualization Index (0) is of no interpretive importance. The value for MOR (2) is slightly higher than expected and may indicate that some of her thinking is characterized by more pessimism than should be the case, but that is a speculative conclusion. The data regarding the Critical Special Scores are of much greater concern. The number of Critical Special Scores (5) is not unusual for an eight, but the number of Level 2 scores (3), and the WSum6 (25) are both substantially greater than expected for this age. Both signal a marked peculiarity in thinking that may not be unlike the type of thinking found in the schizophrenic youngster. However, an examination of the contents of these Special Scores challenges such a conclusion.

The first of the Critical Special Scores, an INCOM, occurs in Response 7 to Card IV. She identifies arms on a big bird. A slip such as this is very common among children. The second is a DR in Response 11 to Card VI. She conveys her awareness of the anus or vagina in a childlike manner. Although the response is somewhat bizarre and reflects a preoccupation, it is unlike the more dramatically bizarre answers given by schizophrenic children. The third is a DR2 in Response 14 to Card VII, in which she mixes her intended words and has considerable difficulty expressing what she perceives. There is a sense of helplessness and circumstantiality in her verbiage, but again, it does not convey psychotic or schizophreniclike thinking. Instead, it probably reflects some of the cognitive handicaps illustrated by the results of the neuropsychological testing. The fourth, a FABCOM2 in Response 19 to Card IX, which is one of her $M-$ answers, is a rather bizarre and unusual combination of a reindeer, hippopotamus, and snail fighting. It is a bad response, but not necessarily schizophreniclike. In fact, had she reported each of the animals separately, only one (the snail) would be minus. The last is also a FABCOM2, in Response 20 to Card X, which is the second of her $M-$ answers, ants and insects waiting for a ride on a merry-go-round. It is a naive and childish answer, but it does not convey the pathognomic features found in psychoticlike thinking.

In general, her thinking is sometimes concrete and naive, and her judgment is often wanting. Nonetheless, it would be erroneous to conclude that it approximates the sort of disturbed thinking found in schizophrenic subjects. For an 8-year-old, her thinking is actually rather sophisticated at times if all six of her M answers are considered (a person standing with a big black coat; witches with their hands touching; someone practicing bowling; a monster laying down; animals fighting; and insects waiting for a ride on a merry-go-round).

There is no question that she is an overly ideational youngster and that more cognitive slippage or poor judgment occurs than should be the case. Her thinking is distorted and counterproductive to her cause much more often than should be the case, but it seems unlikely that she is suffering from a schizophreniclike disturbance. The data concerning her mediational activities may help to clarify her plight.

Mediation—Case 11   The data relevant to the way in which she translates stimulus inputs are shown in Table 95.

The value for Lambda (0.40) is slightly lower than expected for one of her age. In other words, she tends to become more involved with complex stimulus situation than should be the case. This is not a hazard provided that she translates those situations in a reasonably conventional manner and that she conceptualizes her translations accurately. The data concerning her thinking suggests that this is not the case, a postulate that seems confirmed by some of the data regarding mediation. She does give six Popular answers, which is about average for her age and indicates that when stimulus cues are obvious, she will usually give conventional responses.

Table 95.   Cognitive Mediation Data for Case 11

Lambda	= 0.40	OBS	= Neg	MINUS FEATURES
P	= 6	X+%	= .38	4,7,11,12,17,19,20
FQx+	= 0	F+%	= .33	
FQxo	= 11	Xu%	= .29	
FQxu	= 4	X−%	= .33	
FQx−	= 1	S−%	= .14	
FQxnone	= 0	CONFAB	= 0	

On the other hand, the $X + \%$ is only .38, suggesting that when cues are not obvious, her translations of stimuli are quite unconventional. Sometimes the presence of several formless answers account for a low $X + \%$, but that is not the case here. Her $Xu\%$ (.29) and her $X - \%$ (.33) are well above the expected range for her age. They indicate that she distorts the translation of inputs much more than should be the case and that, in many instances, she translates in a manner that does not distort the cues but assigns less conventional meanings to them. This composite of excessive individuality and distortion tends to breed detachment from reality and probably promotes many unwanted and less effective behaviors.

Her minus answers are not very homogeneous although most do involve animal contents. The first, a clown face to Card II, is not uncommon for children. The second, a dead bird to Card IV, is morbid as is the last minus answer, a broken merry-go-round to Card X. This might suggest that a preoccupation concerning self-image is contributing to her tendency to distort. The third, a sex response to Card VI also conveys a preoccupation (a behind) which also seems related to self-image. The remaining four all involve animals that are reported a manner that clearly distorts the use of form. These minus answers are spread throughout the record in ways that are not inconsistent when serious disturbance is present. Yet, almost every answer contains form elements that are easily perceived by even the casual observer. In other words, they do not reflect a wild disregard for reality. Instead they seem to convey issues of self-image, which will be discussed in more detail with the data for self-image. Sometimes, problems in the way that information is processed provoke mediation difficulties. The data for the next cluster should clarify whether that is the case here.

Information Processing—Case 11   The data concerning processing activities for Case 11 are shown in Table 96.

Table 96.   Processing Data for Case 11

L	= 0.40	W:D:Dd	= 16:2:3	Zd	= +2.0	DQ+	= 9
Zf	= 17	W:M	= 16:6	PSV	= 0	DQv/+	= 1
HVI	= No	OBS	= No			DQv	= 0

LOCATION SEQUENCING

I	W,W	IV	W,Dd	VII	W,W,W
II	W,W	V	W,W,Dd	VIII	D,W
III	Dd	VI	D,W,W	IX	W,W
				X	W

The findings concerning Lambda, the OBS, and the HVI are not relevant. The remaining data in this cluster are intriguing because they indicate a strong motivation to process information. The value for *Zf* (17) reveals that most of her 21 responses are organized in some way. This is much more effort than expected from an 8-year-old. The data for the *W:D:Dd* ratio (16:2:3) and the *W:M* ratio (16:6) tend to confirm that she sets substantial objectives for herself when dealing with a new stimulus field and indicates that she may, in fact, try to take on too much from time to time. This may account for some of her mediational problems although it seems more likely that her neurologically related handicaps form the basic source of her mediational and ideational difficulties. In other words, she probably does not retrieve information from long-term storage very well, and/or when it is retrieved, it is not conceptualized or applied very effectively.

Actually, the quality of her processing effort seems quite good, as illustrated by the value for *DQ+* (9) and the absence of *DQv* responses. Similarly, the *Zd* score is well within normal limits, indicating that her scanning activities are not substantially different from most of her age. The location sequencing is reasonably consistent, but it is interesting to note that both of her *D* responses, which are first answers (Cards VI and VIII), yield minus answers. These are sparse data but might suggest that when she attempts to break down a stimulus field, her problems with both short- and long-term memory tend to yield distorted translations. On the other hand, the minus distortions could be the product of ideational impulsiveness. Thus, the issue of her control capacity becomes important in attempting to understand her flawed thinking and mediation.

Controls—Case 11   The data related to her capacity for control and tolerance for stress are shown in Table 97.

Table 97.   Controls and Stress Tolerance Data for Case 11

EB = 6:3.0		*EA* = 9.0		D	= 0
eb = 5:6		*es* = 11	Adj*es* = 11	AdjD	= 0
FM = 5	*C'* = 5	*T* = 1		CDI	= 1
m = 1	*V* = 0	*Y* = 0			

The D and Adjusted D Scores of 0 are somewhat unexpected in light of previous findings and the history. Both are zero suggesting that her capacity for control is not very different from that of most at her age. The validity of the D Scores does not seem to be questionable. The *EA* value (9.0) is slightly above average for her age and it comprises substantial values on both sides of the *EB*. Conversely, the values for *es* and the Adjusted *es* are a higher than might be expected for an 8. In fact, they indicate the presence of considerable stimulus demand which, if increased only slightly, could throw her into a state of overload.

This may be what happens to her in various situations described in the history, that is, those in which her behavior is marked by obvious irritation, oppositionality, and ineffective functioning. Stated differently, she might be considered as a youngster with marginal capacities for control because of her chronically excessive stimulus demands. As a result, she is thrown into overload easily by new, unexpected stimulus demands. Assuming this postulate to be viable, an important consideration for intervention will be a reduction in experienced stimulation. It is clear, from a review of the data for the *eb* that much of her current experience of demand is affect related.

Affect—Case 11   The data concerning affect for Case 11 are shown in Table 98.

Table 98.   Affect Data for Case 11

DEPI = 5				BLENDS
EB = 6:3.0		*EBPer* = 2.0		M.FC'
eb = 5:6		*FC:CF* + *C* = 2:2		M.Fr
		Pure *C* = 0		M.FD
C' = 5	*T* = 1	*Afr* = 0.31		CF.M
V = 0	*Y* = 0	*S* = 3		FC.M.FC'
		Blends/*R* = 8:21		FM.FT
		CP = 0		FC'.FC
				m.FD

The DEPI (5) indicates that she has many features that are commensurate with frequent alterations in mood. In most instances, a DEPI of 5 indicates periodic difficulties in handling emotion and a substantial likelihood of recurrent depressive episodes. The *EB* (6:3.0) suggests that she is not usually oriented to investing her feelings into her thinking. Instead, as an introversive, she prefers to push them aside during problem solving or decision making. At the same time, the *EBPer* value (2.0) reveals that her ideational style is not well fixed, and at times she will be influenced by her feelings when making decisions. Under ideal circumstances, this more intuitive tactic will be used selectively, in light of the demands of situations in which a more trial-and-error approach to decision making seems appropriate. But, the ideal is unlikely in any 8-year-old. In most young children, it is likely that affect becomes merged into thinking in situations that have a high emotional context, and that is probably the case here.

This proposition seems supported by the substantial right-side value of the *eb* (6), which offers reasonably clear evidence of a distress state. The value consists mainly of *C'* answers (5), indicating that she is prone to internalize many of her feelings that she would prefer to release. This is a highly unusual finding for an adult, and more so for a young child. The implication is that she has been taught to contain emotional expressions, and this may have some direct relation to the fact that she has developed an introversive style in which an abuse of fantasy apparently plays a major role.

The data for the *FC:CF* + *C* ratio (2:2) tend to support this hypothesis. Most 8-year-olds give more *CF* + *C* than *FC* simply because they are exuberant and place little value on the containment or modulation of feelings. Most 8's are quite willing to become involved with, and possibly even relish affective stimulation. This youngster does not. Her *Afr* value of 0.31 indicates that she is prone to avoid affective stimulation. When a low *Afr* is noted in the record of a young child, it usually signals some fearfulness about emotion, developed either because of their limited capacity to control their own expressions, or because those around them have offered negative feedback when they express their feelings. The latter is probably the case here. The mother reports many difficulties with the subject during her preschool years, and it seems reasonable to suggest that emotional outbursts, even though natural, were not well received.

There are three Space responses, which might signal an excessive oppositionality or anger, but in this case they all appear to the first two cards, and in the first four responses. They are situationally related. She was irritated by the testing, a predictable factor that she implies by explaining that she had more friends "before everybody started to try to get into my head." The number of blends (8) in the record is much greater than expected for an 8-year-old. Psychologically, she is more complex than most 8-year-olds can handle, and certainly more so than those who are cognitively impaired. Two of the blends involve both chromatic color and achromatic color; they are Color-Shading blends, signifying much confusion about feelings, which probably translates into a great deal of uncertainty and indecision about her emotions.

Overall, this youngster is very uncertain and probably somewhat fearful about her feelings. She keeps her feelings inside and this tends to provoke frequent and probably intense episodes of affective disruption that are likely to occur in the form of depressive experiences. It is interesting to note that three of her four chromatic color answers are minus and that two of the four involve her most serious Critical Special Scores (FABCOM2) and both have $M-$ determinants. Collectively, the data regarding affect leave little question that she is an inordinately inhibited child whose inability to deal with her feelings in a more natural way has created a coping style that is inappropriate for her age. It is even more detrimental to her growth and effective functioning in light of her age and her cognitive handicaps.

Self-Perception—Case 11   The data related to self-perception for Case 11 are shown in Table 99.

Table 99.   Self-Perception Data for Case 11

| 3r + (2)/R = 0.38 | FD = 2 | MOR = 2 | Hx = 0 | An + Xy = 0 |
| Fr + rF = 1 | Sum V = 0 | H:(H) + Hd + (Hd) = 2:6 | | Sx = 1 |

		RESPONSES TO BE READ		
MOR Resp's	FQ − Resp's	M Resp's	FM Resp's	m Resp's
7,20	4,7,11,12,17,19,20	2,3,5,6,20	12,13,18,19,21	16

There is a reflection in the record, indicating an excessive self-centeredness and a tendency to overvalue her worth. This is not unusual for an 8-year-old as more than one third of nonpatient 8's give at least one reflection answer. At the same time, the Egocentricity Index (.38) is inordinately low for an 8-year-old, conveying the notion that she does not regard herself very favorably when she uses significant others as a basis from which to judge her own worth. Collectively, this illustrates a significant conflict state, which is difficult for an older person, but often devastating for a young child. On the one hand, she values herself highly, but on the other, she regards herself poorly. It is a confusing situation and probably accounts for the two *FD* answers that are in the record. She seems to be struggling to understand who or what she is, and probably attempts to compartmentalize the marked disparity in conclusions. The failure to keep these conclusions apart may contribute to some of the defensive aggressiveness that she manifests in school, and possibly at home.

The fact that only two of her eight human contents are Pure *H* answers reveals, not surprisingly, that her conceptions of people, including herself, are based much more on imagination or fantasy than on real experience. This is not unusual for an 8-year-old, but in this instance, it only serves to confuse her understanding of herself and others, and also breeds expectations concerning the behaviors of herself and others that may be quite different from what occurs in the real world.

The two MOR responses have been briefly mentioned earlier with regard to her mediational activities because both are minus. Each conveys an unusual sense of limitation (Card IV, a dead bird with no legs; Card X, a merry-go-round that is broken). In the first, the bird is described as "big," but later is described as "weird." The second may be more important because of the sense of disappointment conveyed, ". . . ants and other insects waiting for a ride," but, ". . . it's broken so they just sit on it." A merry-go-round is a happy place, usually filled with joy and excitement for the young child. In effect, that is how young children view their idealized world. But, in this instance, the idealized world is broken, and the "insects" of that world are left waiting for a happy experience. Single responses should never be interpreted out of context, but this answer seems to convey so much despair that it cannot be ignored. Her world is not a happy or exciting place and she is bewildered because her expectations for life are not being met.

The remaining two minus answers involve shoddy logic. The first occurs as the second answer to Card II. It is a clown's face described as "weird, . . . its black on the face and the red eyes . . ." It is not really a clown as she describes it, but something that is quite unreal. The second, Response 19 to Card IX, includes three types of animals, reindeer, hippopotami, and snails "fighting or squishing each other." The animals, or what they are doing is unreal, even for an 8, but she seems to become very concrete when confronted with the complex, affectively ladened stimulus field, and an aggressive response appears to be her solution.

Her human movement answers also have peculiarities. The first, Response 2 to Card I, is quite unusual. It is a person with a big coat, holding her arms out. The fact that the coat is open seems to be implying a message, *look at me.* The second occurs as the first answer to Card II. Even though the objects (witches) should have an ominous quality, they do not. Instead, they are merely touching hands in an almost hesitant or even timid manner. The third *M* is equally intriguing. It is Response 5 to Card III. Someone is practicing bowling, how to stand when you bowl. It is passive. It involves a reflection. It is preparatory and yet it is also introspective, and may convey her sense of uncertainty about her interpersonal activities. The fourth is even more passive. It occurs in Response 6 to Card IV, a monster laying down, "like a giant that went to sleep . . ." The last two *M* answers have been reviewed earlier as both are minus. They are anthropomorphized animals fighting and waiting. Except for the unreal fighting animals on Card IX, all the other *M's* have a markedly hesitant or passive quality and probably convey very directly her own impressions of herself, that is, hesitant, uncertain, and passive.

The *FM* responses are more distinctive in their actions (a fly flying; a cat crawling along, ready to jump and catch a bird; lions climbing a mountain or rocks; spiders and other bugs fighting with each other). All are active, but only one is domestic (the cat), and two are generally regarded as unliked and unwanted (the fly and the spiders). The single *m* response is a helicopter flying over clouds, "it doesn't want to get down into them or it could get lost." This answer, as much as any of the others imparts her tenuous feelings about herself and her environment.

At least two of her other answers are worth noting for the manner in which they are embellished. The first is Response 11 to Card VI (a behind) in which she shares her preoccupation and also her embarrassment, "its like where you go to the bathroom but

I'm not gonna say it." What might she have said? The second is Response 15, to Card VII (the letter "U," "maybe who made it didn't take her time") which seems to imply a sense of distortion and an implication that someone is at fault regarding her difficulties.

Overall, she seems to be a person who is aware of her deficiencies, but who tries to avoid dealing with them by assuming a rather passive role in decision making that permits her to avoid direct comparisons and/or competition with her peers. At the same time she seems to be struggling with questions about herself and how she has reached this unwanted state. It seems clear that, at some level, she seeks attention and recognition, and is searching for an understanding of herself. At another level, she feels exposed and vulnerable. At still a different, and probably more primitive, level, she strives to achieve a better sense of self and often is aggressive in her orientation to do so. Her interpersonal perceptions obviously play an important role in defining her self-image.

Interpersonal Perception—Case 11   The data concerning her interpersonal perceptions and behaviors are shown in Table 100.

Table 100.   Interpersonal Perception Data for Case 11

CDI = 1	$a{:}p$ = 6:5	T = 1	Human Cont = 8	Pure H = 2
HVI = Neg	Food = 0	PER = 0	COP = 0 AG = 3	Isolate/R = 0.19

RESPONSES TO BE READ

HUMAN MOVEMENT WITH PAIR	*HUMAN CONTENTS*
3,20	1,2,3,4,5,6,10,11

The CDI and HVI are both negative. Interestingly, the $a{:}p$ (6:5) ratio is not larger on the passive side as would have been expected from the data for the $M^a{:}M^p$ ratio. It does not confirm a passive interpersonal behavioral role that has been implied earlier. When these two ratios differ for direction, it usually signifies a distinct tendency to avoid decision making and a tendency to ignore or escape reality through fantasy but also the absence of the more passive or submissive role that often accompanies those features. In this instance, her extreme self-centeredness probably accounts for the unwillingness to assume a passive or submissive interpersonal role. There are no Food answers in the record, but the presence of the single T response, and the presence of a substantial number of human contents (8) are important to understanding the seeming dichotomy concerning passivity. The latter indicates a very strong interest in people. It is much greater than is usually expected in an 8, but as noted earlier, the fact that only two of the eight human contents are Pure H reveals that her conceptions of others are not very realistic. Thus, while the T signals the presence of natural experiences of needs to be close to others, her lack of understanding of them makes this an objective that is difficult to achieve.

Another finding seems to support this notion. The number of PER answers (1) is not significant, but there are no COP answers and three AG responses. The absence of COP and the presence of a significant number of AG responses means that she has a distorted view of the world and people in it and tends to perceive aggression to be a natural phenomenon in everyday interpersonal relationships. This finding is consistent with the history. Sometimes, she is quite aggressive. She attributes this to the fact that her peers tend to avoid her or that they do not always play by her rules. Thus, her behaviors tend to run contrary to her needs, but more importantly, the finding signals that she has no realistic notion about smooth or deep interpersonal relationships.

The Isolation Index is not positive. This could be a false negative, but she is not really isolated. Instead, in her own way, she continues to attempt to achieve interpersonal contact. There are three *M* answers involving a pair (witches touching hands; animals fighting; insects waiting for a ride). None include the sort of positive interaction that might be hoped for in the record of a developing youngster and simply reaffirm her naivety about relations with others. The human contents also tend to convey the confusion that she has about how to conceptualize people (pumpkin; a person with a big black coat; witches; a clown's face; someone practicing bowling; a monster; a vampire; a behind). It is difficult to judge more than one or two (a person with a black coat and a person practicing) as positive, and even those have negative qualities.

In general, this youngster seems remarkably naive about interpersonal relationships. In part, this is because she is confused about herself, but the naivety goes well beyond that and extends into her strange thinking and her unusual and often distorted ways of translating new stimuli. Moreover, her confusion about feelings and the apparent negative reinforcement that she has experienced about expressing feelings contribute enormously to her plight.

SUMMARY—CASE 11

In effect, this 8-year-old, cognitively handicapped child has been taught to be something other than an 8-year-old. The history given by the mother hints at problems early on in the development of this child that have, apparently, been handled quite inappropriately. She continues to harbor the childish notion of being important, but at the same time has come to regard herself as a "bad seed," who is an annoyance in the home and who has difficulty keeping up in school. She has developed an overideational, fantasy-ladened style of coping with life. Her thinking is naive and sometimes detached from reality. Her thinking is a place to hide from an unkind world. She responds very conventionally when convention is precisely defined, but in other circumstances, her fantasy-oriented detachment from the real world causes her to distort much new information, or at best, to attribute features to that information in an unconventional manner.

She is confused about feelings and fails to express herself in a manner that would be consistent with others of her age. She tries to avoid dealing directly with her feelings or with many of the naturally emotionally loaded situations that confront her in daily life. Instead, she tends to bottle up her feelings, and this probably causes much affective disruption, including a vacillation between semireclusiveness, in which some depressive features will occur, and a more aggressive expression of affect that only irritates those around her. She wants contact with others but has no really useful idea about how to achieve this, and in fact, as noted earlier, many of her behaviors cause people to turn away from her.

The referral asks how much of the problem behavior may be attributed to psychological versus neurological factors, and specific recommendations concerning intervention are also requested. The answer to the first question is relatively simple. Most of the problem behavior stems from psychological problems. To be sure, she is handicapped, but it appears as if the reaction of others to her handicaps has led to some substantial impairments to her psychological growth. These include the development of her overideational style, her abuse of fantasy, her confusion about emotion, her confusion about herself, and her difficulties relating to the world. Some of these features have origins in her neurologically related problems, but the way that significant others have addressed those problems has created more current difficulties than the problems themselves.

Intervention planning is, at best, difficult. The parents are obviously embarrassed by this bad offspring and the school really doesn't want her; and many of her strange ideas and unwanted behaviors are now well fixed. Intervention must involve both the parents and the school and special intervention efforts are required for the child. Probably, some sort of family treatment is warranted to aid the parents and the precocious 7-year-old sibling to find different, probably less negative ways to deal with this child. She seems to feel like an outsider in her own home, and that may not be a distorted perception. Intervention in the school is probably more difficult. It seems obvious that she will not be passed to the next grade. The use of the special classes is important to her academic growth, but probably the wrong issues are being focused on. She really needs help in defining conventional responses, especially socially conventional responses, and if the special class work can be altered to this end, it can be useful. On the other hand, simply focusing on academically related material will be of little use, at least for the immediate future. The most important aspect of intervention concerns the child herself and individualized treatment. Her self-image is negative and somewhat chaotic and she does not know what to do with her feelings. Individual play therapy can be quite useful in dealing with both of these problems but quick results cannot be expected, and because of that, the responses of the family and the school are critically important to her immediate future. This is a youngster who is difficult to tolerate, yet a failure to do so will probably relegate her to a continuing miserable and unproductive existence. If family treatment is initiated, a careful evaluation of both parents may provide some useful insights about how best to work with them to become more accepting and encouraging to this child.

REFERENCES

Acklin, M. W. (1990). Personality dimensions in two types of learning disabled children: A Rorschach study. *Journal of Personality Assessment, 54,* 67–77.

Acklin, M. W., & Fechner-Bates, S. (1989). Rorschach developmental quality and intelligence factors. *Journal of Personality Assessment, 53,* 537–545.

American Psychiatric Association. (1987). *Diagnostic and statistical manual of mental disorders* (3rd ed., rev.). Washington, DC: Author.

Anastopolous, A. D., & Barkley, R. A. (1992). Attention Deficit-Hyperactivity disorder. In C. E. Walker & M. C. Roberts (Eds.), *Handbook of clinical child psychology* (2nd ed., pp. 413–430). New York: Wiley.

Barkley, R. A., Fischer, M., Edelbrock, C. S., & Smallish, L. (1990). The adolescent outcome of hyperactive children diagnosed by research criteria: I. An 8-year prospective follow-up study. *Journal of the American Academy of Child and Adolescent Psychiatry, 29,* 546–557.

Beck, S. J. (1930). The Rorschach test and personality diagnosis. *American Journal of Psychiatry, 10,* 19–52.

Bender, W. N., & Smith, J. K. (1990). Classroom behavior of children and adolescents with learning disabilities: A meta-analysis. *Journal of Learning Disabilities, 23,* 298–305.

Brown, R. T., & Borden, K. A. (1986). Hyperactivity at adolescence: Some misconceptions and new directions. *Journal of Clinical Child Psychology, 15,* 194–209.

Brown, R. T., Borden, K. A., Clingerman, S. R., & Jenkins, P. (1988). Depression in attention deficit-disordered and normal children and their parents. *Child Psychiatry and Human Development, 18,* 119–132.

Cantwell, D. P. (1986). Attention deficit disorder in adolescents. *Clinical Psychology Review, 6,* 237–247.

Cantwell, D. P., & Baker, L. (1991). Association between attention deficit-hyperactive disorder and learning disorders. *Journal of Learning Disabilities, 24,* 88–95.

Carr, M., Borkowski, J. G., & Maxwell, S. E. (1991). Motivational components of underachievement. *Developmental Psychology, 27,* 108–118.

Dollinger, S. J., Horn, J. L., & Boarini, D. (1988). Disturbed sleep and worries among learning disabled adolescents. *American Journal of Orthopsychiatry, 58,* 428–434.

DuPaul, G. J., Guevremont, D. C., & Barkley, R. A. (1991). Attention deficit-hyperactivity disorder in adolescence: Critical assessment parameters. *Clinical Psychology Review, 11,* 231–246.

Fischer, M., Barkley, R. A., Edelbrock, C. S., & Smallish, L. (1990). The adolescent outcome of hyperactive children diagnosed by research criteria: II. Academic, attentional, and neuropsychological status. *Journal of Consulting and Clinical Psychology, 58,* 580–588.

Franzen, M., & Berg, R. (1989). *Screening children for brain impairment.* New York: Springer.

Gerstein, A., Brodzinsky, D., & Reiskind, N. (1976). Perceptual integration on the Rorschach as an indicator of cognitive capacity: A developmental study of racial differences in a clinic population. *Journal of Consulting and Clinical Psychology, 44,* 760–765.

Goldstein, S., & Goldstein, M. (1990). *Managing attention disorders in children.* New York: Wiley.

Gottfried, A. E. (1985). Academic intrinsic motivation in elementary and junior high school students. *Journal of Educational Psychology, 77,* 631–645.

Grolnick, W. S., & Ryan, R. M. (1990). Self-perceptions, motivation, and adjustment in children with learning disabilities: A multiple group comparison study. *Journal of Learning Disabilities, 23,* 177–184.

Hammill, D. D., Leigh, J. E., McNutt, G., & Larsen, S. C. (1987). A new definition of learning disabilities. *Journal of Learning Disabilities, 20,* 109–113.

Hirsch, E. A. (1970). *The troubled adolescent as he emerges on psychological tests.* New York: International Universities Press.

Hunt, R. (1988). Attention deficit disorder and hyperactivity. In C. J. Kestenbaum & D. T. Williams (Eds.), *Handbook of clinical assessment of children and adolescents* (pp. 519–561). New York: New York University Press.

Hynd, G. W., Snow, J., & Becker, M. G. (1986). Neuropsychological assessment in clinical child psychology. In B. B. Lahey & A. E. Kazdin (Eds.), *Advances in clinical child psychology* (Vol. 9, pp. 35–86). New York: Plenum Press.

Klein, R. G., & Mannuzza, S. (1991). Long-term outcome of hyperactive children: A review. *Journal of the American Academy of Child and Adolescent Psychiatry, 30,* 383–387.

Lambert, N. M. (1988). Adolescent outcome for hyperactive children. *American Psychologist, 43,* 786–799.

Livingston, R. L., Dykman, R. A., & Ackerman, P. T. (1990). The frequency and significance of additional self-reported psychiatric diagnoses in children with attention deficit disorder. *Journal of Abnormal Child Psychology, 18,* 465–478.

Loney, J. (1987). Hyperactivity and aggression in the diagnosis of attention deficit disorder. In B. B. Lahey & A. E. Kazdin (Eds.), *Advances in child clinical psychology* (Vol. 10, pp. 99–135). New York: Plenum Press.

Mannuzza, S., Klein, R. G., & Addalli, K. A. (1991). Young adult mental status of hyperactive boys and their brothers: A prospective follow-up study. *Journal of the American Academy of Child and Adolescent Psychiatry, 30,* 743–751.

Obrzut, J. E., & Hynd, G. W. (1983). The neurobiological and neuropsychological foundations of learning disabilities. *Journal of Learning Disabilities, 16,* 515–520.

Pihl, R. O., & McLarnon, L. D. (1984). Learning disabled children as adolescents. *Journal of Learning Disabilities, 117,* 96–100.

Pintrich, P. R., & de Groot, E. V. (1990). Motivational and self-regulated learning components of classroom academic performance. *Journal of Educational Psychology, 82,* 3–40.

Ridley, S. E., & Bayton, J. A. (1983). Validity of two scoring systems for measuring cognitive development with the Rorschach. *Journal of Consulting and Clinical Psychology, 51,* 470–471.

Rorschach, H. (1942). *Psychodiagnostics.* New York: Grune & Stratton. (Original work published 1921).

Ross, D. M., & Ross, S. A. (1982). *Hyperactivity* (2nd ed.). New York: Wiley.

Routh, D. K. (1986). Attention deficit disorder. In R. T. Brown & C. R. Reynolds (Eds.), *Psychological perspectives on childhood exceptionality* (pp. 467–507). New York: Wiley.

Salyer, K. M., Holmstrom, R. W., & Noshpitz, J. D. (1991). Learning disabilities as a childhood manifestation of severe psychopathology. *American Journal of Orthopsychiatry, 61,* 230–240.

Siegel, M. G. (1987). *Psychological testing from early childhood through adolescence.* New York: International Universities Press.

Silver, L. B. (1990). Attention deficit-hyperactivity disorder: Is it a learning disability or a related disorder? *Journal of Learning Disabilities, 23,* 394–397.

Stone, W. L., & la Greca, A. M. (1990). The social status of children with learning disabilities: A reexamination. *Journal of Learning Disabilities, 23,* 32–37.

Taylor, H. G., & Fletcher, J. M. (1990). Neuropsychological assessment of children. In G. Goldstein & M. Hersen (Eds.), *Handbook of psychological assessment* (2nd ed.; pp. 228–225). Elmsford, NY: Pergamon Press.

Thompson, R. J., Lampron, L. B., Johnson, D. F., & Eckstein, T. L. (1990). Behavior problems in children with the presenting problem of poor school performance. *Journal of Pediatric Psychology, 15,* 3–20.

Toro, P. A., Weissberg, R. P., Guare, J., & Liebenstein, N. (1990). A comparison of children with and without learning disabilities on social problem-solving skill, school behavior, and family background. *Journal of Learning Disabilities, 23,* 115–120.

Waddell, K. J. (1984). The self-concept and social adaptation of hyperactive children in adolescence. *Journal of Clinical Child Psychology, 13,* 50–55.

Wallender, J. L., & Hubert, N. C. (1985). Long-term prognosis for children with attention deficit disorder with hyperactivity. In B. B. Lahey & A. E. Kazdin (Eds.), *Advances in child clinical psychology* (Vol. 8, pp. 113–147). New York: Plenum Press.

Weiner, I. B. (1992). *Psychological disturbance in adolescence* (2nd ed.). New York: Wiley.

Weiss, G., & Hechtman, L. K. (1986). *Hyperactive children grown up.* New York: Guilford Press.

Wentzel, K. R., Weinberger, D. A., Ford, M. E., & Feldman, S. S. (1990). Academic achievement in preadolescence: The role of motivational, affective, and self-regulatory processes. *Journal of Applied Developmental Psychology, 11,* 179–193.

Whalen, C. K., & Henker, B. (1985). The social worlds of hyperactive (ADDH) children. *Clinical Psychology Review, 5,* 447–478.

Ysseldyke, J. E., & Stevens, L. J. (1986). Specific learning deficits: The learning disabled. in R. T. Brown & C. R. Reynolds (Eds.), *Psychological perspectives on childhood exceptionality* (pp. 391–422). New York: Wiley.

CHAPTER 10

Custody Issues

The problem of forensic issues in the Rorschach assessment of younger clients has not been addressed directly in the preceding chapters. Mainly, the concern is how best to use Rorschach findings in referrals dealing with forensic cases that focus on younger clients. Whether intentionally or unexpectedly, psychologists who do assessment often become involved in forensic issues concerning youngsters they have examined.

In adult cases, forensic issues most commonly involve questions of personal injury, competency to stand trial, and criminal responsibility. When such questions must be addressed, the written report of the psychologist is often supplemented by testimony taken in depositions or given in the course of trial procedures. Although psychologists whose cases come to trial often would prefer to serve in the role of an *amicus curiae,* or friendly advisor to the court, many cases involving adults require them instead to serve as an "expert witness" and come to grips with the often unfriendly aura of the adversarial system (see Brodsky, 1991; Weiner, 1987).

When testimony is given in a trial, whether regarding an adult or a child, psychologists serving as expert witnesses may have to contend with their findings being given short shrift or even being excluded from consideration. Their competence, the validity of the techniques they have employed, and the credibility of their conclusions are commonly subjected to challenge. Psychologists who function as expert witnesses come quickly to realize the importance of being able to support their procedures and statements with solid evidence. Conclusions based solely on clinical impressions rarely carry much weight and can readily be denigrated by competent attorneys, most of whom are well prepared to do so. Only a naive trial lawyer will be unfamiliar with the work of Ziskin (1981; Ziskin & Faust, 1988), who has provided a comprehensive and well-documented reference guide to assist lawyers in refuting psychiatric and psychological evidence. Likewise, only a naive psychologist will go into court as an expert witness without being familiar with what Ziskin has written, especially his argument that psychiatric and psychological evidence often fails to meet criteria for admissibility and merits little attention even when it does.

These introductory cautions are in no way a prelude to depicting psychologists as defenseless in the forensic arena or encouraging them to avoid it. To the contrary, forensic psychology has become a well-established and professionally attractive practice specialty, and competent forensic psychologists can command considerable respect in and out of the courtroom (see Weiner, 1992). Moreover, in addition to an extensive literature demonstrating the soundness of numerous assessment methods, practitioners can turn for guidance to numerous books that delineate effective forensic application of psychological tests and convincing courtroom presentation of test findings (Blau, 1984; Brodsky, 1991; Maloney, 1985; Melton, Petrila, Poythress, & Slobogin, 1987; Shapiro, 1991; Weiner, 1987). Commonly, in fact, forensic psychologists need to be less concerned about being belittled or ignored than about allowing jurists and attorneys to assign more certainty and predictability to test findings than is warranted by our present state of knowledge (see Weiner, 1989).

When a case involves a young person, those who do psychological assessment may find themselves often serving as consultants rather than expert witnesses. Unlike the expert witness, whose testimony is bound by the rules of evidence and who is subject to cross-examination, consultants to the court present and discuss their findings at the pleasure of the jurist; however, their findings may bear on the decision at hand. Consulting to the court more closely resembles the clinical case conference model than testifying as an expert witness and may accordingly feel more comfortable to most practicing psychologists. At the same time, however, consulting typically involves a greater burden of responsibility than sitting on the witness stand. Consultants are more likely than expert witnesses to be encouraged to offer opinions or advice that go beyond the limits of their data, and this can pose some challenging issues.

THE RORSCHACH AND THE COURT

It is important, whether in a consulting role or one that involves formal testimony, to explicate the sources of data/information on which the consulting opinions or testimony conclusions are based. For reasons that are not very clear, many "expert witness" psychologists tend to avoid discussions about their procedures and are satisfied with offering opinions that may seem to be unsubstantiated. In effect, they take on the same role as do psychiatrists or other mental health professionals and usually speak very generally in terms of test findings. In doing so, they often put themselves at a disadvantage, because they tend to cast the findings from assessment in a more subjective light than should be the case. They, or the attorneys with whom they work, tend to dismiss the importance of explaining procedures and, as a result, offer opinions rather than findings. Psychological assessment should not be reduced to that apparent level of subjectivity.

It is unfortunate, but true, that many people, including some well-trained psychologists, have only a limited understanding about psychological testing and how interpretive statements are derived from test results. This naivety seems especially prevalent when findings from the Rorschach are at issue, and as a result, many who offer depositional or courtroom testimony that includes Rorschach findings may be doing a disservice to the client on whose behalf they are testifying. Thus, it often may be important to clarify the nature of the Rorschach and how it works. This will not be true in all cases, but it can be critical in some.

In these instances, it is important to emphasize that the Rorschach is a test, and not simply a procedure. In other words, the empirical basis of the test should be well in place before any testimony and/or opinions are offered, either in a consulting situation or in instances involving formal testimony. To do so tends to clear the air for both judges and juries, and findings often are regarded in the more serious context of scientific findings. It is sad to read trial transcripts in which the psychologist-witness injects the reading of one or more Rorschach responses given by a subject and interprets those answers individually and extensively; yet, this has been a commonplace procedure. In effect, these are witnesses who rely on their own judgments and theoretical orientations and ignore the potential use of the entire array of data generated in Rorschach results. At best, it reflects a poor approach to the use of assessment in forensic psychology situations.

In most forensic situations, it is easy to educate the presiding jurist and/or the jury about the Rorschach, or for that matter, any psychological test, and this should be done whenever it seems appropriate. The reason for doing this is to vigorously refute questions and insinuations about validity of the test in question. As every capable Rorschacher knows, intelligently posed issues of validity that concern the Rorschach are not cast in the all-encompassing question of "Is the Rorschach valid?" Instead, the issue must be formulated in terms of, "For what is the Rorschach valid?" When the question is phrased this way, the expert witness is given a relatively free hand to explain the nature of the test, the test process, and how the data are used. In most situations in which the issue of Rorschach validity is raised, the witness can then respond with a simple but accurate representation of the test and its yield.

The easiest way to explain the Rorschach is to briefly describe the procedure of collecting and then scoring or coding responses. Subsequently, the procedure of tallying frequencies of different response components should be described with an explanation of how these frequencies are converted and translated into ratios, percentages, and summary scores. The easiest way to do this is with a projector onto which two or three of the blots are shown and typical and atypical responses are given as illustrations. Subsequently, a complete Sequence of Scores is shown with a few explanations about some of the symbols such as *W, D, M, FC, P, INC.* This is followed by a slide or transparency showing the top portion of the Structural Summary, with an explanation of the frequency tallies. Finally, the lower portion of the Structural Summary is displayed, and a brief review of some of the ratios and percentages is offered.

Depending on the situation, it may be advisable also to explain how the ratios fall into clusters concerning different features of the person, such as thinking, self-concept, interpersonal relations, and so on. The psychologist must be careful to translate the Rorschach concepts into lay language, but this is not very difficult for the experienced Rorschacher who is accustomed to writing reports for other mental health colleagues or who routinely gives feedback to clients regarding findings.

When the stage is set with an adequate explanation of the Rorschach and how it works, the resulting testimony usually is given much more credence, as the judge and/or jury have become more familiar with the test than most laypeople and, as a result, are prone to weigh findings in the same light that they may/will testimony given by pathologists, or other specialized experts. In effect, this procedure tends to take the Rorschach out of the arena of subjective opinion and place it more directly in the context of empirical findings. Opinions based mainly or exclusively on Rorschach findings are still subject to question, because they contain elements of clinical subjectivity, but the degree of subjectivity perceived by judge and/or jury is far less than might otherwise be the case.

CUSTODY EVALUATIONS

By far, the largest proportion of forensic issues concerning young people involve child custody disputes between parents who are no longer living together. Custody disputes often can go well beyond the simple issue of which parent will provide the best environment for the growing child. They often focus on legal decisions concerning the child, such as payments for support, decisions concerning trust funds that may exist for the child, where the child will live, and the rights of each parent to make decisions about the child's future. As one indication of the frequency with which custodial decisions are made in present-day society, Hodges (1991, p. 1) begins a recent book on children of divorce by noting that 40% of young people in the United States will spend part of their childhood living with just one parent because of divorce. Not all divorces involve contested custody of children, but, when they do, psychologists are often asked to assess the parties to the case and comment on which parent is more fit to have custody. In many instances, the question may be whether either parent would be a suitable custodian or whether instead the parental rights should be terminated, permanently or temporarily, and some other placement should be sought.

Custody decisions are, of course, made by the court, not by psychologists, and there may be occasions when the psychologist-consultant or expert witness is not asked for any opinions concerning custody, but only to provide specific descriptive information (e.g., does this child show any signs of being psychologically disturbed; to what extent are favorable parenting skills present in each of the contenders for custody?). Even then, however, psychologists recognize that certain kinds of personality descriptions are likely to influence the court in certain ways (e.g., other things being equal, a child who is described as seriously disturbed is probably less likely to be regarded by the court as living in a favorable environment than a child who is described as well-adjusted; and a parent who is described as maladjusted is less likely to be viewed favorably than one described as functioning reasonably well).

In this regard, psychologists involved in custody cases can enhance the value of their reports and testimony by taking care to address matters with which the court can be expected to be concerned. For example, virtually all courts regard custodial planning as an interactive affair in which neither children, nor either of their parents alone, hold the key to an optimal arrangement. The success of any particular arrangement for custody will be determined in varying measure by each person's individual needs, attitudes, and personality styles; by the history and current status of both the mother-child and the father-child relationship; and by the history of the marital relationship and the existing accommodations between husband and wife (see Sales, Manber, & Rohman, 1992).

For psychologists, the interactive nature of custodial planning indicates that personality assessment data in cases of disputed custody should be obtained from mother, father, and child, at a minimum, for the evaluation to support any meaningful recommendations. Ideally, if one custodial alternative involves placement with a parent who has remarried or is about to do so, the evaluation should include the present or future stepfather or stepmother as well. Assessment data collected from just one or two parties to contested custody may be informative (e.g., this parent seems emotionally immature). However, such information is likely to be of little help unless comparative judgments can be made (e.g., although emotionally immature, this parent is still more mature than the other one).

As a second consideration in providing helpful information, psychologists should recognize that the courts are generally guided in custody decisions by what is known as "the best interests of the child" doctrine (see Brinson & Hess, 1987; Hodges, 1991, Chaps. 5, 6; Shapiro, 1984, Chap. 5). This doctrine gives precedence to the rights of children to grow up in the most favorable possible environment over the rights of their parents to dictate where and by whom they should be reared; in so doing, the doctrine also asserts the right of the court to make decisions concerning the welfare of minor children and to require parents to comply with these decisions.

In applying the doctrine of the best interests of the child, most jurisdictions assign differential importance to particular environmental circumstances in relation to the young person's age. In the case of infants, courts typically seek to provide an environment that will meet basic needs for nurturance and protection. Meeting these basic needs is commonly referred to as "the mothering function"; although courts may therefore show a strong preference for maternal custody of infants, they are more generally interested in having very young children in the custody of whoever can adequately fulfill this function, which may be a stepmother, an aunt, or a grandmother instead of the biological mother, or may in some situations appear to be the father.

For preschool children after infancy, courts often attend most to the developmental advantages of growing up in a stable, two-parent family and observing positive male-female parental interaction. Other things being equal, and depending on the qualities of the stepparent, a divorced biological parent who has remarried may impress the court as providing a more favorable environment for a child this age than a divorced parent who has remained single.

During the elementary school years, ages 6 to 12, the focus tends to shift toward the developmental benefit at this age of living in a predictable environment. The court is accordingly likely to consider carefully which parent will be more likely to provide a home in which children will know what is expected of them, will be able to depend on their parent or parents to behave in certain ways, and will have good role models available with whom to identify.

When working with adolescents, courts tend to view needs for effective control and adequate supervision as being most important in custodial planning. The best interests of the child at this age are expected to be served by whichever parent seems most able and willing to take on the challenging task of being mother or father to a young person grappling with the adolescent developmental tasks of gaining autonomy, managing complex social and interpersonal relationships, and deciding on educational and career goals.

Finally, for young people of all ages, the courts generally regard the interests of children as being well served by arrangements that encourage and preserve contact with an extended family. In choosing between a mother and a father as the custodial parent, most judges will lean toward the parent who seems more likely to maintain an amicable and cooperative relationship with the noncustodial parent, to comply fully with provisions for shared custody or visitation, and to foster positive feelings by the child toward the noncustodial parent. Similarly, the parent in a custody issue who seems more likely to maintain contact with other relatives and thereby promote the child's sense of broad family membership is likely to be preferred.

Psychodiagnosticians need to appreciate that what the court would like to know prior to making a custody decision typically goes far beyond what psychological tests can show. Most judges are interested in what the parents have to say about whether, why, and under what conditions they would like to have custody of their child; what preferences if any the child can express concerning the custodial arrangement; how mother, father, and child feel about each other, how they in fact get along with each other, and how strongly they are attached to each other, especially the child to each parent; how well or poorly the child is adjusting at home, in school, and in the community; what level of psychological stability and maturity the parents demonstrate; and what resources each parent has for providing the kind of home environment that the child is likely to need now and in the future.

A thorough assessment to answer such questions requires interviews with parents and their children, separately and together; observations of interactions in the office, at home, and perhaps elsewhere; records provided by schools and other agencies that may have been involved with the child or family; reports from the family physician or other medical specialists familiar with the family's health; and appropriate psychological tests (see Blau,

1984; Melton et al., 1987; Weissman, 1991). The psychodiagnostic consultant who provides only the testing portion of this evaluation may have an important contribution to make with respect to the psychological profile of the parties to the case. However, what tests show should be kept in proper perspective as constituting just one of the many pieces of information that the court needs to reach a wise and just custody decision.

RORSCHACH-BASED RECOMMENDATIONS OR TESTIMONY

Turning now to the Rorschach, protocols given by a child and both parents in a custody case can allow the psychologist to inform the court concerning the presence or absence of psychological disturbance in each, the relative levels of social and school or work adjustment each is likely to show, and the personality strengths and weaknesses demonstrated by each. The implications of particular Rorschach findings for personality descriptions of these kinds are discussed throughout the volumes concerning the Comprehensive System. In general terms, information that a parent seems well-adjusted and possesses many personality assets will strengthen that parent's custodial claim in the eyes of the court in comparison with a parent who seems seriously disturbed and to have limited adaptive capacities. For instance, a parent who has a positive SCZI or who is positive on the HVI will be regarded negatively, and the parenting skills of one who has a DEPI value greater than 5 might be questioned.

Once pathology is ruled out, however, there is no personality description that always and automatically determines a judge's decision in a case of contested custody, and there is no personality pattern that has been found to preclude a parent's being granted custody or to prevent him or her from functioning effectively in the parental role. Nevertheless, Rorschach findings may have some specific implications for parental commitment to child rearing.

In that there is no infallible good-parent or bad-parent Rorschach profile, clinicians should be cautious in predicting from personality test data alone whether someone will function well as a parent. On the other hand, it is not unreasonable to suggest that people who are selfish and self-centered and have little inclination to form close attachments to others will often be less likely to shoulder parental responsibilities effectively, especially when doing so requires self-sacrifice, than people who are by nature caring, nurturant, altruistic, and comfortable in intimate relationships.

In Rorschach terms, then, the person with zero T, at least one reflection, and a high Egocentricity Ratio is probably less parentally oriented than a person whose record is free from these deviations from normative expectation. When T-less, high Egocentricity people with reflections enjoy being parents, their enjoyment usually comes from what they are receiving from being in the parental role rather than from what they are putting into child care; such parents are more likely to see and use their children as extensions of themselves than to help them individuate as people in their own right.

Similarly, parents who have few human contents and little Pure H in their records are less likely to be sincerely interested in, or realistic about, the welfare of their offspring. Such a finding could be particularly negative if the record also shows an absence of COP responses. Obviously, parents who show a distinct failure to modulate their emotional expressions, as would be illustrated by an $FC:CF + C$ ratio that is much larger for the right-side value, may have a less desirable feature, a finding that probably would be afforded even greater importance if the record also contains a large number of S responses. In a similar fashion, parents who have Adjusted D Scores that are less than zero, or values for EA that are less than 6.0, will probably be regarded less favorably than parents whose Adjusted D Scores are zero or who have EA values greater than 8.5. But, even if the Adjusted D or EA values fall into the expected range, the favorable nature of the findings would be tempered considerably if the CDI is positive.

The data concerning the personality styles of parents, as revealed by a Rorschach protocol, can sometimes also provide some added clues about the potential for effectiveness as a parent. For instance, an ambient finding is a less favorable predictor of good adjustment than either an introversive or extratensive style. Similarly, a very passive interpersonal style may be less desirable in terms of parenting skills, and this is probably more true when the passive style is combined with a marked dependency orientation.

Overall, the psychologist who uses the Rorschach as a major source from which to offer opinions or testimony in custody cases must be cautious and remember that both good and bad parents come in all psychological shapes and sizes. The psychologist who uses Rorschach data to generate opinions or testimony in custody cases will be acutely aware of the importance of formulating a personality description of each subject that will be as realistic as possible. Each description should give full weight to both assets and liabilities and the summary report should not give undue emphasis to either.

CASES FROM A CUSTODY DISPUTE

The following are data for three subjects, a child and her parents who are in dispute regarding her custody. The protocols of the three subjects, plus their respective histories are included, but unlike presentations from earlier chapters, the Rorschachs are not interpretively dissected. Instead, a Rorschach-based summary concerning each is presented. The data from the Structural Summary and content of each record that relates to statements in the summaries are shown in brackets.

THE ISSUE

The husband and wife in the dispute are both 36 years old. They have been married for nearly 14 years, although separated for about 6 months at the time of the evaluations. The child currently lives with the mother under a formal separation agreement. The father is allowed by the mother to take the child for weekend visits to the paternal grandparents' farm twice each month, and sometimes spends other weekend days with her. The mother and her attorney have assumed that this custody arrangement would continue after the divorce, but recently, a request for a psychological evaluation of the mother was initiated by the husband's attorney, charging that the mother is psychologically unfit and should not be afforded custody of their 12-year-old daughter.

In the petition to the court requesting that the mother and child be evaluated, it is noted that the child's performance in school has deteriorated badly since the separation and that both parents have been called to the school to discuss her problems with a teacher and a guidance counselor. The petition notes that during a previous separation lasting 4 months when the child was in the second grade and living with her paternal grandparents, her performance in school was considered excellent by her teacher. It is suggested in the petition that continued separation from the father has created a potentially serious psychological disturbance in the child.

The mother's attorney has responded to the court with a request for a psychological evaluation of the father, claiming that he has been "mentally" brutal to both his wife and child and arguing that an evaluation of the mother, taken independently, would not approach the issue of the mental health of either parent justly. The court has agreed to hear findings based on the evaluations, asking for any evidence that might support or refute the notion that the child is at psychological risk, and findings concerning the parenting abilities of both mother and father. A psychologist, agreed to by both attorneys, has been approved by the court and assigned the task of evaluating each of the three subjects. The presiding jurist has charged the psychologist to provide separate reports on each of the parents and the child and to be available to provide consultation and/or testimony concerning the findings in the context of a decision that will be in accordance with the best interests of the child. The assessment procedures included interviews, some cognitive testing, the MMPI with each parent, and the Rorschach.

Cognitive testing revealed that both parents and the child are intellectually above average (Mother: Verbal IQ = 113, Performance IQ = 111; Father: Verbal IQ = 117, Performance IQ = 114; Child: Verbal IQ = 115, Performance IQ = 109). The MMPI findings for the mother show that all T scores, except Scales K (74), 2 (72), and 7 (70) are less than 70. The father's MMPI findings reveals T scores higher than 70 on Scales 4 (76) and 9 (72).

CASE 12—THE CHILD

This girl, age 12 years 5 months, is the only child in her family. She was delivered by Caesarean section but with no complications. She walked at approximately one year, spoke sentences before her third year, and was toilet trained during her second year. She attended a nursery school at age 4 and was regarded favorably by teachers there. She entered first grade at 6 and, according to anecdotal reports, was a good reader and an active participant in class. Her report cards through the fifth grade are all filled with good evaluations and very positive remarks from teachers. She is currently in the fifth month of her sixth-grade year. Her sixth-grade teacher complained earlier in the year about her poor performance. After meeting with the parents, the teacher indicates that "some allowance" was afforded for her poor work but that the child has ". . . remained stubborn and rebellious. Her work is at a near failing level and her occasional attempts at improvement are very brief." The teacher predicts failure if the poor performance and rebelliousness persist. The youngster is described by teachers from earlier grades as being outgoing and eager. Two of them state that she was among the top students in their classes. Her music teacher indicates that she is very involved with music and has wanted to learn to play an instrument but has not participated in the school instruction program.

She has no history of major illness, has a very good class attendance record, and has participated in school plays during the fourth and fifth grades. Her mother says that she likes to bake cookies and cakes and has learned to do this independently. The mother also claims that the youngster enjoys helping with housework and that they have established a "very close" relationship since the father departed from the home.

The youngster speaks positively about both parents and cannot account for the breakup of the marriage. She admits that the parents have argued in her presence but suggests that these disputes have always ended in a friendly way. She notes that when her parents separated, when she was 7, she saw both of them frequently and enjoyed staying on her grandparents' farm, which is located only a few miles outside the small town in which she has been residing. She says that she has no memory about that separation and claims that she thought it was due to her father's ill health. During two prehearing interviews, one with a caseworker and one with the presiding judge, she stated that she likes living with her mother but would also like to live with her father. When pressed by the judge to express some preference, she refused to do so.

In the pretest interview she stated that she likes school and has several close friends. She feels bad about the pending divorce and seemed not to accept the fact that she might be placed in the custody of one parent or the other. She indicated that she likes her paternal grandparents very much and enjoys visiting them, but would not want to reside permanently with them. She is acutely aware of her poor school performance but denies that she is stubborn or rebellious ("I just don't do very well. I keep forgetting a lot of things when we have a test. We have too much work and too much homework"). She says that she enjoys cooking with her mother and notes that they spend considerable time together, ". . . shopping and going to the movies and things like that." Currently, she sees her father on most weekends and say that she enjoys staying with him and her grandparents at their farm.

Case 12. A 12-Year-Old Female

Card	Response	Inquiry	Scoring
I	1. It doesnt ll much, mayb a bat E: I thk if u lk a bit longr u'll prob find st else too	E: (Rpts S's resp) S: Well it cld b, it has th body in th cntr hre (points) & big wgs & th antenas too	Wo Fo A P 1.0 INC
	2. Well, up hre cb clouds around a mountain	E: (Rpts S's resp) S: Oh yeah, c ths top prt wld b th mt & all ths prt ll its all around it, u kno E: I thk I c th mt but Im not sur I c th clds all around it S: Well its all grey, c lik clds, lik u realy cant c th mt good, lik u r lkg sort of thru th clouds & thy come out hre too, its lik hazy, th grey makes it ll tht, lik dark clds all around a mt, c som of th grey is darkr & som is liter lik u can c thru thm bettr cause thyr thiner	Dv/+ FC'.FVu Cl,Ls 4.0
II	3. Tht ll a cave, its got th opening rite in th middl	E: (Rpts S's resp) S: Well all ths dark prt wld b lik rock or st & th cntr, hre (points) c th white cntr is th opening tht goes back in E: Goes back in S: Sur thts wht an opening is, a hole, thts wht makes th cave, its an opening of some sort in rock or in a hill E: U said ths ll rock S: Sur, its all dark lik rock, u kno E: I thk so	DS+ FC'.FDo Ls 4.5
	4. Ths mite b a flower petal	E: (Rpts S's resp) S: Well its not really lik a flower, just a petal off of a red flowr, c it goes around lik a lot of flower petals	Do FCu Bt
III	5. Mayb 2 peopl, mayb old peopl thse r pretty stupid u kno	E: (Rpts S's resp) S: Well, thy lk all bent ovr, lik 2 old peopl just standg thre lookg at eo, c th head is here & th legs & thy lk bent ovr, prety dumb	D+ Mpo 2 H P 4.0
	6. Tht cntr prt ll a saddle	E: (Rpts S's resp) S: Well, its lik u lk dwn on a small one, do u kno athg abt English saddles, well thyr vry small & if u lay thm out thy ll ths, we hav som at the farm	Do Fu Sc PER
IV	7. Thts lik a gorilla, lik he's layg dwn or st	E: (Rpts S's resp) S: He's got his big feet stickg out ths way (gestures) & u cant hardly c his head, he's all black & furry lik	Wo FMp.FD.FC'.FTo A P 2.0

E: Black & furry lik
S: Well gorillas r blck, at least all th ones I kno abt r blck & c all thse prts (rubs) thy make it lk kinda lik fur, gorillas hav fur u kno — Ddo mp– Bt

8. If u dont use it all u can mak a tree thre, sort of a droopy one, r we almost thru
E: (Rpts S's resp)
S: Ths is th trunk (points), u tak ths prt away hre (points) & u hav branchs hre, lik thy r drooping ovr, just lik hangg dwn, u understand
E: Thres just a few more
E: Yes, I c it

V

9. Mayb a bf or a moth, I gues just a moth cause bfs r pretty & thse sur r'nt
E: (Rpts S's resp)
S: Well it has th wgs out & th body & th antenas lik hre (points) its just all grey, not a bf but a closet moth thyr grey lik ths — Wo FC'o A 1.0 DV

10. Ths cld b lik th leg of a horse lik hes jumpg or rung behind ths bush
E: (Rpts S's resp)
S: Well, u only c th leg, c th calf of th leg & hre wld b th hoof & hes going behind ths, lik a bush or rock, Im not sur whch it is but it hides th rest of him — D+ FMa.FDo Ad,Bt 2.5

VI

11. Mayb an insect up in ths prt
E: (Rpts S's resp)
S: It has littl wgs & a littl body j lik som littl insect, IDK wht kind, u hav to use ur imagination — Do Fo A

VII

12. Mayb Indians, yeah Indians cause thy got thos feathrs it's just their heads, just lookg at eo
E: (Rpts S's resp)
S: Well thy hav feathrs in thr hair so thy must b Indians, c th nose & th chin & th head & th indentation for th eye, just Indians — D+ Mpo 2 Hd P 3.0 ALOG

13. If u lk at th cntr it cld b an anchor
E: (Rpts S's resp)
S: Ths whole thg coming down in hre, it has th shape of an anchor, c its round & thn goes up, yeah an anchor — DdSo F – Sc

VIII

14. Two bears, but thyr not supp to b pink, thes r pink so thyr not real
E: (Rpts S's resp)
S: On th outsid hre, c th legs & th heads & th body, thy cld ll bears but u'd hav to hav a diff colr for real bears — Do FCo 2 (A) P

15. Mayb a spine in thre too
E: (Rpts S's resp)
S: Lik a straight line up th backbone & c th littl bones in ths space IDK wht prt it mite b but th whol middl thre ll a spine, I'v seen thm in science class — Ddo Fu An PER

IX

16. Mayb thse cld b th horns of a deer lik u c hung on a wall & th cntr is th wood thyr attached to
E: (Rpts S's resp)
S: Just thse orange prts, thy sort of ll big horns, lik u c in a restaurant or somwhre lik tht, thy put thm on a wooden thg lik ths middl prt (D8), I dk wht u call it, but thy hav thse pointy prts on th horns, c (pts) — D+ Fu 2 Ad,Id 2.5

Case 12. (Continued)

Card	Response	Inquiry	Scoring
17.	Mayb its all a bunch of vegetables lik u c at th suprmarket, or mayb lik a salad	E: (Rpts S's resp) S: Well its just a bunch of colrd thgs mayb lik beets & carrots & lettuce, it cld b tht if u use ur imagination E: Beets & carrots & lettuce S: Sur, th pink is beets, th orang is carrots & th green is lettuce	W+ CFu Fd 5.5
X 18.	A persons face	E: (Rpts S's resp) S: Not ths top prt or thse side thgs, but hre, c (points) thse cld b eyes or glasses & th nose & th pink cld b hair & th mouth, pretty dumb lkg E: U said eyes or glasses? S: I thk glasses, thy look more lik tht	DdSo F – Hd,Sc 4.0
19.	It cld all b ocean thgs too	E: (Rpts S's resp) S: I dk wht exactly but I kno tht th green cb seaweed & th pink cld b som ko thg on th botom of th sea & th rest cld just b lik thgs in th ocean E: Thgs in th ocean? S: Lik mayb seaweed & alger or whtevr u call it, just a bunch of diff colrd thgs lik u mite c in th ocean	Wv/+ CFo Bt 5.5 DV

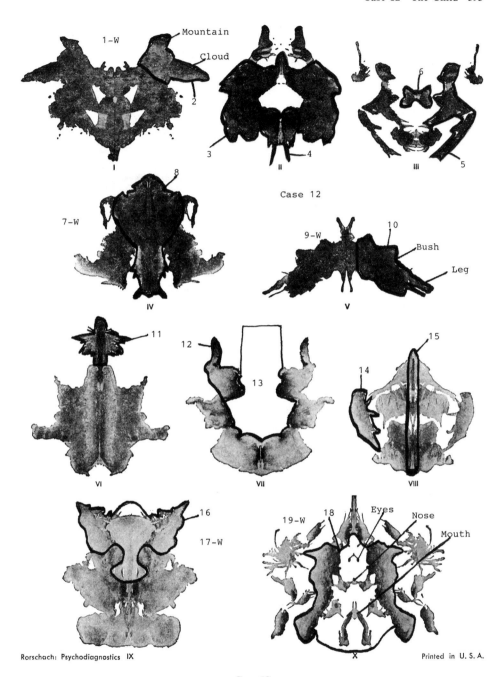

Case 12

Rorschach: Psychodiagnostics

Printed in U. S. A.

Case 12

Case 12   **Sequence of Scores**

Card	No	Loc	#	Determinant(s)	(2)	Content(s)	Pop	Z	Special Scores
I	1	Wo	1	Fo		A	P	1.0	INC
	2	D/	7	FC'.FVu		Cl,Ls		4.0	
II	3	DS+	6	FC'.FDo		Ls		4.5	
	4	Do	3	FCu		Bt			
III	5	D+	9	Mpo	2	H	P	4.0	
	6	Do	3	Fu		Sc			PER
IV	7	Wo	1	FMp.FD.FC'.FTo		A		2.0	
	8	Ddo	99	mp-		Bt			
V	9	Wo	1	FC'o		A		1.0	DV
	10	D+	4	FMa.FDo		Ad,Bt		2.5	
VI	11	Do	3	Fo		A			
VII	12	D+	1	Mpo	2	Hd,Cg	P	3.0	ALOG
	13	DdSo	99	F-		Sc			
VIII	14	Do	1	FCo	2	(A)	P		
	15	Ddo	99	Fu		An			PER
IX	16	D+	3	Fu	2	Ad,Id		2.5	
	17	W+	1	CFu		Fd		5.5	
X	18	DdS+	99	F-		Hd,Sc		4.0	
	19	W/	1	CFo		Bt		5.5	DV

Case 12   **Structural Summary**

Location Features	Determinants		Contents	S-Constellation
	Blends	Single		. . FV+VF+V+FD>2
			H = 1, 0	. . Col−Shd Bl>0
Zf = 12	FC'.FV	M = 2	(H) = 0, 0	. . Ego<.31,>.44
ZSum = 39.5	FC'.FD	FM = 0	Hd = 2, 0	. . MOR > 3
ZEst = 38.0	FM.FD.FC'.FT	m = 1	(Hd) = 0, 0	. . Zd > +− 3.5
	FM.FD	FC = 2	Hx = 0, 0	. . es > EA
W = 5		CF = 2	A = 4, 0	. . CF+C > FC
(Wv = 0)		C = 0	(A) = 1, 0	. . X+% < .70
D = 10		Cn = 0	Ad = 2, 0	. . S > 3
Dd = 4		FC' = 1	(Ad) = 0, 0	. . P < 3 or > 8
S = 3		C'F = 0	An = 1, 0	. . Pure H < 2
		C' = 0	Art = 0, 0	. . R < 17
DQ		FT = 0	Ay = 0, 0	x . . . . . TOTAL
. . . . . (FQ−)		TF = 0	Bl = 0, 0	
+ = 7 (1)		T = 0	Bt = 3, 1	Special Scorings
o = 10 (2)		FV = 0	Cg = 0, 1	Lv1 Lv2
v/+ = 2 (0)		VF = 0	Cl = 1, 0	DV = 2x1 0x2
v = 0 (0)		V = 0	Ex = 0, 0	INC = 1x2 0x4
		FY = 0	Fd = 1, 0	DR = 0x3 0x6
		YF = 0	Fi = 0, 0	FAB = 0x4 0x7
		Y = 0	Ge = 0, 0	ALOG = 1x5
Form Quality		Fr = 0	Hh = 0, 0	CON = 0x7
		rF = 0	Ls = 1, 1	SUM6 = 4
		FD = 0	Na = 0, 0	WSUM6 = 9

	FQx	FQf	MQual	SQx			
					F = 7	Sc = 2, 1	
+	= 0	0	0	0		Sx = 0, 0	AB = 0 CP = 0
o	= 10	2	2	1		Xy = 0, 0	AG = 0 MOR = 0
u	= 6	3	0	0		Id = 0, 1	CFB = 0 PER = 2
−	= 3	2	0	2			COP = 0 PSV = 0
none	= 0	—	0	0	(2) = 4		

Case 12   **Ratios, Percentages, and Derivations**

R = 19   L = 0.58

			FC:CF+C = 2: 2	COP = 0 AG = 0
			Pure C = 0	Food = 1
EB = 2: 3.0	EA = 5.0	EBPer = N/A	Afr = 0.46	Isolate/R = 0.42
eb = 3: 6	es = 9	D = −1	S = 3	H:(H)Hd(Hd) = 1:2
	Adj es = 9	Adj D = −1	Blends:R = 4:19	(HHd):(AAd) = 0:1
			CP = 0	H+A:Hd+Ad = 6:4

FM = 2 :	C' = 4	T = 1
m = 1 :	V = 1	Y = 0

		P = 4	Zf = 12	3r+(2)/R = 0.21
a:p = 1: 4	Sum6 = 4	X+% = 0.53	Zd = +1.5	Fr+rF = 0
Ma:Mp = 0: 2	Lv2 = 0	F+% = 0.29	W:D:Dd = 5:10: 4	FD = 3
2AB+Art+Ay=0	WSum6 = 9	X−% = 0.16	W:M = 5: 2	An+Xy = 1
M − = 0	Mnone = 0	S−% = 0.67	DQ+ = 7	MOR = 0
		Xu% = 0.32	DQv = 0	

SCZI = 0	DEPI = 5*	CDI = 4*	S-CON = N/A	HVI = No	OBS = No

THE RORSCHACH FINDINGS—CASE 12

This is a youngster whose capacity for control has become impaired [Adjusted D Score] because of considerable distress [Adjusted *es*, right-side *eb*]. As a result, she is very prone to impulsiveness, both in her thinking and her behaviors. It might be likened to an overload condition in which she is experiencing much more irritating internal stimulation than is common for one of her age. This affects her ability to concentrate and tends to disorganize her efforts at decision making and some of her planned behaviors. In effect, she simply does not have enough resource readily available to contend with all the things that are going on inside her. The situation is made more complex because she has not yet developed a consistent coping style [*EB*], and even under better conditions, much of her decision-making activity will be less efficient than that of those who have developed a persistent style.

In this instance, many of her current problems have been created because she has difficulty with her feelings. She has several characteristics suggesting that she is often depressed [DEPI], and evidence indicates that she holds many feelings inside rather than express them openly [*C'*]. In fact, she is struggling hard to contain her feelings [*WSumC:SumC'*] and avoid emotionally provoking situations, especially those that might require some sort of emotional exchange [*Afr*]. She has more negativism or anger than should be the case [*S*], but does not seem to know how best to express this. Probably, this relates to some of the reports from her sixth-grade teacher than she seems stubborn and rebellious. It seems clear that her feelings provoke a great deal of pain for her [shading blends] with which she cannot contend easily or directly.

Her self-esteem is quite low [Egocentricity Index], and she appears to be involved in much more self-examination than is appropriate for her age and situation [Vista & *FD*]. Often, when issues of divorce and/or custody are involved, this sort of excessive introspection signals concerns that the subject may be pondering his or her own contribution to the marital discord. Whether or not that may be true in this case, it is clear that she perceives some fairly negative features about herself [Vista]. It also seems clear that she tends to feel morose and is somewhat desperately hoping for greater stability in her life [minus response contents]. She seems confused about the dispute between her parents [content, Response 5] and obviously cannot contend with it [*FM* & *m* answers].

In her effort to avoid emotional provocation, she is withdrawing excessively from others [CDI, Isolation Index] and this has a negative influence on her interest in, and perception of people and her interactions with them [human contents]. She seems to want to be close to others [*T*] and to this end has adopted a very marked passive-dependent form of interacting with others. Thus, ordinarily, she expects and wants others to take responsibility and make decisions for her. She also seems to defend against the harshness of her situation by taking flight into a form of passive fantasy through which she would be able to reconstruct problems rather than deal with them directly. She seems quite uncertain about how to deal with people, and the composite of her passivity and her fantasy life provide convenient ways of avoiding direct interactions.

Her passivity has also created a conservative approach in dealing with new information. She does not want to deal with too much at one time [*W:D:Dd*]. The findings also suggest that she tends to interpret reality more idiosyncratically than is customary for her age [*Xu%*]. This tendency to personalize her interpretations of things can mislead her, and it also may cause others to regard her as unusual or even weird. Her thinking appears to be more concrete than expected for one of her age [special scores], especially in view of her past academic record, and her current state of overload is contributing to this. She is much more defensive than should be the case and is manifesting some of the hostile passiveness that could create much greater trouble in her future.

Overall, she seems to be a youngster who could be headed for a psychological disaster if the tide of current deterioration and defensiveness is not reversed. Much of her current state is a function of the stress created by the problems of her parents and her own indecision about her allegiance and her sources of emotional nurturing. She is bewildered by her feelings and sees no options for handling them except to hold them tightly inside. As a result, they affect her attention and concentration abilities and lead her into a path of potential impulsiveness. She does not understand herself very well and concentrates on features of herself that she believes to be quite negative. In effect, she seems to feel quite helpless and has assumed a very passive-dependent role in her daily life. At the same time, she is an angry child, and this anger contributes significantly to her poor school performance. It seems warranted, regardless of the court decision, for this youngster to enter individual psychotherapy where the major focus will be on her own role identity and her perceived role in the marital dispute. Her self-esteem is far too low for effective survival, and her defensiveness, although somewhat serviceable, may be too great if she is to relate adequately to peers and develop necessary interpersonal skills and confidence in her controls.

CASE 13—THE MOTHER

This 36-year-old is an attractive, dark-haired woman who appeared very neat at the time of the evaluation. She is a high school graduate who married at age 22 shortly before her husband, who was then in the army, was sent to Vietnam. At that time, she was working as a switchboard operator, having held that position for 4 years. She continued to work until she became pregnant about 4 months after her husband returned from overseas. She notes that even before their marriage they used to argue a great deal, ". . . mostly about little things." She described their relationship as being very close after his return from the army: "It was like being on a honeymoon all over again for awhile." She indicates that they did have occasional disputes, however: "He'd fuss over this or that but it wasn't important." She feels that they had a strong love for each other in spite of their frequent arguments. She reports that their relationship became "closer" after she became pregnant and remained so during the first 3 or 4 years after the child was born: "He helped around the house a lot and we did lots of things together. We were a close family, but then it began to fade away. He started traveling more, I was alone more. When he was home we would get into bickering." She reports that their sexual relationship was ". . . always good I guess, he sure never complained about it. That was the one thing he didn't complain about."

Her husband's work as a salesman of parts for farm equipment caused him to be traveling 2 or 3 days per week. He would usually be home at night but often arrived in the evening. ("I could never know when to expect him so sometimes dinner wasn't ready or it was overdone, but even if everything was swell he'd find something to bitch about and I'd always feel like a fool.") She reports that her husband wanted the child to attend nursery school and encouraged his wife to seek employment at that time to help pay for the house that they had recently purchased. She did obtain work selling ladies' wear in a department store, ". . . but that just made things worse 'cause I'd let some things go at home and he'd have something else to bitch about." During the 9th year of their marriage they had a prolonged series of arguments focusing on her care of the home, and at the end of one of these sessions, ". . . he just walked out and said that he was gonna get a divorce." Two days later they agreed to place the child with his parents as transportation to school would then be no problem. ("I should have just quit then and kept her with me, but I was pretty upset and I didn't know what to do.")

They reunited after 4 months. During that time both had spoken with attorneys about a legal separation but without any final conclusion. As part of their reconciliation agreement, she reduced the amount of time that she was working and terminated her employment during the year. In retrospect, she feels that their reconciliation was "a bad move," but she notes that they were being encouraged by most of their friends and family to try again.

She is the second of three children. Her father, age 59, is a plumber, and her mother, age 58, is a housewife. Her older brother, age 38, is also a plumber, married and with two children. Her younger sister, age 33, is also married and has three children. She describes her family as being not very close: "We were all pretty independent. We got along but we didn't do much together. My dad and my brother were always close and so were me and my sister but we never really did a lot as a whole family."

She states that her health has always been good. She began menstruation at age 12 and has not had any problems with it. Her first sexual experience occurred during her third year in high school with the man who was to become her husband. ("We were in a lot of classes together and dated a lot and it just happened.") She reports that she was not orgasmic until after her marriage. She denies sexual relationships with anyone else until after her current separation began. She is currently dating a man who works in a drugstore where she has recently become employed as a cashier on a part-time basis (25 hours per week).

She argues very strongly that her husband has "no right" to their daughter: "I'm the one that's raised her and nursed her and helped her along. We've shared things together. He's gone most of the time and when he is home he's always bitching or watching television. He really doesn't care about her." She admits that she has not been very responsible in handling family funds. They have accumulated a large number of unpaid bills and are 2 months in arrears on their mortgage payments. Many of the unpaid bills are the result of a shopping "spree" that she went on shortly before their separation during which she charged a large number of clothing purchases, mostly for the child. She admits that she did this "out of spite," contending that he had been spending money on other women.

She pleads confusion about her daughter's school performance, suggesting that, "he's got her all upset," adding her belief that when the child is at her grandparents' farm "a lot of talk probably goes on about me." She is rigorous in her contention that she and her daughter are very close and says that she makes sure that her daughter does her homework every school night.

Case 13. A 36-Year-Old Female

Card	Response	Inquiry	Scoring
I	1. It ll a spider to me, ugh, r thre many of these	E: (Rpts S's resp) S: Well hre r th wings & th body & evythg, it just ll a spider	Wo F− A 1.0 INC
	E: Just a few, I thnk if u tak ur tim u'll find st else too		
	2. Well, I supose th cntr cld b a person, mayb a woman, thse r hard	E: (Rpts S's resp) S: It mite b a woman, hres her arms up in th air, lik sbody was pullg a holdup, Im always scared of tht at work E: Can u sho me some of her other features S: Hre r her legs & th skirt going out	Do Mpo H DR
II	3. Two elephants, it ll thyr playg or st thy r touchg thr trunks	E: (Rpts S's resp) S: Not ths red, tht doesnt count hre j th dark prts, thy ll 2 elephants playg, pushing thr trunks togethr, c (points) & hre r th legs	D+ FMao 2 A P 3.0 COP
III	4. Hum, it ll a coupl dancg, thy ll women I thk but its hard to tell	E: (Rpts S's resp) S: Well thy r holdg st between thm lik in a dance way, hre r th bosoms & th long legs thy realy dont ll wm very much, thy cld b men too E: U said holdg st betwn thm S: IDK wht, kinda lik to do w th dance	D+ Mao 2 H,Id P 3.0 COP
	5. Tht red ll bld to me	E: (Rpts S's resp) S: Do we hav to do all of thm again E: Yes, thts how we do th test S: Well its red, thts wht bld is lik, red, hre & hre, just red bld	Dv C Bl
IV	Ths one is terribl, I dont c anythg		
	E: Tak ur tim, we'r in no hurry		
	6. I suppose it cld b a big monstr	E: (Rpts S's resp) S: Its all blk, I always thot of monsters as blk E: Can u sho me som of th features so I can c it S: Thes r th legs & th head up hre & th arms & ths is th tail, weird huh	Wo FC'o (H) P 2.0
V	7. A bat, yes definitely a bat	E: (Rpts S's resp) S: Well it has big wings & a body lik a rat, thts how bats r u kno	Wo Fo A P 1.0
VI	8. A church and a cross	E: (Rpts S's resp) S: Well th shap isnt too good for th church dwn hre, th big prt, but ths cld b a cross & thts a bldg so I figurd it for a church, th cross is more modern lik	W+ Fu Ay 2.5
	9. Tht bottm prt c.b. a skin of som animal too	E: (Rpts S's resp) S: It has ragged edges lik a skin wld b & c thse wld b th legs, bigger in th back lik thy cut th front ones off more	Do Fo Ad P

399

Case 13. (Continued)

Card	Response	Inquiry	Scoring
VII	10. It ll two ladies, thts all	E: I'm not sur abt wht makes it ll an animal skin S: Just th raggd edges, thes r the legs, thts how skins look	D+ Fo 2 Hd,Cg P 1.0
		E: (Rpts S's resp) S: Its just thr faces, up hre & thy hav high combs in thr hair, c th thgs pointg up hre & th nose & chin just two ladies	Wv/+ CF− Art,An,Bl 4.5
VIII	11. Oh, now thts prettier It ll st out of a medical book S: Can I turn it over E: Whtevr u lik	E: (Rpts S's resp) S: Well I dk aythg abt prts of th body, but ths ll one of thos diagrams u mite c in a Drs office, mayb its diffrnt prts of th stomach, yes probably, each color is for a diffrnt prt, lik ths wld b th lowr stomach & th blu mite b another part & th pink is th bld around it	
	<12. U kno ths way it ll a weasel or st crossg a pond & u can c his reflection dwn hre	E: (Rpts S's resp) S: Well hre is th weasel, c th legs & body & he's all reflectd dwn hre, so is th stuff around him	W+ FMa.Fr.CFo A,Na P 4.5
	v13. Ths way it cld b a spidr in his web	E: (Rpts S's resp) S: He's rite hre in th midle, j sort of waitg & th rest wld b th web, lik mayb th sun is hittg it & u c som of th stuff tht collects in a web lik tht E: Som of th stuff S: Nothg special, j thgs tht get caught lik sticks & leaves & bugs, I dont c any bugs, but aftr a spider gets through wrappg thgs up u cant tell wht thy r anyhow, & th way th sun is hitg it is j ll a bunch of colred thgs	Wv/+ FMp.CF− A,Id 4.5
IX	14. It ll an ugly mask of s.s. lik kids wear at halloween	E: (Rpts S's resp) S: Its got all th diff colr, c th big orange ears & th puffy green cheeks & th big pink lip part & hre, c thes white slits, thyr th eye holes & thse othr white prts r whre u tie th elastic thru	WSo CFo (Hd) 5.5
	15. Thse orange thgs mit b sea horses too	E: (Rpts S's resp) S: Thy hav pointd heads & big bellys too, thts whre thy carry th young in th stomach	Do F− 2 A
X	16. Oh, thres a coupl mor spidrs	E: (Rpts S's resp) S: C, thy hav all thos legs & th cntr is th body, I dont c th web tho	Do Fo 2 A P
	17. I dk wht tht pink is, mayb ss of insides, lik an intestines or st, one on each side	E: (Rpts S's resp) S: Well its pink lik it may hav bld on it, I dont thk intestines r realy pink, but thy r long & wrinkly around th edges lik ths	Do CF− An,Bl
	v18. Ths way it just ll an explosion	E: (Rpts S's resp) S: Just lik ethg was going out in all diff ways, all lit up E: All lit up S: Well lik all th diff colrs lik tht happen in an explosion, realy wild lik, going out in all directions	Wv ma.CFu Ex

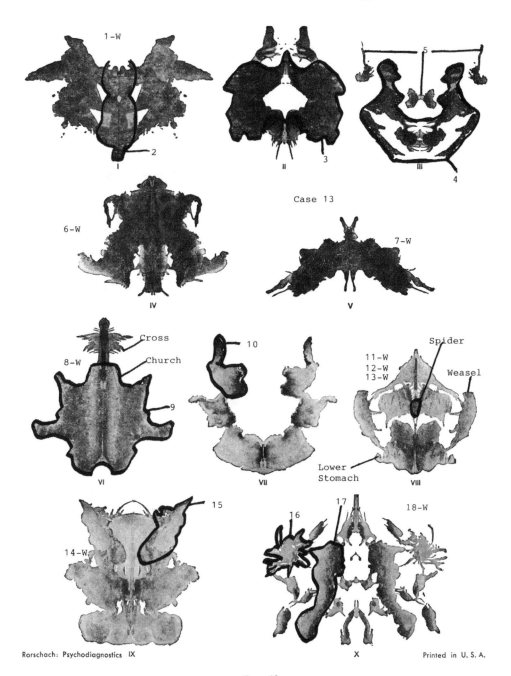

Case 13

Rorschach: Psychodiagnostics   Printed in U. S. A.

Case 13

Case 13   **Sequence of Scores**

Card	No	Loc	#	Determinant(s)	(2)	Content(s)	Pop	Z	Special Scores
I	1	Wo	1	F-		A		1.0	INC
	2	Do	4	Mpo		H			DR
II	3	D+	6	FMao	2	A	P	3.0	COP
III	4	D+	1	Mao	2	H,Id	P	3.0	COP
	5	Dv	2	C		Bl			
IV	6	Wo	1	FC'o		(H)	P	2.0	
V	7	Wo	1	Fo		A	P	1.0	
VI	8	W+	1	Fu		Ay		2.5	
	9	Do	1	Fo		Ad	P		
VII	10	D+	2	Fo	2	Hd,Cg	P	1.0	
VIII	11	W/	1	CF-		Art,An,Bl		4.5	
	12	W+	1	FMa.Fr.CFo		A,Na	P	4.5	
	13	W/	1	FMp.CF-		A,Id		4.5	
IX	14	WSo	1	CFo		(Hd)		5.5	
	15	Do	3	F-	2	A			
X	16	Do	1	Fo	2	A	P		
	17	Do	9	CF-	2	An,Bl			
	18	Wv	1	ma.CFu		Ex			

Case 13   **Structural Summary**

Location Features	Determinants Blends	Single	Contents	S-Constellation

				NO . . FV+VF+V+FD>2
			H = 2, 0	NO . . Col−Shd Bl>0
Zf = 11	FM.Fr.CF	M = 2	(H) = 1, 0	NO . . Ego<.31,>.44
ZSum = 32.5	FM.CF	FM = 1	Hd = 1, 0	NO . . MOR > 3
ZEst = 34.5	m.CF	m = 0	(Hd) = 1, 0	NO . . Zd > +− 3.5
		FC = 0	Hx = 0, 0	NO . . es > EA
W = 9		CF = 3	A = 7, 0	YES . . CF+C > FC
(Wv = 1)		C = 1	(A) = 0, 0	YES . . X+% < .70
D = 9		Cn = 0	Ad = 1, 0	NO . . S > 3
Dd = 0		FC' = 1	(Ad) = 0, 0	NO . . P < 3 or > 8
S = 1		C'F = 0	An = 1, 1	NO . . Pure H < 2
		C' = 0	Art = 1, 0	NO . . R < 17
DQ		FT = 0	Ay = 1, 0	2 . . . . . TOTAL
. . . . . (FQ−)		TF = 0	Bl = 1, 2	
+ = 5 (0)		T = 0	Bt = 0, 0	Special Scorings
o = 9 (3)		FV = 0	Cg = 0, 1	Lv1 Lv2
v/+ = 2 (2)		VF = 0	Cl = 0, 0	DV = 0x1 0x2
v = 2 (0)		V = 0	Ex = 1, 0	INC = 1x2 0x4
		FY = 0	Fd = 0, 0	DR = 1x3 0x6
		YF = 0	Fi = 0, 0	FAB = 0x4 0x7
		Y = 0	Ge = 0, 0	ALOG = 0x5
		Fr = 0	Hh = 0, 0	CON = 0x7
Form Quality		rF = 0	Ls = 0, 0	SUM6 = 2
		FD = 0	Na = 0, 1	WSUM6 = 5
	FQx FQf MQual SQx	F = 7	Sc = 0, 0	
+ = 0 0 0 0			Sx = 0, 0	AB = 0 CP = 0
o = 10 4 2 1			Xy = 0, 0	AG = 0 MOR = 0
u = 2 1 0 0			Id = 0, 2	CFB = 0 PER = 0
− = 5 2 0 0				COP = 2 PSV = 0
none = 1 — 0 0		(2) = 6		

Case 13   **Ratios, Percentages, and Derivations**

R = 18	L = 0.64		FC:CF+C = 0: 7	COP = 2 AG = 0
			Pure C = 1	Food = 0
EB = 2: 7.5	EA = 9.5	EBPer = 3.8	Afr = 0.80	Isolate/R = 0.11
eb = 4: 2	es = 5	D = +1	S = 1	H:(H)Hd(Hd) = 2:3
	Adj es = 5	Adj D = +1	Blends:R = 3:18	(HHd):(AAd) = 2:0
			CP = 0	H+A:Hd+Ad = 10:3
FM = 3 : C' = 1 T = 0				
m = 1 : V = 0 Y = 0				
		P = 8	Zf = 11	3r+(2)/R = 0.50
a:p = 4: 2	Sum6 = 2	X+% = 0.56	Zd = −2.0	Fr+rF = 1
Ma:Mp = 1: 1	Lv2 = 0	F+% = 0.57	W:D:Dd = 9: 9: 0	FD = 0
2AB+Art+Ay=2	WSum6 = 5	X−% = 0.28	W:M = 9: 2	An+Xy = 2
M − = 0	Mnone = 0	S−% = 0.00	DQ+ = 5	MOR = 0
		Xu% = 0.11	DQv = 2	

| | SCZI = 2 | DEPI = 1 | CDI = 0 | S-CON = 2 | HVI = No | OBS = No |

THE RORSCHACH FINDINGS—CASE 13

This 36-year-old female shows no evidence of significant psychopathology. She does tend to value herself much more highly than is realistic, and this feature sometimes causes her to ignore her own shortcomings and blame others for her own failures or mistakes [reflection, Egocentricity Index]. This excessive self-centeredness is not necessarily a major liability, but it tends to reduce the frequency with which she will become involved in self-examining behaviors, a process that often yields greater sensitivity to one's flaws and enhances ways in which people interact with others [no Vista or FD]. She is interested in others [human contents], but to some extent, her self-image is based more on imagination than experience [Pure H]. She also seems to have an unusual preoccupation with her body functions, the cause for which is not very clear [$An + Xy$]. Nonetheless, it seems to have a strong influence on some of her perceptions of reality. This may have to do with a sense of vulnerability or a struggle that she may be having concerning her inflated sense of self. After all, a failed marriage and charges of parental neglect weigh heavily on a person's self-image.

She seems somewhat tentative about her sense of self, that is, not really being secure about being female [human movement contents], and she also seems unsure about her relations with others [FM responses]. Thus, although she seems quite interested in people [human contents], she probably does not understand them very well and apparently does not expect relationships to be close. In fact, she may be more wary of gestures concerning closeness than is typical of most adults [$T = 0$]. In spite of this, she seems to expect that social relations will be marked by positive features, and it seems reasonable to assume that her own interpersonal relations are marked by this attitude [COP]. This could reflect a sort of naivety that is created by her overestimates concerning her worth (I am good so the world around me will be good).

A more significant issue concerns her emotions and how she expresses them. She is a very emotionally oriented person who typically merges her feelings into her thinking, and as a result, her emotions become quite important in her decisions and her behaviors [EB]. In fact, it is probably a rare instance in which she pushes her feelings aside and attempts to address a problem more logically [$EBPer$]. She is not one who contains or inhibits her feelings [right-side eb]. On the contrary, she is prone to express her feelings very directly, and often, they will be much more intense than might be expected for an adult [$FC:CF + C$]. Stated differently, when she becomes emotional, all around her will be aware of her feelings and sometimes they may be disconcerted or irritated by the fervor reflected in these displays. Her failure to tone down her emotions suggests considerably less maturity than might be expected for one of her age and is commensurate with the naive high value that she seems to place on her own worth. On the other hand, she is not a negative person who uses her feelings in vicious or hurtful ways [S], and there is no reason to suspect that her intense feelings have created any more psychological complexity than she can handle easily [blends].

The intensity with which she expresses feelings might convey an impression that she does not have a good capacity to control herself. That is not true. Her capacity for control and her tolerance for stress are, in fact, somewhat better than expected of most adults [D Scores]. In other words, when she releases her feelings in an intense manner, it is not because they have overwhelmed her. To the contrary, these are events that are well controlled and could even be considered stylistic for her. She apparently sees no reason to modulate or tone down her emotional expressions, even though she could do so.

She seems to have adequate reality testing. She works reasonably hard to process new information [*Zf, W:D:Dd*], and there are no indications of negligence when she does so. The way in which she uses new information is less sophisticated than might be the case for an adult [*DQ* + ,*DQv*], but this poses no substantial liability. She does tend to translate information in ways that involve more distortion and/or personalization of reality than common for most adults [*X* + %, *X* − %, *Xu*%]. This seems to relate to her questions regarding her self-image, the credibility of which is an issue at the moment. Her thinking seems reasonably clear [*Sum6, WSum6*] and flexible [*a:p*], and there are no indications of problems with regard to her ideation.

In summary, this is a very self-centered woman who is not very insightful and often will blame others when she is at fault. She seems quite confused about and preoccupied with herself. This preoccupation sometimes causes her to distort reality. Taken alone, this feature may not represent a major problem, but it is cause for concern. She is interested in people and seems to expect positive relations with them. At the same time, she does not expect any of her relationships to involve extensive emotional closeness and probably is more guarded about gestures of closeness from others than should be the case. A much more important problem is the manner in which she handles her feelings, which usually are quite intense. They impregnate her thinking extensively, and she makes very few decisions that are not influenced by them. In addition, when she releases her feelings, she does not control them very much. They are obvious to all around her, and their intensity probably conveys an impression that she is immature. To some extent, that impression is probably correct. Collectively, the way in which she deals with her feelings conveys many immature hysteroidlike features. This kind of immaturity about the use of her feelings and the intensity with which she displays them may cause some people to avoid her or regard her negatively. Thus, although she is sincere in expressing her feelings, their collective mass may well be more than most people want to experience. Nonetheless, she handles information reasonably well, and although her preoccupations with herself sometimes cause her to disregard or bend reality, her thinking is clear and not unlike that of most adults. Overall, this is the type of person who might profit from a developmental form of intervention, provided that she is motivated to do so. There is no reason to question her sincerity concerning the custody of her daughter, but her role as a mother, and as an adult, lacks some of the features that might be perceived as desirable for a parent. Generally, her parenting skills could be enhanced considerably if she were considerably less self-centered and substantially more emotionally mature than seems the case at this time.

CASE 14—THE FATHER

This 36-year-old male is a tall, heavyset fellow who wears glasses and was neatly groomed at the time of the evaluation. He graduated from high school at age 18 with slightly above average grades. During high school, he played on the varsity basketball team and was active in the 4-H Club. At the time of his graduation, he wanted to become an engineer and entered a technical institute from which he received an AA degree at age 20 in mechanical drawing. He worked for nearly two years as an apprentice draftsman before voluntarily entering the army. He decided to volunteer to avoid being drafted. ("It gave me a chance to pick more of what I would do.") His major assignment in the army was in battalion supply for a mobile engineer unit. He served 1 year in Vietnam and was decorated for heroism in action.

He had dated his wife as early as their second year in high school, and after their graduation they saw each other frequently. ("I guess everybody figured that we'd get married someday. I suppose I did, too. If I had only known then what I've learned the hard way, none of this would have ever happened.") Their marriage took place while he was on leave before he was sent to Vietnam. ("It seemed like the right thing at the time. I guess I wanted to know that somebody was waiting too.") After a 2-week honeymoon, he left for overseas. After his return about 14 months later, ". . . everything was great for a while. She had this apartment and had it all fixed up and I got my job real quick. It was nice and I think we were really in love." He confirms his wife's statement that the first three or four years of their marriage after his return from the military were very positive: "We were a young family with a new baby and it was real nice."

He feels that their marriage began to deteriorate as his wife became more and more negligent in her housekeeping activities. ("She just let things go, like she didn't care.") He reports that the frequency of their sexual activities diminished significantly at that time and that he would often find himself in the role of a housekeeper. ("She'd just let things go, and I'd have to do them on my off days.") He finally decided that if they had their own home, she would take more interest, and they purchased a small house. ("I figured that I could work a little harder and we could manage it okay, but then she started complaining about my long hours; and over time things went from bad to worse." He indicates that he thought that if he could interest her in something outside the house, things might improve: "I talked her into a job and it helped a little but not for long. She just turned into a slob and finally I couldn't take it anymore and left. I came back the next day and packed up the kid and took her out to my folks' place. I was really fed up and I wanted a divorce. I think I would have got one too, but my folks really pressed me to try and make it work."

He is the third of four siblings and the second of three males. His older brother, age 41, is a manager of an electrical supply firm. He is married with three children. His younger brother, age 33, is a dentist, practicing in another state. He is also married but has no children. His sister, age 38, is married to a haberdasher and has three children. His father, age 66, is still active in running a large farm, and his mother, age 62, has been the homemaker. He says that he enjoys his draftsman job and has done well at it. He has considered assuming the responsibility for the family farm when his father retires but has not reached a firm decision about it. He suggests that his marriage would have terminated much earlier had they not had the child.

His wife has accused him of seeing other women, but he denies this: "Oh, sometimes I've had a roving eye when things got rough at home, but I've never fooled around since Nam." He feels that his sexual relationship with his wife was satisfying early in their marriage, but ". . . it hasn't been much in the last couple of years." He feels that he might remarry at some future time, ". . . but I'm not sure. Right now I just want to make a good home for my daughter. That's what is important now." He reports that he will probably sell their house to cover the substantial bills that his wife has charged. He is very bitter about this prospect: "I don't know how anybody could be so dumb, but that's how she is."

He feels certain that his wife has had at least one affair during their marriage. ("I don't know with who or for how long but I just know she did.") He denies any drug history and claims that his use of alcohol is "moderate."

Case 14. A 36-Year-Old Male

Card	Response	Inquiry	Scoring
I	I nevr saw nothg lik tht 1. Mayb its lik one of thos masks tht kids wear at halloween	E: (Rpts S's resp) S: Well it wld b a funny one, I dont mean ha, ha funny, but one lik to scare somebody	WSo Fo (Hd) 3.5
	S: It doesnt re me of athg else E: I thk if u look a bit longr u'll find st else, most peopl do	E: Can u describe it for me so tht I can c it S: Well its got thse slanty eyes (points) & thse thgs stickg out wld b th part u curl around u'r head, lik a devils mask, ths is th mouth & its got littl horns	
	2. Well u kno tht cntr prt cld b smthg lik a person, a wm	E: (Rpts S's resp) S: It sorta ll a wm w her hands raised up, l waving or smthg, c hres her legs dwn hre & her waist, I dont c her head tho, mayb its lik she was bending backward so u cant c her head	Do Mao H
II	Wow! 3. Ths ll a cpl of dogs realy tangling it up, at least one of thm is hurt cause thres bld on thr heads & dwn hre whre thr feet r	E: (Rpts S's resp) S: Thy ll big dogs, thyv got big bodies & pretty good sized heads, c hre but thyv got paint or bld all ovr thm & its dwn hre too, mayb thyr bears bc I nevr heard of dogs fighting ths bad E: U said thy hav bld on thr heads & whr thr feet r S: Yeah hre, c all ths red, mayb its paint lik mayb thyr fighting around some paint	W+ FMa.CFo 2 A,Bl AG,MOR
	4. U kno ths littl prt hre is lik stg lik an old arrowhead	E: (Rpts S's resp) S: Th Indians used to make thm of stone & thy wre kinda rough lik ths, sort of pointed but rough E: Im not sur wht thr is thr to mak it lk ruf S: Well its not a straight line, mor lik st carved lik Indians used to do	Ddo Fo Ay
III	5. Well it mite b a cpl of peopl doing st, mayb trying to carry ths thg dwn hre	E: (Rpts S's resp) S: It just ll a cpl of men who r carrying ths thg, c hres thr heads (points) & th long legs, thyr bendg ovr lik thy r carryg ths	D+ Mao 2 H,Id P 3.0 COP
	S: Can I turn it ovr E: Whtevr u lik		
	v6. U kno ths way thse side thgs cb a cpl of bombs	E: (Rpts S's resp) S: Well thyr long & pointed & thy hav ths fin on thm, thts th way thy mak heat controld missils, I saw thm in Nam, missils r lik tht	Do Fu 2 Sc PER

Case 14. (Continued)

Card		Response		Inquiry	Scoring
IV	7.	Thts a big old hulk of a thg, lik st fr sc fict, just sorta standg there	E: S:	(Rpts S's resp) Its just som old furry hulk lik thy mak up for sc fict movies, lik th thg fr th swamp & tht sort of stuff	Wo Mp.FTo (H) P 2.0
			E: S:	Furry hulk Yeah th colrs mak it ll its got fur al ovr it	
	v8.	Ths way ths top prt ll a cpl of camel heads	E: S:	(Rpts S's resp) Well, thy got tht long snout & lik th big eyebrow stickg out & th long necks, c abt dwn to hre (points)	Do Fu 2 Ad
V	9.	Tht ll a big turkey gettg ready to take off <v> S: I dont c anythg else	E: S:	(Rpts S's resp) Well, u kno turkeys dont really fly but thy use thr wgs to help thm run by makg less weight on thr legs, oh thy can get off a bit bit but not for far, Iv seen em do it, any how ths one ll he's got thos wgs spred out & is ready to fly off, c (points) & he's got ths littl head hre & th feet hre	Wo FMau A 1.0 PER
VI	10.	Tht ll a skin, lik som A laid out	E: S:	(Rpts S's resp) Ths top doesnt fit very well, but ths bttm ll a pelt of ss, lik a fox or wolf or st its furry too, lik th other picture, c th colrs, thy ll fur to me	Do FTo Ad P
VII	11.	Gee tht ll a cpl of kids arguing abt st	E: S:	(Rpts S's resp) Well, its lik just thr uppr bodies, frm th waist up, each one has got st in his hair, mayb thyr playg indian & thyr pointg in th opposite direction lik mayb thyr arguing which way to go or st, c th nose is hre & th forhead & th arms r hre (points)	D+ Ma+ 2 Hd,Id P 3.0 AG
	v12.	Tht ll an arrowhead again, thre in th middl, I must hav arrowheads on th brain or st, I havnt seen one in years since my grandady showd me som whn I was a kid, I wondr whtevr hapend to the ones he had	E: S:	(Rpts S's resp) Well, its just got tht shpe to it, lik a point carved out of stone, c u hav to j look at th white cntr (outlines)	DSo Fu Ay PER
VIII	13.	It ll a cpl of muskrats tryg to get at st at th top of ths bush	E: S:	(Rpts S's resp) Muskrats dont realy do tht but thts how it lks, c thre's one on each side (points), thse r th legs & th body & th heads & th rest is som k o bush, its all diff colrs so mayb its a fruit or berry bush & thyr tryg to get at th top prt for som reason	W+ FMa.CFo 2 A,Bt P 4.5

408

No.	Response	Inquiry	Scoring
v14.	If I turn it ths way, ths prt hre s o ll th face of a bulldog	E: (Rpts S's resp) S: Of course th colr doesnt count hre, but if u just lk at th outline, its got thse littl ears & th big jowls & it all has tht sort of droopy shpe l buldogs hav, kinda sad lkg, c thse wld b th jowls (outlines)	Do Fu Ad
<15.	If I lk ths way u can c th whale frm *Moby Dick*	E: (Rpts S's resp) S: Its just ths littl white prt, u kno if u saw th movie tht whale was white, c hre, its white & its sort of shapd lik a whale, lik its got its mouth open, c (outlines)	DdSo FC'.FMpu A PER
IX			
16.	Thse top prts ll a cpl of guys playg th fidl or st	E: (Rpts S's resp) S: Well, thy arnt too clear & I cant figure thos pointd hats, but u get th vague outlines of thm & each one has thr arms out, & ths is th bow & th fiddl, mayb lik at a contest	D+ Mao 2 H,Cg,Sc 4.5
v17.	Ths way it ll a cple of old bear heads, one on each side	E: (Rpts S's resp) S: Its just th green prts, one on each side just th way th snout comes dwn & th littl ears & ths prt, c ths dent hre, is whre th eye wld b	Do Fo 2 Ad
X			
18.	Well thres a cpl of littl ants up hre carryg ths stick	E: (Rpts S's resp) S: C up hre (pts) thy hav th littl antena & thyr pushg lik th devil on ths stick, thy do tht u kno, thy can really carry a lot of weight for thr size, I'v seen em, c th littl legs & th heads	D+ FMao 2 A,Bt 4.0 COP,PER
<19.	Ths thg re me of a potato chip	E: (Rpts S's resp) S: Oh its just tht brown colr & th kinda shap tht thy have, c right hre (points)	Do FCo Fd
20.	Ths littl prt hre re me of th balance governors thy had on th old steam engines	E: (Rpts S's resp) S: Hre ths littl thg, c its weights r on each side & it spins whn th engine turns & th spining action creates a counterforce, u dont c thm much now but thy wre vry common whn I was younger	Do Fo Sc PER
21.	U kno, thse cld b a cpl of dogs too, lik sittg & holdg thr heads up in th air, mayb barkg	E: (Rpts S's resp) S: C one hre & hre (points) hre r th legs out in frnt, & th snout & th tail lik thyr pushg back a bit on th legs & barking in th air	Do FMao 2 A

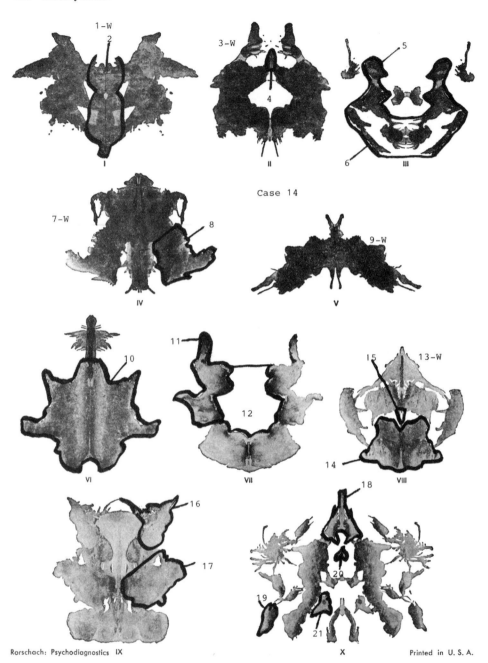

Case 14

Rorschach: Psychodiagnostics   Printed in U. S. A.

Case 14

Case 14   **Sequence of Scores**

Card	No	Loc	#	Determinant(s)	(2)	Content(s)	Pop	Z	Special Scores
I	1	WSo	1	Fo		(Hd)		3.5	
	2	Do	4	Mao		H			
II	3	W+	1	FMa.CFo	2	A,Bl		4.5	AG,MOR
	4	Ddo	99	Fo		Ay			
III	5	D+	1	Mao	2	H,Id	P	3.0	COP
	6	Do	5	Fu	2	Sc			PER
IV	7	Wo	1	Mp.FTo		(H)	P	2.0	
	8	Do	6	Fu	2	Ad			
V	9	Wo	1	FMau		A		1.0	PER
VI	10	Do	1	FTo		Ad	P		
VII	11	D+	2	Ma+	2	Hd,Id	P	3.0	AG
	12	DSo	10	Fu		Ay			PER
VIII	13	W+	1	FMa.CFo	2	A,Bt	P	4.5	
	14	Do	2	Fu		Ad			
	15	DdSo	29	FC'.FMpu		A			PER
IX	16	D+	3	Mao	2	H,Cg,Sc		4.5	
	17	Do	1	Fo	2	Ad			
X	18	D+	11	FMao	2	A,Bt		4.0	COP,PER
	19	Do	13	FCo		Fd			
	20	Do	3	Fo		Sc			PER
	21	Do	2	FMao	2	A			

Case 14   **Structural Summary**

Location Features	Determinants Blends	Single	Contents	S-Constellation

Location Features			Contents	S-Constellation
	Determinants			NO . . FV+VF+V+FD>2
	Blends	Single		NO . . Col−Shd Bl>0
			H = 3, 0	YES . . Ego<.31,>.44
Zf = 9	FM.CF	M = 4	(H) = 1, 0	NO . . MOR > 3
ZSum = 30.0	FM.CF	FM = 3	Hd = 1, 0	NO . . Zd > +− 3.5
ZEst = 27.5	FC'.FM	m = 0	(Hd) = 1, 0	YES . . es > EA
	M.FT	FC = 1	Hx = 0, 0	YES . . CF+C > FC
W = 5		CF = 0	A = 6, 0	NO . . X+% < .70
(Wv = 0)		C = 0	(A) = 0, 0	NO . . S > 3
D = 14		Cn = 0	Ad = 4, 0	NO . . P < 3 or > 8
Dd = 2		FC' = 0	(Ad) = 0, 0	NO . . Pure H < 2
S = 3		C'F = 0	An = 0, 0	NO . . R < 17
		C' = 0	Art = 0, 0	3 . . . . . TOTAL
DQ		FT = 1	Ay = 2, 0	
. . . . . (FQ−)		TF = 0	Bl = 0, 1	Special Scorings
+ = 6 (0)		T = 0	Bt = 0, 2	Lv1 Lv2
o = 15 (0)		FV = 0	Cg = 0, 1	DV = 0x1 0x2
v/+ = 0 (0)		VF = 0	Cl = 0, 0	INC = 0x2 0x4
v = 0 (0)		V = 0	Ex = 0, 0	DR = 0x3 0x6
		FY = 0	Fd = 1, 0	FAB = 0x4 0x7
		YF = 0	Fi = 0, 0	ALOG = 0x5
		Y = 0	Ge = 0, 0	CON = 0x7
		Fr = 0	Hh = 0, 0	SUM6 = 0
Form Quality		rF = 0	Ls = 0, 0	WSUM6 = 0
		FD = 0	Na = 0, 0	
FQx FQf MQual SQx		F = 8	Sc = 2, 1	AB = 0 CP = 0
+ = 1 0 1 0			Sx = 0, 0	AG = 2 MOR = 1
o = 14 4 4 1			Xy = 0, 0	CFB = 0 PER = 6
u = 6 4 0 2			Id = 0, 2	COP = 2 PSV = 0
− = 0 0 0 0				
none = 0 — 0 0		(2) = 10		

Case 14   **Ratios, Percentages, and Derivations**

R = 21		L = 0.62		FC:CF+C = 1: 2	COP = 2 AG = 2
				Pure C = 0	Food = 1
EB = 5: 2.5	EA = 7.5	EBPer = 2.0		Afr = 0.75	Isolate/R = 0.10
eb = 6: 3	es = 9	D = 0		S = 3	H:(H)Hd(Hd) = 3:3
	Adj es = 9	Adj D = 0		Blends:R = 4:21	(HHd):(AAd) = 2:0
				CP = 0	H+A:Hd+Ad = 10:6
FM = 6 : C' = 1 T = 2					
m = 0 : V = 0 Y = 0					
		P = 5		Zf = 9	3r+(2) /R = 0.48
a:p = 9: 2	Sum6 = 0	X+% = 0.71		Zd = +2.5	Fr+rF = 0
Ma:Mp = 4: 1	Lv2 = 0	F+% = 0.50		W:D:Dd = 5:14: 2	FD = 0
2AB+Art+Ay=2	WSum6 = 0	X−% = 0.00		W:M = 5: 4	An+Xy = 0
M − = 0	Mnone = 0	S−% = 0.00		DQ+ = 6	MOR = 1
		Xu% = 0.29		DQv = 0	

SCZI = 3	DEPI = 3	CDI = 1	S-CON = 3	HVI = No	OBS = No

THE RORSCHACH FINDINGS—CASE 14

This 36-year-old male shows no evidence of significant psychopathology. He is the type of person who usually prefers to think things through before making a decision or initiating behavior [*EB*]. He is somewhat more needy [*FM*] than most adults, and at times, these needs tend to cause distractions to his thinking. It seems likely that this unusual excess of neediness is being caused by a marked sense of loneliness that he has [*T*], probably related to the fact that his marriage has dissolved. He is not very flexible in the way in that he thinks about things. Instead, he tends to settle on a point of view about something and sticks persistently to it even though other possibilities exist [*a:p*]. This same kind of inflexibility probably exists concerning his values. Nonetheless, his thinking usually is clear, logical, and reasonably sophisticated [absence of special scores, quality of *M* responses].

He processes information adequately but cautiously, trying to avoid dealing with too much information at any one time [*Zf, W:D:Dd, W:M, DQ+*]. He usually is conventional in the way that he translates or interprets new information [*X + %*] although, at times, some of his interpretations are more individualized than is common for adults [*Xu%*]. However, this has no significant impact on the way that he deals with reality. His capacity for control and tolerance for stress are much like that of most adults [D and Adjusted D Scores], and there is no reason to suspect that he is vulnerable to any loss of control [*EA, EB*, Adjusted *es*].

As implied earlier, he does not like to be overly influenced by his feelings when he makes decisions [*EB*]. There are times when his feelings become influential [*EBPer*], but there is no reason to suspect that his emotions will cloud his thinking or cause him to distort reality. When he expresses his feelings, they may be slightly more intense than would be expected of a thoughtful person [*FC:CF + C*], but not overly so. He is more negative or hostile about his world than are most adults [*S*], but he seems to control these feelings adequately most of the time. He is not a very complex person [blends], but he is slightly more self-centered than is typical for most adults [Egocentricity Index]. This does not appear to be a substantial liability. On the other hand, he is not a very introspective or insightful person [no Vista, no *FD*], and this, plus his lack of flexibility in his thinking, could create a sort of deception about who and what he is.

For instance, at the moment, he is a rather lonely person but probably will not admit to his loneliness [*T*]. Similarly, he is prone to be dependent on others, but it is doubtful that he will concede to this [*Fd*]. His self-image seems to be founded in his experiences [Pure *H*], but his notions about himself tend to include more issues of uncertainty than should be the case [human movement contents], and he seems to regard himself as less capable or secure than he would prefer [other movement contents]. He is very interested in people [human contents] but seems unsure about people and how to interact with them [COP, AG]. In fact, he often defends his sense of insecurity with a kind of authoritarianism that runs a considerable risk of alienating others. It is a feature that many might describe as pomposity and has probably contributed in some way to his marital failure.

In summary, this man presents a picture of a fairly stabilized personality that represents a mix of assets and liabilities. Although his needs, especially his experience of loneliness, are currently creating an added burden for him, he continues to have sufficient resources organized in ways that make them available for most of his routine coping requirements. He is an ideational person who tries to be economical in the efforts that he makes, but he also tries to be somewhat more precise or perfectionistic so that most of those efforts will reflect a thorough performance. His reality testing is good, and his emotional controls are generally commensurate with those of most adults. He is more self-involved than should be the case, probably is not very flexible in his thinking or attitudes, and may be somewhat defensively negative. His self-image is not as sturdy as he would prefer, yet it does not seem to be fragile or diffuse. He tends to defend his sense of insecurity by being overly forceful in conveying his ideas or justifying his actions. Thus, while he is interested in people, it is possible that many of his interpersonal relationships will be more distant and/or superficial because of his tendency to be somewhat pompous or to appear inflexible in his thinking or his attitudes.

COMPARING THE PARENTS

It is not very difficult to see where problems could easily erupt in this marriage. The wife is a rather immature hysteroid person who is very strongly influenced by her feelings and has the potential for being quite disrupted by them. She is extremely self-centered and tends to place a priority on her need to reaffirm her own worth and does not appear to expect close emotional relations with others. This characteristic often causes her to blame others, or the environment in general, for unhappy events rather than to look within herself for possible cause of things that go wrong. In that framework, she is prone to bend and distort reality considerably, and these traits can easily have serious effects on her judgment. For instance, she does not seem to understand that her daughter is doing very poorly in school. She claims that she supervises her daughter's homework each school night, yet her daughter describes their relationship as involving more fun things, such as cooking, baking, shopping, and going to the movies. It may be that the mother is unwilling to face some of the problems that have been created by the breakup of her marriage and is struggling to continue her life in a way that disregards the trauma and realities of the situation, especially as they affect her daughter.

Conversely, the husband is more prone to be an ideational person who likes to plan his actions before testing out his decisions. He is a lonely man who would prefer much closer emotional relationships than he currently experiences. He is also somewhat self-centered, but possibly less secure in his own self-image than his wife. He has developed a somewhat forceful and less flexible role in his values and attitudes, and in his interpersonal world he may be perceived as being more pompous than many can tolerate easily. He wants things to be neat and orderly and probably expects others to want the same. In a marriage to a person who is quite emotional and sometimes very unrealistic, it is easy to see how he would quickly run out of patience, and his defensiveness and inflexibility could often lead to conflict. His wife's reaction to this would, no doubt, include the considerable expression of her feelings, and most likely, he would counter these displays of feelings with his own form of authoritarianism. Thus, it is not difficult to understand her complaints about his "bitchiness" or his complaint that she "turned into a slob."

Neither of these adults represents the ideal parent. The mother appears far too self-involved and too prone to deny or ignore some of the harsh realities and responsibilities of being a parent. She does not handle her emotions very well, and at times, they probably become overly influential in her judgments. Although the father works at being a very thoughtful person, he is burdened by a marked sense of insecurity about himself. Over the years, he has become a dogmatic person who shows little flexibility in his attitudes about the world. Both parents are interested in people, but neither seem to understand how to create and maintain deep relationships with others. Both seem quite sincere about their daughter's best interests, but neither has taken a very realistic view of her problems or their contributions to those problems. She has become the innocent victim of their dispute and now is in great distress and unable to formulate some behaviors or decisions to behavior that will promote relief. She has come to have very low self-esteem, she has numerous features common to depression, and it is likely that she tends to blame herself for some of her parents' difficulties.

THE OUTCOME

The three reports were provided to the presiding jurist and each of the attorneys without specific recommendations concerning custody. The mother's report stressed that if she were to be granted custody, her role as a parent would probably be improved considerably if she entered some form of intervention, oriented mainly toward the development of better control over her emotions. The father's report noted that he also could benefit from some form of intervention but would probably be less willing to venture into any form of therapy sincerely, although if instructed to do so, he would probably comply. It was stressed that, regardless of the custody decision, the child's current state indicated a need for immediate intervention and that the cooperation of both parents might be a crucial factor in determining any progress.

Each of the attorneys requested that the reports be entered formally in the court records, and the psychologist who did the evaluations was required to give depositional testimony before the court. In the course of that testimony, both attorneys pressed for recommendations. Since the original petition to the court was initiated by the father and claimed that the mother was unfit, many of the questions focused on this issue, and the father's attorney pursued the question vigorously. The testimony of other witnesses and the report of a social worker were somewhat damaging to the mother, suggesting that she was socially more active than would be expected of a woman who had her child's best interests in focus.

In an apparent compromise, the court ruled for divided custody for a probationary period of 1 year, with a final decision concerning custody to be rendered at the end of that time. In this arrangement, the mother was to provide housing and care for the child during the week, with the father having custody on weekends and for a 6-week period during the coming summer. The court also instructed the mother to seek psychotherapy at a community mental health center and required that both parents be active in arranging for immediate intervention for the child.

REFERENCES

Blau, T. H. (1984). *The psychologist as expert witness.* New York: Wiley.

Brinson, P., & Hess, K. D. (1987). Mediating domestic law issues. In I. B. Weiner & A. K. Hess (Eds.), *Handbook of forensic psychology* (pp. 86–127). New York: Wiley.

Brodsky, S. L. (1991). *Testifying in court.* Washington, DC: American Psychological Association.

Hodges, W. F. (1991). *Interventions for children of divorce.* (2nd ed.) New York: Wiley.

Maloney, M. P. (1985). *A clinician's guide to forensic psychological assessment.* New York: Free Press.

Melton, G. B., Petrila, J., Poythress, N. G., & Slobogin, C. (1987). *Psychological evaluation for the courts.* New York: Guilford Press.

Sales, B., Manber, R., & Rohman, L. (1992). Social science research and child-custody decision making. *Applied and Preventive Psychology, 1,* 23–40.

Shapiro, D. L. (1984). *Psychological evaluation and expert testimony.* New York: Van Nostrand Reinhold.

Shapiro, D. L. (1991). *Forensic psychological assessment.* Boston: Allyn & Bacon.

Weiner, I. B. (1987). Writing forensic reports. In I. B. Weiner & A. K. Hess (Eds.), *Handbook of forensic psychology* (pp. 511–528). New York: Wiley.

Weiner, I. B. (1989). On competence and ethicality in psychodiagnosis. *Journal of Personality Assessment, 53,* 827–831.

Weiner, I. B. (1992). Current developments in psychodiagnosis. *Independent Practitioner, 12,* 114–119.

Weissman, H. N. (1991). Child custody evaluations: Fair and unfair professional practices. *Behavioral Sciences and the Law, 9,* 469–476.

Ziskin, J. (1981). *Coping with psychiatric and psychological testimony.* Venice, CA: Law and Psychology Press.

Ziskin, J., & Faust, D. (1988). *Coping with psychiatric and psychological testimony* (Vols. 1–3; 4th ed.). Marina del Ray, CA: Law and Psychology Press.

Author Index

Subject Index